DISARMAMENT

The World at a Critical Turning Point

Edited transcripts of the forums held in the United Nations
on 8-9 April, 14 April, 22 October and 27-29 October 1998
and 15 and 22 April 1999 by the NGO Committee on
Disarmament, in cooperation with the UN Department
for Disarmament Affairs and the UN Department of Public
Information, and the 11 May 1999 presentations by NGOs
to the third PrepCom for the Non-Proliferation Treaty Review
Conference in 2000

United Nations   New York   1999

NOTE

This publication contains extensive excerpts from the edited transcripts of meetings held at the United Nations in 1998 and 1999, in cooperation with the UN Department for Disarmament Affairs.

The Department for Disarmament Affairs is publishing the material in collaboration with the NGO Committee on Disarmament Affairs, within the mandate of the United Nations Disarmament Information Programme (UNDIP).

The views expressed herein are those of the participants and do not necessarily reflect those of the sponsoring bodies.

UNITED NATIONS PUBLICATION

Sales No. E.99.IX.5

ISBN 92-1-142231-0

INTRODUCTION

June, 1999

This publication includes the edited transcripts of the panel discussions held in the United Nations by the NGO Committee on Disarmament in 1998 and early 1999 and the presentations made by NGOs on May 11, 1999 at the third PrepCom for the Non-Proliferation Treaty Review Conference to be held in the year 2000. We are very much dependent upon your reactions and suggestions to help us plan what we do in the future. We are now planning the panel discussions for Disarmament Week to be held the week of October 25, 1999. We will also begin planning for the NPT Review Conference in April, 2000 and the Disarmament Commission meeting in the spring of 2000. We need your input. You can e-mail us, fax us, or write us.

*We have a web site on the Internet - **http://www.peacenet.org/disarm/** - on which you will find information about UN activities, the edited transcripts of our forums earlier than we can get them published, and information that comes to us from other NGOs. We intend to provide information about First Committee resolutions and the discussion in the First Committee about them earlier than the UN can do so, with hopes that will help some of you to influence your own governments. We expect a new version of the New Agenda Coalition resolution will be important and so may several others. If you have no direct access to the Internet yourself, and have information you would like to have put there, contact us.*

NGOs need to be much more active, on a much larger scale, to play an effective role at the UN and with their own governments. The NGO Committee on Disarmament welcomes the membership of all individuals and organizations that have an interest in the activities of the UN in the disarmament, international security and peacekeeping areas. We also welcome your subscription to Disarmament Times, published at least six times a year to report on activities at the UN. Our rationale for existence is to inform you of what goes on at the UN, and, even more importantly, to present your expertise, to facilitate your efforts to be heard at the UN, to make your advocacy of specific objectives possible.

Agreement on the agenda and timing of a fourth Special Session on Disarmament (SSOD IV) was not reached by the working group that met for the fourth year during the Disarmament Commission in April, 1999. The Disarmament Commission operates under rules of consensus, and the objection of India prevented a resolution of this issue. It could be resolved by the First Committee, with a vote. The stumbling block has been the differing views of delegations on the importance of the Final Document of the First Special Session on Disarmament. NGO experts could make a very worthwhile contribution to the discussion on nuclear weapons and on conventional disarmament, UN peacekeeping, peacemaking, and peace enforcing that might increase the chances of a worthwhile SSOD IV. We welcome your suggestions.

The major focus of the First Committee discussion in November, 1998 was on the resolution put forth by Ireland, Sweden, Brazil, Egypt, Mexico, New Zealand and South Africa. that called for a new agenda. Much of the discussion in the panel the morning of October 27, 1998 that asked "How Can We Make Greater Progress Towards Nuclear Disarmament and Prevent Further Proliferation?" focuses on the New Agenda Coalition resolution. We also have appended some of the discussion held in the First Committee the day it was adopted. Resolution 53/77 Y was adopted without the support of the US, UK, France, the Russian Federation, India, Pakistan or Israel.

(China abstained.) Nevertheless, 114 countries supported it and discussion continued during the NPT PrepCom and certainly will continue next fall in the First Committee. We think many more need to be aware of this effort to make more rapid progress in achieving the elimination of nuclear weapons.

A number of the other panel discussions focused on nuclear weapons, the Comprehensive Test Ban Treaty, and a beginning discussion of a verification regime for nuclear disarmament. And the NGO presentations to the third PrepCom also focused on nuclear issues.

Several panel discussions focused on a new NGO initiative, Global Action to Prevent War, and there was also much discussion of it in the Hague Agenda for Peace conference that attracted 9000 people. The program, which we have appended, emphasizes increasing the capabilities of the UN to prevent war and reducing the large conventional forces of all countries.

Small arms, or light weapons, were also the subject of two panel discussions. Reducing the havoc caused by light weapons has become an increasing focus of both NGOs and governments and was also a focus in the Hague conference..

We held no panel discussion in 1998 on land mines, but this has been one of the most successful efforts of NGOs and governments. The Land Mines Treaty has now gone into effect, even though several key governments have yet to sign and ratify it: the US, the Russian Federation and China. Clearly the citizens of those countries have a job to do.

The Comprehensive Test Ban Treaty ending all nuclear tests needs the ratification of the US, the Russian Federation, India, Pakistan, Israel, and several other countries to come into effect. 1999 will be a crucial year, because of the provision in the treaty permitting a meeting of Parties to consider further steps to permit it to come into effect.

The NGO Committee is again indebted to the UN Department for Disarmament Affairs and the UN Department of Public Information for facilitating the holding of these panel discussions and for publishing these edited transcripts. We are also indebted to Rissho Kosei-kai, whose financial contribution has again made publication possible. Thanks are also due to the many who helped in organizing the discussions and those who helped Ann Lakhdhir in transcribing, editing and proof reading them, particularly Kathy Uhler, Roger Smith, Caroline Bridgman-Rees, Myrna Pena, Betty Obal and our interns, Brice Friedman, Ilari Marzano, Diana Quintero and Masako Toki.

Vernon C. Nichols, President

Ann Hallan Lakhdhir, Vice President for Program

NGO Committee on Disarmament, Inc.
777 United Nations Plaza, Suite 3B, New York, NY 10017
Tel. (212) 687-5340; Fax (212) 687-1643;
E-mail:disarmtimes@igc.apc.org;
web site: http://www.peacenet.org/disarm/

THE WORLD AT A CRITICAL TURNING POINT

8-9 April, 17 April, 27-29, October, 1998, 15 & 22 April, 11 May, 1999

Edited transcripts of the forums held by the NGO Committee on Disarmament, in cooperation with the UN Department for Disarmament Affairs and the UN Department of Public Information, and of the NGO presentations before the third PrepCom for the NPT Review Conference in April, 2000.

PANEL DISCUSSIONS AND PRESENTATIONS ON NUCLEAR WEAPONS ISSUES:

May 11, 1999: PRESENTATIONS BY NON-GOVERNMENTAL ORGANIZATIONS TO THE THIRD PREPCOM FOR THE NON-PROLIFERATION TREATY REVIEW CONFERENCE IN THE YEAR 2000

These statements were coordinated and drafted by a wide range of NGOs. Each was prepared with the intention of expressing the broadest possible range of views.

October 27, 1998, am: HOW CAN WE MAKE GREATER PROGRESS TOWARDS NUCLEAR DISARMAMENT AND PREVENT FURTHER PROLIFERATION?

Darach MacFionnbhairr talked about the resolution he introduced that afternoon in the UN for a New Agenda for nuclear weapons; Ambassadors Savitri Kumadi, Munir Akram and Ian Soutar indicated their disagreements with the resolution. Norman Wulf focused on other nuclear concerns.

Hal Feiveson talked about de-alerting; Thomas Graham supported pledges of no first use of nuclear weapons; Hiro Umebayashi supported the New Agenda resolution; Arjun Makhijani focused on environmental and health effects of the nuclear weapons complexes.

Jayantha Dhanapala, Masabumi Sato and Daryl Kimball talked about the importance of the Comprehensive Test Ban Treaty; Lars Bjarme and Alyn Ware talked about the New Agenda resolution; Arjun Makhijani criticised Stockpile Stewardship.

Steve Fetter, Chairman of the on-going CISAC project on verification, talked of some of the initial steps; Alan Dowty talked of a ban on the first use of all weapons of mass destruction; Merav Datan focused on the feasibility of a nuclear weapons convention eliminating nuclear weapons.

Bruce Blair and Harold Feiveson talked about de-alerting and the psychological pressures on those called upon to impliment nuclear policy; Admiral Stansfield Turner talked of putting nuclear weapons in storage and the expansion of the NPT into a treaty of no first use of nuclear weapons.

All three panels focused on the progtram of Global Action to Prevent War that in the Hague Appeal for Peace Conference in May, 1999 further expanded its reach to many

As the consequences of the proliferation of small arms throughout the world become more evident, there are increasing efforts by governments to control it. A new network of NGOs, IANSA, has been established.

PANEL DISCUSSION ON OUTER SPACE:

The need to prevent outer space from becoming the locale of future wars.

PANEL DISCUSSION ON SOUTH ASIA:

RELIGIOUS PERSPECTIVES

PRESENTATIONS BY NGOS TO THE THIRD PREPCOM FOR THE NPT REVIEW CONFERENCE, May 11, 1999

TOPIC 1: Evaluation of NPT Compliance and the Review Process to date
PRESENTER: Arjun Makhijani, Institute for Energy and Environmental Research

At this last PrepCom before the Year 2000 review of the Nuclear Non-Proliferation Treaty, we believe that it is important to take stock of the compliance record of the parties to it. We must do so in a manner that is honest and forthright, for the NPT is not in good health. A clear diagnosis of the problem is needed if it is to be saved.

Let us first look at the record of the States Parties that are nuclear weapons states. Whatever their rhetoric, all five of them are modernizing their nuclear arsenals. This is a violation of the clause of Article VI of the NPT that calls for an early end to the arms race. The NPT has been in force for almost three decades now. The Berlin Wall fell a decade ago. Yet, nuclear arsenal modernization continues. This is beyond any reasonable definition of the term "early."

The two countries with the largest arsenals, the United States and Russia, each have about 2,500 nuclear warheads on hair-trigger alert. Despite the rising dangers of massive nuclear war by accident or miscalculation and despite the urging of many recognized authorities, including prominent public figures with military experience, they have refused to de-alert their weapons. On the contrary, both governments have repeatedly and insistently reaffirmed their policy of first use. Hundreds of millions of people, including vast numbers of people in non-nuclear weapons states, would die in case of a massive nuclear launch of the type that may occur as the result of a US or Russian miscalculation. Maintaining any nuclear weapons on high alert, let alone thousands of them, is a violation of the spirit, if not the letter, of Article VI of the NPT and of humanitarian law.

We also see too little respect for international legal institutions. With the notable exception of China, the nuclear weapons States Parties to the Nuclear Non-Proliferation Treaty (NPT) have failed to recognize the legitimacy of the unanimous opinion of the World Court that Article VI requires the actual achievement of nuclear disarmament in all its aspects. Moreover, the United States, Russia, Britain, and France (referred to as the "Four Nuclear Weapon States" below) refuse even to enter into negotiations to achieve nuclear disarmament in all its aspects. Article VI requires "good faith" efforts towards nuclear disarmament. Three decades after the entry into force of the NPT and four years after its permanent extension, when the nuclear weapon States Parties made an explicit renewal of their nuclear disarmament obligation, this refusal is unacceptable.

While the World Court has not set forth the criteria for establishing "good faith" we believe that refusing to enter into negotiations for complete nuclear disarmament, when seen in the context of the failure to accept the World Court's unanimous interpretation of Article VI, is the opposite of good faith. The Four Nuclear Weapon States have repeatedly renewed their verbal commitments to nuclear disarmament in NPT forums. But all too often, even this rhetoric is not repeated in domestic forums where military policy is made. On the contrary, the determination to maintain nuclear arsenals for the indefinite future is emphasized in these arenas, where the money is allocated and the real policy is decided. This is also not in consonance with any reasonable idea of good faith.

As regards China, despite accepting the World Court interpretation regarding disarmament, it continues to modernize its nuclear arsenal. It has also begun to waver in its constantly reaffirmed its no-first-use policy. In the context of the pronouncements of US officials regarding possible installation of missile defenses in Taiwan, it has hinted that it may revoke its no-first-use policy and accelerate its development of nuclear weapons. This again reminds us how frail verbal commitments can be, if they are not backed up by verified actions on the ground.

In this context, it is worthwhile to examine the question of the 1972 Anti-Ballistic Missile Treaty. In one of the most troubling developments since the 1998 PrepCom in Geneva, the United States appears determined to deploy ballistic missile defenses either by forcing an amendment upon an economically weak Russia or, failing that, by abrogating it. The ABM treaty only requires six months notice of withdrawal (the NPT requires three months notice). Like the NPT, there are no sanctions for withdrawal within the framework of the ABM treaty. But Russia and China have jointly announced that "damage" to or violation of the ABM treaty "could generate new factors that may result in regional, even global instability, or provide an excuse to restore the arms race, thus far setting new barriers for the disarmament process." (Beijing Xinhua, English edition, 16 April 1999).

Ballistic missile defenses in the context of a world bristling with nuclear weapons are provocative, since they could be part of a first nuclear strike strategy. The intentions of the party building and deploying them are beside the point. In times of tensions or war, previously announced intentions can change rapidly. Moreover, one might put more stock in announced intentions, if the treaty compliance records of the parties who ask for our good faith merited it. They do not. We believe that this body should examine whether the deployment of ballistic missile defenses in contravention of the ABM treaty would be tantamount to a violation of Article VI, since it would provoke a renewed and re-intensified nuclear arms race.

The United States and Russia keep pointing to START I, START II as well as the reductions in tactical nuclear warheads carried out on a unilateral-reciprocal basis by them in 1991 as evidence of their progress towards disarmament. This was a credible claim in the early to mid-1990s, though restricted to launchers and not to warheads. But the arms reduction process is now stalled. START II has not yet been ratified by the Russian Duma, despite repeated urging by President Yeltsin and his administration that it do so. While it may not have intended it, the United States gravely damaged the process of START II ratification by when it chose to begin its bombings of Iraq in December 1998 and Yugoslavia in March 1999. Both were begun at times just prior to consideration of the treaty by the Russian Duma. On both occasions, the climate before the bombings appeared to favor ratification. On both occasions, it was known beforehand that US bombing would mean that START II would be put on hold again. NATO expansion was also carried out at a time of possible Russian ratification of START II.

The Comprehensive Test Ban Treaty CTBT, the achievement of which was a commitment made by the nuclear weapon states at the time of the indefinite extension of the NPT, has been ratified by only two of them, France and Britain. Further, the United States has already begun a $4.5 billion "Stockpile Stewardship Program" that involves maintenance of design capability for new weapons and of nuclear arsenals for an indefinite period of time. Other nuclear weapon States Parties have begun similar programs, if on a smaller scale.

One analysis indicates that two large laser fusion facilities, the US National Ignition Facility being built at Livermore California and a similar French facility being built near Bordeaux, may violate Article I of the CTBT. These facilities are designed to create thermonuclear explosions that do not fall into the zero-yield-exception claim made for sub-critical testing. In fact, the planned pure fusion explosions would be larger than the four pounds of TNT equivalent fission hydronuclear tests that were clearly banned during the negotiations. Claims that these machines could provide energy sources or that such explosions are allowed under the NPT are irrelevant. The NPT allows nuclear explosions. The CTBT bans them all, including explosions for peaceful purposes.

No real progress has been made on adopting an international, legally binding instrument codifying pledges of non-use of nuclear weapons against non-nuclear weapons States Parties. The nuclear weapons states have also not acknowledged that the assurances made by declaration in 1995 are legally binding. The United States has sought to construe broadly asserted exceptions to this declaration, for example with respect to reprisals against chemical or biological attack. And as have we noted, China's commitment to no-first-use is not as unequivocal as it once was.

There has been no progress towards the goal of a nuclear free zone in the Middle East, a commitment undertaken at the time of the 1995 extension. Finally, we note that the two PrepComs since 1995 have failed to make any headway in persuading the nuclear weapons States Parties to take their commitments more seriously or urgently. The nuclear weapons States Parties are simply not taking the disarmament aspects of the Principles and Objectives for Nuclear Non-Proliferation and Disarmament agreed to in 1995 seriously enough.

Let us now turn to the non-nuclear weapons States Parties. The record of the vast majority of them stands in stark and refreshing contrast. While the nuclear weapons states are violating their commitments in letter and spirit, the record of the vast majority of non-nuclear weapons States Parties is exemplary because they have not made any moves to acquire nuclear weapons. Some of them, notably the members of the New Agenda Coalition, have been in the leadership of trying to persuade the nuclear weapons States Parties to fulfill their Article VI obligations. Several countries that have nuclear weapons capabilities have renounced them unilaterally and joined the NPT as non-nuclear weapons states.

But the situation is not all rosy on this front. The serious violations of their NPT commitments by Iraq and North Korea are well-documented and well-recognized. Yet the States Parties to the NPT have not been able to see to it that the response to these violations was equitable and just. They have not even raised the issue of differential treatment seriously. While the situation in Iraq is admittedly complex, it is clear that it has been the subject of severe sanctions and worse, partly because of its attempts to acquire nuclear weapons. North Korea, which reportedly may have as many as five warheads as well as advanced delivery systems, has been given aid and even the promise of commercial nuclear reactors in return for inspections. Whatever the actual considerations - and neither the people of the world nor the governments of most States Parties to the NPT are privy to them - this difference of treatment creates the impression of legitimizing nuclear deterrence and violations of the NPT when they have progressed to the weapons stage. The harshest treatment appears to be reserved for countries that do not have them yet. This is an unacceptable way to enforce the NPT. It is crucial that the NPT take up the question of enforcement and devise just, equitable, and effective ways to enforce it for all parties.

There is trouble elsewhere as well. NATO reliance on nuclear weapons is problematic in the context of the NPT, to say the least. The Warsaw Pact is no more and Russian conventional capacity is far lower by all accounts than that of NATO. Yet, the NATO strategic doctrine issued on the occasion of its fiftieth anniversary last month re-emphasizes the role of nuclear weapons in any conflict. Its paragraph 46 states:

> "To protect peace and to prevent war or *any kind of coercion*, the Alliance will maintain for the foreseeable future an appropriate mix of nuclear and conventional forces based in Europe and kept up to date where necessary, although at a minimum sufficient level. Taking into account the diversity of risks with which the Alliance could be faced, it must maintain the forces necessary to ensure credible deterrence and to provide a wide range of conventional response options. But the Alliance's conventional forces alone cannot ensure credible deterrence. Nuclear weapons make a unique contribution in rendering the risks of aggression against the Alliance incalculable and unacceptable. Thus, they remain essential to preserve peace."

If nuclear deterrence is needed for NATO members, including the non-nuclear NATO States Parties to the NPT, even though they collectively have the strongest non-nuclear forces, why should other non-nuclear States Parties not want it also? Clearly, NATO members can have nothing to say about proliferation attempts that could be considered non-hypocritical until this nuclear deterrence policy is scrapped. And what can NATO members have to say to India, Pakistan and Israel who have not signed the NPT if they persist in such a doctrine? Continuing to rely on nuclear weapons as an essential part of NATO doctrine means that both the nuclear and non-nuclear weapons States Parties to the NPT that are members of NATO are in violation of the spirit of their NPT obligations.

It should not go unnoticed that the vast majority of violators of the NPT are western governments that often proclaim themselves on the world stage to be the guarantors of international law. Their claims to that role would be more credible if they asked others to do as they do rather than as they say in the arena most urgently crucial to human survival - nuclear disarmament. The catalog of violations of the letter and spirit of the NPT and related treaties is long and serious. It demands a response. Unless the NPT states parties monitor compliance with respect to their various commitments, the NPT is likely to unravel, possibly at a rapid rate. Treaty agreements in many arenas, including other nuclear weapons related treaties, are under serious strain. So it is especially important that the states parties to the NPT, which has more signatories than any other security treaty, should launch an historic compliance assessment review. They could do so by forming an intercessional working group or they could ask the NPT secretariat to produce a review. This review should be completed by the end of 1999, so that there is ample time before the Review Conference for the states parties to take serious steps to remedy problems that the compliance assessment might identify.

We recognize that one or more influential States Parties may block either of these approaches to compliance assessment. A part of the reason that the NPT is in poor health is the failure of the review process so far to produce results. On the contrary, there has been a good deal of backsliding. We therefore urge one or more States Parties to take the initiative to form an ad hoc group of states parties to undertake a compliance assessment. As NGOs who strive for a safe and peaceful world, we stand ready to assist you in the historic and difficult task of compliance assessment before you.

Convenor: Arjun Makhijani, Institute for Energy and Environmental Research
6935 Laurel Avenue, Takoma Park, Maryland 20912, USA, tel 301-270-5500; ieer@ieer.org

TOPIC 2: Analysis of US-Russian Relations with Respect to the NPT
PRESENTER: Vladimir Iakimets, Center for Russian Environmental Policy

Distinguished delegates! The extension in 1995 was to make the NPT review process more effective and to strengthen it. However, both the sessions in 1997 and 1998 illustrated that:

- Larger disagreement among the parties emerged than before 1995.
- The scope of nuclear dangers is greater than before.

Unless there is a strong agreement over the meaning and the content of the strengthened review process, you, distinguished delegates, will face the challenge of many continuing disagreements as happened in 1997 and 1998. Your task for this 1999 Preparatory Committee meeting is to prove that you can do much better with both substantive and procedural issues of both the non-proliferation regime and of nuclear disarmament. If this is not done, then the international events of the last three months could put an end to the NPT.

In the early 1990s, there was extensive cooperation between the US and Russia for nuclear security programs (Bush-Gorbachev Initiative, START I and START II). Such programs as the Fissile Material Storage Facility, the program on Plutonium disposition, the Cooperation Threat Reduction program should also be mentioned. Since 1993, when the START II was signed, the process of nuclear weapon reductions has been hopelessly deadlocked. In the meantime, nuclear dangers, stemming from economic decline in Russia, continue to grow. NATO expansion, US/UK military attacks against Iraq, and the NATO bombing of Yugoslavia without UN Security Council approval, and the passage of bills in the US House and Senate pushing the US closer to a decision to deploy a ballistic missile defense have all provided major disincentives for the Russian Duma to ratify START II. And given the ongoing NATO campaign against Yugoslavia and the negative Russian reaction to it, START II is not likely to go into force anytime soon.

Yet, it is the policy of the US executive branch, with the blessing of the US Congress, to wait on Duma ratification before moving to negotiate deeper reductions under an already agreed outline for START III agreement. In other words, just let the treaty negotiating process run its normal, tediously slow course. This policy falls short of the commitment the US made, along with the other NWS, when the NPT was extended indefinitely in 1995. The second resolution making the NPT permanent binds the P-5 states to make "systematic and progressive efforts" to reduce their nuclear stockpiles. Waiting on START II needlessly prolongs the time that Russia has to keep a huge nuclear arsenal that it can not afford to maintain or safely control. And, even the agreed START III levels, between 2,000-2,500 warheads, remain excessively higher than the levels that Russia will have to reduce to by the early 21st century.

Today, the Cold War threats approach to arms control is ill-suited to address the nuclear threats posed by a politically unstable and economically and militarily weakened Russia. The global landscape, characterized by a lone superpower and an expanding number of nuclear capable states, cannot afford down time for arms control. Although Russian officials have stated that Russia will have to reduce its nuclear arsenal dramatically over the next decade for economic reasons, they have also indicated that they will postpone such reductions for as long as possible, given the US action on ballistic missile deployment. Graver still, there have been reports that Russia might redeploy tactical nuclear weapons to other CIS republics in response to NATOs military campaign in Yugoslavia. It is worthwhile to record the various developments in Russia that have heightened nuclear dangers:

- Russia suspended its cooperation with the NATO Summit and cooperation on Y2K problems was also curtailed (at least with UK).
- The Duma Defense Committee proposed to include preemptive strikes in the Russian National Security Policy.
- In the "Basic Provisions of the Russian Policy in the Sphere of Nuclear Deterrence," approved by President Yeltsin in March, Nuclear Forces are considered as a guarantor of national security and a means to deter aggression against the Russian Federation and its allies.
- Reorganization of the Russian Command Structure for Nuclear Deterrence Forces, which also is experiencing many economic and technical problems, proceeds with the troubling political involvement of many officers and workers in parties across the political spectrum.
- On April 29, at a top-secret meeting of the Security Council on Russia's nuclear arsenal, President Yeltsin signed a decree committing to develop and deploy tactical weapons. He also set out the key tasks for the nuclear defense industry that included developing ways to simulate atomic tests on computers. This is a sign of vertical proliferation. One of the presidential decrees not only contained the concept for the development but also for the *use* of non-strategic nuclear weapons.
- Russian Defense Minister Igor Sergeyev said that NATO military operation against Yugoslavia "may prompt Russia to revise a number of its international commitments, including those pertaining to the Conventional Forces in Europe (CFE) treaty."

The consequences of these developments are very discouraging from the point of view of nuclear disarmament. Instead of a reduction of nuclear arms (and nuclear dangers), we are entering a new arms race. Russia has developed several new missiles, including Topol-27M, and new S-400 system of missile and radar capable of hitting cruise missiles, stealth aircraft, reconnaissance airplanes.

As you may know, at the NATO summit the revised Strategic Concept was unveiled. NATO has decided to conduct military operations outside the Alliance territory. As Kosovo has shown, this is very a dangerous development. As far as NPT is concerned, decisions such as the Weapons of Mass Destruction Initiative (WMD) mean a possible violation of "negative security assurances" guaranteed in the NNWS, which was one of their major arguments in favor of extending the NPT in 1995. The disregard for international law and international organizations, as shown by the NATO actions in the Balkans, sets dangerous precedents:

- The threat or use of force against a sovereign state without corresponding UN authority is incompatible with article 2(4) and 51 of the UN Charter.
- The use of the law of force over international law by three members of the UN Security Council, which are also NWS.

In addition, six NATO member countries are sharing nuclear weapons with the United States (Germany, Italy, Turkey, Belgium, Netherlands, and Greece). In fact, this NATO nuclear sharing policy could be considered as the proliferation of nuclear weapons. Against this ominous backdrop are the very real concerns over safety and control of Russia's nuclear arsenal and vast stockpiles of fissile materials. Bold new thinking and action are needed by the US administration to put nuclear reduction negotiations with Russia not just back on track, but on a course to radically reduce these weapons, ensuring that they cannot be launched on a moment's notice, and safeguarding them and the materials to make them from falling into hostile hands. Time is of the essence. The US administration should act to supplement the traditional arms control process by pursuing immediate, parallel, reciprocal, and verifiable initiatives with Russia that

Reduce nuclear forces to levels far below those envisioned in START III by
- Immediately declaring US intention to reduce, alongside Russia, to 1,000 deployed strategic nuclear weapons within a decade.
- Offering complete transparency on the status of all US and Russian nuclear weapons as the basis for reciprocal reductions.
- Subsequently reducing to 1,000 total nuclear weapons on each side .
- Seeking agreement from other nuclear weapons states on a ceiling on their current nuclear deployments and beginning multilateral talks on reductions.

Take the majority of US and Russian forces off hair-trigger, or quick launch alert status, by
- Immediately standing down, alongside Russia, nuclear forces slated for destruction under START II.
- Declaring US intention, with reciprocal commitment from Russia, to eliminate the launch-on-warning option from nuclear war plans.
- Declaring US intentions, with reciprocal commitment from Russia, to verifiably eliminate massive attack options from nuclear war plans.
- Beginning talks among the nuclear weapons states for verifiably removing all nuclear weapons from hair-trigger alert.

Secure, monitor, and greatly reduce fissile materials and warhead stockpiles by
- Helping to install modern security and accounting systems and providing resources and incentives for sustaining effective security at all Russian nuclear facilities.
- Helping to consolidate Russia's fissile materials into the smallest number of sites
- Promoting alternative employment in Russian nuclear cities.
- Building a comprehensive transparency and monitoring regime for all warheads and fissile materials.
- Negotiating reductions in fissile material stocks in excess of that needed to support a stockpile of 1,000 warheads.

The arms control process has been stalemated for six years and is now in jeopardy of being put on hold indefinitely. To continue to let the formal treaty process run its course (waiting on START II) invites a nuclear accident within Russia and the worst proliferation nightmare imaginable. Distinguished delegates, for the next ten days, it is imperative that you create a list of constructive and politically solid recommendations for the 2000 review conference, as well as your report to that conference. Concerted effort to achieve the goals presented here offer the best hope of not only getting the process moving again, but moving in earnest the two countries toward fulfilling their obligations under Article VI of NPT.

Convenors: Jesse James, Committee on Nuclear Policy, Henry L. Stimson Center, 11 DuPont Circle NW, 9th fl. Washington, DC 20036, tel 202.691.4025; fax 202.238.9604; jjames@stimson.org
Vladimir Iakimets, Center for Russian Environmental Policy, Moscow, Russia iakim@glasnet.ru

TOPIC 3: NATO Nuclear Strategy Review, No First Use, Pre-emptive Counter-Proliferation
PRESENTER: Sharon Riggle, Center for European Security and Disarmament

Mr. Chairman, thank you for the opportunity to address this meeting. It is especially timely to highlight the ramifications to the NPT of NATO's new Strategic Concept, finalized just two weeks ago at the NATO Summit. NATO has announced that it will start a review of its non-proliferation, arms control and disarmament policy, and will provide the initial results of this in December of this year. Until then it is likely that NATO will decide either to increase the role of nuclear weapons in the Alliance, or to decrease this role and make substantive progress on Articles I, II and VI of the NPT. Of these two options, only the latter is compatible with strengthening the NPT.

In this statement we will first comment on the role of nuclear weapons in NATO, the continuation of nuclear sharing arrangements and the possible introduction of counter-proliferation tasks. We will then comment on NATO's new arms control policy review, and finally on NATO-Russia relations.

First, we draw your attention to the role of nuclear weapons in NATO. None of the fundamental principles of NATO's nuclear weapons policy have changed in the new Strategic Concept. Thus, NATO still reserves the right to use nuclear weapons first in any military conflict, nuclear weapons are still considered an essential political and military link between Europe and the North American members of the Alliance, and NATO will continue its controversial and unique policy of nuclear sharing.

It is unacceptable that NATO has not further downgraded the role of nuclear weapons in the Alliance. NATO should make explicit that it has no use for nuclear weapons other than to repel nuclear attack, by adopting a no first use policy. As all Alliance members are states party to the NPT and committed to the aims of the Treaty, NATO should also make clear that its ultimate goal is the complete elimination of nuclear weapons. In the interim, language is required to clarify that nuclear weapons are solely weapons of last resort, spelling out that 'last resort' covers only the one case the International Court of Justice did not definitively rule out as illegal, namely that if the very survival of a state is at stake.

In addition, we draw your attention to the continuation of nuclear sharing within NATO, which is itself a refutation of, and challenge to, the international norm against ownership and use of nuclear weapons. NATO is the only military alliance in which nuclear weapon states and non-nuclear-weapon states participate together in collective defense planning in nuclear roles, in peacetime basing of nuclear forces on [non-nuclear-weapon state] territory and in command, control and consultation arrangements. We raise once again the question of whether NATO's nuclear sharing arrangements contravene Articles I and II. It is clear that there is serious concern about this, as was expressed by the Non-Aligned Movement working paper at last year's PrepCom and the South African statements in 1997. The NPT Review Process is the appropriate forum in which to address this question

The new strategy for the first time commits NATO's military capabilities to playing a role in countering the proliferation of weapons of mass destruction, while stopping short of openly assigning them a role in preemptive military action. We are worried that this could be interpreted in different ways, paving the way to a future expansion of the role of nuclear weapons within the Alliance to explicitly include counter-proliferation tasks. This would violate the negative security assurances of NATO's nuclear weapon states given in UN Security Council Resolutions 984 and 255, which do not exclude biological- and chemical- armed non-nuclear-weapon states.

Moreover, NATO's nuclear and non-nuclear-weapon states would violate Articles I and II of the NPT if nuclear counter-proliferation were officially included in NATO's nuclear strategy. Under NATO's nuclear sharing arrangements, counter-proliferation would require non-nuclear-weapon states to prepare for and participate in NATO nuclear missions against non-nuclear-weapon states believed to own or to have used biological or chemical weapons - a clear violation of the NPT commitment to not transfer the control of nuclear weapons. Even NATO's heavily disputed wartime exemption (which it uses to legitimize its nuclear sharing arrangements) does not allow NATO's non-nuclear-weapon members to participate in offensive nuclear counter-proliferation missions. When explaining the wartime exemption at the time of ratifying the NPT, US officials made it clear that it referred to general war, defined as the time during and after a massive nuclear exchange, not regional wars. Thus, outside of general war the use of US nuclear weapons by an allied nation constitutes a violation of Articles I and II even by NATO standards.

Further, linking military capabilities to counter-proliferation implies that NATO is undermining the Biological Weapons Convention and the Chemical Weapons Convention. Counter-proliferation tasks involve preparing unilateral measures to respond to possible proliferation, instead of promoting the internationally agreed mechanisms to deter and respond to chemical and biological warfare proliferation.

We now draw your attention to NATO's new arms control policy review process, including its nuclear weapons. The Alliance's Summit Communique announces that, in the light of overall strategic developments and the reduced salience of nuclear weapons, the Alliance will consider options for confidence-and-security-building measures, verification, non-proliferation and arms control and disarmament. We strongly support the position of the German and Canadian Foreign Ministries that this process should include a full review of NATO's nuclear doctrine, and emphasize that the review should be as comprehensive and transparent as possible. NATO has pledged to report the initial findings of the review to the meeting of the North Atlantic Council in December 1999. Governments around the world, NGOs and the public will carefully watch the outcome, which may provide important input for the 2000 NPT Review Conference. We are encouraged by the vote on the New Agenda Resolution 53/77Y last year in the General Assembly, especially since it received a margin of support from a majority of NATO states. These states must now make sure that NATO seriously considers the proposals made in the resolution.

Finally, we call on NATO to honor its commitment to develop good relations with Russia. NATO should make its agreement not to deploy nuclear weapons in the Alliance's new member states in peacetime legally binding. In addition, NATO must take care that any possible future enlargement is handled sensitively. NATO should attempt to revive and strengthen the activities of the NATO-Russia Permanent Joint Council, the only body currently consulting on nuclear arms control and disarmament on a multilateral level.

We also call on NATO to end its nuclear sharing arrangements, by withdrawing all its

European-based tactical nuclear weapons. Such disarmament is in the interest of both NATO and Russia for at least three reasons. First, it serves to protect against the risk that Russia may develop its version of a flexible response strategy, a decision which has already been indicated by initial Russian steps to develop a new generation of tactical nuclear weapons. Second, it would give NATO political leverage to embark on new arms control arrangements with Russia, which is especially important now that the START process has come to a halt. And third, it would stimulate comprehensive international disarmament, thereby fulfilling Article VI commitments.

To conclude: More than ten years after the end of the Cold War, it is high time that NATO aligns its nuclear policy with the NPT. The current policy includes aspects out of step with today's security environment. NATO - by far the strongest military alliance in the world - could reduce its reliance on nuclear weapons without any loss of security or cohesion in the organization. The new arms control review is the last opportunity before the year 2000 NPT Review Conference for NATO members to indicate whether they will undertake substantive nuclear disarmament measures, or whether they intend to rely on nuclear weapons indefinitely. Either way the repercussions for the NPT will be great.

Convenor: Henrietta Wilson, Oliver Meier, Berlin Information-center for Transatlantic Security (BITS), Rykestrasse 13, D-10405 Berlin, Germany
tel +49 30 441 0220; fax +49 30 441 0221, e-mail henrietta.wilson@bits.de

TOPIC 4: Regional Proliferation Issues
PRESENTER: M.V. Ramana, Center for Energy and Environmental Studies, Princeton

Exactly one year ago, on this very day, India conducted a set of three nuclear explosions; reverberations from these still continue to affect us all. They were followed shortly thereafter by more explosions at the same site and nuclear tests by Pakistan. The last year has also seen the continued lack of cooperation by Iraq and intransigence by Israel with regard to their nuclear programs. There was also the launch of a new missile, or satellite, by North Korea, and indications from Belarus of renewed interest in nuclear weapons. All of these have made the task of nuclear disarmament even more urgent than ever.

The actions of these states, and those of the Nuclear Weapon States, are quite in contrast to the record of most of the countries that signed the Nuclear Non-Proliferation Treaty. It is clear that the vast majority of the international community rejects the notion of nuclear weapons as providing any kind of benefit. We completely share this sentiment and hope that these few recalcitrant states also realize this soon.

South Asia: The events surrounding the nuclear tests conducted by India and Pakistan are sufficiently well known and it is not necessary to delve into them in detail. There is little doubt that the chief motivations and pressures to conduct these tests were domestic. However, in explaining the decision to test, the Indian Prime Minister and senior policy makers mentioned several external reasons. These included an inequitable international non-proliferation regime and a threat from a nuclear-armed China. Earlier on, India had also pointed to the US stockpile stewardship program, as one of its reasons to vote against the Comprehensive Test Ban Treaty. Regardless of their veracity, these claims allowed the government to justify its actions and the sudden change of policy to its citizens. Recognizing the role played by the nuclear weapon states in India's decision does not in any way legitimize India's actions.

Pakistan, for its part, has firmly tied its own policies to India. This has created a situation wherein two neighboring states, with a history of conflict and an unresolved dispute that has led to two wars in the past, possess nuclear weapons. The recent missile tests only exacerbate the dangers.

While a sustainable solution, here as elsewhere, requires the complete abolition of nuclear weapons from the region and the world, there are some temporary palliatives that could help. The international community must continue to pressure the two countries not to follow the example of the Nuclear Weapon States by deploying their nuclear weapons. Further, the two governments should be encouraged to follow the suggestions of several peace groups in their own countries and stop the missile race as well as move the existing missiles away from their border, thereby lowering chances of misperception and accidental conflict. While the events of the past month have lowered the chances of India's signature to the CTBT before September 1999, the two countries should be invited to at least formalize their existing moratoria on nuclear tests in the meanwhile and sign the CTBT at the earliest possible date. And, last, we also request the international community to help stop the repression of those opposed to the tests and similar developments in the two countries.

Middle East: The lack of any movement in the Middle East with regard to the nuclear question is also troubling. The paralysis of the peace process and the vetoing of any course of engagement or cooperation with Iraq by some of the nuclear weapon states only compound the problem. It is vital that progress be made on the Middle East Resolution that was agreed to as part of the NPT extension package. The countries of the region as well as the Nuclear Weapon States must do their part in ensuring the implementation of this resolution.

The methods used to require compliance in this region also deserve scrutiny. Just as in the nuclear weapon states, these countries also started their nuclear programs in secret; their citizens had little control over the process. Thus, punishing the people of these countries, Iraq in particular, by imposing sanctions for actions of the state is unjust and morally unacceptable. Further, by adding to people's sense that the international system is loaded against them, sanctions only increase support for nuclear and other weapon programs.

North Korea: Another region where little progress has been made is North Korea. The test of a new, multi-stage launcher, and reports of manufacture of several nuclear warheads, transfer of missile technology and building a new underground nuclear facility raise serious concern. We are appalled that with famine threatening much of its population, the government of North Korea would choose to invest its resources on such programs. This tragedy only speaks to the necessity of finding ways of changing the current state of affairs. These require immediate implementation of the 1994 KEDO (Korean Economic Development Organization) agreement with all parties delivering their commitments.

Belarus: The recent statement by the President of Belarus that the decision to withdraw nuclear weapons from his country was a mistake and that he would welcome them back, demonstrates the reversible nature, at least potentially, of NPT accession. Just as in Russia, this indicates the increasing role played by nuclear weapons in the thinking of Belarus despite the end of the Cold War. This statement is also an example of the many non-nuclear factors that influence the nuclear policies of different countries. In the case of Belarus, the statement is clearly linked to NATO expansion. There is little doubt that their desire for nuclear weapons has been strengthened by NATO's bombardment of Yugoslavia without resorting to the United Nations. Such actions must be firmly rejected.

Conclusion: By developing nuclear weapons, investing large amounts of resources into creating huge arsenals, and going to great lengths to preserve these arsenals, nuclear weapon states have set a bad example. Several countries, in particular India and Pakistan, seem to have learnt the wrong lesson from these examples. Despite their treaty commitments, other countries like Iraq and North Korea have also tried, with mixed results, to go the same route. It is clear that unless the nuclear weapon states deliver their Article VI commitments rapidly, the propensity for other countries to acquire nuclear weapons will only increase. Thus, the events of the last year have only highlighted the necessity of achieving a comprehensive nuclear disarmament regime as soon as possible. The time to start on that path is now.

Convenor: M.V. Ramana, Center for Energy and Environmental Studies, Princeton University, Princeton, NJ 08544, USA tel 1.609.258.1761; fax 1.609.258.3661; ramana@princeton.edu

TOPIC 5: Comprehensive Comprehensive Test Ban Treaty
PRESENTER: Tom Z. Collina, Union of Concerned Scientists

Thank you Mr. Chairman and delegates for affording the non-governmental organizations (NGOs) the opportunity to communicate their views and recommendations. We wish you success in your efforts at this important gathering. It is my task to convey to you the views of NGOs on a matter that is central to the nuclear non-proliferation treaty and the fulfillment of obligations made in New York in 1995 - the Comprehensive Test Ban Treaty. The CTBT limits the development of nuclear weapons by all states and is thus vital to the security of all nations.

One year ago this week, India and Pakistan's nuclear tests sent tremors around the globe. Those tests reminded the international community of the continuing risks of nuclear weapons and nuclear war, and the necessity of achieving concrete progress toward nuclear restraint - particularly the Comprehensive Test Ban Treaty.

Fortunately, the nuclear tests in South Asia were short-lived. Additional rounds of testing did not follow. Key to this restraint was the strong condemnation of the tests from the international community and the promises by both nations to refrain from further nuclear tests.

Now, on the nuclear testing front at least, the two nations are moving in the right direction. In statements here in New York at the United Nations last September, Prime Ministers of both nations said they would not impede the treaty's entry into force by September of 1999, when a special conference of CTBT states parties will be convened to expedite the treaty's entry into force. The government of India has since changed. Living up to the promise of its predecessor will be a true test of the new Indian government's commitment to disarmament.

The situation could still spiral out of control if India and Pakistan do not chose the path of restraint embodied by the CTBT. This important norm has been greatly enhanced by the fact that 152 nations have signed the Treaty and 33 have ratified.

The CTBT has a special place here in the NPT review process. You will recall that a central outcome of the 1995 NPT extension conference was a commitment to conclude negotiations on the CTBT by 1996, a commitment that was kept. But the task of realizing the full benefits of the CTBT is not yet complete and it requires your urgent attention and action. Many hope that the CTBT will enter into force - or at least be well on its way - before the fall 1999 CTBT Special Conference or the 2000 NPT review conference, one year from now.

Unfortunately, the prospects for entry into force of the CTBT in the next 12 months are not good. Of the 44 states whose ratifications are required for entry into force, only 17 have done so, and the key nations that should be leading the charge - the United States, Russia and China - have not yet ratified.

You all have no doubt heard about the obstructionist role being played in the United States by the chairman of the Senate's Foreign Relations Committee, Jesse Helms, and the Republican Majority Leader, Trent Lott. But make no mistake, it is incumbent upon President Clinton to take this issue to the Senate and the American public - which overwhelmingly supports the test ban treaty--in order to prompt Senate approval for ratification. However, he has not yet done so.

So we respectfully suggest to you, delegates of non-ratifying nations, do not wait for the United States to take the lead. Move ahead to ratify this important treaty with the goal of safeguarding your own national security and the purpose of isolating those that have not ratified.

We would also like to remind you of the fact that there will be an extremely important event this fall that can help make it clear who has ratified and who has not and to help expedite CTBT entry into force -- the upcoming Article XIV Special Conference on CTBT entry into force.

The powers of the special conference are intentionally vague but potentially far-reaching. If a state wishes to have a voting voice in the outcome of the Special Conference, it must ratify the Treaty. For the special conference to succeed in facilitating the CTBT's entry into force, it must be a large convocation of political leaders, non-governmental organizations and the media.

Two venues are being considered for the Special Conference - Vienna and New York. Vienna is the home of the Comprehensive Test Ban Treaty Organization, the treaty's implementing body. New York is where the CTBT was opened for signature. We believe the first conference must focus on political and not technical implementation. A high-profile Special Conference in New York would be most suitable for this function.

The cherished goal of CTBT entry into force can be achieved by the 2000 NPT review - but only if treaty supporters convene a special conference under circumstances that are likely to accelerate ratifications. We respectfully ask each of your governments and the NPT Prep Com as a whole to express support for a Ministerial-level Special Conference on CTBT entry into force this fall. A group of NGOs have recently released a report on the CTBT entry into force conference to help provide information and ideas on the subject.

The global norm against testing is enhanced by the mere existence of the CTBT. But without entry into force the verification regime cannot be fully activated, and the deterrent effect of the Treaty will not be fully felt. This increases the possibility that a "seismic event" of unknown origin will go unresolved, that suspicions will rise, that nations will break out of the Treaty on the assumption - mistaken or not - that an adversary has cheated.

In this context it is all the more important that the nuclear weapon states refrain from activities that could be confused with underground nuclear tests. "Stockpile Stewardship" activities, such as "subcritical experiments" conducted by the US and Russia, have already led to accusations of cheating. Discontinuing such experiments at the test sites and closing these sites--as France did - would be very helpful. At the least, all weapons states must conduct nuclear weapons research with the utmost transparency to avoid the appearance of violating the treaty.

The CTBT is too important to global security to be cheated out of its rightful entry into force. States that have not done so must stand up and be counted and ratify this treaty. Do not wait for the United States. In fact, isolating the US is the best way to get our obstructionist Senate to take notice.

We respectfully urge this body and individual member nations to reiterate their commitment to the CTBT and take the actions necessary to ensure early entry into force. Thank you.

Convenor: Tom Z. Collina, Union of Concerned Scientists, 1616 P. St. NW, Suite 310 Washington, DC 20036, USA, Tel 1.202.332.0900; fax 1.202.332.0905; tcollina@ucsusa.org

TOPIC 6: Strengthening and Universalizing the NPT: Program of Nuclear Laboratory Testing
PRESENTER: Daniel Durand, Le Mouvement de la Paix

Mr. Chairman, distinguished delgates, permit me to thank you for giving the NGOs who work for nuclear disarmament the opportunity to present their remarks. I will present some observations regarding nuclear testing in the laboratory. We believe that the NPT Review Conference of the year 2000 is confronted with the following challenge: The NPT can only become universal if all its aspects mark substantial advances, including the one about continuing and accelerating nuclear disarmament, as stated in Article VI.

In this respect, we believe that experiments envisaged in projects such as the NIF (National Ignition Facility) or the megajoule laser by some nuclear powers, in particular the United States and France, are likely to:

- Disturb the 2000 NPT Review Conference by slowing down its universalization and putting obstacles to the last non-signatory countries joining in.
- Stop the complete CTBT ratification in 2000: these illegal programmes in regard to the CTBT may also prevent some nuclear threshhold countries to sign it.
- Give a new boost to unnecessary military spending while socially useful spending should be developed instead.

Given these dangers, we suggest, in the framework of a comprehensive approach to nuclear weapon abolition as early as possible, as stated in article 6 of the NPT, that:

- Nuclear powers give international observers free access to facilities and programmes (in the framework of the IAEA), in order to check the stated goals of a mere maintenance of existing stockpiles, set up transparency and confidence-building measures. This could be subject to a recommendation in a CTBT appendix.

- Nuclear powers announce an immediate moratorium on laboratory nuclear experiments, in order to facilitate the ratification and entry into force of the CTBT and universalization of the NPT, until checks are operated and conclusions made.

The previous moratorium on underground tests decided in 1992-94 by Russia, the United States and France greatly helped CTBT negotiations. This moratorium could come together with information policies and a report on experiences already started vis-a-vis States parties to the various treaties (NPT, CTBT). Once the complete universalization of NPT is achieved, as well as the CTBT ratification, this moratorium could shift into a definitive halt, depending on the progress of negotiations for a complete ban of nuclear weapons.

Laboratory testing and the NPT: New Weapons: Today, even though the scientific feasibility of so-called "pure fusion weapons" has not been fully proved, if technical obstacles were overcome, the use of nuclear weapons as war instruments could be fundamentally changed. This development would pose completely new proliferation risks, thus radically reducing the chance to achieve complete and lasting nuclear disarmament. According to official documents of the French Programme PALEN (Program to Limit Nuclear Testing) and US plans for the Stockpile Stewardship programme, these projects aim at maintaining and exercising the capacity to design new nuclear weapons.

It is most conceivable that the scientific experts of these programs may at least carry out preliminary investigations to design pure fusion weapons, once the necessary data are available. If one were to believe the US DOE, it is not only necessary to maintain sophisticated facilities to attract and keep scientists in structures of research, it is also necessary to provide them with the opportunity to practice their designing skills. It is worth noting that the American and French governments deny that they intend to design new weapons. Yet, their current technical work would produce such weapons, since it is compatible with the research and development of pure fusion weapons.

Regarding the proliferation of "sensitive" information: the development of research on inertial confinement and pure fusion can result in the circulation of computer codes and information on the physical aspects of thermonuclear explosives, given that most of these facilities include research aspects with no military objective. For example, astro-physical experiments would be conducted at the NIF as well as at the Megajoule in Bordeaux, France, and experiments conducted in these facilities, which are not completely secret, are then replicated in non-nuclear weapon states such as Germany and Japan.

Laboratory experiments and the CTBT: This aspect is addressed in a specific contribution. According to our fact finding, the NIF, the megajoule laser and all other facilities designed to create thermonuclear explosions, even of a few pounds of TNT equivalent, are illegal in the framework of the CTBT. Even their construction is illegal since the CTBT demands both the prevention and banning of explosions. Signatories also have the obligation not to "provoke, encourage, or take part in any way in the smallest nuclear explosion."

Some nuclear powers act as if their projects were legal with respect to the CTBT. Such an interpretation is clearly unacceptable. An official standpoint by the CTBT Review conference, which would define an explosion with respect to the treaty objectives and set up limits on research based on that definition, is necessary indeed. It should take into account the intention clearly stated in the CTBT to limit the development of new weapons.

Consequences related to the cost of research programmes: Because of their high cost, of the necessary technological standard, these experiments are for a small club of wealthy and powerful countries, which maintain and develop a "technological military gap" that can halt the confidence-building atmosphere which should be broadened. Moreover, this paralyzes resources in work not in conformity with State obligations whereas in these countries, civil research, social needs and education need additional funding.

CONCLUSION: The end of the Cold War has offered humankind a historic opportunity to get rid of nuclear weapons. The question is not only raised in general terms but in a concrete way to speed up the necessary complex elimination process. All development by the nuclear powers of new technological-military nuclear research is antithetical to this process. Declaring moratoria on the work of the American NIF, the French megajoule, and all similar projects would be a sensible proposal and we ask you that you consider it. Thank you again, Mr. Chairman, distinguished delegates, for your attention.

Convenor: Daniel Durand, Le Mouvement de la Paix, 139 bd Victor Hugo / F - 93400 ST-OUEN tel 33.1.4012.0912; fax 33.1.4011.5787 email: ddurand@mail.asi.fr   http://www.asi.fr/~ddurand/

TOPIC 7: Nuclear Energy: We Know Better Now
PRESENTER: Felicity Hill, Womens International League for Peace and Freedom

Article IV of the NPT, the mandate of the IAEA (International Atomic Energy Agency) and agreements made between the IAEA and the World Health Organization are documents of their time and reflect historically specific moments in science and in politics. Assumptions made in 1945, or 1968 about nuclear technology have to be reevaluated in a world that has experienced Chernobyl and Three Mile Island. When the Non-Proliferation Treaty was negotiated, nuclear power was still a relatively new technology. There were high hopes and indeed some assumptions that it would be safe, clean and cheap and that its proliferation risks could be contained. Experience has now given us the data to say that these assessments cannot be supported. Indeed the risks were gravely underestimated.

In 1999, the inalienable right to nuclear energy as enshrined in Article IV amounts to the inalienable right of an expensive industry to massive subsidies, the inalienable right to expose citizens to routine hazardous releases of radiation and the inalienable right to produce a riddle science cannot yet solve: large quantities of radioactive waste. It is inappropriate to define an activity that is limited to one or two generations in benefit, but results in a liability that will persist for thousands human generations to come, as an "inalienable right".

Based on the facts now available to us about so-called peaceful uses of nuclear energy, we will address four areas in this paper: economics, proliferation, releases of radiation and waste.</font>

Economics: Nuclear energy is heavily subsidised for political reasons. On Capital Hill in the United States the estimate for the money spent on building reactors that has not yet been recovered is USD $600 billion. When faced with such enormous figures, in this case a 600 billion opportunity cost, we must wonder what renewable, clean, and democratic forms of energy could have been created with such resources. To give an example, $1.7 billion was spent on doing a feasibility study of a waste repository site at Yucca Mountain in the US, whereas 1.9 billion of public funds was spent on solar energy research between 1970 and 1994.

So has nuclear electricity been "too cheap to meter" as the early propaganda predicted? The answer is no. In many countries nuclear power requires direct taxpayer subsidy to be viable. In the United States, where nearly one quarter of the currently operating reactors are located, electric utility restructuring is subjecting nuclear power to customer choice and competition for the first time. Nuclear power averages at up to 12 cents a kilowatt hour in the US, whereas natural gas and wind turbines are both delivering electricity consistently as low as 3 cents a kilowatt hour - one quarter of the cost.

Industrialised countries are all phasing out nuclear energy facilities or planning to do so, due to well-informed community opposition in the north. The energy assistance offered to the global south by industrialised countries, under the pretext of honouring inalienable rights, is actually debt producing, and has the function of maintaining the wealth of large corporations from the north who have not converted their priorities or technology when faced with the hard economic facts of their industry. We see this in the marketing offensive, especially directed at Asia and former Soviet republics at this time.

The search for electricity free of CO2 emissions has currently revived interest in nuclear technology. Indeed, the discovery of global warming has become a great marketing asset to the nuclear industry, an industry in decline. Global warming is a real problem and one that should be energetically addressed, but this serious problem cannot magically transform a problematic industry into a good source. Nuclear power plant optimisation is a bad solution to the greenhouse problem.

Agenda 21 calls on nations to find more effective systems for producing, distributing and consuming energy and for greater reliance on environmentally sound energy systems with special emphasis on renewable energy. Nuclear power plant optimisation as a solution to global warming will require massive investment which would divest resources from the development of clean and renewable energy, while compounding the threat of nuclear accidents and the problems of nuclear waste management. Mr. Chairman, the inalienable right of all peoples to sources of energy is not being disputed here. If there still needs to be a carrot in the NPT which would reward non-nuclear weapons states for not pursuing nuclear weapons with an energy technology, let that technology be renewable and clean. Nuclear power is neither. With fusion energy development we can expect the same products and by-products and we suggest that based on the facts, we know better now. Research and development into fusion energy should cease.

Proliferation: Let us now turn to proliferation issues. With the CTBT, the separation between peaceful uses and proliferation was defeated as an illogical, unscientific and politically dishonest argument. In effect, the entry into force provision of that treaty acknowledges that nuclear reactors equal the capacity for nuclear weapons programmes. We have seen, with the examples of Iraq and North Korea, evidence of this fact. With numerous sources of clean energy available at a much cheaper cost than nuclear energy - the motivation for wanting a nuclear energy programme must be seriously questioned.

Some positive developments in nuclear safeguards have taken place and should be built on. Agreements such as the 1994 Convention on Nuclear Safety go to the heart of the contradiction inherent in the mandate of the IAEA in recognising the difficulty of simultaneously promoting and controlling an industry. Article 8 paragraph 2 of this agreement states that, "each contracting party shall take the appropriate steps to ensure an effective separation between the functions of the regulatory body and those of any other body or organization concerned with the promotion or utilisation of nuclear energy." This article of the 1994 Convention makes visible the need to structurally alter the mandate of the IAEA on the understanding that history has proved the promotion and controlling function unworkable. If the International Atomic Energy Agency promoted the support of the development of sustainable and environmentally safe energy sources, it would be a mandate that fitted better with the role of safeguarding nuclear materials.

Routine Releases of Radiation: The nuclear industry is not clean. The release of radiation from nuclear testing and the routine release of radiation through reactors have contributed to the cancer plague of the 20th century. Genetic impacts are discussed less frequently than cancer. We now know that radionuclides with a long half-life are cumulatively loaded into the environment and may result in ongoing impacts on health as well as long-term damage to the gene pool. Altering the collective gene pool of life on Earth is not an experiment that is reversible. Science today understands in 1999 what it did not fully comprehend in 1945 or perhaps even in 1968: there is no safe level of radiation.

Waste: And there is no known solution to nuclear waste, all efforts to isolate the material permanently have failed. Therefore any claim for disposal of this material is premature, and must instead be viewed as simply the posture of an industry that must continue to generate this waste as a by-product of its activity. The movement of waste is simply transferring a problem from one place to another, it will not go away. The targeting of less powerful peoples and nations to become dump sites for the world's nuclear waste in the name of economic development is immoral, and should not be tolerated.

No sovereign nation on earth should be made to bear the brunt of the toxicity of the nuclear age. Without consulting the Australian government, the US-based company, Pangea, in partnership with British Nuclear Fuels Limited, has devised a centralised waste repository scheme which would have the hundreds of thousands of tons of irradiated fuel shipped from international sites to the Australian desert for burial. Aboriginal people, citizens and the Australian government have rejected this corporations marketing offensive firmly with Environment Minister, Senator Robert Hill stating," We have said clearly and unambiguously we are not interested in becoming a global waste dump." Two weeks ago, the Australian Senate unanimously passed a resolution in support of this position.

Under the guise of free trade, we are seeing a phenomenon from many industries including the nuclear industry that Hillary Wainwright describes in the following manner, "When multinational corporations don't get their way, the invisible hand of the market turns into a visible fist." The visible fist of the nuclear industry punches notions of democracy in the face as Pangea continues its marketing strategy despite the clear message delivered by this sovereign nation's political mechanism. We all know that the nuclear industry was a necessary component in the development of nuclear weapons, a programme which was conducted in secrecy and in violation of the most basic elements of democracy. How could the history and the culture of the nuclear power industry not be tainted by the fundamentally undemocratic development of nuclear weapons? While the Pangea initiative will fail, it does arouse some concern at the growing stacks of nuclear waste and it does put us all on warning not to repeat the behaviours of the nuclear weapons states in their nuclear inspired assaults on democracy, by truly making decisions about the legacy of the nuclear age in a democratic, open and accountable fashion. Any long-term plan for the storage of nuclear materials from reactors and from dismantled weapons, should not centralise waste, and should not transport waste - the dangers of both are ridiculously high. It should be internationally negotiated and verifiable, and should begin with the only solution to stopping the creation of more waste - closing down the industry as a bad mistake of history, of politics and of science which has since evolved.

Mr. Chairman, through exploring these four elements of Article IV we see it is the fault line along which the non-proliferation function of the Non-Proliferation Treaty cracks. It normalises and legitimises an industry which is economic insanity, environmental suicide, is mutagenic and cancerous.

CO-CONVENORS: Felicity Hill, Women's International League for Peace and Freedom, 777 U.N. Plaza, 6th floor, New York, NY 10017, tel: (212)682.1265; fax (212)286.8211; flick@igc.org
Merav Datan, International Physicians for the Prevention of Nuclear War ,727 Massachusetts Avenue, Cambridge, MA 02139, tel (617)868.5050; fax: (617) 868.2560; datan@igc.org
Mary Olson, Nuclear Information and Resource Service, 1424 16th Street NW, Suite 404, Washington, DC 20036, tel(202)328-0002: fax: (202)462-2183; maryo@nirs.org

**TOPIC 8: Indigenous Peoples Speak Truth to Power: Environmental and Human Health
Aspects of the Nuclear Age**
PRESENTER: Richard Salvador, Pacific Islands Association of NGOs

> Pray that we touch the Earth with kind and gentle hands,
> That Freedom will be found in this and other lands,
> And that Peace will reign all over the Earth.
> May the changing of the seasons
> Bring friends to your fireside,
> Happiness to you heart,
> Peace to your pathway,
> And good health throughout your years.
> May your camp forever be safe and warm,
> Secure away from harm and storm,
> And that good things will come your way,
> To warm your heart each and every day.
> May the warm winds of heaven
> Blow softly upon your house.
> May the Great Spirit
> Bless all who enter there.
> May your moccasins
> Make happy tracks
> In many snows,
> And may the rainbow
> Always touch your shoulder.

Wolf Spirit

Wolf Spirit's prayer, "that we touch the Earth with kind and gentle hands", must also be taken as an admonition to heed the warnings of humanity's combined actions against the Earth; from all corners of our globe, we witness major changes that bode ill for our continued survival. However, the most catastrophic consequences both for the environment as well as human health have been those generated by the Nuclear Age. For many Indigenous communities worldwide, the tale is a grim one, and if we as Indigenous peace advocates had a choice in the matter, we would rather focus our energies on work closer to home, like social and economic development and ensuring access to proper education for our peoples. However, the grim statistics of the Nuclear Age necessitate that we come to regional and international forums like these to continue to "tell the story" of those of us who form the underside of this history.

In spite of having our interests thwarted here time after time, however, we as Indigenous peoples continue to come here to seek redress of the violations of our fundamental human rights and right to self-determination as Peoples. We look to the noble aspirations of the UN Charter and all subsequent efforts to strengthen the resolve of this Institution in our struggles.

Thank you, Mr Chairman and Delegates of this the Third NPT PrepCom, for extending to us representatives of NGOs an opportunity to share our views and offer some of our ideas about ensuring a world without the threats posed by nuclear weapons.

Indigenous peoples have borne the brunt of nuclearism through the nuclear fuel cycle. This begins with uranium mining on their own lands, often doing the mining themselves with little or no protection, to having nuclear tests carried out on their lands, and culminating in their lands being used as radioactive nuclear waste dumps. We recognize that we are not the only ones who have been affected by this process. Nevertheless, with 70 percent of the world's uranium resources located on the lands inhabited by Indigenous Peoples in Africa, Asia, Australia and North and South America, and a vast network of mining extraction of these uranium resources, fraught with racism and irresponsible environmental practices, the net result is a toxic legacy to indigenous communities of genocidal proportions.

For each ton of uranium oxide, several thousand tons of 'tailings' remain behind as low level radioactive waste; just in one single site in Igloo, South Dakota, something of the order of 3.5 million tons of exposed tailings, which remain radioactive for hundreds of thousands of years, line the banks of a river and a creek near the city. Wind and rain spread the carcinogenic dust to the surrounding water, air and soil, thus contaminating agricultural and animal meat by-products and foods for human consumption.

This legacy of environmental contamination has exposed hundreds of indigenous communities to serious environmental and human health hazards. Why is such a legacy justified, and or allowed to exist, even as the United Nations and States Parties to the NPT proclaim the urgency of "curtailing" the proliferation of nuclear weapons?

As the World Uranium Hearing held in Salzburg, Austria in September, 1992, concluded, "The territories of Indigenous peoples, impoverished developing countries, and the global commons are frequently targeted for storage or dumping of waste, thus compounding international injustice."

Injustice is the key word here. Injustice in any part of the world and against any portion of humanity is an affront to humanity everywhere. The injustices of the Nuclear Age must be acknowledged and addressed by the international community. To do violence to the environments upon which Indigenous peoples have lived upon for millennia, is to commit the most appalling injustices against them, for it is by deliberate choice that many of them choose to abstain from industrialization.

Justice considerations also compel us to confront the international political economy of resource extraction and utilization and the attendant violence that is perpetrated against communities standing in the way of such resource acquisition. We see a direct connection between nuclear violations of our lands and colonialism. What we are experiencing is a foreign economic and political regime, imposing itself and depriving peoples of their rights to self-determination.

As Indigenous peoples, our demand for nuclear abolition is also a key component of our struggle to bring an end to the violence of colonial rule. As developments of recent years have shown, the fates of Indigenous and non-indigenous communities are intimately tied together.

It is time that local, national, regional and international bodies own up to the problems created by nuclear weapons and fuel production and begin a healing process that is overdue. States party to the NPT have and should bear the responsibility for ensuring that such a process begin and be supported.

You have before you the task of finding practical ways to stem the tide of proliferation of instruments of mass killing that lie dangerously close to your own doors. But any such effort must also re-visit the roots of nuclearism. We in the Indigenous communities around the world challenge this body to consider the national and global arrangements of power served by weapons of mass destruction.

As you deliberate in this the third year of your preparatory deliberations for the Formal Review in the millennial year, we urge you in the most strongest language possible to speak truth to power, to confront the bases of the threats to our collective security, and to propose radical changes to the manner in which Nations rely on out-dated military strategies that threaten millions of peoples and on the obliteration of our natural environment in order to maintain "security." Thank you.

Co-convenor: Richard Salvador, Pacific Islands Association of NGOs (PIANO), 2424 Maile Way, Porteus 640, Honolulu, Hawaii 96822, USA, tel 808.956.6877, salvador@hawaii.edu

Appendix: We strongly support the recommendations proposed in the Resolution submitted to the European Parliament in October 1997 by the Uranium Tour of Indigenous Peoples. The Resolution called for:

- an independent study about uranium imports/exports, analyzing the impact of uranium mining and processing on health and environment, on the rights of Indigenous peoples and on waste production of the mining operations in regard to the respective country of origin;
- a ban all imports of uranium from mines where the land rights of Indigenous Peoples are being compromised;
- a call to the governments of countries and the private companies involved to respect Indigenous Peoples inherent right to self-determination as well as their right to land, water and resources, including their right to end all ongoing and planned uranium mining activities on their territories or lands, and that the degree of clean-up and/or reclamation be determined and prescribed at the local level and by local people;
- a call for initiatives to reform Article 1 of the United Nations International Atomic Energy Agency (IAEA) and the creation of a new United Nations International Solar Energy Agency, and in any case to repudiate the May 1959 Agreement between the World Health Organization (WHO) and IAEA;
- a call to the international community to halt the construction of new nuclear power plants and to phase out all existing civilian and military plants;
- In addition, we also support the following recommendations put forward by Indigenous Peoples at the World Uranium Hearing in Salzburg, a call upon governments and, within their respective spheres of responsibility and competence, transnational and other corporations, organizations, communities and individuals:

1) To recognize and respect the inherent right to self-determination of indigenous peoples, including their right to determine and control, without external interference, the nuclear process as it affects their societies and territories;

2) To provide reparations for peoples, communities, and individuals victimized by the mining of radioactive minerals, the use of nuclear weapons, or the storage or dumping of nuclear waste. To make every conceivable effort to alleviate risks and damage caused by past and existing uses of radioactive materials.

TOPIC 9: PATHS TO ELIMINATION: QUALITATIVE MEASURES AND POLICIES
PRESENTER: TANYA PADBERG, BASIC (British American Security Information Council)

Distinguished delegates, we must not allow ourselves to be mesmerized and deluded by the numbers game - those vaguely comforting plans about reductions to 1000 warhead, then 200 warhead arsenals, then lower. Pending their complete elimination, it is just as or even more important to focus on *how* nuclear weapons are possessed and deployed, on qualitative disarmament measures and policies that reduce risks and set the stage for abolition.

Existing pledges of non-use against NPT non-nuclear weapon states must be fully respected. The nuclear weapon states should formally acknowledge that their negative security assurance declarations are legally binding - after all, they were given to induce acceptance of the indefinite extension of the NPT. The determination of whether a state is in good standing under the NPT and protected by the assurances is a matter for an authoritative international body, not unilateral decision by a nuclear weapon state. Exceptions should be ruled out. No planning for preemptive nuclear uses against chemical or biological weapon capabilities. No planning for reprisals against chemical or biological attacks. No other exceptions. The security assurances are an integral part of the NPT regime.

The security assurances further should be expanded into unconditional no-first-use commitments as against any state, whether possessing nuclear weapons or not. If nuclear arsenals are held *only* because other states have such arsenals, the logic of eliminating arsenals altogether rather than running the appalling risks that go under the label "deterrence" will become unassailable.

De-alerting of nuclear forces, most centrally through separation of warheads from delivery systems, must commence. This process is vital in its own right, to diminish dramatically the chance of accidental, unauthorized, or miscalculated detonations of nuclear explosives. It would reinforce and actualize existing security assurances and no-first-use commitments. It would allow the cessation of ongoing threats of use of force which would inflict indiscriminate harm, unnecessary suffering, and disproportionate damage to the environment - threats which the International Court of Justice held to be generally illegal. Finally, in lowering the political value of nuclear arsenals, it would smooth the way to reduction and elimination.

The facts regarding de-alerting are nothing less than compelling.

On 25 January 1995, the routine launch of a US scientific rocket off the western coast of Norway set off alarms in Russia, and almost led to global disaster. The first reports from Russia's early warning system indicated the rocket was potentially a Trident submarine-launched missile. For the first time ever, President Yeltsin activated his nuclear suitcase. Russia was literally minutes away from deciding whether to order a retaliatory strike. Finally, Russian officials correctly determined that the missile was not a threat, and the emergency passed. In 1997, reports in the US media indicated that deteriorating Russian command and control systems might have led to missiles switching to "combat mode" without warning. US systems have made related problems in the past, including a 1980 explosion that blew an intercontinental ballistic missile, with its warhead, out of its silo. These incidents demonstrate the dangers of maintaining the high alert status typical of the Cold War era.

In fact, despite the end of the Cold War, Russia and the United States still maintain thousands of warheads on high alert, ready to launch within minutes. A "paralysis of policy" exists in both countries, despite the fact that the two countries now cooperate on a wide range of economic, military, and political issues.

The United States and Russia have already taken steps to reduce the alert status of some nuclear systems, particularly tactical weapons. Thousands of warheads have been withdrawn from Europe and are being destroyed or stored. In Europe, NATO aircraft no longer sit on Quick Reaction Alert, with their electronics preheated and loaded with nuclear weapons, ready for immediate takeoff. The UK announced that its Trident nuclear-armed submarines will now be "routinely at a 'notice to fire' measured in days rather than the few minutes' quick reaction alert sustained throughout the Cold War". According to UK officials, however, this step is not a de-alerting measure. It will not be verifiable externally. Instead, the UK views it as a confidence-building measure, similar to the agreements to de-target nuclear missiles reached with Russia. Because the "notice to fire" status is not verifiable, its benefits are minimized.

Other steps are possible. For example, it is known that US submarines en route to their launch stations are on a modified alert status from which it takes approximately 18 hours to bring the submarine to full alert, ready for launch within minutes. It should be possible to verify this status externally without revealing the submarine's location. Steps to reduce the alert status could include leaving in place the flood plates that block missile launch tubes, removing guidance systems from missiles, or shutting down power to the missiles. These would increase the amount of time required to deliver missiles to their targets by hours or days.

More far reaching steps are also possible, such as removing warheads from missiles and storing them separately.

De-alerting is made more urgent by the well-known problem of the "millennium bug", when computers may be unable to identify correctly the date as the calendar goes to 2000. It may lead to widespread confusion, system failures, and accidents. The danger is not only precisely at midnight of the year 2000. Computer rollover dates can take place at any time, and depend on a number of internal, difficult to verify, timing mechanisms. Problems could occur months or even years after 2000.

Fortunately, the fictional "worst case", where nuclear weapons will explode or missiles launch because of computer failures, is incredibly unlikely. However, there is a substantial chance that some systems critical to maintaining nuclear arsenals, especially communications and early warning systems, may face unpredictable failures. The real "worst case" scenario is that human operators, in a time of crisis, will be given inaccurate or misleading information, and react in ways that only make any problem worse. An "accidental" nuclear war is not impossible. There are also risks associated with maintaining operational nuclear reactors.

Russia and the United States are aware of the danger caused by the combination of nuclear forces on high alert and potential Y2K failures, and were taking steps to attempt to address it. However, following the NATO attacks on Serbia, Russia announced that it was ending cooperation with the US on Y2K issues.

The simplest way to reduce the dangers associated with the Y2K problem would be to take de-alerting steps like those described earlier.

Since of the beginning of the nuclear era, the world has seen the time frame for potential nuclear catastrophe decline from weeks to days to hours to minutes. It is high time that all countries, but particularly Russia and the United States, take steps to remove the threat of global nuclear annihilation. Now, as during much of the Cold War, the chance of an immediate massive nuclear war exists as a policy option. It is time to remove that option, and reduce the likelihood of accident, mistake, or miscalculation, by taking nuclear weapons off alert.

In conclusion, we stress that qualitative disarmament measures and policies like de-alerting and no-first-use commitments, as well as quantitative reductions, can never substitute for the elimination of nuclear arsenals and capabilities. Since the Berlin Wall came down, the demand from all parts of the world for abolition has been escalating. The outrage over nuclear explosive testing after the 1995 Extension Conference is one example. Another is that there are now over 1400 groups who have endorsed the Abolition 2000 statement whose first point calls for conclusion by the year 2000 of a nuclear weapons convention that requires the phased elimination of all nuclear weapons within a time-bound framework, with provisions for effective verification and enforcement.

The civil rights movement in the United States had a slogan: "keep your eyes on the prize". So long as we keep our eyes on the prize of abolition, qualitative disarmament can help create a path to get us there.

Co-Convenors: John Burroughs, Lawyers Committee on Nuclear Policy, 211 E 43rd Street, Suite 1204 New York, New York 10017, tel: (212) 818-1861, fax. (212) 818-1857; lcnp@aol.com

Stephen Young, Coalition to Reduce Nuclear Dangers, 110 Maryland Avenue NE, Suite 201, Washington DC 20002, tel: (202) 546-0795; fax: (202)546-5142; coalition@clw.org

TOPIC 10: MULTILATERAL INSTRUMENTS AND FORUMS FOR NUCLEAR DISARMAMENT
PRESENTER: John Burroughs, Lawyers Committee on Nuclear Policy

Distinguished delegates,

Iin its historic 1996 advisory opinion, the International Court of Justice interpreted Article VI of the NPT and General Assembly resolutions dating back to the very first one, and unanimously concluded: *"There exists an obligation to pursue in good faith and bring to a conclusion negotiations leading to nuclear disarmament in all its aspects under strict and effective international control."*

An essential question to be asked, then, regarding every proposed or actual forum or instrument in this field, is: *Does it contribute to the achievement of "nuclear disarmament in all its aspects?"*

Recent General Assembly resolutions have recognized the imperative of conducting multilateral negotiations with the endpoint of "nuclear disarmament in all its aspects" in view. The resolution on follow-up to the ICJ opinion called for *"multilateral negotiations in 1999 leading to an early conclusion of a nuclear weapons convention."* [1] The New Agenda resolution, sponsored by a grouping of states cutting across traditional boundaries, affirmed that *"a nuclear-weapon-free world will ultimately require the underpinnings of a universal and multilaterally negotiated legally binding instrument or a framework encompassing a mutually reinforcing set of instruments."* [2]

The need to clarify the elements of the institutional framework for a nuclear weapon free world was anticipated by civil society organizations some years ago. This led a distinguished group of scientists, lawyers and arms control experts to draft a model nuclear weapons convention that provides for the prohibition and elimination of nuclear weapons in a series of graduated, verifiable [3] steps. A briefing book exploring the issues raised by the idea of a convention will be available next week. [4]

The New Agenda resolution also usefully identified a number of measures and mechanisms that the nuclear weapon states alone or together could take to diminish present risks as well as set the stage for agreeing upon elimination. These include *"reduction of reliance on non-strategic nuclear weapons and negotiation on their elimination"* and de-alerting of nuclear weapons and *"removal of warheads from delivery vehicles."*

---

[1] 53/77 W (4 December 1998)

[2] 53/77 Y (4 December 1998)

[3] Circulated within the UN as A/C.1/52/7.

[4] International Physicians for the Prevention of Nuclear Qar, International Association of Lawyers Against Nuclear Arms, International network of Engineers and Scientists Against Prolliferation, *Security and Survival: The Case for A Nuclear Weapons Convention.*

In general, the NPT nuclear weapon states, together with at least one outside party representing the international community, should begin now to discuss among themselves such matters as

- Transparency and accounting regarding warheads, fissile materials, and research and production infrastructures
- Verification of actual or proposed de-alerting measures and reductions in capabilities

Such cooperation would enhance present safety and security and facilitate negotiations on de-alerting and reduction and elimination of nuclear capabilities. The early participation of all states possessing nuclear weapons should be a high priority.

Unilateral actions, jointly coordinated actions, and bilateral and plurilateral cooperation and negotiations are all important. But there must also be successful multilateral forums and instruments. Most states are aware of the pressing need for the creation of a forum or forums that explicitly have under consideration the institutional framework for a nuclear-weapon-free-world and how to achieve it.

There are several proposals for an ad hoc committee or working group in the Conference on Disarmament, including two originating from NATO member states.[5] What these proposals have in common is that they recognize the validity of multilateral disarmament talks, if not outright negotiations. Consideration of the verification requirements for the elimination of nuclear arsenals could be one task of such a group.

There also have been proposals for intersessional working groups within the NPT, including a proposal for a working group to address a nuclear weapons convention.[6]

And, both the New Agenda resolution and the Durban Final Document of the 1998 Non-Aligned Movement conference, in different forms, call for the convening of a conference

---

[5] There are five proposals: 1) The South African proposal for an ad hoc committee to "deliberate upon practical steps for the systematic and progressive efforts to eliminate nuclear weapons as well as to identify if and when one or more such steps should be the subject of negotiations in the Conference." 2) The "NATO 5" (Belgium, Italy, Germany Netherlands, Norway) proposal for an ad hoc working group "to study ways and means of establishing an exchange of information and views within the Conference on endeavors towards nuclear disarmament." 3) The Egyptian proposal for an ad hoc committee to "commence negotiations on a phased program of nuclear disarmament with the objective of the complete elimination of nuclear weapons." 4) The Canadian proposal for an ad hoc committee for the substantive discussion of nuclear disarmament issues "with a view to identifying if and when one or more such issues might be negotiated multilaterally." 5) The G-21 proposal for an ad hoc committee on nuclear disarmament "to start negotiations on a phased program for the complete elimination of nuclear weapons within a specified framework of time, including a nuclear weapons convention."

See also the new Agenda resolution, para. 13: "*Calls* upon the Conference on Disarmament to establish an appropriate subsidiary body to deal with nuclear disarmament and, to that end, to pursue as a matter of priority its intensive consultations on appropriate methods and approaches with a view to reaching a decision without delay."

[6] NPT/CONF.2000/PC.1/II (Marshall Islands), para. 13

concerning nuclear disarmament.[7]

The various proposals just mentioned concern multilateral forums that could be employed if there was the requisite political will, especially on the part of the nuclear weapon states. The main item on the actually existing agenda for multilateral negotiations is a fissile materials treaty. These negotiations are critical because they address the key ingredients of nuclear arsenals. Progress is stalled, however, on the link between banning future production of such material and dealing with existing stocks. Both NGOs and governments need to think creatively about possible solutions that would break the impasse and also meet the criterion of effectively contributing to the achievement of "nuclear disarmament in all its aspects."

One approach would be a fissile materials framework agreement, modeled on such agreements as the Vienna Convention for the Protection of the Ozone Layer and the UN Framework Convention on Climate Change.[8] These agreements recorded commitments and goals, and established a process for further review and negotiation that led to agreements on implementing protocols. One advantage of a framework agreement is that it can be finalized within a reasonable period of time, leaving questions of detailed targets and implementation to further negotiation.

Thus a fissile materials framework agreement could include:
- A commitment to the complete elimination of nuclear weapons usable fissile materials and their permanent irreversible disposition under safeguards
- The establishment of formal negotiating machinery for realizing this commitment through a series of phased and interlinked stages, each involving negotiated targets on fissile material stockpile reductions, in relation to reductions and elimination of nuclear weapons arsenals and research and production infrastructures
- The establishment of a process for achieving transparency and accounting regarding existing stocks
- Initial limits on fissile materials stocks
- Targets for a first round of reductions
- A process for public review, reporting, and implementaion assessment

There are other possibilities as well that draw upon existing negotiating forums and instruments. Serious consideration of one such possibility, an NPT amendment conference, is

---

[7] Final Document of the Twelth Conference of Heads of State or government of Non-Aligned Countries, held at Durban, South Africa, 29 Aug. to 3 Sept. 1996, A/53/667, S/1998/1071 (13 November 1998, Annex, para 113. (The Heads of State or Government) called for "an international conference, preferably in 1999, with the objective of arriving at an agreement, before the end of this millennium on a phased programme for the complete elimiantion of nuclear weapons with a specified framework of time to eliminate all nuclear weapons, to prohibit their development, production, acquisition, testing, stockpiling, transfer, use and threat of use, and to provide for their destruction."

The New Agenda Resolution, para. 14, "Considers that an international conference on nuclear disarmament and nuclear non-proliferation, which would effectively complement efforts being undertaken in other settings, could facilitate the consolidation of a new agenda for a nuclear-weapon-free world."

[8] This is an idea developed by Zia Mian of Princeton University, and this discussion draws on his work. See Zia Mian and M.V. Raman, "Diplomatic Judo: using the NPT to Make the Nuclear-Weapon States Negotiate the Abolition of Nuclear Weapons," Disarmament Diplomacy, No. 36, April, 1998, available at www.gn.apc.org/acronym.

supported by some NGOs. An amendment could make the obligation not to possess nuclear weapons apply to all states parties, and a protocol or annex to the NPT could specify the necessary regulatory framework. States now outside the NPT could commit to joining the new abolition regime.

Under Article VIII, the amendment could not be adopted without the consent of the nuclear weapon states. If those states have the requisite political will to abolish nuclear weapons, an amendment conference may be the logical way to proceed. Absent such political will, the conference would at least serve to create a forum in which states could deliberate upon the framework of a nuclear-weapon-free world. If necessary, it could be a recurring process. An amendment conference need not destabilize the NPT. Seeking to make the non-possession norm universal does not imply that states do not value the existing partial non-possession norm. No one thought that if the Partial Test Ban Treaty amendment conference failed itself to produce a comprehensive test ban, states would therefore withdraw from the PTBT.

To summarize and conclude: every action, negotiation, instrument, and forum should be measured by whether it contributes to the achievement of "nuclear disarmament in all its aspects". This presentation should at least have served to underscore that fresh thinking, unconstrained by ideas deformed by the Cold War, is required to meet that criterion.

Convenor: John Burroughs, Lawyers Committee on Nuclear Policy, 211 E 43rd St., Suite 1204 New York, New York 10017, tel: (212) 818-1861; fax. (212) 818-1857; lcnp@aol.com

TOPIC 11: GENERAL AND COMPLETE DISARMAMENT
PRESENTER: Stephanie Fraser, Women's International League for Peace and Freedom

School shootings. Ethnic cleansing. Aerial bombings. Refugees. Cruise missiles. Coiled carbon strand weapons. Depleted uranium bullets. Oil slicks threatening a Bulgarian nuclear power plant. Research reactors on NATO's hit lists. Military domination of outer space. Rape as a weapon of war. Terror as a weapon of war. Mutilation as a weapon of war. These are some of the realities today.

To talk about general and complete disarmament in this time of war in Europe, Africa and South Asia and bombing in the Middle East may seem to be grasping at dreams, but these problems cry out for solutions. It is imperative that the question of general and complete disarmament be understood in the context of planetary survival. The weaponry of today is so powerful and expensive, the targets so utterly toxic, that the world can no longer afford war, financially and environmentally. There are poisonous chemicals and radioactive materials spread across the world. To blow them up with any sort of bomb puts us all at risk. Pollution knows no boundaries. Chernobyl taught us that.

The objective of general and complete disarmament in the NPT began as part of American and Soviet disarmament proposals submitted to the United Nations General Assembly in the early 1960s. It was an intense, dangerous period of the Cold War. Yet, these plans submitted by adversaries were remarkably similar; they both called for a step-by-step decrease in reliance on national armed forces and a parallel increase in UN peacekeeping capabilities. Over the course of time, the radioactive shadow of the Cold War loomed too large and the task of negotiating the goal of general and complete disarmament was broken down into individual arms control components.

The two references in the NPT to general and complete disarmament are used by some as a way to delay real movement forward on all levels of disarmament. There are those, Party to the NPT, who resist mechanisms for achieving nuclear disarmament by claiming that nuclear weapons abolition is to be finalized "pursuant to a treaty on general and complete disarmament..." This hard line position is simply wrong and is disproved by the International Court of Justice when, in its July 8, 1996 advisory opinion, the Court focused on the nuclear dimension and made no suggestion whatsoever that nuclear disarmament is contingent upon general and complete disarmament. Certain nuclear weapons states assert that the ICJ's opinion inaccurately represents the NPT and the state of the law. Why do they continue to resist what they agreed to nearly 30 years ago? Nuclear disarmament is related to but not dependent upon general and complete disarmament, and vice versa.

Electromagnetic weapons. Ionosphere-based weapons Acoustic weapons. Laser weapons. Devices based on nano-technology. Weapons which target one ethnic group based on their genetic makeup. These are only some of the horrifying developments that we need to nip in the bud. New ideas of security need to be fostered. The weapons systems of today are more complicated and their use has far reaching policy and environmental implications. For every dollar or ruble or rupee spent on war-making and death, food, medicine and human rights are stolen out of the lives of children.

New and developing weapons systems change the landscape of disarmament negotiations, speeding rapidly away from the ideal of general and complete disarmament. The weapons being used today are insidious and do not fit neatly into existing weapons categories. The prospect of space-based weaponry raises the specter of an entirely new theater of global warfare. Depleted uranium weaponry - made from the wastes created by the use of nuclear energy - scatters toxic waste and radioactive isotopes across landscapes that may be forever poisoned. This use of depleted uranium in war is antithetical to the ideas of using atomic technology for peaceful purposes. This kind of weaponry is not perceived to be within the scope of the NPT. That Depleted Uranium weapons are proliferating is a cause for concern. The implications of the use of Depleted Uranium should be the subject of discussion in this forum of the NPT review process.

Electromagnetic weaponry may have been employed in the current air war over Kosovo. It has damaging effects and could be developed into high-tech weapon of mass disruption. All the new weapons mentioned, and others not mentioned, are either highly toxic or have indiscriminate effects. If their production, proliferation and use are not opposed on all levels, we face widespread genetic mutations, crop failures due to environmental poisoning and unprecedented control from above.

While the need for comprehensive disarmament must never be allowed to be an excuse for failing to accomplish nuclear disarmament, it is also true that there can and should be a dynamic interaction between the two endeavors. This is well illustrated by the problem of missiles. The nuclear age has been characterized not only by nuclear explosives, but by their combination with missiles and computers. There is now a disturbing and potentially destabilizing resurgence of interest in ballistic missile defense. This ignores that a far more productive approach would be to control and eliminate the missiles actually or potentially posing the threat. Indeed, states urgently need to find a way to commence negotiations on this subject on a global basis. But missiles can carry nuclear, conventional, chemical or biological warheads, so their control will link nuclear and comprehensive disarmament.

Since the birth of the UN, resolutions have been introduced to the General Assembly calling for progress toward nuclear disarmament. They are opposed and sidelined by the Nuclear Weapons States. On the eve of the new millennium, your task in preparing for the 2000 NPT Review Conference is to move forward and put into place the mechanisms and frameworks that are needed to dismantle nuclear weapons arsenals. There are a number of programs and initiatives which aim at building a sustainable peace in the world. The Hague Appeal for Peace, an international conference meeting this week, builds on the First International Peace Conference in 1899 by envisioning an integrated program of disarmament, conflict prevention and transformation, strengthened and enforceable mechanisms of humanitarian law, and incisive efforts to redress the root causes of armed conflict. Governments and NGOs will have to join together in systematically applying conflict prevention and resolution measures and in carrying out the basic concept of the 1960s proposals for general and complete disarmament - a step-by-step reduction of national armed forces to a level where they are sufficient only for the defense of national territory, accompanied by a step-by-step enhancement of multilateral UN and regional conflict prevention capabilities.

In building a secure, just, peaceful world in the new century, we must understand the past and set our sights on the future, while addressing in diplomatic not military terms the difficult problems facing us today. The NPT recognizes that nuclear war is abhorrent and must never happen, and that "every effort should be made to avert the danger of such a war." Make every effort. Create peace. If we can risk global nuclear annihilation, we can surely risk general and complete disarmament.

Convenor: Stephanie Fraser, Women's International League for Peace and Freedom, 339 Lafayette St., New York, New York 10012, (212) 533-2125, sfraser@igc.org

TOPIC 12: NUCLEAR WEAPONS, ETHICS, MORALS AND LAW
PRESENTER: Jonathan Granoff, Lawyers Alliance for World Security

ETHICAL AND MORAL FRAMEWORK FOR ADDRESSING THE ISSUE

In his concurrence with the historic opinion of the International Court of Justice (ICJ) issued July 8, 1996, addressing the legal status of the threat or use of nuclear weapons,[1] Judge Ranjeva stated, "On the great issues of mankind the requirements of positive law and of ethics make common cause, and nuclear weapons, because of their destructive effects, are one such issue."[2] Human society has ethical and moral norms based on wisdom, conscience and practicality. Many norms are universal and have withstood the test of human experience over long periods of time. One such principle is that of reciprocity. It is often called the Golden Rule: "Treat others as you wish to be treated." It is an ethical and moral foundation for all the world's major religions.[3]

Several modern states sincerely believe that this principle can be abrogated and security obtained by the threat of massive destruction. The Canberra Commission highlighted the impracticality of this posture: "Nuclear weapons are held by a handful of states which insist that these weapons provide unique security benefits, and yet reserve uniquely to themselves the right to own them. This situation is highly discriminatory and thus unstable; it cannot be sustained. The possession of nuclear weapons by any state is a constant stimulus to other states to acquire them."

The solution can be stated simply: "States should treat others as they wish to be treated in return."[4] It is inconsistent with moral wisdom and practical common sense for a few states to violate this ancient and universally valid principle of reciprocity. Such moral myopia has a corrosive effect on the law which gains its respect largely through moral coherence. Can global security be obtained while rejecting wisdom universally recognized for thousands of years?

Judge Weeramantry said,"(E)quality of all those who are subject to a legal system is central to its integrity and legitimacy. So it is with the body of principles constituting the corpus of international law. Least of all can there be one law for the powerful and another law for the rest. No domestic system would accept such a principle, nor can any international system which is premised on a concept of equality."[5]

LAW AND VALUES: Law is the articulation of values. Values must be based on moral foundations to have credibility. The recognition of the intrinsic sacredness of life and the duty of states and individuals to protect life is a fundamental characteristic of all human civilized values. Such civilized values are expressed in humanitarian law and custom which has an ancient lineage reaching back thousands of years. They were worked out in many civilizations - Chinese, Indian, Greek, Roman, Japanese, Islamic, modern European among others. "Humanitarian law is an ever continuous development (and) grows as the sufferings of war keep escalating. With a nuclear weapon, those sufferings reach a limit situation, beyond which all else is academic."[6]

In testimony before the Court, then Foreign Minister of Australia Gareth Evans said, "The fact remains that the existence of nuclear weapons as a class of weapons threatens the whole of civilization. This is not the case with respect to any class or classes of conventional weapons. It cannot be consistent with humanity to permit the existence of a weapon which threatens the very survival of humanity. The threat of global annihilation engendered by the existence of such weapons, and the fear that this has engendered amongst the entire post-war generation, is itself an evil, as much as nuclear war itself. If not always at the forefront of our everyday thinking, the shadow of the mushroom cloud remains on all our minds. It has pervaded our thoughts about the future, about our children, about human nature. And it has pervaded the thoughts of our children themselves, who are deeply anxious about their future in a world where nuclear weapons remain.[7]

We must never forget the awesome destructive power of these devices. "Nuclear weapons have the potential to destroy the entire ecosystem of the planet. Those already in the world's arsenals have the potential of destroying life on the planet several times over."[8] Not only are they destructive in magnitude but in horror as well.[9]

Notwithstanding this knowledge we permit ourselves to continue to live in a "kind of suspended sentence. For half a century now these terrifying weapons of mass destruction have formed part of the human condition. Nuclear weapons have entered into all calculations, all scenarios, all plans. Since Hiroshima, on the morning of 6 August, 1945, fear has gradually become humanity's first nature. Human life on earth has taken on the aspect of what the Quran calls a long nocturnal journey, a nightmare whose end one cannot yet foresee."[10]

Attempting to obtain ultimate security through the ultimate weapon, we have failed for, "the proliferation of nuclear weapons has still not been brought under control, despite the existence of the NPT. Fear and folly may still link hands at any moment to perform a final dance of death. Humanity is all the more vulnerable today for being capable of mass producing nuclear missiles."[11] As the General Assembly in its "Declaration on the Prevention of Nuclear Catastrophe" in 1981 said, "all the horrors of past wars and calamities that have befallen people would pale in comparison with what is inherent in the use of nuclear weapons, capable of destroying civilization on earth."

A five megaton weapon represents greater explosive power than all the bombs used in World War II and a twenty megaton bomb more than all the explosives used in all the wars in history. Several states are currently poised ready to deliver weapons that render those used in Hiroshima and Nagasaki small. One megaton bomb represents the explosive force of approximately seventy Hiroshimas while a fifteen megaton bomb a thousand Hiroshimas. Judge Weeramantry emphasized that "the unprecedented magnitude of its destructive power is only one of the unique features of the bomb. It is unique in its uncontainability in both space and time. It is unique as a source of peril to the human future. It is unique as a source of continuing danger to human health, even long after its use. Its infringement of humanitarian law goes beyond its being a weapon of mass destruction, to reasons which penetrate far deeper into the core of humanitarian law."[12] We are challenged as never before: technology continues to slip away from moral guidance and law chases after common sense.

INTERNATIONAL COURT OF JUSTICE: When the International Court of Justice addressed the legal status of threat or use of nuclear weapons members of the nuclear club, which has since grown, asserted a principled reliance on nuclear weapons. The Court held that "the threat or use of nuclear weapons would generally be contrary to the rules of international law applicable to armed conflict, and in particular the principles and rules of humanitarian law" and that states are obligated to bring to a conclusion negotiations on nuclear disarmament in all its aspects[13]

Did the Court open the way for permissible uses of a nuclear weapon by saying that is "generally" illegal and that it could not say that there would never be an attack on a country that threatened its very existence to which nuclear weapons would be necessarily an illegal response? Did the Court acknowledge that there were conceivably hypothetically legally compliant uses? It quoted the UK's statement that "(I)n some cases, such as the use of a low yield nuclear weapon against warships on the high seas or troops in sparsely populated areas it is possible to envision a nuclear attack which caused comparatively few civilian casualties."[14] However, the Court further pointed out that no state demonstrated when even such a limited use would be justifiable or "feasible."[15]

The Court had already ruled unanimously that nuclear weapons must in any and all instances obey humanitarian laws of war. Can our most basic moral judgments founded on "dictates of conscience", "elementary considerations of humanity" which remain "fundamental" and "intransgressible" be squared with these devices?[16] It seems scarcely reasonable with respect to these humanitarian legal requirements that they can.[17]

The Court stated unequivocally that the rules of armed conflict, including humanitarian law, prohibits the use of any weapon that is likely to cause unnecessary suffering to combatants;[18] that is incapable of distinguishing between civilian and military targets;[19] that violates principles protecting neutral states (such as through fallout or nuclear winter);[20] that is not a proportional response to an attack;[21] or that does permanent damage to the environment.[22]

Under no circumstance may states make civilians the object of attack nor can they use weapons that are incapable of distinguishing between civilian and military targets. Regardless of whether the survival of a state acting in self defense is at stake, these limitations continue to hold. For this reason the President Judge stated in forceful terms that the Court's inability to go beyond its statement "can in no manner be interpreted to mean that it is leaving the door ajar to the recognition of the legality of the threat or use of nuclear weapons."[23] He emphasized his point by stating that nuclear weapons are "the ultimate evil, destabilize humanitarian law which is the law of the lesser evil. Thus the very existence of nuclear weapons is a great challenge to humanitarian law itself."[24]

The Court held that no formal testimony was presented that nuclear weapons can meet the humanitarian law requirements for their use.[25] The President Judge along with several other judges undertook to point out the illogic of the situation: "It would thus be quite foolhardy unhesitatingly to set the survival of a state above all other considerations, in particular above the survival of mankind itself."[26] The President Judge said, "Atomic warfare and humanitarian law therefore appear to me mutually exclusive: the existence of one automatically implies the non-existence of the other."[27] The Court said, "(M)ethods and means of warfare, which would preclude any distinction between civilian and military targets, or which would result in unnecessary suffering to combatants, are prohibited. In view of the unique characteristics of nuclear weapons the use of such weapons in fact seems scarcely reconcilable with respect to such requirements."[28]

Discordance between the incompatibility of these devices with the requirements of humanitarian law, the assertion that there could be possible instances in which their use could be legal and the reliance on the doctrine of deterrence compelled the Court to seek a resolution: "the long promised complete nuclear disarmament appears to be the most appropriate means of achieving that result."[29] The requirements of moral coherence and ethical conduct and the need for "international law, and with it the stability of international order which it is intended to govern,"[30] drive the imperative of nuclear disarmament.

ONGOING PROBLEM: Legal and moral questions continue to loom before us. We are not faced with nuclear policies founded on a strategy of dropping depth charges in mid-ocean or bombs in the desert. What the world faces is nuclear deterrence with its reliance on the horrific destruction of vast numbers of innocent people, destruction of the environment rendering it hostile to generations yet to be blessed with life.

Deterrence proponents claim that nuclear weapons are not so much instruments for the waging of war but political instruments "intended to prevent war by depriving it of any possible rationale."[31] The United States has boldly argued that because deterrence is believed to be essential to its international security that the threat or use of nuclear weapons must *therefore* be legal. The United States representative stated: "If these weapons could not lawfully be used in individual or collective self defense *under any circumstances* (emphasis added), there would be no credible threat of such use in response to aggression and deterrent policies would be futile and meaningless. In this sense, it is impossible to separate the policy of deterrence from the legality of the use of the means of deterrence. Accordingly, any affirmation of a general prohibition on the use of nuclear weapons would be directly contrary to one of the fundamental premises of the national security policy of each of these many states."[32]

It is clear that deterrence is designed to threaten massive destruction which would most certainly violate numerous principles of humanitarian law. Additionally, it strikes at generations yet unborn. Even in the instance of retaliation the moral absurdity challenges us. As Mexico's Ambassador Sergio Gonzalez Galvez told the Court, "Torture is not a permissible response to torture. Nor is mass rape acceptable retaliation to mass rape. Just as unacceptable is retaliatory deterrence - "You burnt my city, I will burn yours. "[33]

Professor Eric David, on behalf of the Solomon Islands, stated, "If the dispatch of a nuclear weapon causes a million deaths, retaliation with another nuclear weapon which will also cause a million deaths will perhaps protect the sovereignty of the state suffering the first strike, and will perhaps satisfy the victim's desire for revenge, but it will not satisfy humanitarian law, which will have been breached not once but twice; and two wrongs do not make a right."[34]

Judge Weeramantry rigorously analyzed deterrence theory:

1. Intention: "Deterrence needs to carry the conviction to other parties that there is a real intention to use those weapons in the event of an attack by that other party. A game of bluff does not convey that intention, for it is difficult to persuade another of one's intention unless one really has that intention. Deterrence thus consists in a real intention to use such weapons. If deterrence is to operate, it leaves the world of make believe and enters the field of seriously intended military threats."[35]

2. Deterrence and Mere Possession: "Deterrence is more than the mere accumulation of weapons in a storehouse. It means the possession of weapons in a state of readiness for actual use. This means the linkage of weapons ready for immediate take off, with a command and control system geared for immediate action. It means that weapons are attached to delivery vehicles. It means that personnel are ready night and day to render them operational at a moment's notice. There is clearly a vast difference between weapons stocked in a warehouse and weapons so ready for immediate action.

Mere possession and deterrence are thus concepts which are clearly distinguishable from each other.[36]

For deterrence to work one must have the resolve to cause the resulting damage and devastation. Is deterrence limited to depth charges in the ocean or strikes in the desert? Are we willing to permit global security to rely on a bluff? If it is not a lie but a resolve to be willing to destroy all, are we not reducing humanitarian law to being a mere servant of raw power? Is not the very definition of lawlessness when might claims to make right?

While deterrence continues to place all life on the planet in a precarious position of high risk, one must wonder whether it provides any possible security against accidental or unauthorized launches, computer error, irrational rogue actions, terrorist attack, criminal syndicate utilization of weapons and other irrational and unpredictable, but likely, scenarios. Did the Court undermine the continued legitimacy of deterrence? The Court stated clearly that "if the use of force itself in a given case is illegal for whatever reason the threat to use such force will likewise be illegal."[37]

The moral position of the nuclear weapons states is essentially that the threat to commit an illegal act of massive destruction of innocent people is legal because it is so horrible to contemplate that it ensures the peace. Thus the argument is that the threat of committing that which is patently illegal is made legal by its own intrinsic illogic. Does this engender moral coherence in the youth of the world to whom we must argue that violence and the threat of violence in daily life does not bring human fulfillment?

An unambiguous political commitment by the nuclear weapon states to the elimination of nuclear weapons evidenced by unambiguous immediate pledges never to use them first as well as placing the weapons in a de-alerted posture pending their ultimate elimination will promptly evidence the good faith efforts by the nuclear weapon states to reduce our collective risks. These steps increase our collective security, but are hardly enough to meet the clear decision of the court and the dictates of reason. Only commencement in good faith of multilateral negotiations leading to elimination of these devices will bring law, morals, ethics and reason into coherence. Only then will we be able to tell our children that ultimate violence will not bring ultimate security, a culture of peace based on law, reason and values will.

CONCLUSION: We are heartened by the level of cooperation articulated in the integrated human security agendas that emerged from the world summits of the 1990's which addressed our common environmental and human security concerns. However, it must be pointed out that to fulfill the commitments made at these summits a new level of cooperation is required. It is appropriate, therefore, that the United Nations has declared the first ten years of the 21st century as dedicated to the creation of a Culture of Peace. That Culture of Peace will require a pattern in which trust, respect and transparency will breed disarmament and reverse the pattern of fear and threat which have continued to justify irrational levels of armaments. According to the Brookings Institute the US alone has spent 5.8 trillion on nuclear arms since 1940.[38] General Dwight D. Eisenhower said, "Every gun that is made, every warship launched, every rocket fired signifies, in the final sense, a theft from those who hunger and are not fed, those who are cold and are not clothed. The world in arms is not spending money on arms alone. It is spending the sweat of its laborers, the genius of its scientists and the hopes of its children."

The moral experience of shame has been placed in us along with the moral sensibility of revulsion. What right do we have to organize ourselves such that we might give human beings the Sophie's choice of ending all life on the planet in order to save a human creation, the state. As General Omar Bradley stated, "We live in an age of nuclear giants and ethical infants, in a world that has achieved brilliance without wisdom, power without conscience. We have solved the mystery of the atom and forgotten the lessons of the Sermon on the Mount. We know more about war than we know about peace, more about dying than we know about living."

It is time that we took bold moves to change the moral incoherence of the 20th century for it is now time in which statesmen must delve deep into themselves and become men in a state of grace. Let us grasp this moment of hazard and opportunity with our full humanity. Ultimate hazard and horror is our future if we let it slip away; opportunity to lead the world in fulfilling nothing less than an ultimate moral imperative - nuclear disarmament -- is ours if we meet the challenge. This is a long journey that must take us from fear and incoherence into reason and moral coherence. Let it truly begin with us today. Thank you.

Co-Convenor: Myrna Pena, World Conference on Religion and Peace, 777 U.N. Plaza, 9th floor, NY, NY 10017, tel 212.687.2163; fax 212.983.0566; mpena@wcrp.org

Jonathan Granoff, Lawyers Alliance for World Security, Temple of Understanding, State of the World Forum, One Belmont Ave., #300, Bala Cynwyd, PA 19004, tel 610.668.5470; fax 610.668.5455; jgg786@aol.com

FOOTNOTES

[1] Legality of the Threat or Use of Nuclear Weapons, General List No. 95 (Advisory Opinion of the International Court of Justice of July 8, 1996). Unless otherwise noted, references are to this opinion, which was requested by the General Assembly. The historic importance of this decision cannot be overemphasized for it is the first judicial analysis of the issue by this international tribunal even though the first General Assembly Resolution, unanimously adopted January 24, 1946 at the London session, called for elimination of atomic weapons.

[2] Opinion of Judge Ranjeva, para. 105(2)E1.

[3] Buddhism: "Hurt not others in ways that you yourself would find hurtful." Udana-Varga, 5:18; Christianity: "All things whatsoever you would that men should do to you, do you even so to them." Matthew 7:12; Confucianism: "Do not unto others what you would not have them do unto you." Analects 15:23; Hinduism: "This is the sum of duty: do not unto others which would cause you pain if done to you." Mahabharata 5:1517; Islam: "No one of you is a believer until he desires for his brother that which he desires for himself." Hadith; Jainism: "In happiness and suffering, in joy and grief, we should regard all creatures as we regard our own self." Lord Mahavir 24th Tirthankara; Judaism: "What is hateful to you, do not do to your fellow man. That is the law; all the rest is commentary." Talmud, Shabbat 31a; Zoroastrianism: "That nature only is good when it shall not do unto another whatsoever is not good for its own self." Dadistan-I-Dinik, 94:5.

[4] See, excellent analysis, "Ethics of Abolition" in Douglas Roche's Unacceptable Risk, Nuclear Age Peace Foundation, 1995, p.90.

[5] Opinion of Judge Weeramantry, V4.

[6] Ibid. I 5.

[7] Gareth Evans of Australia, verbatim record, 30 October, 1995, pp. 44-45, 49.

[8] Opinion of Judge Weeramantry, II 3(a).

[9] "1. Nuclear weapons cause death and destruction, induced cancers, leukemia, keloid and related afflictions; 2. cause gastrointestinal, cardiovascular and related afflictions; continued for decades after their use to induce the health related problems mentioned above; 3. damage the environmental rights of future generations; 4. cause congenital deformities, mental retardation and genetic damage; 5. carry the potential to cause a nuclear winter; 6. contaminate and destroy the food chain; 7. imperil the eco system; 8. produce lethal levels of heat and blast; 9. produce radiation and radioactive fallout; 10.

produce a disruptive electromagnetic pulse; 11. produce social disintegration; 12. imperil all civilizations; 13. threaten human survival; 14. wreak cultural devastation; 15. span a time range of thousands of years; 16. threaten all life on the planet; 17. irreversibly damage the rights of future generations; 18. exterminate civilian population; 19. damage neighboring states; 20. produce psychological stress and fear syndromes--as no other weapons do" Opinion of J, Ibid. para. II 4.

[10] Opinion of President Judge Bedjaoui, para.

[11] Ibid. para. 5.

[12] Opinion of Judge Weeramantry II para. 3.

[13] Para.105, the *dispositif* of the Court's opinion. For full opinion and commentary, See, Ann Fagan Ginger, ed. Nuclear Weapons Are Illegal: The Historic Opinion of the World Court and How It Will Be Enforced, Apex Press, New York, 1998; For analysis with excellent bibliography on the opinion, See, John Burroughs, The (Il)legality of Threat or Use of Nuclear Weapons, A Guide to the Historic Opinion of the International Court of Justice, Munster, London, 1997; For opinion available at cost from UN (document A/51/218, 15 October 1996), UN Publications, 2 UN Plaza, DC2-853, NY, NY 10017, 212-963-8302; Also, available at International Association of Lawyers Against Nuclear Arms (IALANA) website: http://www.ddh.nl/org/ialana

[14] Para. 91.

[15] Para. 94.

[16] Paras. 78-79.

[17] Para. 95.

[18] Paras. 78, see paras. 92,95.

[19] Paras 78, 95

[20] Para. 78.

[21] Ibid.

[22] Paras. 32, 33, 35.

[23] Opinion of President Judge Bedjaoui, para. 20.

[24] Ibid. 23

[25] Paras.94-95, see para. 91.

[26] Opinion of President Bedjaoui, para. 22.

[27] Ibid. para 20.

[28] Para. 95

[29] Para. 98

[30] Ibid.

[31] Marc Perrinde Brichambaut, France, Verbatim record (trans.) 1 November, 1995, page 33.

[32] Michael Matheson, US, Verbatim record, 15 November, 1995, p. 78.

[33] Verbatim record, 3 November 1995, p. 64.

[34] Verbatim record, (trans.), 14 November, 1995, p. 45.

[35] Opinion of Judge Weeramantry, VII 2(v).

[36] Ibid.

[37] Para. 47.

[38] Washington Post, July 1, 1998.

TOPIC 13: IN SUMMATION
PRESENTER: Dave Knight, Campaign for Nuclear Disarmament

Thank you Mr. Chairman for this opportunity to express our views and analysis to this important Preparatory Committee meeting. We are pleased that there is agreement here with Under-Secretary-General for Disarmament Dhanapala who stated in January this year: "overcoming complacency and ignorance is a specific area where NGOs can make significant contributions by helping to educate the public and by producing constructive ideas and proposals for national officials to deliberate."

While we do not claim the credit for all the many ideas and proposals that have been elaborated this afternoon we believe that they should be given urgent and due consideration. We wish to have a constructive as well as critical involvement in the Non-Proliferation Treaty process. The NPT has over the years been a valuable instrument in some areas of its work. However it is not at the moment functioning well, as the 1998 PrepCom demonstrated. Clearly therefore decisions need to be made at this PrepCom which will enable the 2000 Review Conference to be sufficiently productive and decisive to save the NPT. The alternative of an ever expanding number of nuclear capable states or even sub-nation groups and of continuing nuclear arms development by the Nuclear Weapon States and others possessing nuclear weapons would have the most serious consequences for global security.

This PrepCom must consider process as well as content for there to be a clear opportunity for the 2000 Review Conference to be successful. That Review Conference must look forward as well as back! It should consider Principles and Objectives for 2000 which would provide a plan for the following five years work and beyond. However compliance, or lack of compliance, with the Treaty should not be ignored and therefore the record of the states parties should be looked at. It is suggested that this PrepCom should set up an Intercessional Working Group to compile a factual record regarding compliance with the NPT and related treaties which would report in advance of the Review Conference. If the formation of such a group is blocked then an ad hoc group of states parties should set up a Compliance Review Coalition.

The record of the Nuclear Weapon States is not good. As well as the continued modernization of their nuclear arsenals they retain, with the exception of China, a first-use policy and sub-strategic policies can be incompatible with the negative security assurances given to the Non-Nuclear Weapon States. Again with the exception of China, they remain unmoved by the opinion of the International Court of Justice and did all in their power to block the New Agenda Coalition resolution in the UN General Assembly.

While none of the NWS are fulfilling their obligations under Article VI of the Treaty clearly the major responsibility is on the United States of America and the Russian Federation to move the disarmament process forward more rapidly and effectively. The end of the Cold War provided the opportunity for a new view of nuclear weapons and arms control and reductions, yet negotiations between the US and Russia are deadlocked in an outdated process based on Cold War perspectives. The blame may well lie mostly with US and NATO actions and intentions, but whether or not that is the case the solution to the logjam in negotiations is for the US and Russia to pursue immediate, parallel, reciprocal and verifiable initiatives, as suggested. None of the preceding should be taken as letting China, France and the UK, or indeed those states possessing nuclear weapons who are not party to the NPT, off the hook. Waiting for START II has been as much misused by them as by the US and Russia. De-alerting and removal of warheads from delivery systems should be carried out by all the Nuclear Weapon States, immediately!

The record of the Non-Nuclear Weapons States parties has generally been one of far greater compliance, with some working very hard to forward the work of the Treaty, and of course some states have renounced nuclear weapons capabilities and joined the NPT. However Iraq and North Korea have committed violations to the Treaty and all NATO states are in violation of the spirit of the NPT and many questions have been raised, inside and outside the NPT, over their compliance with the letter of the Treaty. There would therefore be greater compliance with the Treaty if NATO reversed its first-use policy and US tactical weapons were removed from Europe. These actions would also have wider benefits in the international disarmament process.

In passing it is worth noting the irony in the fact that at the time of the events in Yugoslavia NATO was, through its New Strategic Doctrine, reiterating its commitment to nuclear weapons because they "preserve peace and prevent coercion and any kind of war."

A number of multilateral proposals have been outlined today which states could pursue actively. At the Conference on Disarmament the Fissile Material Treaty needs to proceed, not languish, and the several proposals for an Ad Hoc Committee on Nuclear Disarmament leave those who are stalling its formation with no excuses. The New Agenda Coalition and the Durban Final Document of the 1998 Non-Aligned Movement Conference both call for a conference concerning nuclear disarmament. Within the NPT there have been proposals for Intercessional Working Groups and an Amendment Conference.

The lack of proposals is not the problem. What is necessary for progress and the health of the NPT is fresh commitment to the process unconstrained by Cold War thinking. It is Cold War attitudes that drive the continued development of nuclear weapons and the use of Stockpile Stewardship activities such as subcritical tests and inertial confinement experiments. These activities are not only in violation of Article VI commitments, they clearly undermine the spirit if not the law of the Comprehensive Test Ban Treaty. It is, therefore, proposed that the NWS give international observers free access to facilities and programmes and that they also announce an immediate moratorium on laboratory nuclear experiments. The CTBT is clearly seen as a success of the NPT process even though the prospects for its entry into force are not good. States should not wait for those who are seen as "main-players" to ratify the CTBT but proceed with ratification themselves so that the non-ratifying states become increasingly isolated as the global norm against nuclear testing is emphasized. It is proposed that support should be expressed by this PrepCom for a Ministerial level Special Conference on CTBT entry into force this autumn.

One year to the day India carried out nuclear tests which began the new nuclear arms race in South Asia. While it is extremely important that India and Pakistan sign and ratify the CTBT, the fact that they used the same arguments for having nuclear weapons - "necessary for our security" - as do the NWS indicates so clearly one of the main reasons why the NWS must make significant progress in complying with their obligations under Article VI of the NPT.

No progress has been made towards a Nuclear Weapon Free Zone in the Middle East which shows a complete failure over that commitment from the 1995 NPT Extension Conference. The Middle East resolution should be seriously addressed since it is part of the 1995 extension package.

The work on Article IV, though in some senses a success, is based on outdated assumptions. Experience tells us that nuclear power is not safe, clean and cheap and that its proliferation risks can not be contained indefinitely. Health and environmental impacts both immediate and long term can be enormous and there is no known solution to the major and growing problem of nuclear waste. the positive developments in nuclear safeguards should be built upon and the mandate of the IAEA needs to be changed to separate control from promotion. It has also been proposed that an international energy agency should be established to promote and support the development of sustainable and environmentally safe energy sources.

The elimination of nuclear weapons should not wait on or be conditional on general and complete disarmament. Though the two may both proceed more rapidly if there is interaction where appropriate, the NWS must change the impression that they wish to retain nuclear weapons indefinitely and also, therefore, accept the moral, legal and political imperative of elimination. There are many possible paths to the global elimination of nuclear weapons, with a great variety of steps available which are unilateral, bilateral, plurilateral or multilateral. We urge you to follow the initiatives and proposals which will work best. Take the steps which will provide the fastest possible path! The final step must be a multilateral, verifiable and enforceable Nuclear Weapons Convention and this should be pursued in good faith and with urgency.

I will conclude as I began with thanks for your attention and the words of Under-Secretary-General Dhanapala: "Neither the continued possession of nuclear weapons by those within the NPT, nor these acquisitions by states outside the NPT, serves the cause of international peace and security."Thank you.

CONVENOR: Dave Knight, Campaign for Nuclear Disarmament, 162 Holloway Road, London N7 8DQ, United Kingdom, tel 44.171.700.2393; fax 444.171.700.2357; cnd@gn.apc.org

HOW CAN WE MAKE GREATER PROGRESS TOWARDS NUCLEAR DISARMAMENT AND PREVENT FURTHER PROLIFERATION?

SENATOR DOUGLAS ROCHE, former Canadian Ambassador for Disarmament, and presently a Senator in the Canadian Parliament and Chairman of the Middle Powers Initiative: In opening the NGO Committee's sessions, I thought I would use as a sort of text the words addressed to this issue by the Secretary-General, Kofi Annan, in his most recent annual report. The Secretary-General said:

"We are at a critical moment in the history of efforts to reduce the danger posed by nuclear weapons. Any increase in the number of nuclear weapons States will have serious implications for peace and security. It is therefore of the utmost importance that the Comprehensive Nuclear Test Ban Treaty, together with the objectives agree to at the 1995 Review and Extension Conference of the NPT (Non Proliferation Treaty) become universally accepted. Positive developments this year include the issuance of the Eight Nation Joint Declaration on Creating a Nuclear-Weapon-Free World and the establishment of two ad hoc committees in the Conference on Disarmament, one dealing with assurances for non-nuclear weapons States against the use or threat of nuclear weapons and the other dealing with fissile material cut-off."

The Secretary-General said that he is concerned about the extensions of nuclear testing this year in South Asia. We have representatives of the two states here with us. I am very pleased to welcome to this panel a distinguished list of experts in the nuclear disarmament field who will share their views with us and then we will have a brief question and answer period.

I introduce first Mr. Darach MacFionnbhairr, who is head of the Disarmament and Non-Proliferation Department at the Ministry of Foreign Affairs in Dublin. With an academic background in political science, his career since the mid-seventies has been bound up in security, disarmament and non-proliferation issues. He has represented Ireland at the IAEA (International Atomic Energy Agency) in Vienna, and the OPCW (Organization for the Prohibition of Chemical Weapons) in the Hague and has served as Deputy Head of Mission at the Irish Embassy in Moscow.

Following Mr. MacFionnbhairr will be Mr. Norman A. Wulf, the Acting Assistant Director for Non-Proliferation and Regional Arms Control in the United States Government. Norman has worked on non-proliferation problems for the past 16 years and was the United States representative at the most recent, the second NPT PrepCom in Geneva earlier this year. Then Ambassador Savitri Kunadi, who is India's Permanent Representative to the Conference on Disarmament (CD) at the UN in Geneva, will speak As a member of India's Foreign Service she has served as India's Ambassador to UNESCO in Paris and in Peru and Bolivia. She has also served in Poland as well as here in New York. She previously headed the International Relations Division in the Ministry of External Affairs in New Delhi.

Following her will be Ambassador Munir Akram of Pakistan, the Permanent Representative to the UN in Geneva and the CD since March of 1995. He is Additional Foreign Secretary, has served in that capacity, and also as Ambassador to the EEC in Belgium. He has been Director General of Foreign Affairs in Islamabad and Deputy Chief of Mission in Tokyo and Geneva.Our last panelist will be Ambassador Ian Soutar of the United Kingdom, the UK Ambassador to the CD who has had a distinguished record of service in the diplomatic work for his country since 1968. In addition to postings in various Commonwealth countries, he has served overseas in Brussels, Saigon, Washington, and New Zealand and has been a member of the Royal College of Defence Studies.

DARACH MACFHIONNBHAIRR: By way of background, I would like to make some remarks on the Declaration of the Eight Foreign Ministers and then to turn to the draft resolution introduced by the delegations of the Group of Eight with a number of other delegations. The Declaration has its origins in the evaluation which our Ministers made of the possibilities for action on nuclear disarmament as we approached the end of the nineties, the first decade since the introduction of nuclear weapons which was free from the Cold War. Our analysis of the progress achieved was negative. There had been early promise in the bilateral negotiations between the Russian Federation and the United States, but by the middle of the nineties the signals were that the retention of nuclear weapons was projected for the foreseeable future, the nuclear weapon states focusing rather on new dispositions at lower levels than on elimination. There was an absence of any determination to use the opportunity, which was clearly present, to make that final thrust towards the elimination of these weapons.

There were a number of seminal developments earlier in the decade which form part of the background to this initiative. The outcome of the 1995 Review and Extension Conference of the NPT must be viewed as the most positive of these. The near universality of the Treaty and its indefinite extension were indeed significant achievements. However, the lack of progress in nuclear disarmament since 1995 has engendered the suspicion that another consequence could be the indefinite extension of the possession of nuclear weapons. While we would not concur with this line of argument, it does increasingly inform the debate on the prospects for early achievement of the goal of nuclear disarmament.

The Advisory Opinion of the International Court of Justice (ICJ) and the Report of the Canberra Commission, as well as other initiatives and proposals - governmental and non-governmental - which pointed the way towards elimination, but were not stimulating political action, are further backdrops to our initiative. The failure to build upon the landmark Advisory Opinion of the ICJ is typical in this regard. The ICJ resolution first introduced in the First Committee in 1996 did not succeed in coalescing the international community around its fundamental conclusions, nor, sadly, has it become an impulse for further action. Delegations continue to be locked in traditional and opposite approaches to nuclear disarmament which condemns the international community to inaction even when offered such potential for renewed common purpose as was the case in the Advisory Opinion..

It was in this environment that our Ministers decided that they would try to find some new middle ground less prone to hostile contrary arguments, particularly from the nuclear-weapon States, but also from other States, and which could result in a more forceful commitment to nuclear disarmament.

The range of governments which have associated themselves in the Declaration is broad both regionally and in terms of their respective national approaches to nuclear disarmament. This was indeed intentional: the Ministers wished to cut across traditional barriers and set a new focus in nuclear disarmament. We were successful in that endeavour in the 9 June 1998 Declaration. For each of the participants the initiative represented to some extent at least a stepping back from positions nationally held in order to focus on the essential element, namely the definitive achievement of nuclear disarmament within a reasonable span of time. The governments joined in the Declaration have each in their own right a distinguished track record in the field of disarmament; indeed three of our number have relinquished the nuclear weapons option.

It has been argued by our detractors that this initiative has been inopportune, occurring as it did in the aftermath of the recent nuclear testing in South Asia. There is, however, no relationship between the development of this initiative with that testing, nor indeed in its timing. It did not require the prompting of testing to justify such a declaration. The tests did, however, reinforce the need for the international community as a whole to pursue the goal of nuclear disarmament with a new vigour.

When they launched the Declaration in June, the Eight Ministers decided that they would follow-up with an initiative in the First Committee. The Eight Ministers met in New York on the 22nd of September and launched the text of a draft resolution. In the intervening period there has been considerable further consultation with delegations on the development of the draft and a text was finally presented last evening.

The purpose of this draft resolution is to revitalize the way we approach the nuclear disarmament agenda. Its intention is to galvanize the international community in common action for the purpose of eradicating these weapons for once and for all. It is the prerogative and duty of the membership of the United Nations gathered in the General Assembly to examine and to express the will of the international community on issues of such importance to humanity.

Enacting the proposals contained in this draft would have far reaching consequences: for the nuclear weapon States, for those States which have not joined the international community in relinquishing the option to develop nuclear weapons, and for the international community as a whole, which has the responsibility to bring about the multilateral, non-discriminatory and universal regime for a nuclear-weapons-free world.

The draft resolution proposes an agenda or the contours of an agenda. It does not presume to supplant other resolutions on nuclear disarmament before the General Assembly. It offers a way forward that is contingent on the demonstration of an unequivocal commitment by the Nuclear Weapon States to approach their responsibilities with regard to nuclear disarmament from a novel perspective, namely the speedy and total elimination of their respective nuclear arsenals. This draft resolution calls upon them to demonstrate such an undertaking. Without it we face the prospect of the continued existence and indefinite retention of nuclear weapons.

This draft resolution charts an agenda which in broad terms can and indeed must be addressed if the international community is to seriously grapple with the elimination of nuclear weapons. The agenda focuses on the need to use existing mechanisms and approaches. It provides the balance between bilateral, plurilateral and multilateral approaches, each of which in its own way can and must contribute to the pursuit and achievement of nuclear disarmament.

The effects of following the approach set out in this resolution would be decisive. These weapons will rapidly be relegated as anachronisms, which remain a threat only insofar as the process of their destruction requires cautious handling in conditions of security to be elaborated between the Nuclear Weapon States. The threat of proliferation, which will always remain a concern in a world of Nuclear Weapon States and non-nuclear weapon States, will ease as a result.

The consequences of ignoring the urgency of speedily and totally eliminating nuclear weapons were borne in on us earlier this year. These events should become the defining catalyst for us all to act together now.

This draft resolution provides the outline of a plan of action. Details of this as of any plan can be changed. Timetables can be set. New and alternative approaches can be examined. All of these things we can do. But we can do little until the Nuclear Weapon States have demonstrated an unequivocal commitment to the speedy and total elimination of their nuclear arsenals, to be followed by a new level of engagement in those negotiations which are a first and integral part of the process leading to nuclear disarmament.

In this draft resolution the sponsors attempt - with a reasonable proposal that builds upon existing legally-binding commitments by the Nuclear Weapon States - to secure the final push towards the realization of the Article VI provisions of the NPT, (calling for disarmament) thereby enabling the international community to fulfil the goals of the Treaty as a whole.

The draft resolution is divided into three operational sections. The first section deals with those questions which must be addressed by the nuclear weapon States. The second section deals with those which must be addressed by the States which have retained the nuclear weapons option, and a third section deals with the multilateral aspects of nuclear disarmament. The Agenda captures the entire process leading to nuclear disarmament. It includes calls for interim measures, including de-alerting, and separation of warheads. It calls for the exploration of an undertaking by the Nuclear-Weapon States with regard to non-first use (subsequently eliminated from the resolution) and it outlines the various strands in the multilateral negotiations which are required to complete the nuclear disarmament process.

NORMAN WULF: Let me start by discussing the disarmament half of this agenda and then the non-proliferation portion as well. I think there is a tendency, all too often, to think of disarmament only in what I would call classical terms. By classical terms I mean such things as SALT I, SALT II, START I, START II and hopefully START III. For the past several years the START process has been stalled. It has been stalled in part because our Senate, while it has given its consent to ratification of START II, it is not prepared to see negotiations start on START III until such time as the Russian Duma has ratified START II The Russian Duma has not seen fit yet to do that, although there was some hope that it would do so this fall. We will see.

The preoccupation with START II has I think taken the focus off what else is happening. It is true that when the Soviet Union collapsed, the United States, but not the United States alone, most of western Europe also, and Japan, rushed in to try to make sure that this fissile material in the former Soviet Union that could be used for weapons purposes was not so used. So for the past several years, a number of countries have been spending a significant amounts of money to make sure that all weapons-useable materials is put under some form of safeguards.

I should probably take two seconds to explain some of the terminology for those who may not know some of it. There are two ways you can make nuclear weapons, either with plutonium or with highly enriched uranium (HEU). Plutonium is a by-product of the irradiation of fuel in a reactor and has to be separated out through a process referred to as reprocessing. The other alternative, is highly enriched uranium. Uranium, exists in the natural environment at a very low enrichment level. By running it through centrifuges one can bring it up to a higher level. Very high levels are required before it can be used for weapons purposes.

The former Soviet Union had a lot of this material on hand. The first priority was to make sure that whatever was available there did not become available to other countries in the world through purchasing or smuggling or other activities. These efforts are ongoing. We also have entered into a purchase contract with Russia to purchase some 500 tons of highly enriched uranium. Uranium in this form can be blended down and used as reactor fuel, and that process is underway.

Russia also had significant quantities of plutonium, some of it separated, some of it still being produced, because the Russian nuclear weapons program, unlike the US nuclear weapons program, did not separate clearly the civil from the military uses, so the reactors that are being used to produce electricity also produce plutonium that was useable in their weapons program.

We have entered into an agreement with Russia whereby we will help them convert three remaining reactors that are producing plutonium which is weapons grade and which they are reprocessing because they cannot store it. We are trying to put a handle on that. I might add that that agreement with Russia, the plutonium reactor shutdown agreement, as we refer to it, is a bilateral agreement and has the effect of committing the United States and Russia not to produce any more separated plutonium for weapons purposes.

Plutonium is not as easy to deal with as HEU, in terms of how do you get rid of it, and so there are at least two options that are being examined. One is to convert plutonium to mixed oxide fuel for reactors, basically blending the plutonium with low-enriched uranium to make a reactor fuel which can then be burned. The other option is to take the plutonium, mix it with other waste, and then vitrify it, or make it into a glass solid so it can be stored.

All these processes are extremely expensive. To date the United States has spent over one billion dollars to either make Russian nuclear materials safe or to reduce them. We are also in the process of a budgetary commitment of almost an additional billion dollars towards that continuing process.

No matter how we and the Russians decide to get rid of plutonium, it is going to take a long time. Some estimates are twenty years to burn all this plutonium if it is put in reactors. If it is converted into vitrified waste, it will take perhaps a somewhat shorter period of time, but still in excess of a decade. What happens in that period of time, while this plutonium is sitting around and waiting to either be converted to MOX (Mixed Oxide fuel) or to be vitrified, is a worry.

What the United States has done is to put some plutonium under IAEA inspections with the commitment of the IAEA that their job is to ensure this material is never again used for weapons purposes. We can withdraw it, but it can never again be used for weapons purposes. We are in the process of negotiating with Russia to see if we can get them to do a similar activity. It is not an easy business. It is complicated, hard, slugging work that has been going on since the fall of the Soviet

Union. We have made ,I think, significant progress but a lot remains to be done.

In addition we have done many of the measures that have been referred to by our previous speaker. The other questions, where we go when we get to START III, have already been agreed to to some extent by President Clinton and President Yeltsin with numbers in the area of 2000-2500.

By going to those numbers under START III we are going to go to something that is new and novel in the area of arms control. In the past because of the difficulty and the intrusive verification requirements, we have not used made the warheads themselves what we were verifying. We have used the delivery systems; we count the missiles. We can pretty well limit the damage that the warheads could do if they could not be delivered.

But once you are down to these numbers you have to start looking at a different process. You have to start using the warheads themselves as the unit to count. Going even lower will require even more intrusive measures. It is perhaps one of the real challenges that I think stands in the way of more rapid verification progress towards nuclear disarmament, the verification quandary or challenge.

It is true, for example, in the Chemical Weapons Convention, we have perhaps one of the most intrusive inspection regimes ever devised for an international agreement. But I think it is also true, as the experience in Iraq shows, that no verification regime is perfect. The question then is whether one can take the risks of cheating with nuclear weapons. Certainly cheating with chemical weapons can create a tactical advantage for an adversary. I am not sure that anyone in the United States believes that cheating with nuclear weapons is only a tactical advantage. I am sure you would see it as a strategic advantage. So the question of verification becomes an extremely important issue, particularly as you go to lower and lower numbers. If you are trying to get to zero it becomes a challenge that will I think tax the minds of the best people in the US and everywhere in the world.

Turning to the non-proliferation side of the equation for a few moments, we spent last week in Geneva at what we referred to as the Four Party Talks, talks between the United States, China, and the two Koreas, trying to see if we can elaborate a peace treaty to replace the armistice that has been in place since 1953. I can quickly add that we did not make a lot of progress.

But with respect to North Korea, we have in place an agreement by which we think we have put a cap on their activities in producing materials for weapons purposes. The reactors are all shut down. The spent fuel has been canned and is under IAEA seal, and the IAEA is maintaining a continuous presence. However, there are concerns that there is an underground nuclear facility being built that would, shall we say, frustrate the agreement reached in 1994. We are discussing with North Korea how we can find a way to resolve our concerns about this underground facility. We will be meeting again with them on November 16.

I think, for those of you who spend your time in New York, you are aware of the continuing challenge that Iraq poses to the UNSCOM inspection regime. In addition to Iraq, I suppose we should also raise concerns about Iran's intentions and about Israel's capability. This brings me to the two speakers we have on the podium with us, from India and Pakistan. Needless to say their tests this spring neither helped the nuclear disarmament process nor helped the non-proliferation process. The United States has welcomed the stated intentions given by Prime Minister Vajpayee and Minister Sharif to the UN General Assembly last month to become parties to the CTBT. That intention is welcomed, but we look forward to actually seeing them take the action.

With respect to our own sanctions regime and where we are with respect to India and Pakistan, we also want to see progress on a variety of other benchmarks that have been elaborated by the P5 (the five permanent members of the Security Council) and incorporated into UN Security Council resolutions. Perhaps the largest issue for us is no further progress towards weaponization or production of fissile material. Unfortunately we see no indication of any diminution in the effort by either country to continue producing weapons-useable material, missiles to deliver them, or perhaps even weaponization itself.

The score card, to sum up, from our perspective, is we believe we are making progress on the Article VI requirement toward disarmament. I am personally convinced that President Clinton believes what he says when he says we support the ultimate goal of total elimination. But I don't think anybody in Washington, and I dare say, elsewhere, with all due respect to the previous speaker, has yet figured out how we are going to get to zero. Then the question becomes, do we continue debating the question of how we get to zero, or do we take the available steps that are in front of us at the present time.

My answer is, let's take the available steps and continue trying to elaborate and figure out how we can get to the total elimination of nuclear weapons. In the meantime we are going to continue the program that we have with Russia to try to put fissile material beyond harm's reach and put as much of our own material beyond use for future weapons programs. We are going to continue to work toward the ratification of START II and move forward with START III and hopefully thereafter additional steps. And we are going to continue our efforts to try and prevent the spread of nuclear weapons elsewhere in the world. Thank you.

AMBASSADOR SAVITRI KUNADI of India: ...Needless to say, India attaches importance to the views of the NGO community and we feel that this community is often ahead of what governments think about disarmament matters. Some of the proposals are certainly worthy of serious consideration and support. We also feel that there should be an integrated approach involving NGOs in disarmament work, both in New York and in the Conference on Disarmament in Geneva to which I have the privilege of being India's Ambassador. Our topic today is "How can we make greater progress towards nuclear disarmament and prevent further proliferation?" Given the list of speakers and the time available, I would like to make brief remarks about India's approach to the issue of nuclear disarmament.

India has had a consistent policy since independence on nuclear disarmament, and we remain committed to the goal of the complete elimination of nuclear weapons as we feel that it would be not only in the interests of international security but India's security as well.

Reference has been made to the tests conducted by India and Pakistan. Let me say that the tests conducted by India in May this year were not in violation of any legal commitment entered into by India. There has also been no dilution of our commitment to nuclear disarmament. We will contribute to all efforts for eliminating nuclear weapons globally. While those states possessing nuclear weapons may be interested in using nuclear weapons as currency of power, India has not. India was compelled to exercise its nuclear option to avoid pressures of a nuclearized global order. It has a policy of a minimum deterrent, and fully recognizes that its own interests are served when nuclear weapons are delegitimized and eliminated globally.

Now international efforts for preventing non-proliferation and disarmament of nuclear weapons have been different from those relating to chemical and biological weapons. We believe that the nondiscriminatory approach followed with regard to chemical and biological weapons has given rich dividends. We also strongly believe that there is need to follow the same nondiscriminatory approach with regard to nuclear weapons. I am sure that if this approach is followed, we would succeed in our efforts in this direction.

Unfortunately, however, the nuclear non-proliferation regime, based on the nuclear Non-Proliferation Treaty, has proved to be ineffective. It has legitimized a different standard of national security, allowing the possession of nuclear weapons among a select few. Non-nuclear weapon States, signatories to the NPT, were given security assurances which have remained partial and conditional. Article VI of the NPT remains to be implemented. The basic balance of obligations contained in the NPT have thus not been fulfilled. India remains committed to the goal of a global non-proliferation regime. However, events have confirmed the inadequacies of the NPT.

I would now like to turn to the question of reductions in nuclear weapons. We feel that the promise of deep, substantial reductions in nuclear weapons offered by the end of the Cold War has not materialized. While some reductions have taken place, there is still a long way to go. Reference was made to the START process by the previous speaker. He has of course confirmed that the START process seems to be at a standstill, and this is also our assessment.

Nuclear doctrines have not adapted to the changed political circumstances of the Cold War period. Some of these doctrines espouse first use of nuclear weapons and the hair trigger alert of nuclear weapons poses risks of unintentional and accidental use of nuclear weapons. We feel that this is a very important aspect. Keeping that in view, India this year has introduced in the First Committee a resolution entitled "Reducing nuclear danger" to address this very important issue. I was happy to attend a seminar yesterday on the question of de-alerting. It was very interesting to hear the views of several speakers on this important subject.

We do hope that this initiative which has been taken by India to introduce a resolution on this important subject will receive widespread support. We have been in the process of consulting a number of interested delegations on this resolution. In our view, the essential steps towards nuclear disarmament are the following, and I will briefly list them:

There is need for a commitment prohibiting the use of nuclear weapons. This would have the effect of delegitimizing nuclear weapons in the same way that chemical and biological weapons were delegitimized, starting from the Geneva Protocol of 1925. India has proposed for several years a resolution calling for a convention to be negotiated by the Conference on Disarmament for the prohibition of the use of nuclear weapons.

Next, the goal of global elimination of nuclear weapons is a concern of the entire international community. The tenth Special Session of the General Assembly on Disarmament had entrusted the Conference on Disarmament as the single multilateral negotiating forum to take action on this. For several years India, along with the G28 (a group of non-nuclear developing countries), had been calling for the establishment of an ad hoc committee on nuclear disarmament to negotiate a phased program for the elimination of nuclear weapons. There are of course several other proposals on the table, including the program of action submitted by 28 delegations belong to G28 in 1996. It is unfortunate that some delegations have been opposing any work on nuclear disarmament in the Conference on Disarmament.

We also believe that the indefinite extension of the NPT in 1995, and the measures that have been adopted such as the CTBT (Comprehensive Test Ban Treaty) or those proposed in the FMCT (Fissile Materials Cut-off Treaty), will remain partial measures as regards nuclear disarmament There remains a need for a more focused global effort to give impetus to nuclear disarmament.

India has proposed that an international conference on nuclear disarmament be held with the objective of arriving at an agreement before the end of this millennium on a phased program for the complete elimination of all nuclear weapons. We feel that this conference could enable the international community to seize the opportunity offered by the end of the Cold War for taking decisive steps for nuclear disarmament.

Finally, Mr. Chairman, it is our view that partial and discriminatory measures of non-proliferation must give way to genuine nuclear disarmament. In fact, the attention given to non-proliferation has been at the cost of nuclear disarmament and we would like to stress that nuclear disarmament should be given the priority in international disarmament efforts. We hope that the outcome of the deliberations in the First Committee and in the General Assembly, reflecting the will of the international community, will lead to meaningful steps for the elimination of nuclear weapons.

AMBASSADOR MUNIR AKRAM, of Pakistan: ...I will adopt a different approach from the previous speakers. I would like to address what I believe are the real problems. What is the case for nuclear disarmament? The case can be moral, it can be political, it can be legal and it can be military security. These are all different rationales with different premises which are often put forward, perhaps often mixed together. The rationale which my government uses is a rationale relating to military and security considerations, because that is the duty of every government - to protect national security.

We see the international situation as being extremely disturbing in the nuclear context, and it is disturbing not only because of the South Asian situation, which is of course of direct import for Pakistan. It is disturbing because of at least six different reasons.

Firstly, the global security situation is extremely fragile. There are a plethora of conflicts which have broken out after the end of the Cold War. We cannot pretend that the situation is better than it was at the height of the Cold War. It is worse in terms of the fragility of international security.

Secondly, the international security environment is becoming more and more unequal, with one state having absolute security, its allies having near absolute security but the rest of the world's security situation is deteriorating. For the developing countries security is virtually non-existent. Those with no nuclear weapons, no other weapons of mass destruction, have no security against the major powers. This also increases instability.

Thirdly, there has been very little progress in nuclear disarmament and the prospect for nuclear disarmament is also not very bright. START II ratification by the Russia: does anybody pretend that it will happen very quickly? I think they are fooling themselves if they believe so. They also believe that START III will make rapid progress. I believe that that will require a concerted political effort by the two powers concerned and by the international community. There is no assurance of this. Even if START III is implemented, there will be 2,000 plus weapons with each side, plus 7,500 weapons in storage, which can be deployed at very short notice. 10,000 weapons in the hands of two powers. Given the situation in Russia, is this a situation that the world can feel comfortable with? It is not, I submit.

Fourthly, there is an increasing threat of the use of nuclear weapons. The United States, in ratifying the Pelindaba Treaty (which created a nuclear-weapon-free zone in Africa), stated quite explicitly that it reserves the right to use the weapons in case other weapons of mass destruction are used by any of the parties to Pelindaba. This is an explicit doctrine of the use of nuclear weapons even against non-nuclear weapon states. It has not happened in the past and it can not be ignored. It is a reality. It is a nuclear war-fighting doctrine. And it is even more disturbing that Russia has also given up its no-first-use commitment that it had declared earlier. So the possibility of the use of nuclear weapons has increased.

Fifthly, when and if theater missile defenses are deployed by the United States there will be reactions from the other nuclear weapon States, particularly Russia and also China. The deployment of theater missile defenses will imply two things. First, a multiplication in the number of missiles deployed by these nuclear weapon States. And the most likely militarization of Outer Space. This is happening; technology is driving the United States and the military establishment in that direction. If it is not stopped it will come with a new nuclear arms race, much more dangerous, much more threatening in the future.

And to add to all this, at the top, we have had six or seven years without a major confrontation between any of the Nuclear Weapon States. But there is no certainty that this situation will prevail forever. Thus changes and shifts in Russia and China, and even in the United States, all call for the most circumspect analysis of what might happen in the future. In case there is a confrontation or renewal of confrontation between the major powers, what will happen in a situation where nuclear weapon use is threatened, where a nuclear arms race is threatened, where there is no progress in containing nuclear weapons at the global level? This is the situation one faces.

So when our friends, the major powers, focus on South Asia and the tests conducted by India and Pakistan, we understand their concern and we appreciate their concern, but, excuse me, we believe that in part at least these events are being used by the nuclear weapon States to deflect the world's attention away from the real threat to world peace and security, which flows from the retention of their nuclear weapons in perpetuity, and the threat of the use of those weapons. That is the real danger and let us not be diverted from the real danger that we face.

Now, coming to what can be done. Different methodologies have been proposed. The NAM (Non-Aligned Movement) has one approach, a phased program towards nuclear disarmament, and, of course, one can say very easily this is unrealistic, it is too ambitious, it is not going to happen. But equally we have the P5 program. The P5 says, well let START II happen, START III will happen, and then we will have a process which will involve all the five. We will take care of nuclear disarmament. The rest of you, sit back. And, please don't proliferate in the meantime. We will take care of nuclear disarmament. And it may happen by the year 2020, 2030, it doesn't matter, live with it. The world has been safe for the past 50 years, it will be safe for the next 50 years with nuclear weapons. Nothing will happen to you. If you believe it, we can follow that course.

It is obvious that most of the world does not believe it. And therefore we have the proposal from the G8, the Group of Eight, the Middle Powers, for a New Agenda. I have seen the draft resolution that has been tabled by the G8, I have seen the Declaration. I must confess that I am disappointed, and I would like to say this very openly. I am disappointed because the draft resolution while declaring very sound political and moral principles, does not address the real problems of nuclear threat which I have mentioned. It is a regurgitation of the old agenda, if I may say so, and each one of the provisions that are contained in this draft resolution I am afraid fall short of either being realistic, or being ambitious enough in order to promote real progress in nuclear disarmament. They will ask, what should be done. What is a realistic approach?

Let me outline what I think could be a realistic approach, or at least an approach that may be worth pursuing.

On the non-proliferation front I broadly agree that a major objective should be to contain the proliferation impact of the events in South Asia. But let us not exaggerate what has happened. A nuclear capability has existed in South Asia for the past twenty years. The only thing that didn't happen was, there were no tests and there was no weaponization. Tests have taken place. What is important now is to prevent deployment of nuclear weapons. That is possible. It can be done.

But an agenda that seeks to impose on the South Asian states a situation of inequality vis a vis the P5, that I don't think is possible, frankly, not so much because of Pakistan but because of India. India is a large country. We are not, but India is. They will not be held back. So what is the agenda we have to pursue. We have to pursue a realistic agenda. And here I do not agree with Norm Wulf when he says we are seeking the benchmarks of Res.1172 of the Security Council. That is not true. If it was true there would be no dialogue between Pakistan and the United States. We are pursuing realistic goals, and we will pursue realistic goals, but not unrealistic goals or unequal goals that will be imposed on Pakistan.

Proliferation has to be contained within South Asia, and from South Asia to the rest of the world. And there is also the problem in the Middle East which has to be contained. This is the proliferation aspect.

On nuclear disarmament, what can we do? Nuclear disarmament is necessary because non-proliferation or proliferation cannot be contained forever. It will break out. So disarmament is necessary, so what can we do? Firstly, I suggest a convention committing all states, not only the P5 but all states, India, Pakistan, everybody, to the eventual elimination of nuclear weapons. Pakistan has proposed a convention. It is ready, we intend to table it in the Conference on Disarmament next year. We hope that all the nuclear weapon States, and India and ourselves will be able to sign and ratify that treaty. It is a short convention. It can be adopted within six months. So that is a first step.

Secondly, there must be security assurances to the non-nuclear states from the P5 certainly, and those security assurances must be categorical in providing for non-use of nuclear weapons against non-nuclear weapon States. Those who may have, OK, don't give them such assurances. But for non-nuclear weapon states such assurances must be categorical..

Third, transparency against the qualitative development of nuclear weapons. Open up the stockpile stewardship program. Let us confirm that the nuclear weapon States are not developing their nuclear weapons and not qualitatively designing weapons that can be used on the battlefield.

Fourth, the ratification of START II must be pressed as an international objective by the Security Council, and START III must be pressed also with equal vigor. If India and Pakistan can be pressed in the Security Council to do things, why not Russia? Why is not the attempt at least made for ratification of START II?

Fifth, there must be acceleration of what is called the START III process, negotiations between the two for reduction down below 1500 nuclear weapons. 1500 is too large; it is more than the number of missiles they had in the Cuban missile crisis. 500 should be a better target to aim for in the START III process.

Sixth, there should be an international convention prohibiting the deployment of theater anti-missile systems. This is in my view absolutely essential if a new nuclear arms race is not to be break out. This has to be posed in a multilateral context. We believe that the CD is the right place to do it.

Seventh, once START III is under way and made certain progress, we should draw in the P5 as well as other nuclear-capable states into a multilateral disarmament process.

Here I would like to address a slight difference with the G8 definition of nuclear-capable states. It is not only India, Pakistan and Israel who are nuclear-capable. Germany, Australia, Canada, all these countries could develop nuclear weapons within a matter of months, or weeks, or even days if they decided to do so. I believe that all of them have the right to participate in nuclear disarmament negotiations and have the obligation to give commitments against the possibility of nuclear proliferation and nuclear disarmament in the future.

So the CD negotiations, once they start, should become the apex of all nuclear disarmament efforts and this is where our energies should be focused. It will be a long process, but it should be a honest process. We should stop fooling each other. The nuclear states, the non-nuclear states, and other powers. let us stop playing nuclear disarmament for the gallery, for all you people of good will. If we are serious, we must get down to serious negotiations. That is my hope for this General Assembly.

AMBASSADOR IAN SOUTAR of the United Kingdom: ...I would like to say at the outset that I am very sorry that my other commitments in the First Committee this week prevent me and my colleagues from playing a greater part in your program of discussions this week because I believe that your overarching title is well-justified. We are indeed at a turning point. My fellow speaker, the Pakistani Ambassador to the CD, has spoken memorably in the CD of the fact of Indian and Pakistani nuclear testing having broken the Conference from a long period of slumber. I must say that I agree with that description, although naturally I would have preferred to have been woken a more conventional alarm clock.

But it is certainly true that one of the consequences of nuclear testing has been the establishment of an ad hoc committee to negotiate in the CD a treaty banning the production of fissile in a substantive negotiation. I am not naive enough to think that the negotiating process will either be easy or quick, but the fact that the Conference saw fit to establish the ad hoc committee and indeed expressed a wish for its early re-establishment, merited being included in the CD's report to the First Committee of UNGA (UN General Assembly) over whose adoption I had the honor of presiding and will I hope be welcomed in the resolution on the report of the CD which I have submitted in my capacity as President of the Conference.

Another positive development triggered, if I may use that word in this context, by nuclear testing in South Asia was the welcome announcements here in New York by the Prime Ministers of India and Pakistan of their intentions regarding adherence to the CTBT. Again, this is not a done deal, but it is a step of considerable significance for the non-proliferation regime.

But to return to the theme of this morning's panel, "How can we make greater progress towards nuclear disarmament and prevent further proliferation?" This is self-evidentially a crucial question, but it is one to which the international community has no clear-cut answer. If it had, the debates in the First Committee would be plainer sailing, and the Conference on Disarmament would not find it so difficult to reach agreement on the nuclear side of its agenda every year.

You have heard this morning that among the range of approaches for dealing with nuclear disarmament are two extremes. On the one hand you have the time-bound approach, according to which the international community would agree to lay down a program for the reduction and eventual elimination of nuclear weapons with a predetermined, almost automatic provision for its implementation.

At the other end, as you have heard, there is a preference for a step-by-step approach, which means dealing with discrete and manageable blocks of negotiations on specific areas or topics. This is the approach with which my government,on the basis of our experience over a number of years, feels most happy.

But you have also heard this morning about the New Agenda for nuclear disarmament and non-proliferation which attempts to occupy the middle ground between the two extremes I have just mentioned. As far as the outside world is concerned, and Darach has described this, we first heard about this in the shape of the Declaration the eight countries issued in Dublin in June.

As Darach said, the Declaration places a call on us for a renewed effort to address the problems of nuclear disarmament and non-proliferation. This Declaration, as the outcome of a process of reflection among eight independent countries, two of who were EU (European Union) partners of the UK and one of whom was a candidate for NATO, did not in itself call for a reaction from the UK, although Darach has anticipated my question over the timing of the Declaration and our wondering if there was not a risk that the Declaration might not take the focus off the South Asian nuclear testing.

But the draft resolution, which has now been introduced, does pose more difficult problems, at least for my delegation. As I said, the original Declaration did not call for a response from other states, so that we could let its appearance pass unmarked, at least in public. But of course the introduction of a resolution in the First Committee will require other members of the UN body to take a public position, and I accept that this is the rationale behind the resolution.

least for my delegation. As I said, the original Declaration did not call for a response from other states, so that we could let its appearance pass unmarked, at least in public. But of course the introduction of a resolution in the First Committee will require other members of the UN body to take a public position, and I accept that this is the rationale behind the resolution.

That would not, obviously, in itself have been a bad thing if there were some prospect that the original authors of the resolution would entertain amendments to the resolution which would enable others, if not to support the resolution, at least not to vote against it. Unfortunately, although Darach has spoken of a process of consultation in the course of which the authors of the resolution have shown themselves willing to consider new or amended language, it appears to me that their willingness to accept amendments stops somewhere short of what might be required to secure a positive vote from a number of member States.

I must confess that, like Ambassador Akram, I find the middle way which the authors of the resolution have emphasized something of a chimera. By trying to appeal to both sides of the spectrum they have failed to satisfy anyone, and there is indeed some risk that the resolution will not obtain the support which they might have wished. In many ways that would be a pity, because in the resolution, as indeed in the Declaration, there are many elements with which my delegation sympathizes, and which, were it couched in a separate format, we might have felt able to go along with.

But I would like to turn away from the New Agenda resolution to talk a little bit about what the UK has done, or is doing, to make progress towards the elimination of nuclear weapons. Clearly the Non-Proliferation Treaty is, in the jargon, the cornerstone of the Non-Proliferation regime. We have heard a very clear statement from both Ambassador Kunadi and Ambassador Akram of why their governments feel unable to subscribe to it. We hope, nonetheless, that in the process of time they will come around to the view that this treaty is also in their interest.

But in the meantime the five Nuclear Weapon States are obliged under Article VI of the NPT to progress towards the elimination of nuclear weapons. There is in my view, and I think this was recognized in some of the things that Ambassador Akram had to say, for the time being at least a big distinction between the two largest Nuclear Weapon States and the three smaller Nuclear Weapon States. The main responsibility, for the time being, lies upon the shoulders of the two largest nuclear-weapon States. And I would like to commend the progress that they have made over the past two years in reducing the numbers of deployed nuclear weapons. But, as other speakers this morning have said, that momentum needs to be maintained, if not accelerated, by ratification of the START II Protocol and the early commencement of the START III negotiations.

The role of the smaller nuclear-weapon States is in the first instance not to become larger nuclear-weapon States and secondly, to accept that they too will need to join the larger nuclear-weapon States in negotiations about their nuclear weapons. It is in this context that I would like to talk about what the United Kingdom has done in recent years and is prepared to do now as a result of our Strategic Defense Review.

A decade ago, in addition to operating a system based on four Polaris submarines, the United Kingdom operated systems of land-based nuclear missiles and nuclear artillery. We also had a maritime tactical nuclear capability and we had a significant number of free-fall nuclear bombs in service with our air force. However, some years ago we decided to withdraw from involvement with operation and the Strategic Defense Review took a careful look at the system.

We have decided, overall, that we will maintain fewer than 200 operationally-available nuclear warheads, 192 I believe is the exact figure, compared with the previously announced ceiling of 300. A Trident submarine on deterrent patrol will carry only 48 warheads, again compared with the previous ceiling of 96. And at any one time, only one of the four submarines will be on patrol. And this submarine's missiles will not be targeted and will routinely be at a notice to fire measured in days rather than in the few minutes quick reaction alert common during the Cold War. So these decisions reflect a recognition that there have been improvements for the better in the strategic landscape of Europe and we hope that our announcement will further reinforce these improvements.

We believe that for the last 50 years we have been operating in a world where the dominant concepts were nuclear deterrence against each other, and conventional defense against one another. The time has come to work towards a new world of mutual cooperation with one another and joint partnership with one another. This is not easy but we believe that the steps we have taken are intended to give this process a further push and thus to bring us all closer to achieving the global elimination of nuclear weapons.

I think, Mr. Chairman, we are fast approaching the global elimination of my vocal chords...I did have it in mind to say a little bit more about measures of transparency which we have been taking and which we would like to encourage others to look at, but perhaps I should stop at this point.

DOUG ROCHE:...We have the better part of about 50 minutes for a question and answer session...

BILL EPSTEIN, Pugwash Conferences: I have been at the United Nations 54 years next January and I have spent half a century in disarmament work. I think this was a very good panel. I would like to thank Ambassador Soutar for bringing up the British Defence White Paper. I am a little bit puzzled why it hasn't gotten more publicity because the British government is the first one which has undertaken the de-alerting of all of its nuclear weapons. That is really a big step forward. If the British government could do it, why can't the others all do it? We will be in a much safer world. We won't have to go through another agony such as happened in January, 1995 when they brought the black suitcase to Yeltsin because they misinterpreted a scientific rocket sent up by Norway and we were in minutes of a catastrophe. De-alerting was an easy thing...I cannot for the life of me understand why the nuclear powers cannot agree to de-alert and avoid the dangers of accidental or unauthorized use of nuclear weapons.

Perhaps one of the reasons is that the other side of the coin means no first use, because if you are going to take some days to activate your nuclear weapons, as Ambassador Soutar says, not minutes, then you are obviously not thinking of first use. There was a time when the Soviet Union did agree to no first use as well as China. Then Russia withdrew that pledge in October or November, 1993. I know in 1992 there was serious discussion about it in the United States. I would like to ask Norman Wulf why the US can't agree now to dealerting and to no first use, which would make it a much better world and would be a meaningful step towards the elimination of all nuclear weapons.

NORMAN WULF: The short answer, in respect to de-alerting, is that what the President proposed and worked out at the most recent summit is a requirement, an agreement between us and the Russians, to notify each other of any missile launch, so that the 1995 incident that you referred to may much better world and would be a meaningful step towards the elimination of all nuclear weapons.

NORMAN WULF: The short answer, in respect to dealerting, is that what the President proposed and worked out at the most recent summit is a requirement, an agreement between us and the Russians, to notify each other of any missile launch, so that the 1995 incident that you referred to may be dealt with in that manner. With respect to no first use, I guess the best answer I can give you is Article 2.4 of the UN Charter which says no use of force. But if someone uses force, the United States reserves the right, under Article 51, to exercise our right of self-defense.

PATTY MACMILLAN, Sister of Loretta: I live in New Mexico near the Los Alamos National Lab, and I attend every environmental impact statement hearing. At the last hearing in June the Department of Energy admitted that Los Alamos lab intends to build, produce, 50 to 80 nuclear pits every year. Most of the people in New Mexico, and I think a lot of the people in the country believe that that is in direct violation of the Non-Proliferation Treaty and Article VI if we are planning to build so many more new nuclear pits. The pits are the triggers that make the bomb go off. Also, I don't understand how, if we are doing that, we can expect to ask other nations not to build their nuclear weapons.

NORMAN WULF: I personally don't have knowledge of what you are speaking about, so I can't respond directly to it. The only thing that I can suggest is that I do know that pits need to be reconditioned. If you have a plutonium pit, you have americum that builds up, and that needs to be removed. But beyond that I don't know.

ALYN WARE, Lawyers Committee on Nuclear Policy: Ambassador Wulf, in your comments you mentioned that no one has yet figured out how to get to zero nuclear weapons and as we get to lower numbers verification will be an important problem. On getting to zero there are a number of rough plans, even if they are not specifically on getting towards zero, but getting towards there. One of those is the Model Nuclear Weapons Convention which has been circulated by the United Nations. So the first question is whether you or your colleagues have studied the Convention and what comments you would have on that.

The second question is with regard to your comments that nuclear weapons require highly enriched uranium or plutonium, so therefore the verification of the elimination of nuclear weapons would be much easier than verification of the elimination of chemical or biological weapons, each of which can have hundreds of components or precursors. So would you support the negotiation of an inventory of fissile materials which would help in the verification of the elimination of nuclear weapons? Finally, on verification, a question of Mr. MacFionnbhairr who made a comment on the possibility of verifying nuclear disarmament, because I know that is part of the Declaration of the Eight Nations.

NORMAN WULF:...On the Convention, yes, we are familiar with it and no, we are probably not going to support it. I am with the Arms Control and Disarmament Agency, an agency that is being abolished on April 1 because of the wisdom of our Congress. I don't necessarily support that outcome, I don't necessarily support the outcome of some of our other positions. But the reality is that for some fifty-odd years our national security was defined in terms of nuclear weapons. It is going to take a while for some people to get used to the idea that perhaps one can define national security in other ways.

With respect to getting to zero, I will stand by my concern about verification. The problem, if I understood your proposal correctly on an inventory of fissile materials, is, basically, how do you verify the accuracy of the inventory that the state declares? You have no idea how much they produced. So they could make a declaration of their inventory, but how would you be confident that that declaration was accurate?

I can tell you, in the case of South Africa, which is about the only place where we have actually seen nuclear disarmament undertaken, the IAEA took over 18 months of unprecedented, intrusive measures, to give itself - I think the phrase was "a high level of confidence" - that all the materials that had been in the South African nuclear weapons program had been put under IAEA safeguards. But we don't even know at the present time the Russian inventories, and I am not sure that they know. I think that we know our own inventories, but even there there may be some who would say there is some uncertainty. So I really don't know that a solution based upon a state saying, this is my inventory, if you can't go out and check the accuracy that they have put everything into that inventory, that this solves the problem.

DARACH MACFHIONNBHAIRR: The question of verification is coming very much to the fore in the discussion. During the Cold War, the Western disarmament proposals carried verification benchmarks, which constantly encountered Eastern resistance in view of the levels of transparency contained in such proposals. However, when the then Soviet Union for the first time agreed to this western approach in the negotiations on the Chemical Weapons Convention (CWC) , we were faced with a level of intrusiveness in the field of verification that even its firmest protagonists found uncomfortable. In consequence verification proposals for later multilateral disarmament instruments - the CTBT and in proposals for the BTWC (Biological and Toxin Weapons Convention) Protocols currently under negotiation - have been less intrusive. Even the verification provisions of the CWC itself have now been challenged, for example in the case of the so-called Reservation 18 submitted by the US Administration to Congress and adopted in the context of US ratification of the CWC, whereby US samples subject to inspections may not be removed from US jurisdiction.

MARY SHOIKET, Servas International: ACDA has been eradicated. What agency will exist now? In the light of worry about nuclear terrorism, wouldn't you say that the immediate deactivation and subsequent very rapid removal of all nuclear weapons would be our only true defense against nuclear terrorism? Stockpile Stewardship, we have been messing around there with new designs. Wouldn't you say that other nations might have a legitimate reason for suspecting that the US is not completely honest in what we say about our adherence to the test ban?

NORMAN WULF: ACDA continues to exist until April 1. At that time all the functions that are performed by ACDA and all the personnel at ACDA will be folded into the State Department. I might add, just as a footnote, that in the interagency process leading to the CTBT decision, the State Department supported the threshold rather than zero yield, which was ACDA's position. But so be it, we will be in good hands with arms control in the State Department.

With respect to Stockpile Stewardship, I think it is of course possible that people could misconstrue what is being done. I don't believe there is anybody who was involved in the negotiations in Geneva or subsequently was under any illusion that the United States did not intend to maintain the security and the safety of the weapons systems that we are at the present time keeping.

With respect to Stockpile Stewardship, I think it is of course possible that people could misconstrue what is being done. I don't believe there is anybody who was involved in the negotiations in Geneva or subsequently was under any illusion that the United States did not intend to maintain the security and the safety of the weapons systems that we are at the present time keeping.

Now if and when we get to zero, as your second question implied, regarding nuclear terrorism, we obviously would not need Stockpile Stewardship. With respect to the nuclear terrorist activity, it takes 5-7-8 countries to get to zero. And even if you get to zero, you still have to maintain controls over the plutonium and the highly enriched uranium if you want to make sure that the nuclear terrorists do not have access. When you are talking about that problem, then you have to add in countries such as Japan and France, which have large separated stocks of plutonium.

ALICE SLATER, Abolition 2000 Network: We are working for the negotiation of a treaty by the year 2000 for the elimination of nuclear weapons. One of the points in our abolition statement is the inextricable link between nuclear weapons and nuclear power. There has been reference to the fissile material cut-off treaty. That treaty only cuts off fissile material for weapons purposes. Ambassador Akram discussed how Japan and Germany and other countries, the 44 countries, are required to sign the CTBT because they are all nuclear-capable, because every nuclear power plant is a potential bomb factory. I would like to know from Mr. Wulf how we can reconcile our hopes that some day we can control these materials with the constant production of new materials. MOX fuel won't get rid of plutonium. You will have more radioactive waste anyway.

NORMAN WULF: You will get rid of the weapons grade plutonium but you will end up with plutonium that is not separated. That may not be a satisfactory answer, I concede. With respect to nuclear power plants, it is been the approach and the assumption since 1957 or 1958 that IAEA safeguards were an adequate method of insuring that nuclear power was not diverted to nuclear weapons. With respect to the fissile material cut-off treaty, the assumption there, I think, is that at a minimum you would have IAEA safeguards or some kind of IAEA monitoring on all production facilities devoted to either HEU or reprocessing capability. Whether you wanted to follow that, by going after all reactors as well, is another question that one could debate. There clearly are extremely significant cost consequences when one does so.

One of the things that I have always found embarrassing when I have watched Presidential press conferences, joint press conferences, where he is meeting with a foreign leader and all the questions are asked to the President and the foreign leader is ignored. Usually the questions are purely domestic...

JONATHAN GRANOFF, Lawyers Alliance for World Security (LAWS): During the Cold War it appeared that in the voting in the UN there was often a squaring off between the United States and its allies and the USSR. What we are finding now in the wake of the Cold War is a squaring off between the nuclear-weapon States and the rest of the world. The old doctrine of Mutually Assured Destruction is now giving way to a plethora of new justifications for the arsenals. It seems to me that implicit in Ambassador Soutar's analysis was this spectrum between the developing world, or the nuclear have-nots, and the weapon states. He talked about the need for joint cooperation.

When I look at where we are going, the realities of what the nuclear-weapon States are doing to bridge this, I see NATO expansion, which the UK has been very supportive of and the United States has led, which is a kind of nuclear proliferation because it extends the nuclear umbrella. There is even talk of including the Baltic states eventually in this. I see that the CTBT is not even getting out of Committee in the US, and India and Pakistan may even ratify it before the United States. I see ACDA has closed, that the Senate committee is talking about abrogating the Anti-Ballistic Missile Treaty and we hear no hue and cry from any of the other NATO countries that this would be a provocative and destabilizing position. I see allocations to weaponize space within the Air Force.

I see unified opposition to South Africa's proposal to create an ad hoc committee in the CD which would begin talking about the preconditions for negotiations. I see that the weapons are still on alert and that there is a complete ignoring of the International Court of Justice in interpreting what would be our obligations under Article VI, which is not simply progress but negotiations. So I would like to know, how you can talk about this spectrum, bridging the spectrum? What prospect do we have to see compliance with the ICJ opinion and a new way of looking at things other than what the Eight Nation Initiative has put forth?

AMBASSADOR IAN SOUTAR: ...I'm not sure that all of that question was addressed to me. I think your categorization of opposition in the CD to the South African proposal was exaggerated. There is in fact a spectrum of views in the CD on that proposal. The other question addressed halfway to the UK was a development of new doctrines to justify the maintenance of nuclear weapons. Despite what some of you may have read in the UK Sunday papers over the weekend, I am not aware of the development of new doctrine in the UK. No first use was looked at in the Strategic Review, and the government concluded that adopting a policy of no first use would be incompatible with our NATO obligations.

ANN LAKHDHIR, Institute for Defense and Disarmament Studies and the NGO Committee on Disarmament: I would be interested in having Ambassador Soutar explain what are the parts of the eight nation resolution that cause difficulties for the UK. I would also like the views of the Indian and Pakistani Ambassadors as well. Despite Ambassador Akram's criticism of it for not going far enough, I would be interested in knowing how Pakistan is likely to vote on it, and similarly with India.

AMBASSADOR IAN SOUTAR: ...I will reserve for this afternoon after Darach MacFionnbhairr introduces the resolution in the First Committee a listing of the difficulties which my government feels it must express on the resolution.

AMBASSADOR MUNIR AKRAM: I shan't go into details. I already stated that we are a little disappointed with the draft because it does not go far enough in some respects. In other respects there is a considerable confusion on concepts. For example, withdraw non-strategic nuclear weapons. Why only non-strategic nuclear weapons? The rationale has not been explained. What does it do to the security arguments for Europe, for example, or for other parts of the world? Secondly, de-alerting. The concept of de-alerting covers a range of issues. Exactly what are we talking about? It is not clear. Concept of nuclear-weapons capable states. As I said, you could construe this to mean three or thirty. There is a range of nuclear capabilities. It needs to be clarified. Some of the things that are stated here are kind of dodging the issues.

For example, "calls on the CD to take into consideration both nuclear proliferation and disarmament." Either we want the fissile materials cut-off to be a disarmament treaty or we don't. This is a fudge. Similarly, it "calls upon the Conference on Disarmament to establish an appropriate subsidiary body." There is opposition to an ad hoc committee. If there is an ad hoc committee for other things, the negotiating committee usually is an ad hoc committee. So again, it is dodging positions. There are many other provisions here with which we have problems as a national delegation, but also of a conceptual nature. As I tried to outline in my earlier remarks, we believe that a clear cut approach is required if the political focus has to come on action, rather than on a resolution for the sake of a resolution.

AMBASSADOR SAVITRI KUNADI: Of course we did welcome the joint Declaration which was issued in June by the eight nations. But the resolution which has been introduced by these countries does seek to go beyond the joint declaration. As has been pointed out, it does include a number of provisions with which we have difficulty of a conceptual nature. It would have been better in our view if this resolution perhaps had been more focused on particular aspects which are of immediate concern to the international community and in particular to the non-aligned countries which would lead to the goal of a nuclear-weapon-free world, and this is a goal we all espouse, which we all want to contribute to.

Some of the elements which have been mentioned earlier by Ambassador Akram pose difficulties for my delegation as well. We are not able to understand the exact terms here, nuclear-weapon capable states. This does include not only the three states which have been called upon to undertake certain measures, but in our view it includes a range of other states as well. In particular, then the resolution calls upon my country to adhere unconditionally to the NPT, etc. Now they know very well what India's position on the NPT is. We do hope that it would be possible for all of us to engage in discussions on this particular resolution and to have a text which is then more widely acceptable to all of us.

DARACH MACFIONNBHAIRR: I would also like to refer to the suggestion that measures relating to de-alerting, separation of warheads and no-first use are not the purpose of the process which we envisage here. We do not consider these as disarmament measures because in reality they are not disarmament measures. Nor should we devote more time to negotiate such measures than we devote to the disarmament negotiations proper. It is generally recognized that certain interim steps can be taken at an early date and which would provide greater security and build confidence in the context of the disarmament process which follows from the adoption of the agenda we hope will result from this initiative. It has therefore been our approach in setting out the New Agenda that we should be as comprehensive as we consider necessary for the realization of the goals which underlie the proposal.

Philippines radiological expert: ...I went to the Marshall Islands in 1977 when it was a protectorate of the United States. I was a radiological physicist. We did environmental monitoring...There is a lot of thyroid cancer, abortion, all kinds of cancer in the Marshall Islands and they are very dirt poor...Please get involved with the radiation and public health project all over the world, in Chernoble and at all the nuclear testing sites...http://www.radiation.org

SENATOR DOUG ROCHE: If there are no further questions I will ask the panelists to make a closing statement...

AMBASSADOR IAN SOUTAR: A number of questions have been thrown up. Not everyone will be satisfied with the answers received. I detected some sense of disappointment about the nuclear weapons States agreement to the elimination of nuclear weapons. I tried in my remarks to set out some of the practical steps which my government has undertaken. There are some more in the pipeline. Let me just mention one. I think the question of verification was raised. In the past the United Kingdom has been very much involved in providing technical advice on the detection of nuclear testing, accountancy of nuclear materials. We have launched a new program to build up a body of expertise which we hope will help to wrestle with some of these questions, the verification of the elimination of nuclear weapons. Again, it is not something I went into detail about earlier. But I think it is an indication of some of the practical steps that we should be taking.

AMBASSADOR MUNIR AHMED: It has been an interesting discussion. I am very encouraged by the fact that so many question were directed to Norman Wulf.

AMBASSADOR SAVITRI KUNADI: I would just like to say how pleased I am to be in the midst of people who are very conscious of the subject that we discussed today, namely nuclear disarmament and how to prevent further proliferation. I must say I have benefitted in particular from the statements made by the distinguished panelists who were here today. Also, I was very interested in the nature of questions which have been raised. What I feel, and I think that has come out quite well in the discussion today is that we should not have two types of standards, one for the Nuclear Weapon States, and one for the others. I think India has always tried to highlight this point. We have not turned away from our commitment to nuclear disarmament and we will continue to press forward with these issues at the First Committee and in the General Assembly and of course in the Conference on Disarmament in Geneva.

DARACH MACFIONNBHAIRR: I would like to join the other panelists in thanking the Committee for bringing us together with this group. Indeed, for me it has been a valuable meeting to hear the views of two of the Nuclear Weapon States and India and Pakistan in a setting which is of a reasonable interchange. We will certainly note what they have said and indeed take on board what they have said. We feel that this approach of ours - it is not ideal, as you heard from each of the panelists, who take a certain distance from it - but I think as we progress down the Committee corridors over the next couple of weeks, hopefully we will bring this process closer by the agency of this initiative that we have taken. Thank you.

SENATOR DOUGLAS ROCHE: I want to thank all the panelists for coming here this morning on your behalf...I think it is a great tribute to the NGO Committee on Disarmament that they came and spent the morning with us, so I do thank you very much indeed...

APPENDIX: Resolution 53/77 Y, Towards a nuclear-weapon-free world: the need for a new agenda, and excerpts from the discussion in the First Committee of the UN prior to its adoption on December 4, 1998 by the UN General Assembly.

Resolution 53/77Y was introduced by Ireland on behalf of seven sponsors. It was adopted with a vote of **114 in favor - 18 opposed** (Bulgaria, Czech Republic, Estonia, France, Hungary, India, Israel, Latvia, Lithuania, Monaco, Pakistan, Poland, Romania, Russian Federation, Slovakia, Turkey, United Kingdom, United States) - **38 abstentions** (Albania, Algeria, Andorra, Argentina, Armenia, Australia, Belgium, Bhutan, Canada, China, Croatia, Denmark, Finland, Georgia, Germany, Greece, Honduras, Iceland, Italy, Japan, Kazakhstan, Kyrgyzstan, Luxembourg, Marshall Islands, Mauritius, Micronesia, Myanmar, Netherlands, Norway, Portugal, Republic of Korea, Republic of Moldova, Slovenia, Spain, Tajikistan, The Former Yugoslav Republic of Macedonia, Ukraine, Uzbekistan).

There was intense pressure from some of the Nuclear Weapon States, particularly the US, to vote against this resolution. Slovenia, one of the original sponsors, was persuaded to withdraw its sponsorship. The resolution itself was amended by its sponsors in the First Committee to take out words referring to consideration of pledges of no first use of nuclear weapons. The possibility of first use is still NATO policy. Removing the words in the resolution that referred to no-first-use made it more likely that members of NATO might abstain, rather than vote no. Several NATO members - Canada, Norway, Germany - considered supporting the resolution, but in the end none felt they could with intense US opposition. Those aspiring to membership in NATO, or new members, all voted no. The sponsors have indicated they will continue to press the Nuclear Weapon States to begin serious consideration of nuclear disarmament and are likely to sponsor a similar resolution in 1999.

There were separate votes on operative paragraphs 8, which called for adherence to the NPT, which was opposed by India, Israel and Pakistan, and on which Bhutan and Cuba abstained, and 17, which called for the conclusion of an internationally legally binding instrument to effectively assure non-nuclear weapon States Party to the NPT against the use or threat of use of nuclear weapons that was opposed by the UK. Cuba, India, Israel, Pakistan, and the Republic of Korea abstained. The US, France, China and the Russian Federation did not vote, nor did the Marshall Islands, or Micronesia.

The resolution itself is four pages long. The operative parts:

"1. *Calls upon* the nuclear-weapon States to demonstrate an unequivocal commitment to the speedy and total elimination of their respective nuclear weapons and, without delay, to pursue in good faith and bring to a conclusion negotiations leading to the elimination of these weapons, thereby fulfilling their obligations under Article VI of the Treaty on the Non-Proliferation of Nuclear Weapons;

2. *Calls upon* the United States and the Russian Federation to bring the Treaty on Further Reduction and Limitation of Strategic Offensive Arms (START II) into force without further delay and immediately thereafter to proceed with negotiations on START III with a view to its early conclusion;

3. *Calls upon* the nuclear-weapon States to undertake the necessary steps towards the seamless integration of all five nuclear-weapon States into the process leading to the total elimination of nuclear weapons;

4. *Also calls upon* the nuclear-weapon States to pursue vigorously the reduction of reliance on non-strategic nuclear weapons and negotiations on their elimination as an integral part of their overall nuclear disarmament activities;

5. *Further calls upon* the nuclear-weapon States, as an interim measure, to proceed to the de-alerting of their nuclear weapons and, in turn, to the removal of nuclear warheads from delivery vehicles;

6. *Urges* the nuclear-weapon States to examine further interim measures, including measures to enhance strategic stability and accordingly to review strategic doctrines;

7. *Calls upon* those three States that are nuclear-weapon capable and that have not yet acceded to the Treaty on the Non-Proliferation of Nuclear Weapons to clearly and urgently reverse the pursuit of all nuclear weapons development or deployment and to refrain from any action which could undermine regional and international peace and security and the efforts of the international community towards nuclear disarmament and the prevention of nuclear weapons proliferation;

8. *Calls upon* those States that have not yet done so to adhere unconditionally and without delay to the Treaty on the Non-Proliferation of Nuclear Weapons and to take all the necessary measures which flow from adherence to this instrument;

9. *Also calls upon* those States that have not yet done so to conclude full-scope safeguards agreements with the International Atomic Energy Agency and to conclude additional protocols to their safeguards agreements on the basis of the Model Protocol approved by the Board of Governors of the Agency on 15 May 1997;

10. *Further calls upon* those States that have not yet done so to sign and ratify unconditionally and without delay, the Comprehensive Nuclear-Test-Ban Treaty and, pending the Treaty's entry into force, to observe a moratorium on nuclear tests;

11. *Calls upon* those States that have not yet done so to adhere to the Convention on the Physical Protection of Nuclear Material and to work towards its further strengthening;

12. *Calls upon* the Conference on Disarmament to pursue its negotiations in the Ad Hoc Committee established under item 1 of its agenda entitled "Cessation of the nuclear arms race and nuclear disarmament", on the basis of the report of the Special Coordinator and the mandate contained therein, of a non-discriminatory, multilateral and internationally and effectively verifiable treaty banning the production of fissile material for nuclear weapons or other nuclear explosive devices, taking into consideration both nuclear non-proliferation and nuclear disarmament objectives, and to conclude these negotiations without delay, and, pending the entry into force of the treaty, urges States to observe a moratorium on the production of fissile materials for nuclear weapons or other nuclear explosive devices;

13. *Calls upon* the Conference on Disarmament to establish an appropriate subsidiary body to deal with nuclear disarmament and, to that end, to pursue as a matter of priority its intensive consultations on appropriate methods and approaches with a view to reaching such a decision without delay;

14. *Considers* that an international conference on nuclear disarmament and nuclear non-proliferation, which would effectively complement efforts being undertaken in other settings, could facilitate the consolidation of a new agenda for a nuclear-weapon-free world;

15. *Recalls* the importance of the decisions and resolution adopted at the 1995 Review and Extension Conference of the Parties to the Treaty on the Non-Proliferation of Nuclear Weapons, and underlines the importance of implementing fully the decision on strengthening the review process for

the Treaty;

16. *Affirms* that the development of verification arrangements will be necessary for the maintenance of a world free from nuclear weapons, and requests the International Atomic Energy Agency, together with any other relevant international organizations and bodies, to explore the elements of such a system;

17. *Calls* for the conclusion of an internationally legally binding instrument to effectively assure non-nuclear-weapon States parties to the Treaty on the Non-Proliferation of Nuclear Weapons against the use or threat of use of nuclear weapons;

18. *Stresses* that the pursuit, extension and establishment of nuclear-weapon-free zones, on the basis of arrangements freely arrived at, especially in regions of tension, such as the Middle East and South Asia, represent a significant contribution to the goal of a nuclear-weapon-free world;

19. *Affirms* that a nuclear-weapon-free world will ultimately require the underpinnings of a universal and multilaterally negotiated legally binding instrument or a framework encompassing a mutually reinforcing set of instruments;

20. *Requests* the Secretary-General, within existing resources, to compile a report on the implementation of the present resolution;

21. *Decides* to include in the provisional agenda of its fifty-fourth session the item entitled "Towards a nuclear-weapon-free world: the need for a new agenda", and to review the implementation of the present resolution."

Excerpts from the discussion in the First Committee of the resolution, then titled L.48/Rev.1, on November 13, 1999, the day it was voted on, before and after it was adopted. (Discussion rarely occurs during the General assembly vote on the same resolution later, and did not.):

Darach MacFionnbhairr of Ireland, in introducing the revised resolution (the major change was deletion of the paragraph on no-first- use): In their interventions before this Committee, and from the outset, the sponsors...have promoted dialogue with all delegations wishing to contribute to the further elaboration of this text and they have engaged in a constructive dialogue over the past five weeks with many delegations...This draft does not represent an approach of one delegation. Its sponsors represent the variety of traditions which inform the debate on nuclear disarmament here in the First Committee, at the Conference on Disarmament, in the review process of the Treaty on the Non-Proliferation of Nuclear Weapons, and elsewhere. The sponsors do not expect that they have achieved the definitive determination of the nature or process of nuclear disarmament.The draft proposes an agenda, which is wholly realizable, for which the context and mechanisms are for the most part, already at hand, and which can be infinitely developed.

The dialogue which the co-sponsors have held on this draft resolution - both here and in capitals - has demonstrated that among governments there is a steady awakening to the fact that now is the time to move forward together to eliminate nuclear weapons. It has not been easy for the sponsors to develop such a text and - as the delegations which have engaged with us would testify - the balance we have sought to achieve in our search for a middle ground, drawing together the international community as a whole, has not been easy either. However, the resulting draft, as laid before delegations for adoption, represents a call for action, and the parameters for an agenda required to achieve that goal, which we all declare to be ours.

Ambassador Joelle Burgois of France: Mr. Chairman, France will vote against the draft resolution entitled "Towards a nuclear-weapon-free world: the need for a new agenda." During the debate I explained why we view this resolution as unrealistic and inappropriate. It is unrealistic because it disregards the facts, especially the considerable bilateral and unilateral efforts made by nuclear-weapon Powers with respect to the NPT. It is inappropriate because it seeks, by proposing a new conference and a new agenda, to call into question the achievements of the 1995 Review and Extension Conference of the Parties to the Treaty on the Non-Proliferation of Nuclear Weapons and to cast doubt on the strengthened review process, to which we are strongly committed. Moreover, a future special session of the General Assembly devoted to disarmament will provide an opportunity for a comprehensive consideration of all disarmament issues. France would want this special session to take place in the year 2001.

To continue the process of nuclear disarmament on the basis of Article VI of the NPT requires serious, patient work based on the risks and threats we face. In that connection, it is unacceptable to us that the draft resolution calls into question the principle of nuclear deterrence. Deterrence remains the fundamental element of French defense strategy and an assurance against any threat to our vital interests, no matter what its source or form. It is also a fundamental element in the doctrine of the North Atlantic Treaty Organization (NATO).

France is determined to fulfil its commitments under Article VI of the NPT, putting an end to the nuclear arms race once and for all, negotiating effective measures of nuclear disarmament and working towards general and complete disarmament under strict and effective international control. Because of our desire for international peace and security we must omit none of these elements. For the present, a priority goal must be to negotiate a fissile materials cut-off treaty. For these reasons my country will vote against the draft resolution, which runs counter to these principles.

Ambassador Robert Grey of the US: Since the United States has already spoken at some length on the reasons for its opposition...I will be brief. We have two major concerns. First, this resolution calls into question a fundamental doctrine of our defense, and that of our allies. Secondly, far from advancing the nuclear disarmament agenda, it will in all probability delay it.

As for the first point, the representative of one of the original sponsors could not have been clearer when, in response to a statement of our British colleague, he said that the resolution was intended to call into question the doctrine of deterrence. This doctrine has stood the United States - and indeed the world - in good stead for the past half century. It has kept the peace and ended the Cold War. Along with our allies, we reviewed it recently, and concluded that it should remain the basis for our defense. I note that Article 51 of the Charter gives us all the right to exercise and take measures for individual and collective self-defense, and I want to make it quite clear that my country will continue to exercise this right.

Beyond this, the sponsors of this draft resolution seem to believe that the doctrine of deterrence is a major obstacle to more rapid progress on nuclear disarmament, and conversely, that if only it were abandoned, the nuclear Powers would disarm rapidly. We disagree. Nuclear weapons and nuclear disarmament do not exist in a vacuum. The nuclear disarmament process can take place only in the context of national security interests. The dramatic progress we have made today has been possible because of changes in the international security climate, even as it has contributed to the increased stability and security that makes further progress possible.

The United States intends to continue to move toward greater security and stability at lower levels of weapons in a step-by-step process towards the ultimate elimination of nuclear weapons. But the security and stability would be empty concepts without nuclear deterrence. Let me be perfectly clear: no one will make nuclear disarmament occur faster by suggesting that a fundamental basis of our national security for more than fifty years is illegitimate.

As to the second point, we have already noted that - far from a new agenda - this resolution contains a mix of items already on the arms control and disarmament agenda. Proposals, of which de-alerting is one, which we have already considered and rejected, and suggestions, such as a call for a nuclear disarmament conference that will lead nowhere. Indeed, if the purpose of this resolution is to speed the nuclear disarmament process, it can only be counter-productive.

By lecturing the nuclear-weapon States about their inadequacies, while neglecting to criticize the actions of States that have recently conducted nuclear weapons tests, and have thereby damaged the global non-proliferation regime, the resolution will hardly encourage the entry into force of the Comprehensive Test Ban Treaty (CTBT) or START II. Indeed, it will only give aid and comfort to those that are skeptical about the multilateral role in arms control and disarmament in general. By seeming to require a new commitment to nuclear disarmament as a prerequisite for further steps to reduce nuclear weapons, it will only provide an excuse for delay.

Finally, by proclaiming the need for a new agenda, and for still another conference on nuclear disarmament, it calls into question the agendas on which the international community already agrees, such as the Principles and Objectives for disarmament and non-proliferation. It also intends to undermine existing forums,such as the Conference on Disarmament, the enhanced Non-Proliferation Treaty (NPT) review process, the First Committee and other United Nations disarmament machinery, including a possible fourth special session of the General Assembly devoted to disarmament. We do not understand how this would promote speedier progress on disarmament.

In our view, this draft resolution is still another example of feel-good arms control.The proponents may believe they may accomplish something, but the draft resolution destroys no weapons, prevents no proliferation, and makes the world no safer. My delegation hopes that many of our friends and allies will decide they cannot support this unnecessary and potentially harmful resolution. The United States for its part, will continue to pursue meaningful measures to reduce and eliminate weapons of mass destruction and their delivery systems, as well as preventing the proliferation of such weapons.

Ambassador Ian Soutar of the United Kingdom: The United Kingdom is wholly committed to nuclear disarmament and to our obligations under Article VI of the NPT. This commitment has been restated many times and given practical expression by the measures undertaken in our strategic defense review, which included significant reductions in, and unprecedented transparency about, the British nuclear deterrent and, for example, by ratification of the CTBT.

The 1995 Review and Extension Conference agreed on Principles and Objectives setting the next steps towards nuclear disarmament. We do not believe that the sponsors of the resolution, all of whom are party to the NPT, are, by setting out a different agenda, making a constructive contribution. The agreed next step is the negotiation of a fissile material cut-off treaty, for which an Ad Hoc committee has been established in Geneva. We will work hard for the success of these negotiations.

The draft resolution also advocates measures which were examined in our strategic defense review and which we concluded are, at the present time, inconsistent with the maintenance of a credible minimum deterrent. The draft resolution neither condemns nor even mentions the nuclear tests carried out by India and Pakistan. It is difficult to see how it could be reconciled with provisions of UN Security Council Resolution 1172 (1998) on those tests. The United Kingdom remains ready to support any measure that will make a practical contribution to advancing nuclear disarmament. This resolution does not. We shall accordingly vote against it.

Ambassador Munir Akram of Pakistan: Pakistan strongly supports the objective of nuclear disarmament, and we believe that this draft resolution makes a sincere effort to try to identify the possible elements and approach that could promote the objectives of nuclear disarmament. The draft resolution is more fair and equitable than the one which we have just voted on -A/C.1/53/ L.42/Rev. 1. It is, however, less categorical and clear in its perspective than the draft resolution sponsored by Myanmar and other non-aligned countries which the Committee has also adopted. We see the positive aspect of this draft resolution as being a recognition of the link between nuclear disarmament and non-proliferation, and also a recognition of the realities of the existence of five nuclear-weapon States and certain other States which also have nuclear capability or now possess nuclear weapons.

However, the demands which have been made in the draft resolution on these respected categories of States are somewhat unclear and unequal. Whereas the nuclear-weapon States are asked to conduct negotiations in accordance with Article VI of the Treaty on the Non-Proliferation of Nuclear Weapons (NPT), the two major nuclear Powers are urged to pursue the START talks, to integrate these into a seamless process of negotiations between all five nuclear-weapon States, and to accept a de-alerting of their nuclear weapons.

On the other hand, the nuclear-weapons-capable States are asked to reverse their programs, immediately accept the NPT, accept full-scope safeguards and take measures which are unrelated to their security environment. My delegation does not believe that the steps that are required to be taken by any State - be it nuclear-weapon, nuclear-weapon-capable or non-nuclear - should be unrelated to the security environment and the security compulsions which that state confronts.

In the region of South Asia, we now have a situation where, as a result of the declaration by one State of nuclear-weapon status, and as a result of an acute conventional imbalance, my country is obliged to rely on the deterrence effects of nuclear capability to prevent aggression. Therefore, like the representative of France, I would like to say that deterrence remains a fundamental element of our defense strategy. The representative of the United States has further elaborated on this concept of deterrence and has underlined that this concept has preserved the peace for 50 years. We trust that South Asia, which has seen three wars in the last 50 years, will see no further wars in the next 50 years. We too, Mr. Chairman, have the right, under Article 51 of the UN Charter, to self-defense. That is the right which we exercised when we conducted our nuclear explosions of 28 and 30 May.

It is therefore quite strange that the nuclear-weapon States should nitpick on this draft resolution because it does not refer to these tests. If there was such a reference it would be in the category of the draft resolution that was adopted by this Committee last night - the unfair and discriminatory resolution on South Asia. That would be also in the category of disarmament measures which are meant to make one feel good but achieve nothing.

It is unfortunate that, due to the unacceptable provisions contained in the draft resolution... that my delegation will be obliged to vote against the draft resolution as a whole. We nevertheless appreciate and understand the initiative taken by its sponsors and wish to state this publicly, although we disagree strongly with some of the elements that they have included.

After the vote, the statements in explanation included:

Arsene Millim of Luxembourg: It is my honor to speak on behalf of the three Benelux countries - Belgium, the Netherlands and Luxembourg - as well as Denmark, Spain, Finland, Iceland and Portugal. It is with regret that these eight countries abstained on the vote on the draft resolution...proposing a new agenda for nuclear disarmament. I say "regret" because this draft contains many positive elements which we could subscribe to because we too call on States which have not yet done so to adhere unconditionally to the NPT, to conclude full-scope safeguard agreements with the International Atomic Energy Agency and to conclude additional protocols to those agreements, and to sign and ratify, unconditionally and without delay, the CTBT.

We, too, believe that it is important that the Conference on Disarmament pursue and conclude, without further delay, the negotiations on a treaty banning the production of fissile material for nuclear weapons. We, too, support the proposal that the Conference on Disarmament establish a subsidiary body to deal with nuclear disarmament - a proposal similar to that made by Belgium a few months ago. We, too, support the establishment of nuclear-weapon-free zones everywhere possible. We eight countries thus subscribe unequivocally to the basic objective of nuclear disarmament: the total elimination such weapons. With others, we are tirelessly exploring every avenuethat might lead to that end. But, to arrive there, the consistency of the draft resolution must equal the determination of its sponsors. That does not seem to be the case here. Three imperfections in particular should be emphasized.

The first relates to the alarmist tone of the text, based on an analysis we do not share. By concluding with the need for a new agenda, the draft resolution reveals disatisfaction with the previous one and a lack of faith in the future. Our countries do not share this view. We are pleased to have directly benefitted from the Intermediate-Range Nuclear Forces (INF) Treaty. We appreciate the results of the START process and have confidence in its future. Neighbors of France and Great Britain, we draw satisfaction from their unilateral decisions in regard to nuclear disarmament. We encourage them and China to participate in a plurilateral mechanism, as mentioned in the eleventh preambular paragraph of the draft resolution. It is inaccurate and dangerous to reject the existing agenda on the grounds that it has neither born fruit nor promises to bear any.

Our eight countries believe that progress on nuclear disarmament can only be achieved by means of processes under way - processes founded on Article VI of the NPT and inspired by the 1995 principles and objectives. We cannot support the proposal for an international conference on nuclear disarmament while we have on the horizon the year 2000 Review Conference of the NPT and another special session of the Assembly on disarmament. The present agenda has demonstrated its value, we find it appropriate and we have not ceased to believe that it holds promise for the future.

Finally, it is a matter of concern that a resolution of no fewer than 37 paragraphs says nothing about a major event, the nuclear tests in South Asia, except - and this only makes us more cautious - to introduce, in paragraph 7, an unacceptable ambiguity regarding the status of the "three States that are nuclear-weapons capable." For the States parties to the NPT there can be only categories of States defined by the Treaty: nuclear-weapon States and non-nuclear-weapon States.

I would like to conclude by again emphasizing the firm intention of the Benelux countries, as well as of Denmark, Spain, Finland, Iceland and Portugal, to support any approach that might advance the cause of nuclear disarmament. Without doubt the road is long, but it is clear. It does not seem desirable to call into question the existing processes, which have been effective in the past and hold promise for the future.

Ambassador Li Changhe of China: China fully understands the international community's desire for nuclear disarmament and the importance it accords to the question. China has always supported a total ban on nuclear weapons and their complete destruction so that humanity may be freed from the threat of nuclear war and so that a nuclear-weapon-free world may soon be built.

As a nuclear-weapon State, China has never evaded its own responsibility for nuclear disarmament, and it is ready to fulfill its obligations. From the very day it acquired nuclear weapons China has undertaken never to be the first to use such weapons under any circumstances. It has also undertaken unconditionally not to use or threaten to use nuclear weapons any non-nuclear-weapon State or nuclear-weapon-free zone. China has never participated in any nuclear arms race, and it is against the doctrine of nuclear deterrence based on the first use of nuclear weapons. Our position is an important contribution that China is making in its own way to the final goal of a complete ban on, and thorough destruction of, nuclear weapons.

It is our view that the indefinite extension of the NPT does not imply that the nuclear-weapon States can possess nuclear weapons forever. They should intensify their efforts to fulfil their obligations under Article VI of the NPT. Countries with the largest and most sophisticated nuclear weapons should continue to drastically reduce their nuclear weapons, renounce the doctrine of nuclear deterrence and stop research and development on outer space weapons and missile defense systems that would destabilize the global balance, so that favorable conditions may be created for other nuclear-weapon States to participate in the negotiations leading to nuclear disarmament.

The sponsors of this resolution consulted with the Chinese delegation many times and listened to our views. For that we would like to express our appreciation. China favors the objective of the draft resolution - namely to achieve a nuclear-weapon-free world - and we favor some of the steps mentioned in it. For example, it calls upon the nuclear-weapon States to review their nuclear policies and to negotiate and conclude an internationally legally binding instrument to provide security assurances to the non-nuclear-weapon States, and calls for the enhancement of the NPT's universality. We have also taken note of some other measures in the draft resolution. However, given the great disparities in the nuclear forces, and given that a few countries still cling to the doctrine of nuclear deterrence based on the first use of nuclear weapons, it is premature to ask all the nuclear-weapon States to adopt the same measures. For this reason the Chinese delegation abstained.

Ambassador Mark Moher of Canada: ...After a period of very careful, intense and high-level consideration and consultation, Canada abstained on this resolution. For several weeks Canada worked constructively with the resolution's sponsors. In the course of this work, we were gratified by their determination and by their clear commitment to build the broadest possible base of support. Canada would obviously, also, like to see that objective achieved. While it has come a long way in this direction, on balance our conclusion is that there is still more to be achieved in that respect.

This Committee is well aware of Canada's commitment to arms control, disarmament and non-proliferation as a core dimension of our broader pursuit of greater international peace and security. It is also aware of our unequivocal commitment to all aspects of the nuclear disarmament and nuclear non-proliferation regime - a regime founded on the NPT, and its associated instruments.

The Canadian people are committed to nuclear disarmament and nuclear non-proliferation.

In recognition of this commitment, and of the challenges we face as we approach the new millennium, the Canadian Parliament has undertaken a study of Canada's nuclear disarmament and non-proliferation policy. Its report will likely be tabled in the next few weeks. The Canadian government will wish to take that report into account as it continues to promote the objectives of its arms control, disarmament and non-proliferation policy. Ultimately, the Canadian Government did not wish, by today's vote, to prejudge that process.

As delegations are aware, some countries have raised strong objections to the resolution. *inter alia,* these objections relate to their impressions that the resolution is rooted in "oldspeak," that it does not adequately credit progress made in nuclear disarmament and that it makes no mention of the nuclear tests in India and Pakistan. As a committed member of the United Nations, and of NATO, Canada has examined each of these arguments very carefully. At the same time, we are deeply concerned that the NPT-based nuclear disarmament and non-proliferation regime is now under serious strain. From this perspective, we see the New Agenda resolution as a timely and pointed reminder of the urgent need for further progress on both of these fronts.

While we recognize that progress has been made on the nuclear disarmament front, we think there is both room and an imperative to make more. In the same manner, we have made it clear, that nuclear proliferation is unacceptable. Canada accordingly looks forward to pursuing these issues, actively and forcefully in the coming weeks and months with our friends and with our allies.

We note that the resolution calls for a review at next year's General Assembly. Canada for one looks forward to this review and hopes that all those engaged in this debate will take maximum advantage of the intervening period to pursue the goal of the broadest-based support, demonstrating a common resolve to sustain the NPT-based nuclear disarmament and non-proliferation regime in the face of pressing and potent challenges.

Ambassador Savitri Kunadi of India: ...India positively assessed the Joint Declaration issued in Dublin on behalf of Eight Countries on 9 June this year. There are now, we understand, only seven of the original sponsors. Over the years, India has worked closely with several of the sponsors on disarmament issues in various forums. We have noted that the resolution goes far beyond the parameters of the joint ministerial declaration. It includes extraneous elements and formulations that were adopted in other forums. We reject prescriptive approaches concerning security issues, such as though contained in operative paragraph 7 that are not only extraneous to this resolution but also completely divorced from reality on the ground. The draft resolution also tends to place policy recommendations based on fallacious concepts such as the following in paragraph 7: "those three States that are nuclear-weapons-capable and that have not yet acceded to the NPT." This concept is analytically hollow and does not correspond to reality.

The reference to a nuclear-weapon-free zone in South Asia not only borders on the absurd, but also calls into question one of the fundamental guiding principles for the establishment of nuclear-weapon-free zones, namely, that the arrangements for such zones should be freely arrived at among States of the region concerned. The deliberations of this Committee have once again demonstrated that there is no such consensus on the proposal for the establishment of a nwf zone in South Asia.

On operative paragraph 17, India abstained, as we do not see negative security assurances within the restrictive framework of NPT.

Given the omnibus nature of this resolution, there is a surprising lack of any mention of the doctrines of first use of nuclear weapons, which have been inherited from the Cold War years.

Similarly, the resolution ignores efforts in certain countries, unconstrained by a partial treaty banning nuclear testing, to refine and modernize nuclear weapons for retention well into the next millennium. The on-going effort for building ballistic-missile defenses could well have an unsettling effect on the delicate strategic balance.

There is an intriguing absence of any reference to the Final Document of the Tenth Special Session on Disarmament, which remains the only consensus document on disarmament adopted by the international community as a whole. The Final Document contains a Program of Action which remains only partially implemented. Any agenda for the future would necessarily have to take into account the starting premise for global disarmament contained in the Final Document..

The sponsors of this resolution have sought to portray its recommendations as intended to revive some of the core understandings of the NPT. My delegation's views on this treaty are well-known, and we sympathize with those who have been striving unsuccessfully over the years, including at the second NPT PrepCom this year, to get the self-anointed five nuclear-weapon States to make unequivocal commitments to nuclear disarmament and the complete elimination of nuclear weapons. The draft resolution is silent on the multifarious sources of proliferation which the NPT has failed to stem. We believe that the success of any international effort such as this, however worthy and energetic in its own right, would be limited by the unequal and discriminatory framework of obligations enshrined in the NPT. The New Agenda cannot succeed in the old framework of the NPT.

My delegation has noted carefully the reactions of certain delegations to this draft resolution. The nuclear-weapon States, which are yet to provide the unequivocal commitment to the speedy and total elimination of nuclear weapons, as called for in operative paragraph 1, have sought to justify their opposition to this resolution by citing the lack of any critical reference to the nuclear tests that took place in May this year. This is not a resolution on nuclear testing. Therefore the statements of such delegations, which we reject, are evidence of their desire to use the tests that took place in South Asia as an excuse to oppose any proposal that would invite them to undertake unequivocal commitments towards nuclear disarmament.

The commitment of India to nuclear disarmament, unlike that of the other nuclear-weapon States, remains firm and we remain ready to contribute to universal nuclear disarmament in a non-discriminatory framework. India would have preferred this resolution to include proposals contained in the Final Document of the twelth summit of the Non-Aligned Movement, representing five sixths of humanity, held in South Africa, one of the sponsors of this resolution. This Final Document includes concrete proposals towards a nuclear-weapon-free world, particularly the call for an international conference with the objective agreement on the phased elimination of nuclear weapons. Similarly, we would have preferred the designation of the use of weapons of mass destruction, including nuclear weapons, as a crime against humanity within in the purview of the International Criminal Court. However, India did not press ahead with its amendments in deference to the wishes of some of the sponsors of this resolution and in the hope that these points would find a suitable place in this resolution in the future.

In conclusion, although my delegation also shares the objective of the total elimination of nuclear weapons, and the need to work for a nuclear-weapon-free world, we remain unconvinced of the utility of an exercise bound by flawed and discriminatory approaches of the NPT. We have therefore cast a negative vote on the resolution as a whole.

Ambassador Giuseppe Balboni of Italy: Italy decided to abstain on the draft resolution. Being determined to pursue nuclear disarmament globally, with the ultimate goal of eliminating nuclear weapons, the Government of Italy shares the motivations of the drafters of the resolution. We believe that there is a need to intensify international efforts in this field, in particular by exploiting the momentum created by the achievements to date and the future promise of the START process. However, the draft resolution raises some concerns related to the means it envisages...

Italy is not convinced that the cause of nuclear disarmament, which we fully support, would be advanced by a resolution which has concepts not consistent with the Non-Proliferation Treaty, and which considers strategies which might undermine the Treaty's effectiveness and credibity. Moreover, we believe that a more balanced text, better reflecting the results already achieved in the area of nuclear disarmament, would have been instrumental in intensifying the dialogue between nuclear and non-nuclear states. Italy, for its part, intends to firmly pursue this goal, in line with the perception shared by its Government, Parliament and public opinion that nuclear disarmament is the primary responsibility of the nuclear-weapon States but is also in the undeniable interest of the entire international community. For the reasons I have stressed, Italy decided to abstain, in order to avoid any misunderstanding with regard to our commitment to nuclear disarmament, but also to voice our concern as to the means envisaged by the resolution whose goal we share.

Ambassador Ole Peter Kolby, Norway: Nuclear disarmament and nuclear non-proliferation have been long-standing Norwegian policy objectives. It is necessary to halt the spread of nuclear weapons and to significantly reduce and ultimately eliminate existing nuclear arsenals. Disarmament in general is the responsibility of all states, but when it comes to nuclear disarmament the nuclear-weapon States bear the primary responsibility. It is essential to secure their active participation in any nuclear disarmament and non-proliferation endeavors.

Norway does support the reasoning behind the draft resolution. There is a need for initiatives which can revitalize our way of dealing with nuclear issues multilaterally. We also share the ultimate goal of elimination of nuclear weapons and a desire to approach these issues in a more practical and constructive way. We are, however, not convinced that this resolution in its present form will be as conducive to a more constructive and dynamic climate for multilateral discussions in this field as we have liked. We have in the discussions pointed out several programmatic elements in the text and formulations we cannot agree with. In essence, there are five main reasons why Norway was not in a position to vote in favor of the resolution.

First, the language of the resolution in the preambular as well as the operative parts is too confrontational and categorical regarding the nuclear-weapon States and may not contribute to a strengthened multilateral dialogue on nuclear disarmament issues.

Secondly, the resolution does not duly recognize the significant steps that in fact have been taken by the nuclear-weapon States in the area of nuclear disarmament. We would like to see the reality reflected more clearly and believe that the resolution would then be more likely to facilitate a climate for further improvement in this field.

Thirdly, in our view, the resolution reflects a lack of balance in the sense that it is critical of the way in which the nuclear-weapon States fulfil their nuclear disarmament obligations, while it does not properly address the recent nuclear tests in South Asia.

Fourthly, we believe that an international conference on nuclear disarmament and nuclear non-proliferation to complement efforts being made in other settings, as proposed by the resolution, would be redundant, and that such a conference would have the potential to derail and undermine the strengthened review process of the NPT.

Fifthly, the language of the resolution addressing the possible role of the Conference on Disarmament (CD) on questions related to nuclear disarmament and nuclear arms control is too ambiguous. Like other delegations, we do not believe that the CD should be mandated to negotiate nuclear weapons reductions. Multilateral negotiations would only weaken the responsibility of the nuclear-weapon States to pursue in good faith and bring to a conclusion negotiations leading to nuclear disarmament. On the other hand, we hope that the CD can serve as a forum for exchange and use of information on all relevant issues in this field. We find that more precise language on this point, which clearly excludes the CD from any role in negotiating nuclear forces, is called for.

Ambassador John Campbell of Australia: Australia was not able to support this resolution...we believe the path the sponsors are indicating towards an idea which we share, a world free of nuclear weapons, is not practical or realistic. Regrettably, there are no shortcuts where the balance to verified drawdown of nuclear stocks and systems is concerned. For who would want to add new uncertainties and insecurities to the nuclear dispensation the Cold War bequeathed us. Moreover, we do not accept what appears to be the premise of the new agenda resolution - that the current agenda, the nuclear non-proliferation and disarmament regime as we know it, has failed, or is in dire need of reanimation. In fact, thanks to the dedication and hard work of many States over the past thirty-odd years, the regime is in impressively good shape, has evolved to meet new needs and challenges and has secured the allegiance of the quasi-totality of the planet. This has made possible remarkable progress in establishing and strengthening the instruments that underpin and embody that regime and, since the end of the Cold War, in achieving deep cuts in the numbers of nuclear weapons in the world.

The number of States adhering to the NPT is not only larger than this body itself, but continues to grow, including in this year. Certainly there is no room for complacency, as other events this year have shown, but neither have we hit an iceberg. The approach of the draft resolution is also flawed in that it proposes a new international conference on nuclear disarmament with an ill-defined agenda which we believe will distract attention and energies away from the priority tasks of strengthening the Comprehensive Test Ban Treaty, achieving progress in the new negotiations on a fissile material cut-off treaty, insuring a successful 2000 review conference of the nuclear Non-Proliferation Treaty, and maintaining the good progress achieved to date in nuclear disarmament, notably under the START process.

Finally, Australia remains committed to the twin goals of nuclear non-proliferation and disarmament, as enshrined in the NPT, and will remain active in the pursuit of practical and realistic steps to insure the Treaty's full implementation.

Ambassador Gunther Seibert of Germany: Since the reasons for and against this resolution have already been set out in great detail, I shall heed your advice and be very brief. Germany abstained on the resolution. The Federal Republic of Germany welcomes in the resolution before us the commitment to nuclear disarmament, with the goal of the complete elimination of nuclear weapons. Germany believes that this goal can best be achieved through the speedy continuation of the step-by-step procress of nuclear disarmament.

Ambassador Akira Hayashi of Japan: As a nation who experienced the devastation of nuclear bombs, Japan well shares the long desire to seek a world free from nuclear weapons, the desire that is behind the draft resolution. Thus my delegation has had extensive consultations with the sponsors of the draft resolution, which I believe contains many elements, particularly those in the operative paragraphs, that we can share. In fact, there are a number of common ingredients in this resolution and the nuclear disarmament resolution which we put forward and which was adopted a few minutes ago. Consequently, my delegation's decision to abstain on the current resolution was not easy. We were obliged to do so as, in our view the resolution, in our view, it went just a little too far and contained some elements that are a little bit premature, in spite of the many elements we share.

For example, the resolution speaks in the second preambular paragraph about "the prospect of the indefinite possession of nuclear weapons" and says in the fifth preambular paragraph "the nuclear-weapon States have not fulfilled speedily and totally their commitment to the elimination of their nuclear weapons." The fact is that the nuclear-weapon States have committed themselves, in written documents, to the elimination of nuclear weapons. They have also already achieved a significant reduction in their nuclear arsenals , and there are commitments to further reduction, even though these may not have been to the satisfaction of those who expect even more.

My delegation believes that, given the complexity and the difficult nature of the issue, we should try harder to create a new consensus involving the nuclear-weapon States, so that we can make steady step-by-step progress towards the ultimate elimination of nuclear weapons. Japan believes that the resolution it proposed, which was adopted today, is an effort in this direction. From this point of view, my delegation is also concerned about operative paragraphs 14 and 19 of this resolution. Again, while this delegation was obliged to abstain in the voting on this resolution, we do appreciate the efforts made by its sponsors and look forward to continuing our dialogue with them, with the common objective of a world free from nuclear weapons.

Mr. Fruchtbaum of the Solomon Islands: I take the floor in order to put a proposal to the Department for Disarmament Affairs and others...My proposal derives from the discussion on the resolution "Towards a nuclear-weapon-free world and the need for a new agenda." A number of representatives, particularly from the nuclear-weapon Powers, made the point...that the strategy of nuclear deterrence ended the Cold War and kept the peace. That statement has been made with such authority on a number of occasions, such as this morning, as to seem to indicate that there is no possiiblity of disagreement. As a university history teacher regularly facing young people who ask very difficult uestions, I have long come to doubt the truthfulness of that claim for the strategy of nuclear deterrence. Therefore, I suggest that serious consideration be given to having at the Committee's next session at least a one-day forum, with a morning and an afternoon meeting, at which that issue - how the strategy of nuclear deterrence ended the Cold War and kept the peace - can be debated. Please let those permanent members of the Security Council that make that claim bring their historians, their political scientists and their military strategists to make the argument, and let those of us who have serious doubts about it be able to respond in a very real and serious debate and dialogue. I think and the Solomon Islands delegation thinks, that that would be most helpful in trying to get at some better and balanced understanding about that claim.

HOW CAN WE MAKE GREATER PROGRESS TOWARDS NUCLEAR DISARMAMENT AND PREVENT FURTHER PROLIFERATION: NON GOVERNMENTAL INITIATIVES

JONATHAN GRANOFF: Our first speaker is Professor Hal Feiveson, a research scientist at the Center for Energy and Environmental Studies and a member of the Center for International Studies at Princeton University. He has been involved in research in the fields of nuclear weapons and nuclear energy policy for many years. He, along with Professor Frank von Hippel, is involved in a research program on nuclear policy alternatives. He is involved in a project with Russian scientists as well and is the Editor and one of the founders of a new international journal, *Science and Global Security*.

HAL FEIVESON: ...I will focus on some of the objections to de-alerting. I think the notion of the US and Russia standing down from alert their nuclear missiles is now on the radar screen of policy makers. The US and Russia together right now have maybe 5000 warheads that could be launched within 15 or 20 minutes of an order to do so. Nine years after the Berlin Wall fell, it seems somewhat anachronistic that these weapons should be on high alert. The idea has been put forward in several forums. My colleague, Bruce Blair, Frank von Hippel and I wrote an article last year in *Scientific American*. The latest issue of the UNIDIR (UN Institute for Disarmament Research) newsletter had several articles on de-alerting, including one by Arjun Makhijani, so it has been mentioned at the UN. Ambassador Powar of India mentioned it when introducing an Indian resolution at the UN a few weeks ago, so it is on the radar screen. I am not sure it is on the agenda yet.

A few US and Russian defense experts have talked in support of de-alerting: Sam Nunn, who was the former Chairman of the Senate Armed Services Committee, General Devorkin, a Russian General of note, and other people. But I would say, by and large, the defense experts in the US and Russia have not accepted the idea of de-alerting. Blair, von Hippel and I visited General Habiger, who last year was Director of the US Strategic Command, and he spoke very warmly against de-alerting.

I thought I might briefly review, with the apology that I won't first lay out what the measures are, [1] some of the reasons why the US and Russian military and defense experts, for the most part, up to now, think that de-alerting is not a good idea.

The objections come in two groups. One is that de-alerting is unwise in principle. Even if you could do it technically and verifiably, it is not a good idea. Second is a more narrow set of technical arguments, that you really can't de-alert in a way that is operationally neat, that could be verified and so on. I won't talk, unless it comes up in the question period, about this second group of issues, can de-alerting be verified, and so on, and talk about some of the objections in principle.

One which may straddle the two classes of issues is that de-alerting is a novel concept, and since we are pretty safe now, why bother. Well, it is not really that unprecedented. In 1991, in the wake of the attempted August coup in Moscow and concern over the security of Russian warheads,

---

[1]See the panel discussion on De-alerting in this publication on p.137.

Presidents Bush and Gorbachev took a series of steps to de-alert large parts of the US and Russian nuclear forces. The US took all of its strategic bombers that had been on high alert off of high alert. We disabled 500 Minuteman II missiles that were scheduled to be eliminated anyway under START I years later, and took them off of alert.

The Russians reciprocated similarly and the US and Russia also took out of operation several submarines that were scheduled to be eliminated. They de-alerted them years earlier than they would have had to be eliminated. At the same time the US and Russia withdrew large numbers of naval and battlefield nuclear weapons and put them into storage, a kind of de-alerting of tactical weapons.

More recently, at the Helsinki summit in March, the US and Russia, Presidents Clinton and Yeltsin, agreed that for the multiple warhead land-based missiles scheduled to be eliminated under START II by 2003 the Russians would have another five years to eliminate them, as would the US, but that in the meantime these weapons would be deactivated, which is in some important ways similar to de-alerting, in some ways not quite the same. So it is not unprecedented.

But, of course, these other de-alerting steps did not de-alert the entire nuclear force. Many of the forces still are on very high alert. So if you try to get all the weapons off high alert you run into other objections.

I also should mention that most US submarines are not on high alert. Under START II the US is expecting to have 14 submarines deployed, and only four of these would be on alert, on station in northern oceans, ready to fire within tens of minutes of an order to do so. Most of them are not on station, on alert. So it is not that big a jump to think about of having most of the weapons off alert.

The second objection that has been raised, particularly by the Russians, is that the US and Russia can't stand down their ballistic missiles from alert until the other nuclear weapon states do likewise. But in fact, it may be that the other nuclear weapons states already have their weapons off of alert. The British, in their latest strategic defense review, announced:

We will only have one submarine on patrol at a time, carrying a reduced load of 48 warheads. The submarine's missiles will not be targeted and will normally be at several days notice to fire. This reduced state of alert will enable a greater use of ballistic missile submarines for secondary tasks, such as exercises with other vessels, equipment trials and hydrographic work.

Since France scrapped its land-based missiles, there is some evidence that their weapons also are not on high alert. Recently when President Clinton was meeting with the Chinese leaders, and pressing the Chinese to accept so-called de-targeting policy, the CIA leaked information that Chinese ICBMs, their Intercontinental Ballistic Missiles, were not fueled and did not have warheads on them, that is, that they were many hours or days from being able to fire.

A third argument and principle, which is one of the more important ones, is that the US needs nuclear weapons on high alert to cover a range of what we call counterforce targets in Russia. At the outbreak of a nuclear war, the US wants to have the capability to immediately launch large numbers of missiles at the Russian nuclear-missile complex. That has been a central goal of US strategic force planning for a couple of decades, probably. De-alerting would give that idea up. That I think is one of the strongest reasons the US military doesn't like at the moment the idea of de-alerting.

But there are difficulties with this kind of strategy. A large scale, counterforce attack against Russian missiles would employ hundreds to thousands of warheads. Each warhead on average has about ten times the yield of the Hiroshima bomb and would certainly kill tens of millions of Russians and that would invite retaliation against the US under any reasonable conditions.

When I talked here in April I quoted from the movie, Dr. Strangelove. Let me do it again, because I think it captures the idea of counterforce very nicely. I don't know how many of you remember the movie, but if you remember, the Air Force General, Buck Turgidson, who is played by George C. Scott, is trying to get the President to make a preemptive counterforce attack. He argues:

It is necessary now to make a choice, to choose between two admittedly regrettable but nevertheless distinguishable post-war environments. One where you will get twenty million people killed and the other where you get one hundred and fifty million people killed.

President Merkin Muffly, played by Peter Sellars, shocked: You are talking about mass murder, General, not war.

General Turgidson: I am not saying we wouldn't get our hair mussed. But I do say no more than ten to twenty million killed, tops, depending upon the breaks.

Muffly, angrily: I will not go down in history as the greatest mass murderer since Hitler.

Turgidson: Perhaps it might be better, Mr. President, if you were concerned with the American people, more than with your image in the history books.

That is the US notion of why it is important for counterforce. If you have nuclear weapons, where else can you use them except against the other guy's nuclear weapons? No one wants to use them against cities. So it does go against the grain of the military to think about not using these weapons for counterforce, but I think the logic for counterforce is pretty weak, basically, and I think it will fade.

Finally, in these arguments in principle, there is the argument that de-alerting will undermine deterrence, not just against Russia, but against other countries, weakening US ability and resolve to employ nuclear weapons in general. Let me give you some examples.

When Blair, von Hippel and I published our article in *Scientific American* there was a real counterattack in several quarters. One of them was in the *Wall St. Journal*. I will quote from their editorial and articles:

The biggest flaw in suggestions for de-alerting pertains to rogue states like North Korea, Iran and Iraq, all of them developing long-range ballistic missiles.

The primary reason that US nuclear weapons are on alert is that Russia retains as many as ten times more tactical nuclear weapons than we do, an arsenal capable of destroying the US.

The Center for Security Policy at the same time put out the following:

Messieurs Blair, Feiveson and von Hippel have the cheek to conclude with the assertion that such de-alerting steps would substantially reduce the risk of an accidental nuclear catastrophe, without in any way weakening deterrence. Think about it. These individuals would have us believe that the entire US ballistic missile force could be made incapable of launch in less than one day without having any adverse impact on deterrence whatsoever. Even if the Russians do adopt the measures that the authors airily say they expect President Yeltsin to implement to reduce the readiness of Russian land and sea-based missiles, how can anyone say that the deterrent to acts of aggression by China, Iran, or other emerging missile-equipped nuclear threats currently represented by America's nuclear deterrent would not be degraded?

I think the notion that we have to keep our weapons on fifteen minutes alert because North Korea, Iran and Iraq might in several years' time develop a few ballistic missiles seems a little silly, Or because Russia has some short range tactical weapons in storage. There are other arguments, of course. Let me just quickly mention the second class of arguments, the arguments against de-alerting, not in principle but in practice. I won't try to respond to them, but let me give you the flavor of them.

De-alerting complicates operational control over nuclear weapons and an orderly and sustained implementation of START agreements. De-alerting would not be stable; it would make the strategic forces of both sides more vulnerable and in a crisis lead to a race to de-de-alert. De-alerting, by separating warheads from their delivery vehicle, would make strategic forces more vulnerable by concentrating warheads in fewer targets. (The Russians have made this point.)

De-alerting cannot be verified in a manner that would not also compromise the survivability of the strategic forces being de-alerted.

We can come back to these objections, and you may have some, in the question period.

JONATHAN GRANOFF: I would like to now introduce Dr. Arjun Makhijani, who is the President for Energy and Environmental Research in Takoma, Maryland. He is the author and co-author of numerous books, reports and articles on nuclear weapons and related issues. He has a Ph.D. in nuclear fusion from the University of California at Berkeley. If you look at his newsletters, he goes beyond talking about the technical issues, in which he is an expert, but he gathers relevant arguments from all quarters. In the latest edition you will find the moral argument for the elimination of nuclear weapons put forward by the Catholic Bishops. Dr. Makhijani is kind of a renaissance man.

ARJUN MAKHIJANI: Thank you, Jonathan. I am also affectionately known as "Dr. Egghead." I write a column called "It pays to increase your jargon power, by Dr. Egghead."

I just want to add one thing to the discussion of de-alerting that Hal talked about, and then I will speak about what has occupied me for the better part of fifteen years working with non-governmental organizations, first others, and then the one that I run just outside of Washington.

We have suggested, that in addition to the de-alerting measures that Hal and Bruce Blair and others have written about, that a complementary de-alerting measure be taken by removing all the tritium bottles from thermonuclear weapons. This is a very technical thing, and I want to take just a minute to explain what it is.

Hydrogen bombs have two stages. The first stage has uranium and plutonium in it, and it also has a small quantity of a mixture of two isotopes of hydrogen, deuterium and tritium. These gasses are meant to use the plutonium efficiently. In the designs of most weapons, and I think essentially all weapons in the US and Russia and China, France and Britain, probably, this gas is necessary to make the hydrogen bomb part of the hydrogen bomb go off. It is only about 15% of an ounce, a little more than a tenth of an ounce, 4 grams of tritium gas and a few grams of deuterium gas in each warhead. If you take it out, the hydrogen bomb part won't go off. The primary part of it will go off, so if somebody attacks you, you can still threaten to blow up their cities, but you can't attack them first in the manner that Hal has been talking about, which is blow up their silos. It takes away the arguments for a hair-trigger alert.

It is also very verifiable because once you make the reactor operating records public, how much has been made, you can calculate how much has decayed away, and you don't have to withdraw the weapons from deployment. I am in favor of the kinds of de-alerting measures that Hal has written about, and I have written about them too, and I think they are complementary to what I am talking about. It is something that can be done within a few weeks' time, to convert the world's nuclear arsenals from several thousand megatons to less than a hundred megatons.

I think that it is a very doable technical measure, something that doesn't take away second strike deterrence. It at least ought to be considered by the world's militaries, although a lot of us would like faster progress on a lot of things, and also the disabling of weapons for longer periods of time. It has not been much discussed in the literature, so far as I know.

It has been discussed, sort of in passing, by various people over the years but not considered as the central issue, except a few years back when people were saying we should stop making tritium, which is radioactive and will decay. After some decades we won't have this gas anymore. It will sort of be disarmament by radioactive decay.

I want to talk about another kind of problem with radioactivity and what it had to do with closing down most of the US nuclear weapons complex and has had major effects in other countries, including the former Soviet Union, and specifically Russia. There is no treaty that says US nuclear weapons plants, most of them, should be shut. There is no agreement between countries that required the Hanford reactors and the Savannah River reactors to be shut.

Even as the Cold War was winding down, there were huge expenditures made by the Department of Energy and the US government to try to start the reactors at the Savannah River site in South Carolina. There were many efforts to start the plutonium separation plant in 1989-1990 in Hanford. When we stopped much of the nuclear weapons production in the late 1980s under Presidents Reagan and Bush, the Department of Energy, which owns the nuclear weapons complex, though corporations run it, believed they would soon restart, once the safety issues were resolved.

But a very strange thing began to happen in the mid-1980s. At the global level it had something to do with President Gorbachev and his conversations with President Reagan. It was clear I think as the eighties wore on that the Cold War was winding down, and as the Cold War was winding down, people who lived near nuclear weapons plants began to look more closely at what was happening in their neighborhoods. All of these efforts were made by non-governmental organizations, community organizations as well as national environmental groups. People asked what have we done in the name of national security to our neighborhoods? I'll give you a few examples.

Of course it wasn't new to the 1980s. People have been worrying about this since the testing in the 1950s. It animated global demands for a comprehensive test ban which resulted in the stopping of atmospheric testing in 1963 by the US, the Soviet Union and Britain. But there wasn't an intensive and country-wide movement in every place that had media support and support eventually of a lot of elected representatives. I'll give you the example of the Fernald uranium plant.

It wasn't the biggest in the US nuclear weapons complex but it was something that was very important, I think, in changing the history of how nuclear weapons plants and their operations were assessed. In 1984 there was an accidental release of uranium from the Fernald plant that was reported in the newspapers. It was called the Feed Material Production Center. People thought they were making cat food, or something like that. It had a water tower that looked like a Purina cat chow pattern. I am sure it wasn't deliberate, but if you look at a picture of it, that is what it recalls. People thought they were making some kind of feed. Well, they were making feed materials for plutonium production reactors. The feed material was uranium.

Lisa Crawford, who lived near the plant, asked whether her water had ever been tested. This was in early 1985, and indeed it had, in 1980 or 1981. And the Department of Energy and its contractor, National Lead of Ohio, had found her water to be contaminated. This was in rural Ohio. They had a well in the backyard. She had a small son. She was appalled that the government and her contractor knew for four years and did not tell her, and that she had been giving her son this water ever since he was born and they did not know. I know Lisa very well. She is a good friend of mine. All I have to say to describe her view is two things. She is the most honest person I know, frank, absolutely wonderful. And it is very important in any battle to have Lisa on your side.

She is a perfect fighter for what she believes in. She was not involved in anything environmental or nuclear before. She filed a law suit and it became a class action law suit. My Institute did some of the expert studies for the plaintiffs in this law suit, and we found what later we found to be a pattern throughout the world.

Governments will make nuclear weapons in the name of national security, in the name of protecting the people, as Hal just described, by keeping these weapons on hair-trigger alert. These governments, throughout the Cold War, all of them, were ready to harm the people that they pledged they were protecting. And they contaminated their neighborhoods in secrecy, they operated these plants in secrecy, and when we looked at the environmental science, it was often of poor quality.

I was brought up in Bombay, India, and I went to some of the great universities here and in India, and I never saw bad science as a routine matter in universities. I never expected to find bad science as a routine matter in society, certainly not in the United States. I had lived here for eighteen years before I started finding bad science in a routine way on environmental and health issues related to nuclear weapons production.

I have never come across, and this is a shocking statement to make, a single set of health or environmental data maintained by any nuclear weapon establishment that I have been able to study, that is official, that I would regard as scientifically sound. And I have to say the US is the most open superpower in history, and so it is to its credit that we can actually say these things about the U S. Worse has happened in the Soviet Union, and we don't know much about many other countries. Even Britain has the Official Secrets Act, a sort of anti-freedom of information act.

But I have not come across a single set of health or environmental data that is scientifically sound. On the contrary, I have routinely come across bad data, poor data, incomplete data, even fabricated data, bad algebra, bad arithmetic, complete, total fabrications out of thin air.

We last year published a report on transuranic radioactive waste, highly plutonium-contaminated waste. We claimed that statistics published for guidance of environmental managers inside the Department of Energy, had no technical foundation and were jumping about from year to year, from zero to high numbers, up and down. And we could not find any technical justification for these numbers. Finally the Department did admit this. We had a cooperative review process of our work and we found that there is no technical justification for these numbers, and that the Department doesn't know what is there.

When we looked at the situation in the Soviet Union, I was expecting that it would be about as bad, but we found that it was actually much worse. And there is a reason that it was much worse there. In my estimation, the officials in the United States were constantly afraid of publicity, law suits, investigations by Congress, and protest.

I think the extra-governmental pressures on nuclear weapons states have been demonstrated very clearly and most effectively here. We have most of the nuclear weapons complex shut. Not all of it, but most of it. I think similar things can be done in other countries by people trying to protect their own communities and asking questions of their national governments, why they are engaged in these activities. I think it is also the key to greater openness and democracy because I don't think that the nuclear establishment can stand the scrutiny of sunshine because they have said they are operating for national and global security, but I believe when you look at the details, I do not think that these claims can stand up to serious scrutiny. Thank you.

JONATHAN GRANOFF: Now it is my pleasure to introduce Ambassador Thomas Graham. Ambassador Graham is the President of the national organization that I represent here at the UN, Lawyers Alliance for World Security. He is the former general counsel and the acting director of the Arms Control and Disarmament Agency of the United States. He was instrumental in the START process, the extension of the Nuclear Non-Proliferation Treaty and the Comprehensive Test Ban Treaty. In fact, there is probably no major arms control initiatives within governments in the last 20 years in which he has not played a major role.

And a major role in government means that, within the debates in government, he was one of the voices that I would say was a voice of reason and advocacy for trying to obtain security through promoting the rule of law, rather than what I would call the rule of the threat of violence. Like General Lee Butler, the previous head of the Strategic Air Command, Ambassador Graham knows the inner workings of this system, and so he is a very effective advocate for the step-by-step elimination of nuclear weapons. In terms of understanding how we can be effective in influencing government, I don't think we could get a better speaker. Ambassador Graham.

AMBASSADOR TOM GRAHAM: Thank you, Jonathan...I am going to speak on a somewhat different subject than de-alerting, but a related one: a subject that is essentially associated with the effort to drastically reduce and ultimately eliminate nuclear weapons, that is, nuclear use policy. The Nuclear Non-Proliferation Treaty, the NPT, is the cornerstone of international security. The existence of this treaty is the reason that, contrary to predictions, in the 1960s, we do not live today in a world with scores of nations with nuclear weapons fully integrated into their nuclear arsenals with the survival of civilization in doubt from day to day.

The NPT defined a balance of obligations between the nuclear weapon states and the non-nuclear weapon states. The non-nuclear weapon states agreed to never acquire nuclear weapons. The nuclear weapon states agreed to engage in nuclear disarmament negotiations with the ultimate objective of the elimination of nuclear weapons, and also to share the benefits of peaceful nuclear technology. This is the essential bargain that is the basis of world security today, and which made all subsequent arms control possible.

The 1995 NPT Review and Extension Conference did more than extend the NPT indefinitely. It adopted a statement of principles and Objectives on non-proliferation and a framework for a strengthened review process that will guide our future efforts. The victory in New York in May, 1995, was a common victory. It established a permanent landmark on the arms control horizon that we will be blessed to have in years to come. It represents a change in the conditions under which multilateral discussions on security will occur, broadening the responsibility for security, but also for the opportunities for international leadership.

It also recommitted, pursuant to the statement of principles, the nuclear weapons states to vigorously pursue nuclear weapon reductions, with the ultimate objective of zero. If this commitment is not met, the all important NPT regime will be in jeopardy. In 1995 a number of prominent third world countries privately said, they would re-examine their commitments to the NPT if significant progress toward nuclear disarmament is not achieved in the short to medium term.

More specifically, there could be real trouble if there is continuing dissatisfaction with the nuclear weapons states' compliance with their disarmament commitments at the 2000 NPT Review Conference. In order to avoid disastrous consequences for the NPT regime, and for international security on the whole, all the states parties to the NPT must fulfill their commitments. The nuclear weapons states will continue to be scrutinized, and the health of the regime will be indivisibly linked with continuing progress toward the ultimate goal of a world free of nuclear weapons.

During the Cold War, the era of thermonuclear confrontation between the superpowers, not much could be accomplished to redeem the commitment of the nuclear weapon states. Since the end of the Cold War, much has been accomplished, but much more must be accomplished if the NPT regime is to be preserved as the result of the 1995 conference made clear.

Also during the Cold War, massive conventional superiority of the Warsaw Pact in central Europe was offset in part by the United States and NATO nuclear weapons. This was the rationale of the retention by the United States and NATO of the right to use nuclear weapons first in the case of an overwhelming Warsaw Pact conventional force assault in Europe. But this confrontation and rationale for the first use of nuclear weapons has long since passed into history. It is NATO that has the preponderance in Europe now at a two to one margin over the East.

During the Cold War, in part because of the situation in Europe, the political value of nuclear weapons was very high. Now, years after the end of the Cold War, this value remains very high. If our non-proliferation objective, as set forth in the NPT and the 1995 Statement of Principles and Objectives are to succeed, we, as a world community, simply must reduce the political value of nuclear weapons. Otherwise, they will, over the long run, be too attractive and the fifty-year-old technology involved, too simple to control.

A striking example of the kind of thinking that could ultimately threaten the NPT regime was given by a Conservative Party defense spokesman in the British Parliament when, during a debate last fall regarding the future of the UK's Trident program, it was said "If we are talking about a half-hearted approach to our nuclear deterrent, how seriously will the UN take our continued claim to permanent membership of the Security Council?"

Clearly, the belief in some non-nuclear weapon states that some of the nuclear weapon states claim nuclear weapons as their claim to great power status is not without foundation. However, the survival of the NPT will depend on lessening the perception of the political utility of nuclear weapons. No first use is a good beginning whose time has come.

The United States National Academy of Sciences has suggested in a 1997 report entitled *The Future of US Nuclear Weapons Policy* several important practical steps that the US should take to de-emphasize the role of nuclear weapons and minimize the risk they constitute. The report recommends that nuclear forces be reduced far more, and limited to the core deterrence role of simply deterring the use of nuclear weapons by others. The report urges that the United States and Russia reduce as soon as practicable to one thousand total nuclear weapons, as opposed to 3500 strategic weapons each under START II and 2000 contemplated under START III.

It also encourages that promptly thereafter the other three nuclear weapon states should be engaged in negotiations aimed at a residual level of 200 to 300 total weapons for the United States and Russia, less for the other three, until the world has changed sufficiently for the ultimate abolition of nuclear weapons to become possible.

The Academy further recommends that the United States adopt a no-first-use policy with regard to nuclear weapons as part of the limiting of nuclear weapons to the core deterrence function and downgrading their political value. No first use is a particularly significant issue to focus on because it is very important and it could be implemented immediately. An explicit, clearly enunciated United States policy of not using nuclear weapons first would go a long way to proving good faith with the nuclear arms control and disarmament commitments set forth in Article VI of the NPT and the Statement of Principles and Objectives.

Such a policy would reinforce the defensive posture of US nuclear forces, making it clear that the sole purpose of the nuclear arsenal is to deter the use of nuclear weapons by others. In the past, the possibility that close US allies, especially those considered to be under the US nuclear umbrella, such as Germany and Japan, might consider developing their own nuclear weapons has been used as a rationale for not adopting a no-first-use policy because those countries opposed such a posture. It has been suggested publicly by at least one former senior official that this is the reason that no-first-use was not made part of the nuclear posture review in 1994.

Late last year I led delegations to Japan and Germany to discuss nuclear disarmament, including the issue of likely reactions to the adoption, by the United States, of a no-first-use policy. In both cases government officials were reluctant to make strong statements about what they viewed to be the strategic business of the United States, but they indicated that neither the option of a no-first-use policy or the negotiation of a deep cuts in a balanced context with the other nuclear weapon states would undermine the confidence in the commitment of the United States to their defense. Both governments at that time were absolutely adamant that under no conditions would they ever consider the acquisition of nuclear weapons.

Quite the contrary, it seems clear that efforts to reduce the political significance attached to nuclear weapons, such as the adoption of a no-first-use policy, would serve as an added reenforcement to these countries nuclear non-proliferation commitments. A no-first-use agreement among the five nuclear weapon states would be an even more important step because it would reenforce national political statements and end any dispute over whether or not the first use of nuclear weapons violates international law. Such an agreement would go a long way in demonstrating to the non-nuclear weapons states parties to the NPT that the nuclear weapon states take their disarmament commitments seriously.

Suggestions that nuclear weapons should be used to explicitly deter chemical or biological attacks should not be allowed to justify a failure to adopt a no-first-use policy. Not only would such a strategy be inappropriate and disproportionate, it would endanger the NPT regime.

The 1978 pledge made by the United States, the United Kingdom and the Soviet Union at the first United Nations Special Session on Disarmament not to use or threaten to use nuclear weapons against non-nuclear weapons states parties to the NPT unless they attack the United States in alliance with a nuclear weapon states is an important element of the NPT regime. There is no exception in this commitment for chemical or biological weapons. Numerous non-nuclear weapon states made their decision to join the NPT after this commitment was announced.

This commitment referred to as a negative security assurance was reaffirmed in April, 1995, by the nuclear weapon states in the context of the 1995 NPT Review and Extension Conference. Without it, the indefinite extension of the NPT might not have taken place. The then 178, now 185, States Parties to the NPT agreed to its indefinite extension relying on this affirmation.

The way to deal with threats of the use of chemical and biological weapons is with the overwhelming conventional power of the United States and NATO. It should be insured in the future that any state that resorts to chemical or biological weapons will pay an unbearable price. However, to threaten retaliation with nuclear weapons would only encourage countries who are threatened by chemical or biological weapons to seek their own nuclear weapon capability. Were countries to begin to do this, the NPT would fail, and the existing conventional superiority of the United States and NATO would be neutralized by the widespread proliferation of nuclear weapons.

There is much that non-governmental organizations can do to support affirmative movement toward a more rational and modern conception about the role of nuclear weapons, like no first use. For example, the Lawyers Alliance for World Security, LAWS, my organization, in conjunction with several Indian non-governmental organizations, will be holding preliminary discussions in New Delhi in early 1999 regarding a proposed international conference to consider the possibility of a no-first-use agreement.

Also, LAWS, the British American Information Council (BASIC) and the Berlin Information Center for Trans-Atlantic Security, in conjunction with several other NGOs and with the support of the W. Alton Jones Foundation, will be conducting programs in key NATO capitals with the purpose of avoiding the unrevised restatement of Cold War NATO policy regarding the first use of nuclear weapons at the NATO ministerial meeting this spring.

Both of these initiatives hold promise for near-term progress of the kind that will enable us to move forward, despite the inertia and difficult political circumstances of the moment. We all must do everything we can to support and enhance the NPT regime. If nuclear deterrence is somewhat underemployed, let it remain so. The less dependent we are on nuclear weapons for our defense, the more secure we will be.

The World Court ruled in 1996 that the threat of use and use of nuclear weapons must be subject to international law, which includes the 1995 negative security assurances made by the nuclear weapon states in association with the indefinite extension of the NPT.

The World Court also ruled in 1996 that any use of nuclear weapons would generally contravene the principles and rule of humanitarian law, except possibly in a circumstance - the Court was divided on this - of extreme self-defense. Such a circumstance could not occur for a nuclear weapons state in the absence of a threat or use of nuclear weapons.

Religious leaders have denounced the doctrine of nuclear deterrence in today's world. For example, Archbishop Martino of the Holy See said at the United Nations last fall that "nuclear weapons are incompatible with the peace we seek for the twenty-first century."

No rationale remains for the nuclear weapons states to retain the right to introduce nuclear weapons into a conflict. Clinging to the doctrine of the past supports the political value of nuclear weapons and undermines the NPT. No first use is an idea whose time has come.

JONATHAN GRANOFF: Thank you Ambassador Graham. Dr. Hiro Umebayashi, is the Director of the Peace Resources Cooperative in Japan, a newly-established peace organization for information, education and advocacy. He is a physicist by training, and after resigning from teaching in the university, he has been working for peace issues for more than 25 years. He also serves as the international coordinator of the Pacific Campaign for Disarmament and Security, an Asian-Pacific regional network of grass-roots peace groups. He is one of the key advocates for the Abolition 2000 movement in Japan and also the Japanese representative for the Middle Powers Initiative.

HIRO UMEBAYASHI: What I would like to report very briefly is a new and potentially promising dimension of the dynamics of interaction between Japanese citizens and the government regarding the nuclear disarmament policy of Japan. That dynamic was created thanks to the courageous joint statement of the Eight Nations New Agenda Coalition and the independent activities by the Middle Powers Initiative.

It was a pity, but by no means surprising to most of the Japanese people, that the Japanese government refused the New Agenda Coalition when it was kindly invited to join. If the refusal had happened in a different international environment it would have ended without drawing any further attention, even in the disarmament activities in Japan. In fact, however, it happened just after the series of nuclear tests by India and Pakistan and the Japanese government had already committed itself to an international proposal to respond to the strong public call in Japan for enhanced efforts towards nuclear abolition.

Then foreign minister, and now Prime Minister of Japan, Kazo Obuchi, proposed an international conference to address the new global situation of nuclear proliferation in South Asia. The conference was named at first Conference on Urgent Action for Nuclear Non-Proliferation and Disarmament. The name was changed at the first meeting to The Tokyo Forum on Nuclear Non-Proliferation and Disarmament. I do hope that the elimination of the words urgent and action from the title of the conference will not have any real substance.

The Tokyo Forum planned four meetings with eighteen experts as commissioners. The Tokyo Forum was sponsored by two non-governmental institutions, Japan Institute of International Affairs, and the Hiroshima Peace Institute. The Foreign Minister of Japan serves as the conference secretariat. The first of the series of four meetings took place at the end of August. The second will take place on December 18 and 19, and reportedly the third will be held here in New York around April next year. The final report of the Commission will be issued early next summer.

NGOs in Japan, as well as in many different parts of the world, welcomed this initiative of Japan. At the same time they were aware that the majority of past conferences convened by the Japanese government had only provided opportunities for discussions by officials and experts but lacked the result of political direction of the Japanese government. Given the urgency of issues that confronted us human beings, NGOs thought the Tokyo Forum must be different from earlier efforts.

Therefore, an international NGO letter to the Foreign Minister of Japan was organized to address such concerns and to ask Japan to assume bold leadership in the Tokyo Forum, reminding Japan that it had a special responsibility to humankind as it is the only nation victimized and devastated by nuclear bombing in the war.

Accordingly, the steps that the NGO letter asked Japan to undertake included that Japan should express its support for the Eight Nation New Agenda Coalition initiatives. In combination with the NGO letter, a broad coalition of independent Japanese NGOs held a parallel public conference one day prior to the Tokyo Forum and invited a Foreign Minister official to a panel discussion before the public audience.

After a long negotiation between the NGOs and the Foreign Ministry, the Foreign Ministry decided to send an official to the panel with all the other panelists from anti-nuclear organizations. It was the first occurrence in history in Japan. Under such national and international pressure by NGOs, the Foreign Ministry started to explain publicly why Japan refused to join the New Agenda Coalition.

The crucial point, it turned out, was the request for no-first-use declarations of nuclear weapons by the nuclear weapon states which appeared in the joint statement of the New Agenda Coalition. Japan appears to think that the no-first-use declaration by the United States jeopardizes its security assurance, especially against a North Korean chemical or biological attack. This view of the government was a real surprise for most of the Japanese disarmament workers, not to mention the general public, because the overall understanding of the Japanese government's nuclear policy was that it came from general consideration of the US and Japan relationship, and not from specific local security considerations.

It is a very crude understanding, but it has been a reality. I know we need more deliberation on to what extent Japan has insisted on no declaration by the US of no-first-use and on whether the North Korean threat is real or to what extent it is an excuse. But still, I think it was a very good start for future discussions to know more specifically what the Administration has in mind.

As you might know already, there has been a striking division between the Japanese citizens' strong anti-nuclear sentiments and the passive policies exhibited by Japanese officials in international nuclear disarmament negotiations and discussions.

In my view, one of the key reasons is that there has been very little open argument on security aspects regarding the nuclear policy of Japan. Now the situation is changing. It appears that the emergence of the efforts by the New Agenda Coalition and the activities of the Middle Powers Initiative are changing the framework of dialogues, discussion between NGOs and the government in Japan. Both parties now share the common reference point relative to the arguments which will make their conversation more frequent, specific, and hopefully, deeper.

Recently Rob Green, the major author of the briefing book of the Middle Powers, visited Japan and consolidated constructive relationships with key Foreign Ministry officials and politicians, as well as with NGOs. I hope that the dynamics created by such movement and by ongoing discussions in the Tokyo forum will enhance the whole process of interaction between NGOs and the government, hopefully towards nuclear disarmament. Thank you.

JONATHAN GRANOFF: I was just reminded that several years ago Joseph Rotblatt, who received the 1995 Nobel Peace Award, spoke at an NGO Committee-sponsored meeting, and highlighted what in his opinion was the first and most essential step toward nuclear elimination: no first use. He said that he felt that was the log jam. I found it very interesting that Ambassador Graham highlighted that issue and Dr. Umebayashi highlighted that issue as a key issue. No first use, in the context of disarmament, rather in the context of just changing the nuclear policy, is not something that we, as an NGO community, have focused on. Japan every year puts forward a resolution calling for the ultimate elimination of nuclear weapons in the General Assembly.

I was also in Japan last summer speaking for the Nomura Foundation at a large gathering, and I had the opportunity to speak with the Prince and some of the people in the Diet. I was really surprised that they had not looked at this tremendous anomaly between the government's supporting ultimate elimination and not taking the steps that would help lead it there. I would like to open this up to a dialogue. If there are any NGOs here who want to announce any initiatives that you are involved in that you think would be pertinent, please feel free to do so

RICHARD JORDAN, Co-chair of the NGO Committee on Sustainable Development: Another NGO for which I serve is the Communication Coordination Committee for the United Nations. It has a working group of experts on the year 2000 (Y2K) problem. One of those experts has made the claim that there is a small but finite chance that there could be an accidental launch of a missile with a nuclear weapon due to the Y2K problem. Is anyone at the National Academy of Sciences looking at this problem, and secondly, wouldn't the logical solution simply be to separate all nuclear warheads from all missiles and therefore eliminate that small but finite possibility?

TOM GRAHAM: Many people are studying this problem very carefully. It is a very complex and many-sided one. There is a special commission looking at it. I am sure that the National Academy has people studying the issue. There is a problem in Russia. I am sure everyone is agreed that there is a problem. Precisely what the problem is, there are different views on that.

With respect to the second half of your question, yes, that would be the most logical step. I hope it does happen but I am rather pessimistic that it will before the year 2000.

JIM GARST; Mr. Feiveson, you referred to the more-or-less bilateral agreement in 1991 between the then Soviet Union and the US to do some basic de-alerting. This question is not about the techniques of verification but the process. At that time was there any process, or regime of verification, of the actions of the two powers? Are the recent UK actions accompanied by any process for verification?

HAL FEIVESON: As I understand the 1991 measures, there was no verification immediately. Eventually, with the Minuteman II, for example, the warheads were removed, which is something you could observe, but initially the US and the Russians in a somewhat comparable way, disabled the warheads by flipping a switch which really was not the safety switch. When you go into a silo you want to make sure that nothing happens, so there is a safety switch which disallows ignition. The US did that. It was not verifiable. How much of what the British are doing can be verified? Probably not a lot, unless you contrive new measures, which are contrivable, but as far as I know the British have not offered to do them.

As to the question of process with the 1991 actions, let me just add a word, which goes beyond verification. President Bush, General Scowcroft, the Chairman of the Joint Chiefs, a rather small group, made a sweeping set of decisions without a murmur. Congress didn't say anything, as far as I know, and they swept off the board essentially almost all tactical nuclear weapons, all naval nuclear weapons, except the ballistic missiles, and it was done unilaterally. The Russians did reciprocate. Somehow there is a lesson there, I think. I am not sure exactly how to articulate the lesson, but a lot could be done by courageous leadership of the President, I think.

JIM GARST: Dr. Makhijani, you referred to the Fernald situation and you left us hanging with this very magnificent strong women. What was the outcome?

ARJUN MAKHIJANI: Lisa and her family are well. A lot of the difficulties with drinking contaminated water don't show up for a very long time, because of the latency period. One of the decisions that Lisa made, I think, was not to have any more children, because she was too afraid. They stopped drinking the water relatively soon. The law suit was settled by the government for $78 million. They did not acknowledge that they did anything wrong. The government settled it on behalf of the corporation. It was the corporation that was sued. Senator Glenn was from Ohio, and he got the Congress to ask the Center for Disease Control to do a study of this plant. What they found basically vindicated what we had said. The author of the study in 1995 said publicly that in the 1980s he thought Arjun Makhijani was crazy but now he thought he was right.

Later on we also did a study about the worker dose records. And the workers had been told that they had not been overexposed for the most part. We found that the worst abuses were in the fifties and the early sixties. We found that the uranium that the workers were breathing was not recorded in their dose records. There were urine samples, but that information was not integrated into the records, so if a worker asked he would not get that information.

That turned out to be the case throughout the nuclear weapons complex. We found that most workers in the fifties and the early sixties were over-exposed by then prevailing standards. The numbers fell very sharply with detente and reduced production and also with the environmental movement and very different safety standards. There were not what you would call the best safety standards, but they were much different than the fifties and sixties. So the health of many workers was very seriously affected, I believe. There was a very measurable loss of life expectancy among the workers. We looked at records for the 4000 and we have published our studies...so there has been a fair amount of checking on our work.

TERESA FITZGIBBON, the Religious Society of Friends: Is there is any strategy that we are not trying that we might try in light of your statement that the nuclear establishments can't stand sunshine? In the mid-eighties I was at a demonstration where someone from Germany said if 5000 of us got together at the CD in Geneva, for example, and behind them were 50,000 who said that we will hold you in there until you come out with some really serious solutions to all this...I would like to see something happening in my lifetime, but things move very slowly...When we want to have a war we can do it overnight, but when we want to disarm it takes forever. Two generations have grown up with this and we are leaving an awful legacy to next generations. It seems that when we ask the people, the people want nuclear disarmament. Why can't we move the leaders? Is there some initiative we haven't tried, that our imaginations haven't woken up to yet that would really make a difference? Abolition 2000, which is wonderful, is the only game in town, but we just move very slowly. I would like to move a bit faster.

TOM GRAHAM: That is a very good question. I don't know as anybody has the definitive answer to that. What moves governments, at least democratic governments, is public pressure directly from the electorate, or through their elected representatives. I don't see that public pressure in the United States right now, so how do you convince the public that there is a serious problem? One tries to take the case to the public. But it is a peculiar situation.

I have looked at a number of polls in the last six months. I saw one poll which said that 30% of all Americans believe that all nuclear weapons had already been abolished. I saw another poll, however, which said that two thirds of all Americans believe that terrorists would explode a nuclear weapon in a US city within the next ten years. I don't how you put that together, but it is not a front and center issue that motivates many members of Congress. There is only a very small number of individuals in the Congress that relate to this issue at all. So obviously it must not come up in many states or districts. I would say, what people have been saying for a long time, there is no substitute for trying to energize the electorate through whatever methods seems most appropriate.

Important work can be done working with governments, particularly the United States government, but all governments, by NGO specialists such as Bruce Blair on de-alerting. I would sure like to see more public pressure for progress in nuclear disarmament.

HAL FEIVESON: This isn't quite an answer to your question, but I think the questioner identified herself as a member of the Society of Friends. Several years ago I gave some talks on how the British abolished the slave trade. A committee was formed in 1783 which included 11 Quakers and Thomas Clark, twelve people. They were called the saints, sort of derisively. At that time the House of Commons was against abolition. The House of Lords was dominated by the plantation owners in the West Indies. The King, Admiral Nelson, Liverpool, Bristol, you name it, everybody was against the abolition of the slave trade for various reasons.

In 1787 Wilberforce first introduced the idea of abolition into the House of Commons. By 1792 the country was completely turned around. The slave trade wasn't abolished for another 15 years because the Napoleonic wars intervened. But by 1792 the House of Commons was completely turned around. The Committee's agitation worked in lots of ways, and by 1807, when it was finally abolished and Wilberforce was feted in the House, people didn't congratulate him for doing something that was so amazing. They asked, what took it so long.

I feel a little differently than I did then when I was looking at this. Twelve years ago the lunacy of the arms race, which was still going at full blast, wasn't somehow fully recognized...The notion that the US and Russia should have something like 60,000 nuclear weapons is really nutty, when you think about it now. You still have tens of thousands of weapons. But at least now there is a sense that the whole thing is of lunatic proportions. Maybe few think that abolition is possible soon, but the notion that the US and Russia and other countries have to have thousands of weapons certainly very few believe now. And I think somehow the common sense of the craziness, at least of the dimensions of the arms race, is becoming accepted. I imagine that things like de-alerting, which is opposed now, will become in a few years not look what we did, but what took us so long?

ARJUN MAKHIJANI: One strategy that I think we haven't pursued in this country, which as I said is the most open superpower by far, is that we actually are going backwards in some respects in the nuclear weapons arena, as regards to information, because of what is called privatization. More and more information is being held by corporations, even though it is paid for by taxpayers. I do think that we need some sort of corporate freedom of information act. I think if corporations want to make their money on the free market, they ought to go and do it, but if they want to go to the government for money, then the documents, and information, ought to belong to the taxpayers. I observe that the corporations like government money, and the free market is something to lecture other people about, especially the poor. The documents ought to belong to those who pay for it...

I think openness is even more important in other countries, Britain, for example, France, India, Pakistan, Russia. Many recent Russian successes have been tied to greater information. We know more about Russia now. I think we need openness of information more in China, which is very, very closed. So that is one strategy that we haven't pursued vigorously enough even in this country and certainly not vigorously enough in other countries.

A piece of political analysis that I use to gauge what's winnable and what is not: I think what is winnable usually requires public mobilization, as Ambassador Graham said. Mobilization is very hard when the establishment isn't conflicted. When there is an essential conflict, as occurred within the tobacco establishment when one of the tobacco companies produced documents, saying we did bad, it made the whole situation dramatically different. When men went off to fight World War I, they put women in the factories, who after the war, were unwilling to go home, and demanded the vote.

We think that the Soviet Union lost the Cold War, but we haven't understood that the United States didn't win it. It is not like World War II where the United States after winning could tell Germany and Japan what to do. At the end of the Cold War the Russian economy fell apart, but Russia has as many, or more, nuclear weapon materials than the United States.

I do not believe that the complacency that people feel that nuclear weapons are already gone or no problem is justified by the facts. Ambassador Graham, Bruce Blair at Brookings, Graham Allison at Harvard and others are saying we are in a very perilous time but I don't think we have done enough to understand the nature of this peril. The half life of plutonium is 24,000 years. The half life of a Russian government these days is a few months. That is a very important disconnect that we have created in the last fifty years.

I don't think that we have done much to educate ourselves or the public or our leaders so that we are aware that victory in the Cold War will only come when there is nuclear disarmament. Until then we shall all live in terrible peril. The complacency is there. I am mystified by it. I think we are just not active enough and we are not doing enough.

TOM GRAHAM: There is one thing that might move governments. It is reasonably clear that if the nuclear weapon states do not carry out in a relatively short period of time their nuclear disarmament commitments, if the political value of nuclear weapons is not dramatically reduced, if the nuclear weapons states don't adopt a no-first-use policy and pursue deep and drastic cuts in nuclear weapons, as the years go by, and in only a few years, I believe, it is going to be clear that nuclear weapons are simply going to spread all over the world. The technology is too simple. It is widely available now. To build a crude weapon, if that is going to give a country political status, is not that difficult if they can get the fissile material. Many people say fissile material is for sale in Russia.

If it becomes clearer that nuclear weapons are going to spread, that India and Pakistan are just the first two, not the last two additions to the nuclear club, that the nuclear club may be 20 or 30 ten years from now, with unimaginable effects on everyone's security, as that situation becomes more and more obvious, as I believe it will, perhaps governments will start to move.

BILL SWEET: I am with *Spectrum Magazine*, published by the Institute of Electrical and Electronics Engineers. If you look back at the controversies during the period of the Cold War...that along with many negative developments, precisely because of all the anxieties associated with the Cold War, there was always a powerful dynamic tending in the direction of nuclear disarmament. If one were working in the context of an NGO or as a research scientist, concerned about these matters, one could always find a way of tapping into that inner dynamism to try to get something done.

I share the spirit of the previous questioner. Now that the Cold War has ended, even though the stated rationale for nuclear weapons appears to be atrophying, ironically, at the same time, all the wind seems to have gone out of the counter movement. It seems to me that there is a real need now for some radically different kind of strategy. I wonder if I can needle you into commenting further.

JONATHAN GRANOFF: There is an experiment that we are going to do in Philadelphia. The City Council has declared Philadelphia, America's first city, the birthplace of America, as a nuclear weapon free zone, and unanimously called for the commencement of negotiations on abolition, a no first use pledge and de-alerting. What we are going to try to do is gather the leaders of the city, the leading physicians, the leading business people, the leading politicians, and just lay out for them that we are in an historical crisis. As Ambassador Graham said, if the commitments to the Non-Proliferation Treaty are not fulfilled there will be a review conference, and there are 44 nuclear weapons capable states, countries with the capacity and the plutonium to go nuclear.

Ambassador Roche went across Canada last year visiting 12 cities. I was with him when he presented a report of the 378 people involved to Foreign Minister Axworthy and the Prime Minister, Jean Chretien. I was surprised at the interest. This is something we have not done in America. We have not gone city to city and gathered the leaders and said this is a crisis, what do we do?

As an attorney, when you make a case, you build up your evidence and you build up your witnesses. We now have 61 former generals, General Horner who was head of the air command in the Gulf War, General Butler, who headed the Strategic Air Command, calling for elimination. There are 150 current and former heads of States, such as Jimmy Carter, Mikhail Gorbachev, Pierre Trudeau. This had never happened before. The UN now has a spokesperson, a messenger of peace, Michael Douglas, who is speaking to people in the communications and entertainment industry...

What the abolition movement in America did in the 1850s was to convince people that you couldn't humanize slavery. We have not effectively presented the moral argument about nuclear weapons to the public, that putting all life at risk on the planet is morally unacceptable. I think all of us here have to experiment. We are going to do an experiment in Philadelphia. I would encourage everybody to start experimenting with ways to communicate this message.

TOM GRAHAM: I agree with everything that Jonathan just said. I would like to add one more comment. This is not intended as a political statement; it is intended as a statement of fact. For better or worse, it is the United States that leads on issues like this. It is the United States; it will remain the United States, for at least the current future. What we need most of all is a President who is prepared to take the proper steps, who is willing to face up to the potential criticism, who is willing to make the right moves in the right direction. If you have somebody as President who is prepared to do that, then most things are possible.

ARJUN MAKHIJANI: Let me comment as a member of the Institute of Electronic and Electrical Engineers, since I have belonged to the IEEE for some time...I think the technical troops that provided the technical talent for the Cold War and their professional societies haven't done enough, and that might be one new element in the strategy that is missing. The one constant that is there throughout the world, not a security factor, is money. Right now the main thing I think that is keeping the nuclear weapons business going is the $35 billion a year in the United States that goes into it, and at the head of that there is the several billion dollars that goes into the labs.

We published a report earlier this year on the National Ignition Facility on which we will spend $4 billion building and operating it in Livermore. It is a wonderful technical project. I did my doctorate in fusion; I know how interesting these things can be. However, it turns out that this facility in my very carefully considered view is illegal under the Comprehensive Test Ban Treaty. It has not been ratified yet, but the United States will instantly be in violation the moment it enters into force.

France will be too because they are doing the same thing.

I do not remember reading a thorough criticism of the Stockpile Stewardship program, where nuclear weapons design is in the center of it, even though they say safety and reliability of nuclear weapons is at the center, in the pages of *Spectrum*. I will offer now to write for you a thorough criticism of the Stockpile Stewardship program for my fellow members of the IEEE...

Yesterday I spoke with the manager of the Yucca Mountain project, which I oppose and which he supports, which is a high-level waste depository. We tried to set up an investigation in Yucca Mountain geology that would clarify some issues. I said this is beyond ideological or political issues. Do we know the technical facts?

We got our materials on Stockpile Stewardship from the labs, and that is one of the reasons I really admire what this country is. We put in a request to Los Alamos, and they sent us the data; they compiled it for us. They hated the report that we published, and they probably knew they would, but they still sent the information. When we published the report I got a call from Los Alamos. They said, you are misrepresenting stuff to the public. We don't like your statements. I said, I will send you a copy of the report. If there is an error in it I will publish a correction. They said we have a copy of the report. We have not found an error in the report but we don't like your press release...

SELMA BRACKMAN, War and Peace Foundation: Richard Jordan talked about the Y2K problem. I would like you to comment on the possibility of shutting down the reactors and the weapons for a brief period of a month or so. I also would like to talk about Cassini. The flyby is to be in a year or so with 72 pounds of plutonium...Is the lack of reaction because of the United States position?

JONATHAN GRANOFF: I did a briefing in Congress on the model nuclear weapons convention last spring. There were perhaps 40 legislative assistants of members of Congress present. Congresswoman Woolsey's office had organized it...The ignorance displayed astonished me.

ARJUN MAKHIJANI: The Y2K problem. I think the situation is very confusing because even very knowledgeable people have nothing definitive to say. So far as I understand, nuclear warheads require a positive signal for them to go off. They could go off accidentally if an airplane crashes, for example. There are a fair number of safety mechanisms, so that has not happened yet. So far as I understand, and my understanding is very rudimentary, the danger from the year 2000 problem would come primarily from command and control and satellite systems not functioning properly. I considered for quite a while whether this should be linked to de-alerting initiatives. I don't think it should be put in the middle of de-alerting initiatives because you can do things like stand down for a day and then put them back on alert and you haven't accomplished anything for the long term for disarmament by putting the year 2000 problem in the middle of it.

I think it is an important issue. I think the weapons and warhead-related issues are different from the operational related issues, that, for instance, a chemical plant will confront when they have things with timers and clocks and on line computers that need clocks and timers to operate. I believe they are doing a lot to try and catch the problems beforehand...It would be very difficult to shut off all the nuclear power plants for a month. It is 20% of the power supply of this country...

TOM GRAHAM: Certainly there is no intent to disparage the issue. There are immense resources going into this problem in government and out of government. Former Senator Sam Nunn heads a very large operation in Atlanta that is looking at this question. My understanding is the same, that the principal problem is in the area of command and control, not the weapons or power plants. My limited understanding leads me to understand that the problem in Russia may be considerably more serious. It's not being ignored.

ALICE SLATER, GRACE: ...There are now over 1100 NGOs associated with Abolition 2000...Fortune had a whole long article on Y2K and how it is going to affect banking, etc...There should be more exploration of alternative energy sources. Nuclear power powers the bomb...There are 250 metric tons of plutonium in military stockpiles, and 910 tons in civilian stockpiles...

DIANE PERLMAN, Psychologists for Social Responsibility: ...People are more dangerous when they are afraid...Is there a secret agenda? Is there an economic argument?

ARJUN MAKHIJANI; I don't think there is a secret agenda. I think the agenda is very open. It is one of power and money. The amount of money that is being spent today on nuclear weapons design is slightly more than what we spent during the Cold War, even though there is no actual testing, except some sub-critical testing. The amount of money has stayed remarkably constant...Academia is tied into this money, with a few honorable exceptions like the Center Hal works for...I think it has grossly subverted the scientific academic enterprise. It needs to be discussed.

TOM GRAHAM: I would add one thing. A book has recently been published on the cost of the nuclear arms race, $5.5 trillion, published by Brookings and written by Schwartz...

HAL FEIVESON: A professor of psychology at Princeton recently talked about alcohol use. She used the term pluralistic ignorance. As she defined it, that is where each person thinks that he or she is out of step with what the majority thinks. So at Princeton each student thinks that I don't like to drink that much, but everybody else likes to drink, so to be a real part of the Princeton scene you drink...She found most students she talked to think there is too much drinking...Perhaps that is true here. I think the absurdity of the nuclear weapons, the lunacy of the dimensions I think people basically understand but think that other people don't see it that way...

ARJUN MAKHIJANI: $5.5 trillion is what has been spent. $5.8 trillion includes the future liabilities, the environmental cleanup, that is projected to be spent in the future.

NEWTON BOWLES, UNA, Canada: What struck me this morning were the constrictions of what seemed to be a highly technical approach to what is a deeply human problem. Maybe we put the responsibility for these profoundly human problems in the hands of people whose hands we tie, both technically and politically. What is the basic problem? The basic problem is fear and the lack of trust. And this is pervasive. We have a kind of worldwide xenophobia and paranoia and in this atmosphere it is very difficult to get anything moving...

QUESTIONER, Peace Caucus: I found that this year in the General Assembly there was a big change of focus. Most nations put globalization and the fear of a worldwide economic crisis at the top of their agenda. I feel that we in the anti-nuclear movement have really not tapped into that fear and related it to the huge Pentagon budget...

ARJUN MAKHIJANI: The economic crisis and the nuclear crisis have come together very much in Russia. The main urgent danger in some ways is that Russia has been falling apart. I think the reason there is more attention on de-alerting now is because of this economic crisis in Russia...The robber barons are robbing the country. Banking reform in the international banking system is very much needed to stem the nuclear crisis because I don't think the Russian government or people can have control over their own resources or exports until they can stem this hemorrhage of foreign exchange from their country into foreign bank accounts. And the same kind of reforms are needed for Indonesia or Thailand...a tax on speculation, some accountability in how the foreign exchange goes in and out of a country...

TOM GRAHAM: Shortly before I left government in 1997 I received a briefing from the general accounting office, the arm of the Congress that investigates many things. They had just done a study in Russia on the implementation of the Nunn-Lugar program. Among the things that they did during this analysis was to visit the storage facilities for nuclear explosive material, storage facilities for plutonium and for Highly Enriched Uranium (HEU), both material that came from weapons and material that had never been in weapons. They said they went to one facility where HEU was stored, which is somewhat less lethal than plutonium. The HEU was stored in saucer-like wafers stacked up. The place had two guards who were awake most of the time...When one of the guards went home, he would take one or two of these wafers and just slip them in his pocket as he went out. Now one or two isn't going to make a bomb but if you do that everyday, after a while there is a fair amount of material for someone who wants to make a bomb...There is a tremendous problem of nuclear explosive material getting out of Russia and into the hands of unstable countries, terrorist organizations, religious cults...

JIM GARST: How do we promote conversion to useful activity of these resources and provide employment opportunities for those displaced?

ARJUN MAKHIJANI: The nuclear business is different from other businesses because you are not done with it when you are done with it. I believe that in the process of disarmament, of material accounting in Russia, even in this country, the safeguarding of these materials, the invention of the technologies to clean up these sites, there are immense numbers of problems. I don't think the amount of money required over the next 30, 40, years will be less. So I don't think there is a danger of job loss, but I think this is not well-recognized, and the leading scientists in the nuclear weapons complex don't want to do this work. They are not interested in this work, many of them. Some are. One of the scientists at Los Alamos has played a fine role in helping think through some of the most dangerous problems in the Hanford high level waste tanks...but it requires a firm direction from the top...

CAROLINE BRIDGMAN-REES, Center for International Peacebuilding: ...When I was in England in 1981 War Games, a movie about nuclear war games was shown. There should be an updated War Game...You can use statistics of what is spent, compared with other needs...We have to think of many more practical things that can be done in local communities.

ANN LAKHDHIR, IDDS: In the discussion yesterday on de-alerting, the Russian participant was not particularly enthusiastic. At least he was differentiating his own personal view from what he felt the view of his government would be. I am speculating that part of the difficulty when you get into trying to figure how you verify de-alerting is the great suspicion on his part that it would be much easier for the US to suddenly reverse course and re-alert everything. Has there been any further discussion with Russians since you and Bruce Blair spoke last April on how you could do this feasibly and how you are approaching the problem? Somehow there is an assumption, maybe correct, that the US could reverse course more quickly.

HAL FEIVESON: There has been discussion, and we have talked to the Russian military. The Russians do worry that the US could do everything better than they, so that if there is a de-alerting, the US will figure out how to re-alert quicker than they can. If they take their warheads off their missiles, they will have difficulty finding places to store the warheads, and secondly, they become vulnerable. There are de-alerting schemes that I think they can learn to be comfortable with. But it takes a while for the military to think freshly about issues like this. I think from a technical point of view, that certainly you could invent de-alerting methods, I think we already have methods that would be verifiable, and that would not lead to a re-alerting race.

When I was in the arms control agency I arranged for a showing of the film about an attack on Camp Carey in England that the previous speaker mentioned, and one person came. I thought it was a very interesting film.

CAROLINE BRIDGMAN-REES: We had a big peace meeting in Coventry. On the opposite hill to the march there was a huge number of Nazi youth, British Nazi youth, and after our peace meeting we went to our Quaker meeting house and had a pot-luck supper run by the Campaign for Nuclear Disarmament youth. Somebody knocked on the door and all the Nazi youth were there. The young man who was running the pot-luck supper invited them in. It just so happened that War Games, the simulated nuclear war movie, was being shown just then. So we invited them to watch the movie. They watched the movie and they left without a word, totally silent, totally awed. It was powerful.

ESTELLE EPSTEIN,WILPF: To mobilize, does anybody have any experience with respect to the trade union movement? As you all know, there has been a sizable change in the leadership. Have we tried to counter the religious right with a national campaign for the right to life?

ANN ZANES, Peace Links: ...In 1997 in a poll in the US, 80% of the people would feel safer if no country had nuclear weapons. And 77% want a treaty to abolish them all.

JONATHAN GRANOFF: A year ago I don't think we would have imagined that eight countries from all around the world friendly to the US...would come as a global coalition and call upon the nuclear weapon states to demonstrate an unequivocal commitment to the speedy and total elimination of their nuclear weapons...This is progress, and it is our responsibility to do this. Thank you all...

IMPLEMENTATION OF THE CTBT AND NEW INITIATIVES

Moderator: JAYANTHA DHANAPALA, Under-Secretary-General for Disarmament: On behalf of the newly re-established Department for Disarmament Affairs, may I say how happy we are to cooperate again with the NGO Committee on Disarmament in organizing these activities during Disarmament Week. Today, we have a distinguished panel of experts to discuss the implementation of the Comprehensive Test Ban Treaty (CTBT) and new initiatives. My role here is mainly to set the stage. But, in my task of chairing this panel, may I refer to the fact that the history of the CTBT goes back many years to 1954, when the then Prime Minister of India, Jawaharlal Nehru, proposed a comprehensive test ban treaty.

Ever since then, this has been a clamor on the part of non-governmental organizations and Member States who wanted to see a total ban on any kind of nuclear testing. This was regarded then as a litmus test in the area of nuclear disarmament. In 1963 these efforts succeeded to some extent when the Partial Test Ban Treaty was adopted banning nuclear testing in the atmosphere and every other environment, except underground. We were very close even then to a comprehensive test ban treaty, but unfortunately, lack of agreement on the part of the two Superpowers, the USA and the USSR/Russian Federation, failed to make a comprehensive test ban possible.

We had to wait many, many years after 1963 to achieve a Comprehensive Test Ban Treaty; and this achievement finally took place as a result of the Conference on Disarmament having negotiated a complete text. However, there was no consensus, as you may recall, with regard to reporting that text out of the CD, and it had to be reintroduced into the General Assembly through a special procedure. The CTBT was then adopted by the international community and the resolution on 10 September 1996 opened the treaty for signature. Today we have 150 States who are signatories; 21 have ratified the treaty.

As you know, under article 14, forty-four countries listed in Annex II have to ratify the treaty if it is to come into force. Of these 44, only Australia, Austria, Brazil, France, Germany, Japan, Peru, Slovakia, Spain and the United Kingdom have ratified.

During this General Assembly I think all of us were greatly encouraged when the Prime Ministers of India and Pakistan announced the intention of their governments to sign the Comprehensive Test Ban Treaty. It is therefore the confident expectation of the international community that next year, by September, when the three-year period since the signing of the treaty in 1996 comes up, we will have the treaty coming into force. The Secretary-General, in his capacity as the depositor of the CTBT, will then hold a conference, as requested by the States Parties, in order that they may assess the situation in the event that the treaty has not come into force. That meeting is expected to take place early in October 1999.

With those brief introductory remarks, may I now turn the microphone to our distinguished panel of speakers. I invite our first speaker, Mr. Masabumi Sato, who is the Director of the Legal and External Relations Division of the Provisional Technical Secretariat of the Preparatory Commission for the Comprehensive Nuclear Test-Ban Treaty Organization. Mr. Sato.

MASABUMI SATO: ...It is a pleasure for me personally and my organization to be here and to have this opportunity to address you. In considering the CTBT, first is the basic obligation which States have undertaken to implement the treaty. This is not carry out nuclear explosions and to prohibit and prevent such nuclear explosions at any place under their jurisdiction or control. This is what Article 1 of the CTBT says. The treaty is on our web site, which is **http://www.ctbto.org**

Second point: What makes the CTBT so different from past history is its similarity to its cousin, the CWC, the Chemical Weapon Convention, in that we have a comprehensive global verification system, which is now being implemented. The Comprehensive Nuclear Test-Ban Treaty Organization, which we are working to establish - we are still the Preparatory Commission - is working to establish 321 monitoring stations around the world.

This monitoring system is based on four technologies to monitor the non-conduct of nuclear explosions. As you are aware, unfortunately, our first experience was to monitor the nuclear explosions in South Asia. The 321 monitoring stations specified in the treaty include 171 seismic stations that measure the earthquakes and the earth tremors that result from nuclear explosions. There are three additional means of detection.

A second is through the oceans. We call this "hydroacoustic" monitoring, for which 11 stations have been specified by the treaty. A third is through the air. There are sound waves from atmospheric explosions which will be detected by 60 "infra-sound" stations. These three technologies measure the shock waves from nuclear explosions. I am not a scientist, but scientists will tell you that there are unique signatures of nuclear explosions. They are at some level of magnitude discernible and readily identifiable from normal, other natural or man-made events. If it comes at a lower magnitude, of course, the noise level rises and it becomes more difficult.

The fourth means of detection is radio nuclide technology. We have the capability, and we are expanding our capability, to monitor through radio nuclide stations. There will be 80 stations around the world, 40 with the capability to look for noble gases. When these stations have been calibrated and certified for operation they will give the unique radio nuclide signatures of nuclear explosions, which will be different from those that you get from events like Chernobyl.

That is the global monitoring system. We need your support in working with your governments for them to work with us. The governments have been very forthcoming. As of 24 October, we have been able to collect 63% of our 1998 budget of $58.4 million. This our first full year of operations. Starting from ground zero two years ago, we feel this is a very strong message of support from the Member States. I think we owe a lot of it to the support of NGOs.

The other aspect is non-monetary. As Ambassador Dhanapala said, I have two hats: one is legal, one is external relations. From the legal side, we need framework agreements with some 90 States so that we can establish or upgrade these 321 monitoring stations. We need facility agreements. It has taken some time since the Secretariat started work in Vienna in March 1997. Last week in Ottawa the Canadian government and the Provisional Technical Secretariat, in the person of the Executive Secretary, Mr. Wolfgang Hoffmann, signed our first facility agreement. We are moving forward with other countries. The USA is also close to agreement and there are others. We need these agreements and we count on your support.

JAYANTHA DHANAPALA: ...Our next speaker is Mr. Lars Bjarme, Minister and Deputy Head of the Swedish Delegation to the Conference on Disarmament in Geneva. Mr. Bjarme.

LARS BJARME: I should like to thank the organizers of this meeting for inviting me and thus giving an opportunity to present the Eight Nation Initiative now being discussed in the First Committee. We seem to be in a situation where we are trying to establish a dialogue with all participant States, but some are not willing to listen.

Let me begin from the beginning. The eight States or the Eight Nations are the following: Sweden, Brazil, Egypt, Ireland, Mexico, New Zealand, Slovenia and South Africa. (Slovenia later withdrew its sponsorship.) As you can see, they represent all corners of the world. This was precisely the idea. The initiative did not start last spring. It started during and after the meeting of the First Committee a year ago. Sweden and Ireland started to have bilateral talks about what we could do, because we were feeling that there was a need for action on nuclear disarmament

These two nations made contact with others and the initiative grew. On 9 June of this year our Foreign Ministers launched a joint Declaration which outlined a new agenda and the need for a new agenda. We did have in the 1995 NPT Review and Extension Conference an agreement on objectives and principles, including two major objectives: the Comprehensive Test Ban Treaty and a Treaty on a Ban on the Production of Fissile Materials for Weapons Purposes.

We have the Comprehensive Test Ban Treaty, as previous speakers have noted and explained well. The Conference on Disarmament in Geneva started late this year, one-and-a-half months ago, negotiations on a ban on fissile material for weapons purposes. So, the agenda from 1995 in the Document of the Objectives and Principles is rather exhausted.

What's next? The eight foreign ministers tried to point a way forward. The Declaration has inspired us to present a draft resolution in the First Committee. It is not the same thing. The Declaration is not the resolution and the resolution is not the Declaration, for various reasons.

I said before that when Sweden and Ireland started to talk a year ago, we noted some points. One was, regrettably, a distinct slowdown has taken place in the most recent years as regards future concrete progress towards nuclear disarmament. We noted that the START process is partly stalled. There were other concerns that came to us with events happening this year. Through their nuclear testing India and Pakistan have gravely threatened the international nuclear non-proliferation and disarmament efforts. At the multilateral level, the Conference on Disarmament only recently, after two years of inaction with regard to substantive work, could arrive at the decision to commence negotiations on a Fissile Material Cut Off Treaty. And the challenge remains to get these negotiations off to a speedy and smooth start next year when the Conference starts its work again.

As to the Nuclear Non-Proliferation Treaty, its strengthened review process ran into considerable difficulties at this year's meeting of the Preparatory Committee for the Review Conference in the year 2000. In fact the second meeting with the Preparatory Committee in Geneva could not agree on a document.

So, in our view, a new and forceful political impetus is now needed to reinvigorate and reinforce the nuclear disarmament process. Therefore we have introduced a draft resolution on nuclear disarmament at this year's session of the UN General Assembly. We believe it is of utmost importance that the international nuclear disarmament efforts be pursued expeditiously and with a strong sense of determination, and that the current threats to the global nuclear non-proliferation regime be strongly and resolutely dealt with. These twin objectives are firmly embodied in the draft resolution L.48 (later adopted as Resolution 53/77 Y.)

This draft resolution sets out a clear and concrete approach for taking the nuclear disarmament and non-proliferation process forward. This approach is based on the pursuit in parallel of a series of concrete and mutually reinforcing measures to be taken by the nuclear-weapon-states themselves and by the nuclear-weapon states together with the non-nuclear-weapon states. Together these measures provide a road map for achieving a nuclear-weapon-free world. It must be stressed that the proposed approach does not involve such concepts as a nuclear weapons convention, programs of action or time-bound frameworks. It offers another and, we firmly believe, realistic way of making rapid progress towards nuclear disarmament.

It must also be underlined that this draft resolution is in no way intended to undermine or deviate from the vital work carried out within the framework of the NPT. That treaty constitutes the cornerstone of the global non-proliferation regime and an essential foundation for the international nuclear disarmament efforts. However, we do call for an expeditious implementation of the treaty's article VI. A strong and broad backing of the resolution across all the groupings of the countries will greatly assist in reinjecting a new sense of urgency of the international community to move towards a nuclear-weapon-free world. Thank you, Mr. Chairman.

JAYANTHA DHANAPALA: Thank you, Mr. Bjarme. May I now invite Daryl Kimball of the Coalition to Reduce Nuclear Dangers to speak to us.

DARYL KIMBALL: What I would like to address are the political barriers, political challenges for implementation of the CTBT in the coming year. Mr. Sato described the technical challenges that the Conference and Test Ban PrepCom need to address for the treaty to go into effect. What I'd like to address are the issues relating to the legal entry into force of the treaty.

We are now in 1998 just four or five months after India and Pakistan conducted a series of nuclear weapons explosions that have not only pushed those nations to the edge of a full-scale nuclear arms race but have increased the likelihood of a nuclear conflagration involving one-fifth of the world's inhabitants. We are reminded that much progress needs to be made in the area of nuclear disarmament, including the CTBT. We are reminded of the importance of the CTBT as an important barrier to the development and proliferation of nuclear weapons.

The CTB agreement of 1996, to reiterate this point, which was endorsed by the United Nations and has been signed by 150 nations, aims to "prohibit nuclear weapon test explosions and all other nuclear explosions." This step is extremely important and significant in curbing nuclear bomb work, especially in the declared nuclear-weapon states. This is an issue I've been working on for a number of years. My coalition, the Coalition to Reduce Nuclear Dangers, involves 17 US non-governmental organizations, including Peace Action, the Arms Control Association, Natural Resources Defense Council, British American Security Information Council and many others.

However, as we all know, there are major political obstacles still in the way of full implementation of this treaty. Many people believe that, now the CTBT has been signed, we can rest and relax. The situation is quite the opposite. As Ambassador Dhanapala said, article 14 of the treaty requires that a list of 44 named states ratify the CTBT, in order for the treaty to enter into force. That list of 44 states includes the five declared nuclear-weapon states, as well as India, Pakistan, Israel, and North Korea, countries all of which, except for Britain and France, have not yet ratified, and some of which have not signed the CTBT.

Furthermore, if by September 24, 1999, the third anniversary of the opening for signature of the treaty, all these 44 nations have not signed, those countries who have ratified may, by a majority decision, decide to convene a special conference to evaluate ways to expedite entry into force. And that's something I want to talk about in a few minutes.

So, to date, 150 nations have signed, 21 have ratified, but only 10 of the 44 nations that must ratify for entry into force have done so. In my view, there are three key factors that are going to affect whether or not the CTBT enters into force by the end of 1999. These are not necessarily in order of importance.

The first one is progress toward Indian and Pakistani accession to the CTBT. As Ambassador Dhanapala mentioned, in September Prime Minister Nawaz Sharif of Pakistan and Prime Minister Atal Bihari Vajpayee of India made promising statements about their nations' intentions to accede to the CTBT, by September 1999, the third anniversary date. Other positive statements to the UN, and other statements filled with caveats, have improved the likelihood that the CTBT can enter into force by 1999, if the United States and other nations help lead by example.

It is important to note that just a few months ago, before the Indian and Pakistani tests, it was widely believed that the treaty would not enter into force for quite some time because India and Pakistan had clearly stated since early 1996, on the basis of a number of arguments, that they may not, they would not sign. Well oddly enough, we are now in a situation where these two very important nations may indeed sign, ratify and become part of the regime.

The second key factor, and perhaps this is the most important one and is the one that my organization is working on, is ratification of the CTBT by the United States and the other declared nuclear-weapon states. We are very fortunate to have had the UK and France ratify the treaty, providing important leadership by example to others. Unfortunately, the situation in the United States is that we are quite far from seeing the CTBT ratified, let alone even being considered. It's very important to keep in mind that strong US leadership on the CTBT and ratification is very important to exploit the opening that has been created by the speeches by the Indian and Pakistani Prime Ministers just last month. Otherwise the United States once again becomes part of the problem, not the solution to nuclear testing and nuclear proliferation.

As I said, the Senate has not acted on the CTBT in the year that they have had an opportunity to do so. The problem right now is that the Senate Foreign Relations Committee chairman, Jesse Helms, Republican of North Carolina, who some have said has never seen a treaty that he likes, does not like this treaty and has stated that he will not allow the treaty to be considered by his committee until such time as President Clinton submits a different set of agreements that were worked out with Russia in relation to the Anti-Ballistic Missile Treaty. These are very unrelated issues in some ways, but Senator Helms is trying to link these in order to leverage action on basically destroying the Anti-Ballistic Missile Treaty of 1972.

Just after the Indian and Pakistani tests in May, the Senate Majority Leader, Trent Lott, Republican of Mississippi, unfortunately echoed the same arguments of Senator Helms and expressed his displeasure about the treaty. So, we have the two most important people in the Senate right now opposed to the treaty.

But this opposition can be and will be overcome in my view . Public support for the Comprehensive Test Ban Treaty in the United States is very, very strong. The latest bi-partisan polls that were commissioned, and the Coalition To Reduce Nuclear Dangers commissioned these polls in May, June and July of 1998, show that Republicans and Democrats in all regions of the country support Senate approval of the CTBT in overwhelming numbers. Roughly speaking, three out of every four Americans support Senate ratification. And there are even indications that after hearing about the Indian and Pakistani tests in May, the support for the CTBT is even stronger among American voters, which is exactly the opposite of the views of Senator Helms and Senator Lott. So they are very much out of step with the public on this subject.

And, oddly, Senator Helms and Senator Lott have tried to use the South Asian tests as an excuse for inaction on the treaty, arguing that the CTBT is still not meaningful and that these two nations are not likely to sign the treaty. But with the statements of the Prime Ministers of India and Pakistan last month, that argument has been turned on its head. It's important now, I believe, for the Clinton Administration and other Senate leaders to take the opportunity to move quickly on the test ban. Once brought to the floor, once we overcome the opposition of Senator Helms, based on a reading of conversations and statements by various senators, we believe the treaty will gain the 67 votes, the two-thirds majority necessary for Senate ratification.

However, 1999 is probably the last best chance for Senate approval of the treaty. The year 2000, of course, has the US presidential elections. Historically speaking, no major arms control treaty has been ratified in a presidential election year.

There are several factors, in addition to Clinton Administration leadership, that are important for ratification of the treaty by the United States. There needs to be greater popular support. Grassroots organizations across the United States must be very active on this subject. We must have more support from moderate, especially Republican, senators on this subject to overcome Senator Lott's opposition. There must be progress, or at least signs of progress, of Indian and Pakistani accession to the treaty. Finally, there must be pressure from other corners of the globe to approve the treaty. Also this week there is another very important resolution that's on the floor that is offered by Australia, Mexico and New Zealand on the Comprehensive Test Ban Treaty, Resolution L.11 on the CTBT (which was adopted as a Decision by the UN General Assembly.

Finally, the third important factor that will affect the CTBT implementation is the special conference to which I have referred and others have referred to that is described in article 14 of the CTBT. This conference, if it becomes highly visible, well-attended by high-level representatives of various nations, and if there is talk about this conference in the months leading up to an October conference, could become an important impetus for action by the states, not just those states who have not signed, like India, Pakistan, but those states who have not ratified, like the United States.

Unlike other arms control treaties that we have seen in the past, like the Chemical Weapons Convention, there is no deadline for nations to act to ratify this treaty. So, it's very important that we encourage nations, remind nations about this conference which is intended to explore ways to expedite entry into force. It does not have much more power than that. It can become an important political deadline that's important to force action on the part of politicians who, as we all know, do not like to do anything unless there is a deadline. Maybe that applies to many of us also.

Let's make a final comment on next steps. There's been much talk in the NGO community about the limitations of the CTBT and the fact that the nuclear-weapons states, especially the United States, have pursued a very vigorous program to enhance their nuclear weapons development capabilities. This is known here in the United States as the Stockpile Stewardship Program. Because of the possibility that technological advances will enable nuclear weapons designers to develop and mass-produce new and more deadly bomb types without the nuclear weapon explosives field tests that the Test Ban Treaty prohibits, efforts must continue to ensure that the purpose of the CTBT to end the qualitative improvement of nuclear weapons is fulfilled.

Several organizations inside and outside the US have been pushing a number of measures, one of which is that the costly Stockpile Stewardship in the United States should be reduced in its scope and its cost. And, secondly, that the United States and other nuclear-weapon states should adopt policies that prohibit the design, development or production of new nuclear warhead types or modified warhead types, that provide new military capabilities, such as the B-61 Mod-11.

So, finally, I just remind all of us that the CTBT is not done. There is much more work to be done. We all have a responsibility to follow through on this commitment that was established in the 1995 Review and Extension process. Failure to follow through will open up the possibility that the progress achieved towards the test ban, both real and symbolic, will be lost. Thank you.

JAYANATHA DHANAPALA: Thank you very much, Mr. Kimball. Our next speaker is Dr. Arjun Makhijani from the Institute for Energy and Environmental Research in Maryland. Mr. Makhijani.

ARJUN MAKHIJANI: Thank you, Mr. Dhanapala. It's really a pleasure and an honor to be here on such a distinguished panel. I want to take up where Daryl left off, that is, how do we make the CTBT into a disarmament treaty. That was the purpose of Mr. Nehru's asking the world in 1954 that we should have such a treaty. I want to explore a little bit with you whether we have such a treaty and what we need to do to make a treaty like that.

In case anybody misunderstands the detail that I'm going to get into to provide context, I do support the CTBT. I think it's an excellent treaty in most respects. No treaty can include everything in it, so I accept it for what it is, which is great progress. I would like to see it ratified and enter into force. But, I have great concerns about it and I'm going to devote my talk to sharing with you those concerns. I'm very glad that Mr. Sato is here and I hope that his legal department is going to take up the issues that I mention with some urgency so that they can be resolved before the 1999 Conference of the Parties to the CTBT.

Basically, what we have today is a treaty that puts a moderate amount of restraint upon the nuclear-weapon states in the form of banning explosions, especially the wealthy nuclear-weapon states, the United States, first of all, but, also, Britain and France. I say moderate because it is really necessary to carry out nuclear explosions in order for the military to accept nuclear weapons as workable weapons into their arsenal. Most of the functions of design can still be carried on by the Stockpile Stewardship Program, mentioned by Daryl. Our report on Stockpile Stewardship, which is supposed to be about safety and reliability, is called "The Nuclear Safety Smokescreen." I obviously don't believe the safety rationale. It can be found on the Internet.

I might illustrate it by the Boeing 777. Some of you might have ridden in this new airplane. It's quite nice, I like to ride in it. It was mostly designed in wind tunnels and by computers. The parallel kinds of efforts for nuclear weapons design are still allowed under the CTBT, most of them. There is a particular kind of effort that is not allowed, which is, all explosions are banned. The treaty does not contain any exceptions for any nuclear explosions, whether they are to be conducted in the laboratory, whether they are small or big, whether they are for peaceful purposes or military purposes.

It's quite unlike the Non-Proliferation Treaty in that respect. I think that the first part of article 1 represents great progress over the Non-Proliferation Treaty and fulfillment of some of its objectives. However, the practical effect of allowing laboratory and computer research to go on unrestrained, at the level in the United States of a $60 billion program over the next 13 years, is that what is a victory in the short term is going to create some pretty long-term, dangerous problems.

There is the problem of financial and bureaucratic inertia in the nuclear weapon establishment. Every large bureaucracy seeks to perpetuate itself, and the powerful ones succeed. The amount of money going into the nuclear weapons design and testing effort today, even though explosions are banned, is greater in the United States than the average of the Cold War. Ten or 15 years down the line, even conservatives are going to begin asking, "What are we spending this money for, there's nothing coming out of the other end of the pipeline? We could put this money to better use for fancy gadgets, even military gadgets. There's nothing coming out of this pipeline."

Now, the fatal difficulty at that point - maybe, maybe - but, I think this is a great danger and not a small danger - is that the directors of the nuclear laboratories in the United States, together with the Joint Chiefs of Staff, have been asked as part of the ratification process to certify every year that the US nuclear weapon stockpile is safe and reliable. The definition of reliable is interesting because it really includes the capability of US nuclear weapons to carry out a first strike.

Now, at a certain point, if the existence of the nuclear weapons design establishment is called into question, I would say there would be a natural - there are psychologists among us, so they may correct me if I am wrong - but, I would say the natural, human tendency would be to say "Well, after fifteen years, I can't honestly certify that the stockpile is really reliable."

At that point, the clause of the CTBT which allows for withdrawal from the treaty would come into play in the United States. This is not an easy country in which to maintain adherence to treaties in their strict spirit over the long term. Those who are protesting the CTBT will have a lot of political, social and cultural weapons in their hands. financial.

I think the long-term dangers in this, the clause allowing withdrawal from the treaty, are very grave. If the United States, or any other country that's a party to a treaty that's in force, should test,

I will permit myself to say even in this very distinguished and diplomatic forum, all hell would break loose. I do not believe that the Non-Proliferation Regime could survive, or any disarmament efforts that we have made would survive, a nuclear weapons test by a nuclear-weapons state after the treaty has entered into force. But, that danger does exist not so much because of what's in the treaty, that withdrawal clause does exist, but because, I think, of the amount of money that is going into the nuclear weapons design effort.

The second point is the problem about what is a nuclear explosion and what the United States, France, Germany, Japan and a number of other countries say is allowed under the treaty. There is a newsletter called "Science for Democratic Action" and we have also published a report called "Dangerous Thermonuclear Quest."

I'll just quickly say that Article 1 of the treaty is great progress over the Non-Proliferation Treaty, because it bans all nuclear explosions, including peaceful nuclear explosions. The crucial bit of work that Mr. Sato's organization needs to carry out between now and the end of 1999 is to actually define an explosion. We have suggested a definition of an explosion. I met in a conference a British Disarmament Ministry representative or delegate to a Geneva conference a few weeks ago and he said, "Well, our experts say that we don't know how to define this, but we know an explosion when we see it." I put it to you that this isn't going to be good enough. And I put it to him that it isn't going to be good enough. I handed him a copy of this report and I said, "You can hand this to your experts, and if they can do better, I should be happy to publish your definition or let me know what you think of it." I commend it to you also and we would be happy to hear from Mr. Sato what they think of this definition of explosion.

Why is it important? Right now there are two facilities that are being built. They are billion dollar facilities, one in Livermore, California, and the other near Bordeaux in France. They are gigantic football field - or rugby field size machines which involve a hundred or more lasers which will compress a tiny pellet of radioactive hydrogen, tritium and deuterium and create a thermonuclear explosion in the laboratory. They are designed to create explosions. There have never been man-made thermonuclear explosions without plutonium or uranium, that is, fission explosions going first, because you need them to make it as hot as the sun right here on earth. Thermonuclear bombs really have a primary part that's triggered by plutonium. Plutonium and uranium are very hard to make and they are the mainstays of the successes on non-proliferation. If we can make thermonuclear explosions without plutonium and uranium, you can forget the Non-Proliferation regime.

So far, it has been proved impossible. These laser machines can't be made into weapons. But the scientific data from these can be fed into two other devices, which are now being experimented on in New Mexico, one in Albuquerque. It's an x-ray machine that generates intense x-rays, and another which is being done jointly by the US and Russians at Los Alamos, near Santa Fe in New Mexico, which can be weaponized into pure fusion weapons. No plutonium, no uranium, no fallout. Clean bombs; almost no fallout. Clean nuclear weapons, not big, can be made into twenty-pound explosives, can be made into twenty-megaton explosives. Very nice.

Now, the United States says these explosions are allowed under the CTBT. They claim CTBT exempts these as nuclear explosive devices. I believe that while NPT did exempt these as nuclear explosive devices, that the explosions they are designed to create are illegal under the CTBT.

Moreover, I believe that constructing these devices is also illegal under the CTBT, because article 1 says that each party not only must not carry out the explosion, but each party must prevent any such explosions at any place under its jurisdiction or control. Each party must also refrain from causing, encouraging or in any way participating or in any way carrying out such explosions.

Now, spending a billion dollars on building a machine designed to create explosions, I put it to you, ladies and gentlemen, is not in the letter of this treaty, let alone the spirit of this treaty. We need a ruling from the CTBTO preparatory organization about this issue. If twenty-, thirty- and forty-pound explosions in laboratory devices are exempted, then I think the CTBT effectively contains no upper limit to pure thermonuclear explosions. Pretty soon, if these are scientifically proven, there will be no CTBT left, because thermonuclear explosions will become the center of nuclear weapons development; and plutonium and uranium as weapons devices will become worthless to sophisticated states and useful and relatively cheap for terrorists. This is not a rosy picture. I am sorry to have to present this to you. I do think that we must convert the CTBT into a better instrument.

I will sum up by saying there are two things that are needed for this, and only two, in my opinion. One is that we insure that the withdrawal clause is never actually called upon by any party. That can only be done if the money for nuclear design and lab testing is cut off now.

The other is that we need a definition of explosions that will exclude pure fusion explosions and bring them explicitly within the definition of explosions under the CTBT. Otherwise, if thermonuclear explosions in the lab are proved to be technically possible, within a very few short years after that event, if it happens, I believe we shall have no more CTBT. I'm sorry to have to say this to you, but I believe it is very important that the distinguished people gathered here should know the urgency of this issue.

JAYANTHA DHANAPALA: Thank you, Dr. Makhijani. Our last speaker on the panel is Alyn Ware from the Lawyers Committee on Nuclear Policy.

ALYN WARE: Thank you, Ambassador Dhanapala. I would like to speak about three initiatives today. One is the Middle Powers Initiative, or the New Agenda Coalition, another is progress on the nuclear weapons convention, and the third is a new global movement of citizen weapons inspections.

I'm very pleased to follow some of the previous speakers, particularly Arjun and Daryl, who have indicated some of the urgency for making speedy progress towards nuclear disarmament. I will add some other reasons. I will also follow Mr. Bjarme with regards to the Eight Nations' Initiative for a New Agenda for Nuclear Disarmament. And I will add a couple of extra points with regards to why it's so urgent that we make speedy progress towards the abolition of nuclear weapons.

We've heard about the problems of the continuing research and development into nuclear weapons and the possible development of new, more dangerous forms of nuclear weapons. But, even those that are existing at the moment - we heard Monday about the problems of the five thousand, roughly, nuclear weapons that are still on high-alert status and the great risk of the use of nuclear weapons either by accident or by design, if there is not a move away from that and toward abolition. We know that at the moment there are no negotiations on further reductions in nuclear weapons and no commitment towards the realistic achievement of nuclear disarmament by the nuclear states. So, the initiatives we are talking about today are vital for developing a more secure world.

Firstly, the Middle Powers Initiative. What is this? This is an interesting example of synchronicity between the non-governmental organizations working for nuclear disarmament and some of the key governments. It was about at the same time that the governments privately of Sweden, Ireland, New Zealand, South Africa, Brazil, Egypt, Mexico and Slovenia were discussing the concept of a group of influential countries calling for a new agenda for nuclear disarmament that non-governmental organizations were doing the same thing. The non-governmental organizations called this the Middle Powers Initiative with the idea that a group of influential middle powers could have some positive effect on engaging the nuclear-weapon states and moving them towards an agenda for nuclear disarmament.

The Middle Powers Initiative was launched in March this year. We've now produced a book, "A Fast-Track to Zero Nuclear Weapons." We've swung in behind the agenda proposed by the Eight Nations Initiative, the New Agenda for Nuclear Disarmament, and are fully in support of the UN resolution along this and various other proposals that have come out in the declaration.

We don't see this as the only initiative. The other key one that I want to mention, the progress on the nuclear weapons convention, we feel is very complementary to the New Agenda of the Eight Nations Mr. Bjarme spoke about. The Nuclear Weapons Convention push has really come most strongly after the decision from the International Court of Justice in 1996. Although it had been spoken about beforehand, it wasn't until the International Court of Justice reaffirmed that there is an obligation to pursue in good faith and bring to a conclusion negotiations on nuclear disarmament in all its aspects under strict and effective international control that the proposal for negotiations leading to a Nuclear Weapons Convention got a really large kick-along.

The United Nations, following the International Court of Justice advisory opinion, adopted a resolution in 1996 calling for the implementation of the International Court of Justice advisory opinion through the commencement of negotiations which would lead to the conclusion of the Nuclear Weapons Convention. They repeated this call again in 1997 and the resolution is on the table again this year. It's resolution L. 45 (which was adopted as Resolution 53/77 W).

What the resolution does - the call for negotiations leading to a nuclear weapons convention, similar to the New Agenda proposed by the Eight Nations - is to try to forge a middle path between the extremes of the nuclear disarmament debate. On the one hand, there are nuclear-weapon states who are saying that progress should be made by a very gradual, step-by-step process; and all that you can really do is to concentrate on the next step in that process. And, at this stage, the next step or two steps will be the Fissile Material Cut Off Treaty and further reductions in nuclear weapons.

On the other extreme, you would have the proposed path from the non-aligned movement which calls for a phased program for nuclear disarmament within a specified framework of time. The G-21, the Group of Non-Aligned States, has proposed a sit down at such a time line and they have suggested that in the Conference on Disarmament.

The nuclear-weapon states and other states criticized the time-bound framework approach. There is some justification to the criticism that it's not possible to put down the exact time for all the steps before you enter into negotiations on all the steps. But they use this justification to stop

108

movement forward at all. What we have is that the nuclear-weapon states appear to be traveling down the road to disarmament in an old jalopy with a broken steering wheel, no idea of their final destination and no commitment to reaching the end of the road. The Nuclear Weapons Convention approach is to try to give some idea of what the final destination is. And, I would say the New Agenda program is to provide some idea of the pathway towards that destination. And both of them are trying to upgrade the car, so it can move more speedily down the road.

With regards to the Nuclear Weapons Convention approach, following the UN resolution, a group of scientists, disarmament experts and lawyers drafted a model Nuclear Weapons Convention to take into consideration some of the legal, political and technical considerations that would need to be made for a regime for the elimination of nuclear weapons. This was submitted to the United Nations by Costa Rica and is now being distributed as a UN document, A/C.1/52/7.

Along with that is a growing sentiment around the world in support of negotiations leading to the conclusion of a Nuclear Weapons Convention. We have opinion polls in the United States, in Canada, in Germany, in United Kingdom, in Belgium, all with over 80 per cent support, sometimes over 90 per cent support, for a Nuclear Weapons Convention. And this is just from the nuclear-weapons states and their allies. It's believed that support from the other states would be as high if not higher. There is an international movement, Abolition 2000, which now has the support of over 1,200 organizations. It is campaigning for the negotiation of a Nuclear Weapons Convention by the year 2000. So, there's a lot of support for the proposals and, as mentioned by Malaysia in the speech to the United Nations last week the proposal for negotiations for a Nuclear Weapons Convention fits in with the step-by-step process but just gives it a push along. Malaysia mentioned that the road towards the total elimination of nuclear weapons will be a long and arduous one and will need to be traveled through a series of well-defined stages. Therefore, the approach that they suggest in introducing the resolution for a Nuclear Weapons Convention is not incompatible with the step-by-step and incremental approaches already noted by others.

I'll finish off just with a little mention of the new movement for citizen weapon inspections. This is something which also follows the advisory opinion of the International Court of Justice in 1996. As well as affirming the obligation to negotiate for the elimination of nuclear weapons, the International Court of Justice concluded that the use of nuclear weapons is generally illegal, and the humanitarian laws of warfare apply to nuclear weapons. So, as a result of this, there are groups of citizens around the world who are going to sites where nuclear weapons are deployed or where research and development is being done on nuclear weapons. They are requesting to inspect those sites to determine whether or not the International Court of Justice opinion is being implemented. So far, they are not getting a welcome reception from those sites. In fact, some of them have been a little bit persistent. When they're rejected, they have insisted on their rights to inspect these sites, just as they say it is a right for the international community to inspect the sites in Iraq. The Iraqi sites are in opposition to international law for the elimination of the Iraq's weapons of mass destruction. There are a number of court cases which are coming about following the arrests of these people and this is a growing thing.

These are some of the key objectives. I'd like to finish with a very quick statement from Mohammed Bejaoui, who was President of the International Court of Justice at the time that it gave its advisory opinion on the legality of the threat or use of nuclear weapons. In his explanation of the meaning of the advisory opinion he said that, "The goal of nuclear disarmament is no longer utopian; it is the duty of all to seek it more actively than ever." Thank you.

JAYANTHA DHANAPALA: Thank you, Mr. Ware. The floor is open now for questions.

JOHN LINEWEAVER, Fellowship of Reconciliation: As an observer for about 60 years, I understand that the committees of the United Nations have been unsuccessful in their definition of aggression to this date. I am also impressed with the neglect of of the psycho-social causes of war, the basic causes on conflict, the root causes of the psycho-social pathology of war and the mutual paranoia which is behind these various leaders of the nations who have to have these missiles. Would anyone care to comment on that?

CAROL CHASE, Communications Coordination Committee for the UN: There have been proposals for turning the Trusteeship Council into a People's Assembly, revitalizing it, modernizing it, using broad-band digital technology, and, in so doing, enlisting the peoples' participation. The Canberra Commission, in one of its last conclusions, stated the importance of engendering the public will. I suggest that an international mechanism, this new Peoples' Assembly for the New Millennium, a genuine Peoples' House, would be the mechanism by which to bring about your important Treaty.

PAT KENOYER, Loretto Community and Peace Action: Alyn, I thought your metaphor of the car was good. I think some new push could come from us NGOs; but we can't get to the car to push. Yesterday, we sat here talking about the new Eight Nation Initiative, while in the First Committee they were introducing the resolution. Would it give a push to things if those of us who have members of our organizations in lots of different countries could so structure this Disarmament Week that we would be enabled to talk to the delegates? Surely there is some way where the delegates could hear our concerns. Many of us come from faith traditions and we're concerned about the immorality of these nuclear weapons. But we need to make our voices heard. Polls are fine, but there's something about a face-to-face contact with delegates who are as concerned as we are. So, I would ask you, would that be effective? Would that help give a push? Can you think of a way we could do it?

ANN LAKHDHIR, IDDS: ...Instead of our having a panel discussion at the time the Eight Nation Initiative was introduced, we should have been in the First Committee, if we had known the timing ahead of time. Many of the NGOs who are here could have been sitting in the gallery and listening to the discussion that took place. It was one of the few times when you had a kind of a debate going on in the First Committee. Into the future, I'm wondering if we had had some indication of the timing early enough, we might have at least managed to have many more NGOs seeing what various governments were saying about a key resolution like this one.

JAYANTHA DHANAPALA: The NGO Committee on Disarmament and the Department of Disarmament Affairs consult very closely in the structuring of this Week's events but it is extremely difficult for us to ensure that delegates in the First Committee participate in it. Announcements are made in the First Committee; but, as you know, delegates in the First Committee are engaged in the discussion of the resolutions, seeking co-sponsorship, arranging for amendments. With regard to the timing, arranging some kind of coordination between the events of the First Committee and NGO events, very often delegations themselves do not know when resolutions are being introduced.

And so I think this is a matter where it's necessary for the NGOs to be in touch with the delegations. They don't inform the Department of Disarmament Affairs when they are going to present their particular resolutions. We will explore when we plan next year's Disarmament Week how better to organize things to ensure this interaction between the delegations and the NGOs, because I certainly agree this would be beneficial.

DARYL KIMBALL: We have to make the nuclear disarmament issue more visible and to communicate our concerns to the government policy makers. That won't be solved with these sort of tactical issues of interaction at the UN here. It really goes back to what we as citizens are doing back home. Peace Action, the Loretta Community, Fellowship of Reconciliation and others have a presence here in New York and elsewhere. We need to work together. We need to recognize that this is a difficult time in which to do this because, while support for nuclear disarmament is high among the general public, we also need to recognize that that support is shallow. This is not the issue, unfortunately, that people in New York or Delhi or London are waking up in the morning and worrying about. It is a difficult time and we need to redouble our efforts.

LARS BJARME: On a People's Assembly and new structures, we are certainly willing to look at all new ideas, but can't, however, commit ourselves until we have studied what is proposed. When it comes to the timing of resolutions, we did not quite know until fairly late when we were going to introduce our resolution on the Eight Nation Initiative. And furthermore, it's a bit difficult to know when the debate is going to be because the First Committee at the moment is considering all agenda items on its agenda. So the discussion could jump from one subject to another, as it were.

In the discussion on the resolution, so far there have been a number of speakers in the First Committee and there have been only two negative statements or interventions. We are expecting another, a missile attack this afternoon on our text. But in my personal evaluation of these attacks, what is interesting is that the ability to read the text, which we have presented, seems to be somewhat impaired, or they are reading between the lines or reading other texts which they think they are reading at the same time, because the attacks we have had so far make it very, very clear that we are not having a dialogue but we are having a monologue on both sides. We are trying to reach them but they simply don't answer. Just as an example, we have been trying to convey the message that we are not putting forth an alternative to the NPT, to the CTBT or anything else, and we are told, we are abolishing everything that has been achieved. Perhaps someone from among you could help us to find a way to communicate what we are actually saying, but we are a bit at a loss. Thank you.

MASABUMI SATO: The question raised by the person from the Fellowship of Reconciliation should not go unremarked. We are buried in technical details. I think there is a legitimate reason for that. The question you raise is a question that involves how we make society more just. It really cannot be addressed as an offshoot of the nuclear disarmament question. Nuclear disarmament in many ways is an offshoot of that larger question that you raise. The question you raise is even larger because it involves not only relations between countries, ethnic groups, and so on, but also within the family, men-women relationships, grown-up children relationships, and so on. So it's a very difficult kind of thing. I don't shrink from those questions personally.

But the reason that I engage technically on these questions is I do believe - and one of the reasons I work on nuclear disarmament in this way - that unless we find ways to step back from the brink, we shall not have the time or the luxury or the pain or the pleasure or however you want to look at it to address those larger questions which are going to take a very long time.

I've worked in villages in India, I've worked on problems with poverty; they're still very important to me and I've not forgotten them in the midst of trying to define nuclear explosions and chasing after radioactive materials, and so on, not literally, of course. We are at a time when there is immense peril - a superpower with 20,000-30,000 nuclear weapons has fallen apart and is in economic chaos. The global financial system is in some chaos. We are in a very perilous time, but we are also in a very open time, in which, if we seize the moment, as I think the New Agenda Coalition is doing, then we can accomplish many important things to step back from the brink. I don't believe that the Nuclear Weapon States in their deafness are really in a majority and this voice of the people will become a little bit deafening to them. So, even if they are quite hard of hearing, I believe they will hear, not because of the loudness, perhaps, but because their own security is imperiled.

And, so it's a very important to accomplish some crucial things in the next few years, so that we can step back from this extremely dangerous nuclear brink that we're on and bring these materials under control. My statement to the United States is that they haven't won the Cold War yet. The Soviet Union lost the Cold War. But until there is nuclear disarmament, the countries that will be most imperiled by nuclear weapons are Russia, the United States, and so on. So, this is very important and we can accomplish this. I share your frustration at one level but at another level I don't. I think it's necessary to do this with some discipline and actually accomplish some things.

ALYN WARE: ...With regards to contact with delegations: As Mr. Bjarme noticed, delegations who seem to be responsive to their own NGOs but are also responsive to other non-governmental organizations sometimes are very pressed for time. But if you have information or useful ideas to offer to delegations, you should not hesitate to contact them individually...

With regards to the first question, I think it's very important, these psycho-social causes of war. The UNESCO Charter says that in the minds of men war was constructed, and so it is in the minds of men that the peace must be developed. Now, the sexism may have been intentional, because women don't tend to develop to such a same degree the plans for the destruction of earth as men do. But let's give some men a little bit of leeway here. Before I was working on nuclear disarmament, I was a kindergarten teacher and saw very much the very same sorts of dynamics in the sand pit as I see in the international arena. And I quickly realized that some form of peace education was very important in the kindergarten and that was very much a psychological thing in terms of what Arjun was just saying, I think, which was very important. While it is only a small minority who have this idea that there is some form of security in nuclear deterrence, we need to be able to understand where that's coming from and help them move, just as in peace education we are teaching some of the boys how it's not in their interest to be bullies, in fact it's much better for them if they can cooperate with others. I have attempted to answer some of those questions on the psychological aspects of deterrence in the book *Fast Track to Zero Nuclear Weapons*.

MASABUMI SATO: ...I would like to come back to the question on aggression and Mr. Makhijani's point on definition. I was at a previous meeting in Geneva hosted by UNIDIR where the same issue was brought up. Mr. Makhijani chose on that occasion not to give my organization his ideas for a definition. He has done so now and I will take it back to my scientists for them to look at. But he has,

I must stress, touched upon a very pertinent and difficult point. The clarification I'd like to provide is we are a technical secretariat, so we are, of course, prepared to look at it, but it will be up to Member States, that is you, your governments, to work on this.

A "People's Assembly": I agree fully but these things are more in the realm of the political guidance of Member States. The CTBTO Preparatory Commission has, if I may use your terminology, three people's assemblies a year. It may not be enough, but, in Vienna, you don't get all that many NGOs coming. We organize regular meetings between the Executive Secretary and the NGOs who are registered with the Vienna office of the UN. You are most welcome and I would encourage you to come. On our Web Page at **www.CTBTO.org** in addition to the Treaty, the ratification status, etc., there is a comments page. Send us your comments.

Before taking on this job in the CTBTO PrepCom in March last year, I was the Japanese representative to the Former Yugoslavia. The definition of aggression is painful. The hatred, the mutual distrust, I saw it firsthand. My government reconstructed a school in Sarajevo. I was there; I talked to the principal. She was very happy that we had done this. It was a very small exercise: $10,000. Money is not the point. I saw the children; it was very pleasant.

Then came Dayton; then came the redrawing of the lines. This was a Serb school. We had done it in what is now known as the Federation. We had done it on both sides, but this was on the Serb side, Lukovico, I think the area is called. I happened to go back to a meeting in Sarajevo called by the Bosnian Government, which was Muslim, basically. The school was gutted; burnt out. And that hurt very much. Not because of the money we had put in - these were the Japanese taxpayers' monies - but, it was not so much the money. It was the effort that we were trying to put in, to reconstruct a school, an elementary school. The principal had told me that the children were so overjoyed to have their roof fixed. I went back six months later and it was burnt out. So, you can tell me about aggression and I can tell you about hatred. Thank you.

ANN LEGGETT: Federation of American Arab Organizations: First of all, it would be nice if half or a little more that half of the human race were nicer than our brothers, the men. I was a former kindergarten bully and slightly ruthless type...I recall that one of the objections of India and other countries to the CTBT has been that it tends to freeze the Nuclear Club about where it is now, with the possible exception of its two very newest members. One of the characteristics of this club is that many of its members are either current colonial powers or former colonial powers - and we call this the uni-power world now. We are moving into a situation that's a highly dangerous one, namely, a cold war between the Big Power and the rest of the world. This doesn't bode very well for nuclear disarmament or indeed any other kind of disarmament. As the uni-power world starts to loose its neat construction, if it ever had one, the major power is going to, perhaps, get more inclined to be armed to the teeth, more inclined to violate the letter and the spirit of treaties. What can the rest of the world do to expect the American people to be able to do much about it, except over the very, very long run, considering this is a one party State in which the one party has two names? They don't listen to the people very much anyway. Short of overthrowing the government, which isn't going to happen in a big hurry. What can be done?

JERRY SPIVAK, Millennium Peoples' Assembly Network: The Values Caucus have been meeting with the ambassadors over the past couple of years and we're finding that the ambassadors sound almost like NGO members. So it's not as if we're on two sides of the fence. I think the problem is that we don't have enough communication and the modalities of communication are very different. One question: How do we start moving away from what CNN calls the "bracket mentality", producing lengthy documents and a focus on how you change one bracket, and beginning to utilize the new multimedia, beginning to start talking in terms of visuals? If it's only documents coming out that are of the *New York Times* length, you cannot expect the rest of the world to come on board...

DORRIE WEISS, ECAAR: There are many flaws in the CTBT, as Arjun Makhijani pointed out. The sub-critical testing that is allowed; the fact that countries can opt out when they say that it is because of national security....Why are we chasing other initiatives instead of calling for the implementation of Article VI?

MELISSA BROWN, Reporting Officer for the US Mission Committee on Disarmament: I'd like to address the concern that there is not a communication link between the NGOs and the delegates from the Missions. I'd like to assure you that the proceedings of the meetings are reported on in delegates' meetings and consideration is given to opinions expressed. I'd also like to encourage everyone to contact the Missions themselves.

ROBERT GRANT, International Humanist and Ethical Union:....I'd like to ask Mr. Sato whether they have considered the discussions that are being held in the International Criminal Court. One of the questions that is being raised is whether or not a State can be guilty of criminal conduct.

MASABUMI SATO: The point on visual presentation: We are 155 people; 5 in public information. We are open to ideas. Unfortunately, we may not be the most creative and imaginative people in the world, so, if you see things on the Web Page that you like, tell us. If you have ideas for how we might better present these things, do so. We had a VIC (Vienna International Center) Open House just two weeks ago on Sunday. My children liked it. I went, and to be honest, I was appalled, because my stand was all written material and though it was our first participation, I do take your point seriously.

ALYN WARE: The International Criminal Court is for individual responsibility, not for State responsibility. For State responsibility the appropriate court would be the International Court of Justice. So I refer you in this case back to the advisory opinion, July 8, 1996 on the legality of the threat or use of nuclear weapons.

With regards to the US, those of you who are US citizens will know that there are elections coming up in a couple of weeks, and so, of course, you can consider what your candidates' policies are on this. Also, there's a couple of congressional resolutions: the Woolsey resolution and the Markey resolution, which are both for nuclear abolition. One is for a nuclear weapons convention and the other one is to reorient the Stockpile Stewardship program

. There will be a documentary next year which will be a great opportunity to coalesce action around. It's called "Steep Walk into Armageddon". So watch out for that. It will be a good opportunity to talk with your neighbors and friends and promote the whole idea. And the US campaign for the abolition of nuclear weapons should be established next year.

LARS BJARME: "Why don't we implement Article VI?" This is precisely the question we are asking in our resolution. The first operative paragraph - it's a bit of a mouthful, but please bear with me - calls upon the nuclear-weapon States to demonstrate" unequivocal commitment to the speedy and total elimination of their respective nuclear weapons and without delay to pursue in good faith and bring to a conclusion negotiations leading to the elimination of these weapons," thereby fulfilling their obligations under Article VI of the Treaty of the Non-Proliferation of Nuclear Weapons. This is the first operative paragraph. We return frequently in the text to the Treaty itself but here we specifically mention Article VI and we want this to be fulfilled.

DARYL KIMBALL: We have a very difficult situation in front of us in regard to nuclear weapons disarmament. The year 2000 Non-Proliferation Treaty conference is coming up and the Nuclear Weapon States and others are committed to do a number of things to pursue Article VI to reinforce other components of the NPT Treaty. There has not been very much progress made so far.

What can be done? The Comprehensive Test Ban Treaty is vital but it's not concluded. I would encourage each of you to think how you might be able to engage in that process in each of your own countries. I would also strongly endorse the resolution that has been put forward by the New Agenda Coalition. It provides a very useful framework for how to move forward.

However, the job is not done when the resolution is passed, even if by all the States. It has to be implemented. We need to remind ourselves that statements, laws, proclamations, plans are meaningless unless there are real, meaningful supports behind them. That has to continue over a long period of time. We need to remind ourselves that we need to go back home and tell our decision makers, whoever they may be, that this is what we are looking for them to do.

And, speaking of Web Sites, the Coalition to Reduce Nuclear Dangers Web Site has a web site with links to a number of other non-governmental organizations. We have a section on the Comprehensive Test Ban Treaty. What you might not find on the excellent CTBTO Web Site, you might find on our CTBT section. Our address is: **www.crnd.org.**

ELAINE VALDOV, Chairperson of the DPI/NGO Executive Committee: I would like to express a deep reverence for those who have been victims of nuclear explosions and to add a human face to the wise words that have been talked here today. It reminds me of a story that has been told by, Michio Kaku. He spoke of one day back in the forties when he was talking about his nephew in Hiroshima. He was saying that this little fellow went down stairs in the basement with a chore to do. And there was this large bang, which threw him from one side of this cement basement to the other. He got all bloody. Michio said he came upstairs to find nothing but mass destruction and was walking around to find someone in his pain and saw many, many, many charred women silently throwing themselves into a body of water.

I think what Mr. Sato said he is counting on, and the disarmament movement is counting on to move forward, so we might be able to see a new century that is not covered with the darkness of nuclear destruction, is NGOs. So, thank you, gentlemen and ladies, for the work that you are doing.

JAYANTHA DHANAPALA: ...The Department of Disarmament Affairs also is on the Internet: You can access it from **www.un.org.** May I now thank, firstly, on your behalf, the panelists for their very useful and interesting contributions. I want also to thank the audience for your own participation.

NUCLEAR DISARMAMENT: FEASIBLE? VERIFIABLE?

ANN HALLAN LAKHDHIR, Vice President for Program: In any discussion of a nuclear weapon convention the first question that often comes up is, how would you verify it. Working out how you would verify a convention banning all nuclear weapons is certainly going to take time. We believe it important to begin thinking now about the verification measures that will be needed. I asked the US Ambassador to the Conference on Disarmament last spring whether the CD might establish an ad hoc committee of technical experts to start work on some of the elements that would be required to verify a nuclear weapons convention. An Ad Hoc group of technical experts worked on the verification of a Comprehensive Test Ban Treaty long before the treaty was negotiated, and their work facilitated its conclusion. He responded that some are thinking of that. I hope the some includes the US Administration.

I am going to turn this over to Steve Fetter who, in my thinking, was the start for this panel because I knew that he was a member of the US National Academy of Sciences Committee on International Security and Arms Control (CISAC) which produced a report last year, *The Future of US Nuclear Weapons Policy*, and also knew that he was going to be chairing a further study by the National Academy of Sciences CISAC group on verification. He is a professor at the University of Maryland and has written on this topic. I give this over to him now to both speak and then involve the other panelists.

STEVE FETTER: I will speak first, and then Alan Dowty, who is a professor of international studies at the University of Notre Dame, and then Merav Datan, who is with International Physicians for the Prevention of Nuclear War.

I would like to talk about the verifiability of a prohibition on nuclear weapons, but before I do that I would like to take a step back and ask, why should we worry about nuclear weapons? I think for most Americans the concern about nuclear weapons has faded into the past. It is something that they believe was associated with the Cold War and that has been taken care of. So I do think it important to begin with an explanation of why we should still be concerned.

Most people think, hasn't there been a lot of progress? There has been in the last decade: the INF Treaty, START I, START II, (although it has not been ratified by the Russian Duma), the unilateral reductions of theater nuclear warheads, which in the US case was over 90%, the decision to take bombers off alert and to take the Looking Glass aircraft off alert and to de-target nuclear weapons and the cooperation between Russia and the United States on dismantling, all of these are very significant. Most of us would not have dreamed that we would be sitting here today with all of this accomplished.

And in the international arena, the CTBT has been signed, the NPT was renewed indefinitely, and in many of the regions of the world, in Africa, North Korea, in the Middle East, in South East Asia, there has been progress on limiting the spread of nuclear weapons.

But there are reasons to worry. The first reason is the inherent danger that persists in the US/Russian nuclear postures. The United States retains very large nuclear forces on high alert which are capable of launching on a few minutes' notice even in peace time. Russia similarly maintains a large number of nuclear weapons on high alert: those forces and their ability to provide warning of an attack and the command and control of those forces are deteriorating. This greatly exacerbates the risk of accidental or erroneous or unauthorized use. I worry about that very much.

The second reason for worry is the long-term stability of the non-proliferation regime. The nuclear powers have an obligation under Article 6 of the Non Proliferation Treaty to pursue nuclear disarmament. And that is not a commitment that the nuclear powers seem to be taking seriously, particularly the United States and Russia. Most US government officials believe this situation can persist indefinitely, the situation where a few countries claim the right to hold nuclear weapons forever while denying the right to other countries. I disagree. I don't think this situation is stable indefinitely and that we ought to begin now thinking about ways to take this commitment more seriously.

Furthermore, like biological and chemical weapons, the use or the threat of use of nuclear weapons probably is incompatible with international laws and humanitarian principles governing the use of force.

What do we do? I see both a short term and a long term agenda, with the shorter term agenda focusing on a further winding down of the US and Russian nuclear postures. That was a process that seemed well under way in the late 1980s and the early 1990s. Now it is stalled as we await Russian ratification of START II. We are told that both governments have plans to do lots of things after START II is ratified, but in the meantime nothing is done. There is a program laid out in the National Academy report, *The Future of US Nuclear Weapons Policy*, which can be found on the Internet at http://www.nap.edu/readingroom/books/fun. It focuses on reducing the size, the readiness and the salience of US and Russian nuclear arsenals.

To start with the size: Even after START II is fully implemented, the nuclear arsenals of those two countries would be far too large. The United States, for example, plans to retain over 10,000 intact nuclear warheads, each of which is approximately ten times as destructive as the bomb dropped on Hiroshima. This just seems to be incredibly excessive. I think it is fairly easy for people to agree that at most the United States and Russia should only retain perhaps a few hundred nuclear warheads, and that we should move as rapidly as possible to get down to that level.

On readiness, the United States and Russia still maintain, during peacetime, the ability to launch thousands of nuclear weapons on a few minutes notice. This is a situation which I find mind-boggling after the Cold War. This raises the threat of accidental or unauthorized use of nuclear weapons. To reduce those risks we have advocated a program of de-alerting nuclear forces, taking nuclear forces off alert during peacetime.

Reducing the salience of nuclear weapons is one of the most important tasks. By that I mean several things. Right now both the United States and Russia still retain the right to use nuclear weapons first, to use nuclear weapons against countries that haven't used nuclear weapons. In the case of the United States there have been moves to expand the use of nuclear weapons to deterring and responding to chemical and biological attacks. This mission creep is very dangerous. I see a similar mission creep for nuclear weapons in Russia, whose conventional military forces have been weakened. This of course goes directly counter to efforts to limit the spread of nuclear weapons.

Another worry is "loose nukes" in Russia. What is desperately needed is the accounting of nuclear warheads and nuclear material, inventories of highly enriched uranium (HEU) and plutonium. That is very important also for verification of a prohibition of nuclear weapons.

The United States persists in thinking about the use of nuclear weapons in ways that are virtually identical to how the US thought about nuclear weapons during the Cold War: counterforce, targeting nuclear attacks against opposing countries' nuclear forces very early in a conflict in order to destroy those forces. Of course that poses dangers of rapid escalation. The National Academy of Sciences report advocated that all nuclear powers state that the only purpose of nuclear weapons, while we still have them, is to deter the use of nuclear weapons by other countries. We call that the core mission, the core deterrent role.

The long term objective, nuclear disarmament, needs to be taken more seriously in the nuclear weapon states than it is being taken today. Personally I don't think that a prohibition on nuclear weapons is a near-term possibility. I think it is for a more distant future. Even if the current nuclear powers agreed that this was a desirable objective it would take decades to fully implement a prohibition. The agenda that I just laid out would be a precursor in any case. That has led some people to say it is premature to talk about the prohibition of nuclear weapons because we have this other agenda that will take us at least a decade or more of winding down the overhand in US and Russian nuclear forces. Shouldn't we worry about that first? Regardless of what you believe about the ultimate end state, we have to do this other agenda first.

I agree with that, but nevertheless, it is important for the nuclear powers to demonstrate by their deeds as well as their words that they take the ultimate objective, nuclear disarmament, and their commitments under Article 6 of the Non Proliferation Treaty seriously.

I would like to call attention to one feature in particular, or one condition, that would be required for a stable prohibition of nuclear weapons. That would be the requirement to have a verification system that would not only verify that the nuclear arsenals had been completely dismantled, but would provide an adequate warning of any attempt anywhere to rebuild nuclear arsenals.

How would this work? There would be these two main tasks: one, verifying the dismantling of current arsenals; after that had been done, and during that process, the second task of providing warning of any attempt to rearm, to rebuild nuclear weapons.

Starting with the first task, the first place to begin is with a declaration of what exists. It would be a requirement for all of the countries who now have nuclear weapons to declare their inventories of nuclear weapons, nuclear weapon components and the materials, the fissile materials, plutonium and HEU that are essential components of nuclear weapons. Only after you have this inventory can you really begin the process of verifying the dismantling of those weapons.

And this is something we can begin today. In fact I think it is vital to begin that process today, because if you don't begin when the arsenals are very large, I don't think that you will have the confidence that will be required to go to very low numbers of nuclear weapons and perhaps all the way to zero. Today, as things stand, the US and Russia are dismantling thousands of nuclear weapons without any transparency measures even between the two countries, much less any system of international transparency or accounting or verification.

As long as the nuclear components, the plutonium pits, remain intact, at some future date we can go back and verify which warheads had been dismantled. But as soon as those pits are taken apart we have lost that information forever and it will be very difficult to obtain high confidence about the total inventories of nuclear weapons and fissile materials and to assure that some of that material had not been diverted.

I would like to mention two bench marks for nuclear disarmament, to show how difficult putting into place an accurate accounting system would be. One is the bench mark provided by the US's own effort to inventory how much plutonium it has. A few years ago the US Department of Energy released a report called "Plutonium, the First Fifty Years." It tried to figure out how much plutonium it has. The final answer was something like 99 plus or minus 2.8 tons. Well, 2.8 tons is a lot of plutonium. In fact it is more than the United Kingdom has.

Now that 2.8 tons isn't lost, certainly. It probably is material that was never even produced but was calculated to have been produced, or it probably includes material that is on the walls of glove boxes, and pipes in Rocky Flats. but it is enough plutonium to build about a thousand nuclear weapons. When you are dealing with stockpiles that are as large as those of the US and Russia, accounting discrepancies are going to be quite significant.

Another bench mark is provided by the effort by IAEA (International Atomic Energy Agency) to certify the disarmament of South Africa. South Africa had produced much less material, a hundred times less than the United States or Russia. And even in that case the IAEA was just barely able to say that it has verified the South African declaration of its production to within about one significant quantity, or the amount required to build one nuclear weapon.

Then of course we have the example of Iraq, of how difficult it can be when a country is actively trying to evade detection, how difficult it can be to detect clandestine nuclear activities.

So, although I want to highlight the difficulties, I don't mean to imply by any means that this is impossible. Instead, I want to put the emphasis on the need to get on with it, to begin the research and development program that would be necessary to put in place as accurate a system of accounting as possible so that in the future when the nuclear powers agree to seriously consider a prohibition on nuclear weapons, we will have the solid foundation on which to base that.

NANCY COLTON, International Association for Volunteer Effort: Where is the dismantling taking place?

STEVE FETTER: The US and Russia have dismantling facilities already. The US facility is Pantex. In fact Pantex has given a lot of thought as to how it would dismantle nuclear weapons in a verifiable way, where Russian inspectors could be assured - they haven't thought of international inspectors so far, only Russian inspectors - that a certain number of nuclear weapons is being dismantled without divulging sensitive information. Russia has four such facilities. I think part of any scheme to dismantle nuclear weapons would include some agreement to consolidate those activities at one of those facilities.

QUESTION: Is any dismantling being done in the Ukraine, Belarus, and Kazakhstan?

119

STEVE FETTER: No, all of the facilities for dismantling nuclear weapons are in Russia. In fact the entire nuclear weapons complex for the former Soviet Union is in Russia. There were some non-nuclear components produced in the other republics. I know that Russia had a program to manufacture all of the necessary components in Russia, so none of the other republics are involved. And all of the former nuclear weapons in the republics are now in Russia. Not all of the weapons-useable materials, though, have gone back to Russia. As you may know, there has been a US program to try and get the HEU and plutonium that is scattered about the other republics consolidated.

QUESTION: What about nuclear disarmament in the Middle East and in South Asia?

STEVE FETTER: You have to look at each case individually and try to formulate a program for each region. In the case of the Middle East - I am not the expert here on this, I should refer this question to Alan Dowty who has thought a good deal more than I have about this - I believe that Israel has indicated its readiness to sign a Middle East nuclear-weapon-free zone agreement if there was a comprehensive peace agreement. .

South Asia is more difficult, because Pakistan believes it has no ability to defend itself against India by conventional means. Nuclear disarmament in South Asia would have to be put in the context of a broader security agreement that made Pakistan feel that its security was adequately protected without nuclear weapons. But I am not an expert on South Asia so I wouldn't begin to talk about how you would do that.

MEMBER OF THE NETHERLANDS DELEGATION: Do you agree with those who argue that the fissile material cut-off had to include existing stockpiles of military fissile materials in order to be worthwhile or do you think it would be worthwhile to have an agreement that left out existing stockpiles and merely banned the future production?

STEVE FETTER: I think it would be useful to have as a first step an agreement that simply banned the production of fissile material outside of safeguards. Also I am well aware that the US government and probably the governments of the other nuclear-weapon states are adamantly opposed to a cut-off that includes existing stockpiles of military material. So I would very much like to make progress.

I think that the opposition to including military stockpiles at this point is absolute. I do think it would be valuable to lock in a de facto cut-off on the production of fissile material in part because that would involve a verification system that we could begin putting in place at the production facilities in the Nuclear Weapon States where nuclear weapons materials had been produced. that would be the first time that the Nuclear Weapon States had accepted such international verification. I think that is an important enough step to take that it is worth doing on its own.

It would be terrific if we could take the further step of having some kind of accounting for stockpiles, but I don't see that being the case in the near term. It is worthwhile to go for the more limited agreement now because we can get that now and we can't get the more comprehensive agreement.

QUESTION: Is there any connection between the reduction of nuclear weapons and the use of fissile materials for peaceful purposes?

STEVE FETTER: There is, because you have to use the HEU somehow. The HEU that is being taken from nuclear weapons is being used for reactor fuel, both the HEU being taken from US weapons and the HEU being taken from dismantled Russian weapons. It has been shipped to the US and is being made into reactor fuel. That is a long-term project because there is so much material. The US has agreed to buy 500 tons of Russian HEU over twenty years.

The question of what to do with the plutonium is far more difficult. There are two proposals for that. One is to burn the material as reactor fuel in existing reactors as MOX fuel. I do worry about the implications of that for non-proliferation more generally because the use of plutonium in nuclear reactors is not now economic, not even close to being economic and does create proliferation risks. I worry about the example that this sets for countries that would like to promote the use of plutonium more generally.

The other alternative is to mix the plutonium with waste and to bury it and Russia is adamantly opposed to doing that because it views the plutonium as a valuable resource. It appears that the only way we will persuade Russia to dispose of its plutonium is to dispose of it by burning it in reactors. That is better than leaving the plutonium in the form of nuclear weapons or pits that could be easily recycled.

ARJUN MAKHIJANI: ...when you use plutonium as a fuel, 40 to 75% of the initial amount of the plutonium is still there in the spent fuel, and you have to bury that, so you don't get around the burial problem by using plutonium as a fuel. Burial is a much more complicated problem than the burial of uranium spent fuel. I believe the disposal problem is much less difficult than the MOX spent fuel disposal problem...Vitrification is a far better solution.

STEVE FETTER: I agree with you that vitrification is the preferred route. As you know, I am a member of a committee that has written a rather lengthy report on this and I can't distance myself very far from the position they came to.

We will now move on to Alan Dowty.

ALAN DOWTY: There will be a change of pace because I am not going to be talking about verification. I am going to make an argument for changing the agenda, widening the agenda beyond the nuclear weapons category itself. I will make a case for a universal ban on the first use of all weapons of mass destruction. In order to be as provocative as possible, I am going to do this in the form of four propositions.

Proposition 1: It is time to bring all weapons of mass destruction inside the same tent, from the viewpoint of arms control. As Steve just said, nuclear weapons are still with us and still are a problem. I think it is clear that chemical and biological weapons are going to be with us for some time to come, despite the fact that conventions banning both categories of weapons have been adopted by the majority of the nations of the world. I think 140 countries have ratified the Biological Weapons Convention, and 112 the Chemical Weapons Convention.

But as the case of Iraq demonstrates, adherence to these agreements in itself doesn't necessarily mean that the problem has been resolved. I would submit the experience of Iraq demonstrates that perhaps, in the case of chemical and biological weapons, perhaps nothing short of total military occupation of a country would in fact suffice to guarantee the total elimination of such weapons from a country's arsenal. You might even argue, given the case of Aum Shinrikye in Tokyo, in 1995, that even total military occupation of a country might not be a complete guarantee.

In any case the possibility of the production of these weapons in a clandestine fashion is a rather frightening reality. In fact, the various categories of weapons of mass destruction do already impinge upon each other. We have interdependence here in the unwillingness of countries to contemplate reduction or elimination of one category of weapon without similar progress in the other. Nuclear arsenals are maintained in part as a hedge against chemical or biological attack. Here I differ a bit with Steve's characterization of this. It seems clear in the case of the United States, the possible use of nuclear weapons to deter use of chemical or biological weapons has been operational policy for some time. It is just that in the last year it has become also a declaratory policy.

There are other countries whose nuclear capability has something at least to do with the presumed threat of chemical or biological attack. Israel comes to mind. On the other hand, chemical and biological weapons are often defined as the poor man's nuclear weapon. Apart from the Arabs who maintain chemical capabilities to counter Israel's nuclear capability, a surprising number of the non signatories to the Chemical Weapons Convention are also countries that could be characterized as facing as they see it at least some sort of nuclear threat: North Korea, Viet Nam, Ukraine, Kazakhstan, some of the Arab states - Iraq, Libya and so on.

There was an anemic response by the international community to the actual use of chemical weapons over an extended period by Iraq against Iran and against its own population. There is of course also fear that the use of chemical weapons has become almost routinized. By the end of the Iraq-Iran war the Iraqi army was in fact using these weapons in a routine way. It had a lot to do with the collapse of Iran at the end of the war. One report is that the number of countries developing chemical weapons has doubled since that time as a result of that.

But we have to recall that considerable progress has been made toward stigmatizing all weapons of mass destruction, beginning in 1925 with the Geneva Protocol. The fact that countries still try to conceal chemical and biological weapons indicates some recognition of this fact. I am arguing that from here on further progress in any one of these categories is likely to depend upon making progress in tandem across the board. One reason for the lack of progress which Steve has described so well on the nuclear front, not the only reason, is the risk of chemical or biological attack.

Proposition 2: The best approach may be a universal ban of first use of any weapon of mass destruction. We should continue to try to eliminate chemical and biological weapons, and nuclear weapons, but the focus also has to be put on preventing their actual use. This recognizes the fact that weapons of one type are in fact used to deter attack with weapons of another type of weapon of mass destruction. What the no-first-use ban would do would be to limit all of them only to that role of deterring weapons of mass destruction. What these weapons all have in common, apart from their genocidal capacity, is that their use is irrational if they are faced with the threat of retaliation in kind. So even in the current militarized environment, and even among the most hard-nosed advocates of national defense, a no-first-use policy now makes eminent sense.

It is clearly increasingly irrational to consider any possible first use of nuclear or chemical or biological weapons against conventional weapons. The NATO position of reserving the first use of nuclear weapons because of the presumed inferiority to the Soviet Union in Europe on the conventional level is obviously no longer relevant. The entire NATO position here on the implied first use of nuclear weapons is no longer relevant. The uses of ambiguity, not saying that you wouldn't use them first because it leaves some degree of doubt and uncertainty in the minds of the opponent, what is called broad deterrence, is much harder to argue for in a post-Cold War environment.

Even in some of the other nuclear weapons states, the threshold states of India, Pakistan and Israel, it could be argued that the risk of conventional defeat, the risk to national survival from defeat by conventional weapons is receding, and that the risk of destruction by weapons of mass destruction is growing. At some point a simple calculus of national interest, even in these cases, would argue for adherence to a universal ban on first use of all such weapons.

Proposition 3: A universal no-first-use ban may be the best platform for reduction and eventual elimination. Once you reduce the role of all weapons of mass destruction to a deterrence of other weapons of mass destruction, it becomes easier to envision a future step. These weapons have been reduced simply to deterring themselves. They are no longer being introduced into operational planning for ordinary, regular warfare. All of the justifications for various refinements become irrelevant because if the role of such weapons is simply to deter the use of other such weapons, the operational requirements are quite minimal.

This requires the acceptance for the time being of the second use of weapons of mass destruction, at least in theory, but again this recognizes a simple reality, that states like the United States already are using nuclear weapons to deter chemical or biological attack. Deterrence is also essential during the transition period because defense against biological and chemical weapons, even more than with nuclear weapons, is practically impossible, so that the problem here of preventing their use really comes down to the critical issue of deterrence.

However, eventually one could imagine that countries in the position of the United States in particular, relying on massive conventional superiority, could dispense with even this first use of weapons of mass destruction. We should recall that when General Horner, the Commander of the Air Forces of the coalition in the Gulf War was asked his response to a chemical attack by Iraq, it was we would not nuke them, but take the country apart, one brick at a time. In other words, that the United States and the coalition would rely on overwhelming conventional superiority to solve the problem at its roots rather than engaging in senseless retaliatory attacks. Furthermore, modern technology obviously does increase the value of conventional superiority in many ways, even in this capacity of deterring weapons of mass destruction. So the ultimate aim, it seems to me, would be to rely on conventional strength and the international community acting together to eliminate even the remaining part of first use.

Proposition Four: Such a ban would force a change in US policy which is long overdue in any event. We have a current contradiction in our posture. We have renounced chemical and biological weapons. At the same time we have implied that in response to a chemical or biological attack we would respond with nuclear weapons, or we would reserve the nuclear deterrent in this case. The threat was delivered by Secretary of State Baker to Tariq Aziz on the eve of the Gulf War and the Presidential Decision Directive of last year which explicitly reserved this option.

The problem here is that this pledge directly contradicts another presumed cornerstone of US nuclear policy: a pledge, dating back to 1968, never to use nuclear weapons against a non-nuclear country that was a party to the NPT and which was not allied with a nuclear power. So Iraq, which is a party to the NPT, acting alone, and remaining non-nuclear while launching a chemical attack against the United States or another country, would be covered in theory by this pledge. I would again submit that in fact US operational policy has not followed this guideline. A universal ban of first use of weapons of mass destruction would, among other things, resolve this contradiction by essentially revoking that pledge, which is taking one step backwards in order to be in a better position to move forwards.

The change in US policy toward no-first-use of nuclear weapons against conventional attack is certainly long overdue. It is very difficult to describe any reasonable scenario under which the United States would actually consider the first use of nuclear weapons in a conventional setting. Former Secretary of Defense McNamara has said that he recommended to both Presidents Kennedy and Johnson, that the US in fact not make use of first use of nuclear weapons in Europe or anywhere else and that in his view they accepted this recommendation.

Certainly in the post Cold War environment, with a defense budget equal to that of the next six countries combined, four of whom are allies, it is very difficult to imagine that a first use of nuclear weapons in any conventional setting would make sense. You could also of course convert this to an argument that might even appeal to some of our hard-nosed defense supporters. If the United States is in fact the leading conventional power in the world by a wide margin, it ought to be, by logic alone, the leader in the fight against weapons of mass destruction which erode this natural advantage.

STEVE FETTER: Are there any questions directly on the points raised?

CAROLINE BRIDGMAN-REES, Center for International Peacebuilding: What are the countries, besides Iraq, that have used chemical weapons?

ALAN DOWTY: There are confirmed cases of Egypt using chemical weapons in Yemen. If you want to go back to the thirties, there are cases of Japan using chemical and biological weapons. The cases that have taken place are characterized generally by the fact that they took place in wars in which the target did not have any means of responding in kind and generally in remote circumstances where it was difficult to get outside confirmation of what took place, typically in Egypt's use in Yemen. What really amazes me about the Iraqi case is that this use of chemical weapons took place over a period of about five years. By the end of that time it had become a routine part of the Iraqi strategy and the international response to this, both by the United States and the United Nations, was anemic, by anybody's definition, for a weapon that had presumably been stigmatized repeatedly. I have no real explanation for that, but I think that the Iraqi case in the 1980s is very frightening for that reason.

MERAV DATAN, Director of Programs for International Physicians for the Prevention of Nuclear War in Cambridge, Massachusetts, and formerly the Research Director for the Lawyers Committee on Nuclear Policy: We heard a little bit about long term and short term steps towards nuclear disarmament, the elimination of all weapons of mass destruction. I am going to take it a little bit farther. I think that the ground has been laid well in the sense that what to my mind links both the previous presentations is the psychological component, the role of confidence, confidence in verification, and confidence in no first use. To me that is a relevant setting of the stage because I am going to talk about a nuclear weapons convention, a treaty for the elimination of nuclear weapons, and that's a goal that will require a significant psychological shift at all levels, governmental and non-governmental, although most of the people in this room would probably support such a goal.

I will start with a recent statement by the delegation of the United Kingdom to the last NPT Preparatory Committee meeting in April. The Ambassador was addressing the question of the elimination of nuclear weapons and the different approaches to that. He identified two different approaches, and I will read from his statement to the PrepCom.

> If we look beneath the surface of the debates on the elimination of nuclear weapons, I believe we can discern two major currents of thought about the best way to proceed towards our shared goal. On the one hand there are those who believe that the key point is to know the destination we are aiming at and to concentrate on taking the next manageable steps towards it, knowing that as we move forward the subsequent steps will become clear. On the other hand there are those who before going any further want to have a much clearer map for the entire journey, preferably along with a firm indication of how long it will take. In our view, that is the view of the United Kingdom. The basic difficulty with the later approach is that it does not do justice to the complexity and variety of the problems we face in moving towards elimination. To assume that all these can be foreseen at this stage, let along solved, and then neatly encapsulated in a rigid time frame or single convention seems to us to smack of unrealistic idealism.

Starting with that I would like to make the case for an exercise in unrealistic idealism, and why such an exercise is useful. I don't mean to underestimate and I probably don't grasp as fully as the Ambassador might or as Steve Fetter might just how complex the problem is, but I think that precisely because the problem of large-scale nuclear disarmament is so complicated, we need to get the discussion going now at all levels. And this was the purpose of developing and distributing a model nuclear weapons convention. Over the last few years the calls for a nuclear weapons convention at governmental and non-governmental levels have been increasing. To my mind in the long run it doesn't really matter if it is one convention, one treaty, or a framework. There are resolutions being discussed by the First Committee of the UN calling for a nuclear weapons convention and another one under the New Agenda Coalition, sponsored by seven nations, that mentions a framework. To my mind it doesn't matter in the long run. A nuclear weapons convention is a convenient shorthand way of citing the goal and pointing to the need to develop a comprehensive plan to work towards that goal.

Why do I think it important to at least attempt to develop a comprehensive plan, rather than focus only on the next manageable steps? For a couple of reasons. Some of these may be obvious, but I think they are worth repeating. There is in the first place a legal obligation to negotiate nuclear disarmament. The step-by-step approach, START I, START II, START 17, doesn't guarantee that in the end we actually will achieve nuclear disarmament. We face the danger that while the right hand is negotiating the START process and the CTBT, the left hand is developing Stockpile Stewardship, or deepening its understanding of nuclear weapons and simulation technology. So only, to my mind, a focus on the goal will ensure that the steps that we take in that direction do lead towards that goal.

Besides that, the incremental steps are linked. A comprehensive plan can help identify some of the early steps that need to be taken. A perfect example of that is something that echoes what Steve Fetter mentioned, the need for an inventory of fissile material. We can't even begin to think about elimination of nuclear weapons without a sense of what is out there now. And so work on that should begin as soon as possible, without even necessarily agreement among those who are taking part in the process as to what the final goal will be. But there will be no possibility of achieving nuclear disarmament without some sense of what is out there now and what form it is in, what form it would need to be stored in, how it would be handled for how long.

I also think that an exercise in developing a plan, designing the elements of a plan for complete nuclear disarmament, is a good way to engage the participation of governments and non-governmental bodies early on because it will require coordination across different industries and across political bodies at a level that probably we haven't seen yet, so the sooner we can get everybody thinking about it, the weapons labs, among physics students, and at the governmental level, the better.

As many of you probably know, a model nuclear weapons convention was released about a year and a half ago, in April of 1997, with the idea of stimulating discussion along these lines. It was submitted to the United Nations as a discussion document by Costa Rica about this time last year, in November of 1997 with the UN citation A/C.1/52/7. It is meant as a discussion document. It is far from the correct plan. It has problems, but the point of it is to raise the issues. It also mirrors many of the topics that would need to be addressed. It was an NGO initiative, but it included former arms control negotiators. It is also available on the web. Try doing a nuclear weapons convention search. I will mention a little about the content and the approach that we took.

Steve is the expert on verification, but I want to highlight some of the specific requirements for verification. Because this was meant as a discussion document, I will devote some time to the responses we have received to the convention. Those responses highlight the areas where the political will or technical knowledge is lacking. We don't have answers to some of them, but we think it is important to get the discussion going.

The general obligations, some of which will seem obvious: Negative obligations will be that States Parties undertake never to use or threaten to use nuclear weapons, or to engage in any military or other preparations to use nuclear weapons. A controversial one: not to research (we have learned we need to refine that more carefully) to develop, test, produce, otherwise acquire, deploy, stockpile, maintain or transfer nuclear weapons or delivery vehicles for the purpose of delivering nuclear weapons. And never to produce, stockpile, retain, transfer, use nuclear weapons-grade fissionable or fusionable material. There would be exceptions for defined quantities for medical, agricultural or research purposes. Those would also apply to nuclear weapons components or equipment.

Among the affirmative obligations: To destroy nuclear weapons and destroy or convert facilities involved in the production, testing, and research of nuclear weapons, as well as nuclear weapons delivery vehicles. To participate in activities aimed at transparency and education for purposes of detecting and preventing prohibited activities. I don't mean this in a KGB kind of sense, that you must participate. The idea is to encourage active participation at all levels.

There are also obligations to report violations of the convention, to cooperate with the implementing agency, and to enact domestic legislation that is necessary for the implementation of the convention.

The approach that this model convention took is not the time-bound framework that some of you are familiar with. Our thinking was that that had already developed a resistance. The point isn't so much to have a fixed time-bound framework as to change the path that we are headed on, to change the direction, and go in the direction of nuclear disarmament in a universal way. The emphasis should be more on security and safety and irreversibility rather than sheer speed for the sake of it. What we would propose are phases that would coordinate the various activities.

The phases that were laid out, and again, they are far from perfect, far from the ideal, but a first attempt to try and think about the steps that need to be taken and their sequencing. These phases are aimed at reversing the armament process, so that would mean starting from the very end and working backwards, de-targeting, de-alerting, removal from deployment, separation of warheads from delivery vehicles, and in conjunction with that, deep proportionate reductions among the nuclear weapon states. Obviously it would have to start with the US and Russia. And all these measures would be verified, starting with initial declarations, to be regularly updated and followed by on-site inspections and challenge inspection, remote and on-site monitoring and surveillance, accounting and control measures that relate to nuclear weapons, nuclear materials, facilities and delivery vehicles.

One of the innovations in this proposed treaty is the rights and obligations of persons. Persons means natural and legal persons. That includes corporations. It would include responsibility to report crimes under the convention and protection for persons providing information. International law seems to be moving in this direction, with the International Criminal Court holding individuals responsible, but it is something of an innovation.

The agency proposed to implement the model convention is modeled on the agency that is implementing the Chemical Weapons Convention, that is the Organization for the Prohibition of Chemical Weapons because that was an institution that was developed for the elimination of an entire class of weapons.

Our proposal has no withdrawal clause. As far as I know, it would be the only treaty that would have no withdrawal clause, but it seemed to us that there would be no point in an agreement like this if States could pull out.

The responses that we have received highlight some of the more difficult questions. The areas of greatest debate this document has inspired have to do with areas where the knowledge, the technology, or the political will are lacking. They are open questions. We don't have complete answers to them.

By far the most prevalent question is, how would you enforce something like this, how would you enforce a nuclear weapons convention? The problem has to do with the centrality of nuclear weapons in security thinking today. Enforcement I think will be the Achilles heel of any security system that relies primarily on threat, or on the use of force, on military might for security. The real security issues are human issues, problems of development and health, and the focus on seeking security through the ability to dominate, rather than prevent a conflict, is something that will only lead to further development of weapons or a greater reliance on weapons and arms races. I don't see a way out of that unless we change the way that we think. I come back to the issues of confidence that are the key to changing reliance on weapons for security.

The model that we propose doesn't exceed today's security regimes, that is the United Nations Security Council. That is because we meant it to be relevant, idealistic as it is. Perhaps some think it reads like science fiction. We are still starting with the world that we are in today, and the Security Council is the body that is meant to be responsible for security. We don't propose the reform of the Security Council in this document. And we don't propose a change in the international security system, although we recognize that that would be necessary for the elimination of nuclear weapons. Instead, the idea would be that as something like this develops, it reinforces those elements of security that are based on genuine human needs and reduced reliance on policies of military might as a way to security. In any case, a nuclear weapons convention should emphasize compliance rather than enforcement. Compliance should be made more attractive than non-compliance. There should be incentives to comply. These might be in the form of humanitarian assistance, assistance in alternative energy possibilities because of the proliferation risks associated with nuclear energy or other forms of development, because those are often behind armed conflict, or the threat of armed conflict.

Another key question is how to prevent breakout, or cheating. There is no magic formula to this, but the key is in the irreversibility of the armament process, dismantling of the nuclear weapons industry. The farther away you move from the armament process, and from where we are today, the more difficult it will be to conceal a program of nuclear weapons. One of the questions that keeps surfacing in my mind in this context is why do we seem to be so much more worried about the possibility of one nuclear weapons being hidden away in somebody's basement than we are about thousands of weapons today on hair trigger alert? I say this because this is posed over and over again as a threshold question, how could we be sure that we had achieved complete nuclear disarmament? Well, wouldn't we be better off in a world where that is the concern, rather than in the world that we are in today, or the direction that we seem to be heading in today?

Another question that surfaces quite often, perhaps the one that is the most divisive, even among supporters of nuclear disarmament, is the question of nuclear energy. There isn't any agreement as to whether a nuclear-weapon-free world is possible in a world where there is still nuclear energy. Even among the peace activists there is disagreement about this. In any case, I think we could say that the viability of complete nuclear disarmament, or adequately verifiable nuclear disarmament will turn on the degree of surveillance and accounting and control that States are willing to tolerate.

The final question that I will mention has to do with the different roles of the nuclear weapons States and the non-nuclear weapons States in a regime of nuclear disarmament. This is relevant because the regime that exists today is seen as overtly discriminatory between the nuclear haves and the nuclear have-nots. The question of verification and of the disarmament process will aggravate some of those concerns because in the process of disarmament there is going to be an unequal sharing of information. There won't be equal access to the materials or the technology and this might aggravate the discrepancies that already exist. I think that different responsibilities and different roles of the nuclear weapons States and the non-nuclear weapons States are inevitable. There needs to be attention paid to the concerns of the non-nuclear weapons States and perhaps they could have some part in the verification process, in the way, for instance, that Richard Butler comes from a non-nuclear weapons State but heads UNSCOM. It would have representatives of the non-nuclear weapons States taking part in the verification process, without access to the types of sensitive information that in the long run we would like to see destroyed.

There is a danger in all of us talking to each other when for the most part we tend to agree. We may disagree on the details or on exactly what is feasible and what is not feasible, but the danger is that unless there is much broader concern about these issues, and much greater awareness, we are not going to get anywhere. We need more awareness both at the government level and at the public level to bring pressures on governments.

With that in mind, IPPNW has put out a book that is meant not so much for this kind of audience, but for your friends, your family, to try to undermine the perception that Steve Fetter mentioned at the beginning, that we are better off now, the world is secure, the Cold War is over. That is not true. We have put together a book of photos and quotations from the media that pretty much speak for themselves about where we are, and what the myths are about nuclear disarmament, as opposed to the realities. It is something that I think is fairly easy to read through and to reach a state of enlightened panic and will help push the agenda forward, bring more pressure on the government. The book is titled Is Everything Secure? The Myths and Realities of Nuclear Disarmament. It costs $10 and is available from IPPNW, 126 Rogers St., Cambridge, MA 02142 .

STEVE FETTER: Are there questions for Merav?

NANCY COLTON, International Association for Volunteer Effort: ...How would the verification regime relate to the IAEA, and what would be the cost to non-nuclear weapons States? We want to encourage all nations to join, because if some do not join, non-parties could build nuclear weapons...
MERAV DATAN: On the question of costs: We would propose that the costs be proportionate to the stockpiles. Most of the costs would be borne by the nuclear weapon States. They have the facilities, like Pantex, where they assembled them. Those facilities would be turned into disassembly facilities, so the costs would be borne in proportion to the stockpiles of the state.

The IAEA is the organization that has done the work on fissile materials and safeguards. The problem is that the mandate has them both promoting nuclear energy and safeguarding and the emphasis has been on detecting diversion rather than on preventing diversion. We don't mention the IAEA in this document, but one possibility would be to split the function of the IAEA and have the central implementing organization, which is modeled on the Chemical Weapons organization, have that take over the verification part. In the recent IAEA 93 plus 2 program they had some developments that were in the direction that we would like to see. Those include increased environmental monitoring, a shift from emphasis on routine on-site inspections to broad access, interactive no notice inspections, challenge inspections. We would include a focus on prevention rather than detection. I think in the 93 plus 2 program they also appreciated that the big picture is important, not just what is going on at one facility, but what is going on across the network of facilities, so that you can put together the pieces. The importance of that became really clear in Iraq.

NANCY COLTON: Can you have a Secretariat which would have all the data? Where would the Secretariat be, and how would the monitoring be set up?

MERAV DATAN: We envisioned a single central technical Secretariat, not regional bodies, although

129

in the Middle East nuclear disarmament is only likely in a regional agreement, and so there may be some regional agreements that would fit into something like this, but we envisioned a central technical secretariat. It would include a registry of the publicly available information. I emphasize that we mention transparency as a good thing but I don't think it is always the right approach. I think some of this information we would want to hold on to for as long as it is necessary to dismantle and destroy the weapons, and after that, to destroy the information. Some of this information, design information of nuclear weapons, we would not want to have publicly available because it would make developing nuclear weapons that much easier.

It will be quite difficult to strike a balance between secrecy and transparency and openness. Do you want it known exactly where fissile material is stored, or where warheads are stored? I think there needs to be confidence among the states that are taking part, and among states that don't have the weapons, to insure that disarmament is going on. One proposal that we would make, when it comes to physical access to material, that that access not be exclusively national access but under a two key system, the nation itself that formerly owned the weapons or material, and the international body which would have representatives from non-nuclear states.

STEVE FETTER: I think you would want to separate two kinds of verification activities, those that don't involve technical nuclear weapons information, and those that do. And the activities that don't involve that information, such as trying to detect any attempt to clandestinely produce highly enriched uranium or plutonium, those activities could be conducted by inspectors from any state. On the other hand, activities that involve the dismantling of nuclear weapons or pits, those would have to be, I think, restricted to nationals of nuclear weapon states in order to prevent the dissemination of information on how to build nuclear weapons. There is a precedent for that in the IAEA, the "technology holder" principle which has been applied where only nationals from countries that have a sensitive technology would be allowed to contribute inspectors.

ANN LAKHDHIR: What do you see in the second stage, what happens when all the nuclear weapon states have declared what they have and even to agree to reduce it or maybe to eliminate it altogether, what do you see at that point to verify that nobody develops a new capability?

STEVE FETTER: Let me outline that briefly. It follows what is established by many arms control treaties. You start with a declaration of what you have. The next step would be baseline inspections to verify that declaration. There would be a process of systematically going to all of the locations where you had declared that you had nuclear weapons or nuclear weapon materials and verify the number that you say are there are in fact there. Perhaps then going to other places and verifying that prohibited activities are not going on at other locations. There would be this series of base-line inspections to verify that declaration.

After that had been done you would proceed to verifiably dismantle nuclear weapons and to dispose of the nuclear materials, the fissile materials, in them. I think this is a fairly straightforward process that people have been thinking of in the US government, for how to do this with participation by Russian observers to verifiably dismantle the nuclear devices and then dispose of the uranium and plutonium in ways that would not easily be reusable in nuclear weapons.

And of course you would have a similar process for delivery vehicles which has already been worked out in the START agreements for the warheads themselves and for the fissile materials. It could take years to work out the details and many more years to actually implement this process for the tens of thousands of nuclear weapons that are still stockpiled. But that would be the process in outline.

Then after you had verifiably dismantled the stockpiles you would have to maintain a verification system to detect any attempt to build nuclear weapons. This would be based on the same techniques and technologies that are now used by the IAEA and that had been proposed with the 93 plus 2 program, a system of monitoring existing nuclear facilities, nuclear reactors, and so on, to insure that no material has been diverted. We know how to do that pretty well.

The harder task is to verify that none of those prohibited activities are going on anywhere else, that nuclear reactors, reprocessing plants, or, more difficult to verify, that no enrichment plants are located anywhere or activities to maintain nuclear weapons or build nuclear weapons. As I say in the report that Ann referred to earlier, I think the hardest step in all of this is to assure that you have got everything in the beginning, that there weren't any nuclear weapons or, even harder, any stockpiles of fissile materials hidden away someplace. Given the magnitude of the stockpiles that exist in the United States and Russia it is hard to imagine that you will ever have an accounting system that is so precise, that is so accurate, that you would be sure that you had found every last nuclear weapon, and accounted for every last kilogram of plutonium or highly enriched uranium. So naturally you would have to have mechanisms in place both to dissuade any country from violating the agreement by hiding material. You don't want countries to have incentives to cheat in the first place, but you would also want mechanisms in place to deal with cheating if it did occur.

That is it in briefest summary. If you are interested in more details, more of the technical details, I would be happy to provide you with the report.

CAROLINE BRIDGMAN-REES, Centre for International Peacebuilding: I was intrigued by your use of the word irrational. We all feel that all of this is irrational. My question is, where is the irrationality most prominent? In the military-industrial elite, in the government, in the military, among the civilian leaders? How can you break down this irrationality?

ALAN DOWTY: I was using the term "rationality" in a minimal sense, referring to the use of weapons of mass destruction against other weapons of mass destruction. Most people would regard as "rational" the implicit threat of responding in kind. In the real world you won't get most countries to surrender that minimal usage of their weapons of mass destruction. I don't mean to say that the result could be described as rational in any sense. But it is a way then of pointing out that using weapons of mass destruction in a different role, beyond that, as a response to conventional attack or threat of any kind simply doesn't meet even the most minimal military definition of rationality.

Where is this prevalent? Where is it not prevalent? In my thinking, even at the peak of the Cold War, threatening the first use of nuclear weapons against conventional attack, by Soviet tanks in Europe, was irrational. And it is certainly even more so today. It is difficult to imagine any kind of argument for retaining that particular reserved right of first use of nuclear weapons. But that argument wasn't accepted by most people in decision-making positions then, even though, I would point out that there have been some important people who, at the peak of the Cold War, made this

131

argument. Robert McNamara and the "Gang of Five," in their article in *Foreign Affairs*, also argued for no first use during the same period. So everybody was irrational.

ROGER SMITH, NGO Committee on Disarmament: My problem might be the inverse of Caroline's problem. We are seeing what might be called excess rationality. There is no doubt that the causes of the nuclear arms buildup and the retention of nuclear weapons are beyond irrational. They are simply Freudian. But I am not convinced that what we have been listening to is anything more than an academic debate of decreasing relevance. I wonder where the signs of political progress might be expected to come from that would make this remarkable detailed work, creating a nuclear weapons convention, devising plans for verification and monitoring of a political outcome which is so far removed from what the nuclear states are currently seeing as relevant.

Where is support going to come from? Where is the support within the nuclear weapons states, any of them? You are saying that the costs of eliminating nuclear weapons should be proportionate to the stockpiles. If I were a Russian hearing that, that would make me go through the roof. There is no way that they could take on that responsibility, given the economic chaos going on in that country. You might be able to find allies among the Chinese, given the Chinese position officially on nuclear disarmament, but is there really support for any discussion of this type? When will there be any sign that things are moving in the direction you advocate?

MERAV DATAN: I couldn't agree with you more that progress is too slow. I do think that we see some promising developments these days with the New Agenda Coalition. I would expect that that is going to lead to something. As I said, I think the lack of public concern on these issues is really distressing. Maybe everybody is in a state of denial. We need to get people to panic about these issues, because that is the only way that I see things moving forward.

ROGER SMITH: Did you have conversations with people currently in governments in any of the P5 (the five permanent members of the Security Council) when you were working on the model nuclear weapons convention?

MERAV DATAN: Not at that time. There were former arms control negotiators. Since then we have had some feedback. We have had more feedback from the former threshold states, the former three thresholds. There have been some off the record comments that this is the right direction, though idealistic. Nobody is willing to say they don't support this goal, so that is something to work on. I think it is valuable to get governments to say we do support the goal. Maybe we get sick going to NPT PrepComs and hearing the nuclear weapons states say we support elimination, but the more they keep saying, the more maybe they will work in that direction.

ALAN DOWTY: I want to come to the defense of my fellow panelists. I was thinking earlier about the division of labor that seems to have developed here between those who are looking at where we ought to be headed, the end state that we are aspiring to, and my role: how do you get there. I don't think there is anything incompatible. I would argue that you still have to think about the linkage to chemical and biological weapons from this point on to make any progress, and I was trying to make a practical suggestion on the first step, something that could and should be taken right now, that is overdue, and that would improve the chances for progressing further.

Let me add that it seems to me that we might move beyond the treaty model, the voluntary adherence of different states to a convention, to the legislative model. We do have a precedent for that. The Security Council in 1968 legislated that an attack on a non-nuclear state by a nuclear state would be met by Security Council sanctions. It didn't spell them out, but in a sense it made such an action illegal, and legislated that for all states, without requiring their individual adherence. I would pursue that model to outlaw all first use of weapons of mass destruction, as something that would be imposed on all states without their voluntary adherence. Moving into the legislative model and Security Council powers also takes us a step closer to the ultimate goals.

TRACY MOAVERO, Peace Action: There is the Abolition 2000 network which focuses on a number of things. We can have the academic discussion and the public outreach at the same time...Peace Action is the largest disarmament organization in the US. We feel that we need to hold our leaders accountable, and be very creative about that. We miss a lot of opportunities. Peace Action has started to focus on using the election process in the US as the moment to catch people's attention, because that is when people are talking about some of these issues in a way that they don't at other times. For the 2000 election, Peace Action will be building up to a major campaign, putting abolition out there, through radio ads, through print ads, through voter guides. This year Peace Action is reaching about 6 million voters in targeted races for Congress on a number of peace issues, including military spending and land mines and UN debt. the kind of creativity we need is to start taking advantage of the opportunities that we have been missing.

ROB WHEELER: I am the coordinator and chair for the Millennium People's Assembly network. I am also on the interim steering committee for the Millennium Forum. If people aren't aware, the Millennium Forum is the primary event that will be held at the UN in 2000 as a follow up to Kofi Annan's invitation to civil society. Coming out of that there will obviously be thematic reports from the forums that are held around the world as well as the global forum at the United Nations. But it is likely that we will cover so many thematic areas, and address so many issues that it will be incomprehensible to the public to make sense of what that whole report is. My network, the Millennium People's Assembly network, realizes that if we really want to make changes it will take an ongoing effort over many years, as well as looking at the primary issues in a concise way that grabs the public's attention.

We are promoting both ongoing people's assemblies or civil society forums and also launching an initiative for a people's agenda for the twenty-first century. We are working with the Hague Appeal for Peace Project, and intend to hold sessions there, focusing how the peace agenda that comes out of the Hague Appeal can be united with the other aspects of environment, human rights, economics, so that we have a concise People's Agenda document that has the key things that must be done, the abolition campaign, the disarmament of chemical weapons, land mines and nuclear weapons and what must be done in each of those areas in a very strong statement. We are looking to the disarmament community to join us in this effort so that we can come up with something strong and powerful to present to the world in the year 2000 and beyond.

Related to this, I have become increasingly aware that there seems to be a conflict resolution of peace and disarmament, people who are working to bring public attention to peace initiatives, peace day campaigns, and there seems to less cooperation between those who are working with the political system and those that are trying to build a mass movement. I would like to see more unification within that. One initiative that I would like to see our network give some leadership to is to have one web site where we can have an overview of the various projects that are being launched and make this information easily available to the public. We are a strong movement that is moving towards a new way of life, new opportunities into the next century.

MERAV DATAN: An initiative that was started by some abolition groups is a resolution before the House of Representatives in the US Congress, Res. 479, that calls on President Clinton to initiate multilateral negotiations leading to the early conclusion of a nuclear weapons convention. So the concept of a nuclear weapons convention has been introduced into Congress as a concept. It also welcomes the model nuclear weapons convention and requests further progress, according to the United Nations General Assembly. A very simple step that people could take is to ask their representative to co-sponsor it. At this point there are 28 co-sponsors of the resolution, introduced by Congresswoman Lynn Woolsey, Democrat of California.

QUESTIONER: Would you say more about how nuclear power relates to the nuclear weapons convention?

MERAV DATAN: This was a divisive issue. We decided in this model convention not to take the question of nuclear energy head on because the focus was on nuclear disarmament, which is difficult enough. But we included an optional protocol that would offer assistance in alternative forms of energy. That would be our recommendation, to promote alternatives. I think, as I mentioned earlier, that there is an inverse relation. The more nuclear energy facilities you have, the more dependence on nuclear energy, the more difficult nuclear disarmament will be.

JIM GARST: ...In all proposals presented, government action is required. Would unilateral steps and the promotion of a campaign of unilateral steps by the US be useful in Alan Dowty's proposal and Steve Fetter's? The setting of a model unilaterally might lead to momentum internationally.

STEVE FETTER: That is a good question. I think a lot of progress could be made by beginning unilaterally and then challenging others to follow. That is possible in some areas, but not in others. For example, in reducing the size of the US arsenal, it is not possible because Congress passed a law prohibiting the President from reducing the size of the nuclear forces until Russia ratifies START II. But in other areas it would be quite possible. The President could order the nuclear forces to stand down in peacetime tomorrow. He could do that on his own authority. The President could declare a policy of no first use of nuclear weapons, or no first use of weapons of mass destruction on his own without consent by Congress, although maybe it wouldn't be politically wise for this President to do anything without the consent of Congress. We could also challenge Russia to follow suit in both of these cases.

Also, in the case of transparency of nuclear weapons and fissile materials stockpiles, the United States has already done this to a small extent with its plutonium report, but we could do a better job by simply announcing the US holdings of nuclear weapons and fissile materials and challenging Russia to do the same. I know that has been discussed in the government and rejected because the argument is that it would take the pressure off Russia. It turns the argument on its head. They say that if we give up our leverage then there will be no reason for the Russians to agree to do the same thing because they have already gotten it out of us for free. But I rather think that it is the other way. If the United States proposes to do these things, then the pressure would build on Russia to reciprocate. I think it is an excellent way to proceed.

ALAN DOWTY: That is an easy question in my case, because the United States could tomorrow declare against the first use of nuclear weapons in response to conventional attack, a step that many of us think would have been logical and useful even in the Cold War and certainly now can be presented as a step that, taken unilaterally by the United States, improves American security. Some people on the right are saying that as well. Sooner or later it may even penetrate to the government. In addition to that, we could change the negotiating framework to some extent. I have argued for the linkage of these different categories of weapons of mass destruction. Obviously the United States could take the lead in doing that, since the United States plays a major role in defining the frameworks for those negotiations. Obviously this requires a new way of thinking. One other step that the United States could take unilaterally to reach this platform would be to give conventional guarantees to countries that may be unwilling to surrender weapons of mass destruction because of the conventional threats that they face. The US is certainly in a position, if it is willing to make such commitments, to make it easier for states in that situation to forswear the use, if not the possession, of these weapons.

MARGARET MELKONIAN: I am working with the Hague Peace Appeal. You discussed the gap between incremental movement towards the elimination of nuclear weapons and the comprehensive plan. How do you bridge that gap? How is the work of the NAM and the New Agenda Coalition being integrated with the work plan you have sketched out that will take us ten or twenty years to get us closer to the goal?

MERAV DATAN: Focusing only on the incremental, as opposed to a comprehensive approach, is a way for the nuclear weapons states to drag their feet. They say that they can only move incrementally and that it is premature to discuss how we get to the end goal because things will change. One way to bridge that gap is to acknowledge that things will change, but to start talking now about the first steps towards that goal with that goal in mind. We have mentioned that an important essential threshold move in that direction is an inventory. Why not begin now? A lot of the solid work that has been done, at least the questions that have been raised, have been by non-governmental organizations. Governments often rely on the non governmental organizations. In the development of the Comprehensive Test Ban Treaty, some of the work on verification that was done by NGOs was very important in developing the confidence that a Comprehensive Test Ban was verifiable. I think, on the question of inventory, for example, or material accounting and control, there has been some good work done at an academic level, but it is not something that NGOs have taken up. I think it is a pretty simple concept. An inventory. How much of this poison is out there? That is something that it is not difficult to grasp. I think the pressure has to be on governments, from the non nuclear weapons states, and from citizens within their own countries.

I think the New Agenda, and the NAM resolutions, are fairly new ideas. My sense is that even the states behind the New Agenda Coalition resolution aren't yet sure where we would be two or three years from now...We talk about the model nuclear weapons convention being a road map, but the course we are following might change...We are highlighting the immediate steps that might be taken, like de-alerting and the inventory. When change comes it might very well be surprising,

135

sudden, unexpected. It doesn't seem to be in the minds of the nuclear weapon states now. They are talking about reducing at the same time that they are developing. There has to be a serious shift.

ALYN WARE, Lawyers Committee for Nuclear Policy: We did raise this question about an inventory with Norman Wolfe in the US Arms Control and Disarmament Agency a few days ago. He mentioned the problem with an inventory, as Steve Fetter mentioned, is that it is very difficult to determine exactly how much fissile material there is, and where it all is. To some degree there is a reliance on declarations, and the validity of declarations, but that is not a reason for not going ahead with it. That is just a statement that one can't be 100% certain with regard to the amount. But it is much better to have an idea of where 99.9% of the material is, and you have much greater confidence if you have an inventory than if you don't have one. It would be a very important step.

STEVE FETTER: I agree with that, and I should say that it is the position of the US government that there should be an inventory, although an inventory that is only shared between Russia and the United States. But the US did make a formal proposal to Russia in 1995 that was rejected by Russia. Russia has since refused to discuss the matter except to agree in the Helsinki Declaration that this matter will be an issue for discussion as part of START III. That was in a sense a step backward, because before that time there had been an agreement that it would be an immediate step, or a near term step. I am afraid, if we ever get to START III, it would be left out even in that discussion. But it is the position of at least the US government that there should be an inventory of warheads and fissile materials. Although the current thinking is that it would only be shared with Russia, I think you could see how that could readily be broadened, moving on to the other nuclear weapons states, and then eventually in the context of a nuclear weapons prohibition, shared internationally.

STEVE FETTER: Any more questions? No? In that case, thank you.

DE-ALERTING AND "NUCLEAR ESCROW": ENDING THE SPECTER OF SURPRISE NUCLEAR ATTACK

JONATHAN DEAN: We have a remarkable opportunity this afternoon to learn about what is probably the most promising and interesting new development in the nuclear arms field in many years, de-alerting, and also Admiral Turner's program, strategic nuclear escrow. Our highly qualified speakers are, first, Bruce Blair, of the Brookings Institution in Washington, DC, who is a former nuclear missile control officer. He has almost singlehandedly made the US, Russia and the rest of the world aware of the continuing dangers of the deterrent alert posture. I know the others on the panel will attest that to be the case, and that we owe him a real debt of gratitude for this service.

Our second speaker will be Professor Harold Feiveson of Princeton. He has been on the forefront of nuclear disarmament for many years. He is the man to turn to if you want serious, well-informed advice, plus imagination.

Our third speaker is Admiral Stansfield Turner. Among many other assignments he commanded a US fleet equipped with nuclear weapons and he was also the Director of the CIA. Among the senior military officers who support radical cuts in the United States and Russian nuclear weapons, he has put forward an extremely good plan for deep cuts in nuclear weapons which complements, as he will explain, the de-alerting approach. The message of our speakers is extremely important for us all. Please lead off, Bruce.

BRUCE BLAIR: That was a very generous introduction, and I don't want to be too much in the limelight on this. I just want to acknowledge my deep gratitude to others who have been slugging it out on this agenda as well, including Hal Feiveson and Admiral Turner, who both have had leading roles in pushing this agenda.

I would like to try and make the case for taking all US amd Russian nuclear weapons off alert, standing down the forces completely, extending the time needed to prepare nuclear forces for launch, now literally a few minutes, to hours, days, weeks, eventually longer, even months. The case for de-alerting really begins with the observation which may not be news to many of you but is always worth repeating, that both the US and Russia have continued the alerting and targeting practices of the Cold War. Thousands of strategic weapons are poised for immediate launch, even under the normal peacetime conditions today. If Presidents Clinton and Yeltsin gave the order to launch right now, in three minutes, missiles would be leaving their silos and thousands of warheads on each side could be flying to targets half way around the globe. This is referred to as a hair-trigger posture. That phrase gets me into trouble in Washington. I believe it is a fairly accurate characterization of these postures.

I think this posture is clearly not in keeping with the end of the Cold War. It is incompatible with the political relationship that we established between Russia and the United States, and clearly incompatible with the direction we want to take in that relationship in the future. Furthermore, it is inherently dangerous, although this common sense observation is not shared very much within official circles. It is clear to me it is dangerous, and it is becoming more so as Russia relies more on nuclear weapons and their early use, first use, even, in a crisis or in a conventional conflict. As you know, Russia has dropped its previous no-first-use pledge in response to the collapse of its conventional forces. The country is increasingly relying on nuclear weapons to compensate. At the same time that Russia relies more than ever on nuclear weapons, its early warning networks are deteriorating and that makes the situation doubly dangerous.

De-alerting would address some of the problems that currently plague the relationship. I will mention two of the most fundamental and later I will raise a few other ones. Russia's strategic forces depend today more than ever, since the early 1960s, on early use. Those forces cannot wait out an attack and therefore Russia is put in a position today of having to launch their forces on warning of an incoming attack. Because of the Russian economy, shortages of defense money and other problems, they are unable to disperse their forces into the sanctuaries of the seas and the forests to put them into an invulnerable disposition. Today they might have one or two submarines at sea and one regiment of land-based missiles out of 350 in the field; that would be nine missiles out of 350 in their inventory. Essentially, their forces are acutely vulnerable to attack. To compensate for that weakness, Russia has their forces poised for immediate launch out of their silos, even out of the launch tubes of submarines that are sitting at dockside. They literally have more submarines on alert at dockside, on the surface, ready to fire their weapons in a matter of a few minutes than they have submarines at sea on patrol.

This is a classic problem of stability that we heard so much about during the Cold War. If there is an acute imbalance, a lopsided imbalance in the strategic forces, there is a potential danger that results from the pressure that it puts on rational leaders to use or lose their nuclear forces. This may seem somewhat of a moot point, an academic point, at the end of the Cold War, but I would remind us all that the prospect of a return to the past, to the Cold War tensions of yesteryear, is the rationale given for our keeping so many weapons in our arsenal and on high alert to hedge against a reversal in the relationship, to hedge against future hostilities and crises with Russia. If such a development comes along, then, we would find ourselves in a strategic situation that would be acutely unstable in classic terms.

The second concern, which is more pertinent to the immediate circumstances, is that this hair trigger on US and Russian forces could lead simply to a loss of control over those weapons, even under normal peacetime conditions, resulting in an unauthorized or inadvertent or mistaken launch. Clearly I think this danger today is a much more relevant, serious one than the danger of a cold-blooded, deliberate attack. Almost certainly it is a greater danger today than it was in the Cold War.

This problem is largely a reflection, again, of Russian weakness and the deterioration of its nuclear control and early warning network, a deterioration that is not only physical but also organizational and human. I won't serve up a litany of all the problems that plague the Russian nuclear systems. They range from crumbling nuclear command posts to worn out communication networks. Even the famous nuclear suitcases carried by Yeltsin and the other top nuclear authorities have fallen into some disrepair. I am thinking about organizational problems, including the fact that Yeltsin has failed to replace the Communist Party apparatus with a new institutional mechanism to insure military subordination to civilian control and of the fact that the military leadership in Russia is significantly corrupt and incompetent, that there is inadequate training of nuclear commanders, little time training the forces, flying the planes, and therefore less proficiency in the handling of nuclear weapons safely.

In the human category I am thinking of the obvious problems of the decline of morale and motivation that has attended the collapse of the Russian military. The food shortages, housing shortages, pay arrears, lack of training, corruption and all the rest I think must have a serious effect on the motivation of nuclear weapons personnel to operate their weapons in the safest possible way, to adhere to safety rules. It also leads me to worry about an impulse to vent their frustration in ways that could increase nuclear danger.

Now, this is not a line that is especially welcome in Washington or in Moscow. Both the Clinton and Yeltsin Administrations' official line is to deny that any problems along these lines are noteworthy. We have the Commander of the US Strategic Command kicking the tires at a Russian ICBM land-mobile intercontinental base and declaring that the Russian nuclear control system is safe and secure. I would urge all of you to be sceptical of these assurances. I think that very clearly all of the trends pertinent to the functioning of Russian nuclear control and early warning are negative.

The situation reminds me a lot of the circumstances in the late 1980s when we could see adverse trends working on the Soviet Empire. In political, military, economic, social terms, any terms you can think of, the trends were adverse for the Soviet Empire. Almost no one, though, grasped the imminence or the magnitude of the quake that brought the Empire down. Yet, when it happened, we look back in hindsight and say it was quite predictable, because of all of these trends. I think the same situation applies currently in Russia. There is a very serious problem of internal disintegration. All the trends are adverse, and if something happens tomorrow, if there is a nuclear incident, we will look back at it and say this was an accident waiting to happen. It was predictable, and we could have done a great deal more to address it.

I can not predict when a nuclear incident might occur, or what form it could take, whether it is some terrible consequence of a coup-like episode at the top of the chain of command or a breakdown of control at intermediate or lower levels, or a launch on mistaken warning similar to the episode in January of 1995 when a Norwegian scientific rocket triggered a false alarm of the Russian early warning and command system that actually activated Yeltsin's nuclear suitcase and initiated the whole launch-on-warning decision cycle, or whether it is some other unpredictable, unexpected event. I am not prepared to say, but I do think that it is clear that we can do something about the two problems that I mentioned - the instability that exists in the strategic balance, and the danger which I think is growing of the breakdown of control over nuclear weapons, particularly in Russia.

I don't want to single out only Russia. What is on a hair trigger in the US arsenal is also inherently unsafe. We have had some experiences with our forces and command systems that are not very heartening ones, including two major false alarms in 1979 and 1980. They led to the de-certification or the firing of the duty officers at the early warning station in Colorado and the supporting crew on both occasions because they made such terrible mistakes in assessing these false alarms. The problem is a two-sided one. I don't mean to focus exclusively on Russia, but there the deterioration of warning systems I think is clearly rather more alarming.

What we need to do to address these two particular problems is to take all the nuclear weapons on both sides off alert so that they are taken out of play, so that they are not susceptible to launch on warning or to unauthorized or inadvertent launch, so that these forces could not be pulled out of the quiver and used quickly, under any circumstances. This would buy time. It would give a buffer against some of the more untoward scenarios that we can imagine that could greatly enhance

139

the operational safety of nuclear forces on both sides.

Of course, this will have to be a reciprocal process on both sides. It would build on the de-alerting agreement, the spirit of the agreement of 1994 which we have heard so much about from President Clinton in recent years. Clinton was quick to point out that the US and Russian missiles are no longer aimed at each other's countries. Of course that is a gross misrepresentation of reality. That agreement was entirely symbolic and cosmetic. It takes literally a few seconds to reverse. In fact, that agreement would not add a single second to the amount of time either Russia or the United States needs to launch a strategic attack.

We need to push forward with very concrete, practical steps that disengage these two coupled arsenals on high alert and put them into a much safer posture. Our immediate goal is to remove launch on warning. By that I mean launching our own force in response to detecting an appearance of enemy attack, before the arrival of those incoming weapons which could be ten to twenty-five minutes later, depending on the launch location. We would eliminate launch on warning from the repertoire of the strategic organizations on both sides. Currently that is the principal option on which both sides rely. We need to get rid of that.

The de-alerting measures that we would institute would extend the preparation time to launch by hours, instead of the current few minutes. Our more ambitious goal then would be to institute measures of de-alerting that would move us toward more and more lengthy periods of re-alerting, before weapons could be used. Hal Feiveson is going to describe some of those measures in more practical or technical detail.

Let me just close my presentation by noting that this agenda is much broader than the question of US-Russian relations and the operational safety of our two arsenals. It is an agenda that I think has large global implications that everyone should be able to support.

First of all, if Russia and the United States adopt serious measures of de-alerting, if we stand down our nuclear arsenals, I think it could create an international norm of operational safety that could be applied universally to all nations, making it absolutely taboo for any country to put nuclear weapons into a launch-ready configuration. I think that could be a very important international norm in the future in other parts of the world, particularly the Middle East and now, given the recent political developments in India, in South Asia as well, and other places.

Secondly, de-alerting, though it doesn't imply the permanent elimination of nuclear weapons, and it does allow for re-alerting under some circumstances of national emergency, it does, at the same time, I think, project elimination of nuclear weapons in the sense that Jonathan Schell writes about in *The Nation* article. De-alerting measures could be made ultimately to take months and months to reverse, to re-alert.

Studies by the US government have shown that the US, if it undertook a crash nuclear program from scratch, without any nuclear weapons infrastructure or complex in place, that is, if we dismantle all of our nuclear weapons infrastructure but have access only to nuclear fuel from nuclear power reactors, we could, on a crash basis, within a few months build an atomic bomb from scratch.

I can imagine de-alerting measures that would take longer than that to reverse. The warheads that are coming off the Minuteman missiles under the START II agreements, two warheads per missile, 500 missiles, a thousand warheads, are being put in the hedge inventory, that inventory of weapons that might be returned to delivery systems in the event of a breakdown in relations with Russia. The US Air Force estimates that to put those thousand warheads back on the missiles would take them three or four years. So that is the idea. It stretches it a bit, to make the comparison with a crash nuclear program. I think that comprehensive de-alerting converges on elimination in the time dimension at some point.

Finally, de-alerting, to the extent that it leads to removing warheads from missiles, the ideal de-alerting solution, would promote the establishment of a system of international monitoring of warhead storage, of warhead stockpiles. It would be very important for purposes of securing those stockpiles against theft or diversion to other states or terrorists. Just as importantly, it would begin the process of acquiring experience managing these stockpiles and keeping tabs on these inventories, creating confidence in an international monitoring system that would give us more confidence that we could move toward elimination with less fear about the existence of covert stockpiles.

My point, in wrapping up, is that this agenda is broader than it may seem, in the way that it is often caricatured in some of the media and in some of its political opposition camps.

JONATHAN DEAN: Bruce has succeeded in taking over the entire nuclear reduction agenda in his program. I had confidence that he would be able to do this. Please, Hal:

HAROLD FEIVESON: While Bruce has made the case for a stand down in the alert status of nuclear forces, the question that I am going to take up is how to do this. First, let me say that we - when I say "we" I am referring to Bruce, Frank von Hippel and myself, who did an article in the November issue of *Scientific American* in which we advocated a de-alerting scenario. It is this scenario, elaborated by some further thinking that we have done, that I want to talk about.

We realize that de-alerting causes problems for the nuclear commands of both the United States and Russia. At the moment neither command is much of an advocate. The US Strategic Command, for example, worries that de-alerting measures will be complicated, difficult to verify and that conceivably if you try to re-alert, the reliability of weapons systems will be undermined. They at the moment are much more comfortable with a gradual but quite substantial reduction in the numbers of the weapons on alert that would come out of the START process.

For example, at the height of the Cold War we had something like 4700 warheads on this hair trigger alert. Today it is more like 2700. Under START II the Strategic Command estimates that it would be about 980. Under START III, which they are very comfortable thinking about, it would go down to maybe 600. That is the idea that they would like to see go forward, a kind of gradual reduction in numbers of deployed weapons and numbers of weapons on alert.

In any case, it is important, as we think through how to de-alert, that we take the sensitivities of the strategic commands, both here and in Russia, into account. Let me put forward a scenario in some detail. Bruce has emphasized the starting point of a de-alerting scenario. It has to address the vulnerability of the Russian nuclear forces today, at least, the theoretical vulnerability. The key to a de-alerting program is to stand down the forces sufficiently so that Russia will no longer fear a kind of bolt out of the blue attack that leads them to keep their weapons on launch on warning. That was our starting point.

We imagine that in the first wave of measures the US President would first direct the US Strategic Command to remove to storage the warheads on MX missiles. We have 50 MX missiles, 10 warheads on each missile, which are our chief threat to hardened Russian ICBM silos. We would disable, in that sense, the MX missiles. We would also remove to storage the higher yield submarine missile weapons that we have. They are called W-88s, which are silo killers. The MX and the W-88s were deliberately deployed to be able to threaten Russian silos. We would replace the W-88s with lower yield weapons.

The second step: The US now has 17 ballistic missile submarines. It is about to have an 18th. Four of these will be retired under START II. Our plans for START II are to go from 18 to 14, and to reduce the number of warheads on each sub-launched ballistic missile on the submarines. We advocate doing that immediately. Essentially, bring to dock the four submarines that we plan to retire anyway, and down load the warheads on the missiles and put these warheads in storage.

These actions would deactivate a large number of warheads that now threaten Russia. We use the word deactivate somewhat differently than we use the word de-alert, or stand down and de-alert. By deactivate, I want to emphasize these weapons would effectively be taken out of the US operational arsenal. They could be thought of as a hedge, as Bruce said. If matters worsen again in the future, over a period of two or three years, the weapons could be brought back. But they are essentially out of the operational arsenal, so that the US Strategic Command is not, on the one hand, taking the weapons out, and then, on the other hand, sort of working to see how fast we could get them back, how fast we could re-alert them. So basically they are out of the plan, and that is what I mean by deactivation.

It would be a head start toward START II by this deactivation. Those are the first two measures. The third is that the US should put all its submarines on a modified alert. Right now the US keeps roughly, it varies a bit, but roughly, four of these 18 submarines I mentioned on what they call a high alert. They are in the northern oceans, ready to fire within minutes, maybe tens of minutes, of a order to do so. They are basically on battle station. All the other submarines are either in port or they are going to and fro these battle stations in a modified alert status. It would take on the order of a day to ready the missiles to fire, even if they were within striking distance. That is modified alert. Our third plank is to put all our submarines on modified alert. In a sense it is not such a big deal. In effect, instead of having all your submarines, minus four, on modified alert, we are saying, have all your submarines on modified alert. There is a question how easily this could be made transparent to the Russians. How do they know our submarines are on modified alert? I will come back to that.

Finally, as the initial part of our scenario, the US could somehow disable our ICBMs in silos, the Minutemen. I will come back to that.

In response to this, it is our hope that the Russians will move away from the launch on warning status, and in particular would do the following:

They have something like 36 multiple warhead missiles that they imagine to be put on trains. These are 10 warhead missiles, called the SS-24. Ten of them are also in silos. It looks like the 36 that were supposed to be on trains are no longer there, they are in a base. Some of them may be in this launch on warning status. We advocate, as a first step, the Russians withdraw the warheads from these weapons, to deactivate them.

We also think that they could deactivate the submarines that would be eliminated under the START II agreement. This would parallel the US deactivation. Remove the warheads from those roughly 15 submarines that they plan to eliminate under START II.

And then, two other actions. As Bruce said, the Russians now keep their submarines in port, or some of them, in launch on warning status, on high alert. We want them to stand down those submarines in port from this alert status, something we could verify.

We also want them, in ways that I will have to talk about in a little more detail, to take off high alert their warheads in their land-based ICBM silos, the SS-18s and SS-19s, which are multiple warhead missiles which are scheduled for elimination, for the most part, under START II but where the preponderance of the Russian nuclear force is now located.

And also, we want them to disable the launchers on their mobile ICBMs, of which they have many, even though only a few are typically in the field at any time.

As I mentioned, the deactivation of the SS-24s and the fifteen submarines scheduled for elimination can be done pretty straightforwardly by removal of warheads. The de-alerting of submarines in port would take some thinking, which we haven't looked at in detail. We believe that the Russians could take sufficient action - these submarines are under constant surveillance by US satellites, and also various kinds of electronic communication surveillance - that the Russians could make apparent the alert status of these weapons.

The multiple warhead ICBMs represents a particular problem. One way to proceed is to remove the warheads from these missiles, but the Russians are nervous about doing so for various reasons. One, they say they don't have storage space for all these warheads. They could take off some warheads from some of their weapons systems, but most of their warheads are on these SS-18s and SS-19s. They say they don't have storage space for them. If they did have storage space, they might be afraid that the warheads would be so concentrated that the stores themselves would become a possible target of a US first strike. Right now the warheads are in hardened silos. If you take the warheads off and put them in a central place they may be vulnerable, they worry.

Thirdly, they worry that even if they could be put the warheads in dispersed sites so they would not be targetable, that if there were a race to re-alert, the US could do things quicker and better than they can, that they would never get the warheads back on the missiles.

At the Helsinki Summit a year ago the US and Russia agreed that the Russian SS-18 missiles, the ones I am mostly talking about here, would be de-alerted in some way to give the Russians an extra five years to actually eliminate the missiles. START II says they have to be eliminated. The Russians say it is too expensive and too time-consuming to do it by 2003, so we are letting them stretch the elimination until December 31, 2007 so long as these were systems de-activated by 2003.

The Russians have said that they don't want to do it by removing warheads. They would rather do it by other means that leave the warheads in place. So they have suggested that other de-alerting ideas be examined for these ICBMs. Several alternatives have been mentioned.

143

One is to remove the batteries in the missile guidance systems. Another is to remove the gas canisters that are used to explode open the lids of the ICBM silos before they are launched. A third idea, not raised by the Russians, as far as I know, is to replace the aerodynamic nose cone of the missiles (which is important as the missile moves to the atmosphere when it is launched) with a non-aerodynamic nose cone. That would make a launch impractical. Another idea which has been mentioned, which has a kind of clear simplicity about it, but which sounds funny, is to pile tons of dirt on top of the silos. It would take bulldozers to get the silos ready to launch.

These ideas and others should be studied in detail by the US and Russian militaries. But none at present seems completely satisfactory. The battery removal and the removal of the gas canisters that explode open the lids may not be so easy to verify in real time. You could come and visit the silos, over some extended period, and see that they are not there, but if they could be put back within hours, each side will be nervous that they are not able to monitor that in real time.

The replacement of the nose cone, and the piling of dirt on top, I think the nuclear commands worry about. They don't fit into a neat operational scheme. They are exercising the possibility of re-alerting these things. They might be an asymmetry in how quickly the US and Russia could put nose cones back on or how quickly they could bulldose away the dirt. I am not saying that these measures, which sound a bit unwieldy, can't work, but I think they do give the strategic commands some nervousness.

In these circumstances, I think there are two somewhat different approaches that one could take. One is that you could just take the ICBMs out of the operational force. They are going to be eliminated anyway; let's get a head start on these things. Maybe you don't destroy the silos immediately, because that will take some time and money, but you do it by this nose cone removal or some other way. Once it is out of the force the US and Russian strategic commands won't be spending all of their time thinking how quickly we could put them back on. They are just out of the force, sort of out of sight, out of mind. They could be thought of as a hedge, if things go bad in five or ten years, but they are really out of the force. That is an attractive way to think about it.

A less drastic alternative would be to effectively down-load the missiles so that each missile has only one warhead, instead of multiple warheads. In the Russian case, they could replace the SS-18 10 warhead missile by something called an SS-25 which is a single warhead missile. Once the missiles are single warhead, even if in some sense they are on alert, the incentive of a launch on warning is much reduced. It would take one side many more warheads to destroy the warheads on the other side than would be destroyed. It would take more than one US warhead to destroy one Russian warhead.

One de-alerting measure that Bruce has advocated and others have suggested is a rather nice one. It is to take the US submarines, when they leave port, and instead of going north, have them go south. The submarines would patrol mostly in the southern oceans. That is a great de-alerting scheme because the survivability of the submarines is in no way diminished. In some ways it is increased. It is a vast ocean area, it is concealed, far from Russian borders. They would be effectively out of range of accurate attacks on Russian missile silos. So the question is, how can we assure the Russians that our subs are 18,000 kilometers away, not 3,000 or 4,000?

This will take new verification arrangements, but there are ways to do it. One way, for example, is for Russia to interrogate at some regular interval, once a day, or every three days, say submarine number 12, tell us your location. That submarine will get the message, it won't be under water all the time. It will then send a coded reply. This response could be delayed for hours, so that it would not give away the precise position of the sub, by loading the response message into a buoy released by the sub.

Another de-alerting measure would be to remove the guidance systems from the missiles and store them on board the sub, with a seal installed so that the guidance systems could not be restored without breaking the seal. Again, on a random basis, the subs could be interrogated to assure that the seals had not been broken. (Unfortunately, Russian submarines lack this option as their missiles are not accessible from inside the boat.)

These kinds of verification measures don't sound very familiar, but they do not appear to be technically daunting. They will nevertheless require time to work out and implement. For this reason, we believe that the US and Russia should not delay the initial stage of de-alerting, while the modalities for de-alerting the submarines are fully worked through.

Let me conclude with some questions and comments. Will the stand-down of US forces that I have somewhat summarily outlined be enough to get Russia to take its forces off launch on warning? I would say we don't really know for sure. But for the US to move down this route makes sense. Even if the Russians did not stand down their nuclear forces, it is in the US interest that we relax the preemptive threat that we seem to hold over the Russians. We don't want them to feel trigger-happy, that they are under a constant possibility of a US preemptive attack. Even if we completed all the de-alerted measures that Frank von Hippel, Bruce Blair and I have outlined, the US would still have something like 600 warheads at sea, completely invulnerable, not ready to fire within minutes, but invulnerable. So there is really little risk in the US stepping down this path.

What the US loses by this is the possibility of a rapid counter-force attack against Russian missiles at the very start of a nuclear war. That may be one reason why the strategic command will be reluctant initially to move to this stand-down Bruce has argued for.

In conclusion, there are a lot of details of de-alerting that are yet to be worked out. They have to be worked out by the militaries, not by independent analysts such as Bruce and myself. But in doing so, in thinking about how this will be worked out, it is important that we keep in mind the basic absurdity of the present situation, almost ten years after the collapse of the Berlin Wall, that the US and Russia have close to 5000 warheads on high alert aimed at each other.

JONATHAN DEAN: Thanks very much, Hal, for a clear presentation of a complicated subject. Admiral Turner, would you like to speak?

ADMIRAL STANSFIELD TURNER: I want to start by saying how much I agree with both Bruce and Hal on the whole de-alerting process as a way of avoiding accidents and miscalculation. I would like to build on the warhead de-alerting aspect of their program to construct a regularized, verifiable process by which the United States and Russia, initially, can accelerate the planned reductions in the START process. We are all very enthusiastic, and we are only here I believe because we support START and various other arms control treaties, but I think it is time that we made a realistic reappraisal of the START and other treaty process. It really is moving very, very slowly.

START I got us down to something like six thousand warheads per country, In START II will get us to 3500, START III, if it comes about, they are talking about 2500. Some people talk about a START IV to a thousand, and then maybe something beyond that which would get all the way down to zero.

Let me suggest that I think anyone who hopes we can accomplish these four or five steps downward in a reasonable period of time is doing wishful thinking. As has been noted already, a year ago March, the two presidents, Yeltsin and Clinton, delayed the full implementation of START II by five years to the end of 2007. I don't think that is an aberration.

I don't think it is just due to the conditions in Russia today. It is systemic with arms control treaties. As the numbers get lower, the resistance gets greater. And this is reflected, if you think about it, in the difference in the negotiated number of 3500 for START II and the proposed Yeltsin/Clinton agreed number for START III of 2500. A reduction of 1000 is almost insignificant. It doesn't make the world safer. The reason they had such a small increment, in my opinion, is that it would be very complicating to go much further. You would meet much more resistance from the military and you would have to bring in the other nuclear powers. It would be a more difficult process.

Now, on top of all this, let me suggest that we should be aware that the numbers that I have been referring to are all phony. As has been mentioned by Bruce, when we take our warheads off our multiple warhead ICBMs we are going to put them in storage, we are going to hedge. The United States has said publicly that START II covers only intercontinental weapons with the warheads actually mated to the delivery vehicles. We are going to take those un-mated warheads and keep them, one for one, in reserve. In short, 3500 mated, 3500 hedge.

Because the treaty doesn't cover non-intercontinental warheads, we are free to keep whatever we want of tactical warheads, and we have said we are going to keep another 3000 of those, shorter range ones. That adds up to 10,000 warheads. So what we are talking about today is the United States, and presumably Russia will do something similar, ten years from last December, will still have 10,000 nuclear warheads in our arsenal.

I think the citizens of the world ought to be indignant that 10,000 nuclear warheads ten years from now is the best the two nuclear superpowers can do. The process is not only slow, but it is also problematic. We all are wondering whether the Duma will ratify START II. We certainly haven't seen any easy way to get all these other treaties negotiated thereafter.

I suggest, particularly sitting here in the United Nations, with all the countries of the world represented, we ought to recognize that every country in the world should be interested in accelerating this process from 10,000 warheads to something else. There is not only the risk of accident, but I particularly want to focus on the risk of proliferation of these weapons, because once proliferation starts, it is going to spread. When China got weapons, India got weapons. India got weapons, Pakistan got weapons. It has a cascading effect.

As long as nuclear weapons are as important to the two nuclear superpowers, wanting to keep their arsenals for another decade in the tens of thousands, wanting to maintain a first-use policy - as Bruce noted the Russians backed away from a no-first-use policy a few years ago. I think it is very difficult for either one to contend that they aren't important to lesser countries. And therefore we, the

United States, are getting rather unenthusiastic support for our efforts to counter proliferation in these weapons. Look at the struggle over the last several months with the mandates on Iraq. Look at the United States sanctions on Iran, which nobody else in the world supports.

My suggestion is that the superpowers can move in two constructive directions to make nuclear weapons not as important to them, and therefore be more persuasive in getting other countries to support anti-proliferation efforts. The first is what I call strategic escrow, and builds directly on de-alerting warheads. One or the other of the two nuclear superpowers would simply take a thousand warheads and move them at least 200 miles away and put them in storage. I suggest 200 miles because I think we want a few days of separation, not months, not years, but days, enough that there would be time for diplomacy to take effect if someone started recombining them and bringing them back. Whichever side put them into storage first would invite the other to put observers on the storage site. The observers would have no control whatsoever. They would only count what went in, and count if anything went out and send up a message if they did.

If the initial country put a thousand in storage, and the second country reciprocated by doing the same, and they each had observers of the other's storage, we would have a process going, one thousand, two thousand, three thousand, four thousand. Let me suggest this isn't a ten year process. This is a matter of a few years. There is a problem of storage, but that is solvable. Storage only has to be in concrete bunkers. They are not something that takes centuries to build if they don't exist. I believe, and none of us can get classified information to verify this, that a US arsenal that once had 32,500 warheads, can find enough storage for these things today. And you can take the storage for the warheads for ICBMs and you put them in storage for SLBMs, the submarine missiles, and vice versa. It is only the separation you want. You want them to not be immediately available.

Until you get to very, very low numbers, it really doesn't make any difference if the other side is holding something out, not telling you about it, hiding it. Why? Because it is very important that we begin to understand that first strikes have never been viable, and they are not viable today. The United States of America is not going to initiate nuclear war against Russia in the hope that it could knock out 100% of the Russian retaliatory nuclear capability. Which American in this room would want to lose one city in the United States, to achieve what?

We are under no threat from Russia today. And it is impossible to think that Russia would initiate an attack against us, and lose Moscow and St. Petersburg and a few other cities, which they have to count on no matter what our targeting strategy is. They have to count on the worst. We have to count on the worst. And with weapons of this magnitude you don't need to threaten thousands of detonations in order to deter somebody from starting a war. This is not related to the Russians being willing to burn Moscow before Napoleon. Napoleon was there. We are talking now about whether the Russians deliberately calculate that they would come out ahead if they tried to knock out the US strategic nuclear capability. One of our submarines on patrol is all that is needed to deter them from ever starting a nuclear war.

We ought to get off this kick of making our calculations based on who is vulnerable to a first attack. If we can do that, this process of strategic escrow, of getting those warheads off and into storage, could move very rapidly, because you are not asking those strategic commanders to divest themselves. You are asking them only to put in a delay factor. As the warheads go into escrow, we keep the START process going, and it destroys the weapons, in accordance with those schedules, 3,500, 2,500, and so on. In the meantime we have greatly reduced the dangers to the world. More importantly, we demonstrate to the world that these are not that important to our military planning, and therefore we enlist greater cooperation against proliferation of these weapons to other countries.

I call this escrow because of an important element. Maybe one of the only places where I diverge from Bruce and Hal is that I think it is positively important to keep an ability to quickly reassembly some nuclear weapons. That is your assurance against cheating. That is your assurance that if a Saddam Hussain suddenly gets some weapons and starts threatening the world and we are down to zero, that you can bring them back together and say to a Saddam Hussain, "You use your nuclear weapons at your own peril." Or, if one of the nuclear powers had cheated and held some out, the other nuclear powers could reassembly enough to constitute a counter to that.

The second step that I would suggest is that the two nuclear superpowers quickly make a statement of no first use. We have never done that. The Russians have until recently. There would be no need for a negotiated treaty on this. They could be unilateral statements that simply lower the importance of nuclear weapons to these two countries.

Once that is on the table, I would suggest the United Nations should expand the NPT into a treaty of no first use. We would have up to 185 signatories, 180 of whom don't have nuclear weapons and therefore ought to be willing to pledge they would not use nuclear weapons. It seems rather simple. But what you want from that 180 or whatever number you could get to sign up, would be a commitment to counter proliferation, because these countries would pledge, in addition to not using nuclear weapons first themselves, that they would conduct economic and political sanctions against any country that did become a nuclear aggressor. And therefore you not only put some pressure on a would-be nuclear aggressor but you begin to commit these nations to the fact that they want to insure there is no use of these weapons.

How do we get moving in these directions? We surely are having trouble in this country. We are not seeing much progress in Russia. I think we have to get outside pressure on the two nuclear superpowers to move much more rapidly to reduce numbers and to eschew first use.

For instance, I think the NATO countries today should take the initiative and say to the United States, we no longer want your first-use guarantee, the nuclear umbrella. We don't need it. We are not under any threat. I am talking only about a nuclear umbrella that we put out in 1952 against a conventional attack on western Europe, not a response to a nuclear attack, but a response to a conventional attack. It is nonsense that we maintain that today when there is zero conventional threat against western Europe. We pay a price of being inconsistent with respect to nuclear weapons and their importance when we insist on maintaining that.

I was in Europe not too long ago, in Norway, where they are very anti-nuclear. I held a seminar on this subject and at the end one person said, well, everything you say makes sense, but we don't want to get out from under the nuclear umbrella. We have to change the intellectual foundation here. People don't understand the significance of being inconsistent in this situation.

I close by saying the world community has a big stake in all of this. We do not, any of us, want a world in which there are more nuclear powers than we have today, because the more nuclear powers there are, the greater the risk of actual use. In my view the world has changed from the threat of a nuclear Armageddon to heavily armed nuclear superpowers who were reasonably responsible and cautious because they understood the consequences of using thousands of these weapons to a world in which we might have multiple nuclear powers with small numbers but much greater probability that a Sadam Hussain or such would be irresponsible and actually employ them. It would be a world in which there were occasionally uses of nuclear weapons would be a very different world than the world we live in today. If we don't want that kind of a world for our children and grandchildren, I think we have to move faster than ten thousand warheads ten years from now. Thank you.

JONATHAN DEAN: I think we are going to have a very active discussion. I am going to take the privilege of the Chair and ask Bruce a question. You mentioned the possibility of extending de-alerting to countries like India. I think that is a good idea. Would you explain a bit more how that might work.

BRUCE BLAIR; He always comes up with a question I haven't thought through yet. I have observed that China is modernizing its nuclear forces and I believe is moving in the direction of putting its nuclear weapons on alert status. I think presently they are de-alerted. India and Pakistan I think have a dynamic that, unless there is powerful civilian restraint put on their programs, on both sides, it has a dynamic that will inevitably move in the direction of the weaponization of their systems, moving toward a higher alert status over time. I think that is the general case for all nuclear powers. People may not know this, but the Soviet Union, until 1966 or 1967 kept all of its very large strategic arsenal off alert. It had all its warheads for its intercontinental missiles and its theater missiles in the custody of a special custodial unit in bunkers. In a crisis they would plan to mate up the warheads to the missiles. They were de-alerted in the mid to late sixties. And so it is not as though the Russians have no experience with this kind of a posture.

Given the trends that I am projecting here in South Asia, and possibly in the Middle East, there is pressure to move in that direction for any proliferant state and for China. We need to try and quickly establish for everyone a norm, a norm that prohibits categorically keeping nuclear weapons in any kind of launch-ready configuration. This is about as far as I have sorted this out. There would have to be some kind of regime of de-alerting, preferably of the order of Admiral Turner's strategic escrow, something transparently clear to everyone that no one is in the game anymore. If there were violations of this norm it would be understood that the rest of us would gang up on the violator.

JONATHAN DEAN: I think you are closer to success than you think. If first Russia and the United States adopted a de-alerting regime, and it is spread to the other nuclear-weapon states, then you have a very powerful argument to spread it to the threshold states, with the modification you were speaking of, some kind of monitoring of the warheads. I think, in the case of the threshold states, it would probably end up with having to monitor the delivery systems because of their desire to keep their holdings secret, but I do think it is extendable and I am enthusiastic about that possibility.

JOHN LINEWEAVER, Fellowship of Reconciliation: I have been listening to these discussions for 16 years. I have an uncomfortable feeling I am listening to cave men talking about anthropocide. In 1970 Anwar Sadat spoke in Jerusalem. He said 70% of our problems with Israel are psychological. The American Psychiatric Association described at that time that war is a plague, a public health problem. Since then I have heard no discussion in these panels of the psychological aspects that we

149

are concerned about: fear, anxiety and trepidation. I think this topic has not been discussed. There is a body of knowledge available on these subjects. I suggest a panel that includes psychologists...

QUESTIONER, Physicians for Social Responsibility: Bruce Blair, why wasn't the 1994 de-alerting more than cosmetic? And do you have Russian counterparts?

BRUCE BLAIR: I think John made a very good point, and I would like to make a comment on your statement. I am in total agreement with the point. There is the psychological and psychiatric aspects of living under the threat of holocaust for ordinary citizens of our country and the rest of the world. There is also the issue of fear and panic and other psychological issues related to the management and control of nuclear weapons. This is an area, although I don't underscore it here sitting on this panel, which is an underlying factor of enormous importance in the way I think about this problem. I share Admiral Turner's views about deterrence and how low we could go with our nuclear arsenals and still maintain an adequate deterrent. We could go practically to zero, if not to zero. Deterrence isn't a problem. The problem has to do with breakdowns of control. This is my own take on this. It is very much related to these issues.

For example, launch on warning is a psychological problem of the first order. There is a deadline in the Russian command system that a decision on whether to retaliate to an incoming strike must be made ten minutes after the initial detection of attack. That means that the early warning operators have to detect the attack, assess it, and forward the information. There has to be an emergency conference involving the top advisors. The commander of the Strategic Command in the United States is allowed 30 seconds to brief the President of the United States about his recommendation about the kind of response we should make to an attack. The Commander of NORAD, the duty officer who is responsible for sitting in Cheyenne Mountain, Colorado, is responsible for collating and assessing censored data from satellites and radars that might indicate an incoming attack. He is allowed three minutes from the time the initial sensor reports a possible threat to the time he has to give his assessment to the higher ups as to whether North America is under attack. This is an incredibly stressful, time-compressed, psychologically impossible situation. So what you see is people enacting scripts. They are not thinking. To the extent that psychology is at play, it is only because it has been stripped out of the whole process by checklist.

I used to do this myself. I had a three minute drill to fire 50 Intercontinental Minuteman Ballistic Missiles. From the time we received the message and authenticated it, using codes, retarget the missiles, and go through a big coordination procedure with other launch control centers, and turn keys, we were allowed three minutes. This concatenation of time-compressed procedures is obviously not a rational process. Deterrence is based on the idea of a rational interaction between countries. But that is not really what the heart of the problem is in this relationship. It is a very major underlying factor. This is what motivates many of us to take on these issues. If everyone is rational, it doesn't really matter if there are tens of thousands of nuclear weapons out there or not.

The 1994 de-targeting agreement grew out of an idea whispered into Yeltsin's ear by a person from the arms control branch of the Soviet Foreign Ministry by the name of Sergei Kortunov who now works in the Security Council of Russia. He got the idea of de-alerting about two weeks earlier at a conference at Brookings, at which several of us advocated this same agenda, in January of 1992, including Fred Ikle, who was Reagan's Under-Secretary for Policy, who is an advocate of this. We argued that both sides should take all their nuclear weapons off alert in 1992. Sergei Kortunov went back, proposed this, and a week later Yeltsin came out with a statement, as he is wont to do, that we should stop aiming missiles at each other. Kozyrov, the Foreign Minister, presented the same idea in a little more elaborate form to the UN in February, a couple of weeks after that. The next thing you know we have some sort of big momentum here to stop aiming missiles at each other. Of course, the spirit of the idea I think was on the right track, but no one applied any adult supervision to the actual process of implementation, and so you wound up with an amazing product, which was zero, except for a symbolic adjustment made in the computers on both sides for the missiles. It is called zero flight plan on the Russian side. We call it Broad Ocean Targeting here.

The Air Force guys who cooked this up realized we could aim our missiles simultaneously at Moscow and the oceans without having to change the trajectory except a little bit in the elevation angle. When the missile fires, if you just tip a little further down, like when you lower a hose, so that you can go farther, the missile will fire at Moscow, as part of our war plan. Otherwise the missile is lofted, and kind of goes straight up, to land in the Arctic Ocean. It was very clever. So all the missiles ocean targets are on the same path as their wartime targets. It is only a slightly different elevation. It takes a computer zero time to figure this out and reprocess it. And the Russians did something similar. It basically was a prostitution of the concept. I had to admire the ingenuity of these guys, though. They did enough to persuade Clinton that he would not be mendacious to say that we had stopped aiming missiles at each other...

Yes, we have spent a lot of time talking to the Russians. As I said, the 1994 agreement came out of a dynamic in the conference at Brookings on this subject. We have pursued it with lengthy discussions on the topic, including with some influential ones. There is some support for this idea over there, or at least interest on the part of one person in the Defense Council and with some people in the Strategic Rocket Forces. In the Russian case the opposition is quite strong to the idea of disarmament for the reasons that I outlined in my talk. They rely more on nuclear weapons than we do. This is their psychological crutch. Their conventional forces have declined to the point where they can't perform the traditional missions of protecting Russian territory. As a last resort they have seized on nuclear weapons as a psychological crutch. It is going to be a hard sell to get them to completely de-alert, much less completely abolish nuclear weapons, a harder sell than our side, I think.

DORRIE WEISS, ECAAR: Everyone agrees that there should be a build-down. But I haven't heard any real questioning about deterrence...which leads some to say we still need some nuclear weapons...

BRUCE BLAIR: I think that deterrence remains a valid concept but it is vastly overrated. What we need to do in our strategic policy is to strike a far better balance between deterrence, reassurance of Russia, which is desperate for assurance of its security, and operational safety. In fact, I think operational safety of nuclear forces should be the centerpiece of our nuclear agenda and our arms control agenda. Deterrence is all you hear about in Washington. It has a long way to fall, but it needs to be subordinated to these other issues because it is so easily satisfied at very low numbers. It is almost not an issue in my mind.

DORRIE WEISS: To talk of reassuring Russia, and talking at the same time about expanding NATO, it seems to me is contradictory.

JONATHAN DEAN: All on the panel agree with you on this. Admiral Turner has signed a letter, as did I, from Susan Eisenhower to the President opposing the enlargement of NATO.

ADMIRAL STANSFIELD TURNER: I would just like to say that many of us would like to get away from Mutual Assured Deterrence, but I don't see that as practical at this time. It seems to me that what we want to do is understand that you can have Mutual Assured Deterrence at very low numbers and that those numbers don't have to be instantly available. That moves us into a much better realm, but I don't see us escaping the ultimate threat of nuclear retaliation until we can go to total disarmament.

JONATHAN GRANOFF, LAWS: What are the economic aspects of this? Aren't the Russians going to have to come down to lower numbers just because of the economics of this?

BRUCE BLAIR: It is clear the Russian economy is in dire shape. Between the lack of money to build new weapons, and the fact that their older weapons are reaching a point of block obsolescence, in terms of their expected life span, in the next ten years, the combination of those two factors, mass obsolescence approaching in the next five to ten years and no money to replace them, means that the Russian strategic arsenal is headed into a huge tailspin.

I have done projections that would indicate that a thousand weapons in the Russian arsenal by the end of 2007 would be a plausible number, and 500 by the end of 2012, with the help of a colleague at Princeton, Josh Handler. Those are really incredible numbers. START II and III are completely unrealistic for Russia. We have to fast forward START, probably engage the other countries in multilateral arms control, and look toward a ceiling of a thousand weapons for the next round of START in order to be in the feasible ball park of discussion. Otherwise START talk is out in the ether, and has nothing to do with where Russia is headed. They are broke, and the economy is in terrible shape. We have to realize that we either follow them down to very low numbers, or figure something else out, if we are not willing to go down that low. If we want them to de-alert we will probably have to subsidize weapons storage facilities.

START II was unrealistic, so we agreed to go to 2,500 in START III. But those numbers are also unrealistic. When you see a collapse happening it usually goes much faster and harder than anyone expects or predicts, and that is what I think you are looking at here. We have an opportunity to go down as low as the Russians and we should, I think, and have parity. But that means a huge stand-down is going to happen naturally that should be controlled, that shouldn't just happen by spontaneous combustion. It should be regulated, and warheads that are coming off old delivery systems should be put in safe storage, and there is a price tag associated with that. I think it is going to be fairly expensive.

WILLIAM EPSTEIN, Pugwash: ...The first UN resolution called for the elimination of nuclear weapons. Then the Cold War started...Unless we make getting rid of all nuclear weapons a crusade, we are not going to succeed...

JANE FIX, League of Women Voters: How far have the ideas we have heard this afternoon spread? Have they been heard by people in the military?

ADMIRAL STANSFIELD TURNER: I have been out of the military a long time, so I really can't answer your question authoritatively. Very few senior military officers are enamored with nuclear weapons. The challenge of being a military officer is to develop tactics and have your operational unit tactically ready. When you introduce tactical or strategic nuclear weapons into your tactical equation it just goes to hell, so they don't like them.

The feeling in the Pentagon today, from what contacts I have had, is that there is an openness to change in this area and to reductions. There is not an openness to no first use, because when you tell a military officer we have just invented the ultimate weapon, but we are going to renounce it, and not keep it in our back pocket for an emergency, it is tough to get through to them. Finally, if START II does not pass the Russian Duma, the Congress has mandated that the military stay at START I force levels. That is probably a billion dollars a year out of the military budget, so we have leverage on that. They don't want to stay at START I levels. They want to put their money into other things.

HAROLD FEIVESON: After Bruce, Frank and I wrote our *Scientific American* article, General Habiger, who is the Commander in Chief of the Strategic Command, invited the three of us to go to Omaha to talk about this. So, in the sense of being open to discuss it, they are. In that sense, ideas are percolating. He didn't agree with us. They see stand-down and de-alerting as muddying up the operational clarity that they would like to see. But at the same time there was a really striking support of deep reductions in nuclear weapons. We are at a kind of cusp.

There is a striking relationship that General Habiger, for example, has with his counterparts in Russia. It sounds to me it is becoming rather close. They visit each other. Habiger described with appreciation a visit to Omaha by Sergeyev who, at the time of the visit, I think was the Minister of Defense. Before that he was the head of their Strategic Rocket Forces. There was a sense of friendship between them.

BRUCE BLAIR: This relationship between the two sides militaries is really almost getting a little out of hand. When we were in Omaha I got into a debate with the Commander of StratCom, General Habiger, over how long it took Russia to re-target their missiles. He was so anxious about the outcome of this debate, he picked up the telephone after we left the office and called the commander of the Russian Strategic Rocket Forces to get him to side with him against the position I was taking. Anyway, the military, as Admiral Turner said, except for the specialized nuclear operators, StratCom, abhor nuclear weapons, I think. The Army hated them because of the safety rules. It drove people crazy. They spent all their time worrying about nuclear weapons safety and they were happy to get rid of them.

In StratCom it is not the same. This is the essence of the organization. Nothing disturbed StratCom more than the 1991 agreement between Gorbachev and Bush that you may recall de-alerted a large number of strategic weapons and brought back all of our thousands of tactical weapons from all over the globe, except for a couple of hundred in Europe. There was nothing more unpopular for Strategic Command, because the launch officers, what I used to do, had to sit in the bunkers watching over missiles that had been de-activated. The warheads were still sitting on them, but they had even taken the launch keys away from these guys. It is a very emasculating step to take for these people. In fact, General Habiger mentioned that as a good illustration of the effect on morale that de-alerting would have. It is something to reckon with.

153

When men of such stature and credibility as Admiral Turner and Sam Nunn take a position on de-alerting, as they have, it gets the attention of the Pentagon. Their collective influence has instigated a very serious analysis of de-alerting within the Pentagon and the Joint Chiefs, as well as the creation of an interagency working group on de-alerting. They did a very serious analysis. I haven't seen it, so I can't speak that authoritatively about it. It provides options to Secretary Cohen, and an options paper that supposedly was transmitted to Secretary Cohen about a month ago. He sent it back to the interagency for further work.

Senator Nunn and I have met with General Ralston, who is the Vice Chairman of the Joint Chiefs, and other senior military officers on more than one occasion to discuss de-alerting. My sense is that they are very sincere in looking into this and are taking it very seriously. We expanded those meetings to include Senator Daschle, the Senate minority leader, who is a champion of this idea of de-alerting. He gives a floor speech every couple of months touting the virtues of de-alerting. Sen. Bingaman is big on it. He had a hearing last week that he managed to finagle from Republican control where Admiral Turner and I were able to testify on behalf of de-alerting in front of Sen. Bob Smith of New Hampshire, not a particularly strong proponent. But Sen. Bingaman is strong, and these meetings have expanded to include Daschle, Bingaman, Lugar, Levin. There is a constituency here. Domenici, from New Mexico, is showing signs of support for this idea, which would mean, along with Lugar, two Republican backers, potentially, on the Senate side. So it has percolated somewhat.

ANN LEGGETT, Federation of Arab-American Organizations: If they re-target away from Russia, might they target others, such as Iraq?

ADMIRAL STANSFIELD TURNER: I don't think that it enters into the thinking of policy makers, with a couple of exceptions. That is the strong feeling in policy circles that we must maintain ambiguity, at least, as a way of deterring the use of biological and chemical weapons. I don't happen to agree with that, but that is very much there. You occasionally read about policymakers thinking they might want to use a nuclear weapon against Libya's underground chemical weapons factory, or things like that, where there is a contrived situation, and they think a conventional weapon won't do the job. I don't think those are terribly serious situations. Finally, there is what I mentioned earlier: This feeling that if we were ever, in extremis, in a conventional war, we would not want to have given up the option of using a nuclear weapon to get us out of that extremis. Again, I don't agree with that argument, but I am giving you the extent of policymaker thinking. No one I know thinks this is the way to keep the rest of the world in line. That is implicit in our having nuclear weapons. I don't think we say a country ought to be worried about us because we have these weapons.

HAROLD FEIVESON: I don't think there is any logical connection between the stand-down on alert and other countries. That comes into no first use. However, the first public sort of attack on what Frank, Bruce and I did was in the *Wall St. Journal*. They said the main reason we have to have weapons on alert is because of Libya, Iraq and Iran maybe at some point getting ballistic missiles. So in the minds of some people who don't like a stand-down on alert, they try to put "rogue" countries at the forefront. But it doesn't make any real sense.

BRUCE BLAIR: I have never talked to a policymaker who imagined any conceivable circumstance for nuclear weapons to sort out a problem in the Third World. What gets translated through the bureaucracy might be something else again. You hear Gen. Habiger saying flat out that we now have a policy that allows us to use our nuclear weapons in response to the use of weapons of mass destruction by other countries. Targeting these countries has become something of a cottage industry within the planning community and it has been going on for a long time. It goes back to the eighties. Iran was the target of our strategic planners in Omaha in the 1980s. But the rationale has changed in the nineties and the momentum has given impetus to this activity. You now have a mission that can justify a substantial amount of activity and weapons and targeting and alerting. It does add to the complication of de-alerting and elimination and deep cuts.

JONATHAN DEAN: There is also reason to believe that what Admiral Turner referred to, ambiguity, is a deliberate policy of the Administration, and so that keeps it cooking.

PETER DAVIES, A SaferWorld and Peace Action: ...I would be very interested in your comments to the Stockpile Stewardship Program and sub-critical testing.

HAROLD FEIVESON: I edit a journal called *Science and Global Security*. Last year we published an article on sub-critical testing, by Frank von Hippel and Suzanne Jones. In the next issue, which is about to be sent to the printer, there is an article by Jones and von Hippel on the testing of pure fusion devices, and also an article by Christopher Paine and Matt McKinzie of the Natural Resources Defense Council on the US Science-Based Stockpile Stewardship Program.

I don't know what one could say in a word about the sub-critical tests, except that it would be a good idea to put certain constraints on them, making them as transparent as possible, so that you could see that new devices aren't being tested, and that the tests are really sub-critical. There are also experiments going on at Los Alamos. These might not be their overt purpose, but they raise the possibility that one could move toward pure fusion weapons. It is important that those experiments be constrained in various ways that will be put forward in the article on pure fusion testing. The other side of the story is that the Science-Based Stockpile Stewardship Program is the price that had to be paid to get support for a Comprehensive Test Ban Treaty.

JONATHAN DEAN: The President, in following the action of the Congress in declaring the unilateral moratorium, and then saying it should be extended with the Nuclear Test Ban, was faced by a very powerful coalition of the weapons laboratories and the professional nuclear group in the Pentagon, and by very strong Republican senators. This Stewardship Program is what he and his staff figured they had to do to buy them off. It is a makework project, as you were saying this morning. But I don't think the original decision was wrong. It does have to be kept under control, and checked, as time goes on. As you are aware, a lot of people are suspicious and are raising questions.

QUESTIONER: ...What role would you see for the United Nations, for non-nuclear countries and for NGOs? And what role for the International Court of Justice? Isn't the Cold War over?

JONATHAN DEAN: Let me try to answer that first. I think many of us feel the NPT review process is the place for concentrated pressure on the weapon states. The dream of many of us has been to form a broad coalition among the non-weapon states, over 180 of them, behind the same kind of program. That has not been possible up to now because of very deep divisions of attitude. The US allies don't want to offend their protector and they restrict their proposals to rather limited ones. On the other hand, the non-aligned continue to demand rapid satisfaction, in terms of time-bound commitments to abolition.

Ideally, you should be able to form a program which has in it a serious demand for abolition plus a specific program of steps. What many of us are urging now for content of such a program are de-alerting plus a final deep cuts position, what I call the last negotiated reduction before elimination. If we could get a broad coalition backing that kind of approach, then the weapon states would have to pay serious attention to it. As some of you know, Ambassador Roche of Canada is proposing a move in that direction with his middle states project. A lot of people are thinking of it. I hope it will be possible. It is my conviction that we are not going to get progress unless you can combine the pressure for elimination with agreement on some specific steps, not many, that the weapon states should take in moving towards elimination. I think the NPT process is the best vehicle. We are moving now to a further review conference in the year 2000, as Ambassador Dhanapala mentioned this morning. One could maximize that pressure. At this year's PrepCom, they could move towards a bigger coalition and then launch it in the year 2000 review. Then we would have a lot of external motivation for the weapon states to move more rapidly, and a path which could be indicated by the coalition which I hope will come into being.

ANN GERTLER, Project Ploughshares, Canada: It was a surprise to find that the NGO Committee on Disarmament was focusing on US and Russian problems. They are very important but other views should be included. Canada is involved with NORAD as well.

JONATHAN DEAN: The US and Russia have the most nuclear weapons.

BRUCE BLAIR: I met with the Defense Committee of the Canadian Parliament and gave a briefing on de-alerting and related topics. I am working for their staff that is putting together a report that will include Canada's role. The heart of it is at NORAD, and Canada is a partner with the US in this hair-trigger system. We are all in this together.

On whether the Cold War is over: When I point out that there is this imbalance in strategic capabilities, and that Russia is quite vulnerable, and that is why they are on launch on warning, people say, how can the Russians worry about an attack from the US? At some level that is certainly true. We are not enemies anymore, but the fact is we haven't really changed the paradigm of our planning systems, and operational systems. We still operate under this umbrella concept of deterrence, the instrument of containment, and we operate the forces in exactly the same way. The people who are responsible for national security, in the military in particular, still act as though the Cold War never ended. In fact you can find a fair amount of sentiment in attitudes along these lines as well.

I also point out that the threat isn't just theoretical. It is actually manifested every day in concrete terms. We still, for example, operate RC-135 reconnaissance airplanes off the coast of Russia all the time. They are called Rivet Joint Missions and we send them up there to probe Russian air defenses. Sure enough, we are finding gaping holes in their air defense and the Russians worry about this. They see us coming. They also see our anti-submarine warfare operations haven't really changed. In other words, there are concrete, visible manifestations of the old Cold War operations that sort of bear down on both sides, but mainly Russia, and to them it doesn't look like a radically changed circumstance from the Cold War, I think.

HAROLD FEIVESON: Let me add to that. One of the reasons the US has the launch-on-warning capability, and keeps its weapons on high alert, is the notion that at the start of a nuclear war we could respond very rapidly to limit damage to ourselves by striking a whole spectrum of Russian targets. There is a lot wrong with that, but that is still the kind of philosophy we are going on. Thinking through this I was reminded of the scene in the film, Dr. Strangelove, which I hope most of you have seen. Let me go through the scene very quickly.

If you remember, George C. Scott is playing the Air Force General, Buck Turgidson. He confronts the President, when it looks like a Soviet attack is under way.

Buck Turgidson says: "It is necessary to make a choice, to choose between two regrettable but nevertheless distinguishable post-war environments, one where you get 20 million people killed, and the other where you get 150 million people killed."

President Muffley (Peter Sellers), shocked, says: "You are talking about mass murder, General, not war."

Turgidson: "I am not saying we wouldn't get our hair mussed, but I do say, no more than 10 to 20 million killed, tops, depending on the breaks."

Muffley, angrily: "I will not go down in history as the greatest mass murderer since Adolf Hitler."

Buck Turgidson: "Perhaps it might be better, Mr. President, if you were concerned with the American people more than with your image in the history books."

That logic is still there.

JONATHAN DEAN: Our thanks to all of you...

DISARMAMENT AND UNITED NATIONS REFORM: JAYANTHA DHANAPALA, UN UNDER-SECRETARY-GENERAL FOR DISARMAMENT AFFAIRS

and

NUCLEAR ABOLITION:THE GIFT OF TIME: JONATHAN SCHELL

LYUTHA AL-MUGHAIRY, Chief, Public Liaison Service, UN DPI: Today's briefing is on disarmament and UN reform. This program is sponsored in cooperation with the NGO Committee on Disarmament. We have two distinguished speakers today, Mr. Jayantha Dhanapala, who is the United Nations Under-Secretary-General for Disarmament Affairs, and Mr. Jonathan Schell, author of The Fate of the Earth and The Gift of Time, who will make a presentation entitled Nuclear Abolition: The Gift of Time. Welcome.

We will start with Mr. Jayantha Dhanapala, who was appointed by the Secretary-General, Kofi Annan, to be Under-Secretary-General of the newly created Department for Disarmament Affairs. He assumed this position on 1 February, 1998. Secretary-General Annan also recently appointed Mr. Dhanapala as Commissioner in UNSCOM, as Head of the Special Group visiting the Presidential sites in Iraq, in connection with the implementation of the Memorandum of Understanding.

Prior to joining the UN, Mr. Dhanapala was diplomat in residence at the Center for Non-Proliferation Studies of the Monterey Institute for International Studies in California. He first became associated with the UN in 1984, when he was appointed Permanent Representative of Sri Lanka to the United Nations in Geneva, with concurrent accreditation to the UN agencies in Vienna. In 1987, UN Secretary-General Perez de Cuellar appointed him Director of the Geneva-based UN Institute for Disarmament Research. In 1995 he served as President of the Review and Extension Conference of the Treaty on the Non-Proliferation of Nuclear Weapons (NPT). Mr. Dhanapala joined the Sri Lankan Foreign Service in 1965. Between 1965 and 1983 he held diplomatic appointments in London, Beijing, New Delhi, and in Washington, DC, where he also served from 1995 until 1997 as Sri Lanka's Ambassador to the US, with concurrent accreditation to Mexico. Welcome, Sir, and I give you the floor.

JAYANTHA DHANAPALA: Thank you, Madame Chairman and ladies and gentlemen, for your warm welcome. It is a great pleasure for me to be present at this seminar which has been organized by the NGO Committee on Disarmament, an organization with which I have had very close connections long before I assumed my present position.

I am particularly glad, so soon after my assumption of duties, to be able to talk to you about the subject of United Nations reform and disarmament. It is also a particular honor for me to be sharing the forum with Jonathan Schell, an author of great repute, whose imaginative genius has helped the cause of disarmament for a very long time.

My subject today is a very relevant one. As you know, the General Assembly of 1997 was very much the reform assembly, as a consequence of the July, 1997 reform document, A/51/950, put forth by the Secretary-General. The fact that disarmament was placed in such a key role in the reform program is not a surprise because in the post-Cold War situation that we are in, it is clear that the UN is uniquely positioned to play a positive role in disarmament and security matters. Disarmament is a key component in international peace and security, and the recognition of the importance of multilateralism in the post-Cold War disarmament situation has led the Secretary-General to a vision as to what the UN can do in this field.

You are aware of the details of the reform proposal as they were contained in the Secretary-General's reform document. It is also appropriate to mention that, in the same document, the Secretary-General made a very detailed reference to the need for the UN to reach out to civil society. Clearly, NGOs are the embodiment of that civil society. So my presence here today to talk about reform is in pursuance of both the Secretary-General's policy with regard to the importance of civil society in the role of the UN in global affairs and the importance of the UN in disarmament affairs.

I have long believed that the participation of NGOs in disarmament affairs should be far more active than it has been in the past, and this relates to the structures of UN organizational procedures, where multilateral conferences are concerned. I believe it is important that NGO participation in disarmament conferences should be as active as it is in the human rights field, in the environment field and other fields. There has to be an end to the disparities that exist with regard to the participation of NGOs in disarmament fora, however inconvenient it may be to certain Member States. I believe that the more we hear the voice of civil society in multilateral disarmament fora, the more likely we are to have action pursued in very important areas in the multilateral disarmament agenda.

Let me begin by saying that disarmament as it was featured in the Secretary-General's reform package was, in fact, a recognition that it is time that the central issue in the international peace and security agenda should also take center stage in the UN itself. It was also a recognition that reform is not merely a question of downsizing or a reduction of jobs or programs, but also a refocusing on the priorities of the UN. The re-establishment of the Department for Disarmament Affairs after a lapse of six years, during which it languished as a Centre within the Department of Political Affairs, was therefore symbolic of the Secretary-General's vision that the United Nations should play a central role in the future as far as multilateral disarmament is concerned. Today, as a result of the reform package being discussed in the General Assembly, on the basis of both the original document, A/51/950, and the companion document, A/52/CRP.3, it has been possible to reestablish the Department with an Under-Secretary-General at its head.

This means that disarmament has a visible role in the higher echelons of the UN Secretariat. It is present in the Senior Management Group and the Secretary-General has a team of expert advisers in the Department who are able to keep him abreast of contemporary developments in the disarmament field and serve as his spokemen in this very important area of our work. My commitment to translating the Secretary-General's vision into practice has led me in the last few weeks to try to restructure my deparment in such a way that we will be able to fulfill the role he has in mind for us.

We do not intend to play any evangelical role, but we will objectively and resolutely pursue a UN agenda with regard to multilateral disarmament. We are in fact, with a strength of 45, both

Professionals and General Service, the smallest Department in the Secretariat. But I think we are the smallest Department with the largest potential to be able to serve the cause of multilateral disarmament. I am not here to empire-build, I'm not here to engage in turf battles, but I believe with a small core of dedicated professionals in the Department, many of whom have long experience in the UN, we will be able to fulfill the vision of the Secretary-General.

The functions of the Department were explained by the Secretary-General in a statement that he delivered to the Advisory Board on Disarmament Matters in Geneva last month. In discussing the re-establsihment of the Department as a key element of his program of reform, he talked about disarmament work in the Department having four main components.

Firstly, he mentioned preventive disarmament measures such as dialogue and transparency and confidence-building measures. He identified the Register of Conventional Arms as one such measure. You are all familar with the Register that has been maintained, and continues to be maintained, in the Department for Disarmament Affairs. He also referred to regional forums such as the Standing Advisory Committee on Security Questions in Central Africa.

A second element of the work of the Department is norm-setting. The creation of norms in the deliberative bodies of the First Committee and the Disarmament Commission, and thereafter given treaty form in the single multilateral disarmament negotiating forum, the Conference on Disarmament, plays a very important role in the work of the Department for Disarmament Affairs. Not only must we preserve and protect the existing norms and the existing treaties and nuture the treaty regimes that exist, but we must also try to move towards a situation where fresh norms are created. I do not believe that we have reached the end of the road in this very important task for the Department for Disarmament Affairs, because there are a number of areas in which norm-creation is possible.

A third component consists of practical measures carried out in post-conflict settings. This includes the question of disarming former combatants, re-integrating them into civil society and cleaning up the remnants of war. Mali has been a triumphant example of where this has been possible. In 1996 a bonfire was made of the weapons that had been collected and held in Mali, and this has become symbolic of what can be done with regard to the destruction of small arms and light weapons. Last month the Secretary-General launched a book issued by UNIDIR (United Nations Institute for Disarmament Research) on the Mali experience. This area of small arms and light weapons has therefore become a very important element in the work of the Department for Disarmament Affairs.

Fourthly, there is the post-conflict enforcement of disarmament to ensure that hostilities do not arise again. The work that is going on in Iraq is an example of this, and the Secretary-General's appointment of myself as a Commissioner in UNSCOM and the head of the Special Group that recently conducted the visits to the eight Presidential sites has a logical link with the agenda of disarmament.

Let me now move to the fact that the UN as a consequence has a very definite approach, a very clear-cut, moral approach, to the question of disarmament. We are not apolitical and detached when it comes to the subject of disarmament. We are very much engaged. The Charter is our manifesto. The UN therefore is pro-disarmament; it is pro-non-proliferation of weapons, it is pro-international peace and security. In my view, disarmament and non-proliferation go hand in hand.

They are two faces of the same coin. I do not believe that we can achieve one without the other. Therefore, this two-dimensional approach to non-proliferation, both vertical and horizontal, whether it is weapons of mass destruction or conventional arms, is a very important element in our philosophy.

Looking at the general agenda of disarmament, it is clear that we must continue with our old mandates, and until such time as there is a fresh consensus document emerging from a special session on disarmament, we still look upon the Final Document of SSOD I of 1978 as being the source of the mandate that we have - together, of course, with the UN General Assembly resolutions. We will continue to implement these resolutions and these targets that have been arrived at through multilateral consensus.

In addition, in the field of weapons of mass destruction, we continue to regard nuclear disarmament as one of the priority issues, and the support of the NPT regime, greatly strengthened after the 1995 conference, remains an important responsibility of the Department for Disarmament Affairs. We will have the Second Preparatory Committee of the 2000 conference take place in Geneva shortly and my Department is very much involved in that task.

Early ratification of the CTBT (Comprehensive Test Ban Treaty), which was greatly encouraged by the ratification of the UK and France recently, is another important target for us to move towards, bearing in mind that next year we will have a conference which will consider the entry into force of that important treaty. We continue to maintain close relations with the Chemical Weapons Convention regime, set up in the Hague, and we will continue to work closely with them as well as with the Preparatory Commission of the CTBT Organization in Vienna.

With regard to the Biological Weapons Convention, you are aware of the hard work that is going on in order to create a verification Protocol so that this important convention can be given teeth and can allay the suspicions and fears that have arisen recently about a resurgence of these odious weapons that we hope we have banished for all time.

In conventional weapons, certainly there is a great deal to be done, and the Secretary-General has repeatedly called attention to the importance of action with regard to small arms and light weapons. He has stated that there have been four million deaths caused by small arms and light weapons in conflicts that have taken place after the fall of the Berlin Wall. This is a stark reality that we must address, and while we continue with our work with regard to weapons of mass destruction, we must also make parallel progress with regard to conventional arms.

There are a number of other issues that have to be undertaken: the prevention of an arms race in outer space, Nuclear-Weapon-Free Zones, continued work with regard to verification and confidence-building measures, and a host of other issues that you are familiar with in the disarmament agenda. I see the Department as a consensus-builder. We will try to provide objective information and background material so that Member States will have this information available to them as they approach the disarmament agenda, both in the deliberative bodies and the negotiating bodies.

There are a number of specific issues that will arise in the near-term. The first, of course, is to address the remainder of the Secretary-General's ambitious program of reform as far as disarmament is concerned. He has requested Member States to look into the work of the Disarmament Commission, and the First Committee of the General Assembly with a view to updating, rationalizing and streamlining their work. As you know, the Disarmament Commission has already begun its work and is taking an introspective look so that it can make recommendations regarding the improvement of its working methods.

I'm sure you, as the NGO community, deeply involved in the work of multilateral fora in disarmament, have your own views, and will share them both with the Member States and with us, so that together we can collectively achieve what the Secretary-General has requested. We have ourselves conducted some brainstorming within the Department and we'll try to encourage Member States to make reforms that will serve the cause of multilateral disarmament. Next, there is the NPT review process, which is well underway. The review conference in the year 2000 will be the first review conference after the indefinite extension of the NPT. It is very important that the strengthened review process be realized. That process is evolving, with the second PrepCom taking place at the end of this month in Geneva.

In the Conference on Disarmament, many Cassandras have been very active in predicting its demise. I believe this view is gravely mistaken. The fact that we have had one and a half years of a drought after the rich harvest of the Chemical Weapons Convention and the CTBT is no cause for hand-wringing. There have been longer periods of inactivity in the CD, particularly during the Cold War. There is no need to apportion blame, it is not unusual for the CD to have periods when it is not as active as it should be.

I'm happy to report, however, that on the 26th of March, the CD did adopt a modest program of action. That program provides for the creation of an ad hoc committee of negative security assurances, which hopefully will negotiate working arrangements in order to give non-nuclear weapon states guarantees against the threat or the use of nuclear weapons - a long-held demand of the non-nuclear weapon states.

SSOD (Special Session on Disarmament) IV is another important upcoming event, although no date has been set. However, at the last General Assembly session, as you are all aware, consensus was reached on the need for such a special session in order to review the situation of disarmament internationally and set commonly agreed targets in the field of disarmament for the new millenium. My hope is that the Disarmament Commission, which is in its final year discussing the SSOD IV, will be able to reach agreement on its objectives and agenda so that the task of setting a date will be facilitated as we come to the General Assembly session later this year.

Ladies and gentlemen, I do not wish to take more of your time. I believe that we are at a very crucial and important stage with regard to multilateral disarmament. We have unique opportunities, and it is for the Member States to grasp these opportunities. You, in the NGOs will be there providing us with your enthusiasm, your dedication, and your ideas. The Department for Disarmament Affairs will, to the best of its professional ability, help to respond to the needs of the Member States, but it is ultimately the Member States that have to take the decisions.

The Secretary-General, in his last report to the General Assembly, stated very clearly that in this era of realignment, variously described as the post-Cold War era, or an era of transition, multilateralism has the capacity of tipping the scales, of tipping the balance in favor of the positive over the negative. And it is out of that conviction that the Department for Disarmament Affairs has been re-established, so that the UN can play a more assertive role in the field of multilateral disarmament.

The Duke of Wellington said that beginning reform is beginning revolution, and the Secretary-General, in his own words, has begun "a quiet revolution." A quiet revolution without arms is what we want. The Department for Disarmament Affairs remains, therefore, dedicated to the cause of multilateral disarmament, and we'll do what it can, with your help and the help of the Member States. Thank you very much.

LYUTHA AL-MUGHAIRY: Thank you very much, Mr. Dhanapala. It is a pleasure to see you here with us and thank you for having found the time to come and talk to us. I would like now to introduce Ann Lakhdhir, who does not need introduction, from the NGO Committee on Disarmament, who will introduce Jonathan Schell to you.

ANN LAKHDHIR: I am sure many of you saw the special issue of *The Nation*, the special issue that came out in February, and perhaps many of you know that in May it will result in a book, *The Gift of Time*. I am sure many of you have read some of Jonathan Schell's prior books. I had not realized, until I read his bio, that he has already written ten books and many articles. *The Nation* article and the book about to be published is based on many interviews, from General Lee Butler, to Robert McNamara, to Bruce Blair, whom you will have the opportunity to hear speak this afternoon, and Rolf Ekeus, Joseph Rotblat and Gorbachev and many others. I found it very interesting.

What I didn't know, until I read his bio, was that he was the primary writer for the Notes and Comment section of *The New Yorker* over practically a twenty-year period. Nor did I realize that one of his languages is Japanese, and that he not only has a Harvard degree but also did work in the graduate school focusing on Far Eastern history.

For decades, Jonathan Schell has been one of our most articulate and thoughtful writers. We are delighted you can speak with us today.

JONATHAN SCHELL: ...For many centuries the international sphere has been a rather bleak and stony place. At best you had diplomacy, at worst war. Recently it has occurred to individual citizens to intervene, and thus we have NGOs and meetings like the one today. With all respect to the diplomats among us, I regard this new intervention as sort of what the French used to call a *mission civiliatrice*, to introduce the ways of civic society into the international sphere.

I want to add that it is an especially great honor for me to share this platform with Under-Secretary Dhanapala, whose work on disarmament has long been a legend in this organization, and now it is becoming a legend in the world at large. I will take exception with him on one point, however. He seemed to seek to reassure us that he would engage in no empire-building. I personally would like to encourage him to build an empire, because I am confident that the sort of empire that he would build is the kind we need. It is the only kind of empire we need.

My subject today is the abolition of nuclear weapons. In order to get at it I am going to step back for a moment and examine the historical moment in which we find ourselves. I have just been through this process of conducting many dozens of interviews with people around the world on the subject of abolition, and perhaps I can share with you today a few of the conclusions I have drawn from these conversations.

We are coming to the end of the bloodiest century on record. I don't mean the century that began in 1900. I mean the one that began in 1914 with the beginning of the First World War which turned first Europe and then the rest of the world into a slaughterhouse. This period was above all a period of unparalled mass killing in war, mass killing in revolution, mass killing in concentration camps and finally mass killing in atomic attack.

That First World War, we are now in a position to see, touched off a chain reaction of bloody events, both within nations and between them, that has continued down to virtually today. Tsarist Russia was swept from the stage, to be succeeded shortly by Stalin's gulag. The harsh and unjust peace at Versailles set the stage for the rise in Germany of Nazi totalitarianism, and thus for a Second World War, worse than the first, in which the totalitarian behemoth fought with the democracies, allied with the Soviet Union.

And so to Stalin's camps were now added Hitler's, and the genocidal attack on the Jewish people, the worst crime of which history has record. And the final chapter of this tale, of course, was the construction of nuclear machinery for mass killing which was never used to the full, but that, if it ever were to be used, would kill without limit, possibly extinguishing our very species.

Historians call this period the short twentieth century, to distinguish it from the longer actuarial one that began in 1900. This short twentieth century, they are saying, ended in 1991 with the dissolution of the Soviet Union and the end of the Cold War. But I have to disagree with this dating. How can we accept it as long as long as the most lethal instruments of them all remain in abundance, ready for use at a moments notice. Our self-congratulations, I suggest, are premature. Until those nuclear arsenals are destroyed that bloody era will not truly have ended.

I haven't come here, though, to complain, or to tell you that nothing has changed. Quite the contrary. I believe, in fact, that part of the problem we face now is a curious incapacity to absorb good news when it comes along.

Let us consider for a moment that great windfall that has been handed to us by history, the end of the Cold War. It came as a complete surprise. Wasn't the almost universal failure to predict this epic-making event due in part to a deeply ingrained pessimism which teaches us that gigantic systems based on force are almost in their nature unchallengeable and bound to defeat all efforts to bring them down, and to endure forever?

I am the first to admit that this pessimism, after the two world wars, after the concentration camps, has profound cause and justification. But I want to suggest today that it may be misleading us. I accuse us, in fact, of the sin of ingratitude. Having accustomed ourselves to terrible news for so long, we seem to have lost the capacity to receive the good. Aren't we, perhaps, all guilty of this mistaken pessimism when, without sufficient thought, we make the assumption that the system of global nuclear terror is unchallengeable, that it must last forever? What warrant does anyone have, after all, to declare that it is impossible to abolish nuclear weapons?

I'll tell you what seemed impossible. Dissolving the Soviet Union from within, and without violence, seemed impossible, something that was really out of the question. I don't mean to underestimate the difficulties ahead of us, but abolishing nuclear weapons is highly practicable by comparison.

In 1945, our short twentieth century reached an abrupt turning point when the first nuclear weapon flashed over the city of Hiroshima, destroying it. One person who understood the magnitude of that event almost immediately was an American writer, James Agee. Just a few weeks after Hiroshima he wrote "All thoughts and things are split."

What did he mean? I think he meant that for the nations that possessed nuclear arms, we were divided down the center of ourselves. The reason was quite simple. Mere possession of nuclear weapons committed us, in some circumstance or other, to killing tens of millions, hundreds of millions, of human beings, most of them entirely unengaged in any combat. But such conduct could not honestly be justified by any civilized moral code or moral feeling.

Thereafter, the possessors of nuclear weapons were condemned to live in a split world, in which moral feelings existed in one sphere, and strategy existed in another, and never the twain shall meet. As the arsenals grew, and it became clear that an attack would spell the ruin of the attacker as well, common sense had to join morality in the discard pile. Mutual Assured Destruction became the watchword of the day. From that point forward, we were faced with the question that Albert Camus, in the late 1940s, said was henceforth the only serious question. Shall we commit suicide or not?

Now to this dark picture of life under the shadow of nuclear danger during the Cold War, another important element must be added. This was the widespread conviction, especially among nuclear powers, that any escape, any hope of actually eliminating these weapons, was impossible. Here in the United States the syllogism went as follows: Disarmament required inspection. The Soviet Union was a secretive, totalitarian state that wouldn't permit inspection. Therefore disarmament was ruled out. I am sure that in the Soviet Union they had a parallel syllogism to resort to.

This belief, so difficult to shake off, that nuclear disarmament was impossible under the conditions of the Cold War, was the most agonizing part of the split that Agee foresaw. It meant that even people of good will felt paralyzed. They scarcely dared even to mention the goal that alone could deliver us from the intolerable position of threatening the mass slaughter of millions. Yes, many might call out to ban the bomb, but how many believed in their hearts that this would happen? this perceived impossibility completed their despair. It is one thing to believe that one's species has wandered into a suicidal trap. It is another, much worse thing, to believe that no escape is possible.

If we place this terrible predicament into which we have wandered into the history of the short twentieth century we see that a paradoxical thing had happened. On the one hand, the mass killing on that global scale had slowed down some. On the other hand, the potential for slaughter swelled a thousandfold, until all earthly life was in its shadow. And nuclear arsenals, you might say, permitted the actual, practiced terror of the twentieth century to be distilled in its most concentrated form, increasing immeasurably in virulence, though placed in a kind of temporary storage, ready for use at all times, and yet not, thank God, actually used. And so we lived for fifty years.

And then, at the beginning of this decade, against all expectation, a great windfall was suddenly handed to us, the end of the Cold War. A new age suddenly opened, catching everybody by surprise. As a great American President, who happened to be an abolitionist in another sense of the word, I mean Abraham Lincoln, said, "As our times are new, we must think anew." We sit today, bewildered, in the rubble of the Cold War world. It is time we picked ourselves up and began to think what kind of a new world we want to be living in. Not everything, after all, consists of corporate mergers, exchange rates and capital flows. Politics still exists, and so does nuclear danger. For while the Cold War ended, the great nuclear arsenals that were built to wage that conflict did not, and today almost 40,000 of those weapons still remain in the world.

I said that history handed us a windfall. But that, of course, was only a manner of speaking. Strictly speaking, history does nothing. Men and women do. In the case of the end of the Cold War, the men and women in question were very largely those in the former Soviet Union and in Eastern Europe, who, at exorbitant personal cost, resisted, and finally defeated the system under which they lived. They included, for example, Alexander Solzhenitsyn, Andrei Sakharov, in Russia, Vaclav Havel in Czechoslovakia, Lech Walenca and Adam Miknik in Poland, to name just a few.

And the battles in that war seemed at the time quixotic gestures and only now can be understood as stages along the path to a success. They included the Hungarian revolution in 1956; the Prague spring in 1968; the solidarity movement of 1980 in Poland; and finally the successful resistance in 1991 to the attempted hardline Communist putsch in Russia against Boris Yeltsin and Mikhail Gorbachev.

It was not the intention, in most cases, of these reformers and fighters for freedom to advance the cause of nuclear disarmament, but that, as things have turned out, was one of their achievements. It is a pleasant paradox of the time, that the end of the totalitarian movements did more for nuclear disarmament, perhaps, than we in the West who resisted nuclear arms directly.

Important consequences, historically, flow from this realization. If we suppose that the most important task before us is to dismantle the unprecedented systems of indiscriminate mass killing that in our century fastened themselves in the form of totalitarian regimes on entire nations and empires, and then, in the form of the system of Mutual Assured Destruction, upon the entire world, then the cause of nuclear abolition must be seen as the second stage of a world movement whose first stage was the campaign against totalitarianism.

Just as the peoples of the East found a way to dismantle the system of terror under which they lived, so now it is the responsibility of peoples of East, and West, and South and North alike, together to dismantle the system of nuclear terror under which we all still live.

What of nuclear danger, though? Broadly speaking, I would say two things have happened. The first is an immense and welcome reduction in nuclear danger. True, the arsenals remain, still on hair trigger, still poised to turn us to dust in half an hour. And yet we would be fools not to acknowledge that, with the end of the Cold War, the danger of their immediate use has sharply declined.

The second development, however, cuts in the opposite direction. It is the spread of nuclear weapon technology. And this spread, something quite unstoppable in our so-called information age, greatly increases the danger that a so-called regional war will break out somewhere, or that one or a few bombs will be used, removing London, or New York, or Delhi or Moscow, from the face of the earth.

To sum up the matter of nuclear danger, you might say we have traded in some of the peril of a full-scale apocalypse for a greater peril of local catastrophe.

But none of this is the main point. The main point today concerns something else, not danger, but opportunity. The essential point is that the end of the Cold War cleared away the barrier of political impossibility that for fifty years stood in the way of nuclear abolition and was the source of our tacit despair. Now that Gordian knot has been dissolved. Russia welcomes inspection, perhaps more than the United States does. The advocates of nuclear arms have been forced to repair to a far weaker line of defense, having to do chiefly with the danger of cheating, or so-called breakout from a nuclear abolition agreement.

I am not going to enter into the thicket of argumentation on that point. I can just refer you to the interviews I have done in which I think it is taken care of decisively by such people as General Lee Butler and the UN's own Rolf Ekeus.

So I propose that we begin our stocktaking of the present opportunity by counting our blessings. And the first of these is the fact that, broadly speaking, the international conditions are more favorable to peace today than they have been since the nineteenth century. In fact we have to go clear back to 1815, when Napoleon was defeated and the Congress of Vienna was meeting, to find conditions remotely comparable.

Consider: no defeated power threatens to upset a victor's peace, as Germany did after 1918. Further, no ideological rivalry threatens to divide the world, as the Cold War did almost immediately after 1945. Or consider the following remarkable fact: there is no full scale war being waged between any two full-fledged nations in the world.

Now I don't mean to paint a utopian picture. Terrible slaughters, including episodes of attempted genocide, have erupted again and again, in the post-Cold War period. But when we speak of nuclear weapons, our concern must be above all with the international sphere, strictly speaking, not the domestic one, in which, all agree, nuclear weapons have no use. No one has ever stopped a revolution with the use or threat of use of a nuclear bomb.

My point is that those of us that have opposed nuclear weapons during the Cold War have been sprung from our trap. Our despair has lifted. We have reason to believe it can lift altogether. For the first time since the bomb flashed over Hiroshima 53 years ago, we can, at long last, call for the abolition of nuclear arms and believe in our hearts that it will happen.

The revolution that has occurred, therefore, is a revolution in possibility. I want to tell you that I, for one, feel exuberant at the change. I feel a confidence that I have never felt before, that if we can rouse ourselves to action, no insuperable obstacle stands in our way of eliminating every nuclear weapon from the face of the earth.

What would that mean? It would mean, above all, getting out of the filthy business of threatening to kill hundreds of millions of people. On a deeper level, it would mean that we were turning away from the whole business of mechanized killing that began in 1914. It would mean washing our hands of all that. Most important, it would mean knowing that life could go on, and that we who are alive today had had a hand in that. It would mean placing hope first, and fear second. It would mean that we could offer participation in a great and positive enterprise that has every chance of succeeding, not just some desperate makeshift that will buy us a few more days or weeks reprieve from annihilation.

Frankly, sometimes it seems to me that we who oppose nuclear weapons fail to acknowledge this change. Sometimes it appears that we conceive our job as keeping the level of alarm at maximum pitch in order to stir people into action. This seems to me a mistake. If we who oppose nuclear arms don't seem to know that the Cold War is over, and that there is a measure of safety that we didn't have, say, 15 years, it may look as though we are not really serious about nuclear danger, or glad when a reduction in it occurs. Or as if we were asleep somewhere when the Cold War ended and don't know yet that it occurred. If we let this happen, then we become strangely akin to those characters in the government who, for their own quite different reasons, in effect deny that the Cold War is over or invent new terrors for the world to fear, rogue states and so forth.

So two approaches are possible. One is to claim that nothing has changed, or that things have gotten worse. That is to try to go on to frighten people into action. The other is to fully acknowledge, that by some miracle we have, through the end of the Cold War, got half way to our goal, and that our responsibility now is to take the logical next step, which is abolition. And that second path seems to me the right one.

We have to awaken people all over again. But this time we must awaken them to hope, not to terror. This is something new for those who oppose nuclear weapons. It is uncharted territory. This is new work for our intellects, but also for our imaginations and our hearts, and above all, for our practical capacity for action. Fear is indeed inherent in the nuclear dilemma, but there is a wisdom in the old saying, "Do not take counsel of your fears." Feeling hope, we can give hope. Full of confidence, we can inspire confidence. Moved by love, love of the life we seek to preserve, we can move others to that same love. We can stand on the solid ground of faith, not the trembling, uncertain ground of fear.

Heaven knows, the aching world is full of sorrow, with starvation that is present and real, not merely potential, like nuclear danger, with violence, insult and wrong that are happening today, as they happened yesterday and will happen tomorrow. I know that ridding the world of nuclear weapons will not vanish these things from the earth. At the same time, though, I don't know how we can even begin to make sense of our world, either in our thoughts or in our deeds, if, now that the Cold War is over, we permit this universal peril to persist. We can heal the split world. The gate is open. Let us walk through. Thank you.

LYUTHA AL-MUGHAIRY: Thank you very much, Mr. Schell. We will now take your questions., Mr. Dhanapala first, since he has another commitment...

JOHN LINEWEAVER, Fellowship of Reconciliation: My question is in the area of psychology and philosophy...When I was a child there was a War Department, and they changed it to the Department of Defense...Nuclear missiles are called Peacekeepers...The UN Department for Disarmament Affairs should be renamed...Changing the name to prevention, to inspection, or security for justice and peace, would be an important change...

JAYANTHA DHANAPALA: We can certainly examine it, but I think we have had over the centuries a number of accumulated ideas on this question. Firstly there are the ancient words, "Civis pacem, para bello." In other words, to prepare for war as a deterrent in order to achieve peace, has long been a practice of states. I would like it to change into "civis pacem, para pacem."

But we need to have an attitudinal change that is very widespread. As long as Article 51 remains in the Charter, providing member states with a right to self-defense, and the right to self-defense using arms, we will continue to have nation states, with the sole exception perhaps of Costa Rica, having standing armies in order to protect their national security and their sovereignty. What we must do is to have some kind of regulation of arms, arms that will not be used as a projection of force beyond the national borders of countries, arms that can only be used for the protection of citizens in the normal civilized governments of countries. We need, as you quite rightly say, to change the language of discourse with regard to peace and security. We need to insure that a new culture of peace is created. This will take time, and I believe that while your suggestion is certainly well-intentioned, we need disarmament, we need to reduce the level of arms, and we need to have international peace and security at the lowest possible level of arms. That will continue to be the immediate objective.

ALYN WARE, Lawyers Committee on Nuclear Policy: Ambassador Dhanapala, I would like to thank you for raising the example of Costa Rica. I believe there are 23 countries that don't have standing armies. My questions have to do with treaty negotiations this year that you didn't mention. First, on the draft convention on nuclear terrorism. I believe that this convention will only apply to non-state actors. Given that the International Court of Justice decision made no distinction between the threat or use of nuclear weapons between state actors and non-state actors, is this an appropriate path to follow, to just condemn nuclear terrorism by non-state actors in this draft convention, and is the Department playing any role in this? Another negotiation taking place this year is on the statute for an International Criminal Court. There is a proposal from Germany and other NATO states that the use of chemical weapons, biological weapons and dum dum bullets be criminalized, but not the use of nuclear weapons or land mines. I am wondering if the Department is playing a role in that. The final question is in regard to Resolution 52/38 O, the resolution following up the ICJ Opinion. It requests member states to make a report to the Secretary-General on the implementation of this resolution and progress towards nuclear disarmament. Is the Department playing any role in encouraging states to make reports, and the follow-up report on this?

JAYANTHA DHANAPALA: On the question of the draft convention on terrorism. this was an initiative that arose in the Sixth Committee, the Legal Committee, as you know. It is a continuation of the work that this Committee has been doing with regard to the convention on terrorist bombings. We are present at these discussions, but as you know, the main impetus comes from a different department. We will certainly be present and convey our advice from time to time. The Advisory Opinion of the ICJ, as you know, is an Advisory Opinion. While there may be differences of opinion among international jurists as to what weight it has, or whether it in fact constitutes international law, or whether it is part of the body of practices and opinions that are influential but are not necessarily mandatory, without going into that debate, I would imagine that there would be some concern about extending the convention to member states because the thrust has been to address non-state actors in the context of terrorism.

On the statute of the Criminal Court, you know discussions were concluded at the end of last week. The question of whether or not nuclear weapons could be included as a crime against humanity, again, is very much a question for the member states to decide. We have a CWC and a BWC which explicitly bans those categories of weapons of mass destruction. We do not as yet have a convention banning nuclear weapons. The NPT refers only to the non-proliferation, both vertical and horizontal, of nuclear weapons but it does not specifically ban nuclear weapons. So there is no treaty regime yet which would be comparable to the CWC and the BWC. Until that is achieved I would imagine a criminal court would find it difficult to include nuclear weapons.

The Advisory Opinion and the follow-up: Yes we will be receiving the views of Member States and when they are received we will compile them and present them at the next General Assembly session.

ROGER SMITH, NGO Committee on Disarmament: ...I would like you to elaborate on your comment that the NPT Review process has not arrived at its full potential. Are you foreseeing the possibility that under the NPT process substantive negotiations would take place, either in intercessional bodies, or in a special session of NPT States Parties, or do you have something else in mind? My second question has to do with depleted uranium weaponry, which creates a sort of hybrid between conventional weaponry and nuclear weaponry. It was used in the Gulf War to a huge extent. We have just heard that NATO forces employed depleted uranium ammunition in Bosnia as well, irradiating the battlefields and causing symptoms of radiation poisoning to both combatants and civilians. So far depleted uranium weapons are having a difficult time entering the UN process. A sub-commission of the Human Rights Commission has included them in their study on indiscriminate weaponry. Do you have a suggestion how this issue might arrive on the UN agenda?

JAYANTHA DHANAPALA: On the first, I was not suggesting that the full potential of the NPT review process had not yet been realized. I was expressing the hope that we would be able to make use of the preparatory process in order to insure that the strengthened review process really was in fact utilized by all member states. We have only had the first preparatory committee meeting in April of last year. So the process has only just begun. There is no way in which the process could be prevented from reaching its full potential. I believe that already consultations are going on between the Chairman of the second PrepCom and member states in order to insure that there will be a full discussion on the substantive issues. This is what distinguishes the review process from previous review processes. It will no longer be a purely procedural preparatory committee but will be discussing substantive issues. There was an exchange of views last year. I think that there will be a full exchange of views and an attempt to formulate recommendations which will go to the 2000 review conference in some kind of a rolling document which will contain all the recommendations of the PrepComs.

On depleted uranium weaponry: I have seen the reports that you refer to. I imagine that the way in which it could be brought into the UN process would be to have a resolution in the General Assembly. If there are member states sufficiently concerned about this issue, who have evidence of its effects, this could be a subject for discussion in the First Committee.

NANCY COLTON, International Association for Volunteer Effort: ...Could thr Department for Disarmament Affairs be involved in regional Middle East security and disarmament issues?

JAYANTHA DHANAPALA: Regional disarmament is a very important area of our work. In the restructuring of my department I have in mind the establishment of a regional disarmament branch which will not only coordinate the activities of our Lima, Lome and Kathmandu regional Centres for Peace and Disarmament but will also monitor developments in all regions of the world, exploring what fresh initiatives can be taken and exploring how the experiences of one region could possibly be used in another region, mutatis mutandis.

I think it is important, in the context of the Middle East, to remember that we have a proposal for a zone free of weapons of mass destruction that was made some time ago by the President of Egypt. Studies called for by General Assembly resolutions have focused on confidence-building measures in the Middle East and the achievement of this zone and been the subject of much discussion. We are also aware that in Resolution 687 of the Security Council with regard to Iraq there is a specific mention of a zone free of weapons of mass destruction in the Middle East. These subjects are very much on the discussion table and will be pursued at the appropriate time.

QUESTIONER: How do we deal with the arms industry and weapons contracts?

JONATHAN SCHELL: Weapons contracts are an important fact of life. I do not believe that they will be decisive, especially in view of the fact that the expenditure on nuclear weapons is far less than that for conventional weapons...The people who are earning their livelihood by it defend it. My point is that we need to win the substantive argument and the substantive argument for abolition is incomparably stronger today in the aftermath of the Cold War than it was during the Cold War. Poll after poll has shown that the public supports abolishing nuclear weapons by percentages like 87% in the United States and England and in Canada the figure is 93%. I don't imagine that the public is very fervent about this now. I think a movement is only just beginning to draw public attention to this question, but it definitely shows that there is no great obstacle in public opinion. If there is one thing that politicians are responsive to in a democracy it is public opinion...They are elected, or not elected, according to whether they pay attention to it. I think there are reasons for hope, even though you are quite right to point out the weapons contracts and the influence of the industries is a very powerful one. It need not be decisive.

ANN LEGGETT, Federation of American-Arab Organizations: My organization objects to the use of the term rogue states...Basically it means countries that the US doesn't like. It further means, disarm the natives, but let the white folks keep theirs...Shouldn't this term be dropped?

JONATHAN SCHELL: Yes.I hope you detected that I used it ironically and in quotation marks.

JERRY SPIVACK, CCCUN: You have made me rethink the words "Cold War." I believe, in fact, that it did not end. The Cold War really represented the ability of peoples to destroy one another, using nuclear bombs. The mere fact that you change governments in Russia and that we say we are friends is a peculiar way of saying we have ended the Cold War when all of humanity is in fact still faced with this. When we were about to go to war with Iraq one of the things that was said in this country was that if they were to do anything with biological weapons we would consider hitting them with nuclear weapons...The mere fact that we have nuclear weapons and there is no willingness on the part of any of these great countries to give up nuclear weapons really puts us in the same situation as we have always been during the Cold War...Do you agree?

171

JONATHAN SCHELL: There is among governments a definite desire, whether it is habit or conviction or a deeply ingrained belief, I don't know, to hold on to these weapons. Among the public I think it is a different matter. For the public in the US the Cold War was real, and it is over. I think that lays the basis for a very important shift in public opinion, whatever the governments may be doing, and the task now is to bring that public opinion to the surface, to organize it, to bring pressure to bear on the governments to take the next step, which I think is to get rid of nuclear weapons.

KATHY UHLER, Franciscans International: ...It seems to me the right of self-defense is not an absolute right, whether it has to do with the individual, or a country. I wonder if you agree and if you would develop that type of argumentation in terms of abolishing nuclear weapons.

JONATHAN SCHELL: If by saying the right of self-defense is not absolute, you mean that it certainly should not include endangering hundreds of millions of people, I emphatically would agree. There is a sort of bitter irony in using that term, even if you accepted its validity when speaking of a doctrine such as Mutual Assuring Destruction which actually envisions and depends upon a threat of the annihilation of one's own country. Whatever validity it has in fields other than the nuclear, it certainly has very little in this very paradoxical strange world that is created by the presence of nuclear weapons. But your question is a deep one, and I don't think I have done justice to it. I would like to take it up with you some time.

QUESTIONER, Soka Gakkai International, Japan: I am sure you are aware that there is a global campaign called Abolition 2000. We have over 13 million signatures for abolition. Outside Canada, the US and the UK there is a feeling about the opportunity that exists in civil society.

JONATHAN SCHELL: I think it is tremendous, and the kind of effort that you described is the sort of thing we need. In the United States a conviction has settled in, and it runs rather deep in official circles, that it is impossible to get rid of nuclear weapons. That somebody would cheat. That it cannot be done, or should not be done, even if it can be. This runs very deep. It is connected with the deterrence doctrine which in this country has gained such a deep grip on the official mind. However, it is perfectly obvious that there are some 180 countries who have foresworn nuclear weapons. Far from thinking it is impossible to do without them, they have sworn to do without then. And so opinion in those countries would be warmly supportive, I would imagine, of this goal, since they too are at risk. The potential is tremendous, if it can be galvanized, and that is the work ahead of us.

PETER DAVIES, Oxfam International, A Saferworld and Peace Action: Congresswoman Woolsey has introduced in the US Congress a resolution regarding the Stockpile Stewardship Management Program on sub-critical testing of nuclear weapons. One portion reads "Whereas the proposed Stockpile Stewardship Program is provocative to both nuclear weapon states and non-nuclear weapon states, and it runs counter to the obligations of the treaty on the Non-Proliferation of Nuclear Weapons to pursue negotiations in good faith on cessation of the nuclear arms race and nuclear disarmament..." It proposes that sub-critical tests should not be conducted. I wonder if you would comment on the US nuclear position that somehow it is OK, despite the NPT, to, in effect, continue to upgrade and test higher forms of nuclear weapons.

JONATHAN SCHELL: ...I think what we have is an example of a kind of pork barrel legislation. In my judgement that program is chiefly a political one to buy off opposition from the weapons labs and the weapons community to the test ban. I think it should be opposed.

MIRANDA SESSIONS, The 1999 Hague Appeal for Peace: We agree very much with the vision you hold up. In the civil society process that we are trying to organize, which is to galvanize both governments and non-governmental organizations on humanitarian law, against nuclear weapons and other weapons, with a series of conference, what are the main opportunities, the main norms, the points that we could push? How would you concretize the agenda at an international level? Can you give us one or two suggestions of the critical issues to be pursued?

JONATHAN SCHELL: Yes. I won't surprise you very much. By way of preface, I want to emphasize again that radical newness of our situation, the fact that the path is clear to move ahead in the post-Cold War environment. I don't think we have woken up to this fully, and I don't think we have awakened the public to the fact that something really wonderful can be done. It is a radically new fact and we should go for that opportunity.

What it comes to specific steps, I would join very enthusiastically many that have been offered. My favorite one is de-alerting, because I think you get a real measure of safety through de-alerting, a real increase in safety in very short order. Secondly, it involves all nuclear weapon states, immediately. It gets away from this bilateral business. I would also favor the speeding up, the continuation of cuts. There are many other things I would mention. I think you could make your own list. A fissile material cut-off ban, transparency, nuclear-weapon-free zones...I was talking to Jonathan Dean earlier. Sometimes an argument breaks out between those who are supporting these more limited measures and those who want abolition. To me this is absurd. If you have a goal you can't get there without steps. When you get to the top of the stairs, but on the other hand, if you don't have a goal, you don't know where your steps are going, so it is just obvious to me that both of these things are needed and there should be no argument between the two schools.

TOM MASON: I represent probably the most unpopular NGO in the UN, the National Rifle Association. It is interesting listening to a former writer for the New Yorker speak to an extremely liberal group. I spend most of my time out in the hinterlands where this is not a burning topic. How do you intend to get out to the First Congressional District in places like Oregon, where I live, where this is not a burning issue?

JONATHAN SCHELL: All the instruments of democracy lie open to us. It has been done before, if we speak of the United States. The freeze movement got out there. It achieved great popularity among the public at large and I think had a decisive impact on policy and was very instrumental and important in the whole turn around that happened around 1985. Again, I don't have anything magical to offer. I will note that a campaign is beginning in New England, in Maine and Vermont where I am going to visit in May to bring the question of abolition to town meetings, just as once before the freeze was brought to town meetings. This was very effective politically. You can't determine what other people are going to think. You just have to go out there and offer it to them and hope for the best reaction you can get. If you don't run anything up the flagpole there is nothing to salute, so that is what we are about.

LYUTHA AL-MUGHAIRY: Our thanks to all of you.

GLOBAL ACTION TO PREVENT WAR: HOW TO PREVENT FUTURE KOSOVOS AND RWANDAS

PAUL HOEFFEL, new Director of the NGO section of the UN Department of Public Information: I am turning over this morning's briefing to Ann Lakhdhir, who has been representing the Institute for Defense and Disarmament Studies at the UN for more than 15 years. She is the Vice President for Program for the NGO Committee on Disarmament, which is cosponsoring this morning's briefing.

ANN HALLAN LAKHDHIR: Thanks, Paul. Many of you heard Randall Forsberg and Jonathan Dean several months ago when they talked about this program, so to some extent this morning will be an update on what has happened since then and a plea for all of you to get involved. The new version of the program was put on the IDDS Internet site yesterday. I would recommend those of you who have a computer to access the web site, which is global action at www.idds.org.

Randall Forsberg will be the first speaker. She is the Executive Director of the Institute for Defense and Disarmament Studies, a research organization in Cambridge, Massachusetts. Her Institute has done a great deal of work both on nuclear and conventional weapons. Jonathan Dean is the arms control advisor for the Union of Concerned Scientists. His background includes many years in the US diplomatic corps, with postings in many different areas, but I think most relevant to the proposals for reducing conventional arms is his past role as the head of the US delegation for many years in the Mutual and Balanced Force Reduction talks.

The UN Disarmament Commission began meeting on Monday this week, and will conclude on April 30. There are three Working Groups. The three topics are nuclear-weapon-free zones, conventional weapons, and finally deciding the timing and agenda of a fourth Special Session on Disarmament. The topic on conventional weapons is focused on small arms. Our two speakers this morning are going to be talking about a much broader range of conventional weapons. I think our topic fits into what might be on the agenda of a fourth Special Session on Disarmament, both its program for reducing conventional weapons and its suggestions for strengthening the UN role. The Indian delegate in the Disarmament Commission said that no military action such as the bombing over Kosovo should be taken without the approval of the Security Council, and that this topic should be before the fourth Special Session on Disarmament. I now turn this over to Randall Forsberg.

RANDALL FORSBERG: We are looking at issues of war and peace from a large-scale, long-term point of view. If we stand back, I think that there is a good news-bad news story. There is some good news. First, there is the end of the Cold War. Secondly, there have been really huge cuts in the arsenals of nuclear weapons in the United States and Russia, at least in terms of pulling the warheads off weapons and putting them back in a storage area if not actually dismantling them. From an even longer term point of view, the world has moved beyond world wars, or great power wars, in which the most heavily armed countries fight with each other in order to seize control of each other's territory and build empires. So there is a decline in the nature of war, the form which we can expect it to take, and central to that is the decline in the acceptance or tolerance of war.

The bad news is that, on average, over half a million people a year have been killed in war since World War II, so we are far from ending war even though we seem to have ended one very terrible form of war. The resources allocated to the military have declined, but they are still huge, especially in the United States. Now, for the first time since the end of the Cold War, it looks as though the US is heading toward real increases after inflation in military spending. The level of spending on the military today is the same as it was from the end of the Korean War until Reagan. The resources allocated to the military are also very large in many third world countries that desperately need these resources for other ends. They are substantial in Europe, in China, and other places. The production and trade of major weapons systems - tanks, aircraft, ships and missiles - continues, even though there is no prospect of their being used on a large scale.

It goes on throughout the world, but particularly in the United States and Western Europe, which are competing to export these systems to third world countries, particularly countries in regions of conflict, where there is a greater risk of a major war. They are being sold to Greece and Turkey, who both receive weapons from the United States and other NATO countries, which they acquire primarily to deter and threaten each other. In the Middle East, they are being sold to Syria, Iran, Israel, Egypt and Saudi Arabia; in Asia, to India and Pakistan, South Korea, Taiwan and China. These countries are involved in long-standing regional conflicts which have involved wars and which involve the prospect of involving wars on a large scale. They account for more than two-thirds of the world trade in armaments, so all the arms that we are producing and exporting in this country are going primarily to countries where there is the greatest risk of use.

Associated with these continued high levels of military spending in regions of conflict, and in some industrial arms-producing countries, notably the US, is the spread of weapons of mass destruction. All of the countries which have acquired nuclear weapons since the end of World War II, starting with the United States and the former Soviet Union, are countries with very large, costly, standing conventional armed forces. Nuclear weapons have been acquired as a deterrent, not to nuclear war, but to non-nuclear war, because we have not found effective international means of preventing war in a reliable way. So, following the industrial countries, India, Pakistan, China at an earlier period, Israel, potentially Iran, potentially North Korea, are the proliferating countries - the same countries that are the big importers of conventional weapons.

And there are potential new threats. It is possible, if things continue as they are now, that over the next several decades China is likely to become a major military power, in terms of conventional navy, army and air force capabilities, and possibly also additional nuclear weapons capabilities. The likelihood of rivalries and military arms races and militarized confrontation between China, Japan, Russia, Taiwan, the United States, in a new theater of conflict that resembles Europe, shifted to the Pacific, is very great, if we continue as we are.

Finally, all of this is associated with an archaic approach to military security, to threats of war, which stresses reliance on individual nation-states, individual governments, national means of deterring and defending against war and looking after national interests, rather than on the United Nations system, on international cooperation and international organizations. This continued reliance on primarily national means undermines the rule of law in the international system. It sets precedents, which encourage actions like Iraq's invasion of Kuwait, because the great powers are constantly looking out for their own vital national interests when they justify the use of force internationally. They do not refer to the rule of law, the body of international law, the critical importance of establishing non-partisan, non-self-interested standards of behavior within and among countries, of limiting the use of force to enforcing these standards - defending against aggression, and stopping and preventing genocidal internal violence. This archaic approach to security also blocks and undermines the spread of democratic institutions, which ultimately must be the foundation for a peaceful and thriving international system.

Global Action to Prevent War is a response to this bad news. It represents an effort to use the highly limited resources of those who are deeply concerned with this problem in a more effective way, by working together more effectively. It focuses on what we can do together, which we can't do separately as organizations, as bodies within countries, even when represented among transnational and international organizations. What we could do far more effectively than we have is to share priorities, coordinate actions, and lend mutual support to each other in working for a very different kind of future. The future that we are looking for in Global Action to Prevent War, the end-point, is something we can't describe, because none of us knows how the world could conceivably evolve. But we can conceive of a desirable future world that we would like to head toward, contrast it with the one we are living in, and think in a reasonable, clear, way about what would have to happen to get from the world we are in to that alternative future.

The future that I have in mind lies, in Phase 5 as we describe it, beyond the end of our plan. It is a future in which countries have nothing more than something like the Coast Guard, and the United Nations has a police force, and that is it. There is no war, there is no threat of war, there are no resources allocated to the military, a very, very, different world.

What would have to happen to get to that world? How could we possibly be working more effectively in a concerted way to move in that direction? The Global Action plan groups together priorities for change into four phases:

- Strengthen institutions and mechanisms for conflict prevention, for preventing conflicts from turning into armed conflicts, and build confidence in those mechanisms

- Then reduce armed forces.
- Then another period of strengthening institutions and building confidence.
- Then reduce armed forces further.

What this four-phased plan does is to bring together different components, advocated by many of the organizations in this room, that are necessary and important to move toward a long-term demilitarized peace. They are currently pursued separately, independently, without coordination, without thinking about how they might fit into a larger program that would have the support, in terms of popular support of numbers of people, but also the concepts and the mechanisms to actually lead, step by step, toward that future.

These many different components include reform of the United Nations and the strengthening and reform of universal membership regional security organizations that are counterparts to the UN security organizations. The prime example today of such a regional security organization is the Organization for Security and Cooperation in Europe, the OSCE. The regional security organizations should resemble the UN. Every country in a given region should be a member of the organization, and actions should not be taken with respect to a country when that country is not a member and does not have a voice, does not have a vote, does not have an ongoing relationship. (The action that has been taken against Yugoslavia by NATO, a security alliance, would not be permitted.).

So we advocate reliance on the United Nations and on regional security organizations in which all of those involved have a voice and have a role. We advocate reform of the United Nations, reform of the Security Council and of the regional organizations, so that they can be both impartial and nonpartisan, not loaded in favor of one side or another. They must also become effective, and not have their hands tied so they end up doing nothing in situations of crisis where rapid action is needed to prevent an impending disaster of human violence before it actually happens.

A second element is strengthening conflict-resolution and conflict-prevention institutions, mechanisms and skills, reliance on them and awareness of them. There are many organizations today that are working on nonviolent conflict resolution in one form or another. Generally speaking, both non-governmental organizations and governmental organizations work in complete isolation from the people who are working on disarmament, military confidence building, arms reductions in the regions concerned, and the reform of the international institutions that would be the ones to take responsibility for conflict prevention and rapid intervention.

We need to have available the skills for early warning of conflict. We need to be aware when a situation is moving toward violence. We need to have people in place, at the disposal of the Secretary-General. We should have a standing mediation corps, not individual diplomats who are called on in an ad hoc way, but a corps of trained people familiar with the regions, the regional problems and special regional issues. They should be experienced in many different mechanisms of diplomatic intervention and mediation, ready to go in at a moment's notice. We should have a humanitarian corps who are ready to go in and help, human rights monitors who are ready and experienced in monitoring adherence to the human rights conventions that most countries have already signed which include provisions for monitoring and for compliance but which are currently not being implemented. There are no demands for implementation, no awareness of the need.

Another major area is the reduction in standing conventional armed forces and the production and trade of major weapons systems, as well as in small arms and land mines. The standing armed forces that exist today, as I have underscored before and will stress again and again, account for well over 95% of world military spending, probably closer to 98 or 99%. Weapons of mass destruction, while individually costly, account for a tiny fraction of military spending. We cannot make the deep cuts in the resources allocated to the military even if we completely eliminated all weapons of mass destruction. The only way to make deep cuts in the resources of the military is to make deep cuts in conventional military forces, in armies, navies and air forces, and to make deep cuts in the arms industries, in the arms production, the arms trade. We must cut the armed forces and the arms industries, the whole shebang. How do we cut these? .

Why didn't they decline at the end of the Cold War all by themselves? One of the pivotal reasons, critical in terms of creating political will, is that the United States, and other countries in Europe and throughout the world, following the lead of the United States, continue to rely on an archaic concept of security. It is a concept of security that involves maintaining armed forces that have the capability to intervene in virtually any armed conflict anywhere in the world, and to prevail, in the sense of being able to destroy everything from the air, in a matter of a few weeks. That does not mean prevailing politically, as we have seen.

Militarily, the United States has arrogated to itself military decisions, and the European members of NATO are supporting the United States in this role. Indeed they are happy to allow the

United States to use its own resources and its own political capital. They prefer not to be put in the position of having to do so themselves, to make the decision when the use of force by the international community is warranted for the purposes of defending against aggression or preventing or ending genocide. The United States has taken it upon itself to do this, and to maintain armed forces that are capable of doing this anywhere in the world and in several places simultaneously, without any loss of life on the part of the US.

That is the ostensible political reason for the scale of military spending in the US. We have miniature versions of this approach to security in those regional armed conflicts where, instead of cooperating for a secure and reliable defense, countries are involved in armed competition to beat each other, to be superior, to be able to prevail in a war. Cutting conventional forces and cutting military spending means ending reliance on exclusively national means of defending against aggression and preventing genocide. Instead, it means turning toward nonpartisan, just, multilateral deterrence and defense, when necessary, and establishing norms against genocide and ethnic conflict, and defending against those when they occur.

Why is transfer to this view of security so critical? Because if many nations are involved in doing this together, then each nation can put fewer resources into the military. Then then they are not arming against each other, they are arming only to the extent that is jointly needed to deter against defection of a country or a leader. If countries have made a commitment to global security, to global peace, to the global absence of armed violence, then it follows from that commitment that they all benefit from the lowering of the levels of armament. The fewer national armed forces that are out there, that are not part of the multilateral peacekeeping capability, the less risk there is that there will be a major armed conflict. And the smaller the scale of the conflict, if it occurs, smaller the forces required to deter such a conflict and to intervene to end it.

What we propose in this plan is the strengthening of the capabilities of the United Nations and regional organizations, building on the many good existing conventions and treaties, the dimensions of international law, and many aspects of the UN Charter that exist that are being ignored. We propose to strengthen these, to give them more clout, to make them more meaningful. The global agreements on human rights, the capability of the International Court of Justice to be used by nations to resolve disputes between them that could otherwise lead to armed conflict, the establishment of an International Criminal Court, the UN readiness brigades, post conflict measures and the diplomatic intervention capabilities are all good existing beginnings.

What can and should be done as soon as possible in the first phase is to improve on these by creating regional counterparts to the UN in all parts of the world where they do not exist and then by strengthening, in both the UN and the regional organizations, conflict early warning capabilities, and by creating a professional mediation corps and a pool of civilian police or readiness brigades which can move in very rapidly when situations like that in Kosovo are obviously evolving. We need to have countries make participation in the mediation corps and the humanitarian aid corps alternatives to military conscription. We need to strengthen the existing human rights convention by establishing a code of minority rights, to insure that any treaties that countries sign include a provision that if there are disputes about what is going on under the treaty, they must be referred to the International Court before any other action is taken. We must begin to make the International Court and the idea of adjudication central to the rule of law.

We need to have the UN be much more pro-active in intervening at an early stage in conflicts before they become armed conflicts by having human rights monitors. We need to take steps such as warning and advising governments that they are moving in a direction which will require international intervention if things keep going the way they are.

We need to increase the impartiality of the UN, possibly by expanding the membership of the Security Council or perhaps, more importantly, by restricting the use of the veto to what it actually says in the UN Charter, to threats to the territorial integrity of the countries which have the veto power. So if the Security Council is about to send forces into Russia, Russia could veto that. But there would be no other use of the veto. This is a reform that is already part of international law that is being ignored and not pressed for. *(Wonder what you mean here. AHL)*These are only a few examples of ways of strengthening conflict prevention and early conflict resolution capabilities of international institutions.

In the second phase, our stress is on an initial round of confidence-building reductions in armed forces which is prorated so that the countries with the biggest forces, the US, Russia and China, cut by a third, the next group of countries, Britain, France, Japan, cut by a quarter, and all other countries cut by 15%.

In the third phase, having done more to strengthen international institutions and having made these initial cuts, what we would do is have a trial period of relying exclusively on UN and regional security organizations for multilateral action for intervention to respond to cross-border aggression or internal, genocidal violence.

In the fourth phase we would have another round of cuts like those in the second: a third, a quarter or 15% in the armed forces. They are no longer needed because the capability of the international system and confidence in the international system to deter and defend against threats have been so greatly strengthened.

The idea that deep cuts could be made in standing conventional forces and in the conventional arms production and trade relies entirely on transferring that sense of responsibility and authority for action in the event of violence from individual nation states to the UN and its regional counterparts. This is why we need a concerted action that brings together the human rights components, the conflict resolution and prevention components and the international institutions and disarmament into a single coordinated campaign. Thank you.

JONATHAN DEAN: I would like to discuss with you what the Global Action to Prevent War program could have done in helping to prevent the Kosovo crisis, what contribution it might still make to a solution there, and what it could do to prevent future Kosovos and Rwandas. This is a practical way of reviewing the content of Global Action to Prevent War as it deals with preventing internal conflict and of eliciting your suggestions to improve the project.

The purpose of Global Action in crises like Kosovo is to enhance the capabilities for conflict prevention of the UN, regional security organizations, the international judicial system and human rights institutions, as well as of NGOs, and to bring them all more fully into an active conflict prevention role. To do this, we envision fifteen or sixteen individual measures, which I would like to describe briefly. Please bear in mind that it is unlikely that any of these measures alone could have decisive effect. They have to act together.

(1) For countries that have already signed human rights covenants, Global Action foresees a treaty commitment to admit official human rights monitors immediately on request to the host country and to facilitate their visits. We know that acute Serb abuse of the Kosovars has been going on for at least ten years since Milosevic revoked the autonomy of Kosovo in 1989. Yugoslavia is a signatory of the Universal Declaration of Human Rights, of the International Covenant on Civil and Political Rights, and many other human rights covenants. Many of these covenants and treaties do have provisions for compliance and inspection. These are very often ignored in practice. They have been violated by the Serb authorities.

The Organization for Security and Cooperation in Europe has an agreed but complicated procedure for admitting human rights observers even when the host government is reluctant. I do not believe it has ever been invoked. What we are proposing here is a worldwide commitment that will make entry of monitors to check compliance with existing human rights commitments a right. If human rights monitors had visited Kosovo early to investigate abuses there and immediately publicized their findings, reporting them to the UN High Commissioner for Human Rights, to the international courts, and to the Security Council, and had done this repeatedly, this would have inhibited Milosevic. Many NGOs and diplomatic observers were in Kosovo, and reported a remarkable campaign of nonviolent resistance by the Kosovars, but their reports did not get action out of Western governments.

Remember that the explicit standard for existing human rights covenants is that the status of human rights within a given country is not solely a matter of national sovereignty, but a legitimate interest of the international community.

(2) Another of our measures, an international treaty on minority rights, could have had even more effect. This treaty would have promoted Kosovar autonomy and protected that autonomy, once granted, against arbitrary change. And its terms would have given the Kosovars status to complain to the international community and places to lodge these complaints: the UN Human Rights Commission, the International Court of Justice, in future, the International Criminal Court, and ultimately, the Security Council.

(3) We would back this treaty on minority protection by a commitment to teach non-violent conflict prevention and productive intergroup relations in every participating country at every level of education.

(4) Global Action foresees the establishment of a professional mediator corps of the UN, with counterparts in regional security organizations.

(5) To feed into these positions and to provide the trained peacekeepers I will mention later, we also propose that, in UN member states, service in mediation, humanitarian aid, and peacekeeping be an accepted alternative to military conscription. Where armed forces are professional and there is no conscription, we ask governments to set up a career public service in these fields and to place these practitioners in senior government positions.

(6) We foresee that the trained mediation professionals at the UN, at the disposal of the Secretary

General and Security Council, would collect and analyze information about potential trouble spots and also about proven methods of conflict prevention. They would be sent out individually or in small teams to areas where conflict might develop. Their status would be protected and all UN member states would be committed to receiving them on their territory and facilitating their stay.

Small teams of professional mediators could stay on site for months, becoming acquainted with the local population, working with local and foreign NGOs, trying to bring hostile groups together, proposing solutions, investigating incidents and, if helpful, making their findings publicly known. The OSCE (Organization for Security and Cooperation in Europe} already does valuable work of this kind. Our proposal is that the work be intensified and be carried out by trained professionals with a reputation for institutional neutrality rather than by OSCE member state diplomats. Today, the Secretary General sends out small missions of this kind, but he has neither permanent professional personnel nor adequate funds for this function. These professional mediators in the field could warn UN Headquarters if there is a real possibility of armed violence.

(7) They could also alert the Conflict Mediation Panel of the General Assembly that we propose. This open-ended committee of General Assembly members would be a less formal, more flexible conflict prevention group than the Security Council. It would not be subject to the veto and could set its own agenda by majority vote.

In this case, the General Assembly Conflict Mediation Panel would send a team to Kosovo composed of UN representatives from various countries and it would hold on-site hearings, publicizing them if it seems desirable. In the Panel's sessions in New York, as many as possible of them public sessions, it would invite Kosovars and the Yugoslav diplomatic representatives, and perhaps some Serb officials, to tell their story, and to listen to the Panel's advice on what to do.

It would be the obligation of this Panel to give the UN and the world public comprehensive, balanced information on the disputed issue and to propose possible solutions.

One of the big problems in conflicts like that in Rwanda and Kosovo is that, although government officials are often aware of these conflicts at an early stage, they do not publicize their reports and media coverage in these early stages is often sporadic. As a result, the conflicts often hit an unprepared world opinion only when they are at an advanced state and organized killing has already begun. To give civil society a chance to do its job, it has to be brought in early. The same goes for governments in other areas and for national legislatures that may have to decide on aid, sanctions, or peacekeeping operations. The work of the professional mediators and of the Conflict Prevention Panel would alert the international community, along with NGO's and the public in major UN member states, to the Kosovo problem. The media would intensify its coverage of Kosovo, and the political opposition in Yugoslavia would have grounds early on to question the actions of their government.

(8) A main feature of our proposal is a reformed Security Council, expanded in membership and restricted in use of the veto through an informal understanding among the permanent members of the Security Council. We suggest that this reformed Security Council should make a deliberate decision to undertake a highly pro-active role in conflict prevention and should make the commitments in professional backup and financing needed to carry out this role.

In the Kosovo case, backed by information from the Mediation Corps, whose personnel would serve the Council as professional staff for this program, and by information from the General Assembly's Conflict Mediation Panel, the Security Council would invite the Yugoslav government to appear before it in a series of hearings to explain its policy in Kosovo.

The Council would present the reasons for its own concern over the situation. It would give its advice to the Yugoslav government on treatment of the Kosovars and offer its assistance, both in personnel and money, to carry out this advice.

If the problem continued, the Council would invite the Yugoslav government to appear before it again and would warn it of the probable future consequences of its anti-Kosovar practices, and would point out to the Yugoslav government and the world public that the problem in Kosovo was becoming a threat to international security.

This activity by the Security Council would prepare the road to further Council action, including the possibility of full negative publicity, the use of emissaries to Yugoslavia's leaders, carefully selected economic sanctions, or peace enforcement. The international community would be alerted at each step.

(9) We believe the Security Council and the main UN member states should move step by step toward an agreed concept for humanitarian intervention based on the idea that governments are entrusted with stewardship of the welfare of their people, especially their human rights, and that when this stewardship is misused or abused in an extreme way, the international community should be prepared to intervene in some form. The Council would decide in the individual situation whether this is the case and what action should be taken. Actual practice of the Security Council is moving toward this concept. A clear statement of it would have advantages for member state governments and publics.

If the Security Council is blocked from action by vetoes, then resort should be made to the General Assembly by shifting action to the Conflict Mediation Panel or, in extreme cases, through the Uniting for Peace resolution. I should point out that these proposals for a General Assembly Conflict Mediation Panel, for a pro-active role for the Security Council, and for resort to the Uniting for Peace procedure are not future possibilities. They could be invoked today.

(10) Another proposal of Global Action is that the President of the General Assembly or his representative should participate in meetings of the Security Council to report on Assembly views and keep the Council engaged and accountable.

(11) This is a logical point to mention that the Global Action program foresees the establishment of universal membership regional security organizations in each major region, each with conflict prevention capability. When intervention is carried out by a regional security organization, the Security Council should give its approval.

We do not know the long term future of NATO. It may merge with OSCE or both may finally be absorbed into the European Union structure. But according to our approach, NATO's membership would have to become universal and NATO would have to recognize the authority of the Security Council.

(12) We propose in the Global Action program that all newly concluded treaties provide for referral of disputes to the International Court of Justice for adjudication, giving the court a more active role in conflict prevention. These activities need not be limited to interstate disputes: Under the minority rights treaty we propose, the UN Human Rights Commissioner and the Kosovar community in Yugoslavia would both have status to bring complaints to the Court.

(13) We also assume effective operation of an International Criminal Court and authority under its procedures for the Kosovars to inform the court's prosecutor at an early stage that abuses of their human rights are taking place. Effective operation of the Criminal Court will mean that the Court's existence and practices would have a deterrent effect on actions and practices like those of the Yugoslav government against the Kosovars. We believe other aspects of the Global Action program will also have deterrent effects.

(14) The Global Action program foresees the existence of full-time UN volunteer peacekeeping forces, a brigade in each major geographic region, with the capacity to call on member states for backup forces. These units would be financed by the proceeds of an international tax. If the Yugoslav government was prepared to accept the force, the Security Council could propose preventive deployment of this force in Kosovo, stating an emergency was beginning to emerge. If the Yugoslav government refused, the Council could call for further steps, including carefully articulated economic sanctions and the use of military force. In contrast to the present situation, these pre-financed peacekeeping troops would be ready to move on a few hours notice.

(15) They would be backed by a standing UN police force composed of volunteer personnel who could also take on the job of maintaining order in Kosovo. There are many occasions, including Kosovo, where inviting in a police force poses much less of a challenge to national sovereignty than an outside peacekeeping force and could therefore be more acceptable to the host country and to the Security Council. If either of these forces had already been available, they might have provided a vital component for a negotiated solution of the Kosovo problem.

In fact, I am proposing that a United Nations peacekeeping force be substituted for NATO troops as an international peacekeeping force for Kosovo. A proposal to do this could bring about earlier agreement to end the Kosovo crisis than may be achieved otherwise.

What about the question of political will? Would governments and institutions really act to give real effect to this institutionally-improved international security system?

We believe so. First, authority in the system we are describing would be widely dispersed. There would be many separate decisionmakers: NGOs, human rights officials, UN officials and representatives and governments. Above all, the potential victims themselves would have a much louder voice.

What about timely decisions by regional security institutions or the UN Security Council to send peacekeepers? The issue of political will might become critical at this point.

As regards the Security Council, I believe that the five permanent members, in their own self-interest of saving the Council from the oblivion it would otherwise suffer and of preserving their own international influence as members of a functioning Council, will ultimately agree informally among themselves to restrict use of the veto. This restriction could be very limited or general. Resort to the Conflict Mediation Panel of the General Assembly or to the Uniting for Peace procedure are possible alternatives.

Speaking more generally, when we raise the issue of political will, we are talking about education. A large part of what we call political will is learned behavior.

(16) The Global Action project includes an intense education program for political leaders at all levels, government officials, military officers and NGOs on recognition of the signs of possible conflict and the logic of determined early action to prevent conflict.

For Kosovo, we know the lesson already: the costs of failure to intervene early in the Kosovo crisis include the costs of the current NATO military campaign, the costs of caring for the refugees, the costs of an international force, the costs of rehabilitating Kosovo, as well as possibly Serbia, a total which will probably exceed $50 billion for all NATO countries for the next two years.

Governments do not like to take early action. By and large, they believe that most incipient crises will dissipate and that there will be no need to incur the political and economic costs of action to cope with them. That is one lesson from experience. The lesson is wrong in the field of internal conflict. Here, governments have to learn that when certain indicators are present, it is a necessity to pay for the insurance policy of early preventive action. Doing so will save more lives and be cheaper to pay these costs than to risk the heavy costs of waiting.

Using round figures, the maximum cost of applying all the measures proposed by Global Action for Kosovo and described in this paper would perhaps have been $300 or $400 million - excluding the standing peacekeeping brigades, $100 million - as contrasted to the loss of life and uprooting of thousands of lives and costs of at least $50 billion in the belated action now going on.

This lesson about the need to act early can in fact be learned. A whole generation of Westerners went through World War II and came out with one lesson: the danger of allowing the human and material resources of Europe to fall under hostile hegemony. Without real hesitation, they followed that lesson into the cold war. Debate during the cold war was mainly about the methods.

To cite another example, in the century between the end of the Napoleonic Wars and World War I, the British political class learned the lesson of early warning and early intervention and acted on these lessons scores of times. Sometimes the objective was laudable, sometimes not, but the point is that this kind of alertness can be learned.

That is the kind of political understanding and political will that must ultimately arise with regard to prevention of conflict. It must be part of the training of every NGO, legislator, diplomat, and soldier on the planet to recognize and react to these symptoms early on. It is a central part of the job of supporters of Global Action to help to carry out this educational task with their political leaders and government officials.

Let me draw a conclusion from these comments: This list of preventive measures is not and cannot be complete. We need the help of everyone who has ideas on this issue and of the many experienced workers in this field. Please give us your suggestions and help us make the Global Action approach better. Our argument is not that any single one of the 15 or 16 measures I have described today would have prevented the Kosovo disaster.

It is that, working together, these measures, combined with the widespread conviction that armed conflict can in fact be prevented, and combined with insistent pressure from civil society from all of us can be a powerful force in drastically reducing the outbreak of armed conflict and in preventing future Kosovos. This is what the United Nations and world civil society should be working on in its preparations for the agenda-setting Millennial forums next year and it is what the United Nations should be working on today.

RANDALL FORSBERG: I am going to focus on what you can do. Up until now we have been preparing, developing, trying to think through how to do this. We are now about ready to get going. We have set for ourselves a deadline at the time of the Hague Appeal for Peace that we will be participating in very actively in the Hague and afterwards. We are about to create a coalition. The title of our effort has been changed to "A Coalition-building effort to stop war, genocide and other forms of deadly conflict." I will describe very briefly different ways in which people could get involved.

First, we would like you to join Global Action to Prevent War, to become a member. What is really important is to get your organizations to become organizational members of this coalition, to see themselves as part of a larger coalition effort to prevent war and to define their tasks not as the single tasks of the organization, but to define your own agenda, to recognize it, to tell other people that this is part of a larger agenda that is shared of efforts to prevent war. To do that we need you to give our statement to the Board of Directors of your organizations, to send it out to members, to put news of this in your newsletters, to get people to talk about it, to think about it, to understand it. We need you to know it like the back of your hand so that you can persuade other people that this makes sense, that united we are going to be a lot stronger than we have been separately.

This is intended as an over-arching coalition, and we hope that you will want to join it and be part of it and that you will spread that message. Besides having your own organization involved, we would like you and your organizations to reach out to other organizations and get them to be involved. Among other things we think that this campaign has the potential to interest and engage organizations which are not traditional peace organizations, organizations that work in the area of development, humanitarian relief, environmental protection. All would benefit tremendously from the success of this program. If we could get those organizations on board, think about the combined political influence and outreach effectiveness of such a coalition. So we need your help in reaching out to organizations in those areas which are not traditionally involved, even though they are sympathetic to peace efforts, that don't see themselves as being directly involved.

We have two categories of membership. One is for people who do see themselves directly involved, either individual or organizational members. We have another category which we are calling affiliates. That is for organizations like the Red Cross, or a church, organizations which are in and of themselves peace organizations, but which want to be affiliated with Global Action to Prevent War. Contact us for as many copies of the program as you would like, and/or to join us.

As a coalition, we do not have a predetermined agenda. As many of you know, this document has been evolving. We are calling this the tenth version. It has been evolving over the last two years. It is designed as an open-ended document, open to input from new and old participants, and it will keep changing as the world changes and as the participants change. We want your input into program. We want your suggestions, your comments, things that we have left out. We want you to identify parts of the process of working for peace that we have overlooked so that we can add them. We want you to identify yourself in this program. One of the things we want to put up on the web is a list of those organizations which are working on each of the different pieces, so that people who want to be involved in working on a specific piece can see what their options are, in terms of where the organizations are located and what their particular orientation is.

Thirdly, we would like you to use the coalition. We are going to have a board on the Internet where you can post notices and we will also have a newsletter version of the same thing of actions and information and priorities. We are going to have a Council of Member Organizations and a Council of Affiliate Organizations which will be an environment in which you can meet with other people who see themselves as part of this effort to promote your initiatives and your priorities and try and see if other people will get on board. We would like you to use Global Action to get that additional outreach and visibility that the coalition is designed to bring.

Finally, there are no organizations that I know of which are working on large-scale conventional disarmament, which is a very central part of this plan for both Jonathan and me and was an important component in why we wanted to bring this about and launch it. We think that conventional disarmament is important. It is important to save resources, it is important to transfer the locus of authority, it is important to change peoples' view about the legitimate use of armed force, which should be never. If you are interested in getting involved in that component, or any other component of the program on which there is not currently an organization focusing and working effectively, we would be thrilled to have your support and help in trying to launch an education and outreach effort on those topics. Please let us hear from you by mail, by fax or E-mail. Our web site on the Internet is **www.globalactionpw.org** It can also be reached at globalaction@idds.org Our E-mail is **info@globalactionpw.org** Our telephone number is (617) 354-4337. Thank you.

Questions:

NANCY COLTON, International Association for Volunteer Effort: Regional human rights organizations and centers have been pushed by many on the Human Rights Commission for years. That has not taken place, but similar organizations to OSCE could be quite effective, as you have mentioned. Also regional military organizations could be involved in humanitarian efforts, environmental cleanups and disasters. This might bring nations together to work together, to depend on each other and lessen these terrible hatreds. You might also get all the CONGO NGO Committees to sign on to this, disarmament, development, human rights. The Human Rights Center has people who report on human rights offenses, and these often are behind the conflicts...

RANDALL FORSBERG: We hope you will help us involve the NGO Committees.

HARRISON HOFFMAN, Center for War/Peace Studies: My impression was that Global Action was a design for a world that would start to exist long after I had died, rather than one which could be implemented while the present problems are presently understood by presently living people. I don't think we need to have a design which waits for future generations to bring into being. I think what we need is activity that can be taking place while the crisis is understood by the people who suffer it.

JONATHAN DEAN: Most of the things we have in mind can be done now by decisions of existing organizations. The Security Council can decide to play a pro-active role. The General Assembly can decide now to set up a committee. However, I understand your point.

JOHN LINEWEAVER, International Fellowship of Reconciliation: ..There has been subtle ethnic cleansing that the Serbs have experienced at the hands of Tito and others in Kosovo. 700,000 were killed in the concentration camps during World War II... In your review you use the word universal membership for regional security organizations. Nowhere else in the document do you use the word universal to modify regional organizations. The one would imply universal membership. The other would cover NATO. I wondered why the difference, dropping the word universal.

RANDALL FORSBERG: It is just because it is a very long phrase. But wherever we use the word regional organization, we mean specifically a universal membership regional organization and not a subsidiary organization that is partisan.

JONATHAN DEAN: Yes, there are grievances on both sides in Yugoslavia. I think our preeminent interest was to stop the killing and to find ways of doing that. No reconciliation is going to be possible while that goes on, no economic development, desperately needed in the area is going to be possible while it goes on, and so I don't think it is necessary in order to act effectively in a program like this to have in mind the ultimate solution of the individual problems that we are tackling. Those ultimate solutions ought to be approached. But what we want to do is restore peaceable conditions and some kind of human environment where people can begin to get together with each other.

MARGERY COHEN, League of Women Voters: In your presentation you mentioned something which seems to me very troubling and very crucial, and that is the arms manufacturing and selling, particularly in the United States. This is a very big industry, it benefits a lot of people, and they are involved in campaign funding. The League of Women Voters is involved in campaign finance reform. Given this reality, how would you answer this particular problem?

RANDALL FORSBERG: That is a good question, and I agree with you about campaign finance reform. My first response is that this sector of arms production is a great deal smaller than people realize and has in fact shrunk enormously since the end of the Cold War by about half. There are about half as many people employed in arms production today as there were in the late 1980s in the United States, and the number of companies, of course, has shrunk because they are consolidating to try to stay as big units. They have less clout than people think. I agree with you, however, about campaign finance reform. These organizations do command a lot of resources. And there is the pressure of constituents employed in the industry on members of Congress. Virtually the only way that members of Congress can support employment in their home constituences is to give them a defense contract.

This will not happen until the 97% of the American population which is not employed for military dollars has an interest in changing national policy and overcoming this resistance, mobilizes and has an education campaign in a large-scale, coalition-building effort that we are talking about. Piecemeal campaigns, on land mines, on the Law of the Sea, one issue or another, are never going to engage enough of the population to outweigh the organized lobbying and leaning on members of Congress of those who are supported by the defense budget. That is a critical reason why a campaign of this kind is needed.

DORRIE WEISS, Economists Allied for Arms Reduction: I don't think that any of this is going to work unless nations are prepared to yield some measure of sovereignty...Nations can say we will not admit human rights monitors or we don't want resident mediators. How do we address this?

RANDALL FORSBERG: When you ask "Will the US yield sovereignty to the UN?" we all know the answer is no. Will the current or next US Administration make a major policy change on their own initiative because it is good for us? No, that is absolutely not going to happen.

But if you ask "Would the American people be willing to share the burden of keeping the peace around the world if it meant that their tax bill would be cut by 30%?" I think the answer would be yes. The American people could influence what the Administration does and how it defines sovereignty. We need to take possession of these issues. They do not belong to the bureaucrats in Washington. It is only when we say this is not the kind of world we want to live in, this is not our view of national sovereignty, and we represent the majority, that we will succeed.

KATHY UHLER, Franciscans International: Would you comment on the withdrawl of the UN preventive peacekeeping force from Macedonia about three weeks ago?

JONATHAN DEAN: That withdrawal took place because of the veto by the Peoples' Republic of China of the continuation of the force in Macedonia. The precipitating factor was the agreement by Macedonia to have bilateral diplomatic relations with Taiwan, which is providing a large sum of money for development. These circumstances are part of the complications of international life. We do have in mind a method of getting around that kind of problem in our proposal, first for an informal understanding among the five permanent members of the Security Council, including China, to exercise the veto less and less in their own interest in an operating body. We are faced, if the vetoes continue, with a degradation of the Security Council's effectiveness, and I think it will be found to be in the interest of many of the permanent members to have an operating body from which they themselves gain a good deal of international status. China is quite disciplined about the way it exercises its veto, dealing mainly with questions of direct concern to it. So I think that we could get an understanding among the permanent members which would cut back on the vetoes.

But we also propose two other methods of dealing with the situation where there is a veto and a prevention of action. One of them is the Conflict Mediation Panel in the General Assembly. The GA can set up any committee it wants to. It could do it tomorrow. The other is resort to the Uniting for Peace resolution, used at the time of the Korean War and of the Congo peacekeeping exercise. You may recollect that when Ambassador Lavrov brought in a resolution last month condemning NATO action that it was defeated by a vote of 12 to 3 in the Security Council. That indicates to me that a positive General Assembly vote supporting this action would have been possible.

JERRY SPIVACK: We are living in a surrealistic universe in which the US is doing whatever it wants, and we are acting as if we can propose all sorts of marvelous fixes with the UN. Very strange.I was also distressed about your comment about taxes. We can talk about enlighted self-interest, and we used to talk about altruism as being the way we thought about self-interest. We are currently trying to get rid of taxes and get rid of education and other worthwhile government expenditures. For us NGOs to play to that and argue that we can cut back on our taxes, when we are the richest nation, making money on the stock market hand over fist, when worldwide everybody is losing their money, is extraordinarily distressing. I think it is the wrong direction.

RANDALL FORSBERG: The current United States role in the world is very clearly a central object, if not the central object of this campaign. If we did not label this as a response to the current US military policy, that is because in order to have the situation of hegemony you have to have people who let themselves be told what to do as well as people who do the telling. I think the relationships within NATO are a good example of that. The problem with the United States is not only the United States. It is all the other countries that say, well, what can I do? So we need both a greater sensitivity and a retreat by the US, but we also need a stepping up to the plate by other countries to say we are also responsible for what goes on the world and for how problems are dealt with. It isn't sufficient to dismantle the US role in the world. It is important to have that role be transformed and replaced by an active and effective international community. I don't think this is only the problem of the US.

On tax cuts, in our proposal we say that the savings achieved should be redirected to nationally adapted objectives. It depends on which country what combination of tax cuts, domestic programs, international debt relief and development aid are adopted, all of which have claims. It is not just our domestic programs that have been wiped out in the US, but the extent of US debt relief and development aid is really shameful. When you see something moving towards a billion dollars being spent bombing people, what you would like is a billion being spent on aid to create an internal economcy and politics where the violence that is going on would not be happening.

So I agree it is disheartening to be confronted with a gap between what you read in the paper and what we have been talking about here. We are trying to mount an effort to close that gap, instead of just falling back in the face of it and picking a little piece and chipping away.

ELAINE VALDOV, Chairman of the NGO Executive Committee: Thank you very much Ann, Randall and Jonathan. It is most important that we all join together in this endeavor.

*****

The conclusions of Jonathan Dean in mid-June, 1999, after the bombing had stopped and NATO and Russian peacekeeping forces were moving into Kosovo:

Clearly there are and must be better ways of dealing with human rights abuses and of carrying out humanitarian intervention than destroying the entire material base of a country, killing perhaps 6,000 soldiers and 2,000 civilians, and then spending the 100 to 150 billion dollars the NATO and European Union countries will have to make available tin connection with this intervention.

My conclusion is that the Kosovo crisis could have been prevented, that the military campaign could have been better run, and that a political settlement would have come earlier if the NATO countries had agreed to accept a UN-controlled intervention force for Kosovo.

But on the other hand, I also conclude that the NATO intervention in Kosovo was justified, that it was legal, if only barely, and that it was in fact generally well conducted. It will probably go down in history as a success, but a very costly one, and with worries about using bombing as a method.

The real conclusion is that these humanitarian interventions cannot be fought without human and material losses that have to be weighed against their benefits for human rights, making military intervention truly a last resort. Consequently, these crises have to be prevented.

APPENDIX II: GLOBAL ACTION TO PREVENT WAR, A COALITION-BUILDING EFFORT TO STOP WAR, GENOCIDE, AND OTHER FORMS OF DEADLY CONFLICT

web site: http://www.globalactionpw.org/   E-mail:info@globalactionpw.org

April 1999, Rev. 10

Organization Members *(in formation)*

International Alert, Kevin Clements
International Alliance of Lawyers Against Nuclear Arms, Phon van dan Biesen
International Peace Bureau, Colin Archer
International Physicians for the Prevention of Nuclear War, Victor Sidel
Earth Action, Lois Barber and Nicholas Dunlop
Hague Agenda for Peace, New York, Cora Weiss
State of the World Forum, Alan Cranston
Toda Institute for Peace Studies, Majid Tehranian
World Order Models Project, Saul Mendlovitz

Coordinating Committee *in formation, organizations for identification only*
Canada
Douglas Roche, Member of the Senate, Ottawa
Denmark
Bjorn Moller, University of Copenhagen Peace Research Institute, Copenhagen
Egypt
*Mohammed Sid-Ahmed, journalist, Cairo
France
Genevieve Schmeder, University Professor, National Institute of Arts and Crafts, Paris
Germany
Hans Gunter Brauch, Arbeitsgruppe Friedensforschung und Europaumlische
  Sicherheitspolitik, Mosbach
Dieter Lutz, Institute for Peace Research and Security Policy, Hamburg
Great Britain
Kevin Clements, International Alert, London
Nicholas Dunlop, EarthAction
Scilla Elworthy, Oxford Research Group, Oxford
Owen Greene, University of Bradford Peace Studies Program, Bradford
Mary Kaldor, London School of Economics Project on Civil Society and Sussex University
Daniel Plesch, British American Security Information Council, London & Washington DC
*Joseph Rotblat, Pugwash Conferences on Science and World Affairs, London
Greece
Panayotis Tsakonas, Hellenic Ministry of Defense, Athens
India
Vandana Shiva, Research Foundation for Science, Technology & Natural Resource Policy
Israel
Merav Datan, International Physicians for the Prevention of Nuclear War, Jerusalem
  and Cambridge MA

Japan
Mitsuru Kurosawa, Osaka University, Osaka
Akiko Yamanaka, Member of the House of Representatives, Tokyo
Lebanon
Afifa and Boutros Arsanios
SOS Children's Villages, Beirut
Netherlands
Phon van dan Biesen, International Lawyers' Alliance against Nuclear Arms, The Hague
Nicaragua
*Alejandro Bendana, Center for International Studies, Managua
Philippines
Walden Bello, Focus on Global South, Bangkok & Manila
South Korea
Yong-Sup Han, Korea Peace Research Association, Seoul
South Africa
Jacklyn Cock, University of the Witwatersrand Peace & Security Project, Johannesburg
Spain
Mariano Aguirre, Center for Peace Research, Madrid
Switzerland
Colin Archer, International Peace Bureau
Andreas Gross, Member of Parliament, Geneva
Patricia Lewis, United Nations Institute for Disarmament Research, Geneva
Russia
Vladimir Sliviak, Socio-Ecological Union and Center for Russian Environmental Policy, Moscow
Roland Timerbaev, Ambassador of the Russian Federation (Ret.), Moscow
United States
Lois Barber, EarthAction, Amherst
John Burroughs, Lawyers' Committee on Nuclear Policy, New York
David Cortright, Fourth Freedom Foundation, Goshen
Alan Cranston, State of the World Forum, San Francisco
Jonathan Dean, Union of Concerned Scientists, Washington, DC
Randall Caroline Forsberg, Institute for Defense & Disarmament Studies, Cambridge
John Fousek, World Order Models Project, New York
David Krieger, Nuclear Age Peace Foundation, Santa Barbara
Susan Collin Marks, Search for Common Ground, Washington, DC
John McDonald, Institute for Multi-track Diplomacy, Washington, DC
Saul Mendlovitz, Rutgers University Law School, Newark
Jonathan Schell, writer, New York
Victor Sidel, International Physicians for the Prevention of Nuclear War, New York
Majid Tehranian, Toda Institute, Honolulu
Cora Weiss, Hague Agenda for Peace, New York
Yugoslavia
Radmila Nakarada, Institute for European Studies, Belgrade   **invited*

GLOBAL ACTION TO PREVENT WAR
A Coalition-Building Effort to Stop War, Genocide, and Other Forms of Deadly Conflict

Overview

GLOBAL ACTION TO PREVENT WAR is a comprehensive project for moving toward a world in which armed conflict is rare. The program envisions four phases of change, each lasting 5-10 years, to fully implement a wide array of measures to prevent international and internal war, genocide, and other deadly conflict.

GLOBAL ACTION TO PREVENT WAR addresses the global problem of organized violence The world also faces fundamental crises of poverty, human rights violations, environmental destruction, and discrimination based on race, gender, ethnicity, and religion. To meet these challenges, many efforts must be pursued: No single campaign can deal effectively with all of them; but efforts to address such global problems can and should complement and support one other.

The GLOBAL ACTION program focuses on violent expressions of conflict, which obstruct efforts to get at the roots of conflict. Specifically, the program increases early warning and early action, such as mediation, to prevent the escalation of disputes into armed violence; it minimizes the mistrust fueled by arms races and offensive military strategies; it guards against genocide; and it builds commitment to the rule of law and the peaceful resolution of conflicts. When implemented, this program is likely to make war rare, saving many lives. At the same time, by increasing respect for human dignity and saving billions of dollars for productive uses, GLOBAL ACTION will reduce structural violence. It will strengthen efforts to meet basic human needs, build tolerance, and protect the environment; and it will foster the democratic institutions that must ultimately replace armed force in achieving justice and fulfilling human needs.

Substantial efforts are now underway to reduce and eventually abolish nuclear arms, but there are no comparable efforts to reduce conventional armed conflict and conventional arms. Yet nuclear disarmament and a comprehensive program to prevent armed violence are both indispensable requirements for practical progress to peace. Each program must support and invigorate the other.

The GLOBAL ACTION program is a coalition-building platform for peoples and governments everywhere. Some components of the program, such as conventional arms cuts or multilateral action against aggression and genocide, concern mainly governments. Other components, such as those dealing with nonviolent conflict resolution and peace education, can be implemented by individuals and state and local communities as well as by national governments.

The GLOBAL ACTION program is a work in progress. The current phase is one of strengthening and disseminating basic concepts, and recruiting coalition members. Concerned individuals around the world are invited to make suggestions and report activities. News will be reported on a web site and in occasional newsletters. Every six months or so, a coordinating group will publish updated versions of the program materials. These drafts will be distributed globally to organizations concerned with peace, development, humanitarian aid, and the environment, and to all governments. The goal of this process is to support and supplement the many efforts for peace already under way by adding important elements and uniting all components in a common program. The sense of common action, in turn, will reinforce the separate projects and facilitate coordinated efforts.

The ambitious goals of the GLOBAL ACTION program cannot be achieved quickly. Building support for the program will take several years, and launching the first phase will take some years more. But sustained, coordinated efforts *can* stop the killing, and the GLOBAL ACTION program has the potential to mobilize and focus such efforts.

Phases

The GLOBAL ACTION program proposes three initial phases of change, which last 5-10 years each and which, taken together, lay the foundation for a fourth phase that establishes a permanent global security system. The goals of the successive phases are as follows:

I. Reduce *internal warfare* by greatly strengthening a reformed UN, universal-membership regional security organizations, and institutions to protect human rights and enforce the rule of law on genocide and crimes against humanity. At the same time, begin to reduce the risks of *major international war* with talks on cuts in military forces, military spending, and arms holdings, production, and trade; and build confidence with a commitment to provide open information on these elements of armed forces, and not to increase them while talks are under way (or for 10 years). Progress in this and subsequent steps will foster steps toward nuclear disarmament. But nuclear and conventional disarmament, while interacting, should move at their own speed.

II. Further reduce the risks of *major international war* by making substantial global cuts in armed forces and military spending (up to one-third of the largest forces) and in arms production and trade, and by mandatory submission of international disputes to the International Court of Justice. Further reduce the risks of *internal warfare* by continuing to strengthen UN and regional conflict-resolution capabilities and the international courts, using a tax on international financial transactions to support these activities.

III. Building on the improved means of avoiding armed conflict developed in the first phases, deepen confidence in the international community's ability to prevent war with a watershed commitment by participating nations, including the major powers, not to deploy their armed forces beyond national borders except in multilateral actions under the auspices of the reformed UN or its regional counterparts. This commitment, undertaken on a trial basis, will test global and regional institutions while participants still have national means of action as a fallback.

IV. Complete the process of making war rare and brief by permanently transferring to the reformed UN and regional security organizations the authority and capability for armed intervention to prevent or end war and genocide. To support this shift, expand the individually-recruited all-volunteer forces of the UN and regional organizations and make another round of deep cuts (up to one-third, compared with today's levels) in national armed forces. The remaining national forces, at most one-third the size of today's largest forces, will be limited to defense of national territory, and will be restructured to focus exclusively on this role.

In a final phase of change, expected to evolve later, national armed forces will be cut back to defense of borders, coasts, coastal waters, and air space; and UN and regional security forces will have the police functions of guarding against rearmament and against transnational violence by terrorists or criminal syndicates. That future world - where arms are minimal and defensively oriented, and armed conflict is rare, brief, and small in scale - can be characterized as a world where war has been abolished.

The Need and Opportunity for Change

The UN and its member states are failing to prevent new outbreaks of armed conflict, and the entire world is paying huge costs for this failure. The statistics are dismaying. According to some estimates, up to 35 million people - 90 percent civilians - have been killed in 170 wars since the end of World War II. Thirty wars are now taking place, most inside national boundaries. In addition to the tragic loss of life and limb, these conflicts breed international terrorism and they have huge economic costs. War's damage to productive economic activity is immense: it lasts for decades, sometimes generations, multiplying the human costs of conflict. (In Lebanon - one case where hard figures are available - 20 years after civil war broke out, the GDP was still only half of its previous level.) Moreover, the large standing forces maintained to deter or intervene in wars cost hundreds of billions of dollars per year.

Despite their enormous resources and vast spending on armaments, governments around the world have been unable to prevent frequent outbreaks of armed conflict; instead, they react to them. Responding to dislocation, destruction, and loss of production and trade, the industrial countries and voluntary organizations spend billions of dollars on economic rehabilitation of war-ravaged areas, humanitarian aid, refugee relief, peace-keeping forces, and in some cases military intervention. Instead of repeatedly financing these costly post-war remedies, which are usually too little and too late, governments and voluntary organizations should invest in *war prevention*.

Today we have a rare opportunity to mobilize government and public support for a comprehensive approach to war prevention. Working relationships among the world's top military powers (the United States, Russia, France, Germany, Great Britain, Japan, and China) have created an unprecedented opportunity for cooperation to strengthen UN and regional conflict resolution and peacekeeping and to reduce global arms deployment, production, and trade.

This may be a waning opportunity. Unless preventive action is taken over the next 10-20 years, we may see renewed armed confrontation between the most heavily armed nations (the USA, Russia, and China). Moreover, other nations are poised to acquire armaments that neighboring countries may find threatening. Today, when there is no near-term risk of major war, is the time to prevent the rise of new military threats.

In addition, innovative concepts for war prevention, forged during major conflicts ranging from World War I through the Cold War, offer powerful new tools to help prevent war. These include confidence-building measures, transparency and information exchange, mutual constraints on force deployments and activities, negotiated reductions in armed forces, and restrictions on arms holdings, production, and trade. Equally important are constructive new measures for peacekeeping: preconflict early warning and action, including diplomatic intervention, mediation, judicial processes, and preventive deployment of armed force; and post-conflict peacekeeping and peacebuilding. Another innovation is the trend toward linking international loans to limits on military spending. Thus far, these useful approaches to preventing war have been applied separately and incompletely; none has been fully successful, and none is likely to be so if they remain separate projects, unconnected by a larger framework.

In the 1960s, the United States and the Soviet Union proposed plans for general and complete disarmament combined with improved UN peacekeeping; but these plans were shelved in favor of separate programs for partial arms limits and reductions. For nuclear arms, this approach has begun to work because the many issues into which nuclear arms control has been divided - testing, bilateral

194

reductions, nonproliferation, ending production of fissile material, and disposing of fissile material - are all supported by strong public rejection of nuclear weapons. For conventional forces, in contrast, the disaggregation of disarmament into separate projects has fragmented interest, dividing support among many worthwhile measures, such as limits on arms transfers or cuts in military spending. Moreover, while nuclear war is considered avoidable, many people and governments have an anachronistic attitude toward the inevitability of "conventional" war. Peacekeeping has been completely separated from efforts to reduce conflict through arms control. The areas where there has been some progress - the 1990 Treaty on Conventional Forces in Europe, and recent efforts to ban landmines and control small arms - have been exceptional in generating broad support.

Now, instead of striving for peace in fragments, it is time to bring together these diverse approaches - conventional force cuts, limits on arms production and trade, cuts in military spending, measures to stop proliferation and build confidence, training for peaceful conflict resolution, and means for peacebuilding, and peacekeeping - in a unified program to prevent war.

A comprehensive approach is needed both to be effective in reducing armed conflict and to mobilize sustained public pressure for new policies. Such an approach will strengthen existing peacemaking and arms control programs by building a broader coalition of interested publics and government officials to support them. Once convinced that a practical program to prevent war exists, people and governments will eagerly champion it.

Equally important, by significantly lowering the world level of armed conflict and greatly reducing the world's largest conventional military forces, the GLOBAL ACTION program will create an environment in which it will be possible to eliminate all nuclear weapons. Neither nuclear disarmament nor the effective prevention of conventional warfare can be fully implemented without the active contribution of the other. One the one hand, the abolition of nuclear weapons will require reduced levels of conflict worldwide and deep cuts in the conventional forces of the major powers. Among other things, China, Russia, and India will not relinquish their nuclear arms if the main effect of doing so is to enhance the already large conventional superiority of the United States. On the other hand, the governments of the most heavily armed countries will not drastically cut national conventional forces unless nuclear weapons are on their way to elimination.

A Phased Process of Change

To succeed in mobilizing broad support, a program of action to prevent deadly conflict should meet several criteria: it should be careful not to inadvertently increase some risks of war while reducing others; it should strengthen commitment to nonviolent conflict resolution; it should offer substantial economic benefits; and it should include means of overcoming domestic resistance to change rooted in inertia, ignorance, and vested interests.

The GLOBAL ACTION program seeks to meet these criteria. Militarily, it proposes a series of gradual changes, carefully designed not to create new situations of uncertainty in which the risk of war might rise. Morally, it underscores commitment to the rule of law and peaceful dispute resolution in international and domestic affairs in three ways: it radically enhances institutions for war prevention; it limits the accepted uses of armed force to deterring and defending against aggression, genocide, and other forms of mass violence, and it replaces national armed forces for use in what may be arbitrary, self-interested ways with UN and regional forces for use in a nonpartisan fashion.

Economically, this program should bring major savings both to the potential victims of armed conflict and to the potential donors of emergency relief and reconstruction aid. In addition, by cutting the world's largest conventional armed forces and major weapon systems - which take 95 percent of world military spending - the program should release enormous resources for non-military uses. In the case of the United States, which accounts for one-third of world military spending, initial cuts in conventional forces and weaponry could save $90 billion per year (out of the current $270 billion annual military budget), and longer-term reductions could save close to $200 billion per year. Other countries, including both industrial countries and developing "middle powers," would save comparable proportions of their current military budgets - which in many cases are now higher than their budgets for health or education. After an initial period of transition and conversion, these savings could be directed to nationally-adapted combinations of tax cuts, domestic programs, international debt relief, and development aid.

With respect to potential internal obstacles to change - employment in defense-dependent communities, profits in arms industries, the careers of senior military officers, and so on - a gradual process of change will enable a smooth transition to non-military employment and production. It will mobilize local as well as national support by ending local boom-and-bust cycles of funding for arms production, strengthening economic growth, and releasing a large fraction of government spending for other needs.

Phase I. Strengthening UN and Regional Means of War Prevention

Phase I seeks to reduce the frequency of genocide, ethnic conflict, internal wars, and border wars by strengthening global and regional institutions for preventing and ending organized armed violence. It also address the longer-term risks of major international war by starting negotiations on global cuts in military budgets and conventional arms holdings, production, and trade, while instituting a freeze on these elements of military power, and requiring a full and open exchange of information about them. The two approaches are mutually reinforcing. Reducing the frequency of internal warfare will reduce the intervention of great powers and facilitate cuts in their large standing armed forces; this, in turn, will facilitate cutbacks in arms transfers and help defuse regional conflicts.

There are several reasons to begin by stressing efforts to reduce internal wars: They are the main source of bloodshed today; measures to prevent such wars, though well known, are underdeveloped and sporadically applied; and success in strengthening these measures will build confidence in the ability of the international community to prevent all types of armed violence.

Phase I would begin with an initial Treaty to Reduce Armed Conflict (TRAC I) in which participating nations promise to work to reduce organized armed conflict by enhancing means of conflict resolution and limiting national armed forces.

To prevent and end internal wars, genocide, and other large-scale armed violence, a range of steps to strengthen global and regional war prevention and defense capabilities are feasible and urgently needed:

POLICY PROGRAM I: Measures to Prevent Internal War and Genocide

Expanding Global and Regional Security Institutions
1. Establish universal-membership regional security organizations in the Middle East, South Asia, and North-East Asia comparable to those in Europe (OSCE), Africa (OAU), the Americas

(OAS), and South-East Asia (ASEAN); and strengthen the conflict-prevention and peacekeeping capabilities of all regional security organizations.

2. Ensure that regional security organizations remain effective through oversight by the UN Secretary-General in consultation with a reformed Security Council.

3. Strengthen the conflict-prevention role of the UN Security Council, and build confidence in its efficacy and impartiality, through several means, including expanded Council membership, restricted use of the veto, *ex officio* membership in the Council of the President of the General Assembly, and Security Council authorization for the Secretary-General to rapidly deploy small peacekeeping forces to prevent the outbreak of armed conflict in situations of crisis.

4. Increase dialogue and cooperation on peace and security matters between nongovernmental organizations and the UN and regional security organizations.

Strengthening Nonviolent Means of Preventing and Ending Armed Conflict

5. Strengthen the UN's conflict early-warning system, which collects and analyzes information about potential trouble spots, and about effective methods for preventing the escalation of disputes into armed conflict.

6. Create a professional mediation service and a civilian humanitarian aid corps which are available for use by the UN Secretary-General and Security Council.

7. Create a Mediation and War-Prevention Committee in the UN General Assembly.

8. Move toward establishing an agreed framework and criteria for humanitarian intervention in the UN General Assembly and Security Council.

9. Create standing contingents of civilian police trained for peacekeeping missions to accompany peacekeeping forces, undertake peacekeeping missions of their own, or conduct other tasks at the request of the UN Secretary-General, the Security Council, international courts, or the regional security organizations.

10. Refer international disputes to the International Court of Justice, moving toward compulsory submission.

11. Bring into force the 1998 reaty creating an International Criminal Court to prosecute war crimes, genocide, and other crimes against humanity.

12. Include a provision in all newly-concluded treaties requiring referral of disputes about their implementation or interpretation to adjudication and arbitration in the International Court.

13. Begin international negotiations to establish an international code of minority rights.

14. Admit UN observers immediately and unconditionally to assess the implementation of commitments under existing human rights conventions, when requested to do so under the authorized process.

15. Bring into force the UN General Assembly convention on international cooperation to prevent terrorism.

16. Initiate or expand domestic programs for training in the nonviolent resolution of disputes in all schools and for dispute-resolution mediation and arbitration services in all communities.

17. Institute service in peacekeeping and mediation corps as an alternative to military conscription, career military service, or other national service.

Refining the Military Means of Last Resort for Preventing and Ending Armed Conflict

18. Create readiness brigades in Africa, Latin America, the Middle East, and Asia, matching the brigade that now exists in Europe, and make these brigades available for UN and regional peacekeeping and defense missions.
19. Establish several mobile headquarters units at the UN to permit the rapid establishment of new peacekeeping operations, and create a $500 million fund for such operations.
20. Create all-volunteer armed forces for use under the aegis of the UN or its regional counterparts.

Since many of the procedures and institutions proposed for Phase I already exist in some form, GLOBAL ACTION TO PREVENT WAR will not be starting from zero, but rather building on positive recent developments. For example, there are global agreements on human rights, on dispute resolution by the International Court of Justice, on cooperation to prevent terrorism, and on the establishment of an International Criminal Court. Many countries have begun to institute programs on nonviolent conflict resolution in schools and local communities. The UN Secretary-General has an informal system for diplomatic intervention to prevent disputes from escalating into armed conflicts; the UN Security Council has considerable experience with peacekeeping; and a few initial international readiness brigades and headquarters units are being prepared for intervention to deter or end aggression or genocide. There are also universal-membership regional organizations in Europe (OSCE), Africa (OAU), and Latin America (OAS), which provide a start for building effective regional security organizations on all continents.

Existing war-prevention institutions and processes can and should be greatly strengthened. The network of regional security organizations should be filled out and each organization should develop some mediation and peacekeeping capability of its own. The UN should expand its early warning capability, establish a professional mediation corps and humanitarian aid service, and increase the pool of civilian police trained for peacekeeping and related missions. Service in peacekeeping and mediation corps should be made an alternative to military conscription or, where appropriate, to professional military service. An international treaty on minority rights should be adopted; and this treaty as well as other future treaties should provide for participants to submit disputes about them to the international courts for arbitration or adjudication.

Nongovernmental organizations (NGOs) have programs in several of these areas, including mediation, arbitration, and the unarmed intervention of peace brigades. Such activities, which have been growing rapidly, are likely to be increasingly useful in future as NGOs become more experienced and innovative.

Building on these measures, the Security Council, **the Secretary-General, and the universal-membership regional security organizations should undertake a pro-active role in preventing armed conflict.** The UN and its regional counterparts will be expected to act quickly to advise, warn, and assist governments encountering difficult political and economic problems, and to assure that the UN Human Rights Commission and regional commissions are active in easing ethnic and minority frictions. Governments will make a renewed commitment to fulfill their obligations under existing human rights covenants by unconditionally admitting observers when requested to do so. At the same time, the UN General Assembly will set up a Mediation and War-Prevention Committee to supplement the work of the Security Council on a less formal plane. Operating by majority vote and not subject to veto, the Committee will hear and advise citizens and government officials from areas in crisis, and inform the international community of its findings.

As the role of the UN and its regional counterparts in preventing war grows, it will be essential to take steps to build widespread confidence in the impartiality of these organization's decision-making on matters of war and peace. One way to do this may be to make the UN Security Council more representative of the international community by expanding its membership, and more likely to undertake decisive, impartial action by restricting the use of the veto. An initial informal agreement among the five permanent members of the Security council to use the veto sparingly could lead eventually to a situation in which the veto is restricted to threats to the territorial integrity of the country issuing the veto. Another way to achieve impartial action, also without changing the UN Charter, would be for the Security Council to establish new committees or agencies to deal with specific aspects of security, replacing the veto with "super majorities" in these organizations. Similar steps could be taken by the regional security bodies. If action by the Security council remains blocked, the "uniting for peace" procedure used in the Korean War and the Congo peacekeeping mission could be employed.

For fuller accountability in the UN, the President of the General Assembly should have a seat on the Security Council, allowing him to report Assembly views to the Council and vice versa. To further enhance accountability, a practice of judicial review by the International Court of Justice over precisely defined areas of Security Council and regional security organization competence could be gradually introduced.

Finally, steps should be taken to strengthen dialogue between government representatives and officials at the UN and its regional counterparts and NGOs and people's assemblies, which are playing an increasingly important and useful role in shaping government security policies.

To reduce the longer-term risks of major international war and to further reduce the risks of internal war, TRAC I participants will take several additional major steps:

- Begin talks on global reductions in armaments, and make a commitment not to increase any key element of military power (current and planned future armed forces, military personnel and spending, and arms holdings, production, and trade) while the talks are under way or for at least 10 years;

- Support the talks by providing full transparency (open information) on the same key elements of military power;
- Apply a prescribed set of confidence-building measures, including constraints on force activities, in bilateral relationships that have the potential to lead to war; and,
- Establish a coordinating committee to oversee implementation and verification, patterned on similar committees in START I and II, the CFE Treaty, and the Chemical Weapons Convention. The responsibilities of this committee will increase in later phases.

Phase II. Cuts in Forces, Spending, Arms production, and Trade

Phase II will continue to strengthen the means available to the international community for preventing and ending genocide and internal warfare. For example, governments will commit themselves to obligatory arbitration or submission of disputes to international courts. This phase will, however, place greater emphasis on steps to reduce the risks of major regional or global war. A second Treaty to Reduce Armed Conflict, TRAC II, will make substantial global and regional cuts in key elements of military power (force structure, military personnel, and spending), and in the holdings, production, and trade of major weapon systems. (Major weapon systems are combat aircraft, armed helicopters, tanks, armored personnel carriers, heavy artillery, missiles, and naval ships over 1,000 tons.)

Aiming ultimately at low levels of national armaments in all parts of the world, TRAC II will make proportionately larger cuts in countries with larger armed forces. For example, countries with aggregate inventories of major weapons numbering over 10,000 (the USA, Russia, China) might reduce their forces by one-third, while those with inventories totaling 1,000-10,000 would cut by one-quarter, and those with inventories under 1,000 by 15 percent. Following this guideline, the United States, Russia, and China would cut by 33 percent. About 20 military "middle powers" would cut by 25 percent: In Europe, Germany, Britain, France, Italy, Greece, Turkey, Poland, and Ukraine; in Asia, Japan, India, Pakistan, North and South Korea, and Taiwan; and in the Middle East, Israel, Saudi Arabia, Egypt, Iraq, Iran, and Syria. All other countries (about 170), which have very small armed forces, would cut by 15 percent.

These global cuts will be supplemented by additional confidence-building arms reductions and defensive-oriented restructuring in areas plagued by long-standing regional conflicts. Obligatory cuts in arms production and trade will accompany the global and regional cuts in forces. During reductions the need for replacements for older systems will be minimal. As a result, there will be more than proportionate cuts in arms production and trade and in the size of remaining arms industries. Reduced armaments will be destroyed unless they can be used to replace permitted but unserviceable weapons, thereby avoiding production of replacement systems.

At the same time, participants will finally implement their obligations under Articles 43 and 45 of the UN Charter to make available to the Security Council pre-designated trained and equipped ground, air, and naval personnel, ships, and planes. An individually-recruited all-volunteer force will also be established; and the standing peacekeeping forces at the disposal of the UN and regional security organizations will begin the process (to be continued in Phase III and completed in Phase IV) of making a gradual transition from national contingents earmarked for multilateral use to the growing all-volunteer force. Little by little, reliance on national military contingents will be phased out except for large operations.

Participants will also implement their obligation under Article 47 to establish a functioning Military Staff Committee to provide strategic direction of these forces on orders from the Security Council, and will establish regional Military Staff Committees.

It will be essential to strengthen the UN’s capability to head off incipient armed conflict, and not be blocked from taking any action either by a threatened Security Council veto or by lack of political will among Council members. To this end, the Secretary-General of the UN will be authorized by Charter amendment or by Security Council decision to deploy military or police forces of limited size for peacekeeping only. For the deployment to continue beyond 30 days, it would have to be confirmed by the Security Council.

More generally, a major goal of GLOBAL ACTION TO PREVENT WAR is to make clear to national leaders at all levels - that is, elected officials, military officers, and civil servants - and to society at large the inescapable need for identifying brewing conflicts at an early stage and take action to prevent them from becoming armed conflicts.

Efforts will continue during Phase II to strengthen institutions for war prevention and conflict resolution, and to prevent the outbreak of civil wars, violent ethnic conflicts, and genocide. The entire program up to this point - including the cuts in arms holdings, production, and trade - will support a shift in Phases III and IV from national to multilateral means of military intervention to preserve or restore peace.

The growing international means of war prevention will be funded starting in Phase II by a tax of one/one-hundredth of one percent of all international financial transactions over $10,000.

Phase III. Trial Ban on unilateral Military Intervention

In a third Treaty to Reduce Armed Conflict (TRAC III), participating countries, including the major powers, will test the effectiveness of the expanded global security system by making a provisional commitment not to deploy their armed forces beyond national borders except as part of a multilateral deployment under UN or regional auspices. This commitment appears far-reaching, but it corresponds to obligations under the UN Charter which member states undertook when they joined the UN.

By the beginning of Phase III, the UN and its regional security counterparts, which will have expanded their peacekeeping capabilities in Phases I and II, should be willing and able to take responsibility for these tasks. In other words, they should be prepared to take steps, authorized by the Secretary-General or the Security Council (or a regional counterpart), to launch rapid multilateral non-military intervention or, as a last resort, military action aimed at preventing or ending the outbreak of war, genocide, and other forms of deadly conflict.

When considering armed intervention in internal conflicts, the Security Council will decide on a case-by-case basis whether intervention is justified, using criteria such as the threat of genocide, threats to international security, or the far-reaching failure of governments to meet the requirements for stewardship of their citizens' rights, security, and welfare.

At any time during Phase III, if participating nations conclude that their security is endangered by a failure of the global security system, they will have the right to withdraw from TRAC III; and since TRAC II cuts will reduce national forces by no more than a third, capabilities for unilateral national military action will still exist. Withdrawal from TRAC III will not vitiate the commitments made under TRACs I and II.

A successful TRAC III trial - a decade with no withdrawal and no unilateral military action by nations with large armed forces - will be a prerequisite for proceeding with TRAC IV. During the TRAC III trial, talks will take place on another round of cuts in conventional forces and military spending to be carried out in Phase IV, when there is full confidence in the effectiveness of the global security system.

By the time the TRAC III is agreed, nuclear disarmament should have reached a point at which the small remaining stocks of warheads and delivery systems have been immobilized by being placed in internationally-monitored storage - that is, the last step before the complete abolition of nuclear weapons. In this case, the TRAC III trial transfer of responsibility for military action from national to global and regional hands, preceding the permanent transfer, would parallel the trial immobilization of nuclear weapons preceding their complete abolition.

Phase IV. Permanently Transfer Defense Assistance to International Means

Following the trial run in TRAC III, the TRAC IV agreement, a treaty of indefinite duration, will complete the transfer of the responsibility and capability for international assistance in protection against genocide and aggression from individual nations to the global security system operated by the reformed UN and universal-membership regional security organizations. This transfer will permit and require further cuts in national forces like those in TRAC II (one-third, one-quarter, and 15 percent, respectively, for countries with very large, large, and small forces). Force-projection capabilities - air, naval, and logistical forces that permit military attacks far from national borders - will be dropped from national arsenals, in whole or in part.

At the same time, the scale of the peacekeeping and defense forces maintained by the UN and regional security organizations will grow, as these organizations complete the transition from use of earmarked national contingents to reliance exclusively on all-volunteer forces. Production of major weapons will be restricted to systems needed by individual nations for defensive security (defense of national territory) and those needed by the UN and regional organizations for peacekeeping and for multilateral defense against genocide and aggression.

Ultimate Goals - Phase V

As confidence in the global security system grows and military threats diminish, further changes will be desirable and should be possible. These changes, which may occur quickly or slowly, can be considered to comprise the fifth and final phase of the multiphase process.

The initial goal for the final phase is for all nations to convert fully to defensive security, by limiting national armed forces strictly and narrowly to territorial defense (air defense, defense of coasts and coastal waters, and border defense), and by making the UN and regional security organizations alone capable of large-scale military intervention beyond national borders.

Efforts to achieve this goal are likely to be mutually reinforcing. As confidence in the global security system grows and national armed forces shrink, the multilateral forces needed to deter and defend against cross-border aggression and other forms of large-scale violence will be both smaller and more likely to succeed. At the same time, as expectations of peace grow, nations and national leaders will become more comfortable with the idea of limiting their armed forces to defense of national territory. In particular, the major military powers (especially the United States), which would be giving up their capabilities for large-scale military action beyond national borders, will have concluded that their security is better served by the new system, and will actively support it.

Eventually, the world's nations may reach a degree of commitment to peaceful conflict resolution such that the UN and regional security organizations will have only police functions: verifying adherence to defensive security limits by individual nations, and preventing the use of violence for gain or for political intimidation by nonstate actors such as terrorists and criminal syndicates. At this point we could reasonably describe the situation as one in which war had been abolished.

A Plan for Action

Near and Medium-Term Goals

GLOBAL ACTION TO PREVENT WAR sets out a comprehensive approach to war prevention, with a plan to reduce the frequency and devastation of war and the scale of preparations for war throughout the world. Most experts believe that once implemented, GLOBAL ACTION will achieve these goals - but that implementation could be slow and difficult, especially at the outset. That is why GLOBAL ACTION has a plan for a long effort, which will be sustained by a very broad coalition of groups and individuals until the program wins the support of the governments of many countries, especially the most heavily armed countries, including the United States.

Coalition-building among organizations and individuals:Supporters are now in the initial stage of disseminating the GLOBAL ACTION concept and beginning to build a coalition. Those who are already committed ask interested individuals, groups, and organizations to discuss the GLOBAL ACTION program in detail and give it the widest possible distribution–to friends, relatives, colleagues, religious and political leaders, and others.

GLOBAL ACTION's first goal, to be achieved in two or three years, is to establish an international coalition of groups and individuals who are sufficiently committed and influential to make GLOBAL ACTION known worldwide as a serious long-term enterprise with increasing visibility and momentum.

The next goal, to be reached within five years, is to get name recognition and understanding of GLOBAL ACTION roughly equivalent to what exists today for the campaign to abolish nuclear weapons. Once many committed people throughout the world conclude that GLOBAL ACTION entails a practical and effective program to make armed conflict rare, this effort will tap into the universal desire for peace and support for GLOBAL ACTION will spread much more rapidly.

Developing support among government officials: Key government officials in several countries have already expressed serious interest in and support for the GLOBAL ACTION program. GLOBAL ACTION needs supporters who are willing and able to help circulate the program in the higher ranks of government in every country, soliciting favorable endorsement by working level officials. In addition, other near-term goals for work with governments include finding one or more friendly governments to introduce the GLOBAL ACTION program into the agenda of the UN General Assembly (as Costa Rica did with the Model Nuclear Weapons Abolition Convention); and persuading various government leaders to make positive public mention of GLOBAL ACTION at suitable times, for example in annual speeches to the UN General Assembly.

Within five years, it should be possible to gain wide governmental acceptance in different parts of the world of specific components of the Phase I GLOBAL ACTION program, such as strengthening means of multilateral war prevention, conflict resolution, and peacekeeping; securing verified commitments from individual governments to freeze or reduce military spending, production, and trade; and providing full transparency on their military forces and spending, and arms holdings, production and trade. One important step toward these goals would be to establish a working group at the Conference on Disarmament to discuss a possible GLOBAL ACTION Treaty or, alternatively, to have several governments to convene a special conference on the GLOBAL ACTION program. Other feasible mid-term goals are:

- Establishing new regional security organizations, and strengthening existing ones;
- Regional discussions of a no-increase commitment for armed forces;
- Discussion of a worldwide no-increase commitment on armed forces, including arms transfers (an important symbolic beginning for negotiated reductions);
- Agreement on a comprehensive global exchange of information on armed forces;
- A strong General Assembly vote for a resolution urging unconditional acceptance of outside observers to confirm compliance with human rights conventions; and

- A decision by the UN Security Council to take a systematically pro-active role in preventing internal armed conflict, to empower the Secretary-General to take early action (as noted earlier), and to fund the information gathering and staffing needs implicit in this decision.

While implementation of the full GLOBAL ACTION program lies far in the future, the components of the first two phases are politically modest and feasible within a few years. They involve strengthening war-prevention and conflict-resolution mechanisms that are already exist, initiating similar new ones, and taking modest steps to reduce the longer-term risks of major international war, including cuts in armed forces built up during the Cold War. Most of these measures can be put into effect independently of one another.

What is needed to launch the GLOBAL ACTION program is the formation of a broad, powerful coalition composed of concerned individuals, private voluntary humanitarian and economic development organizations, peace, disarmament and religious groups, businesses, political parties, and supportive government officials. Such a coalition can bring pressure to bear on governments to acknowledge the need for a comprehensive approach like that offered by the GLOBAL ACTION program, and to start by taking the modest steps outlined in Phases I and II. The remainder of this section describes how such a coalition might be created, and the kinds of action participants might take.

Just as the environmental activists of the 1970s and 1980s made environmental protection a near-universal goal, GLOBAL ACTION participants now seek to make war prevention a nonpartisan goal that is widely perceived as part of the general good. Today, grade schools teach environmental conservation; when GLOBAL ACTION TO PREVENT WAR has mobilized a global movement, grade schools will be able to teach peacebuilding skills and policies as an equally nonpartisan, nonpoliticized matter.

A Multi-issue Campaign with Shared Priorities

The GLOBAL ACTION program covers the whole spectrum of issues relating to nonviolent conflict resolution, peacekeeping, demilitarization, and disarmament - but it is much more than a catalog of actions to prevent war. It is based on a "living" platform that is constantly being updated and improved, with input from new and old supporters. Because it delineates a practical route to a substantially different world, starting with modest steps that are politically feasible today, it combines vision with practicality. Its in-depth analysis clarifies the synergistic relationship between various steps to reduce the risk of war, such as reductions in standing armed forces and military spending, limits on arms production and trade, a new balance between military and nonmilitary means of preventing aggression and genocide, confidence in international peacekeeping capabilities, and a greater role for the international court system in resolving conflicts and preventing war. Finally, the GLOBAL ACTION problem distinguishes between near-term and longer-term goals in these diverse yet linked aspects of efforts to prevent war. Without prescribing rigid coordination, it takes into account the need for progress in certain areas to permit progress in others.

These features of the GLOBAL ACTION program facilitate independent yet mutually supportive efforts by members of the GLOBAL ACTION International Network (GAIN, described more fully below). Organizations can choose the issues on which they focus. Within the broad framework of the GLOBAL ACTION program, they can usefully focus on specific short-term goals, or work to make the overall program better understood and more widely supported, or foster broad, long-term moral and cultural change. They can work against nuclear proliferation, or against violence in children's TV programming, or for universal school education on nonviolent conflict resolution, or for prompt payment of UN dues, or for tolerance and respect among sub-national groups –and equally well identify themselves as active participants in GLOBAL ACTION TO PREVENT WAR. There are many component areas in which grassroots and governmental effort for change and improvement are needed. These include but are not limited to:

- Arms control and disarmament, including measures to reduce and eliminate weapons of mass destruction (nuclear, biological, and chemical), and to reduce conventional armaments, land mines, small arms, and handguns.

- Confidence-building measures between and, where needed, within nations.

- Nonviolent means of conflict resolution, promoting a culture of peace, and opposing the culture of violence.

- Conflict early warning to prevent the escalation of disputes into armed conflict.

- Reform of the UN and the development of new or improved universal-membership regional security organizations.

- Improvement in multilateral means of peacekeeping.

- Education for the prevention of violence and the nonviolent resolution of conflicts in schools; and programs for violence prevention and nonviolent conflict resolution in communities.

- Global and regional means of assisting post-conflict rebuilding and reconciliation.

- Steps to strengthen international law and the role of international courts in preventing and ending armed conflict.

Organizations that work in any of these areas are urged to become Members of the GLOBAL ACTION International Network; and those working in or familiar with areas of activity that are useful for preventing organized armed conflict but not noted in the GLOBAL ACTION plan are requested to send suggestions to the Coordinating Committee.

Because various regions have diverse security concerns, stemming from differences in history, size, culture, and resources, different aspects of the GLOBAL ACTION program will be most pertinent in different states. In parts of Europe, Africa, and Asia, stopping the bloodshed will be the highest priority. In Latin America, there are urgent needs for greater openness of information on armed forces and military plans, and for steps to strengthen the security role of the Organization of American States. For conflict-prone countries in the Middle East, South Asia, and North-East Asia, the top priorities may be confidence-building measures, such as defensively-oriented cuts and restructuring in armed forces perceived as threatening by neighbors, and the establishment of universal-membership regional security organizations. In the United States, support must be developed for many near-term steps, including participation in the International Criminal Court, global talks on cuts in conventional forces and on the abolition of nuclear weapons, unconditional payment of UN dues, and the strengthening of the war prevention and peacekeeping capabilities of the UN Security Council and Secretary-General.

The Phase I goals of GLOBAL ACTION TO PREVENT WAR - strengthening multilateral war-prevention, peacekeeping, and defense capabilities, and talks on global conventional arms cuts, supported by full transparency and a no-increase commitment–are sufficiently diverse that nongovernmental organizations and individuals in every country will find useful areas for public education and national political debate. On certain issues, however, transnational mobilization may be most effective. For example, a global campaign supporting the development of rapid response brigades, building on current efforts by the government of Denmark, Norway, and Netherlands and others, would be extremely useful. On issues where the GLOBAL ACTION program calls for steps to be codified in international treaties, national and transnational organizations might press their governments to show leadership by acting unilaterally.

What will give GLOBAL ACTION unity and focus - and what will give GAIN global clout - are the shared objectives for near- and longer-term change in a common program. What participants will share is a commitment to the goals of delegitimizing violence as a means of achieving various ends, strengthening nonviolent means of meeting basic needs, and providing political empowerment, dignity, and equal opportunity to all.

GAIN - the Global Action International Network

The core program statement of GLOBAL ACTION TO PREVENT WAR is constantly undergoing revision, update, and improvement. Organizations and individuals reading the statement for the first time are invited to send comments and suggestions to the Coordinating Committee. Revised drafts, published every 3-6 months, take into account suggestions from supporters and changes in the world. This keeps the program statement up-to-date, relevant, and open to input from members of an ever-expanding coalition. Until all phases of the GLOBAL ACTION program have been implemented, GLOBAL ACTION will be coalition-building "network-in-formation," inviting the active participation of old and new supporters, and gradually evolving from a campaign to a global movement. The basic structure for creating this movement is provided by the GLOBAL ACTION International Network, GAIN, a worldwide association of groups and individuals who support GLOBAL ACTION TO PREVENT WAR. GAIN offers a capacious umbrella for coalition-building. It allows individual and organizational members of the network to work for diverse goals while identifying themselves as part of a truly global effort.

GAIN welcomes organizations which relate to the GLOBAL ACTION program in different ways. "Members" of GAIN are organizations and individuals involved in *like efforts* by groups such as the Hague Appeal for Peace, Earth Action, or the European Conflict Platform, which have multi-issue campaigns to prevent war; and *component efforts* by groups working for specific goals within the overall GLOBAL ACTION platform, such as Abolition 2000 (advocating government commitment to talks on a plan to abolish nuclear weapons) , the campaigns against landmines and small arms, or efforts to cut military forces and spending, limit the arms trade, promote education and training in nonviolent conflict resolution, strengthen the UN, or increase the use of the international courts.

"Affiliates"of GAIN are organizations and individuals involved in *related efforts* in fields which would benefit from the success of GLOBAL ACTION TO PREVENT WAR, such as humanitarian aid, refugee relief, development, human rights, the environment, economic justice, women's issues, domestic abuse and youth violence, and businesses seeking stable markets and currencies and peaceful environments for international finance and trade, tourism, and transnational extraction and manufacturing industries. Affiliates can of course become Members at any stage.

The first step for organizations that are considering GAIN membership or affiliation is thorough dissemination and discussion of the program among their own members and, where needed, formal agreement by members or boards to endorse the GLOBAL ACTION program and to join GAIN. Four Councils - for individual members, individual affiliates, organizational members, and organizational affiliates - let participating groups and individuals work together on joint GLOBAL ACTION projects...

Groups and individuals can choose their own degree of involvement in GAIN. You can indicate interest in being informed about GLOBAL ACTION without endorsement or active participation. Members and Affiliates, who in joining indicate that they support the general thrust of the GLOBAL ACTION effort, can participate in GAIN Councils and use the public areas of the GLOBAL ACTION web site. Greater degrees of participation include education or lobbying on specific components of the GLOBAL ACTION program or the program as whole, offering input into the evolving program, or, for those most active, becoming an organizational GAIN network node for multi-faceted GLOBAL ACTION activity and support.

How GLOBAL ACTION TO PREVENT WAR Can Support Your Efforts

The GLOBAL ACTION coalition will support participating organizations in two ways: it will give broad support and visibility to the many existing efforts for war-prevention and disarmament; and it will spur new initiatives that would benefit existing programs, such as new pressure for deep cuts in conventional arms and military spending. Specifically, as members of GLOBAL ACTION, you can:

1. **Spread information about your programs**: Organizations which are Members or Affiliates of the GAIN, the GLOBAL ACTION International Network, can disseminate information about their goals, events, and priorities through GAIN. GAIN will provide links to the web sites of associated organizations, listed by sphere of activity or interest. An index of the areas of activity or interest covered by GAIN appears on the GLOBAL ACTION web site, www.globalactionpw.org. You can request links by as many topics as are relevant; if you plan listings under several topics, please try to give links directly to the most relevant pages in your web site. For organizations that do not have web sites, GLOBAL ACTION has a web page which lists participating organizations with descriptions of organizational concerns and goals, and posts notices of events and priorities that are sent to us by email. Please take advantage of these web-based means of spreading information about your related activities and priorities!

2. **Use the GLOBAL ACTION coalition forums to set priorities**, launch initiatives, debate issues. The GLOBAL ACTION Councils provide forums at which you can introduce others to your initiatives and recruit partners.

3. **Help shape the GLOBAL ACTION program, priorities, literature & web site** : The GLOBAL ACTION Coordinating Committees will regularly review proposals for additions and revisions to the GLOBAL ACTION program and related literature. New and old supporters are welcome to submit suggestions at any time via mail or fax or by email to suggestions@globalactionpw.org

GLOBAL ACTION TO PREVENT WAR

There were two earlier panel discussions, one on the Global Action program, one on April 8, 1998, and another on October 22, 1998, with Jonathan Dean, Randall Forsberg and Saul Mendlovitz. It seems more important to include the full program in an appendix as it had evolved by May, 1999, than to include a full transcript of the earlier discussions here. We have cut out the description of the various stages, because you will find it in the prior panel discussion, and in the appendix. We present other excerpts from both. We believe that the questions raised focus on some important issues, so we are including many of them, and the replies they elicited. Anyone interested in the full transcripts should contact the Committee.

VERNON NICHOLS, President, NGO Committee on Disarmament: ...We have three speakers this morning who have been working together on a project entitled Global Action to Prevent War. The first speaker is Ambassador Jonathan Dean. He is Advisor on International Security Issues for the Union of Concerned Scientists, and President of the United Nations Association of the Washington, DC Metropolitan Region. In addition to his distinguished diplomatic career, he is the author of several books, the most recent of which is *Ending Europe's Wars*, published in 1994 by The Twentieth Century Fund.

Our second speaker, Dr. Randall Forsberg, is Executive Director of the Institute for Defense and Disarmament Studies in Cambridge, Massachusetts. She is the author of many publications, including the Non Proliferation Primer. She received a five year MacArthur Foundation fellowship as well as other rewards for her work.

Dr. Saul Mendlovitz is the Dag Hammarskjold Professor of Peace and World Order Studies at Rutgers University. He is also the UN representative of the International Association of Lawyers Against Nuclear Arms. Among his publications is the book, *Preferred Futures for the UN*.

JONATHAN DEAN: *(April 8):* I will begin by describing some of the reasons why we turned to this idea. and will then go on to outline the content of its first phase. Looking at today's situation, all arms control and disarmament programs are motivated by the underlying desire to decrease the frequency of armed conflict. However, there is no major program among UN member states that directly pursues this aim of preventing war. We believe there should be such a program. Humanity is moving to a new, more hopeful millennium at the close of its bloodiest century. After learning a good deal during that century about how to prevent armed conflict, it's time to think in more ambitious terms. We are trying to do this with our program.

And there is real need to do this. Today, the United Nations and its member states are not doing well in their main Charter task of maintaining international peace and security. In spite of their enormous collective resources, they are failing to bring the level of armed conflict in the world under effective control. And they are paying the high costs of this inefficiency. A new approach to this problem is needed. that is our subject today - better ways to stop armed conflict.

The statistics on this subject are truly dismaying: According to some estimates, up to 45 million people, 90% of them civilians, have been killed in over 170 wars since the end of World War

II. Thirty major wars are now taking place, most of them inside national boundaries. In addition to tragic loss of life, the damage to productive economic activity and the setbacks to economic and social development are immense. They last for decades, sometimes generations, multiplying the human costs of conflict. Twenty years after civil war broke out in Lebanon in the seventies, Lebanon's gross national product was still 50% lower than before the fighting.

Despite their own enormous resources, the governments of the industrialized countries do not seem able to control this situation, only to react to it. Yet these same countries are almost always called on to pay both in public funds and voluntary donations a large part of the economic costs of these conflicts, measured in billions of dollars.

War has many causes - each war has many specific causes - but we can surely do better than we are doing now, especially in controlling the frequency of these small wars, both in the interests of the victims and in our own interest. Our current approach, coping with conflict, is not effective. Why is that so?

In 1962. as the Cold War was peaking, the US and the Soviet Union each presented to the UN plans for general and complete disarmament which combined the two approaches of peacekeeping and disarmament into a single integrated program. Under both plans, national armed forces, both conventional and nuclear, were to be reduced step-by-step, and, as this reduction process went on, the peacekeeping capabilities of the UN were to be built up. But as the Cold War continued, these plans for general disarmament, which were deliberate efforts to integrate the problems of peace and arms, were abandoned and disaggregated into separate programs. This disaggregation was intended to make the underlying problems more manageable.

It has achieved some progress with respect to nuclear weapons, partly because each of the many individual programs into which nuclear arms control has been divided - the test ban, bilateral reductions, non-proliferation, and ending production of fissile materials - was supported and sustained by strong public rejection of nuclear weapons.

But for conventional arms control, this disaggregation has had the negative result of dividing public and governmental interest and support, along with dividing up the subject matter. Dropping an integrated approach and segmenting these programs has resulted in a multitude of weakly supported programs - conventional disarmament, regional arms control, transparency, arms transfers, defense budgets and confidence-building measures.

Conflict with conventional arms has become so frequent and so usual in our time that these individual programs are not supported by the enormous public and governmental concern that comes with every aspect of nuclear weapons. Where there has been success, as in the Conventional Forces in Europe Treaty and with anti-personnel landmines, it has been because these subjects generated great public support. But they have been exceptions. In contrast to the integrated approach taken in the sixties, peacekeeping too has been handled completely separately from disarmament.

Today we have an unparalleled opportunity to do better than was possible in the last two or three decades, because of the more positive relationship among the major powers, and because we also have effective methods for preventing conflict. We have to use this opportunity before it is too late. We have to put these methods and these individual programs of conventional arms control

209

together into a more effective overall approach.

As regards methods, in the seventy years between the end of the World War I and the end of the Cold War, a lot of people worked to develop control over conventional weapons and armies in all the aspects that we are familiar with today: confidence-building measures; transparency and information exchange; mutual constraints on force activities and deployments; negotiated force reductions, and agreed restrictions on arms production and transfers.

Yet these procedures cover only one portion of the wide spectrum of conflict prevention and reduction measures that have been developed in this century. The remainder of that spectrum is covered by peacekeeping in its various forms, conflict prevention, mediation, arbitration, preventive deployment, post-conflict peacekeeping, peace building and, occasionally, peace enforcement.

The trend in international lending to raise conditions with regard to the level of military spending and even the direction of national military policy has also been useful. Recently, there were reports that the IMF blocked purchase by Romania of a large number of attack helicopters.

In past decades, these approaches, especially disarmament and peacekeeping, have been applied separately and incompletely. None has by itself been fully successful. Nor are they likely to be successful as long as they are applied separately and as individual components. In other words, our governments have been practicing peace in fragments. We believe that, instead, it is time to think about joining all these approaches and all these measures together, in a single unified program, with an initial focus on conflict inside national borders, a comprehensive program that can combine and increase public and governmental support for all these programs.

If governments throughout the world can act together to combine the two approaches of disarmament and peacekeeping into a single integrated program - and if governments can act to apply more systematically and consistently the whole spectrum of conflict reduction and conflict prevention measures - and also integrate the work of international financial institutions - then it should be possible to prevent an increasing number of tension areas from erupting into armed conflict, to make conventional warfare less frequent, and to limit conflict when it occurs. This is the objective of **Phase I** of our program and we think it can be achieved.

Yet no comprehensive program on coping with organized armed conflict now exists anywhere. This topic is not being discussed by individual governments, by the General Assembly, by the Conference on Disarmament, or by NGOs. The need is there; in fact, it is acute; the means are there, but no effective action is being taken. This is a serious omission.

We think this first phase can be achieved. But let me make clear that we are talking in Phase I about what the Carnegie Commission on Preventing Deadly Conflict calls "operational methods" of conflict prevention, not what the Commission calls "structural" means of preventing war - sustainable economic development, promotion of human rights, and social justice." These programs must be pursued in parallel, but they are not the subject matter of this first phase of our project, which is to get more control over the killing.

Let me summarize our main points. First, in the process of breaking down and dividing the subjects of conventional disarmament and conventional armed conflicts into individual programs, we have gone too far. We can get better results and gain greater public and governmental support through supplementing current programs with an overall integrated approach that combines arms control and peacekeeping, that adds a top-down approach to existing individual bottom-up approaches for constraining conflict. These individual programs must of course continue, but we want to bring their supporters together into a bigger, broader coalition.

Second, the objective of this combined approach should be to reduce the frequency of armed conflict throughout the world, a goal that is achievable through more systematic application by more countries of the broad repertory of peacemaking measures developed in this century.

Third, as a vehicle for this new approach, we need an international treaty to pull together these efforts and to motivate continuing onward action, the equivalent for conventional arms and conventional conflict of the Non-Proliferation Treaty for nuclear weapons. Only a treaty of global scope can provide the systematic worldwide action over many years that is necessary to bring results on this problem. In other words, we need a global non-proliferation treaty approach that combines conventional arms control and peacekeeping into a unified whole.

It is relevant here that reducing the worldwide level of conventional conflict and conventional arms is likely to be a requirement of the nuclear weapon states and their allies for making deep cuts in their nuclear forces or for seriously considering their elimination. If we can make headway on this project, this will mean progress toward fulfilling the obligation in Article VI of the Non-Proliferation Treaty to move toward general disarmament...

JONATHAN DEAN: (*October 22*) Today, we want to give you a progress report on the program called Global Action to Prevent War. As some of you know, we started this project about a year ago, it has been changed considerably as the result of comments we have received, many of them here in this room. It is appropriate that we report to you in this building, because Global Action to Prevent War aims to fulfill the first mission of the United Nations, to prevent war and to maintain international peace and security, by building up in phases the still rudimentary machinery of multilateral conflict prevention, peacekeeping and the rule of law.

The subject matter of the Global Action program is the wars that are going on, wars that we see, hear or read about every day in the public media - wars in Angola, Congo, Sierra Leone, Algeria, Sudan, Eritrea, Kosovo, Turkey, Afghanistan, Kashmir, Sri Lanka, and many other places. Some of these are internal conflicts, some are interstate wars, many are a combination of the two. But, however we classify them, all of these wars share one obvious characteristic: Thousands of people are dying in them, mainly old people, women and children. Many more are being wounded, many crippled for life.

Beyond this, the productive economy of the victim countries is destroyed and social and economic growth is set back for decades and decades, breeding hopelessness, a pervasive culture of armed violence, terrorism, and still more wars. We all know these facts. It is appalling to compare the scientific advances of our time with this grossly anachronistic continuing bloodletting. But, unless something decisive is done to change the situation, there is every indication that this tragic process will continue and that millions more will die in the next century.

Of course, a large number of programs to deal with this situation are in fact underway:

conventional force reductions, limits on arms production and trade, cuts in military spending, measures to stop proliferation and build confidence, measures for peaceful conflict resolution and for peacebuilding, peacekeeping, and peace enforcement. These programs are valuable, but they are not doing the job. What we are proposing is to bring these approaches together in a more effective, unified program to prevent war, and to incorporate this program in a treaty structure that assures its enduring implementation all over the world.

This comprehensive program to prevent war is also an indispensable counterpart to efforts to ban nuclear arms. I visualize it as the equivalent for conventional arms control and peacekeeping of the Non-Proliferation Treaty, which has moved slowly, but which has focused the actions of member states for thirty years...

When this program is implemented, it is likely to make war infrequent. It will save thousands of lives and huge sums of money. At the same time, it will foster the democratic institutions and the rule of law that must ultimately replace armed force in resolving conflicts, achieving justice, and fulfilling human needs.

Up to now, we have received over 200 written and oral comments on this project. One frequent comment was that we should deepen our treatment of internal conflicts. We have done that in our most recent version. We have added six measures which will strengthen the role of the international community, the UN and regional security organizations in preventive action to avert internal conflict.

The second area of frequent comment was that we should make more explicit the relationship of the Global Action program and programs of nuclear disarmament. We have done this, making clear that each is indispensable to the other, while avoiding lockstep.

I want to mention some distinctive features of the Global Action program. It is important to keep them in mind because they are more important in their essence than the individual details of what we are proposing. First and foremost, this project tackles head-on the central problem of human society - organized armed conflict and bloodshed. Other programs with the same aim are either indirect in their effects, for example, human rights programs, which tackle some of the injustices leading to war, or they are partial, for example, the very successful and useful Campaign Against Landmines. These programs are very valuable and they must be continued and furthered. These partial programs save a lot of lives. But they do not stop new wars from erupting. Nowhere - either at the UN, among governments, or among NGOs - is there any comprehensive program that has the direct aim of trying to stop the killing.

This is a big goal, but perhaps not as big as it looks when you try to deal with it in practical terms of reducing the frequency of war. And that goal can be carried out. The post-cold war situation is uniquely favorable for this project and the measures and procedures to do the job are available. The Global Action program combines conflict prevention, peacekeeping and conventional disarmament, hitherto pursued separately, in a more effective, integrated program. The treaty structure we suggest provides a framework that can link the efforts of many governments and NGOs and individuals toward a common goal over a long period of time. This job needs to be done. It will be done, sometime. The longer we wait to begin, the more people will die.

Second, as I have mentioned, this program is an essential counterpart to programs of nuclear disarmament. Unless nuclear disarmament comes as the result of a nuclear weapons catastrophe, its achievement will require reduced levels of conflict worldwide. Weapon states will not decide to eliminate their weapons when there still is a high level of violence throughout the world.

Nuclear disarmament will also require some effective and acceptable way to reduce the conventional forces of the major powers, especially their force projection capability. Countries like China, Russia and India will not relinquish their nuclear weapons if doing so has the effect of consolidating the conventional superiority of the United States.

Third, this Global Action program will get a better grip on all main types of war. For internal conflicts, it proposes an array of conflict prevention measures and a proactive role for the UN and for regional security organizations. For possible conflict between neighbors, it proposes force reductions, moving toward defensive defense, and a prescribed set of confidence measures and constraints on force activities in all situations where there is bilateral friction. It deals with the possibility of conflict among the major powers by fostering their cooperation in preventing smaller wars and through step-by-step force reductions that reduce their capacity to attack each other. In particular, this program will enable the step-by-step elimination of the possibility of foreign military intervention by large powers acting on their own which, historically, has been the source of many wars. I believe it is clear that elimination of nuclear weapons is a prerequisite for this.

Fourth, this program would establish a comprehensive, robust world security system composed of a well-financed UN with its own readiness forces, and a fully developed network of regional security institutions, each with some peacekeeping capability of their own, plus strengthened international judicial institutions and procedures. All of this would be developed step-by-step with reductions in national forces - but with an escape hatch for withdrawing from the scheme if the system does not perform effectively, with adequate national forces still intact.

Finally, if this program - or something along these lines - is carried out, it can in fact prevent the tragic loss of millions of human lives and the vast waste of productive resources which the armed conflicts of the next century will otherwise surely bring.

That is a brief summary of our program. Now, I want to turn to some questions that are often raised about it.

First, some believe the objectives of this program are highly desirable, but also rather unrealistic because, they argue, war is part of the essence of human society, will always be with us, and it is futile to try to stop it. As you know, this view on the genesis of war is far from agreed. But the short answer to this argument is that we can as a practical matter reduce the frequency and incidence of conflict and that we do have the tools to do this. We can tackle the question of whether war can be eliminated completely after we have made it infrequent.

I have mentioned that up to now, we have had over 200 oral or written comments about this project. None of them has argued that what we proposed would not work if it were fully put into effect. But several have referred to the difficulty of getting the plan adopted by governments. What about that question: Can a project that is so ambitious get off the ground? Is it unrealistic in the sense of its prospects for implementation?

213

I should make clear that we are thinking here of a twenty to thirty year effort. In the first few years of dissemination and discussion, we believe a sizable group of supportive governmental officials, NGOs and individuals will identify themselves and that this group will be large enough for the project to become widely known and influential, and to start making incremental progress, perhaps at the UN, perhaps in various regions. In particular, we believe we can attract the interest and support of governments and large humanitarian and private voluntary organizations, which have shown through their actions in peacekeeping and humanitarian relief that they have a built-in interest in reducing conflict and bloodshed.

On the same issue of feasibility, people also ask us, can you realistically expect the United States to relinquish its predominant military power through accepting this scheme? The answer to that is - at the outset, surely not. Before that happens, it has to be demonstrated convincingly that, with this program, the United States - and other industrial countries as well - can save very large sums of money otherwise spent for its own forces and for paying for the consequences of wars elsewhere and that it can live in a more secure international environment without being called on to continually function as the world's policeman, without its substance being nibbled away by all these demands. In time, this argument will have real impact.

Another key question: Most people would agree that the machinery for conflict reduction can be improved, but many point out that, even then, the problem will remain, how to get political decision makers to use the machinery before it is too late. We see that again and again. We agree this is a serious problem. This is the question of political will. It is a major goal of the Global Action project to help political leaders come to the realization that they have to act decisively when the indicators say trouble is ahead, to realize that, unless they do act, people will die and that their own governments will pay and pay - and that those governments will also endure serious damage to their own reputations as competent and effective governments.

One last point that is sometimes made about the Global Action program: Some people argue from the point of view of realpolitik that a few thousand war dead a year is the normal condition of humanity, a reflection of the first argument I mentioned, and that we should count our blessings that no world war with millions of dead is in the offing at the moment. To this view, I would respond that this kind of historical normality is far more dangerous now in an era of weapons of mass destruction, and that a world of expanding population and numbers of poor simply cannot afford the human and economic costs of frequent wars and preparation for war.

Finally, we believe something that I think many of you will share. We think it is immoral not to act against the killing when we almost certainly have available the means of sharply reducing it.

RANDALL FORSBERG: *(April 8)* I would like to begin with a brief review of the trends that are already underway in the incidence and scale of large-scale conventional warfare. It is useful, when trying to get a handle on this topic, to divide the kinds of wars we would be concerned with into two main categories, great power wars and major regional wars that are not great power wars.

The difference between these is that in a great power war typically there are only a handful of countries, sometimes two, sometimes three or four or five in the entire world which have the economic resources and the military means to bring warfare to distant regions, not only to attack one another but to spread war over great areas of the earth, in the twentieth century, to create world war.

Great power wars have been fought since the time of the earliest civilizations when there were wars of empire. But over the last five centuries, in particular, there has been a marked pattern of the world being dominated by a handful of great powers who competed with one another for land and for the population and natural resources and wealth which control of land brought with it.

In the nineteenth century the great powers which competed with one another were Britain, France, Germany and Japan. In earlier centuries there was another group of countries: Spain, Portugal, Italy and the Netherlands, all of which were great seafaring nations, and Sweden, all great powers with expansionist aims and colonial empires. In the twentieth century the United States and the former Soviet Union, now Russia, have joined the group of great powers which have waged war with one another around the world.

What is remarkable and important from the point of view of a long-term plan to reduce the risk of war, all kinds of war, is that since the end of World War II there has been a marked change in the legitimacy and expectation and nature of great power war. This is due to a combination of things, first and foremost the fact that the entire world has been mapped out into constitutional states which have their own constitutional governments recognized in the UN system. In the twenty years after the founding of the UN, with the decline of the legitimacy of colonialism and empire, and the rise of virtually universal support for self-determination, the idea that a large, powerful nation could undertake a plan of territorial expansion, or deliberate military aggression with the idea of seizing and incorporating territory into its political control, has been thoroughly de-legitimized, totally rejected, not only in idealist rhetoric but in the rhetoric and practice of nation states themselves.

This is a major change of behavior. The idea, to take the World War II examples, of German or Japanese expansion of spheres of influence as a deliberate policy, pursued by military means, is now inconceivable in the policies of the great powers since World War II. It has been replaced with the practice of military intervention. You can see, in the words that we use, aggression and intervention, the difference.

In the case of military intervention, military forces go into another country and intervene in a conflict in that country with the goal that when the conflict ends in the way that they favor, they will remove their military forces. Countries influence, shape, perhaps attempt to control developments with military force, but don't actually appropriate the territory and make it part of their empire. Intervention is a lesser form of military aggression than the outright empire-building aggression.

I will come back to aggression in talking about major regional wars, but to conclude on great power wars, there is no longer present today to any significant degree fear of a great power war or a world war started deliberately as a matter of policy, as a means of achieving economic or political ends, by any of the great powers against one another.

But there is still fear of great power war and I think it is an important driving component of what is perpetuating the system. For the near term that fear rests entirely on the military capabilities for great power war, which still exist. That was particularly true during the Cold War.

I was quite shocked to discover that some of the most hawkish US military analysts actually felt that, while the risk of war in Europe was very high, the possibility of a Soviet attack was very high and we had to be heavily armed to deter this, they completely agreed that such a war would not be started as a matter of rational policy to gain ends through it.

What they feared was a crisis escalating out of control and a preemptive attack that was actually a defensive move. One side would start the war by attacking the other side's forces so they would not be as vulnerable to being attacked as if they went second. The war would then escalate out of control and become a major war. They feared war by accidental escalation or miscalculation.

The deployment of forces that make such wars possible and that make potential military opponents fear and suspect each other remains a major source of fear of war. In Europe it has gone down. Obviously the countries that were great powers, Britain, France and Germany, have been approaching the process of ending fears of great power war in a much more radical way through integration, a marvelous idea that arose at the end of World War II and that we see unfolding today as the new Euro currency is moving along. Among those countries obviously there is no fear of great power war, nor do we have any fear of war between the United States and Europe or the United States and Japan or Japan and Europe.

There is, however, some remaining concern about the potential of a renewal of confrontation between the United States and Russia or between Russia and China, or conceivably China and Japan. While these concerns are extremely low, from the point of view of the public, from the point of view of the military planners they remain very salient. As far as I have been able to determine from talking with people directly, including Ted Warner, who is in charge of the threat assessment area for the US Defense Department, the concept behind the US forces is in the near term to be prepared to fight two major regional wars.

But that is not really what justifies our large standing forces in the United States. The real justification is the fact that sooner or later we can expect Russia or China to acquire major military forces and to represent the threat of great power war. If and when that happens we need to be prepared. We can't disarm and then expect to rearm in ten or twenty years. So we need to maintain all these forces in the meantime for future great power war scenarios.

If there were an arms control regime which dealt with the main military as opposed to political sources of fear of war and fear of escalation and armed conflict, that would address the strongest argument that is being made for military readiness. Military fears create a need for military readiness. This is an ideal situation to intervene with arms control and disarmament. If it is the military preparedness that is making you fear war, then let's get that to a state where you don't fear war.

If we look at the main factors that lead people to worry about a large scale war, either globally or regionally, they tend to be large standing armed forces which can go to war immediately, forces which have long-range offensive attack potential to attack an opponent's forces as a means of winning the war. They may be offensive in the tactical sense but still are considered defensive in the strategic sense. But from a possible opponent's point of view, such a capability is offensive.

The constant innovation in armaments creates technological uncertainty about potential war outcomes. Open arms production lines mean that in time of war much larger forces can be mobilized rapidly. These four aspects: the size of the standing forces in peacetime; the open arms production lines which permit rapid expansion in wartime; technical innovation in armaments; and offensive strategies and aspects which encourage preemptive attack and escalation, are components which are prominent among the great powers, and also in the major regional conflicts. If they were reduced or eliminated, they would reduce the fear of war, not as the product of a deliberate attack but as the product of an inadvertent escalation of a political crisis situation into war.

When we look at major regional wars, people tend to think that there are all kinds of risks of war which could crop up who knows where at any time. In fact, if you are considering large-scale wars, by which I mean wars in which thousands, or tens of thousands of major weapon systems will be employed on the two sides combined, not hundreds, and wars in which tens of thousands or hundreds of thousands of uniformed military personnel are involved, there are only a handful of areas around the world where there are both conflicts and capabilities for major regional war. They are all well-known to us. We can track them and know where we are because they are in fact so few.

There is the potential for war between China and Taiwan, which is remote at least for the near future; the potential for war between the two Koreas, which is somewhat closer but may disappear altogether in the next decade in an integrated fashion; the very long-standing conflict between India and Pakistan over Kashmir, which has led to several wars and could do so again; the on-going conflict between Greece and Turkey, which has also led to war, although not recently, and considerable arms buildups of the two NATO countries. That is eight countries, and four pairs.

Then there are six countries in the Middle East which have the capability for major war and have gone to war since 1945. These are Egypt, Israel, Saudi Arabia, Syria, Iraq and Iran. So fourteen countries, six in the Middle East and eight in other regions are all of the countries in the world, outside of the United States, Russia and countries in Europe, which have the capability for a major conventional war.

So the largest military forces, those of the United States, in particular, and secondarily Russia and to some extent China, are being maintained in the first instance, or in the long run, to deter great power conflict with each other, and secondly, for the potential to intervene in these regional conflicts which I have just listed. The regional conflicts, in turn, where large wars could occur, are long-standing conflicts where the issues are well-known and where it is also well-recognized, both in the regions and in the international community, that war is not the answer. There are routes to conflict resolution which can, should be and are, to a greater or lesser extent, being pursued.

What is important, with respect to the armaments in these regions, is to try to remove the military sources of fear, confrontation and suspicion, and to create a situation in which it is militarily difficult to attack and easy to defend, in which there is high confidence on both sides that attack is extremely unlikely and that thoughts of war as a means of addressing the conflict are constantly declining.

RANDALL FORSBERG: *(October 22)*: I would like to begin by giving you the punch line, which is this. At the end of the Cold War the world has changed so radically that we do have an opportunity to make a difference in the outbreak of war, its frequency, its scale, and the attitudes that people have about the normality of war, or the expectation of war. We all know, I think, that we have that opportunity, and yet, so far, neither governments nor we, the non-governmental community, have risen to that occasion. We have not come together and said, OK, the time has come. Enough. We tried this before the First World War, after the First World War, before World War II, after World War II. Then the Cold War came in and we stopped trying for fifty years to end all war, except for trying to stop the nuclear arms race and trying to cut back on the level of military spending.

We are now in a completely new era in which all the ground rules have changed, in which the opportunity that people on the panel, and I think all of the people in the room have sought and longed for for decades. This opportunity has now presented itself to us. Jonathan and I and Saul Mendlovitz and others who have begun to join in with us would like to invite you and encourage you and press you to join with us in trying to rise to the occasion, not just to chip away in the smallest and the most incremental measures that can ameliorate the human condition but to try and go to the heart of the problem and say that human beings can do something about this problem, that it is not beyond us, it is not undoable, that this does lie within the human capacity.

The program that we are suggesting has two aspects. One of them is a sort of umbrella aspect. it is a very large and comprehensive program which has room for and encompasses many of the activities that are already going on to support peace and disarmament. What it does is try to bring them together and integrate them in such a way that people can see themselves as working toward a common end in a common enterprise and both recognizing themselves and being recognized by other people as working together towards the abolition of war. Right now there is a sort of loose idea that there is a peace movement that opposes war, or an anti-war movement, that there are peace people, disarmament people. But we have no sense that there is a global movement to end war, and that this movement is widely supported, widely believed in, pursued with deep commitment and conviction on the part of hundreds of thousands or millions of people. We all know that people with those values are out there. What we want to do is to crystallize and mobilize that energy and that commitment that exists against those traditional realpolitik values.

The other aspect of the program is that it is not just an umbrella bringing together many different diverse pieces. It also includes some pieces that are not already being pursued. Rather than pulling them out separately, I will just give a sense of the main phases and components and of the integration of existing and new elements. There are four phases in the policy program that we have proposed. I think it is useful to think of them as sort of steps in a sort of stepwise reduction toward the abolition of war. Not all of them are reducing, Some of them are building up. To begin with it is useful to think of them as four steps which go like this: build confidence, reduce, build confidence, reduce. That is the program.

The part that is being reduced is national armed forces maintained for national unilateral use of force, nations arrogating to themselves the decision-making to intervene in wars in other nations. What is being built up is the UN's capability to address war, to prevent it if humanly possible, and if we don't get there in time and war breaks out, to help end it as quickly as possible with the least possible loss of life. So the concept is that we are building confidence in the ability of the international community to take effective action according to the rule of law, that is according to the Charter of the United Nations, and specifically the commitment of individuals and nations not to use violence or armed force, except for the purpose of self-defense, under any circumstances, that rule of law which is shared within our nations and within the international community in the form of the UN Charter. We are building confidence in the commitment and the ability to live by that rule of law in the confidence-building steps that we are undertaking. At the same time we are decreasing reliance on the national capability for security, for humanitarian intervention, for intervention against aggression. We are strengthening the international community's capabilities and the reliance of nations on the international bodies for doing those same functions, for preventing war, for preventing genocide, for ending genocide, for protecting against aggression, and, generally speaking, trying to prevent and end non-defensive uses of armed forces where people are trying to accomplish certain political or economic ends by means of using armed force.

In the First Phase we look specifically at strengthening confidence in the ability of the United Nations and of comparable regional organizations like the Organization for Security and Cooperation in Europe, the OSCE, and creating new organizations of that kind where they don't already exist in the Middle East and South Asia and East Asia. We are strengthening the security role of the organizations that do exist, the Organization for African Unity and the Organization of American States, so that we have not only the United Nations but also regional counterparts to the United Nations, which can function in the first instance and more close at hand to potential conflicts, being aware of their roots and organization and of potential means of resolving them. In the first stage we are looking at a variety of means of strengthening the ability of the United Nations and of non-partisan, regional security organizations to prevent conflict or to end it quickly if it breaks out...

SAUL MENDLOVITZ: *(April 8)*: In the March, 1997 issue of *Arms Control Today* Michael Mandelbaum wrote in "The Post-Cold War Settlement In Europe: A Triumph Of Arms Control" the following:

The military capabilities of the countries of Europe are less threatening now than in the past, and this has been accomplished by arms control. Specifically, it has been accomplished by the remarkable series of accords that were signed beginning with the Intermediate-Range Nuclear Forces (INF) agreement of December 1987, and culminating with the START II accord of January 1993. These arms control agreements are similar in appearance to those of the earlier part of the Cold War, but they differ in content in two truly revolutionary ways...

First, the later series of arms reduction agreements is characterized by 'defense dominance.' That is, they have reshaped military arsenals to make them more useful for defense than for offense in the case of conventional forces, and more useful for deterrence than for actual war fighting in the case of nuclear armaments...

The second revolutionary feature of the post-1987 arms agreements, both conventional and nuclear, is that they establish transparency. That is, all the countries of Europe and North America now can know what armaments all the other states have, what they are doing with them, and whether they are violating the agreed limits - and they can know this at all times.

In 1996 and 1997 Romania signed treaties with both Ukraine and Hungary with the following wording:

The contracting parties on a bilateral and multilateral basis, shall actively contribute to the further reduction of the armed forces and armaments to levels corresponding to their defense needs.

In 1993, perhaps more significantly, there was a study that came out of the United Nations from the Office of Disarmament Affairs, entitled "Study on Defensive Security Concepts and Policies." It was a study which was initiated and promoted by the Gorbachev Administration. It had a group of arms experts and diplomats. After some two years of meetings, they issued this document in which they set forth the possibility of establishing a regime, a military regime, a military way of looking at the world, based on defensive security.

What they meant by defensive security was what, in our terminology, would be called a border defense order. That is, every state in the world would have only those weapons, ground, air and sea, which would be capable of defending their own territory, but which would not have the capacity to engage in a long-range, enduring strike against the territorial integrity of another state.

I bring this document to your attention because I believe that defensive security may be, to the abolition of war, what the elimination of the slave trade was to the abolition of slavery. That is to say, can we conceive of a world in which all the unilateral systems of the world are geared to defense, and that that defense is so unthreatening that no other state conceives of itself as ever having to go to war?

This study, which came out in 1993, never was promoted within the system because of the changes which took place in the Soviet Union at that time. Gorbachev left, Yeltsin came in, there was the breakdown of the Soviet Empire, so-called, and we moved into a world in which the post-Cold War seemed to eliminate the immediate threat of nuclear weapons, the immediate threat of large-scale warfare, even regionally. So it didn't seem like something we had to be looking at.

One of the things that our movement could take on is this notion of defensive security. The reason I selected this UN document is because it comes out of the UN, and in that document it calls upon the states of the world to carry on intensive dialogues, and to bring to the UN plans for restructuring their armed forces so that they will be in a defensive posture.

We have called the project we are working on "Global Action to Prevent War." I have a different title for my speech. My speech, "The Campaign to Abolish War, Genocide, and Other Deadly Conflicts." The reason I tell you about my title is two fold.

To begin with, I am an abolitionist. I believe it is possible to abolish war as a human institution. That is why I use the metaphor and the analogy of the abolition of the slave trade with regard to slavery.

Number two, in addition to that, I believe that those of you who are in the audience, who have other views of what ought to be done next, vis a vis moving us towards a more safe, sane, sensible defense system, or security system for the globe, can enter into our project without committing yourself to the entire enterprise. That is to say the three of us are very strong-willed people. We have very strong views of what to do next, but we believe that we are at a moment of history where those of us who are at various parts of the movement are able to come together to put together a coherent scheme. While I am an abolitionist, and it makes one of my colleagues shudder if I say it aloud too much, because it seems utopian, I nevertheless am convinced that global action to prevent war is a realistic political project.

So let me give you a second sub-title. This is a realistic political project, from what I would call from the middle. We are used to talking from the top down, and from the bottom up, but we do not talk about from the middle. I see Jim Wurst here in the audience. In preparation for this talk, about three weeks ago I called him, and I said to him, Jim, what is on the arms control and disarmament agenda. He gave me something. Then, I asked, is there a peace movement? And he hemmed and he hawed, and then he said, no, there is no peace movement. I said to him, that is an interesting answer. I then called nine other people. I did not call my colleagues. Only one other person agreed with me, Johan Galtung, that there is a peace movement.

What do I mean, there is a peace movement? Let me quote Jim Wurst again in writing about the Ottawa signing which was coming up. He says "The Austrian text represents an unprecedented openness and cooperation between governments and non government people." I have given that some thought. I believe it is inaccurate, at least in general. It may be accurate with regard to the particular text. But what I want to argue is that the peace movement is alive and well, and that what has happened is that we have gone from the streets to the bargaining tables, to the political pressure groups, to the bringing together of various interest groups around particular issues.

I am here to profess law, and 1899 was the first Hague conference. I want to stretch us into the year 2020, and what the law might look like then. If you begin in 1899 you will see that that original Hague peace conference came about because of the pressures of so-called NGOs, what I prefer to call citizen's organizations in society. If you look at it closely it turns out that there were many women involved. They were not even voters, but if you look at where the impetus came, there was a Jewish merchant in Belgium named Immanuel Block, who wrote a six-volume work on war, there were women's organizations who were in touch with one another, who brought people together to talk about, not eliminating war, but laws regulating war. The first two conferences, in 1899 and 1907, talked about the rules of war on land. They were not attempting to end war at that point, although they set up international arbitration.

The point I want to make is twofold. There is the possibility of moving towards a plateau in the war system towards defensive security, and secondly, we in this room can help bring it about because we are helping bring it about. Let me state it in another way. "If it exists, it can happen." What I attempted to do, in quoting Michael Mandelbaum on NATO and western Europe and the former Soviet Empire, the treaties which have been signed by Romania, and the defensive security notion, and then beginning to look at the rest of the globe, is to demonstrate it is already beginning to operate. More and more states are moving into a force posture in which defense is what they are concerned about.

Let me move on before I come back to whether there is a peace movement and to what extent the NGOs and the governments are operating with one another. I want to move on to what I would call peacekeeping, and for the moment I am going to call it constabulary forces. I don't want to call them armed forces. I don't want to call them police because I still have my sixties mentality about the police. What I want to do is talk about constabulary forces, and be very specific about them.

We need to begin to think about standing forces of the UN, of individuals who are recruited as individuals and not as members of nation states, who owe their commitment and their loyalty to the UN as a civil servant. They are recruited and trained by the United Nations. They are placed into a standing constable force, let us say initially of some 15,000 individuals, maybe in four or five regions of the world. Each of these individuals should speak at least two languages of the big five languages. On the other hand you might want to add Swahili, Hindi, Arabic.

They should be paid rather well, and they should not be permitted to stay in the constable forces for more than twelve years, and they should be given some sort of opportunity when they get out. I would start with that kind of force now. I am supposed to be talking about long-range objectives, but I want to start with a group of some ten to fifteen thousand now, who would be called out by the Secretary-General.

There is the big political issue. When you look at the establishment of standing forces, the three big problems that seem to be involved are sovereignty, states are afraid they are going to lose control, nationals dying, the political problem back home in case any of your boys or girls get killed, and money, who is going to pay for it. I believe the creation of a standing force of some ten to fifteen thousand will overcome all of these issues. If the standing force is not made up of US citizens, or Russian citizens, or Belgian citizens, but are made up of UN officialdom who are police, or constables, that is different than calling on the US to send in a battalion. It is regrettable when there are any body bags, but when the body is killed it is the body of a policeman, and maybe Mayor Guiliani will show up and lament that, but it is not the body of a US citizen from the US armed forces.

The money issue: It appears to me that you can get a state of the art global force of the sort I am talking about for somewhere between $1 billion and $5 billion a year. $1 billion would give it to you in the sparse, lean form. $5 billion would give you the operation you need for air and all that.

In the early stages of setting this up you would obviously have to rely upon the major armed forces of the world to supply some of the equipment. But you can envisage a period in which we are capping what other states can have and bringing them down in which some of the materials which are being used by those major states are given to this new UN police force, or constable force.

Control is a major issue. I would to go into the present circumstance. I believe Randy was right in analyzing the likelihood of war between and amongst the major powers and the major regional powers. I do not believe we are likely to have a major war in the near future. On the other hand there are some 35 internal wars taking place, and we do have a fair amount of genocide taking place. I would propose that we start with an international genocide police force. The reason for that is that genocide is an international crime. It is already an international crime. What it lacks is enforcement machinery. I would provide the Secretary-General the capability to call out the international genocide police force on the suggestion and advice of an advisory council, that advisory council having been appointed by the Security Council.

I would use the Singapore formula, as put forth by Singapore in discussion of the creation of an International Criminal Court, in dealing with the question of whether or not the Secretary-General can trigger that force without the Security Council. The Singapore formula says that the independent prosecutor can go forward as long as no state, or no two states, says you cannot. We would have the

Secretary-General, on the advice and recommendation of the advisory council, move forward. Within sixty days, if the majority of the Security Council decided they wanted the forces withdrawn, they could withdraw them.

I would initiate that within the foreseeable future. I do not see that as a long-run issue. I think that the genocide issue is sufficiently poignant, sufficiently moving, so that we should begin to think about that now.

As we went through phases II, III and IV, that Randy has outlined, I would begin to increase the numbers of individuals in that international police force, remembering that we are also moving towards border defense, defensive structures of weapons and military arrangements, so that the number of people that would be needed for that transnational UN police force might be no more than a hundred or a hundred and fifty thousand, again, dispersed according to the same criteria that we used before in selecting, training and paying them. I believe that that is foreseeable. I would not see that as being fifty years down the line. I see that as being somewhere like twenty years down the line, building on the experience we have had with the genocide police force.

Now my title, The Abolition of War, Genocide and Other Deadly Conflicts, picking up on the Carnegie study of deadly conflicts. But what I really have in mind is internal civil war. I believe permitting internal civil wars to continue is an extraordinary way of creating the legitimation of violence. Let me make a couple of points.

Sunday's *New York Times* had an article from Oslo saying that a group had come together around small weapons. It said "Nations Endorse Moves to Eradicate the Plague of Small Arms." They quote Jan Egeland, Director of the Norwegian Initiative on Small Arms Transfers, which convened the meeting along with the UN Development Program. "It is a dream come true," said Mr. Egeland, a Norwegian diplomat who two weeks ago was the key speaker at a conference at Columbia University on controlling the light weapons trade.

Michael Klare in 1994 wrote a report saying we really don't know what is going on in small arms. In December of 1997, speaking to the same group that came together in 1994, he said, we now have a hold on that program. We actually know what is going on with regard to small arms. What I want to argue is that the movement is moving. It has taken itself from the streets to the conference table to the drafting of a document. We have a document. The document at the moment has the lugubrious title of "Global Conflict Resolution: Comprehensive Arms Reduction and Defensive Security." It is a 35 page draft treaty. It is being offered as a vehicle for beginning to discuss the various points that have been raised by my colleagues and by myself. It is a way of promoting a comprehensive, integrated approach to the whole war system, arms control, disarmament, peacekeeping.

I want to wind up with one other point, and that is the rule of law. This past three weeks we have had the sixth prepcom on the International Criminal Court. There will be a five and a half week period between June and July in Rome where the decision as to whether to go ahead with the Permanent International Criminal Court will be made. My guess is it's fifty-fifty, but certainly by next year we will have it. We may not have it this June, but we will have it next June. The crimes are war crimes, crimes against humanity and genocide. Those three for sure. The question is whether we are going to have aggression. The United States says we should not have aggression because the term is too murky and nobody knows what it means. It is like pornography, as we say in the Supreme Court. I know it when I see it, I don't have to define it.

What is happening with the establishment of the International Criminal Court is a reshaping and remolding of the notion of sovereignty. It began in 1899 and 1907, when the laws and customs of war were established, with individual responsibility for what you do on the battlefield. It went through the League of Nations, to the Pact of Paris, to the United Nations Charter, to the Genocide Convention which we are celebrating the fiftieth year of, to the 1949 and the 1977 protocols; all of those are the rule of law, making individuals responsible for what they have done to one another in conflict and violence. I believe the rule of law is something that our movement, which is alive and well, is capable of carrying on.

QUESTIONS: *(April 8):*

JIM WURST, Council on Economic Priorities: Saul didn't quote me enough. The broad grass roots public mobilization that defined peace movements in the past, the Ban the Bomb movements in the late fifties and early sixties, the anti-war movement, the anti-nuclear campaigns in the 1980s that brought out a million people to Central Park in 1982 and three to four million people across Europe, that helped establish free civil societies in the eastern countries, that movement does not exist. I was a part of two of those three. I am not happy to say that but I do believe that that is the case.

If we did have this broad grass roots, public constituency then we wouldn't be having some of the insane policies we have today. It would not be a matter of debate whether the Comprehensive Test Ban Treaty should be signed, NATO expansion would not be an issue, it would be considered far too absurd to pursue. You would not have politicians and other public figures acting with impunity in favor of UN bashing or the unrestrained proliferation of small arms. Just recently we had a member of the US Congress saying the UN Secretary-General should be horse-whipped. If there were a true broad-based peace constituency in the United States the political price of that sort of madness would be too high and it would not exist. That is what I am talking about when I say there is no peace movement.

In terms of the smaller, concentrated constituencies for certain policies, like some of the things you have mentioned, the International Criminal Court, landmines, yes they do exist, and they do continue to build, and every once in a while something, hopefully, will continue to push in the direction of a peace constituency. I am not saying there is no peace movement. If that were true, I have wasted my entire adult life.

Every one of the ideas you raised is very good, very useful, but this is not the sort of thing that will get a million people out to Central Park. Your ideas are viable, some of them will work, but you have to make a distinction between the massive, popular peace constituency and constant, hard, consistent, lobbying on these issues...

SAUL MENDLOVITZ: Jim is right that there is no broad-based, on the street movement. And it would be nice to have them around particular issues. But it is not clear to me that every moment in history needs people in the street in order to effectuate change. As someone who marched in those streets and actually went to jail, I don't say it is nostalgia in wanting to go back, it is another form of the social movement. I believe that the form of the social movement we now have is where skilled individuals all over the world are working on these issues. I am going to be sitting in another couple of weeks on an International People's Tribunal where people who have environmental issues, or human rights issues, are coming to discuss the claims they have against Brazil, or the claims they have against China. I am saying that the movement has variegated itself, and there are many more rivulets in the stream. I think the strength of what Randy, and Jonathan and I are doing is to find the place in which the various members of this movement can make a contribution of their own.

RANDALL FORSBERG: I didn't disagree with anything Jim said, except the implication at the end. I think it is entirely true that this kind of approach that we are still groping toward is not the kind of approach that is going to get a million people to Central Park. However, it is also not another piecemeal effort to lobby government officials. The intention of this approach is to encourage people who support peace and disarmament, but have not found a sufficiently broad and compelling platform to be active around, and who are not motivated by piecemeal efforts, to become more active, with the goal of having a hundred thousand people, instead of a thousand people in the US, working day in and day out on peace issues. To do that by bringing together people who are currently active in many different organizations to see themselves as being part of a larger movement with more comprehensive goals which I think have been taken for granted but are not articulated for the people who aren't active yet.

I think there is a different kind of activism. There is something in between the million people in the streets and piecemeal efforts, an informed mass movement which can debate these proposals, make variations on them and try to propagate them and get them into popular debate but may not decide to have a public demonstration on a large scale. That would still be different from the hitherto fragmented efforts. At least that is our hope.

JOAN DAVIS, Gray Panthers, New Yorkers Against Violence and Peace Action: I have seen young people try to keep young people out of jail, trying to keep young people from violence. Whenever we talk about disarmament in this country some big arms manufacturer says, but look at how many jobs we create. Have you been able to see the real cause of war? We have to see it in relation to the ordinary person, and I don't think you have represented the ordinary person yet. You have represented governments.

JONATHAN DEAN: I think there is a lot to what you say. We have deliberately stuck to what the Carnegie study calls operational methods, that is controlling violence in direct ways. The other programs of getting to the root causes of war have to go on simultaneously, but without some modicum of order in conflict areas, you can't really get at root causes. You can get at them of course by anticipating comflict, and that is what we have in mind, prevention and triggering these other processes for social justice and economic development.

RANDALL FORSBERG: I have a slightly different view. I think that there are many causes of war, just as there are many causes of violence within communities and in families. There isn't one cause. There are so many causes. But I personally think about war in analogy to interpersonal violence as something which isn't really caused. It is a behavior. There are many causes of conflict. There are many problems. The question is, do we respond to these causes and problems with violence, or do we find other ways. I think there is a lot of room to apply that analogy in the international arena, and not just in relations between husbands and wives.

It doesn't matter what the cause is. Violence is not the answer. War is not the answer. In fact, we know that the war system, the mentality that goes with it, and the resources it absorbs, undermine and block and weaken our ability to address the problems that are stimulating wars and feeding and fueling wars. I would not concede to the thrust of your non-question, that what we need to do to end war is to get to the root causes of war. I think that the root causes of war, in one sense, are the human condition. There is never going to be total justice, and total equity. What we need is to get people to make a commitment to non-violence in trying to make the most out of life for the most people. We can do that before we have succeeded in addressing many of the more profound and far-reaching, destructive, aspects of human life in today's world.

GAIL COLBY, Coalition for Peace Action in Princeton: ...I especially like the idea of the international genocide police force...I do have a concern that your ideas could be used to preserve the status quo. You could sacrifice social justice to preserve peace at any cost. How do you propose to find a mechanism to solve real issues of self-determination? They are often classified as "internal" issues. What about East Timur? What about Tibet? What about the internal colonies of Russia's current empire? How do you resolve these potential conflicts in a peaceful manner?

JONATHAN DEAN: That is a very difficult question. I have proposed that the OSCE, the Organization for Security and Cooperation in Europe, which has among its 53 members a lot of these groups that you mentioned that are seeking self-determination, establish a commission to which people can turn and set up a procedure by which they can achieve at least a great deal more autonomy and self-government. That would require them to undertake a commitment of non-violence in their approach and to go through a series of votes and plebiscites to ensure that there is real public support for autonomy. They would have to put forward a program for taking care of the minorities in their areas, if they become more autonomous, and they would also have to put forward a program for paying the cost of greater autonomy, sharing those costs. The governments, for their part, would have to make clear the rights that they are going to give and also engage in power-sharing. I don't think the creation of a lot more independent states is the answer to this kind of a problem. In fact, I think it is a recipe for disaster.

SAUL MENDLOVITZ: The issue of self-determination is one of the most vexatious that we are going to have to face. On the other hand, we have some normative order with regard to self-determination and how it might be played out, and we also have some covenants that deal with how individuals ought to be treated. What needs to be done now is to have a group put an annex to our document that looks at those issues where people are arguing that they are enslaved, that they would like some authoritative hearing, in some place, so that their complaints might be listened to and adjudicated. And so my sense is that as we continue - this is our first road show together, we have done a couple binaries - we need to develop an annex that would be part of our treaty that would deal with this issue and we would love to have you start it for us.

RANDALL FORSBERG: Your question, like Joan's, suggests that our proposal is going to preserve too much of the status quo, and not deal with injustices. We think that if you could get the governments with the largest military forces to disarm according to the terms of our plan, that would strengthen efforts for justice, not only in a broad social and economic sense, but also in the sense of

226

practicing participatory democracy. The central concept of this proposal is that groups renounce the use of force as a means of obtaining their ends. To have governments do that means that governments are not going to be thinking about using force repressively to impose regimes.

On the constructive side, I think generally speaking those groups that are seeking more rights or more recognition are much more likely to succeed if they use non-violent means than if they use violent means. We now know that there is a wide repertoire of non-violent means available, including non-violent direct action, civil disobedience, and civilian resistance, which are three different forms, all highly developed, to wrest away rights from the opponent, without using the tools of the oppressive opponent. This system is designed to complement the implementation of rights. You dismantle the government means, you empower the people's non-violent means of taking back those rights which they should have.

Finally, to generalize from Jonathan's comments, this would be the kind of thing that would be referred, not just in Europe, but globally, to a regional security organization that could say, this isn't fair, military means are being used to deprive us of basic human rights. One of the primary functions of a regional security organization would be to say, how can a claim of that kind be adjudicated and addressed without resort to military means? So building up organizations to protect human rights and recognize violations, as well as keeping the peace, would be integral, the other side of disarming.

CORA WEISS, Peace Action: ...Jim, I think we have to all agree that when conditions become outrageous enough, people become enraged and go to the streets. We can see that now with growing public opinion opposing NATO expansion...despite the absence of street action, but the presence of forums like this, so I agree with Saul that the peace movement is taking different forms, or forums...The Hague Appeal for Peace will be an end of the century conference in the Hague, celebrating the centenary of the first Hague Peace Conference which Saul Mendlovitz referred to and which calls for the abolition of war. It also calls, in one of its tracks, for a discussion of the root causes of war. So it will be the root causes of war, disarmament, including nuclear abolition, humanitarian law, and what changes need to be made in laws to protect the peace and prevent the conflict and promote reconciliation. The addition to what you have proposed today is the concept of a culture of peace, trying to create and inject into the new century a new way of living and to lift up the idea that a culture of peace is the way to go...Will you accept an invitation to bring your road show to the Hague and to integrate our work together, because clearly it is the same thing?

SAUL MENDLOVITZ: ...There is this culture of peace notion. Randy has been running a seminar with Elise Boulding, and she has been talking about preventing and abolishing war, and Elise has been talking about building the culture of peace, so we are very tuned into that. The question is what do you put into a document, how comprehensive should it be, especially if you are putting it in treaty form...We will definitely be at HAP. *(All three were.)*

RANDALL FORSBERG: I am thrilled that there is going to be a hundredth anniversary, even though it is a kind of perverse anniversary. For a hundred years we have been trying to end war, and we are going to cheer because we haven't succeeded yet? I think it is an important anniversary to mark, and to draw strength from. This was the first hundred years, but if we look at slavery, we are on the right track, and it will probably happen in the next hundred years, and that's great.

ANN LAKHDHIR: I have two questions. One was provoked when I was watching India's Republic Day parade on January 26 in New Delhi, where two-thirds of it focused on the Indian military. It ended up with the fighter aircraft that India has dropping flower petals on everybody, and all the Indians certainly exulting. When nationalism is so much defined by your military capability, how do you get a handle on that?

The second, and more difficult question is the product of having watched NOVA on public television last night. It focused on weapons of the future, focusing on what weapons the US would need to develop that would be more effective, more accurate, than the weapons the US used in the Gulf War. How do you defend against missiles, that may have biological, chemical or nuclear warheads? It is another dimension to protecting your borders. The focus was on the need to develop still more effective weapons. How do you put some limit on technological developments into the future? Do you ban certain kinds of weapon systems, like missiles?

JONATHAN DEAN: The Vienna document of the OSCE and also the CFE Treaty provide at least an opening on this issue. They provide for advance notification of new models or types of weapons. They provide for advanced viewing of prototype tests by all of the members of this treaty who can then presumably join together if they think a development is threatening, to argue with the originator and then perhaps to suppress it. So there is a literature on this subject of controlling technology. We did have in the US a system of evaluations by the Arms Control and Disarmament Agency of new weapons and their potential effects. That too is an obvious field in which this could work.

As regards missiles, it is my opinion that this is indeed a neglected field. We should begin to think in the next START negotiation of an agreement between the United States and Russia, to be expanded to others later, to destroy the surplus missiles. That is not the case now. To limit their production in the future, with verified exceptions for space and satellite launch. I think as reductions go on it will be possible to put up quite a convincing case for a worldwide treaty in this field, but the actions I have described would already bolster the Missile Technology Control Regime, the suppliers regime which does exist. So yes, I think it is better to go after the missiles than to put up missile protective systems, which has been the answer. I think you are on to a very important area.

RANDALL FORSBERG: Weapons of mass destruction, combined with missiles, is a particularly bad recipe. But the thing about weapons of mass destruction is that they don't have to be combined with missiles in order to be devastating against civilian populations on a large scale. The idea that we can develop better defenses against chemical and biological weapons or even nuclear terrorism, really this is an area for prevention and not military defense. Of course the kind of defense that was being referred to there was not defense, but preemptive attack, which should be replaced with another form of prevention than a partisan military attack.

Regarding the issue of nationalism that is reflected both in the Indian example and also in the television program, I will make two comments. Disturbing as it is, it is only one part of contemporary culture. As an example, in late September there will be a Frontline program called Sleepwalking to Armageddon, which is about the dangers of the nuclear weapons in the former Soviet Union getting into terrorist hands. These are examples of popular culture that take on that military nationalism and says it is not in our interest, this is not a good thing. I think it is a constant on-going struggle between these cultural perspectives. I don't think there is a short answer, a quick remedy.

In terms of the larger picture of how to address the fears without that kind of NOVA response, the oh dear, the threats are getting worse, we need more arms: I would like to underscore for this audience in particular the reason for the stress the three of us have put on strengthening the military capabilities of the UN and the regional organizations. It is to offer a concrete alternative which we have many reasons to believe will be more constructively used and less frequently than the national means of preemptive attack used as defense.

If it were not for the tendency to say in this country that the US and a few others, should sort of arrogate to themselves the responsibility to protect everyone in the world from those things we decide are military threats, then there might not need to be that degree of stress on the military component of the disarmament approach. Given that there is that stress on threats, I think there needs to be an essential component to create a large-scale public campaign for disarmament in which people can have confidence that that disarmament is not going to leave them defenseless, with no way of addressing new threats in the world. We need to offer a different response, which is more constructive, and more likely to prevent those threats from arising anew.

PETER DAVIES, Peace Action, A Safer World: First of all, congratulations for the diversity of views...What concerns me most is that in your presentation, Dr. Forsberg, you in effect said there are two types of war, the great powers and the regional. It seems to me, picking up from Saul Mendlovitz, it is terribly important that this comprehensive approach address three types of conflict, which includes the internal, indigenous civil war that we see as so prevalent. I don't think you can sweep under the rug the root causes of land pressure, of population, and all the others, because basically that third type of ethnic conflict, and I have lived and worked in many of these countries, is because politicians use those root causes in order to gain power and keep power. How do you reduce the opportunity for evil men, if you like, to exploit that situation? Saul, how do you get an international standby force, given the structure of the Security Council today where you know that there will be a veto by the great powers?

RANDALL FORSBERG: ...It is not the case that our proposal only addresses large scale conventional war. While Jonathan and Saul are focused particularly in their presentations in addressing ethnic conflict and genocide, my aspects of the presentation focused on the large scale conventional war. We are in agreement that you should not limit this proposal to the risks of large-scale conventional warfare. Let me turn your questions around: Ethnic conflicts don't necessarily arise from the root causes of war but from the tendency of evil people to exploit those causes and turn them into war. That question I would like to turn over to my colleagues.

JONATHAN DEAN: We did try to deal with this issue, perhaps not adequately. The various devices for prevention, better mediation, better warning, and direct international attention to these efforts, like that of Milosevic, to deliberately foment nationalism and hatred group feeling, must be used much earlier, to cope with that before a conflict stage is reached. There has to be organized effort on this. You don't go after this after it happens and then bemoan the fact.

SAUL MENDLOVITZ: ...We see the war system and the conflict system and the violence system at the level of organized violence and large-scale violence as being part of the same parcel. The problem is what are the strategy and tactics for moving forward with regard to these different kinds of violences. With regard to the specific issue of the internal civil wars, the difficulties have to do with how we move forward, not whether we move forward. I have only spent 50 years studying the root causes of war, and I refuse at this point to tell you what they are, because I don't know what they are. We know Freud tells us that human beings have an aggressive impulse. They also have a compassionate impulse. On the left hand side there is love, passion, and on the right hand side there is ugliness and aggression. What is going to be socialized, and then what that socialization is going to work out in terms of human institutions, that is a cultural matter, and we just don't know how that is going to work. What we are attempting to do, as Jonathan pointed out, is to get an operational way of dealing with this.

RANDALL FORSBERG: That is a purely inadvertent association between left and right?

SAUL MENDLOVITZ: Well, I happen to be right handed, but I am a lefty, as you know. As to the Security Council, my experience in talking to the people at State and Defense, they haven't thought much about an interventionary force around genocide. That is not an issue that they have looked at. You didn't need any early warning system for Rwanda and the former Yugoslavia. Everybody seems to believe that with regard to Rwanda, somewhere between 5-10,000 troops would have stopped the butchery...The really crucial thing is to send people in immediately...

TITUS PODEA, International Fellowship of Reconciliation: ...I have just returned from Stockholm where there was an international conference on the power of culture, but first, something on self-determination...France took the attitude that human rights could evolve up to a certain point. When they become group rights, they become minorities, and the minority problem has to be treated differently than human rights...President Wilson said that well-identified groupings should self-determine, but when they are not well-identified, there is another problem...France brought the southeast Europeans to Paris, and said, engage in negotiation and in neighborhood treaty-making. You have to learn how to live with your neighbors before you come into NATO, or the European Union. Hungary, who for 700 years has had claims on a province of Romania, Transylvania, signed the treaty saying we have no territorial claims on this territory, and Romania gave up her national rights to the province of Moldova, all to enter the European Union and NATO. So if there is some enticement, you can move minority groups to learn how to live with your neighbors...

In Stockholm 170 governments were present. It was not heads of state or prime ministers who were the predominant representatives, but Ministers of Foreign Affairs and Ministers of Culture were highly represented. It ran in parallel with another conference, not an NGO forum but a business UNESCO forum. UNESCO invited the business community to participate in a conference on culture...Can you give a definition of culture? Culture is the way we look at life. We are the product of a cultural environment. Business representatives said in Stockholm that culture is moving from the margin to the mainstream of life...One of the main themes was mini-banks...The eight days of discussions resulted in a document I recommend you look at...We need a holistic approach, development and culture, not just disarmament...

HARRISON HOFFMANN, Center for War/Peace Studies: Is not a chapter of great importance missing from your presentation this morning? You have gone, quite thoroughly it seems to me, in realistic terms, to describe a process of disarming. What you have not described is what the world does as a replacement for what it used to use arms for. How does the process of settling disputes go along with the process of taking away the military way of doing that?

SAUL MENDLOVITZ: Under the rule of law, when we finally get to it, there would have been compulsory jurisdiction before the Court at the Hague for disputes between and among states, compulsory jurisdiction. There would have been the establishment of a Permanent International Criminal Court under which people would be apprehended, tried and convicted or found innocent. So the whole rule of law notion is an essential element of what we are about as a way of resolving disputes before they break into violence. In Jonathan's fix on this there is a good deal of preventive work that goes on before matters go to a court. You only go to a court if you can't solve it at the local level, or the level of negotiations and mediation. But you are absolutely right, there is a triad. There is the normative order, the legislative capacity, there is an enforcement order, the police, and there is a judicial order. Those three have to be part of what you are talking about if you are going to eliminate conflict and violence. There is no question about it.

NEWTON BOWLES, Canadian United Nations Association: It struck me from the beginning of my association with the NGO Committee on Disarmament that our approach was a piecemeal one. I think this is a very healthy attempt to revive a more comprehensive attack on what you might call the war system. If we try to do everything, of course, we could end up doing nothing. From a Canadian perspective, is the US in the United Nations or not? If the US isn't going to pay its assessed contribution to the UN, what is the point of our discussion today?

SAUL MENDLOVITZ: The landmines treaty went on without the US signing it, and there is a landmines treaty. I believe that the US will sign it in the next few years. I believe, looking to the US to be part of every ratification, to be part of every regime on the globe is a mistake. I don't want to isolate this polity, but I don't want to make it the superhegemon, and if it doesn't come along we can't do it. Now I want to go to the money. Let's say the US owes a billion four hundred million. That's pipsqueak money. That is not a lot of money. The fact is, I believe the other states of the world are remiss in not providing the moneys that are needed to run this organization. We are talking somewhere like ten billion dollars a year for the entire UN system, and that is very little money. Yes, the US is behind in its dues. Throw them out. Don't let them vote. But do not hide behind what is a minuscule amount of money and say that the system can't work.

QUESTIONS *(October 22):*

KEITH SWARTZENBERGER, Mennonite Central Committee: First of all, let me express my gratitude to the panelists. The work you have done is invaluable and will definitely contribute to a world that has at least lower intensity conflicts. That having been said, I want to offer a criticism as well. You spoke, in your closing comments, of the desire to draw in NGOs and other groups which work with poverty and refugees. Yet I see nothing within the action program to actually deal with the root causes of war which are poverty, refugees, human development in general. If this truly is to be a global action to prevent war, I might offer the suggestion that this be included as part of it, some program for human development as well. If you do that, these other groups would be more than willing to join in.

RANDALL FORSBERG: We have heard this comment before, and we have responded to it in our statement by expressing the view that we hold that the causes of war can be addressed much more effectively if war isn't going on. Of course it is a chicken and egg problem. But the point is that human development, economic development, social development, political development, is a vast, vast project which is going to take a very long time. We are convinced that we can have war get out of the way of that project with greater focus and in a much shorter period of time. What we have here is a thirty year plan. Obviously it is not that we oppose and don't support the human development efforts. It is just that what we have taken on is the specific question of how to get war out of the way. I think that we need to keep that focus because that is the task that we are trying to accomplish.

KEITH SWARTZENBERGER: You talk about getting war out of the way, ending war. I really don't think that you are going to be successful in doing that without dealing with human development first. The very most that you can hope for is reducing intensity, which would be extremely helpful in dealing with these problems, but you will still have poverty and human rights abuses, you will still have people running around with baseball bats beating each other if they don't have weapons.

JONATHAN DEAN: I take very seriously what you are saying. We are a coalition, and I find it difficult to talk about the abolition of war because I see it at the end an enormously difficult task of affecting human nature and human psychology which, for our purposes, we shouldn't have to undertake. Here we are really talking about reducing the frequency of conflict. I think we can do this with this program. That will permit the longer-term efforts, the more fundamental efforts to get at the root causes, to operate more effectively.

MICHELLE PEPPERS, Ribbon International: Do you address economic conversion specifically in your plan?

RANDALL FORSBERG: Obviously we can't give in a short statement any kind of detailed plan that would apply to many different countries and circumstances. We do discuss the transfer of resources from military uses to non-military uses, and we do discuss re-employment possibilities for people and that there would be more vigorous economic development if we weren't involved in the boom and bust investment in military production and instead were working on civilian production.

MIRIAM MENDELSON, UN intern: This question is going to sound a little abstract. To anyone who has tried to start a car on a cold day, there is a moment at which the spark catches and the engine turns over, and from that point on, the engine goes. I am hearing a plan and a lot of desire. I wonder how any one of you would envisage what single force, what single person, what combination of circumstances might produce that moment where this actually catches and starts to go.

JOHN LINEWEAVER, Fellowship of Reconciliation: I have two books. One is *The Psychoanalysis of War*. I can't get anyone in the peace movement to read it. There is another book, *Enemies and Allies*. These present a diagnosis of the psychosocial aspects of the pathology of war. We mentioned here the normality of war. War is a psychosocial pathology. And we must emphasis that and substantiate that diagnosis. Sometimes we need treatment rather than treaties. I think parallel to your one third reduction in arms, twice, we need one-third progress in social economic justice. That would balance out your effort. But it has to be a parallel effort. We last week talked about poverty. This week we talk about disarmament. They must be in a coherent way integrated. I agree with Keith.

JONATHAN DEAN: Yes, we are confronted with starting a car on a cold day. I said that reducing the frequency of war is a task that needs doing. That is the car. You and everyone else in this room I think would agree with that statement. And I think many of us can feel that there is a growing movement, very slow, in that direction, so that you could even share my statement that this task will be done some time in the future. We want to start doing it now. That is the purpose of our entire activity, because all of us here can say we have got to reduce the frequency of war, and we have got to believe that it can be done eventually. Our objective in starting this organized effort is indeed to begin the process and to warm up the engine. We think that within two or three years we can make this idea so current throughout the world, that people know that this idea exists, that they come to it with the desire to stop conflict, to get people to support it. We think that in three or four years this idea can penetrate the upper ranks of government. They begin to talk about it, they begin to introduce resolutions here at the United Nations, we can get action in the Conference on Disarmament ultimately in talking about this problem. We can assemble all of the components that we have put together and start putting them, piecemeal, in different areas. We think that if we put our backs into it and really get the thing moving that we will really start the engine within the next five or six years. We do have a fairly lengthy program that we describe to accomplish this fundamental change.

RANDALL FORSBERG: Let me try to do better about poverty. I made a mistake. It is hard to be part of starting something that you are able to keep and also let go of at the same time. This is genuinely intended to be a sufficiently skeletal and flexible program so that people can flesh it out in the way that makes sense to them. The more appropriate answer would have been, we would like you to write the part of the program that has to do with poverty, and put it on the bulletin board and show that it is an important part of the solution to address the roots of the problem. This is not intended to be exclusionary. I was just saying that my focus needs to be on the ending war pieces that have to do with organization for protection and militarism. That doesn't mean that this program isn't a sufficiently large umbrella to encompass justice and equity and basic human needs that people feel are tremendously central to this issue. I mean that seriously. I am inviting you and others who feel that we have left out a crucial part of the program. It is not that you disagree with what we have put in but that we have left something out, send us what we have left out. Allow us to add it on and to make it a more complex reality.

We need to address the pathology. I was using "normality" specifically in that sense. I was saying it shouldn't be. War is treated by the society and the culture as normal, but it shouldn't be. It should be treated as an aberration, as a barbarism, that doesn't belong in our world, ever, under any circumstances. From that point of view the most important change is the change in people's hearts and minds. It is not the change in the hardware or the institutions. Those are roots to changes, paths to changing hearts and minds. You give people a structure where they have to make a decision, they have to make a choice for one thing or for something else, and you use that decision-making as a way of pulling people and coalescing them around the moral choice against violence and for non-violence. From that point of view I do think that there is another dimension to the poverty issue.

I think about an analogy, the situation in which you have husbands beating wives and people trying to get that to stop. You know that in that situation, you never say "you should stop beating your wife after your salary is high enough, after you have a decent place to live, after you don't have a million kids screaming all the time and upsetting you." What you say is "first, you stop beating your wife." Then you deal with those other things. So I think there is an important component of the war problem that does not have to do with its roots or the things that people fight about, that has to do with the commitment to solve the problems not by fighting but by non-violent means. Our program is trying to build and develop and strengthen the commitment and the belief that that can happen.

233

ANDY SIKORA, International Physicians for the Prevention of Nuclear War: Earlier this year I had the opportunity to spend two months in Sri Lanka where I got to see up close the world's number one form of warfare, internal civil conflict. Could you describe a little more what exactly your proposal contains to address internal conflict and what may be some of the criticisms on that topic?

JONATHAN DEAN: Let me try. The initial comments focused exactly on that problem. Some people said we had a formula adequate to deal with inter-state war but were not talking enough about internal conflict and so we added some elements. We are talking about a pro-active role for the UN and for regional security organizations. One of the things we are asking for is a professional conflict warning and mediation service at the disposal of the Secretary-General. We are talking about, as Randall said, establishing regional security organizations where they don't exist, building them up where they do exist, infusing them with the idea of conflict prevention and arbitration, mediation, all of the things that they should be doing, giving them some peace-keeping capability, putting them under the oversight of the Security Council and the Secretary-General, invigorating the Military Staff Committee to think also about domestic conflict and what can be done about it.

We suggest readiness brigades for preventive deployment, as it is being practiced in Macedonia. A move towards a more compulsory jurisdiction of the International Court of Justice and to give it some domestic edge. We talk about beginning international negotiations to establish an international code of minority rights. We want the signatories of this treaty to agree to unconditionally and immediately admit and facilitate visits of UN observers to check compliance with human rights obligations. As you know, there are about 60 treaties on human rights, and if you heard Secretary-General Annan speak in September, he complained about the good paper record and the poor actual performance record on human rights.

We think a device of this kind will oblige countries to live up to those obligations. We also want to initiate or expand - this is supposed to be an obligation of every country, in our concept - nation-wide domestic programs for training in the peaceful settlement of disputes in schools and communities. We want the Security Council and the regional organizations to take a pro-active role when they see trouble in a country, to advise that government sometimes when it is justified and to help them in solving these potential conflicts before they erupt. There is no perfect answer to this but we think we have a more effective approach to this than we had before, but with your experience, look at this program and give us your suggestions. We will certainly take them very seriously.

BETTY REARDON, International Peace Research Association: I also want to express, on behalf of my organization, thanks for doing the hard, detailed work and to re-enforce the invitation from Randy and Jonathan for us to become involved in the process. I want to reinforce the importance of focus. There is an element that I would call war-readiness. I think you have got the element of war itself and the alternatives for security, but there is a great deal of what people have been referring to here in terms of causes that are actually consequences of war-readiness: the erosion of the environment, military spending. There is a very important area too, the security of women, and war-readiness and the long-term stationing of forces of forward-defense bases undermines daily the security of women. We would be glad to help link that up.

BETH LAMONT, American Humanist Association: In July 120 nations signed a draft document for an International Criminal Court. The US did not sign. When Ambassador Sheffer of the US reported to Congress, one of the reasons he cited was that it would interfere with US responding militarily to crises around the world. I see this as a major problem What say you.

JONATHAN DEAN: It was a great advance when 120 countries gathered in Rome and developed the treaty and a very severe disappointment when the US failed to sign. I think that was a real error on the part of the Administration for not having seen this question coming long in advance and not having developed an acceptable compromise formula. As it now stands, most observers do expect the US Administration to come along with this treaty in the course of time, as it did with the Law of the Sea Treaty. I think the general expectation is the court will be established and will function, and after a time, the US will join. We of course will do our level best, along with you, to accelerate that.

RANDALL FORSBERG: Among our first phase measures we call for nations to join and support the International Criminal Court. We also call for the creation of a civilian police force trained for peace-keeping missions at the disposal of the UN Secretary-General and the international court system so that there is a mechanism for enforcing the use of the International Court of Justice and the International Criminal Court.

DAVID BURLESON, UNESCO adviser to UNICEF, retired: I laud you on your 30-year project. When I am not busy being a peacenik I try to be an anthropologist. I wish to offer you an icon for peace. Extend your time frame a bit. On the second floor of the United Nations opposite the entrance to the Security Council there is a magnificent icon of peace. It is dated 1269 BC and it is the first known peace treaty in the human experience. If you do some simple arithmetic, take 1269 and 2031 AD, add them together and you can have the 3300th anniversary of peace.

RANDALL FORSBERG: In the last formal stage we speculate what might happen after nations are left with forces which are only capable of defending their own territory and not capable of moving into the territory of other nations. That means that they end up with border guards, a coast guard, air defenses but no large standing armies which have the logistical ability to move out into other nations.

MARIA MALAMAN, Legion of Good Will in Brazil: I love your words. The Legion of Good Will preaches understanding among all religions and people. We think this is the most important problem in the world. We understand that love is important, spirituality is something special in the hearts of people. How is spirituality being addressed in a global way to prevent war?

JONATHAN DEAN: I think the global effort to prevent war is going to be fueled and driven by spirituality. We think that along with the desire to survive, the desire for peace and an end to conflict is probably the most basic emotion of society and we feel that if we can release it and we have presented a vehicle that people think will do the job that we will have tremendous outpouring of spirituality and support for this undertaking.

EMERGING PARTNERSHIP ON SMALL ARMS

JIM WURST, Council on Economic Priorities, Chairman: Multiple initiatives are emerging on the control of small arms. This is a pervasive problem that has no single solution. No one country, no one agency, no one Non Governmental Organization can come up with everything. We will look at several ways of addressing this issue. With us we have two governmental representatives, Ambassador Johan Nordenfelt of Sweden, Mr. Fernando Chomar from the Mission of Mozambique, Swadesh Rana from the UN Department for Disarmament Affairs, and Loretta Bondi of Human Rights Watch, Arms Division.

Ambassador Nordenfelt, since early 1997, has been the Swedish Ambassador for Disarmament in Stockholm. He was the Director of the UN Office for Disarmament Affairs in the early 1990s. Ambassador Nordenfelt.

AMBASSADOR JOHAN NORDENFELT: Thank you very much. When it comes to small arms and light weapons, there is no one problem, no one solution, no one way to go. It is an immensely complex and complicated problem. There are figures that speak their own language and, although one must be very careful with figures, it has been suggested that up to 90% of all casualties in armed conflicts in our decade have been victims of small arms and light weapons. This of course would necessarily include victims of anti-personnel mines. But it is a staggering figure. Even if it is not 90 per cent it certainly is enough for one to realize that it is a problem to tackle even if it were only 50, and surely it is much more than that. And we know that up to 80 percent of all casualties and victims are civilians and we know that a great number of these are women and children.

So these are weapons that are actually in use. These are the ones that kill and maim and make societies in reconstruction dangerous places to be in. We have to look at a whole range of ways to tackle it. We certainly need to do it in an integrated way and try to work out an action plan. But we cannot wait until we have it all together. We must start now because the problem is here right now. So whereas we should strive for an overall strategy, and we should strive for looking into the many components of this problem and study it closely, we also must not hesitate to start where we can start. I mention this because we have already started in certain areas. The Mali initiative for a small arms moratorium is a start that deserves the full support of the international community. It is not only a program for Mali, where it started, it is also a program that has been expanded to involve all the West African states. We are waiting for them to adopt formally the Declaration on the Moratorium which is applicable to all of them, on the transfer and the circulation of small arms in their countries.

The vast amounts of small arms in illicit circulation is a serious problem and we need to help those states that need and ask for help in this area. It is not only a matter of tackling such things as customs control and legislation for the transfer and the possession and use of weapons and to help those who request technical assistance and economic assistance in doing it. It is also a matter that requires a great deal of cooperation.

But that is only one side; the other side is where do these weapons come from? A large number of the weapons that are now in circulation, and move from one area to another, have been in circulation for a great number of years, but there are also new weapons. And we have to look at ways of checking the sources. We have to be able to establish rules of constraint when it comes to transfers from the producing and exporting states. In Europe last April a Code of Conduct in the European Union for transfers of arms was adopted which covers, to a very large extent, small arms and light weapons. It is a system that requires Member States of the Union to consider a number of criteria for when and how they should allow the transfer of small arms and light weapons and other weapons. They include the recipient country's human rights situation, an assessment of the likelihood the weapons might move on to other recipients, and the risks of creating instability in the region.

The European Union has also adopted an active program to assist countries in the area of small arms and light weapons. This is only a beginning. This has to do with the collection of surplus weapons and their destruction. It has to do with helping them construct safer structures for handling small arms and light weapons, and with assistance to internal law and order reform within the framework of good governance. We need to get to this problem because it is not only that the weapons are used in conflicts, but when you arrive at a peace settlement between parties to a conflict, that peace agreement is often very fragile if you have not been able to collect weapons. When the combatants are demobilized they need assistance and help to reintegrate into society. Their weapons need to be collected, but all those other people, who in the course of a conflict have acquired weapons for their own security will, of course, feel hesitant to give up their weapons unless there is a basic law and order structure which may allow them as civilians to feel reasonably safe in society. So assistance is needed in all these areas to make it work.

My country, Sweden, has participated through many decades in peace-keeping operations, together with other Nordic countries, and we have built up a fair amount of experience in this area. We believe that in peace agreements and settlements and peace missions intended to support an internal settlement, small arms and light weapons need to be highlighted; what to do with them needs to be a part of the agreement between the parties and it also needs to be part of the mandate for peace mission. Some guidelines for peace operations need to be developed which will assist them in working with the parties to collect and destroy surplus weapons.

We intend to organize, in Sweden, a seminar on this aspect in March of next year which will be a complement to a seminar that has already taken place here in New York. Another seminar is being organized in Guatemala around the same set of problems. We believe that this is an area that needs to be further studied so that we can arrive at practical guidelines, a manual, if you wish.

The problems cannot be dealt with the way we dealt with anti-personnel land mines. Here the answer was a total prohibition. It is a great stride forwards that we have the Ottawa treaty and that so many states have already signed and ratified it that it will enter into force and the first meeting of States Parties will take place in Mozambique in May. But we cannot approach small arms the same way. They cover such a wide range and are not of a nature to be completely prohibited. Many small arms are considered to be reasonable and legitimately acquired for purposes of national defense and maintenance of citizen security through a well functioning law and order system. So we have to go about it in a more complex way through a series of meetings, a series of projects, a series of activities, and hope that we have an international conference and come up with an action plan that will facilitate coordination between us.

FERNANDO CHOMAR, Permanent Mission of Mozambique: We believe the issue of small arms is not only important for governments but also for the NGO's to overcome the problem of small arms.

In my own experience I have seen have seen small arms with my eyes in the hands of those that can use them to threaten the peace and security of the country and the people. Small arms can be put in one's pocket. While walking in roads one can grab someone and ask for money. Which means the person can be in danger if he does not accept what the holder of the small arms is asking. Small arms can be used to go to everybody's house at night when not expected to ask for the keys to the car or to take the television or other goods. You have worked hard for those goods and then they are taken. But we are considering small arms in the international dimension.

Small arms in the hands of the government can still be dangerous because someone can go to the storage and organize people to use them and a conflict can erupt. If those people who are taking guns from storage go to government and ask to be appointed as minister and are not appointed they will threaten government with those weapons. The conclusion is that the use of small arms constitutes a serious threat to national and regional security. It aggravates internal conflict and increases crime banditry and civil disobedience not only in affected countries but in neighboring countries.

In the case of Mozambique, the long-lasting conflict resulted in the combination of large quantities of weapons out of governmental control. Weapons were in the hands of private people and hidden throughout the country. Many of these weapons were brought to the country illicitly. The issue of arms collection and destruction was one of the major responsibilities of the UN operations in Mozambique within the framework of the Rome agreement which was signed in 1994. Most of those tasks were to be obtained though disarmament and the demobilization of forces to ensure a peaceful transition, especially during and following the general elections of 1994, in Mozambique. The accomplishment of these tasks was regarded as vital, taking into account the lessons that had been learned from peace processes in Angola. The partnership we are talking about here is of interest for those who are suffering from small arms.

To overcome the trends that I have mentioned I would like to share some humble suggestions aimed at reversing these trends and insuring international security: 1). The international community should promote and ensure an exchange of material of national and sub-regional experiences in the collection, control and disposal of small arms; 2) the programs of reintegration of former combatants into civil society at the end of armed conflict, including the legal framework for reducing the excessive accumulation and transfer of small arms, should be established under the guidance of the United Nations; 3) the United Nations should include all kinds of weapons as integral parts of peace accords where the international community is involved in putting an end to armed conflicts and in consolidating peace processes to prevent their re-emergence; 4) in affected regions or countries, states and regional organizations should also take immediate steps to stop the inflow of small arms and light weapons through increased cooperation, harmonization of transfer procedures, control and intelligence sharing.

Mozambique, located in the southern part of Africa, is a member of the Southern African Development Community. Measures are being taken by this organization to make sure there is police coordination. Small arms cause a lot of problems for development in that region. In this region, we have already established a mechanism to avoid the transborder movement of small arms and light weapons and to combat smuggling, money laundering, stock stealing, drug trafficking, and vagrant theft and to harmonize national regulations in order to ensure that criminals escaping from justice in one country with stringent laws do not find shelter in our region. We are also encouraged by other initiatives in the continent of Africa.

I would also like to provoke a discussion by putting a question forward. I think we are here not only to listen to what some of us have experienced but would like to get from you the experience you can contribute to our respective countries. The question is how do you, as NGOs, as a civil society, feel about the production of small arms? In our respective countries we don't have industries to build small arms, but we do have the industries to use the small arms which are coming to our countries, illicitly, sometimes, but also for the sovereignty and the security of the country. And if it is not well controlled by the government, it causes a lot of problems. The question is up to you and should guide this forum into discussing the ways in which we can deal with the issue.

The second question is: do you think that the collection of small arms is the unique solution for the problems of conflict in these countries or in all countries ?

SWADESH RANA, UN Department of Disarmament Affairs:...As Johan has pointed out already, in our search for the perfect partnership that would do for small arms what has been done for land mines, we seem to forget that small arms are not land mines. It is not a category of weapons which can be banned because these weapons are a part of the armory, a part of the arsenal of national security of every single member of the United Nations. All the 186 Member States of the UN have some quantity or quality of these weapons. There is no possibility that these weapons as a category can be banned.

Second, this is not a new category of weapons that has been introduced on the horizon. In some form or shape, small arms and light weapons have existed ever since the beginning of humanity; they took the form of machetes and spears which are still used in places like Rwanda. This is not a category of weapons whose use and production can be banned because police officers, law and order and maintenance officials, need them, as well as border security forces. So there is nothing particular about these weapons to put them in a category where production can be banned, where their use can be banned. Can their transfer be banned? No, because of the 186 member countries, 117 members of the UN do not manufacture weapons. Bravo for the disarmament community; it is a great achievement that these 117 countries do not manufacture weapons. But they do have legitimate international security and national security concerns, so they import these weapons. If somebody comes up with forbidding all transfers of small arms to every place in the world, then the chances are that out of these 117 countries, quite a few might be forced to start manufacturing weapons themselves because they have got legitimate concerns of maintaining internal law and order and of protecting their frontiers. Having said that the manufacture of these weapons cannot be stopped, their use cannot be stopped, their transfer cannot be stopped, what are we worried about now?

This is where the NGOs can be very helpful in putting this question in the correct framework. This issue is a must in the disarmament agenda because these weapons are killing people in the thousands. There is a concern that these had become the real tools of armed conflict in which the United Nations is involved. But then the issue is no longer confined to the disarmament agenda. It is no longer confined to an arms control issue. It has become an issue in which the humanitarian, the developmental aspects and the criminal linkages between these weapons and violence and drugs and terrorism have given this issue a totally new perspective. And if you understand this, then it will be easier for you to craft the emerging partnerships. These partnerships that are emerging to do something on this issue, as I see them, are of three types: those partnerships which are emerging within the UN system, and I am sure you are familiar with the various organs of the UN that deal with matters pertaining to disarmament, to security, to economic and social issues, and to General Assembly affairs. The partnership that is emerging in small arms now involves all these organs.

The Secretariat, headed by the Secretary-General, is usually the implementing authority of the mandates that are given by the General Assembly or the Security Council. But the Secretary-General himself, in his latest report on Africa, has very strongly favored doing something to stop the illicit flux of arms to Africa. So the Secretary-General has taken the initiative to talk about the subject because he feels it is very seriously affecting the security of Africa.

The Security Council usually deals with matters pertaining to threats to international peace and security. Cruel and unkind as it may sound, although the devastation, the deaths, the destruction, the displacement, the uprooting caused by small arms in parts of the world has been enormous, it really has not been considered as the kind of threat to security that was posed by the possibility of a nuclear war. Even so, the Security Council has started taking an interest in the matter. They are currently in the process of drafting a resolution from the Security Council in response to the Secretary-General's report in which they propose certain measures on how to deal with the issue of arms in Africa.

Then you have the ECOSOC, which deals with the economic and social issues traditionally. ECOSOC, in February this year, adopted a resolution asking for a convention to be signed by the year 2000 which would restrict illicit traffic and prevent transnational transfer of firearms. So, from the view of preventing crime, the ECOSOC has taken interest; from the viewpoint of preventing conflict, the Secretary-General himself has taken interest; from the viewpoint of emerging threats to international peace and security, the Security Council has an interest; and the General Assembly at this session had several initiatives on the issue of small arms. So within the UN system there is a partnership among various organs of the UN which are looking at the issue from different sides but they are zeroing in on doing something in this area.

The second partnership I see emerging is within the Secretariat; the various departments which deal with disarmament, with peacekeeping, with political affairs, with humanitarian affairs, all from their different perspectives have an interest. The Secretary-General, in his wisdom, has decided to designate my department, the Department of Disarmament Affairs, as the focal point for coordinating all action on the issue of small arms within the entire UN system to avoid duplication and encourage a coherent and coordinated approach to the subject.

Then there is a third type of partnership which is emerging which is outside the UN; it is among the donor countries, the affected countries and the international developmental and financial institutions, none of which deal with the issue of disarmament per se. Yet some of the major donors to the development countries feel that the results of years of developmental assistance have been negated by certain outbreak of violence and armed conflict in places like Rwanda, Burundi, Liberia, Somalia and there are so many other places where years of developmental achievements have been negated by the upsurge of the violent conflict fought with small arms. And they are concerned that these conflicts should not reoccur so that the developmental aid that is provided reaches the objectives, the targets, without being interrupted.

Then you have the affected countries themselves. By my last count there were almost twenty-three countries where the United Nations has intervened, where the United Nations was actively involved in peace operations, whether in Central America, Africa, or in parts of Southwest Asia. And there are some countries which have been very badly affected by the phenomena of the use of small arms, whether for violence, for armed conflict, or for linkages between violence, armed conflict and illicit trafficking in other types of goods.

These countries don't have time on their side. My colleague from Mozambique has referred to the experience of Mozambique. When we were in Pretoria last year, or the year before last, one of the questions that was repeatedly asked from the participants from Africa was: it is good that peace accords are going to be signed and protracted conflict in Angola and Mozambique is going to come to an end, but what will happen to those millions of weapons which have been used in these countries? They will be released into civil society and in countries where fragile political institutions and the judicial system are in the process of formation, and the internal law and order situation is poor, how are they going to deal with it?

So the countries that are seriously affected are either those which have gone through a protracted periods of war or internal unrest, or national liberation or political revolt. These are one set of countries and then there are the countries on the borders. The neighboring countries are seriously affected when refugees from these countries move in, taking with them some of the unresolved tensions they have. If they happen to be inside a country where they have some ethnic affinity, then you know what the problems are.

So, there are the donors, there are these affected countries, and there are the international, developmental and financial institutions like the World Bank, like the International Monetary Fund. I think the World Bank has established a unit called the Post Conflict and Reconstruction Unit, precisely because donor countries are worried that unless something is done to stop the flow of weapons to these countries, the availability of weapons, or the use of weapons, it will be difficult for them to achieve their developments. So, this is the third type of partnership which is emerging.

If I were to try to draw certain conclusions which are commonly shared by all these partnerships, I would point out three on which there is a consensus. One is that there is an interface between crime violence, illicit arms traffick, trafficking in drugs and some types of terrorism. The second area is that weapons, small arms and light weapons, by themselves do not constitute a huge threat to international security. They are part of the national security arsenal of the member states of the UN. They become a problem when these weapons are used or traded without the legitimate control of state authority. Some of you are dedicated to the idea that the state itself can sometimes become a source of illegitimate use of these weapons. We should not forget that there are some states that have, themselves, used these weapons for violence. I am not commenting on that; I am commenting that there used to be a fashionable phrase about societies like Liberia, Somalia, Haiti a few years ago, Rwanda, Burundi or Albania:- "failing state structures," "failed states."

It sometimes intrigues me that those who are first to analyze the issues dispassionately or passionately are not necessarily those who are affected by these issues. Even I feel very self conscious that among all of us in the panel, only one of us comes from a part of the world that has actually experienced it. It is very easy for the rest of the world to tell a government how to have a good judiciary system, a good system of legislative organizations, a good system of education, and then talk in terms of controlling the weapons and to say you have no right to do anything unless you have all these institutions which have been time tested, which have worked in Europe, in America, in parts of Asia. First, concentrate and then give them the human rights, the good human rights, the right to speak, the right to write, the right to express themselves. If you went and talked to some of the women, the children, the elderly, the family members who are running away from areas where weapons have been used, and you put the microphone in front of them and said, "Don't you think human rights are a good idea?" What do you think they would say?

When translated into the language they understand and asked "What is the most important human right you want?" And they would say, "The right to live! I must live first! I must eat, I must have a shelter over my head before I can decide whether or not I have free expression." That is not a human right they are asking for. So when we try to tell these countries that there are a certain set of rules by which they must abide before the international community can come to their assistance, they will listen to you; but then they are not going to wait until all these procedures have been established, democratic institutions have been established, because they have to live. And this is where my optimism is, because they have to cope with this problem on a daily basis, they are not going to wait for mega-international conferences to come to an agreement on how to stop the import/export of weapons to some part of the world. They are already entering into partnerships with each other; the society with the government, the government with the neighbors, the neighbors with sub-regional groups, and we have an excellent record of initiatives coming from the affected parts of the world on what to do about this problem.

When I said that they are not going to wait for mega-conferences, by no means am I saying that in mega-conferences the subject of small arms is not needed. A declaration at a high political level of global commitment, a global denunciation, a global understanding to do something about this is called for. All that I am saying is that until that happens, to expect that the affected countries will wait is not a very good idea. So one should not feel upset, one should not feel offended if while a community is waiting to come up with a very perfect agenda on what to do about small arms, some modest initiatives are being taken in various parts of the world in order to deal with it on a daily basis. And those are the kind of initiatives also which we in the UN follow with a great deal of joy, and in our way we try to encourage them; in my grant, the Congressional Arms Grant, to keep evolving the text of new initiatives.

When we started a year ago, it took three pages; today, it takes forty-six pages to list the new initiatives, and the initiatives keep on coming. Those partnerships are not reported in the western media, they are not recorded in the newspapers or in your televisions. They are taking place when family elders, clan leaders, school teachers, students, ordinary men and women whose life is affected come to some kind of agreement. This is what my Secretary-General calls, "involvement of civil society." This civil society is much larger than the NGOs; NGOs are a good part of it, but that civil society is not organized does not mean that it does not have a voice and you don't have to listen to them. That is why my department is making a lot of effort to reach that civil society through tools which that civil society understands, not Yale and Princeton analyzed books, not excellent articles in some of the prestigious journals, not workshops which are conducted in superb fashion with the best minds on the subject, but simple things. Even people who do not know how to read or write like inviting pollsters from the local community to express themselves. To involve civil society in this part of the world which is affected by the small arms is something to which the Secretary General himself attaches a lot of importance. This is where, I think, the larger the public awareness of what this problem is, whom it affects most and how to make it possible for those who may not be participating in the grand partnerships, to make them aware of what we are doing, needs to be encouraged.

If there is a journalist among you, I will make an appeal to him or her. Let that story be of the women who took out a procession in the streets of Sierra Leone when they were told, "If you go to vote, we are going to shoot you." They said, "Okay, go ahead, shoot us; we are going out and voting." The story of a little child with a begging bowl, crying; I don't want stories of despair, I want stories of hope. This is what my department is trying to do; this is where NGOs can help us.

Let me conclude by saying that within this framework there are broad agreements among partnerships that this issue does not affect every country in the world in the same fashion. But for those countries whom it affects, it's a matter of life and death. Something must be done.

Second, among all the aspects of small arms, the worst is the linkage between violence, criminality, armed conflict, drugs and terrorism.

Third, until the time when we have state institutions in perfect order all over the world, it is safer to restrict the possession and use of this weapon to legitimate state authority rather than let arms be distributed to everybody. Within this framework, we at the United Nations are hoping that in coming years until the global community decides how to best handle this issue in a single global forum we follow every single initiative, every single partnership that is making a difference. We are going to concentrate our efforts in three areas: a) is it possible to, as the Secretary General says, to spotlight on illicit arms traffic. Because nobody is really going to tell us how many manufacturers are there in the world - I believe in the United States there are more manufacturers of weapons than there are McDonald's, or something to that effect. There are 70 countries in the world where these weapons are manufactured. If the Member States could give us information about those companies that are licensed manufacturers, we will publicize them. We can't tackle the problem, but we can go around it. The illicit arms traffic is one issue.

The other issue is to give help to those countries that ask for help, as Albania did. My Under-Secretary General was there to make an evaluation and he has made a proposal, which is to say that instead of offering cash to buy back weapons, he has   ?   Buy back is a big craze; every rich country is entitled to believe that if you throw enough money into the problem, it will go away. But there are some problems in which money might create more problems than it can resolve. If you publicize the idea of buy back without really going into the internal situation of that country, there is a fair chance that some young kid, between the age of 12 and 18, might steal a weapon for free from a police officer who is sleeping and then want to sell it for two hundred dollars. In the mountainous region of Southwest Asia where single missiles were sold many years ago, or maybe they were given free, they disappeared. And then they reappeared at a cost that was 10 times more than what they were bought for when news went around that they could be bought back. So buying back is a good idea, but it needs to be looked into a little more seriously so that it doesn't send out a wrong message.

Albania is one country which has sought assistance; Nigeria is another, Sierra Leone is a third. There are at least 20 countries in the world where conflicts have, happily, wound down. And the civil society now has to deal with the issue of former combatants, demobilized soldiers. The army officer who fought for whatever good or bad reason, when he is demobilized, he still has a family to support, probably a larger family than you are aware of here. They need bread to eat and a place to stay. These people need to be reintegrated into civil society instead of being stigmatized. The former combatants need to be reintegrated.

I was told a story in Pretoria, and the story was repeated to me in Central America and even in Kathmandu, where Indians and Pakistanis do not normally agree on anything. There was agreement that one of the worst fears is drugs from Afghanistan on one side and Burma or Myanmar on the other. These are the high ranking producers of opium in the world. The illicit arms traffic and sale of drugs is such a threat to their youth, and don't forget South Asia has one fifth of the world's population. They were worried. That's why I am really optimistic that these emerging partnerships among people who are affected, among international development agencies, among the donors, and among NGOs like you, would lead us to a happier future.

JIM WURST: Thank you. Our final speaker is Loretta Bondi. Loretta joined the arms division of Human Rights Watch as an advocacy coordinator in July 1997. Previously Loretta was a foreign correspondent for major publications, including Corriere Della Sera, Italy's leading newspaper, and a foreign news analyst for Rai, Radiotelevisione Italiana. As a journalist she was based in South East Asia, Europe and the Middle East. Loretta currently lives and works in Washington and she holds a Masters degree from the School of Advanced International Studies of Johns Hopkins University.

LORETTA BONDI: Thank you, Jim. I would like to speak about another major angle of partnership, and that is the partnership that is emerging among NGOs all over the world, and the partnership these NGOs are trying to build with governments and international institutions. As you mentioned, the proliferation of small arms is an enormous problem which has been evident for quite a long time. But only in the last few years this problem has started to permeate international consciousness outside of the regions of conflict, outside of the circles where the issue had been traditionally tackled and analyzed and studied and investigated. The proliferation of small arms affects entire communities and entire countries. Much more needs to be done to achieve a further understanding of the problem and elevate the level of consciousness in the international community.

One of the problems that NGOs have faced from the very beginning is that the issue of small arms proliferation seemed really intractable. As Ms. Rana has described very effectively, light weapons are a different beast than landmines. They are not inherently indiscriminate and they do not constitute a discrete weapons system. We are speaking of an enormous quantity of different weapons with different specifications. An early realization among the NGOs was that in our work we may not achieve an all-encompassing, cathartic outcome as the landmines campaign achieved, such as a treaty or an overarching convention. But we realized that we have to do something and do something quickly to help curb the trade and proliferation in small arms that emboldens human right abusers; we have to act on the information that is already available. And we have to react especially to the request for action from people against whom abuses are perpetrated.

So we started working in a more systematic manner across the ocean and across continents. And finally last summer about thirty NGOs came together in Toronto and an embryonic worldwide coalition was started. This coalition is an international action network on small arms.

Recently we met in Brussels and this time 200 NGOs participated. We put together a program of action that is undergoing a redrafting process. In a nutshell, we realized immediately that what should be central to our efforts is the protection of human security and human rights, both jeopardized by the proliferation of small arms. We also realized that a partial approach to this problem would be unproductive. There are several aspects of it that are interconnected. We should take a hard look at the supply or demand for small weapons, legal or illegal transfers, state or non state actors as recipients and suppliers. All these dimensions required a comprehensive evaluation of small weapons trade entailing a cross-section of specialization. At the conference in Toronto the NGOs came from the human rights community, the development community, the humanitarian and relief community, the gun control community, the disarmament and victim assistance groups. with all of us at different junctures, of course. We were clear that all these different facets must be tackled not only in a comprehensive way, but also in a simultaneous fashion. This is also because, on the part of governments, there are currently many efforts underway to curb illicit trafficking in weapons. Comparatively, there is scant concentration on the legal transfers of these weapons.

One instrument that has been thoroughly debated and which finally came to life last year - after relentless NGO pressure - is the Code of Conduct on arms transfers . It's a very valuable instrument and is the only cross-national instrument that is actually tackling states responsibility in the trade vis-avis their international obligations to uphold human rights. The European Code of Conduct is not a binding instrument. However, I think that the Code of Conduct will eventually evolve.

The Code has broken a major taboo in Europe by bringing about a common understanding that arms exports, previously regarded exclusively as a domestic domain, actually pertain to international frameworks as well. The Code is already working in its stated direction. I have been told that exchange of information and notification of denials of arms transfers have been circulated among the members of the European Union. There will also be an annual review. We believe that instruments like the Code of Conduct in Europe should be replicated elsewhere in the world. In the United States NGOs have been very actively engaged in a similar effort. A Code of Conduct on Arms Transfers passed by a voice vote in the House of Representatives. Unfortunately it was killed in conference , but it remains the standing position of the House .

Codes of conduct on arms transfers put the responsibility squarely where it belongs, that is with government because the lion's share of weapons transfers to abusive forces and irresponsible beneficiaries is still played by the trade governments allow both overtly and covertly. Most governments, however, do not seem to be receptive to NGOs' sentiment on this issue. For example, at the beginning of this month in Brussels a conference, organized by the Belgian Ministries of Cooperation and Foreign Affairs attracted participants from 98 governments and about 200 NGOs.

At the end of the conference the chairman drafted a call for action on small arms which was pretty comprehensive. The problem there is that individual governments that have endorsed the

Brussels call for action can pick and choose from the list. They are not bound to follow any particular policy in any particular order. There are already indications that governments do not intend at any time soon to translate into concrete measures the responsibility and accountability in state-sponsored arms transfers, advocated by the Brussels document. It's our responsibility as NGOs to make sure that we define the order of priorities on the basis of the indications that would come from the regions and the countries, including this one, where the proliferation of small arms is jeopardizing human rights and human security. NGOs are working now to persuade governments that Codes of Conduct, stricter export controls of weapons, measures for tracking the illicit trafficking, the creation and support for conditions in which demand can be curbed, are essential and must be developed simultaneously. The UN, as Ms Rana has illustrated, has already taken important steps in this direction.

Given the penury of systematic data collection on the topic of small arms proliferation and its effects, we would certainly like the UN to play a role in putting together scattered data. We do know that small arms are the major culprit when it comes to civilian casualties. Their proliferation is fueling conflicts and making them go on for a long time. What we do not know is the exact breakdown of the impact that small arms have on the civilian population and the impact that these arms have on particular categories of population, such as women, children, elderly people. The UN can help clarify the picture. Another step that the UN can take is to support and advocate follow-up action on the recommendations that the UN panel of experts on small arms have put together. These recommendations should now be implemented.

A third area in which the UN can certainly help us redefine and tackle the problem is by taking a very very close look on how to implement and enforce arms embargoes. Arms embargoes, besides legal domestic controls, are the only instruments that preclude arms transfers to abusers. However, arms embargoes seem to have only a symbolic value, in that they have hardly been implemented. They have hardly been monitored or enforced. One instrument that could help in the enforcement of arms embargoes is the creation of regional registers for small arms movements. There is no other way to create a semblance of accountability, especially in regions where conflict is ongoing.

As Ms. Rana has mentioned, I think that the Bretton Woods institutions should play a role as well. National budgets should be analyzed a little bit more closely. In Burundi, for example, 36% of the total budget goes to defense, while 24% goes to agriculture, health and education combined. I think the Bretton Woods institutions should take a very hard look at national budgets and their breakdown. The World Bank, as Ms. Rana has illustrated, is already putting together ideas and thoughts on how to tackle these impossible problems.

Another international organization that has responsibility in curbing or helping to curb the proliferation of small arms is NATO. The new members and partners have reduced and will modernize their arsenals to meet NATO standards. This joint process creates a problem that we have already monitored for quite some time. That is the freeing up of surplus and obsolete weapons. Human Rights Watch has brought this issue to the attention of NATO's Secretary General. We believe that NATO has the power and the influence to demand better accountability of how the excess and obsolete weapons are disposed of.

JIM WURST: Before we start the question and answer session, I would like to see if any of the panelists wish to comment on anything they've heard from the other panelists.

SWADESH RANA: I am very grateful to the previous speaker and I would like to say something that is relevant to the request that has been addressed to the United Nations. First of all, we are very aware of the international network that has come into being in Toronto. We are in touch with them and we wish them great success. And we will follow their progress with a great deal of enthusiasm and see how we can join hands in this partnership which is emerging between the UN and the NGOs.

On the specific request that you have made on the issue of data collection, there are two resolutions currently being considered which would give the UN greater responsibility in the area of collecting, exchanging and disseminating information on arms transfers. Our capacity to collect data independently of what governments give us is somewhat limited.

That's where my request is going to be addressed to all the NGOs, particularly those in the business of collecting information: A Saferworld, ICRC, the Quakers, BASIC, Human Rights Watch and others who have access to publicly available information. We will be happy to tell you the categories under which we are looking for information. If you would pass on that information to me in the Conventional Arms Branch we would be happy to register it in our data bank and then make it available to all those who want it. We do not need brilliant analysis of why information is not available. We know why it is not available. But if you have data about the number of people who have been affected in a conflict, we'll give you the categories. Briefly, we are keeping data on the following categories and you are welcome to have access to it.

We are keeping:

1) an evolving text of all the major initiatives by governments and organizations.
2) a list of all the research institutes around the world who work on this subject.
3) a roster of individuals who have now developed expertise in this area.
4) the facts and figures for ready reference from sources like SIPRI, the US Arms Control and Disarmament Agency, ISS, or individual resources like Ed Lawrence at the Monterey Institute. We retrieve from it information like how many countries are manufacturing weapons in the world.

With the encouragement and support of the Under-Secretary-General my branch has created a two page description of categories of weapons which does not exist so far. It categorizes those seven major categories which are covered by the UN Arms Register. It also covers what are small arms? What are light weapons? What are ammunitions and explosives? What are firearms? What are homemade firearms? And what are weapons which were not intended to be weapons but are used, like spears and machetes? It gives you a plain description. You are welcome to have access to that. And please pass on to us whatever data information you think would be of interest.

Second, when you are talking in terms of a closer look at the embargoes, the Security Council is drafting a resolution on the subject. When it comes to regional registers of arms transfers, this is among the recommendations emerging out of the Secretary-General's report.

AMBASSADOR JOHAN NORDENFELT: I also would like to take this opportunity to say how important we think it is that the NGO community is engaged in this. And we realize how difficult it is because it's so complex and has so many aspects. So it is indeed very encouraging that an umbrella organization has been set up. We were very glad to contribute money towards holding the meeting in Toronto and the meeting that took place in Brussels. I mentioned the Mali Initiative and the moratorium that it has spawned among the African countries. Ms. Rana informs me that it was adopted this morning. The Swedish government has contributed a million US dollars towards the realization of the Mali Initiative.

It's worth mentioning also that Mozambique and South Africa have a very interesting field project developing in the collection of small arms that merits study and support. The Dutch are contemplating an initiative within the framework of the Organization for Security and Cooperation in Europe to work out a convention on the illicit transfer of small arms and light weapons between countries inside the area covered by the organization. And from countries in that area into other areas. And that is an interesting project that we hope to be able to develop...

LORETTA BONDI: Concerning NATO, I was there recently and I was told that in 18 years the issue of small weapons had never surfaced in a NATO discussion. Not even once. Although NATO is an alliance, it has no power to oversee national domestic controls. However, we believe that NATO has the influence to stimulate, at the very least, a debate on this issue.

JIM WURST: We will open the floor now to questions.

NEWTON BOWLES, Canadian UNA/USA; Ms. Rana, there are two pioneering studies, one initiated by the UN from the military standpoint and the other a civilian, firearms study. The firearms study was initiated by the Commission on the Prevention of Crime; the other came from the General Assembly. Eventually, everything goes back to the Assembly. Those are converging, complimentary studies and its encouraging to know there was some consultation between the people who did the studies. I think its important that the findings should be brought together in terms of a comprehensive policy. I wonder if that in fact is being done. And would your department be handling that? And second, you referred to the remarkable initiatives being taken at the local level by community initiatives. Among those being supported by the UN is the UNDP support in Mali and contiguous countries. Is that pattern of UN support being extended or is that an ad hoc thing that just happened to come up in West Africa?

KEITH S, Mennonite Central Committee: Ms. Rana, I found some of your comments honestly to be a bit depressing. Your comments especially on establishing a register of manufacturers of arms within states and allowing them to continue their manufacturing. That's one area where we have some difference. I think that a lot of the private manufacturers don't necessarily have the best motives in mind when they're selling arms abroad. They have profit in mind. So I would be a bit more strict than just knowing that they are there. And also, you seem to highlight the illicit transfers which is extremely important and it does fuel a lot of conflicts; but more important, as Ms. Bondi stressed, is the legitimate state-to-state transfers. Examples just from recent past: The Iran Contra state transfers of arms were very illegitimate. Throughout the Cold War the fighting was by proxy wars by both the former Soviet Union and the US and a number of different third world countries which today has let loose a cache of weapons which rotates around to different conflicts.

So my question is, taking a look at the ECOWAS moratorium, which seems to suggest there exists some willingness for a moratorium on legitimate arms transfers, is that a possibility on a global scale? Establishing some sort of a moratorium on state-to-state arms transfers? It seems you speak of the need of light weapons for state security. I would think the ultimate state security is not to have weapons to threaten other people to begin with. Short of that, though, what would your views be on extending the Malian initiative, the ECOWAS Moratorium, to more of a global scale?

DORRIE WEISS, Economists Allied For Arms Reduction: You said that the problems of conventional arms are essentially interrelated and have to be dealt with on a number of fronts. And I absolutely agree with you. While all issues of war and peace are also issues of poverty and development and environment and water and the interweaving of many things, it seems to me that it is also a disarmament issue, and that setting it up as something that must be dealt with on other fronts, but not calling it a disarmament issue, is like a setting up a false dichotomy. Can't we, in addition to using all of the other initiatives, look for an overarching convention on conventional weapons that would be an international norm, a standard set up internationally through the UN?

VINCE COMISKY, Pax Christi International: Just a note to all of you about the increased amount of awareness on this issue. Last week before the First Committee, Archbishop Martino, of the Holy See, devoted about half of his talk to the issue of small weapons, a hopeful thing to know about. I appreciate, Ms. Rana, your linking this issue with other issues. One of those issues that Pax Christi International has been making the linkage with is child soldiers, the increasing number of youngsters being brought into warfare and conflict because of the proliferation of illicit weapons. Do you find this emphasis of any use? Is it playing out in the field in any positive fashion? Could you define the difference between light weapons and small arms?

NANCY COLTON, International Association of Volunteer Effort: I would like to know if it would be possible to include in a conference on small arms, destruction of obsolete weapons by governments and corporations? We could have a fund to pay to buy these weapons, because a lot of them are sold by countries who want to make hard currency on sale of obsolete weapons. But the fund could be an international fund that could buy these weapons for destruction purposes.

SWADESH RANA: I will work my way backwards, starting with the destruction of weapons. It may be good for you to know that the government of Norway has recently announced the establishment of a fund for weapons collection. If I am not mistaken, they have initially contributed close to about three million dollars for efforts by the UN and its associated agencies to collect and destroy weapons.

The questioner asked about the difference between a small arm and a light weapon. A small arm essentially is a weapon which is used by one person and is non-portable. A light weapon could be used by a crew, or it could be mounted on a light vehicle. What was used in Somalia was a weapon that was put on a jeep and used with devastating effect. That is a light weapon, whereas an AK47 is a small arm. You can dismantle an AK47 into 12 different parts and a ten year old can put it together. It's very easy to assemble and reassemble.

The third question was about child soldiers. You are absolutely right, in fact it has been very much on the minds of those in the UN who want to come up with a convincing strategy, because not only the children are the victims of conflict. They are also participating in conflicts. And perhaps it should be known that in cooperation with UNICEF my department is planning to put together an exhibit on children and small arms. And if we succeed in getting across the message we will portray children in three ways: As victims of conflicts fought with small arms; as participants in conflicts fought with small arms; as born doing conflicts fought with small arms, where women, whose husbands were killed by soldiers, were violated and carried the babies of these soldiers they couldn't get rid of because there were no hospitals and facilities for them.

These are the kinds of issues that will be covered. You know the Secretary General has designated Ambassador Olara Otunu as a special representative on this issue, and we are in touch with his office as a part of the coordinating mechanism. We are hoping that in this exhibit their input will be very important, both to get the facts and figures and the message that we want to portray.

On the question of an overarching convention which would cover all the categories of weapons, my suggestion would be to pick up the two page description we have given of the various types of weapons, those which are covered by the conventional arms register, and the other categories of weapons. Then it may be easier for you to appreciate that at the moment I think it would be a bit too utopian to think in terms of an all arms convention that would cover all categories of conventional weapons because some of these weapons are not even weapons. They are used as such.

The question raised about the ECOWAS Moratorium: I think it would be useful for you to know that the member states of the ECOWAS have agreed to impose upon themselves a volunteer moratorium to stop the import, export and manufacture of weapons. And they have been given support by the Nordic countries. The Wassenaar Group of countries I believe is also among the group. That is a supply side group which will help them to uphold this volunteer moratorium. It is a declaratory moratorium and I think its a major step forward. It has been called a breakthrough and it has the full support of the Secretary-General. It seems to me that it will be a while before the other member states would look at the operation of the moratorium and make up their mind as to whether and if this is applicable to all regions of the world.

The question on the two pioneer studies; one which has been conducted under a mandate from the ECOSOC on firearms and the other in the area small arms: Within the coordinating mechanism we are in touch with them. In fact, when we were putting together these categories of weapons, we consulted them to see what they think of firearms. And among the various initiatives which have been taken there is the very serious awareness that in the activities in the area of small arms and in the area of firearms are likely to converge when it comes to trans boundary movements of each types of weapons because in many cases they use similar routes and actors.

JIM WURST: I have a question for Mr. Chomar. In the beginning of your remarks you referred to the collection of weapons as a "unique" solution. I would like you to elaborate on what you mean by a unique solution, as opposed to something that would be done in isolation. And tell us what you are thinking of in terms of NGO help in general and on this question.

FERNANDO CHOMAR: Collection by itself should not be the solution for these problems in an armed conflict. I think just to collect means nothing. Those who are going to collect the arms are going to stockpile them and they will reemergence. Collection has to be combined with destruction. After collecting and destroying you have to have enforcement laws which can make sure that nobody is going to have illicit arms. I believe the arms which cause the most problems are those which are coming into the countries illicitly.

JIM GARST: I was interested that you described the procedures used in Mozambique as modeled on those in Angola. In Mozambique it appears to be working and in Angola it does not work. And I would appreciate some elaboration on how that came about.

FERNANDO CHOMAR: In fact, what we are talking about here are interconnected conflict solutions, the collection of small arms and light weapons combined. The experience of Mozambique always is considered a success in the United Nations and worldwide because, first, of the political willingness of both parties in the conflict. There was a time where the two parties in fighting had no means of meeting themselves and to come to the conclusion of the conflict itself. But, the international community as well as the United Nations made efforts to make sure that the two parties in the conflict can meet. And they can be committed to the peace agreement. In 1992 the two parties signed the agreement and both parties were committed to it. There was a political willingness to settle the problem.

What is happening in Angola, from personal perception, is that both parties lack political willingness. If there is no political willingness to settle the differences between those who are in dispute no international effort can dictate to them what to do. We all know that in Angola they have resources. The government has resources and UNIDA also has resources and utilizing the resources they can continue fighting because they still have resources. But the international community can advise them and make sure they can meet their concerns.

DAVID JACKMAN, Quaker UN Office: This is the first small arms session you have had here in the last year that does not involve the NRA, or some other arms industries spokesperson. But I'd like to ask the question for them. Are the interests of arms manufacturers easily compatible with the contemplated restrictions on illicit weapons trading? Does anyone contemplate an extensive dialogue with legitimate manufacturers? I am often curious about whether there really is an issue of difficulty between those wanting to ban illicit trade and the manufacturers or whether this is a somewhat trumped up difference. So, perhaps Loretta has some thoughts about this.

LORETTA BONDI: From the Human Rights Watch point of view we don't have anything against the legal manufacturers or the legal transfer of weapons per se. It is when it appears that these transfers are directed to forces that abuse human rights and international humanitarian law that we have a problem. Legitimate manufacturers are undoubtedly aware that the wide proliferation of weapons is accompanied by the proliferation of not always legitimate centers of production.

Let me narrate an anecdote. I was a journalist in the Philippines and I came across a village which was called Danao in the island of Cebu, where a big chunk of the population was involved in producing so called "paltic." Paltic means "counterfeited" weapons production there involving small arms. Different people produced different parts of different weapons and they were quite good. Their clients ranged from criminal organizations such as the Japanese Yakusa and the Chinese Triad, to assorted rebel movements in the Philippines and elsewhere. I don't think legal manufacturers would be very happy with that kind of configuration. I am sure you are well aware that is only one case. Cottage industries producing small arms are mushrooming in several other countries, outside of their government's purview, or because of those governments'tolerance or lack of enforcement capacity all over the world.

I do think the legal manufacturers have an interest in curbing this kind of proliferation. It's in their own interest to take a very hard look at what's going on and lend their support to our effort. In a sense this is already happening. In Europe, for example, with regard to the discussions that went on concerning the Code of Conduct, some arms manufacturers have come forward in support of it. And this is understandable. The bigger perspective there, which is somehow different from what's going on in the United States, is that the defense industry is undergoing a reorganization and so the very fact that a Code of Conduct is in existence somehow guarantees that there will be an instrument there to watch over each other's shoulder.

JIM WURST: It is an interesting idea that it is possible that the legal manufacturers of weapons in the United States might have more common ground on this than the NRA would want us to believe. Because you have to remember, in the US context the arms manufacturers have taken positions, small arms manufacturers - I am not talking about Boeing - opposed to restrictions. The NRA has opposed, for instance safety locks and the ban on certain types of ammunition. So the domestic gun control folks like Handguns Control in Washington are a part of the national NGO campaign. There is a common interest between international arms control and domestic gun violence and I think this is probably part of their campaign. But, of course, I am in no position to speak for them. If it isn't already being pursued, it will be soon.

BOB LARICK, Interfaith Business/Security Alliance: I thought you brought up a good point about the national situation in terms of the NRA. But has this ever been developed in terms of a mental health issue? What has been done to tie in with UNESCO's peace and non-violence campaign? Which is how I see it. What is a weapon? It's any object that is used to kill someone, which could be a handgun; it could be a rock, anything. So the real issue is not as a discouraging fact but as an encouraging fact that all the laws for non-proliferation, etc., are really part of a need for a sense of peace and justice. And the idea of hostility within the individual or the psycho-spiritual healthy civil society orientation. Building a central authority in civil society brings up what you were saying about the US problem, some of the kids 11 and 12 years old shooting up other kids in schools in this country, as well as the problems of drugs. And the need for better psycho-spiritual orientations and working together with the mental health society and with the educational systems in this country and overseas. To make it an educational psycho-spiritual problem and not just a legal problem of how do you develop more peaceful human natures?

LORETTA BONDI: If that question is for me, I couldn't agree more. And in fact within IANSA, the International Action Network on Small Arms, there is a very strong component that addresses precisely a public health dimension. As I said, IANSA is a coalition of networks and there are several levels in which NGOs with different priorities are working, but the public health dimension, whether you belong to a human rights NGO or humanitarian or development NGO, is very much on this network's agenda. Just to spell out some of the issues that have been connected with the public health approach, the IANSA draft founding document outlines the necessity of reversing cultures of violence including social conditions that inform male-attitudes towards violence.

Or the portrayal of violence by the mass media. This NGO network also believes that in terms of public health you have to address the problem by creating norms of civilian non-possession of weapons should be studied. Efforts will be made to discourage the perception that weapons do not protect against guys knocking at your door in the middle of the night, as my distinguished co-panelist was describing. According to many observers, more weapons in the hands of civilians exacerbate insecurity.

BOB LARICK: I know in some of the women's issues that the idea of gender issues and the idea of male identity and female identity becomes an important issue. If we can develop areas of independence and mutual empowerment, we tend to be better off. Have the spiritual faith groups also been involved?

LORETTA BONDI: Absolutely. Yes, we have a number of groups as part of IANSA which come from these walks of life.

JIM WURST: As it was pointed out, the Archbishop, the Representative of the Holy See, gave a very strong statement on light weapons and Pax Christi, the Catholic Peace organization, is one of the groups involved in the international and various national campaigns.

VERNON NICHOLS, NGO Committee on Disarmament: In a number of regions of the world this problem is exacerbated by the breakdown of civil order; the inability of countries to establish very much control within their own borders, and this of course raises issues of sovereignty as far as what others can do and I realize complexity. And I wonder if either of the panelists would like to comment on ways that they see such situations may be helped.

LORETTA BONDI: It's a very complex problem. I feel I cannot tackle this in a few words. But again, my first instinct would be to mop them up. Just take them out of circulation. I don't think that weapons trigger conflicts. I do think that weapons availability prolong and exacerbate those conflicts. And as long as these weapons are in circulation, peaceful solutions will be less forthcoming. This is my personal view. Peace and security zones which have undergone protracted violence and which are isolated are more difficult to achieve. Even after peace is obtained, other problems are only compounded by the ready availability of weapons which feeds criminality, violence against women, and so forth. This answer in a very unsatisfactory way to address your very complex question.

FERNANDO CHOMAR: Yes, the question is too delicate and it has no answer. But, collecting small arms from people is not easy and we are pessimistic on achieving the global understanding on ending small arms. For it is a state security matter. But I foresee that the First Committee in this General Assembly maybe will come with some formulas which are going to stimulate us and try to being us to optimism. They are trying to come to a resolution on small arms to call the international community to come together to discuss the problems of small arms. If the agreement is there in Geneva in the year 2000 or 20001 we will be having an international conference to deal with this issue. But still the problem will remain because we are all covered by pessimism.

LORETTA BONDI: May I just add something? I recently read an article in the Economist about the situation in Phnom Penh. According to the article, there are currently in circulation 500,000 weapons of this kind. 250,000 in the hands of the security forces and the army. Only 10,000 of them have been regularly registered. Now, the mayor of Phnom Penh, discouraged by the fact that his appeals for the collecting of these weapons have resulted in only one AK47 being turned in, is going door to door and personally trying to collect the weapons. Good luck! Certainly these initiatives need all the support we can give them.

QUESTION: What is the current role of the United States in Angola?

LORETTA BONDI: Perhaps I could add something. During our investigations in the Great Lakes region in Africa, we were informed by diplomats there that the US had exercised quite a lot of pressure not to pursue illegal traffickers' networks which were activated during the Angola war by the US in order to arm UNITA, and they were now providing weapons to the belligerents in the Great Lakes region. According to these sources, the US had asked the governments in the Great Lakes region not to go after these traffickers because they were now serving the SPLA in Sudan. This kind of ramification is not at all surprising.

JIM WURST: Officially the US recognizes the government of Angola. It does not recognize UNITA. It supports the arms embargo against UNITA because those are the UN Security Council Resolutions, and of course the US has voted for those. That's the official position. But UNITA uses its money not only to fuel arms purchases but also to buy public relations. They spend millions of dollars a year on public relations firms in Washington and remarkably enough they still have allies in Congress, including a senior Senator from North Carolina.

BOB LARICK, Interfaith Business/Security Alliance: You brought up a good point. Have the Southern Christian organizations, these family-focus and character building organizations been made aware of the need to control arms around the world?

JIM WURST: You mean the Southern Christian coalition? That's pretty far out of their field. There have been progressive Christian groups working in the failed states like Pax Christi.

ANN HALLAN LAKHDHIR: It seems to me governments are much happier talking only about illicit arm. I am wondering how Human Rights Watch and other NGOs are approaching this and how do you make it broader than the question just of illicit arms.

LORETTA BONDI: We have made very strong representations, both in our reporting and our advocacy to the governments that it is their responsibility to control legal transfers. There is a dimension that is often ignored when we speak of illicit trafficking in weapons. A lot of this trade doesn't start as illicitly. But often weapons traded legally , continue their itinerary illicitly. This is because end user certificates are falsified and weapons are transferred to third countries without previous authorization by the supplier. However, the failure of supplying countries to monitor what happens to the weapons they or their nationals sell, and where they end up, is a government

FERNANDO CHOMAR: Thank you. This constructive dialogue will lead us somewhere soon.

In May, 1999, the International Action Network on Small Arms (IANSA) was launched in the Hague. IANSA now comprises 200 NGOs from Africa, Latin America, Asia, North America, Europe and New Zealand. The areas of activity of these NGOs spans from human rights to development, from peace to victim assistance. Some of these NGOs are international, some others are community-based. IANSA will campaign to reduce the proliferation and misuse of small arms. You can visit IANSA on the Internet web site at www.iansa.org

HUMANITARIAN AND DEVELOPMENT IMPLICATIONS OF SMALL ARMS PROLIFERATION

Moderator: LORA LUMPE, The Federation of American Scientists: Throughout the Cold War, the disarmament community focused principally on nuclear, and to a lesser degree on chemical and biological weapons, because of their potential for mass death and destruction. When the spotlight occasionally shown on conventional weapons, that is bombers, tanks, jets, etc., it was these high end weapons that were the focus. Scant attention was paid throughout the Cold War to limiting the production and traffic in small arms and light, man-portable weapons, like assault rifles, mortars, grenades and landmines. In fact the military powers distributed such weapons with abandon.

Increased attention is now being paid to the devastation wrought by on-going, rather than potential, armed conflict around the world. Previously referred to by official Washington, where I am based, as "low-intensity conflicts." These wars have resulted in the death of well over one million people this decade. The vast majority of these casualties, as many as ninety per cent, are believed to be civilian victims. They're victims of indiscriminate warfare. The International Committee of the Red Cross has determined that small arms are the principle cause of death in these conflicts. In fact, these arms are thought to be responsible for as much as ninety percent of the recent war casualties. Small and light arms are cheap and portable and are used by all combatants, state militaries, militias and insurgents alike.

It's the prevalence, the widespread proliferation of these arms, combined with their indiscriminate use, that renders them responsible for so much of the killing in recent wars. Many private groups and governments, inspired by the success of the recent campaign against anti-personnel landmines, are now lining up to challenge policies that proliferate widely guns and grenades around the world.

For example, four non-governmental organizations in Norway, including the Norwegian Red Cross, recently banded together to launch a campaign against small arms. This initiative was launched on the one-year anniversary of the killing in Chechnya of several Red Cross nurses in 1996. The Norwegian and Canadian governments have expressed support for tackling this complicated issue, as have several other governments and several major non-governmental organizations.

There's been much work undertaken on the issue in the last couple years. The UN Small Arms Panel issued its report last summer with several very good recommendations. A second phase of this panel will begin its work in May of this year and will report in the summer of 1999. In addition, many initiatives have been undertaken on the illicit side of the small arms trade.

We have an excellent panel today to talk about and make very clear the connections between this issue - the spread of these weapons - development and humanitarian interests around the world. First will be Michael Renner, who has just written an excellent monograph, *Small Arms, Big Impact: The Next Challenge of Disarmament*. Michael is a senior researcher with Worldwatch Institute, which is a non-profit organization based in Washington. Before joining Worldwatch in 1987, Michael was a Corliss Lamont Fellow on economic conversion at Columbia University. Prior to that, he was a research associate at the World Policy Institute in New York.

255

Next will be Joost Hiltermann, who's the Executive Director of the Arms Division at Human Rights Watch, based in Washington. He was the primary researcher of the Iraqi genocide of Kurds for Human Rights Watch; and has worked for Palestinian human rights organizations on the West Bank for five years in the 1980s. Joost recently oversaw the research and publication of an excellent study on the arms flow to Burundi, and before that several studies on the small arms flow to Rwanda and elsewhere.

Following Joost, Ivor Richard Fung will speak. He is presently the regional advisor on governance and peace building with the UN Development Programme. He was previously political affairs officer and acting director of the UN Regional Center for Peace and Disarmament in Africa in the UN Department of Political Affairs. He served as secretary of the working group on security assistance to non-nuclear weapons states during the 1995 NPT Review and Expansion Conference. Dr. Fung has been playing a central role in the conception and negotiation of the proposal by West Africa on the moratorium on import, export and manufacture of light weapons in West Africa. Many of you probably just read about Dr. Fung's excellent work a couple days ago in a major article about his work in the *New York Times*.

MICHAEL RENNER, Worldwatch Institute: I will give a fairly broad overview but also focus specifically on the issue of surplus small arms and some of the underlying problems that lead people to use the small arms that are available so easily.

By all indications, the number of small arms worldwide is enormous, but nobody really knows what the quantities involved are. One estimate, about five hundred million military-style small arms, mostly firearms, is I think fairly broadly accepted. If the figure were four hundred million or six hundred million, or even one hundred million, that may not make that much of a difference, because relatively small quantities of these arms can have devastating consequences, certainly on societies that are under enormous pressure and that are becoming fragmented. This five hundred million figure is sort of a rough indicator.

As Lora said, particularly during the Cold War, vast quantities of these arms were distributed primarily by the two Superpowers, but also by other governments. With the end of the Cold War, this practice has not changed. Perhaps the quantities now being shipped are smaller, and at least the Cold War motivation is gone. But there is clearly no sense that there is any restriction, any restraint, any real norm that we can work with. There is a growing awareness, but that's about it.

Because small arms are so sturdy and therefore so long-lived, weapons produced and shipped in the past still are of great concern. It is a cumulative problem, like a snowball, continuously gaining in size and strength. The longer the issue is not being seriously addressed, the larger the problem gets.

Surplus arms are very often transferred from one hot spot to another. There are two primary sources: one is the armies of the former Cold War protagonists in Europe, Russia, and North America. These armies, and their arsenals, have been and are shrinking, and so a fairly large share of the excess equipment, and that includes both major arms and small arms, are now being given away or sold very cheaply. In some countries - Russia in particular - there is very grave concern about theft from military depots. There is very poor control over where the weapons are, where they are going, and there is every indication that poorly paid soldiers have a real incentive to steal weapons and to sell them to supplement their meager incomes.

The second source is mostly in developing countries, as many civil wars - thankfully - have come to an end. Government armies, but also opposition forces, are being demobilized, or in some cases they really just disintegrate, as is happening in Somalia. So again, large quantities of weapons suddenly become surplus. There is, on the one hand, this positive trend of demobilization and relative disarmament. Yet, in trying to deal with the consequences, we find that there are a lot of still unresolved problems.

I want to address two issues. One is efforts to collect the weapons that were in the hands of soldiers, guerrilla fighters or even civilians, to put them in secure storage, and avert them from falling into the "wrong hands." What happens, though, is that very often a large quantity of these weapons is retained by former fighters, put in hidden caches, or smuggled. They find their way into the black market, both within these countries, but also across borders.

During the past decade peacekeeping operations, both UN and non-UN, have been involved in various ways in trying to secure these small weapons. These efforts have a mixed record at best. Some of the reasons for this spotty record are that the peacekeepers being engaged in these efforts never really were able to work with a reliable inventory. What's really out there? Where are these weapons? Who has control over them?

Second, with very few exceptions, there is no clear mandate to disarm the portions of the civilian population that, during the civil wars, were often armed, either by the government side, the opposing side, or by both.

And third, there has been more of an emphasis on weapons collection, and temporary storage, without trying to dismantle or destroy the arms. And so, often the weapons are stolen and enter into circulation again. There is a sort of a Sisyphus syndrome: You first make efforts to retrieve these weapons, but then you don't follow through and destroy them, and you have to start all over again.

There has been some partial success in the Central American nations, as far as weapons collection and destruction are concerned, but by and large failures in countries like Somalia, Mozambique and apparently also in Angola.

Another challenge, closely related, is to reintegrate the former combatants into civilian society. A lot of these fighters do not possess any really meaningful civilian skills. And so, many of them fight with unemployment or underemployment, particularly since the countries that they live in have almost been drained by long years of warfare. But also, the programs, to the extent that they exist, to help them reintegrate have often not been effective. Either there is not enough funding or the programs haven't been planned or thought through well enough. Again, there is a mixed picture so far and there are lessons to be learned.

To the extent that reintegration doesn't work terribly well, there is a temptation to engage in criminal activities, banditry in the rural areas, or for these former fighters to sell off their weapons to supplement their income. In addition, small arms have become a form of currency in a lot of these societies.

Certainly the black market is well-fed. Nobody really knows how big the black market is, but anecdotal evidence collected by researchers certainly indicates that it is increasing in importance relative to other means of transfer. And that is a problem domestically in these countries that have just come out of civil wars. Countries like South Africa, El Salvador and others have seen a transformation from political violence to criminal violence. The level of armed violence in those two countries is about as high today as it was when "there was a war, a civil war, going on." So, this is clearly an enormous concern.

In addition to just a purely domestic situation, again and again we find that small arms are being transferred very easily from one hot spot to another. Let me give you a few examples. Weapons left over from the Vietnam war were transferred to Cuba and then went to Central America. Weapons left over from the conflict in Central America now find their way into Panama, Colombia, Peru, Mexico and some other countries. Weapons left over from Mozambique and Angola go into Namibia, Zimbabwe, Botswana and South Africa. Weapons that were provided to the Mujahadeen resistance to the Soviets in the 1980s in Afghanistan now often are found in Pakistan, India, Tajikistan, and Sri Lanka. Leftover weapons from the civil war in Lebanon from the '70s have also made their way into Bosnia. As these examples show, the patterns are essentially global. Where there is a conflict, where there is somebody who wants small arms, there is always a way to get weapons to these people.

There is what one would call most appropriately a ready market for surplus small arms, but also for newly produced small arms. As Lora alluded to in her introduction, internal conflict, what often is called civil war, is what most of the conflicts nowadays are all about. We see very few interstate wars, such as the Persian Gulf war or the border conflict between Ecuador and Peru. The internal conflicts pit governments against opposition forces, different ethnic communities or, perhaps warlords' criminal bands. These are the very types of conflicts where small arms are essentially ideal. It just doesn't make sense to fight these wars with a tank or an F-16 fighter jet. It makes sense to fight with AK-47s, Uzis and so on. Small arms really are the weapons of choice.

Let me say a few words about the background to these conflicts, because I think it's an important issue to be born in mind when we talk and think about small arms. These internal conflicts are often rather simplistically called ethnic conflicts, implying adversarial ethnicity, culture, religion, what have you. One of the problems is that some people say there is very little that they can do about these. These are people who want to kill each other, these are ancient conflicts and all we can do is watch and just ring our hands and say how awful! We can do something about the flows of small arms. I think we can do something, at least in terms of recognition and awareness, of what triggers or what aggravates these conflicts very often. That awareness has to be part of the solution to the small arms problem.

Some research I and others have done shows that very often, beyond the surface, are social and economic disputes, and worsening environmental and resource pressures which often drive and maintain the momentum behind these conflicts.

Disparities in power and economics are growing certainly in many, many countries. And these kinds of equity issues, in combination with population growth, also interact with growing resource scarcity. In particular, there is a depletion of water resources and a degradation of arable land. Both are playing an important role in generating or aggravating conflict, particularly in countries where the majority of the population is crucially dependent for its livelihood on the integrity of the natural systems that they are so closely bound up with, certainly in rural and agricultural areas.

In societies where there are significant economic and inequality issues, massive poverty and unemployment, where environmental degradation puts enormous pressure on rural communities, where the social fabric is under severe strain, and, of course, where strong ethnic or class animosities persist, it's very often likely that these disputes fester and don't really get resolved, particularly because political institutions are not very strong or don't even attempt to resolve these issues.

With the very easy availability of small arms it is so much easier to seek a violent resolution to these conflicts, rather than try to figure out another way. The massive availability of these kinds of arms literally invites violent responses to unresolved problems.

Let me end by saying a few things about what should be done. What strikes me is the small arms issue is like the landmines issue in many ways. It is not a traditional arms control problem, where you could have delegations from different governments sitting around a table and hammering out some kind of an accord to say, OK, you get to deploy 100,000 AK-47s and you get 150,000, and you monitor each other.

Obviously that just doesn't work. It is not government troops facing each other but all kinds of non-governmental actors that are involved. I think what is related to past disarmament issues is clearly the need to deal with the unrestrained small arms trade, particularly the illegal portion. But I think it would be a mistake to limit it to the illegal portion and just say whatever governments approve of is fine and there's no problem, because very often government transfers started the problem in the first place. For example, we see weapons that the US and Soviet governments sent to Afghanistan are now ending up all over South Asia.

So we need to address the arms trade, certainly, and I think we also need to think about the continued production of these arms. The small arms issue is different from traditional arms control in the sense that a lot of things can and need to be done on the national level, within countries.

And things are being done, such as buy backs of weapons, which Australia and England have done; stricter licensing, the kinds of discussions we have seen in this country to some extent; improvement in ways of dealing with the leftovers of the civil wars, vis-a-vis the active combatants who are having a hard time finding a livelihood after wars end in economies that are in shambles and invite crime.

These kinds of policies are very important pieces of the puzzle. But beyond them, if the social and environmental issues underlying these conflicts are not being addressed, we can do all we want with regard to buy backs, and monitoring trade, and so on, and I don't think we will get very far. We will be on a treadmill, and we'll get somewhere, but there will be continual new problems cropping up. So, I think we need to look at it both in terms of the way problems have been looked at traditionally with regard to arms control and disarmament. But we also need to recognize that without social, economic and environmental policies, that deal with the root causes of what makes people use these sorts of small arms, we are always going to be facing the same problem. Thank you.

JOOST HILTERMANN, Human Rights Watch Arms Division: I want to focus on the situations of conflict, not the situations after conflicts that Michael has talked about. My organization, Human

Rights Watch, looks at the situation during conflicts which leads to exactly the kinds of problems that Michael has outlined. Human Rights Watch is an international organization that seeks to promote human rights around the world and it has had a long-standing interest in the kinds of weapons that are used in conflict and how they are being used.

About six years ago my division, the arms division, was set up. We have worked on the plague of landmines, focused on the trade of arms to forces, be they government or irregular, that abuse human rights, and international humanitarian law, and we have looked at other weapon systems, like blinding lasers, that constitute specific problems under international law.

The standard that we employ is international human rights and international humanitarian law. Humanitarian law is the laws of war, like the Geneva Conventions and other instruments that have been drafted really to govern the conduct of parties to a conflict and includes both governments and guerrilla forces. Under these standards, fighting forces cannot just use any weapon they like. And even weapons that they can use - they cannot use them in any way they like.

Weapons that are used cannot be inherently indiscriminate, like landmines which will kill innocent civilians for decades after a conflict is ended. They cannot cause what is strangely called "unnecessary suffering." This sounds strange because, of course, in war what everybody does is suffer a lot. What is meant by unnecessary suffering, in the concept that is being developed, is the kind of injury that is irreversible, permanent physical damage, that cannot easily be overcome. For one weapon system that we have worked on, the blinding lasers, blinding is seen as one such disability.

Fighting forces cannot also use weapons indiscriminately, so even though the Kalashnikov is not an illegal weapon in international law, and neither, unfortunately, is a cluster bomb, you cannot use these weapons just in any way you want. You certainly cannot target civilian population centers and there are a number of other restrictions.

In preparing this presentation, I decided to highlight a number of myths and half-myths. And in doing so, I am going to repeat a couple of the things that Michael has already so ably pointed out. One is a half-myth, not a full myth. It is often said - we get this from governments in Africa where we do a lot of work, "Listen, the arms trade, the influx of weapons, is not the problem at all. The weapons are already here. The region is awash in arms and there is nothing you can do from the outside. It's a problem of internal circulation."

Michael talked about the circulation of small arms on a regional basis, or from conflicts in one continent to conflicts in another continent. I'm not talking about that. There is, in fact, an influx of weapons into a conflict area. I'm talking about weapons that have been in a place for a long time and are being used in a conflict. You may think of the Balkans or countries in Africa.

The second myth is that when it comes to civilian suffering, it is only the large weapon systems that matter: artillery, aerial bombardments, carpet bombing, etc.

The third myth is that arms supplies to, say, continents like Africa are part of a fiendish, neo-colonial plot to continue Western dominance.

The fourth is that weapons don't kill people, people kill people. You've all heard that one. And Michael has already said that many say these are all local problems based on age-old ethnic hatreds that we cannot really do anything about, that require local solutions.

The fifth myth is, what about Rwanda? After all, what killed half a million people was machetes and not people with Kalashnikovs or other weapons?

And the sixth myth is that there is nothing governments can do about this anyway.

I'll address each one of these very briefly. Of course, there is a problem with local circulation, and Michael has pointed out that after a conflict has ended, weapons stay in a country for a long time and end up in the hands of the civilian population. If a country remains unstable, which is likely, and reverts to a situation of armed conflict by, say, a rebel force against the government, then obviously these weapons are going to be used again.

But that is not the only problem, and that is why it is a half-myth. The main problem is that new supplies of weapons are always coming in. I'm not saying new supplies of new weapons, I'm saying new supplies of weapons. And to the extent that they are new weapons, as a considerable portion of them are, they also tend to be more lethal weapons, more sophisticated weapons. You see automatic rifles coming in and sophisticated mortars and rocket-propelled grenades. And they can do a lot more damage. They are a lot more deadly than the weapons that have been in circulation for years and for decades.

That's one important thing. The second thing is that the influx of weapons itself emboldens the recipients of the weapons. To the extent that the weapons were supplied by a government, or outside power, rather than by a private entrepreneur, they constitute a form of political and military support, which is what they need in order to fight their conflict. So the external supply becomes a lifeline and becomes a source of encouragement.

The second myth, about the large weapons: obviously large weapons can do a lot of damage. The carpet bombing in Vietnam made that very clear. Where a mix of weapons was used, you'll see that heavy artillery bombardments and aerial bombardments and strafing by helicopters did a tremendous amount of damage and caused civilian suffering. But in Iraq, for example, if you look at the Allied bombardment, you see in fact that there was very little direct civilian suffering from that. Civilian targets were largely avoided. Of course, the flip side is that there was a huge amount of indirect civilian suffering, but it was not caused by the bombing directly but by the targeting of electricity stations, which then caused the water supply to run dry, and that triggered numerous diseases.

But it is clear that the proliferation of small arms and light weapons has increased the lethality of the large number of post-Cold War, more regional conflicts. These weapons, as Michael mentioned, are causing the largest portion of civilian suffering. This is certainly true for conflicts in Central Africa, the Balkans and Central Asia.

The assertion that arms supplies are a Western plot: there's no doubt that some of the neo-colonial powers, the former colonial powers, continue to meddle in their old dominions, especially in Africa. You see, for example, France, Britain and Belgium still being involved on the side of some of their local allies. But, it's very important to also understand the role of the market in the post-Cold war era in a continent like Africa. It's very clear that if the private traders are involved, ferrying weapons to where the demand is high, then the demand is in fact high, because supply is plentiful and the prices are, therefore, relatively low.

Weapons don't kill, people do. Well, obviously they do: it's people. But, as I said before, the main problem is that the influx emboldens people and the influx then increases the lethality of the conflict and may even increase the size of a conflict. So even though weapons are not the cause of the conflict, they certainly compound the problems of the conflict and increase its scope and size.

Machetes were mostly used in the genocide in Rwanda, causing the death of over half a million people. That's true, too. But civilians wielding machetes killing other civilians who similarly had machetes could not have killed that many if there hadn't been a security environment created by the Rwandan government and the militias that it controlled who were heavily armed by outside parties in the years leading up to the genocide.

And the sixth myth, that governments cannot do anything about this because it concerns small arms and they are hard to detect and that there is not good documentation amongst private traders - that's all hogwash! Governments can do a lot about it. And more importantly, they have a huge responsibility in this, because as Michael also pointed out, they are often the first ones to distribute the weapons.

They start circulating to private traders, too, because this is the era of privatization. They hire private contractors to get the weapons to the recipients. In many cases, the governments are the arms suppliers themselves. They, therefore, can reasonably anticipate what the consequences of their transfer is going to be, if the transfer is to a government or other forces that are involved in a violent conflict.

All governments must join in international codes of conduct, now being discussed within the European Union, within the framework of the United Nations and also in the United States. If these governments are sovereigns of territories that are used as transshipments for weapons, which you often see in Western Europe or South Africa for weapons coming from Eastern Europe and elsewhere, then they have the means, the customs authority, the mechanisms in their hands, to regulate this trade and they must do so.

I want to add three realities. The first one is that civilian casualties now vastly outnumber military casualties in conflict. This is very important from an international humanitarian law perspective, because under international standards, it is legal to target soldiers and to disable them. It is not legal to target civilians.

The second reality is that international relief agencies are increasingly coming under fire from both sides to the conflict, by government forces and by irregular forces. They are being threatened by landmines, both anti-vehicle mines and anti-personnel mines. They often have been forced to withdraw, or to suspend operations for periods of time. This has compounded the sufferings of people who were dependent on food delivery or medical care, etc.

And the third reality, which Michael has already pointed out, is that the longer conflicts last, the more weapons come in and rotate down towards larger groups of the population and cause huge post-conflict problems. And, of course, landmines stay in the ground as well.

I want briefly to talk about one experience that we have done a lot of work on, which is the Great Lakes in Africa. We investigated the supply of weapons to the conflict in Rwanda in 1993. Rebels who are now currently in power had come into the country from Uganda in 1990 and entered into conflict with the now ousted government.

We found that a number of countries were fueling the fires: France, South Africa, Egypt and others. We published this material in early 1994, about two months before the genocide broke out. The report was ignored, which is not so surprising. Now it is a standard reference, unfortunately a little bit late. I'm not suggesting that we could have prevented the genocide. That would be naive. But if there had been heightened awareness at the time of the importance of the international role in stoking the fires in Rwanda, prior to the genocide, the international community might have reacted much faster and might have contained the damage. Maybe not so many people would have died. Of course, our report wasn't the only signal that was being sent out at the time about what was going to happen.

Then the genocide broke out in April 1994, exactly four years ago. The international community pretty much withdrew from Rwanda and then imposed an international arms embargo on 17 May. This is now the response of choice of the international community. Just slap an arms embargo on the area and hope that no weapons go in. There's absolutely no follow-up. The committee set up at the highest level, including the members of the Security Council, does absolutely nothing.

So weapons continue to pour in and this is why we continued with research in Rwanda in 1994 and 1995. A researcher went to the region and discovered that there were continuing inflows of weapons in clear violation of the international arms embargo on Rwanda, and that in fact countries like France had continued to send weapons to the Rwandan government at the height of the genocide in May and June of 1994.

When we published that information, we made an instant enemy, that was the government of France. And they still don't really like to talk to us about this. But because it was so intensely embarrassing, the Security Council did take notice of it. It was intensely embarrassing only because we are talking about genocide. Your run-of-the-mill gross human rights abuses don't get that kind of attention, unfortunately.

But Rwanda did in 1994 and 1995, and we tried to capitalize on this. The Security Council passed the resolution in June 1995, sharpening the embargo or clarifying the embargo to make clear that [it] applied not just to the government of Rwanda, because by now that government had changed, but also to the former Rwanda government, which was in exile in neighboring countries and still causing a lot of trouble. It continues to do so today.

The resolution also said that the issue of deploying international monitors at airfields and other ports of entry in the region should be considered to monitor the influx of weapons. A special envoy was sent to the region to discuss with governments how this deployment should happen. Well, the envoy came back with the message that none of the leaders of the states in the region was willing to host international monitors on their soil. This was a sovereignty issue. This was not surprising. The government of Zaire, at that time under Mobutu - and Zaire was one of the main parties accused by us - made very clear that all of this was hogwash. They said: Why would you listen to an NGO anyway? Zaire was never a haven for forces that were attacking a neighboring country, and no arms were being transshipped. Why don't you come and look for yourself? Why do you have monitors? There's no need. Why don't you have an investigation?

Well, de facto, that's what happened. That's certainly not what we had wanted, but the whole monitors idea was shoved off the agenda. Something else happened that was one step down but was still very significant and we supported that effort. In September 1995 the International Commission of Inquiry into Arms Trafficking in Violation of the Arms Embargo on Rwanda was created.

This Commission was called UNICOI, a typical UN designation, United Nations Commission of Inquiry. It started its work in October 1995 and completed its work exactly one year later. It prepared three reports. Two were made public in the spring of 1996.

One third report, which was not made public when it was completed at the end of October 1996, was forwarded to the Security Council and then disappeared somewhere. Nobody knows what really happened with it. Well, somebody knows, but I certainly don't know what happened with it. And the public doesn't know. But it was finally released. It was basically resurrected in January of this year and released out of the blue. There was never any reason to suppress it, because there was nothing in it that in any way added to the two previous reports, except that it was a nice history of what had happened. It didn't implicate anybody to any further extent. So, it's quite a bit of a mystery.

The Commission, in any case, in its one year of work and two or three reports did some very useful work. It did find clear evidence of violations of the international arms embargo. It was the first time that the UN actually had sponsored an in-depth investigation of an international arms embargo that it itself had imposed.

It focussed on one particular arms deal that involved a South African ex-official and a Rwandan leader of the genocide. In an addendum to these reports released in January of this year, in fact, the Banque Nationale de Paris, a major French bank, was implicated in this particular arms deal. It became all very "John Le Carre-like" and interesting and exposed a very shady deal.

This Commission was able to bring that to the surface. It was a very healthy, useful exercise in the end. I say in the end because the Commission died at that time, or maybe it was frozen. It was not really clear and I don't have the latest news. Today, supposedly, it was recreated after a lot of pressure from us and other organizations, who had an interest in the continued life of this Commission. The Security Council today was supposed to reactivate this Commission. (The Commission was revived on April 9.)

We had also fought for an extension of the Commission's mandate to include all of the Great Lakes, especially Burundi. I don't think that is going to be quite explicit in the final language. We hope that this Commission will, in fact, look at the issue regionally, because the problem is not confined to Rwanda only. The rebel forces are still based in what is now Congo and in Tanzania and they are receiving military support from certain international sponsors.

So, it is very important that this sort of Commission continues. Why? Because when it does, these little effects come out, like there's a French bank, not a small one, a big one, involved. That implicates French policy and it may implicate the policy of other countries. That is intensely embarrassing. We have found that what works, in the final analysis, is not the laws and the arms embargo so much, even though they are very important, but the embarrassment that you cause when you show that a government has continued to supply weapons to forces that are involved in very serious human rights violations, including and most seriously genocide.

Our approach is that, yes, we must fight for better regulations and codes of conduct which are critically important. Yes, treaties or conventions against illicit arms trafficking are very important. We support these. But, even when you have these, and the same thing is true for the landmines treaty that now exists - it's great to have it, we had to get to that point - now that we have it we must continue to investigate violations because they will happen. They will happen routinely unless we are watching. So, we must investigate. We must be out in the field. We must look at what is happening, what is being imported, what is being exported, what is coming into a country, and who is doing what. What are the channels? What are the mechanisms? Who are the actors?

We must use that information, publicize it, get the press involved and embarrass the hell out of the governments that are implicated in one way or another, either because they are direct suppliers or because they are closing their eyes to the transshipment of weapons through their territories, or because they are thoroughly corrupt.

I want to alert you to one potentially very grave development which is the consequences of the expansion of NATO to include three countries in the former Warsaw Pact: the Czech Republic, Hungary and Poland. The expansion itself falls outside our mandate as a human rights organization. What it will entail is that these countries need to upgrade their weapons systems to NATO standard. What that may mean is that they will end up with lots of weapons in their hands, old stocks that they need to get rid of. There is no provision in the expansion of NATO for the disposal of these weapons. The likelihood is that these weapons will be thrown out onto the open market. Because these are huge amounts of weapons, they're going to be very cheap and they are going to go to conflicts where demand is extremely high.

These weapons, which are very sophisticated weapons, are going to create real havoc in conflicts in Africa, in Central Asia, in the Balkans and elsewhere. There is already a bit of a coalition building to address this particular question. If there is any way you would like to be involved in that, then there are organizations like BASIC in the US and in Britain, Human Rights Watch and others that are focusing on this issue.

IVOR RICHARD FUNG, UN Development Programme: ...I will be speaking from a very practical, field-oriented approach, having been involved for the past five years or so in the field, trying to come to grips with these issues. I am now managing a project at the UNDP, UN Development Programme, which seeks to integrate security issues and development. That is the reason why I will be putting a lot of emphasis on the development side of this. There can be no development if there is no security. Small arms is an integral part of that.

Let me start by trying to understand with you what the concept of small arms means. There is no generally agreed definitions of small arms. However, the ones that are being used contain some of the following elements. These elements are drawn from a recently concluded international conference in Oslo on the small arms moratorium in West Africa.

What is understood by small arms is, first, the focus is on legal equipment, weapons and the ammunition generally used by military and paramilitary forces, excluding items such as knives and hunting rifles. This is important because the last speaker just referred to the war in Rwanda, largely fought not with firearms but with machetes, domestic tools.

Second, the emphasis is on weapons that are man-portable or transportable by light vehicles.

Third, this equipment is easy to maintain. It can function without much logistical backup and it requires little training to use.

Fourth, to be militarily and politically relevant, the definition comprises weapons that are in frequent use, weapons that kill.

We have in West Africa reached a practical understanding of these weapons. We have categorized them in seven areas: (1) pistols, which includes revolvers, semi-automatic; (2) shotguns; (3) submachine gun; (4) rifles; (5) machine guns; (6) anti-tank mortars; (7) landmines. We have things like flame throwers and other explosives.

In Africa this is a growing phenomenon. I remember when I was growing up, it was very difficult to talk of weapons because we never saw them. Pistols - we never saw them. But today when I go back home, I see children, teenagers, with grenades. This is a very new phenomenon which has created a big concern in Africa today. Cities are growing, so too is the rate of crime and banditry. That is the reason why today in Africa everybody is concerned: politicians and people in civil society everywhere are trying to come up with solutions which would bring this problem under control.

Why is it important to curb the proliferation of light weapons in a region, like Africa, for instance? What is the purpose?

There are three main objectives of particular importance. One of them is conflict prevention and the prevention of arms banditry. To have a fair chance of success, strategies of conflict prevention and post-conflict peace consolidation have to be comprehensive.

Six components should be considered whenever such a strategy is being devised, though not all of them would necessarily be relevant to every situation. Disarmament has a place in two of those situations, establishing security first and disarmament in the context of demobilization, when the conflict is coming to an end.

Another objective is to pave the way for socio-economic development in general and for donor-supported development projects, in particular. The latter are particularly sensitive to incidents of violence.

The fundamental condition for development in any country is that an adequate level of security is maintained by the state. In 1994, the Security-General of the United Nations put together an advisory mission for West Africa. I was part of that mission. One of our major findings was that there can be no development in an insecure environment.

This conclusion came as a result of the realization that in the northern part of Mali, where an armed conflict had been raging, in Liberia and in Sierra Leone, all development projects were stopped. Nothing could happen. In Mali we discovered that more than two hundred million dollars worth of development projects were frozen in the bank and that money could not be used because of insecurity in those areas where the project was supposed to take place. So, it is very important to note the impact of small arms circulation on development in Africa in addition to the other dimensions which have been outlined by the two previous speakers, the humanitarian part of it.

The idea of the security first approach is taking root in many development projects. I mentioned the project I'm managing at the UNDP. The World Bank, too, has started integrating into its work the need to come to grips with issues of proliferation of small arms. In the field we work very closely with NGOs, civil society. What is happening now is that everybody is gradually understanding, even those who in the past felt that the proliferation of small arms was not part of a development project but part of a disarmament project.

I remember in the '80s when Colombia brought a resolution on the illicit circulation of small arms to the First Committee where I served at that time. It was very difficult for people to accept it. They said, small arms - that's a non-issue. But today, because of the havoc everybody is witnessing in Bosnia, in the Great Lakes region, which my previous colleagues have so elaborately spoken about, it is glaringly clear that the issue of small arms has to be on the table of the international community as a major security question.

It is therefore important to convince donors that in many countries part of the development aid may be invested in a more effective law and order mechanism to be developed under international supervision. It is only when functional substitutes are offered for the role that weapons now play, for instance, in the form of sub-defense groups, that incentives to collect arms can work well. It is only when arms have been brought under control and the security environment has become stable that development can be conducted. Hence, the quest for an integrated and proportional approach to security and development. That is what we call a security first approach.

The third objective is to come to grips with crime and banditry. This is often a big problem in states where civil society is poorly developed and the social fabric is in dismal condition. Furthermore, it is almost a law of nature that when internal wars come to an end, there is a burst of crime and banditry in the aftermath. I was involved in Mozambique, in Angola and presently in Liberia. What the UN has done in Liberia is to provide support to ECOMOG, to go through the disarmament and demobilization process of the ex-combatants. But what has been collected so far is not even one tenth of the weapons that are presently proliferating.

This applies to what the previous speakers have said about surplus weapons. Surplus weapons are in some of these countries; and there is a need to mop up those weapons. We are presently, as part of the project I am managing, trying to create what we call a trans-border grassroots security dialogue. This is aiming at creating conditions for the grassroots population, who most of the time are not only the victims of small arms proliferation but also the primary actors of this phenomenon. What we are trying to do is engage them in a dialogue so that they can tell us what can be done in order for them to surrender their weapons. Part of the problem is extreme poverty. People resort to weapons, to small arms, as a way to survive. It's like an income for many people there.

This is where the notion of armed banditry comes in in the rural areas in most African countries. We have started a pilot program in Mali. In addition to the three thousand weapons which we collected two years ago, we have collected about six hundred more just by going to the rural areas, talking to people and hearing what their problems are which prompted them to carry weapons. Then we will try to find solutions to that.

One of the primary responses is, "Listen, we resorted to weapons because we needed to survive. There is no development, there's nothing, there's absolutely nothing. So, we needed to stand in the highways to trap anybody passing and take whatever he has."

We are now working with donors as part of the development approach to see that some of the remote areas have equitable development distributed which would give some jobs to those people that are idle and can find no other way but to resort to carrying weapons. It seems to be succeeding in the case of Mali where we have already collected many weapons.

What is more important in this connection of security and development, the human beings, the combatants, or the weapons that they carry? It is more important to address the humans behind the guns than to eliminate the material vehicles of violence. This comes to the question my friend was asking that it is not a gun that kills, it is the person who carries the gun who kills. So, it makes sense in all development approaches today to target not just the weapon. Taking the weapon away is not enough, because they will always get another. Try to look into the problems of that person who has the weapon and see what can be done.

African countries, being as poor as they are, can not do this alone. They depend very much on the international community of donors, NGOs, etc., to work with them. It is not a matter of either/or; both are important. Many other factors can also help produce the crime and banditry that disrupt so many societies. If there are a lot of arms around, easy access to weapons invites violent solutions to problems. By implication, acquisition of arms for self-defense invites violence since there may be no effective police to rely upon.

The proliferation of arms breeds cultures of violence. If arms are carried in public places, this tends to stimulate violent behavior. If a peace operation deployed to a country in conflict winds up before measures have been taken to control the flow of arms, post-conflict construction may be jeopardized. In Africa some governments, because of the political situations in which they find themselves, resort to providing weapons to people who are from their region and who are ready to defend them. We end up in the situation that is very, very delicate, with everybody carrying weapons. The mere fact that those weapons are being given them by the authorities in power gives them some legitimacy. They believe they have the right to carry weapons.

This brings us to the problem of the legality of the weapons and the legality of some of the governments. That's why one should not lose sight of this other dimension, the political dimension. There is the need to combine all these efforts with the process of democratization in many of these countries.

It is not an easy task, but I can tell you that many NGOs are down there and are trying to see how they can be useful to these governments. Some of these issues are very political and they require some very daring solutions to convince some of the governments to do their work as they should.

I mentioned why we are targeting the grassroots. It is because for some time now we have realized that this dialogue, this conversation or discussion about small arms, about disarmament in general, is at a very superficial level in the states with the people in power. We often forget that the victims have something to say about all this and they can contribute to the solution. I'm sure my friend, who has been working in the Great Lakes, in an area I know very well, can testify to this.

I remember when the first Commission - I was part of the group that put together that Commission - went down to Zaire, to the Great Lakes. It wasn't an easy thing. I was in Togo not long ago and I spoke with the president of that Commission. He told me that when they went to Kissangali, they were driven away because it was claimed that some of the population, instigated by the government, accused them of doing things which were not legal. It is always good to bear in mind that the local populations have a contribution to make that can be very, very important.

Let me touch on another dimension of control, regional approaches. Some countries see international efforts to come to grips with the proliferation of light weapons as interference into their domestic affairs, and, therefore, something they cannot go along with. They are afraid that their sovereignty may be compromised. This is not difficult to understand since monopoly on the physical means of control goes to the core of what states are about. States of South Asia see it in this way. My colleague, working on these issues in South Asia, knows this type of problem.

The political vision in Africa is different. I'm going to get to some of the daring proposals which have been made in Africa to control small arms. In many parts of Africa, governments take the opposite view. Here efforts to mop up light weapons and curb illicit flows of arms are seen as a welcome contribution to the reconstruction of states and something that may help them establish real sovereignty. It is new. Five years ago one could not easily go to any state in Africa and talk about how to mop up small arms.

In 1994 I was rapporteur of a working group in Southern Africa on demilitarization and disarmament of civil society. We started working with several governments, including Zimbabwe, South Africa, and Swaziland. The end result of our work was a proposal that the frontline states alliance at that time, which has been dissolved, become a security mechanism within the Southern African development community. This could become a permanent institution in the framework of which some of these issues could be discussed and ways to address the problems could be found. Fortunately, some of our recommendations were taken into consideration, because South Africa, Swaziland and Mozambique established a trilateral commission to look into the proliferation of small arms in their neighborhood. This is a welcome development.

In that meeting we discovered that just in that Southern African region there were, if one included landmines, over fifty-six million light weapons proliferating in the region. This is enormous! Mozambique and Angola, states that have been going through armed conflict for several years, were the greatest holders of these weapons.

Let me go directly to this exciting proposal that is coming out of Africa. Countries in Western Africa have realized that there is a need for political action in this field. They have proposed to declare a moratorium on the import, export and production of light weapons in Africa. This would be a three-year moratorium, at the end of which there would be an assessment conference, an evaluation conference, which would determine whether the moratorium could be continued or whether in its place one could work out some sort of a permanent legal instrument, which would be a step towards having a legal framework in this field in that part of the continent.

The moratorium is open to all African countries that are interested in this issue. It is not a binding mechanism. It is only a political measure to translate the good will, the good faith of those countries who have become aware of this problem. They feel that in order for them to make any progress, there is a need for a voluntary abstention from importing and exporting and producing weapons and ammunition in the area.

This is considered a major thing at the political level. It is supported by the Norwegian government which organized in Oslo an international conference which brought together 13 African countries, members of the Economic Community of West African States (ECOWAS) and 23 member-states of the Wassenaar Arrangement. One of the novel aspects of this moratorium is the expression of the members to engage in a dialogue with arms suppliers of the Wassenaar Arrangement, so that the moratorium proposal, when it is declared, hopefully in July when the heads of state of ECOWAS will be meeting, would be respected by suppliers.

It is a major thing. When we started, I went to Vienna to talk to the secretariat of the Wassenaar Arrangement. I was told that they do not deal with small arms. They had not integrated that into their structure as one of the primary things with which we should be working. But because we insisted, in December last year they issued a statement. In their final document they included this concern about small arms. They were represented at the Oslo Conference by the chairman, who made a statement The moratorium would be on the seven categories of weapons I earlier listed.

PETER DAVIES, A SaferWorld: A SaferWorld has a publication on light weapons, small arms, written by Owen Green last July. I want to congratulate all three panelists but particularly the exciting information on the moratorium. I think this is a wonderful example of transparency.

I am very interested in the issue of how you take the experience of the landmines campaign, which many of us have been actively engaged in, and translate this into a campaign on small arms, light weapons. The experience, as I see it, has been one where the landmines campaign started small but proliferated into national campaigns in every country with over one thousand NGOs involved. They came together as a unified campaign in forty countries. It was successful in focussing on a single issue. It seems to me that while it may be more complex than I heard Lora relate at Columbia University a couple of weeks ago, it may be possible to organize a similar type of campaign. I would very much appreciate Michael's, Joost's and Dr. Fung's comments on whether and how you see this moving. Part of the problem, however, is certainly the attitude of some southern countries. I was delighted to hear what you had to say about the changing attitude in Africa towards this issue, that is that it not the North saying you should do this as opposed to a felt need.

IVOR FUNG: Let me say that this is an issue that has been under discussion among some of us who have been involved in efforts to control small arms proliferation. Starting from 1994, when we went to Africa as part of the mission of the Secretary-General to advise on how one would control this, the idea, of course, at that time, was not clear in our minds but gradually taking shape. Recently, when I went to Oslo to receive the one million the Norwegian government was contributing to our efforts on this moratorium, we did discuss on a more practical and concrete manner how one could start a campaign, an international campaign. This was in October of last year.

In December the Norwegian Red Cross, the Norwegian Institute of International Affairs, the Oslo Institute of Peace Research and the Norwegian Church all came together to launch a campaign on small arms. That campaign has started its work with the Oslo Conference I just returned from. We believe it is a very complex issue, very fluid, and a very large concept. It is not as precise in its operationalization in the field nor in its content as landmines. It is going to be very difficult to wage the type of campaign that we did for landmines. But nevertheless, in Oslo we came up with the Oslo Platform for a Moratorium on Small Arms in West Africa, which is going to serve as a pilot program.

KATE JOSEPH, BASIC: My two questions to Dr. Fung relate to the Mali Moratorium. Firstly, I think it was Joost who talked about the need for comprehensive verification of these types of agreements. I wonder what proposals there were to ensure compliance with the moratorium. Secondly, you said that this is a pilot project and it'll be investigated to see if it really works. I wondered what your ideas were about the possibilities for replication of this moratorium in other regions all around the world? That's a valuable idea.

IVOR FUNG: What I didn't mention in my presentation, because there wasn't much time, was that the moratorium regime would be supported by a secretariat, a mechanism called, Program for Coordination and Assistance on Security and Development. Now, there are many activities, many programs, such as: the control of border areas; provision of assistance to member states in their revision of relevant legislation bearing on weapons; establishing regional registers on small arms and data bases, etc. Some of these practical issues would be addressed in the context of that program.

Of course, what we are talking about is a political will. It is voluntary, so it is very difficult to monitor, to verify. It is very difficult to go to the government of Mali or to any government and say, "but you said you were not going to import or to export weapons but we have seen some movement in your neighborhood." What is happening? We have come to realize it is a very sensitive and delicate issue. However, this secretariat has made the provision for monitoring and verification, which will consist in working very closely with the government. All weapons which were ordered before this moratorium are exempt from this. Also, there is a provision that they work with the government in constantly reminding them of this commitment not to import. That would be the political dimension of the work of this secretariat. To sum it up, it is difficult but it will be taken care of in one way or the other and provisions have been made for that.

To the other question re the exporting of this pilot case to other regions. In Oslo, we had presentations by Ed Lawrence of the Monterey Institute on Latin America and Central America. The idea was to see which are the factors which may favor or not favor the export of this type of experience to that part of the world. What we are thinking is that it would be possible, but, of course, we would need this international campaign. Our efforts are for a specific region, and we do not have the mandate to extend them to other regions. If there is an international campaign, it would make it possible for other countries, for some daring ones, Colombia, for example. The government of Colombia has been very active in this field when they sponsored about three resolutions in the First

Committee. If we have one government that can start, then it could go like wildfire.

LORA LUMPE: Let me use the chair's prerogative and to ask you two questions. One, do you have any sense of how many countries you expect to endorse the moratorium in July? Secondly, is the one million dollars from Norway to support the moratorium enough, or is this initiative looking for more money from the international aid community?

IVOR FUNG: When we started with the moratorium idea, it was something very crazy. I remember very well when I first spoke of it to the President of Mali. He laughed and laughed for about fifteen minutes. He told me, Are you mad? Don't you see, in the culture of Mali, it is forbidden, it is an abomination to destroy a weapon? It is an abomination, because most of them, about 70 per cent of the population of Mali, are nomadic. They move from one area to the next and in that process they carry weapons with them.

However, we succeeded with the government of Mali and the issue defines the foreign policy of Mali today. We worked with the President of Mali and government of Mali. We went to the OAU, to ECOWAS, the Economic Commission of West African States, to talk to the other governments. We based this conviction on the Flame of Peace Ceremony, which we had staged in Mali.

Fortunately for us, our diplomacy worked in bringing a number of countries on board and the idea was recently endorsed at the ministerial conference of the Economic Community of West African States, which brings together 16 countries in West Africa. In principle, all 16 countries have accepted and they are expected to declare a moratorium in July. At that meeting, a conference of ministers, the ECOWAS secretariat, was mandated together with our support to come with a text for the declaration. This would be endorsed and used by the heads of state in July.

So, Lora, the optimism is there and I feel that at least ten countries, if not more, would be able to declare a moratorium in July. As far as the question of money is concerned. I just spoke to you about this implementing structure of the moratorium, the Programme for Coordination, Assistance on Security and Development. It is a five-year UNDP project, which will require close to 7 million dollars to function. For now, we have pledges. In fact, Norway is the only one that has actually paid. They pledged two million; they have paid one million. We have the support of the US Government. They will be contributing but on the condition that there is a declaration.

The State Department and the Department of Defense told me at a very high level they were going to support it. Since then they have been doing a wonderful job. The list of weapons which I read to you, the seven categories, they sent a colonel to help us in working out this. We have really been working together with the US Government and, more than that, they have also been convincing other governments, like the UK, like Canada.

I just got a call from Canada; they are ready to contribute. We have not been there but it's the US that told them this is a very good initiative. I think that they cannot do all this and then end up by not putting money into it, hopefully. We have the UK. Last week in Oslo the representative of the UK announced half a million dollars contribution to this mechanism. We also have some good commitments from the Dutch, the Swedes and maybe the Japanese.

UNDP is going to put some money into it too. For those of you who may be interested to know how it will be functioning - the idea so far is to combine this mechanism with the UN Regional Center of Peace and Disarmament in Africa, which is located in Lome. This is a disarmament issue and it may be appropriate for it to be hosted by that UN institute.

JOOST HILTERMANN: We have been extremely active in the landmine campaign and I see the campaign as *sui generis* and unique. Even though I would like to see the campaign replicated in the campaign against small arms, I think it is impossible. That's because landmines are an indiscriminate weapon. It is a single system and the major casualties are clearly people after conflicts are over and they are completely innocent, having nothing to do with the conflict itself.

With small arms it is much more difficult. Small arms are not in and of themselves illegal. It's their use that is the problem. We're not talking about a single weapon system, we're not talking about a single treaty. It's not really clear what the goal is of the campaign. It involves a number of organizations that have entirely different agendas and mandates and it might be very difficult to come to that single goal. Yet, it's worth looking for one. But, I think what's more important is that there is some momentum that has been created by the landmines campaign. We must capitalize on that. If there are now governments that are saying we have to do something about small arms, that's great! We need to use that energy, and the momentum and, maybe, the money - definitely the money. The question is what do you use it for? How do you use it? That is going to be a lot more difficult.

What has already happened in the last few months because of this sort of energy is that a lot of the organizations that are doing something about small arms and light weapons have gotten together more and have started talking to each other. That is really very important. There is more coordination now and there's maybe less overlap in work. I think that is one very good thing. Then maybe a number of concrete objectives will emerge. Whether that will translate into a campaign, I don't know. It really doesn't matter so much. Maybe it's not a campaign we're after but a number of loosely coordinated separate campaigns, each having very clear objectives. Maybe that is something to aspire to. If that comes out of the landmines campaign, then I think that's already a great victory.

MICHAEL RENNER: What strikes me about this issue is that, going from country to country and region to region, you have slightly different situations and slightly different problems. I think with landmines more than with any other type of weapon, you have a very clear kind of problem that, no matter whether you are in Central America, Africa, Cambodia, whatever, there was a similar sort of issue at hand. With small arms, I guess, it's a different situation with a country that comes out of a civil war than, say, with the United States or any other country. I think recognizing that means that the local and national and regional campaigns obviously are more tailored to what makes sense in that particular context. So maybe that too, which is in a way a strength and not a negative, makes it more of an issue of coordination rather than an issue of whether there is one global campaign.

Peter also said it's the sort of thing that the North imposes on the South. I think what's encouraging are the initiatives coming from the South: the Mali initiative, Colombia has been on the forefront, Mexico was really the lead country in pushing the recent OAS convention on combating illicit trafficking of small arms, also South Africa, Mozambique, and Swaziland, I believe, have been very active in their region. I think countries, meaning both governments and NGOs, recognizing what the issue is leads to a lot happening on the ground. I'm not too afraid that this is going to be seen as the West again telling the rest of the world what to do.

JOOST HILTERMANN: In fact, I think it's up to the West to tell itself what to do, because a lot of the weapons are coming from here or from the former Warsaw Pact countries that are now being integrated into NATO. We have a very important role to play here. Obviously, there is also a role to play for the countries where the weapons are being used. The moratorium discussed by Dr. Fung is extremely important, but we have a role to play as well that is focused inward, not outward.

LORA LUMPE: Absolutely. I would just add to that some recent research I have done. I was able to find about the US $530 million worth of US small arms exports licensed by the State and Commerce Departments in 1996. If you divide that by $200 or $300 as an average price per weapon, which is random but in the ballpark of the price, that's coming up to several hundred thousand guns being exported. That's totally aside from the weapons that the Department of Defense exported from the United States in 1996. We're talking about hundreds of thousands of guns being exported from this country in that one year alone.

TOM MASON, NRA: I'm Tom Mason and I represent the National Rifle Association. I am also speaking on behalf of the World Forum on the Future of Sport Shooting Activities, a new NGO just formed to a great extent in response to what has been happening. That organization, the World Forum, includes the European Association of Ammunition Manufacturers, the American Association of Small Arms and Ammunition Manufacturers, the Italian Small Arms Manufacturers, the South African Small Arms Manufacturers, Safari Club International, the National Rifle Association, the British Shooting Sports Council, the German, French, Danish, Italian and Spanish Hunting Associations and several other organizations.

Let me preface my questions with a comment that, throughout your whole presentations, there's not been one mention of hunting or self-defense. Ms. Lumpe just mentioned the export of American arms. I hate to tell you but most of those were hunting weapons. The United States is the largest manufacturer of hunting weapons in the world.

Let me ask you three questions. Mr. Renner, you talked about limiting production of small arms. How would you limit production of small arms and still preserve production of civilian weapons, weapons that are currently held by civilians for legitimate civilian purposes, if I can use a broad term? Or, if I can rephrase the question, how would you differentiate between a medium-calibre, self-loading hunting rifle and a medium-calibre, self-loading military rifle? We have had a problem here, especially in the United States, with definitions and when we have accepted a definition, it seems that the definition isn't quite good enough. The people want to go back on the definitions. How do we know that you are not going to go back on the definitions?

Then, let me ask you this. I did not hear one mention here of the role of self-defense. It's an historical fact, there's never been genocide against an armed population. Indeed, do we totally submit to the idea that all security flows out of the state? Is there any role here for the personal right of self-defense? The UN Charter represents the right of nations having self-defense. Do you see any role here for people defending themselves?

MICHAEL RENNER: In the first place, you are creating a one-stop shop for all of us who want to address the manufacturers. If you all come together, we just need to go to one place and say, Please, here are some of our ideas. In a sense, I guess I am glad to hear that, although on our side of defense, so to speak, I hope we can similarly be well-organized.

When I talked about limiting production, I'm probably too far out there. I think a lot of the people who have gotten themselves into this issue in various ways are saying, there's this enormous quantity of weapons that's already out there. That's the first order; we've got to address that. So, in that sense, I'm probably a little ahead of myself by saying we've also got to think about production.

I don't mean to get away from your question. Clearly, yes, the question of the definition is many ways is key, as Ivor Fung was actually pointing out. The problem clearly is it's very, very difficult to define what is small arms and light weapons. No matter how you think about these issues, you can come up with x number of different ways of defining it.

To me what really makes sense is not to get lost in technical distinctions. I think that is part of what the US discussion is about. You have a law, a 1994 law, that defined very, very narrowly what's outlawed and what's not outlawed. I think that just didn't make any sense. If we were to go on in the same way on an international or regional level, the same problem would obtain. I think you clearly have to say, Yes, this is the class of weapons, clearly defined, that we are addressing.

What I am concerned with is that there may be an easier way to say let's talk only about military small arms that are clearly defined and recognized as such. I think one can draw somewhat of a line there. Clearly, there is a gray area, no matter where you draw a line. So, what we need to do is to step back and say clearly there is not a black and white distinction between military and civilian types of weapons and also military and civilians owning or controlling these weapons. One of the problems in so many countries is because there is such an enormous quantity of weapons. People do feel, yes, I have to go out, too, and get in on the act. I'd better be armed because so many other people are armed, government or not government.

I think that's the very problem. You seem to be saying that, if everybody is allowed to own arms, then there's no problem. Look around. There is a problem. Right? We really need to recognize that in many societies, I'm not saying in all societies but in many societies, there really is in effect a domestic arms race going on. Where is that going to lead? Is there a logical conclusion? Are we all going to deter each other, if we are all well-armed?

I think these are questions that may be hard to answer, but I just want to say that if we put restrictions perhaps on the production but certainly the circulation and transfer of arms, that may cause one set of issues to be addressed. But, if you don't do it, there is a whole range of other issues that we need to deal with. I'm not going to say nobody has the right to self-defense, but what does that mean in a country, in a situation that has so many arms that you're not going to get anywhere with that, basically. You end up with everybody armed and everybody very distrustful.

JOOST HILTERMANN: The NRA and manufacturers in this country and in other countries are in the business because it is extremely profitable. The more you are into a profitable business, the more distant you are from the facts. It's clearly not an historical fact that genocide has only happened against populations that were unarmed. Just look at the genocide of the Kurds by Iraq, for example. The population was a heavily armed population that was protected by a military force that was defeated. That is simply not a fact at all, it's a non-fact.

Aside from that, I didn't mention the right of self-defense because for my organization it is not an issue. The issue is not whether people have weapons but how these weapons are used. This is a state responsibility in international law. If people have weapons but then proceed to commit crimes with them, the state has the responsibility to do something about that. It has various mechanisms at its disposal and the laws. It can confiscate a weapon, it can make licensing more strict, etc.

The point is that there has to be very strict controls on how weapons are used. If you send weapons into areas where you know weapons are going to be misused because there is serious conflict going on, then that is a very irresponsible action. I think it is very important that these kinds of supplies, these kinds of transfers are stopped. This can be done through codes of conduct. Codes of conduct are not designed to stop the arms trade. Codes of conduct are designed to make sure that weapons do not fall into the hands of forces that you know are going to be abusing these weapons and killing civilians.

SONYA OSTROM, Peace Action: I work with students in the Brooklyn House of Detention and I used to wear a pin that said "No arms." My students would say to me, "You're right. We don't believe in guns. We wish all guns could be gotten rid of. But, because everyone has them, we have to have them, too. There's no way we are going to walk out on the street without a gun in this neighborhood." I think if we don't understand that that's what's happening to our society and societies all over by the proliferation of small arms, then I think that we're blinding ourselves to the reality.

LORA LUMPE: I think that's the point that Mr. Fung made very well, that you've got to look at the root cause and address why people are feeling that they need to be armed. I think we would all agree very much with that.

TRACY MOEVERO, Peace Action International Office: Are there some positive, successful examples on which we can build?

LORA LUMPE: I would say that Dr. Fung's story about the Mali Moratorium is a very positive one. There are several recent initiatives having to do with the illicit arms traffic, which have been alluded to.In November of last year, 28 countries signed a treaty in Washington, negotiated through the Organization of American States, which curbs the illicit manufacture, production and transfer of weapons. In a sense, it's making it illegal to illegally transfer weapons. It has some very practical mechanisms, though. It actually promotes cooperation between Customs. It promotes the ability of governments in the hemisphere to trace illegally obtained weapons back to their source, promotes greater cooperation between states in the hemisphere on combating this. I think that's a positive example. Anything else?

MICHAEL RENNER: There's the landmines treaty, of course. The 1995 treaty to ban blinding laser weapons also is very important. Even though they're not being used today, if they hadn't been banned, they'd be out on the streets pretty soon.

JOOST HILTERMANN: There is a sort of a similar effort on the European Union level comparable to the OAS agreement. There are similar objectives.

TOM MASON: The OAS Preamble states right up front that it's not meant to interfere with hunting, sport shooting or the lawful possession of firearms by civilians. At first it did. And it wasn't until we participated and wrote that language that it was put in. We would like that same type of language to be acknowledged in this conference. I don't see that in any of this dialogue.

LORA LUMPE: I think Dr. Fung said very explicitly that in the definition of the weapons that were included in the Mali Moratorium that hunting rifles and knives were exempt.

TOM MASON: The same rifles we use for deer hunting in my state are the military sniper rifles, so you loose any meaning to that.

MARY SHOIKET, Servas International: Everyone who has a job and needs it wants to keep it. That would go for all the people who work in factories making guns. Perhaps these manufacturers might profit from someone coming to discuss conversion with them...

MICHAEL RENNER: I think you're quite right. The conversion idea per se is not a new one. The problem that really has thwarted progress on that issue is that there really has not been a whole lot of political will behind it. Certainly in this country; in Europe, in any country that has an arms industry, this issue has been discussed into the 1980s, into the 1990s. The problem has been the political support for it...It makes a lot of sense to me to offer alternatives and it certainly is an idea that has been addressed, not just with regard to small arms. It has actually arisen from, as you probably know, the areas of weapons-making that have been concerning us much more, - the big tanks, the helicopters, the submarines, etc. Clearly, if you can address the big industries, those kinds of things, then those making small arms ought not to be a problem. Unfortunately, there has not been that kind of political support for the concept.

ROGER SMITH, NGO Committee on Disarmament: ...The information you have presented makes it clear that we have a steep learning curve to climb. Toward that end, I'm going to take the liberty of asking a couple of questions, which you may consider stupid questions. First, I am really seeking to understand whether the phrase "small arms and light weapons" is completely redundant or only partly redundant or whether Dr. Fung's breakdown of the categorizations used in West Africa helps in answer to that.

The second question is a little deeper and may reflect some of the concerns that Mr. Mason brought up about self-defense. In the discussion this morning about cutting back on war, there was a question raised about self-determination, which I think may be another vexatious problem for those attempting to campaign on this issue. I can easily see situations where you have governments that may perhaps be victorious in civil conflicts seeking the help of the UN and the donor community to complete the disarmament of a rival who has been defeated. I wonder to what extent the small arms efforts are going to play into the hands of these kinds of governments, and whether this presents problems in terms of the UN Charter or other principles of international justice? To what extent has this been thought of and are there ways around it?

LORA LUMPE: I use small arms and light weapons basically interchangeably. I think the general, broad working definition, surely what I consider either one, is a manned, portable weapon, a personal, portable weapons system. I think his working definition of the categories of arms matches very closely with the small arms panel's definition of small arms, with two exception, ammunition and grenades, the things that actually go in the grenade launchers and the guns. I use them fairly interchangeably to liven up a speech.

MICHAEL RENNER: Small arms, light weapons, explosives and ammunition are four related categories. It's everything that's not in the UN Register for Major Weapon Systems. That's the other way of looking at it.

JOOST HILTERMANN: The question about how governments might benefit from the UN helping them disarm, concerns of justice and survival, and the question of self-determination, the right of peoples to take up arms against repressive governments, in many ways the same question Mr. Mason was asking, is out of our mandate. Our issue is how the weapons are used; it's not the disarmament issue. All I could say is that so far as the peacekeeping mission is concerned, it is an issue that has not come up because the UN is only expected or allowed to go in once there is an agreement.

LORA LUMPE: ...We should be embargoing weapons to repressive states that might be giving cause to insurgents to take up arms. The international community should be encouraging states to negotiate and find political solutions. That might sound idealistic but I think certainly that would be my preferred alternative to arming sub-state groups to form nations through the force of arms. I think it's a code of conduct approach. The international community ought not be arming repressive and human rights governments. If that were happening, then political processes and negotiations should find space to operate instead of armed conflict.

REGINA MURPHY, Interfaith Center on Corporate Responsibility: ...ICCR is a church-related group that tries to coalesce church organizations and their pension funds to address as shareholders the corporations that are involved in military production and sales. We've traditionally, for the past twenty years or so, addressed the corporations that are dealing with larger arms. Economic conversion has been a constant refrain. We had several shareholder resolutions years back with companies like Grumman and Boeing, etc. When these companies had to scale down considerably because of financial difficulties, we felt like saying, We told you so! But, by then it was somewhat late and we hadn't gotten a very attentive hearing from them.

I assure you, the small arms question is on our agenda for discussion. I think it is important that we get the research and I applaud all the mentions of reports. I agree with Michael that until there's political will it's an uphill battle. Not only the political will of the citizenry, but the also the political will in the corporations. I think as long as the shareholders and the corporate entities continue to make profits, it's very hard to convince anybody that they should either corporately or individually change their ways.I'd also like to applaud mentions of coordinated programs that we've heard this afternoon, and also this morning. Those who are working in UN groups, those who are working on the political agenda, as well as addressing the economic structures, need to work together and create that groundswell that perhaps we do not have as we did in the '70s and '80s.

NEWTON BOWLES, UNA Canada:I noticed on the report that went to the General Assembly last fall of the panel on small arms that one of their recommendations was that there should be an international conference specifically on ammunition and explosives. I understand that at least seventy countries and maybe as many 100, actually manufacture ammunition. It must be an extremely difficult thing to get a hold on. Do any of our panelists have some ideas on how to move on that? What could come out of a conference?

MICHAEL RENNER: This is certainly an idea that has been mentioned by a lot of people. If I'm correct about this, the ability to manufacture ammunition is not as widespread as the ability to manufacture the actual guns. So, you could narrow the problem in the sense of how many parties you need to address and get on board for whatever you want to do.

But, also ammunition is probably somewhat harder to destroy because it is bulky. If you want any meaningful amounts for military or military-type operations, you need pretty large quantities. There's a lot of weight involved. I'm not aware of any particular efforts to really push that more beyond the idea stage.

KATE JOSEPH: We have a study coming out in about a week or so on this subject. It will examine the production of ammunition and whether or not there are viable means for its control. I think, probably, the most promising recommendation that came out of that was the idea of tagging ammunition, so it can be traced more easily. That seems to be the most realistic policy proposal.

PETER DAVIES, A Safer World: I think we must answer Roger's question. I think the answer is, let's take the example of Angola and the Lusaka Agreement. Let's take the example of Liberia. Basically, the UN view has been that after a conflict, it is necessary to disarm both sides to have a reconciliation programme to collect arms from all sides. The problem has been the lack of funding available to the UN Peacekeeping and the Department of Humanitarian Affairs to carry out these types of programs. I don't think it's correct to posit that there is, if I understood your question correctly, a sort of legitimacy in the same way as the right to self-determination. Conflict is bad in itself and if you can lower the threshold by reconstruction and disarmament, you're going to get a much better resolution of conflict. If I understood your question, I think it's not really a relevant one.

French Official from the UNDC Working Group on Small Arms: I have just two remarks. The presentations were very interesting, but I was surprised by the mentioning of specific countries or even the responsibility of specific countries regarding some African conflicts. I really don't see what this has to do with a general presentation on the issue. France did not ship arms to Rwanda during the genocide.

JOOST HILTERMANN: It is entirely appropriate for a human rights organization at this kind of forum to name names. We carried out an investigation and uncovered clear evidence that France had sent arms to Rwanda at the height of the genocide...

LORA LUMPE: Our thanks to all of you...

PREVENTING THE WEAPONIZATION OF OUTER SPACE

CHAIRMAN: RON CLEMINSON, Senior Adviser for Verification in the Canadian Department of Foreign Affairs: Ladies and Gentlemen, I'd like to welcome you to this session on Preventing the Weaponization of Outer Space under a rather interesting title, Emerging Disarmament Issues, because outer space is very much an emerging issue. I spent a life in the Air Force so I do not consider myself to be a diplomat, but I have had fifteen interesting years in arms control and disarmament. Some say if you've spent your life in the military, arms control is going against the military. Of course it isn't. Arms control and disarmament are basically to maintain peace and security. NATO for many years, though many never recognized it, had a motto: "undiminished security at lower levels of armament." The CD Treaty has underscored NATO's motto and countries generally have now subscribed to security at the lowest levels of armament. This is particularly apropos in terms of outer space.

Outer space has been an interest of mine for many years. Why? In all the arms control and disarmament issues which we face, outer space is unique for a number of reasons. First, it is the fourth environment in which we live. We've been engaged for centuries intellectually with outer space but we have attempted to operate and live within it for less than fifty years. And we're seeing history happening with NASA, with the space station, with space probes. We're interested in exploiting space for the betterment of mankind. It is the environment in which we have the least idea of how we will develop it and live with it but we know that it is the future as far as the world is concerned.

It's unique also because it is the only environment which is weapons-free. We have over a period of time, on land, sea and air, armed and rearmed to an extreme degree. And we're seeing in our arms control treaties the results of that in the hundreds of millions of dollars being spent to disarm.

A two star Air Force General told me you cannot talk about arms control in space until you have arms there. Then you can control them. I thought that was a joke but in fact he believed it. Surely we have learned there is such a thing as the prevention of weaponization. That's what we're talking about. So, space is the fourth environment we're living in; it is the only weapon-free environment, and, third, it has a dual purpose as far as arms control and disarmament is concerned.

We talk about "weaponization of space" and "the use of space for military purposes" but it is also indispensable to the whole arms control process. Without the use of space-based imagery, without the use of space-based monitoring, we would not have any significant arms control treaties. In the early days in the Cold War between the US and the Soviet Union, the major arms control treaties, the SALT treaties, the ABM Treaty, were monitored and verified by the use of space-based equipment and space-based sensors only. This is now evolving as we now have commercially available imagery which is moving this into the multilateral sphere. It's really in the multilateral aspect of outer space that we have the challenge to keep space as a weapons-free environment.

In the multilateral framework there are two organizations which deal with space. The first is the Committee on the Peaceful Use of Outer Space (COPUOS) and the second is the Conference on Disarmament, which has a committee to consider space issues. I look at them as mirror images. I've always thought that the Conference on Disarmament would make sure that space was not armed, that space was not used for hostile purposes, and that COPUOS would have the function of using it

280

properly for the peaceful use of outer space.

We have a number of treaties which provide the legal framework: the United Nations Charter, the 1967 Outer Space Treaty and more recently the Comprehensive Test Ban Treaty. But there are also bilateral treaties which are of significance from a multilateral perspective though they are bilateral in nature. Through customary law the ABM Treaty, the SALT treaties, the START treaties, set a certain level of customary international law which gradually becomes the purview of the international community. Some say the legal framework is at the present time sufficient, others say it is not. That will be discussed increasingly.

We need to understand what we're talking about. Central to that are the definitions of what we're talking about. There is a lot of work that can be done whether there is a negotiating mandate in the Conference on Disarmament, whether there is a mandate just to discuss, whether there is a mandate at all. The CD does not need a mandate in order to discuss an issue. Central to that are the definitions of what we are talking about. As you may know, there is no definition of outer space, or of a weapon, no definition of a lot of things and some use this as a reason not to discuss. It is a reason to understand things better than we do at the moment. I am going to take three examples of the sort of things we should understand. You will often see the phrases "the military use of outer-space," "the militarization of outer space," and the "weaponization of outer space." Some consider these three to be synonymous. In many UN documents you will see "military use of outer space" and "militarization of outer space" used almost in the same sentence. But they are not the same thing at all.

The military use of space can have a pejorative meaning but it can have a reassuring meaning also. Without the use of military satellites there would not be an ABM Treaty, SALT or START treaties. So from an arms control perspective the military use of space can be beneficial. At the other end of the spectrum is the weaponization of space, the placement of a weapon in space. How do you define a weapon? A weapon is something designed to kill someone else. The prevention of the weaponization of space is something the international community should recognize as a worthy objective. As I mentioned earlier, the other three environments have been weaponized to an obscene degree. Outer space should not be.

In between that comes militarization, more pejorative perhaps than military use and less pejorative than weaponization. Militarization is something that some people say has happened, some people say it hasn't. I would think that if space were militarized, in order to use space you would have to go through some sort of military organization to be able to put a satellite in space, to be able to use space. That is not the case, and in fact the use of space is increasingly becoming commercial. There are now more commercial satellites than there are military, a big change from fifteen years ago. I think that it is reasonable to say that space is not militarized at the moment and that's something we have to ensure doesn't happen. I don't think we have to ensure it. Many commercial companies will ensure that it doesn't happen.

Is the non-weaponization of space enough? Is that a final goal in and of itself? The answer is clearly it is not, but it is an achievable end. It is now a non-weaponized environment. If you can keep the status quo, you can achieve one end. Most people say that's only a small part of it, but why not take it one step at a time? This is one thing that is achievable through both COPUOS and the Conference on Disarmament action, which regrettably is not discussing this. Certainly, the history of the Conference on Disarmament on Outer Space in the last ten years is a miserable one. We have looked at all other things; chemical weapons, nuclear weapons, but not the use of outer space. We have treaties in three of the four areas of mass destruction, the CTBT, the NPT on nuclear, the CWC for chemical, the BWC for biological. The last weapon of mass destruction is radiological weapons, and there is not an agreement yet.

The single most important issue in the next ten years in arms control and disarmament will be related to outer space. Our countries, individually and collectively, and through the United Nations, should be moving to ensure that outer space is dealt with, and dealt with in a reasonable fashion, with the objective of reaching a level playing field. There are some who will say that countries will be placed under a disadvantage if space cannot be weaponized, if weapons can not be placed in space. But it is difficult to see that if you can have a verifiable agreement that applies to all nations equally, how any one nation could be disadvantaged with the status quo or with a level playing field.

Pierce Corden, of the US Arms Control and Disarmament Agency, will be our first speaker.

PIERCE CORDEN: I have been in the United States Arms Control and Disarmament Agency for about 27 years now. I am a physicist by training, I suppose you would say an arms control specialist by practice, so maybe I can exclude myself from just being a pure diplomat. At the moment my responsibilities in Washington include some oversight for our delegation to the Conference on Disarmament. I have also worked on the nuclear test ban agreements and other arms control issues. I have done work on the bilateral side but some of my work has been on the multilateral side. I have also had a stint here in New York with the United Nations, working on the Special Commission for Iraq. It is a pleasure to be back. My task today is to set the stage for the discussion from the perspective of the US approach to the use of outer space, the arms control arrangements for outer space, and the question of the weaponization of outer space.

I will make three points, and elaborate on them. The first one is, to pick up on what Ron has already indicated, that the use of outer space is not only of considerable importance to the United States, from the standpoint of maintaining strategic stability, it is also a very complicated one and has many different facets. The second point is, as Ron has indicated, there is already a wide spectrum of agreement to regulate activities in outer space, both military and civilian, peaceful activities. The third, and the one that undoubtedly will prompt some reaction and discussion, is that the US has not been persuaded that the multilateral arms control regime as it impacts on outer space should be augmented in order to maintain the strategic stability that I mentioned in the first point.

The use of outer space goes back four decades to the first launch of a satellite in the late fifties, Sputnik. That is a rather short space of time, and yet in that time we have gone from a situation where there were no satellites orbiting to the more than 500 satellites that are in space now, not to mention quite a few space probes extending all the way from the sun to beyond Pluto. Of those 500-some satellites, some 40% are owned by the United States. Looking in some of the trade journals, you will see that over the next 10 years or so it is anticipated that another 1800 or so satellites are likely to be orbited.

Satellites and space as a whole are utilized across a very wide spectrum of endeavors that the United States has a strong interest in. Starting from the security end, Ron has already mentioned the indispensable role that satellites play in verifying arms control agreements. The SALT I treaty, and the Interim Agreement from 1972, and now the START I and START II Treaties, the Limited Test Ban Treaty of 1963, all depend to a great extent on our ability to use satellites to observe the earth's surface, and outer space itself, to ensure that an agreement is not being violated. As Ron has noted, more recently the Comprehensive Test Ban Treaty, which will extend to space as well as to the other three environments, will be verified in part, from the United States side, by our own national technical means of verification, which are largely satellite-based.

In a broader sense, we acknowledge that we use space assets for gathering intelligence. It is indispensable for global stability and for US security that we be able to do that. If you expand that notion of remote sensing to gather intelligence to the civilian environment, you understand that the applications that satellites can be used for is even broader. We rely quite heavily on satellites to provide early warning against a possible missile attack against the United States, the possibility of which is still real, though thankfully less than it was 15 or 20 years ago. The use of satellites to provide navigational capabilities, both military and civilian, is now heavily integrated into both the national and international systems. The use of satellites for communications is almost a given, again, both military and civilian, and for science and exploration. In sum, you see that space is being used by the presence of man-made objects in space for commercial activities, for military activities, and in many respects, these are being carried in a dual-use mode. It is almost impossible to separate some of these uses. For the United States, strategic stability requires that those capabilities be sustained and advanced and certainly not damaged. Again, given the international nature of that environment, and the increasingly international approach to putting satellites in orbit, it is also an environment and an enterprise that has become remarkably internationalized.

From my personal appreciation of the situation, what we are faced with now is a period of some change. I think it is going to take the US government some time to sort out how we are going to approach some of these issues. One example is the recent relaxation of the rules about the ability to image the earth. It used to be that you couldn't release an image with a resolution of less than about three meters. That is now down to one meter. Another example is the heavy reliance upon the Global Positioning System and the capability that that can give to either a friendly force or an adversary who can go to a hardware store and buy a GPS receiver. Perhaps equally important, the military establishment in the United States, and I assume in other states, is turning increasingly to the civilian sector to provide certain services, like communications, that they rely upon, if not in a World War III-type situation, certainly in implementing military policy, military activities, and in peacekeeping, peacemaking situations like those in Bosnia and Haiti. Our military forces will contract with civilian organizations to provide those capabilities.

Over the last several years the Clinton Administration has looked at its approach to space policy. It published in the fall of 1996 an interesting document on national space policy. In reviewing it, I am struck by its breadth and complexity. It deals in some detail with all of the issues I have just addressed. It starts by talking about access to and use of space as being central for preserving peace and protecting US national security, as well as civil and commercial interests. It says:

> The United States will pursue greater levels of partnership and cooperation in national and international space activities and work with other nations to ensure the continued exploration

and use of outer space for peaceful purposes. The US is committed to the exploration and use of outer space by all nations for peaceful purposes and for the benefit of all humanity. Peaceful purposes allow defense and intelligence activities in pursuit of national security and other goals. The US rejects any claims to sovereignty by any nation over outer space or celestial bodies or any portion thereof, and rejects any limitations on the fundamental right of sovereign nations to acquire data from space. The US considers the space systems of any nation to be national property with the right of passage through and operations in space without interference. Purposeful interference in space systems shall be viewed as an infringement on sovereign rights."

To somebody reading this who has thought a little bit about how we've dealt with other environments this sounds very much like the way we deal with the high seas. They're available for our use, they're common property, but as a nation we retain the right to freedom of action in that environment. The document has a long section on civilian uses and then there's another long section on national space guidelines and I will quote some of those:

National security space activity shall contribute to US national security by providing support for the United States' inherent right of self-defense and our defense commitments to allies and friends: deterring, warning and if necessary defending against enemy attack; assuring that hostile forces cannot prevent our own use of space; countering, if necessary, space systems and services used for hostile purposes; enhancing operations of US forces; ensuring our ability to conduct military and intelligence space-related activities; satisfying military and intelligence requirements during peace and crisis as well as through all levels of conflict; supporting the activities of national policy makers.

Under another section it gives guidelines for the defense space sector and I would stress the first words. It says:

Consistent with treaty obligations, the United States will develop, operate and maintain space control capabilities to insure freedom of action in space and, if directed, deny such freedom of action to adversaries. These capabilities may also be enhanced by diplomatic, legal or military measures to preclude an adversary's hostile use of space systems and services. The US will maintain and modernize space surveillance and associated battle management command, control, communications, computers and intelligence to effectively detect, track, categorize, monitor and characterize threats to US friendly space systems and contribute to the protection of US military activity.

In another section which deals with overlapping matters, under international cooperation, it states that "we will enhance relations with our allies and with Russia while supporting initiatives of other states of the former Soviet Union and emerging space war nations." Under "arms control" it points out that "we will consider and, as appropriate, formulate policy positions on arms control and related measures governing activities in space and will conclude agreements on such measures only if they are equitable, effectively verifiable and enhance the security of the United States and our allies." One other section deals with space debris. It points out that we will seek "to minimize the creation of space debris and develop guidelines to minimize and reduce accumulation of space debris, consistent with mission requirements and cost effectiveness." I mention that because as a scientist it's interesting that the consequences of your actions in space are governed by Newton's Laws, not Einstein's but Newton's. If you blow something up there it creates a lot of stuff and it stays there until the atmospheric drag finally causes it to decay.

That sets the framework for the US approach. Ron's already talked about some of the current agreements. I think it would be fair to say that the US considers the existing legal regime to be rather far-reaching and robust. Ron's mentioned the UN Charter, I've already talked about the Limited Test Ban Treaty and the CTBT. The Outer Space Treaty puts celestial bodies off limits to all weapons, so we're not looking at any additional need to ban weapons on celestial bodies. That's already been taken care of by the Outer Space Treaty. The moon is free, asteroids are free, Mars, Venus, and other galaxies. The Outer Space Treaty also makes that environment free of mass destruction weapons, be they nuclear, chemical, biological, toxin or radiological, and that's a pretty far-reaching non-proliferation measure where the starting line, as opposed to the earth's surface, is zero, not the possession of weapons by some number of states.

The Anti-Ballistic Missile (ABM) Treaty, Ron has already noted, rules out any anti-ballistic components in outer space. The United States, as recently as last fall, re-affirmed that this treaty is the cornerstone of strategic stability between ourselves and the Russian Federation. Last fall an additional arms control arrangement that impacts on the outer space environment, a United States agreement with the successor states of the Soviet Union, was concluded in which Russia, Belarus, Ukraine, and Kazakhstan are recognized as the successor states to the Soviet Union for the purposes of maintaining the Anti-Ballistic Missile Treaty in force. The demarcation agreement that we reached with respect to separating out theater missile defenses, which are not prohibited by the ABM Treaty, and strategic anti-ballistic missile capabilities which are governed by that Treaty, has an additional agreed statement, an undertaking in which we have agreed that we will not pursue space-based anti-theater ballistic missile capabilities. In other words, we have agreed that we will not put in space what I think Ron would call "weapons" for theater missile defence purposes, even though the ABM Treaty would not prohibit that. We also agreed not to put those kinds of capabilities in space with respect to lasers or sophisticated new technologies, what are called, "other technologies based on other physical principles."

One final point on the current legal regime: you also have to have a look at some of the agreements that govern civilian uses of outer space. Some of the commercial communications satellite capabilities are governed by international treaties, in particular the treaty that established the International Satellite Organization, Intelsat. There is also Immarsat and other organizations that govern communications.

My third point is that we have not been persuaded that the existing arms control regime, which we see as pretty far-reaching and robust, requires any augmentation by multilateral agreement. Ron mentioned that the CD has for a number of years had a subsidiary body, a committee that had a mandate to consider the question of expanding the regime. I happen to have been present at the creation of that body back in 1985. For quite a few years it looked at the existing regime. It considered other possibilities. But the Conference on Disarmament works by consensus. And a consensus was not reached on the necessity to expand the regime. Indeed, in the last couple of years, there has not really been a strong conviction that the committee should continue under its previous

285

mandate. This spring the Conference on Disarmament agreed to appoint a special coordinator to give further consideration to outer space by consulting with the membership on ways that the CD might organize its work. As Ron knows much better than I, Canada has already spoken at some length about the issue in the CD this spring. Our delegation will listen extremely carefully to what other delegations have to say and be responsive, as best we can, to see what the next steps should be.

In brief, our view is that outer space is a vital environment for us, a very complex one. There is a broad legal regime that already exists which the US supports very strongly. The 1996 US National Space Policy certainly doesn't rule out further steps, but we have not been persuaded that such steps would be useful to take at the present time. Thank you.

RON CLEMINSON: Thank you very much. Is there an immediate question?

JONATHAN GRANOFF, Lawyer's Alliance for World Security (LAWS). A very simple question. What weapons are permitted under the existing regime?

PIERCE CORDEN: I don't know that you could say that there's a formal permission to deploy weapons to outer space. Usually international arms control law

works the other way. You formally "prohibit" things. It would be fair to say that it is not prohibited to put a rifle in orbit. I suppose it would not be prohibited to put some kind of missile up there that wouldn't have an ABM capability, although, as I noted, we have ruled out putting anti-theater missiles up there. If you think of anti-satellite weapons, it is not prohibited to put a launcher on the surface of the earth that could launch an anti-satellite warhead to knock down a satellite, or notionally to orbit such a system. That's not prohibited. But, it doesn't, I think, technically make sense to say that it is "permitted." It is the obverse of that. But you would have to be careful not to give those systems the types of capabilities that are ruled out by the ABM Treaty.

DORRIE WEISS, Economists Allied for Arms Reduction (ECAAR) and the NGO Committee on Disarmament: Since the US classifies information technology and encryption as munitions and they come under the heading of "Munitions Exports," can it not be argued that we have already militarized outer space?

PIERCE CORDEN: I suppose you could make that argument. But I don't think that, regarding encryption, which is of course something that banks and others use for legitimate purposes for protecting information, you could really conclude that that has militarized outer space. The military's uses of outer space in a direct sense are much more significant in terms of early warning, communications, observation and navigation.

DORRIE WEISS: The only reply that I would have is that while encryption has commercial uses, the US controls those commercial uses by withholding patents for anything that it wants to keep. And so what can be used for military purposes is denied for industry.

LOUISE MILLS, Florida researcher: I hear what you're saying. I've done a lot of reading in the last couple of years. My heart and my mind don't want to believe that the US has any intention of developing space-based weapons. Then I went to Colorado Springs last week for the International Space Symposium, and found that the US is developing a space-based laser weapon.

TINA BELL, Woman's International League for Peace and Freedom (WILPF): To follow up on that point, you said the 1996 US document said that the US is committed to the peaceful uses of outer space and that it would be available for all countries. However, in the latest US Space Command brochure, they talk about how the US is going to "dominate outer space and fight in outer space." So, I am not sure how this goes along with the 1996 document.

PIERCE CORDEN: I am not sure that I can shed much light on it either. I think, typically, a military organization, when it describes its objectives, is doing so in the context of what its job is, which is to defend the national interest. And when you want to defend the national interest, you do so by being there firstest with the mostest and being prepared to win. That's being translated, I suppose, in their terminology into a military situation, to a military confrontation, to coming out on top. I don't think it would necessarily be fair to say that means that we anticipate running outer space for everybody. I don't really think that's a fair conclusion from what you're reading.

RON CLEMINSON: Our next panelist will be Bill Sulzman, who head the Global Network Against Weapons and Nuclear Power in Space in Colorado.

BILL SULZMAN: I also was in Colorado Springs. In fact, I have lived there for twelve years and followed the development of the US Space Command over that time. A lot of you probably picked up a little one page brochure that we developed a couple of years ago that is, not surprisingly, already out of date. It says "hidden in plain sight" and it goes into a whole view of the US's military use of space, contrary to what has just been presented as being the US position. That is so out of date, I would take the word "hidden" off that title. It is in plain sight now that the United States has published a series of documents paid for by taxpayer money, which openly talk about "control of outer space," "domination of outer space," "superiority in outer space," "denial of outer space."

We just saw depicted in a poster distributed at the space symposium in Colorado Springs one of the explosions as the result of the firing of a weapon in outer space. A retiring general from the Space Command two years ago talked about "fighting war into space, in space and from space" as being something people don't want to hear about but which is already in the planning stage. Falcon Air Force Base, which opened as a Star Wars base, the test facility of SDI, converted that to something called "The Space Warfare Center." There is an interesting disconnect when you hear something like this and you hear and see "Space Warfare Center, War Plan 2000, War Plan 2010, War Plan 2025." When it gets to how you're going to use space in future wars, all of a sudden it's war, it is not "defending interests." It's not "legitimate military use," it's war. It's as if they haven't caught up with the change of the War Department to the Defence Department in 1951. When it comes to these matters, it is seriously a disconnect. It's like somebody needs to get the semantics going in a consistent direction.

I'm here as the activist, somebody who has worked in the grass roots end of organizing about space issues. As you might guess, it is difficult to do, although it has been getting easier as we get in touch with more people in something called the Global Network. Space is certainly global. There are no boundaries up there. There are no ethnicities, no difference of language naturally occurring up there. It is above us all and because of the way physics works it is a common heritage. Naturally it has been that way, and as Ron mentioned, the spiritual side of us has often looked at space and the figurations up there for inspiration and for helping us to look within ourselves to the spiritual side.

287

But from the beginning space has been also a consumer thing for us. It has been the cutting edge of our science and technology. It's often been beyond our ability to figure out how things work that go up there and to do things up there. This has been highlighted in the military area, because it has been so secret. The largest two military operatives in space have been the National Security Agency and the National Reconnaissance Office, both of which have been on the shadow side of our governments, spending tens of billions of dollars per year for a long time, much of it in space. So we have had this natural tendency to be just consumers of space.

In 1992 people who had been following this and noticing some dangerous trends got together and said we can have a role in deciding some of this stuff, not just looking at it on television. We want to be on television sometimes about this stuff. Thus the Global Network Against Weapons and Nuclear Power in Space. I alluded to a couple of these documents. One, put out by the Air Force Space Command, which has a whole a section in it on the Space Warfare Center, and some of the war gaming stuff that they do there every day, scripting future wars and the space dimension of those future wars. The US Space Command a year ago put out "Vision for 2020" which goes into some detail about the four military uses of space. For me it is a phony distinction between weapon and military in space when the United States can brag that the 1990-1991 war against Iraq was the first space war. They understand that when you collect information, select targets through the use of space, and then direct weapons to targets using space, you have the equivalent of a piece of the weapon being in space. A gun sight is a part of the gun. A spotter, who in the old days targeted artillery, was using a weapon and shared responsibility for the deaths that were caused. And so space already, in current military jargon and practice, has an important piece in the weaponized part of warfare, getting people killed and getting explosives sent to targets. In effect, already, there is a major piece of the business side of warfare conducted from space.

A year later we have "Long Range Plan" of the US Space Command. It came out a week ago. You can get it on the web. They show a lot of things blowing up in space and they tell you how that is going to happen. They talk about some of the things that stand in the way of future plans for using space militarily for conducting war, for enhancing the productivity of weapons. Nowhere do they mention the Outer Space Treaty as being anywhere a deterrent to that. They do mention that we need to fine tune a little bit the ABM Treaty, not to tighten it but to allow some of the things that the United States wants to do.

We had a workshop at this recently concluded conference in Colorado Springs which helped connect a few dots for me about why the Outer Space Treaty has been so long absent, except from the 1996 overview. Professor Ved Nanda of the Denver University Law School talked about some of the things that have happened since the 1967 dual declaration that space is for peaceful purposes and a common heritage with no boundaries, no private property, no rights to sovereignty. He explained that that principle evolved through the seventies in a series of follow-on agreements, worked out at the UN.

Finally in 1980 a treaty about the moon was concluded and signed by many. But not a single space-capable country has ratified it. It was becoming clear that the big players didn't want to give up sovereignty over space resources. In the last 18 years that has become ever more true. It is not the policy of US corporations, nor of the US government, to recognize the principle of common

288

sovereignty in practice, not that they would not say, as this 1996 document does, that we still believe in common heritage. But Vision 2020 says one of the jobs of the US Space Command is "dominating the space dimension of military operations to protect US national interests and investment." This is far beyond any notion that this is common heritage. Now one of the jobs of space forces is to protect US national interests and investments.

Professor Nanda said one of the reasons for the US getting worried by commercial development is that it is hard to control it. You don't have the need for the Marines if you don't have anybody there that owns property. We can look at our own development westwards. The forts had to come in after the settlements, and after gold was discovered. It explained for me why the US is so bent on controlling space. Pete Warden, who used to command the Air Force base where the space warfare center is, was in the space symposium with his name tag. He is the kind of guy who is not afraid to dialogue with people on the opposite side. The theme of the conference was "Take Up Space" and his badge read "Deputy Commander for Space Domination." Domination to me is a step beyond mastery. It is even a little beyond control. Domination makes it very clear. You can't dominate if you are clearly reserving yourself to peaceful uses, or there is common heritage. So I would argue that common heritage over the last 20 years has become a fiction, useful to pull out when you are talking against Russia, who, when it was the Soviet Union, was charged with having a plan to dominate the earth.

Professor Nanda quoted from a speech on the common heritage of the oceans that Kissinger gave in the 1970s that is often used as a paradigm for what is going on in space now. Kissinger talked about the oceans as a common heritage and that that was a model. The other example that is often cited is Antarctica where the US had to be shamed into getting on board. The Outer Space Treaty is dead. It needs to be revived. We do need serious new initiatives to prevent an emerging problem in space.

I haven't talked about something that was the subject of an Aviation Week series of articles, "Information Warfare: Could the US Strike First?" Satellites would be a major player in information warfare. My answer to this question would be in the past tense. The US is already doing this.

There is a serious issue developing in England around the Menwith Hill spy base which is a major US base which intercepts commercial traffic, satellite transmitted traffic. It has become an issue because people are asking, is the commercially useful part of this information getting fed to certain select US corporations to the disadvantage of European corporations? The tentative answer is yes.

Could the US strike first in information warfare, using space assets? Not only could they, they have been, I believe.

JOHN PIKE, Director of the Space Policy Project of the Federation of American Scientists in Washington: For the last 15 years I have been the designated critic on Star Wars. I have been the guy who in the third paragraph of the *New York Times* magazine is the one who is quoted in the paragraph beginning "The critics charge it is a bad idea..." I have been saying it is a bad idea for the last 15 years. The US government hasn't always been listening to me. I think we find ourselves, today, fifteen years and a few weeks after President Reagan first made his Star Wars speech in a situation that for me is clarified not by going back 15 years but by going back 2500 years to the history of the

Peloponnesian War by Thucydides. If you will bear with me for a moment I would like to read you some very old history that I think has some profound relevance to describing the current political situation...It seems to me that Thucydides, chapter 17 of the fifth book in the Melian dialogue, lays out the essential condition we find ourselves in today with respect to the United States' military activities in space. The setting of the Melian dialogue is that Athens has laid siege to the city of Melos and the Melos city fathers come out and try to persuade Athens to please go away and don't burn down our city. The Athenians respond to the Melians' sweet reason by saying that

> Of men we know that by a necessary law of their nature they will, whenever they can, and it is not as though we were the first to make this law, or to act upon it. We find it existing before us, and shall leave it to exist forever after us. All we do is make use of it, knowing that you, and everyone else, having the same power as we have, would do the same as we do. For ourselves, we shall not trouble you with specious pretense, either of how we have a right to our empire because we overthrew the Mede or are now attacking you because of a wrong that you have done us, and make a long speech which would not be believed. In return we hope that you will aim at what is feasible, holding in view the real sentiments of us both since you know, as well as we do, that right, as the world goes, is only a question between equals in power, while the strong do what they can and the weak suffer what they must.

The fundamental thing that has changed about the question of military use of space over the last five or ten years is that during the Cold War era there was a question of right between equals in power. The debate in the United States concerning the Star Wars program or missile defense or space weapons or other military space capabilities was basically defined in terms of how this is going to interact with another roughly equal in power, namely the Soviet Union. With the demise of the Soviet Union, the end of the Cold War and the emergence of the United States as the sole remaining superpower, it seems to me that questions of right, with respect to military space activities, have largely evaporated, in the absence of countervailing power, and that now we are in the situation so classically defined 2500 years ago by the Melian dialogue, that the strong do what they can and the weak suffer what they must. In this case the strong is the United States Space Command and the weak is basically everybody else.

How this works out in practice I think was articulated very clearly by a fact sheet that the Ballistic Missile Defense Organization had on its web site describing the space-based laser program. I was rather surprised to see some of the phraseology in this fact sheet. I was not terribly surprised to see that adult supervision intervened and a new and improved fact sheet was put on their web site a few months ago that removed the uncharacteristic candor. It describes the utility of the space-based laser in terms of making a reliable space-based defense system would induce potential aggressors to abandon ballistic missile programs because they would be rendered useless. Failing that, the creation of such a universal defense system would provide the impetus for other nations to expand their security arrangements with the United States, bringing them under a United States-sponsored missile defense umbrella.

Pete Worden has already been mentioned. Pete's a real good guy and we've been drinking buddies since he was present at the creation of the Star Wars program. You don't have to get very far into the second pitcher of beer before it becomes clear what the agenda is. These military space systems are viewed as being the hallmark, the preeminent instrumentality of the proposition that the US is the sole remaining superpower. They are the instrumentality of the imposition of American political hegemony. The agenda, the centrality with which these weapons would be used to achieve the basic goal of current American military strategy is very clear.

American military strategy currently consists of achieving what is called in the capstone military doctrinal statement, "Joint Vision 2010." The American military objective is no longer one of achieving either military parity with the Soviet Union or military superiority with respect to the Soviet Union, but rather of achieving full spectrum supremacy with the rest of the world. Full spectrum supremacy is defined as a military preponderance so overwhelming that no other country would even think about possibly acquiring the capability of challenging the United States militarily and obviously the ability to deny the country's access to space.

I confess, however, that this rendition of what is going on with America's military space capabilities may impose slightly greater rationality on the process than in fact is the case. I am glad Bill brought up the question of information warfare because there is currently a very serious debate within the military space and the national intelligence community as to precisely what the proper paradigm or doctrinal framework is for understanding how to use these new military and intelligence space capabilities. The one that thus far has been preponderant is the aerospace doctrine which essentially views air and space as a single continuous medium and basically is of the view that everything that we have traditionally done with air power is also something that we ought to be doing with space power. Just as we have had ground to air missiles, we ought to have ground to space missiles. Just as we have had air-to-air missiles, we ought to have space-to-space missiles. Just as we have had air to ground attack capabilities, we ought to have space to ground attack capabilities. As a result, there is this very strong doctrinal presumption that anti-satellite capabilities, that space-to-space weapon capabilities and that space to ground attack capabilities are something that can and should be part of our normal military operations, which is where you get some of the exciting art work in the US Space Command brochures.

There are basically two practical problems with this. The first one is that the aerospace power community has been trying to get these weapons into the operational inventory for about the last four decades or so, and unfortunately Mother Nature has proven extremely resistant to the practicality of a lot of these ideas. The notion that we should have space fighters, for instance, is extremely thrilling to the pilots who might be able to fly around in them. The problem is that the US Air Force has spent billions of dollars on developing such capabilities off and on for the last four decades and still has not been able to figure out how to make the frisky things work, and still hasn't been able to figure out how to use them in a meaningfully operative military sense.

We have spent $60 billion over the last 15 years working on ballistic missile defense, and as a report recently released by the Ballistic Missile Defense Organization, prepared by a number of former heads of missile defense research organizations in the US, concluded, after 15 years and $60 billion, we still can't hit anything. We have had over a dozen tests of these anti-missile interceptors over the last five years. The Navy's interceptor, for instance, has had an extremely successful test record with over 41 out of 42 test objectives achieved. The only problem is that the 42nd test objective, the one they have not achieved, is to intercept an incoming missile. The rest of the experiments succeeded, but they could not actually hit anything.

All of these difficulties have further reinforced the alternative information warfare view of what we ought to be doing in military space, one that was certainly given a lot of emphasis by Operation Desert Storm. When you look at the military and intelligence capabilities that the US had, the capabilities that were widely regarded as being decisive in that operation, which have certainly been of increasing importance in peace keeping operations since that time, the things that are notably present have a lot more to do with information operations, have a lot more to do with finding out what is going on and preventing battles from happening, or ending battles very quickly at relatively low cost, and have very little to do with Luke Skywalker and Darth Vader dog fighting up there in the cosmos. There is a growing sense within the military space community that aerospace power doctrine really isn't terribly informative of how these forces ought to be organized, trained or equipped and that doctrinal precepts derived from information warfare would be far more informative in terms of how US military space and intelligence organizations ought to be formed and operated.

The problem is the Air Force has seen this movie before. They themselves starred in this movie back during World War II when, as part of the Army Air Forces, the Air Forces said that air power is separate and distinct from land power, that there is a separate and distinct body of doctrine called air power doctrine, and that since air power is different from land power, operationally different, doctrinally different, it should also be organizationally different. Low and behold, at the end of World War II air power doctrine led to the formation of a separate air force. So the people in the Air Force know that when a separate doctrinal body emerges, a separate organization inevitably emerges. Since the Air Force leadership would like to keep space power institutionally within the Air Force, they continue to mandate that the Air Force Space Command be an aerospace power doctrine organization within the Air Force rather than an information warfare organization that unavoidably would very rapidly evolve into a new military service that would be totally outside the air power community and totally outside the Air Force.

But as long as American military space operations are informed by aerospace power doctrine we are going to continue to have this very strong institutional emphasis on space weapons. And, unlike during the Cold War when American national interests had to be balanced by concerns about countervailing space weapon activity on the part of the Soviet Union, I think that what is going to happen over the next five or ten years with respect to American military space capabilities, is going to be driven much more by the fact that this is dreadfully expensive and very difficult to do, and the fact that there are countervailing doctrinal formulations which would suggest it is not only expensive and difficult, but it is operationally irrelevant and actively counterproductive to be worrying about these things, as opposed to important things. With any luck it is also going to be constrained a little bit by brother Sulzman's capability to get people better educated about what is going on. But I think we have a long row to hoe. I have been hoeing this row for the last 15 years. I don't think that I have gotten to the end of the row and I don't think I am going to get there anytime soon.

QUESTION: How do you get information about the US Space Command?

BILL SULZMAN: You can get information from their web site: www.spacecom.af.mil/usspace, though it is not as good as the hard copy. The address is US Space Command, Director of Plans, Peterson AFB, CO 80914-3110.

A quote I left out: "Although unlikely to be challenged by a global peer competitor, the US will continue to be challenged regionally. The globalization of the world economy will also continue with a widening between haves and have nots." For context I also like to quote UNICEF's report of December, which talks about how bad it is already between haves and have nots. It says that more than half of the 12 million children under five die in developing countries each year from preventable causes or as victims of malnutrition. So an increased projection of power from space is seen to operating over the next 25 years is one in which this gap gets worse. That, more than anything else, is what motivates me to say, time out. This notion that the strong dominate the weak and that is just the way it is needs to be challenged here.

RON CLEMINSON: Our final speaker is Ambassador Changhe Li of China. He is the Ambassador of China at the Conference on Disarmament in Geneva.

AMBASSADOR CHANGHE LI: I am pleased to have this opportunity to meet all of you this afternoon and to share some of my views on the issue of outer space in terms of arms control and disarmament. First, I would like to say, starting in the fifties and sixties, human beings have achieved great successes in outer space science and technology. These achievements were led by both the United States and the former Soviet Union, now Russia. I think we should all be proud of the great achievements in space throughout the world. This is a demonstration of the wisdom of the great people of America and Russia in developing the capabilities of human beings to explore space. This is equally true in the nuclear field. Many achievements have also been attained in nuclear science and technology. We can peaceful use of these sciences and technologies to resolve the enmities of the future generations.

However, as always in the universe, there are two sides of a matter. While these sciences and technologies can benefit mankind, on the other hand, they can also be used for military purposes. I would like to share the feelings not only of my country but of almost all countries. I come from Geneva. I am the Permanent Representative to the Conference on Disarmament. The membership of the Conference is 61. Almost all the member states of the CD are concerned with the recent developments in military activities in space.

Generally speaking, the common view of all countries is that outer space is the common heritage of mankind. It should be used solely for peaceful purposes for the benefit of humanity. It is also the view shared by almost all countries that the development of space weapons is contrary to the peaceful use of outer space. It would certainly upset the global strategic balance and jeopardize international peace and stability. It is also a commonly shared view that to deploy weapons in outer space would trigger a new arms race. That would hamper the international arms control and disarmament process. Different countries have different levels of development in science and technology. But sooner or later, science and technology will be known to many countries. Some may take the lead to build something in outer space, while others may have to wait for some time. But if weaponization starts, it will trigger an arms race eventually.

My country, China, stands for the prevention of an arms race in outer space. We hope that all countries, especially those with the most advanced space capabilities, will refrain from developing outer space weapons and to take concrete measures, first and foremost to prevent the weaponization of outer space. Those countries should keep themselves from testing or deploying outer space weapons, including anti-missile weapons or anti-satellite weapons. If there are such devices, they should be abolished. Unfortunately, in recent years there are some activities in that regard. If any country wants to do that, it has to be based on tremendous financial expenditures and advanced science and technology. Some country with such capabilities, in disregard of international opposition, has intensified the research, development and testing of space weapon systems. That is certainly against the aspirations of most countries and runs counter to the trend of the times. These developments have aroused serious concern among the entire international community.

At present, there is one country which has such capabilities, and it also enjoys advantages in other military fields. In a military sense, there is no reason for this country to develop such new weapon systems to enhance, and to increase even more, the military superiority it now enjoys. It is irrelevant for a country like the United States, which already has great superiority in the military field, to try to seek absolute security.

In Geneva many countries believe that the prevention of an arms race in outer space has become an urgent issue for international arms control and disarmament. If we do not address this issue, we will have to negotiate on "disarmament in outer space" or "prevention of the proliferation of outer space weapons" in the near future.In that respect we can draw lessons from the nuclear field. Now we talk about the non proliferation of nuclear weapons.

I think the United States, as the most advanced country, in terms of space capabilities, should take the lead in that exercise, for the benefit of humanity and for international peace and security. We should not repeat what we have in other fields of disarmament, notably in the field of nuclear weapons. As some previous speakers pointed out, although there are a number of international legal instruments related to outer space, none of them is adequate to keep outer space free from weapons. It is high time for the international community to work together to find a way out, to conclude international agreements with a view to preventing an arms race in outer space. This is just a brief introduction of the views of my country on this issue. It is not only the view of my country. I come from Geneva and know that this is the view that is shared by almost all the member states of the Conference on Disarmament.

RON CLEMINSON: Thank you, Ambassador. Are there any questions?

NEWTON BOWLES, UNA, Canada: I happen to have been born in Chengdu. I wonder if you could elaborate a little bit on what is happening in Geneva on this issue at the CD.

AMBASSADOR LI: In Geneva the CD has worked for the past one year and a half to identify what could be the next goals in the field of arms control and disarmament. Different countries have different priorities in mind. Most non-nuclear states would like to have nuclear disarmament as the highest priority. The strongest view is that this is the time to talk about a time-bound phased program for nuclear disarmament with the eventual elimination of nuclear weapons. Some countries do not think this is the time to do that in the multilateral forum. Outer space is also a major agenda item. Having worked for a year and a half, last month the member states of the Conference finally reached agreement to appoint a special coordinator to facilitate the exchange of views on the prevention of an arms race in outer space. Starting from next month the member states will exchange their positions on this issue. It is still far from entering into the negotiating stage. As I said, basically the vast majority of states thinks that we should now begin to negotiate an international agreement for the purpose of preventing an arms race in outer space.

ROGER SMITH, NGO Committee on Disarmament: ...It is clear that the Chinese government has a strong and to my mind sensible position on this issue and clearly you have given the matter a great deal of thought. I wonder if you and the Chinese delegation intend to take a leadership role in the process that will be developed by the special coordinator and whether at this time there is anything substantive that you can say about the kind of framework or points that you would like to see optimally in any international agreement.

AMBASSADOR LI: As I said, many countries have strong views. No matter who is going to be the special coordinator, the subject will enjoy wide support. This is at the stage of exploration. When we consider this item, many countries, including my country, will send their specialists on this issue. All countries share a common concern.

JOHN PIKE: ...I would like to clarify where the United States has taken the lead over the last several years and why it is a question now of a multilateral response to what has thus far been essentially a bilateral arms control regime. It is particularly timely now because for a very long time the question of weapon activity in space was largely governed by the Anti-Ballistic Missile Treaty that was negotiated in 1972 and that essentially remained unchanged until very recently. Last fall, here in New York, the United States and Russia and all the successor states came up with a very elaborate series of demarcation protocols that have substantially revised the scope and nature of the treaty regime. Among other things what they have done is significantly expand the scope of activity that is permitted under the ABM treaty. Specifically they have generally significantly revised the premise by which anti-missile capabilities are evaluated.

Previously the criteria for evaluating whether something was treaty-limited was whether, one on one, a single interceptor could intercept a single missile. Now the criteria has been changed to a many on many or force on force capability. It is no longer a question of whether an individual laser can shoot down an individual missile. It is a question of whether all of the lasers the United States has in space are capable of shooting down all incoming missiles that Russia has. As long as we can't shoot down all of them then it is pretty much OK.

Through the negotiations that we have had with Russia over the last five years, I think a presumption has been created in Washington that, regardless of what the Russians currently object to, that eventually they can be brought around to just about anything that the US proposes. If one looks at the extremely vigorous opposition and skepticism that one saw out of the Russian government since the early 1990s on most of the provisions that they eventually agreed to at the Helsinki Summit, it is certainly no longer politically realistic for anyone to suggest that the Russians will not agree to any further revisions to the ABM treaty that the US might have in mind. If there is anything that is viewed as not being permitted by the treaty, and it is very difficult to see what the US is not currently free to do under the treaty, it is probably to deploy more than 100 interceptors at a single site.

But if anybody were to say today that we are not going to be able to change that a couple of years down the road when we might want to deploy at a second site in Alaska, because the Russians won't go along with it, I don't think anybody would believe that. The Russians have clearly demonstrated that regardless of how much they complain, eventually they will agree to whatever it is the US proposes. The basic nature of that treaty regime has changed radically, compared to what it was in the previous 25 years, and the trajectory of that treaty regime, rather than being static or more restrictive, has, in a very real sense, changed in the direction of suggesting that over time the few remaining bilateral restraints on American freedom of action with respect to space weapons are something that could be reasonably expected to go away.

KARL GROSSMAN: I am the author of a book, *The Wrong Stuff: The Space Program's Threat to our Planet*, and narrator and writer of a TV documentary called *Nukes in Space, the Nuclearization and Weaponization of the Heavens*. What we have heard in this building and in Geneva and Washington doesn't cover what I saw last week in Colorado Springs. The United States is clearly trying to dominate space. In the next two decades, new technologies will allow the fielding of space-based weapons with devastating effectiveness, space-borne lasers with reasonable mass and cost to effect many kills. It is a problem putting lasers in space, getting power for them. So a natural technology to enable high power is nuclear power in space. That is why the group is called the Global Network Against Weapons and Nuclear Power in Space. At this conference it was announced by the Department of Energy that the TRW Corporation had been granted a $10 million contract to develop a pilot program for a space-based laser. It is happening. It unfortunately has not been on the radar screen of the peace movement or others concerned about peace all over the world.

The Outer Space Treaty is the bedrock. It says states shall not place nuclear weapons or other weapons of mass destruction in orbit. Is not what the United States is up to now certainly in violation of the intent if not the letter of the law of the Outer Space Treaty?

JOHN PIKE: These are not weapons of mass destruction, and so they are not governed by the Outer Space Treaty.

BILL SULZMAN: This gets a little beyond my expertise. Customary international law, I think, would say the Outer Space Treaty is still in effect. John may be right that these are not weapons of mass destruction. But the treaty in a broad sense says peaceful purposes and clearly these things are not peaceful in nature. And people understand that once you break through a barrier, others will follow. Clearly in that regard they violate the spirit of the treaty. The treaty is very general in nature. It needs tuning up. I think it needs a major rewrite because it is only handy to pull out when you want to make a general statement. Then you go into the 44 exceptions to it and then there is nothing there. I clearly do believe that space should not be seen as a new frontier for nuclear energy, for whatever reason. It is still dangerous to produce it, it still has leftovers that we don't know what to do with, and on and on. I agree with you that it violates peaceful purposes and common heritage. Unless we rescue them they are pretty much gone.

PIERCE CORDEN: I don't think the Administration would consider the Outer Space Treaty a dead letter. The US is committed to adhering to its provisions, finds it in its interests to do so, supports global adherence to it. I think it is correct that it relates to weapons of mass destruction as they are understood by the international community over the last 50 years, stemming from the 1948 delineation of nuclear, chemical, toxin and biological, and radiological. To that I would add, by virtue of the Environmental Modification Treaty of 1977, certain types of geophysical manipulation. It might be possible to understand that to be even broader if other new types of weapons come along. One of the points the Administration would recognize and understand, is that the Outer Space Treaty, with respect to what it addresses as peaceful purposes, and I already quoted this, allows defense and intelligence-related activities in pursuit of national security and other goals.

LILLIAN ROSEN, Voice of Women, Canada: I am unhappy that intelligent men defend the posture of the US which is putting the whole world at risk. What can we do to change this?

JOHN PIKE: The short answer may be nothing. The longer answer is that it is very important to understand the political context in which a lot of these things are happening. There is a strong tendency to regard this as being a series of technical questions or strategic military questions. It is basically a set of political questions about America's role in the world. It is basically a question of whether the American republic is in a position to run the world on a day to day basis in the way that is implied by the expressed need to acquire these military capabilities.

The clear presumption of the current US military strategy, Joint Vision 2010, that this requirement for full spectrum supremacy of space systems comes from, is the proposition that the US government is going to be focused on military operations around the world to keep the whole planet in running order. That the development of the global economy and the global society has outpaced the development of global governance institutions. That until such time as the United Nations is able to evolve into an effective world government that the US government is sort of going to step in and run the world until the UN can, at some point in the third millennia when the UN has matured to the point where it can take over that responsibility, recognizing that not everybody may accept the role of the United States as the world government so they need to develop all these military capabilities.

To me the basic questions very clearly posed by these systems is whether the American people have any day-to-day interest in running the planet, whether the American government has the wisdom to run the planet, whether the American republican form of government can survive the burden of running the planet. Personally I think it is no accident that we have seen this incredible upsurge about political influence-buying in Washington because basically every government now knows that they have to come to Washington in order to get a piece of the action. It think those are the questions that are being raised by lasers running around in space. I don't think the debate is currently being framed that way. I think that we are going to be in real trouble unless it is framed that way.

QUESTIONER: To paraphrase what you said, unless we can make the UN stronger, unless we can mobilize the American people to see that they have to be interested in this, that we are up the creek without a paddle.

JOHN PIKE: We are not necessarily living in a happy ending story.

GEORGE KELLEY, Veterans Against Nuclear Action: I served in two wars that I guess were regarded as conventional. What can we do to counteract the power of the media and the tabloid press with the glorification of Star Trek and Rambos and combat in outer space.

BILL SULZMAN: I guess I will take that as being like the last question. What is the hopeful side of this? I have been a peace activist for 30 years. I don't want to be cast in some sort of martyr role. Ultimately I think there is more good in human beings than there is bad, and that there is hope when people are properly informed and motivated. We are in a world of six billion, soon to go higher, and we know environment truths have taught us we have to be more cooperative. In 1967 people looked at the beginning of the space age and said, let's not make these same mistakes again in space. Let's keep it for everybody as best we can and let's keep war out of it. Given that that is still an option today, that is what people would finally chose to do. It is just that there are many other competing forces, economic ones, and nationalism is resurging in this country to our detriment. We are backing ourselves into a corner. By defining much of the world as our enemy we are creating our own monster. We must latch on to some of these cooperative images, use education, and go back to our spiritual traditions... It is work on many fronts that is going to unglorify war and suggest some way out of this box. I think this thing is stuck and people have to stand out from the crowd sometimes to get it unstuck. Business as usual is not going to do it. We all have ways of pointing in a positive direction and cooperatively moving in that direction. There aren't any magic solutions.

JOHN PIKE: The basic thing that I find in talking with our mutual friend Pete Warden is that we have a very different image of the Star Wars movies. I think that the rebel alliance and Luke Skywalker are the good guys and he thinks that Darth Vader and the Emperor are the good guys. I think if one looks over the last dozen years about things in American movies there are not very many themes in which the dark lord and the emperor are the good guys that the American public is being asked to identify with. So I think that we have some very rich cultural materials to get started with. Glorification of empire is not a very strong theme in American popular culture.

CAROLINE BRIDGMAN-REES, Centre for International Peacebuilding: I have watched Star Trek very little and all I remember is that I missed trees and flowers in nature. Thich Nhat Han, at the end of his book *Lotus in a Sea of Fire,* mentions a Vietnamese legend called the elephant with the brain of a shrimp. I think our government, particularly at this point, is such. We have elephant's power but we haven't the knowledge and wisdom to use that power. Even if the government wants to support peaceful outer space the lords of profit do not. There seems to be no organization controlling who goes up. I make two suggestions. One is that we have a conference like this for the Thursday briefing or a big conference, and there should be a new law of outer space, and that we challenge the whole idea of consensus in the CD, because you say, Ambassador Li, that almost everybody supports a peaceful space. But consensus is the rule and so we get nowhere.

AMBASSADOR LI: You raise a profound question that diplomats have been wrestling with for many years regarding the rule of consensus. For an international agreement to be effective, it has to be accepted by all states. If you conclude a treaty without consensus, then it is not going to be supported by significant countries. Consensus is upheld by all the members of the CD. Everything has its advantages and disadvantages. We should seek a common ground, such as with the Comprehensive Test Ban Treaty (CTBT), or it will not come into effect.

ANN LAKHDHIR, Institute for Defense and Disarmament Studies and the NGO Committee on Disarmament: Nova, on public television, had a program on weapons in the future. It was focused on weapons improvements over those used in the Gulf War, especially those that made targeting ever more precise. I am sure most of the Americans watching it certainly saw this as a great advantage, that if weapons were more accurate you could hit only the target you not cause as much damage to civilians. This is a capability all countries would like to have. It strikes me that this is something that would be very difficult to control. You are talking about using satellites also for rescue operations. How would you ever be able to control using satellites to provide even more accurate targeting information? It is certainly a way in which space would be involved in any wars in the future.

RON CLEMINSON: What you are talking about is dual use, and dual use is a problem, in and of itself, which has to be addressed in a lot of contexts.

SELMA BRACKMAN, the War and Peace Foundation and the NGO Committee on Disarmament: About a week ago we published in our digest an article by Dr. Rashmi Mayur called "Joint Vision 2010: US Blueprint for World Domination." Two of the speakers today referred to this.

RON CLEMINSON: I suggest many people in the US government do not know about it. Space Command has been redesignating their commands from Air Force commands to space wings. There is a lot in profile, there is a lot in the words you use. I sort of admire the way they are doing it. Quite obviously they have someone packaging this well for them.

ROGER SMITH: We have a representative of the Arms Control and Disarmament Agency who assures us that the kinds of activities that have been mentioned would not be prohibited by the existing treaty. What constraints are there? Cassini, the space probe that went up in October with the plutonium radio-isotope thermal generators, is not seen as a military issue. But the need for nuclear power to power some of the systems on the drawing board leads me to the thorny question, will there be a need, given the threat, to use some means to prevent future launches with those plutonium generators?

JOHN PIKE: Under the Outer Space Treaty weapons of mass destruction, in practice nuclear weapons, are prohibited from being placed in orbit. There are currently no restrictions on ground-based anti-satellite systems. That is why we have an overt laser-directed energy anti-satellite capability at the White Sands Missile Range, Miracle Laser. That is why we have an unacknowledged high-powered micro-wave anti-satellite capability. Some people are saying we need yet a third rocket anti-satellite capability, all of which I find curious because there are no adversary satellites for us to be shooting at, so why we need all these weapons I am not clear. Everything in between that, space lasers, a lot of the missile defense stuff, is more or less up for grabs. The presumption is that we are either currently permitted to or could rearrange the ABM restrictions to facilitate deployment of just about everything as long as it was not a nuclear weapon in space. I would say that part of the problem right now with the legal treaty regime with respect to anti-missile deployments is that arms control, simply considered as a predictability measure, has certainly diminished in value because of the unpredictability of the direction in which the regime is going to evolve. But I would say that, apart from nuclear weapons in space, the US can pretty much either do what it wants to do or reasonably believe that it can change the treaty regime to accommodate it well in advance of the ability to actually do so.

JOHN PHELAN, Union of Concerned Scientists: I have always been impressed by the specificity of knowledge that is displayed at these me etings. I have a comment and then I have a suggestion. My comment is this. Precision-guided munitions have to be counterforced by precision-guided protest. My feeling is that too many people say the United States wants to do this, the government wants to do that. It seems to me the United States and the government, without a doubt, is very plural, and there are contending forces within the government who want contradictory things. I think that it would be most useful for people not to protest against the United States government in general but to go after very specific people and agencies who are pushing a particular agenda.

What sort of allies should we try to enlist in this cause who previously seem not to have been tapped? It seems to me that the multinational corporations have an extraordinary stake in world peace and yet the narrow interests of these multinational corporations are pushing the limits of a peaceful infrastructure and creating tremendous problems for themselves. If we could get Microsoft, TRW, if we could get to these people and show them something that I am sure they recognize, that it is in their own interest to censure the peaceful use of space. It certainly is in the interest of a man I don't admire very much, Rupert Murdoch. If we get Rupert Murdoch worked up about how important it is for satellites to be safe so that he can broadcast whatever he wants to the world, then maybe the *Post* and some of the media that he controls, and others that others control, would show people the specific dangers to world peace.

TINA BELL. WILPF: Pierce Corden, the 1996 document that you read I understand is a US government document, so all departments of the government must abide by this document. You stated that the US government would or could deny freedom of access to adversaries in space if they were doing something the US doesn't like. Does that mean the US government would go against the peaceful uses of outer space whenever an adversary does something that the US doesn't like? I also have a question for Ambassador Li. You stated that China would not want the anti-satellite weapon to be developed. I am wondering what this would force China to do, or the international community to do, if they were developed. How would that affect international peace?

PIERCE CORDEN: I tried to make clear that peaceful purposes allowed intelligence activities in pursuit of national security and other goals. You can extend the dialogue about how one interprets peaceful uses or peaceful purposes and I am not an international lawyer. I think it would be fair to say that the Outer Space Treaty does not preclude military activities in Outer Space. We are doing that now, as other commentators have said. We use outer space to operate the Global Positioning System which is a large group of satellites which allow you to navigate your airplane or your jeep. This can also be used to help guide bombs to their targets. You can argue about that if you don't agree. Certainly that is one of the privileges of living in a democracy that we can have a debate like this. I don't think, realistically, that you are going to get any space power - and the US is not the only one, the Russian Federation remains one, Israel has assets in outer space, so does India, so does France, Japan, China - I don't think you are going to get any of those states to agree for the foreseeable future that certain activities that have a clear military benefit, like observation, communication, navigation are going to be precluded by the fact that those countries are party to the Outer Space Treaty. It is indeed an open question about what one ought to do about weapons in outer space. This is a healthy discussion we have had about it today.

AMBASSADOR LI: This is still at the stage of identification. What kind of activities does the international community think is appropriate for military purposes? In fact you cannot exclude the military use of outer space completely. There is some difference between militarization and weaponization. Satellites have multiple purposes, both civilian and military. The idea floating now is that weaponization means deploying weapon systems themselves in outer space, either weapon systems as a whole or their parts. Satellites can be used for some legitimate military purposes. The anti-satellite weapons could create more problems than satellites themselves. What does weaponization mean? Some of my colleagues describe that you place a pistol in space, this is a weapon. But if you place targeting components of a weapon system in space, is this something to be permitted? Is it helpful for maintaining strategic balance and stability? This is a question for exploration.

BILL SULZMAN: The UN Charter in its wisdom after World War II said that all aggressive war, space or earth-bound, is illegal. Isn't that a founding principal? The problem is who gets to define.

JOHN PIKE: When you are talking about anti-satellite weapons China is really a clarifying scenario. The most popular scenario in Washington among the Star Warriors for why we need anti-satellite weapons is so that we can destroy Chinese reconnaissance satellites when we fight a war with China over the liberation of Taiwan. I have a number of problems with the scenario but it is interesting to juxtapose that with an information perspective on the problem. China puts up one reconnaissance satellite for about a week every year, and so it is not as though China was presenting us with a target rich environment. On the other hand, if I was the sole remaining superpower and was worried about asymmetric responses in which an adversary was placing at risk things that I valued a lot without having to breathe terribly hard, China's anti-satellite capabilities would be something that would leave me awake at night, because anti-satellite capabilities are not that difficult to have. Unlike China, the United States is presenting an extremely lucrative, extremely rich environment. If I were a Chinese military planner determined to liberate Taiwan the first thing that I would do would be to use my anti-satellite capabilities to shoot down all the American spy satellites. I would have to say, however, that until there is a clear and present danger of the Chinese having an anti-satellite capability like that, and until the United States understands the jeopardy that that would create, I can see no incentive whatsoever for worrying about anti-satellite weapons arms control in Washington, unfortunately.

RON CLEMINSON: I heard General Horner, who was head of the Space Command some years ago. One lesson he learned from the Gulf War, he said, was what's an enemy satellite? He said the coalition forces were using channels on Arabsat, and Saddam Hussein was using channels on Arabsat. If we had considered that to be an enemy satellite, who would have suffered the most? He said, probably us. So there is a whole dynamic out there, as more military functions come to depend upon commercial satellites that it would be difficult to identify. Some could be identified, but the vast majority up there are doing an awful lot of things. The man who made the statement earlier about international corporations I think made a good point.

JONATHAN GRANOFF, LAWS: I asked earlier what weapons were permitted. It is clear, as the afternoon has gone on, that there is a really great difference of opinion that appears to be coming out of ACDA and the State Department and the kind of programs that were articulated as being promoted in Colorado, laser-based weapons, and space weapons. I wonder if there is a robust debate going on in Washington, and if there is, who are the people engaged in this. If there is no debate, than why not? Because it is clear that what Pierce Corden put forth is a regime that circumscribes activities that are quite at odds with what the Air Force wants to do.

PIERCE CORDEN: I tried earlier to make the point about what is permitted. I think it is important not to disparage the existing legal regime, which in my opinion is robust and far-reaching. Anyone who spent time trying to work on nuclear disarmament ought to thank their lucky stars, pardon the pun, that outer space is forever free of weapons of mass destruction. That is pretty important and it is worth sustaining. I won't claim the level of detailed knowledge that John has to address the questions as to his judgements as to what is feasible with the existing legal regime. But I would say that the United States remains convinced at the level of national policy that the ABM Treaty is a cornerstone of our strategic stability. I know of no present effort to try and adjust it beyond those changes that we have made and that the Russian Federation has agreed to with respect to TMD (Theater Missile Defense). I pointed to the additional constraint on TMD that relates to space-based missiles. It seems to me that is a significant point. The future, from my perspective, will have to unfold for itself. I simply can't comment on John's assessment of the trends.

JOHN PIKE: I think that the most significant change that it looks like the Senate may be ratifying later this year is basically the change in the definition of the capabilities that have to be demonstrated, the way in which you would find what is accountable under the treaty. There basically have been two changes. Previously there were two criteria that one could use to decide whether, for instance, a space laser had sufficient capabilities so as to be prohibited or limited under the treaty. Those two criteria were that it either had to be capable of substituting for an ABM interceptor, that is to say, your theoretical analysis, how bright the laser is, how long the range is, tells you whether this is something that could shoot down a strategic missile, or it has to be tested in an ABM mode. That means not that it has to have a theoretical capability to shoot down a strategic missile but that you actually have to go out and do it. The first change that we have made in the treaty is that we have eliminated the capability of substituting for criteria and now the only criteria is a demonstrated capability rather than a potential capability. So we could put Battle Star Galactica and the Dark Lord's Imperial Death Star in orbit and throw in the Starship Enterprise with all its lasers and photon torpedoes just for good measure and as long as we did not actually shoot at a strategic ballistic missile it would be permitted under the treaty because the first criteria is simply so long as it has not been tested in an ABM mode. So long as it is not tested in an ABM mode, whether it is capable of substituting for an ABM interceptor is no longer a criteria.

The second thing that has changed is that previously the criteria was basically one-on- one. We were looking at what, in terms of what was a treaty accountable item, could be limited under the treaty, or prohibited. If one interceptor looked like it could intercept one strategic missile then it was treaty accountable and if it was space-based the laser was a no no. We have changed that criteria to a many-on-many or a force-on-force criteria so that now it doesn't matter how capable the individual laser is, as long as all of our lasers put together do not have the ability to shoot down every missile that the Russians might launch in a first strike. Then it does not meet the force-on-force criteria for what constitutes a problem under the treaty. So the new and approved copy of the treaty says that as long as I don't test it against strategic missiles, and as long as I have got enough to soak up the second strike, but not quite enough to robustly soak up a first strike, then I can at least claim deployment is permitted under the treaty, without thinking that I was actively making that up out of whole cloth. So when the space laser people say that they can sort of see their way forward to how they can get those lasers to defend America without the ABM treaty being much of a problem, I don't think they are making that up. It sounds good. Reasonable people may disagree about what is currently permitted under the ABM Treaty. Twenty-five years ago everyone was reading from the same copy of the treaty. It was kind of open and shut what was permitted and prohibited. I would say today that the thing has been fiddled with so much and has been creatively developed so much that I think nobody knows what the treaty means anymore, apart from you can only deploy 100 interceptors at one site. That is the only bright line restriction we have left and that is the problem. Totally apart from controlling weapons capabilities, even the more modest goal of arms control as improving predictably and enhancing certainty, even that has been undermined.

JONATHAN GRANOFF: Given that ambiguity, aren't people putting forward another treaty regime that specifically addresses this? Is there a debate going on? And how would we identify the parties so that we could engage them?

JOHN PIKE: Senator Kyl, a Republican Senator, is putting forward an alternative approach to dealing with this, and I think that it is going to be the focus of a debate later this year because, if and when the Duma ratifies START II, then that triggers the United States government submitting to the Senate the demarcation protocol of the ABM Treaty and the succession protocol with all these other things I have been talking about. Senator Kyl's view is that the ABM Treaty is basically an obsolete relic of the Cold War, that it no longer bears any resemblance to the way the world is working and that it would be better to clarify the situation by just saying that this ABM Treaty stuff is no longer relevant and that we are perfectly capable of doing whatever we want to do with the Russians without having to confuse things with this unnecessarily complex and ambiguous ABM Treaty. I have to confess, that after spending the last 15 years saying that the ABM Treaty is a good thing, Sen. Kyl may be on to something. I think there is certainly the merit of clarity and candor. It perhaps would be better to have no ABM Treaty at all and let everybody be aware of that fact than to think that we have an ABM Treaty which in fact obscures rather than clarifies and makes the situation less predictable. I would rather have it clearly on the table that apart from putting nuclear bombs in orbit the US can do whatever it wants to rather than having this regime that nobody knows what it means.

KARL GROSSMAN: If Cassini on its fly-by in 1999 does hit the atmosphere, and disintegrate and there is the kind of disaster that occurred to Canada in 1978, a nuclear-powered space device splattering radioactivity over a large area, only much worse, the space nuclear power agreement entered into by NASA and DOD would limit liability to the US to $100 million to all nations other than the US, which would pay $8.9 billion to its people. This is in violation, it seems to me, of the Outer Space Treaty which says that states should be liable for damage caused by their space objects. I would recommend a book, *The Future of War: Power Technology and American World Dominance in the 21st Century*, in which the authors, think tank people, write that the US is expanding its power into space. Just as European powers redefined relations among nations with their fleets, American power is redefining those relations...Who gave the US the authority to control space?

RON CLEMINSON: As a Canadian, trying to understand how the US government operates - we see the Administration on one side, the legislature on another side and the bureaucracy on the third side, and know they aren't all in step. You see people, such as the Vice President of the US, make some very good statements about outer space. Statements made in the Congress are on both sides and the bureaucracy does not seem to change. I remember a Canadian bureaucrat saying, with the politicians it isn't having them make a decision. If they say yes, then we are going to do it thatway, and if they say no, we are going to do it our way, but if they don't make a decision we have to stop.

I think bureaucracies around the world are all the same. You have your bureaucracy, your legislature and Administration. The person with the greatest sense of humor in the entire world, looking at the expenditures on this, must be the United States taxpayer. The answer is the United States taxpayer...

BILL SULZMAN: Canada, as part of NORAD, is pulled into being part of dominating space as a significant partner in the US Space Command. I don't know if that has really been decided in Canada.

RON CLEMINSON: We have an Ambassador in New York who answers things like that. There is certainly a concern. Canada is a part of NORAD, not of the Space Command, and certainly within the mountain there are sections which are US Air Force Base Command and there is NORAD. They are not tied in. I am sure there are Canadians who would like to be, and there are Canadians who don't want to be. NORAD has been extended for two years, and each time it is extended that comes up. The Canadian policy has been no weapons in space for the last 30 years. Prime Minister Pierre Trudeau suggested in 1980 that the Outer Space Treaty was 15 years old and should be renewed. He suggested then that other nations should follow Canada's lead and review the treaty and renew it. It is now 30 years and the Outer Space Treaty has not been reviewed or renewed. There are some suggestions, including the simplistic suggestion that you remove the word "of mass destruction" and it would be weapons that would be banned in space. That is obviously too simplistic for diplomats or politicians or anyone else to accept. But most certainly there will have to be reviews of this. It is a sensitive thing in Canada and in the US quite obviously.

Vice President Gore was the one that when they were discussing the resolution that would be permitted publicly, and the US Air Force said absolutely never, under any condition, could resolution below five meters be permitted, Vice President Gore said one meter. The Air Force Command comes under the US government, and the wisdom of the people of the US usually comes out in the end.

I want to thank the panel on your behalf, and thank you for being here.

AN INTERNATIONAL SATELLITE MONITORING AGENCY: THE IDEA WHOSE TIME HAS COME

The following presentation was made during a Department of Public Information briefing at the United Nations focusing on UNISPACE.

COLLEEN DRISCOLL, Professor of International Relations at Villanova, and representative at the UN of the Common Heritage Institute: In 1985 I published a monograph entitled"An Idea Whose Time has Come: An International Satellite Monitoring Agency." Many States did not agree that the time had come, and thus no serious work ever took place on establishing such an agency. However, in March 1999 Under-Secretary-General Dhanapala said to a group from the NGO Committee on Disarmament, ISMA (International Satellite Monitoring Agency) is "an idea whose time has come." And in the January 27, 1999 Report of Secretary-General Annan to the UN Conference on Disarmament, the Secretary-General discussed the ISMA idea, stating that

> I therefore believe that Member States should now give serious consideration to the feasibility of establishing an international satellite monitoring agency to improve the transparency of military operations, in space and on the ground, and to improve the international community's capabilities for monitoring disarmament agreements, crisis areas and the proliferation of military space technologies.[1]

Thus, perhaps now the time has come to reassess and give serious consideration to the concept. To begin, here is a brief history of the concept of an International Satellite Monitoring Agency, and of what it might do for the cause of peace.

It begins with the story of a flyer who, having experienced the horrors of World War II, observed, when it ended, what he termed "the beginning of the next world war" in a May Day parade of military might in Moscow, and in the laboratories and testing grounds of the US. So he took his knowledge of military strategy, of flying, and of ground control systems for aircraft, and began to create a strategy for peace. Together with his wife, a Unitarian Minister, he studied and learned, then wrote of how the new satellite reconnaissance technology could be used to create peace systems. He dreamed of the positive use to which that technology could be put in the interest of the people of the world through an international satellite monitoring system. His name was Howard Kurtz.

In 1975 President Giscard D'Estaing of France established a committee which was given the task of devising new ideas through which France could play a leadership role in the world. Robert Muller, Assistant Secretary-General of the UN, who believed that ISMA was an idea worth pursuing, gave Howard's writing to D'Estaing. France then made a proposal for the establishment of an ISMA at the General Assembly's First Special Session of Disarmament in 1978. France proposed that ISMA be used to monitor arms control agreements and crisis situations.

The General Assembly made the proposal part of the Final Document adopted at the end of

---

[1] Report of the Secretary-General. International Cooperation in Space Activities for Enhancing Security in the Post-Cold War Era. DCF/335, January 27, 1999

the Special Session, with study of the idea deferred to the thirty-third regular session of the GA.[2] At this session the GA adopted a resolution requesting the Secretary-General to get the views of States and to authorize a study of the feasibility of such an agency. A group of government experts conducted the study on the financial, political and technical aspects of such an agency. Their report was submitted to the Second Special Session of the GA devoted to Disarmament and to the thirty-seventh regular session of the GA. The General Assembly adopted a resolution supporting the concept of an international satellite monitoring agency with the United States abstaining and the Soviet Union dissenting, together with the socialist bloc nations.

Howard's idea of ISMA was that it would provide the world a shared access to information for monitoring arms control and crises but also for a variety of other uses: monitoring cease fires and peacekeeping missions, refugee movement, environmental studies, search and rescue missions, crop studies, land use... The data which would be acquired would make the world transparent, and thus any State or international organization - and possibly NGOs and any part of civil society - would have access to quality data. And the sharing of that data would bring the world together, working for peace rather than preparing for war. Since this peaceful, positive use of space and of satellite technology would add to, encourage, and perhaps assure peaceful and positive uses of outer space, an attempt was made to bring a discussion of ISMA into UNISPACE "82. However, both of the space powers - the US and the Soviet Union - opposed such discussion.

In February 1985 Switzerland suggested to Sweden and Austria that they cooperate with other neutral countries to establish a satellite monitoring agency themselves, and to offer it to any State wanting to use it. They suggested that it might operate within the framework of the Conference on Security and Cooperation in Europe. Sweden had taken a very positive view of the concept, with its government and research institutes conducting studies of the concept.

At the 1988 Special Session of the General Assembly devoted to Disarmament the Soviet Union proposed the establishment of an ISMA. Then, at the 1989 meeting of the Ad Hoc Committee on Prevention of an Arms Race in Outer Space of the conference on Disarmament, the Soviet Union presented a Working Paper on the Establishment of an International Space Monitoring Agency. [3]

At the same time, various countries, scientific groups, and scholars were studying the concept. On January 21, 1988, Argentina, Greece, India, Mexico, Sweden and Tanzania issued the Stockholm Declaration: The Six Nation Initiative. In it they

> recognize the need for the establishment of an integrated multilateral verification system within the United Nations, as an integral part of a strengthened multilateral framework required to ensure peace and security during the process of disarmament as well as in a nuclear-weapon-free world.

---

[2] Final Document, Special Session of the General Assembly on Disarmament, 1978, United Nations, Department of Public Information. E.83.IX.3. 23 May-1 July 1978.

[3] Conference on Disarmament, Ad Hoc Committee on Prevention of an Arms Race in Outer Space. CD/OS/WP.39, 2. August 1989.

In the United States, in February 1988, a House of Representatives Resolution was introduced on an "International Security and Satellite Monitoring Act of 1988." Then, in August 1989 Ambassador Morel of France introduced a Working Paper into the Conference on Disarmament entitled "Space in the Service of Verification: Proposal Concerning a Satellite Image Processing Agency."

Throughout the 1990s, at intervals, France or some other country would mention the concept as still being valid, and something to reconsider. Many private groups did studies of a possible satellite monitoring agency, with varying potential names. What Howard Kurtz had called "Life Support Systems for Planet Earth" the Canadian Government called Paxsat, a Swedish institute called International Satellite Surveillance, while others referred to a UN Satellite Agency, an International Verification center, or an international Space Monitoring Agency.

Just as the potential names may have differed, so did the possible roles for the agency. Some scholars suggested that a Regional Satellite Monitoring Agency might be the best way to begin, with regional groupings of States cooperating and sharing data. Some concentrated on the arms control verification potential, with ISMA offering an ongoing, established mechanism which might make future arms control agreements easier to conclude. As a crisis monitoring system, ISMA would be readily available whenever and wherever a crisis might break out. Others took the broad view that data useful for one purpose could also be used for other purposes, such as environmental monitoring. It was seen also as a way of giving the Secretary-General and the Security Council continual and immediate information to deal with crises and to fulfill their Charter-mandated roles.

In Europe, serious consideration was given to the ISMA concept. In 1983 the Council of Europe had recommended, based on resolutions from UNISPACE '82 and the European space program, that the European Ministers take new initiatives for the establishment of an ISMA. At the Third Special Session on Disarmament in 1988 the French Foreign Minister proposed a United Nations facility which would process and interpret data acquired by civil satellites. In the Lisbon Declaration, resulting from a Conference on North-South: Europe's Role, the States of Europe proposed that the cause of development could be promoted by cooperation with the developing world on projects such as ISMA.

Whatever the name of the monitoring agency, its role, or its final configuration, there are reasons why it deserves serious attention by the United Nations and its Members States in 1999.

- The world has made significant strides in the progression of arms control treaties, and of the verification of such treaties. The Chemical Weapons Convention, with its intrusive verification, is a clear example of this progress. A satellite monitoring agency would provide verification for present and future treaties using nonintrusive space systems.

- A satellite monitoring system would, at one cost, serve many purposes. A United Nations-owned satellite system which could monitor a military crisis could also monitor the environmental effects of that crisis.

- An ISMA would give both the Secretary-General and the Security Council real time, ongoing data without their being dependent on national systems.

- ISMA would create a level playing field where high quality, high resolution satellite data would be available for use by all States, developing as well as developed.

- The same high quality data would be available to UNHCR, FAO, WHO, UNICEF and all the UN departments and specialized agencies to use in handling human disasters, movements of people, and the human effects of armed conflict.

- And, of considerable importance, a satellite monitoring agency under international control would add to the maintenance of peaceful uses of outer space. By recognizing in practical and functional ways, the principle of use of space for the benefit of all humanity - as mandated by the outer Space Treaty - it would help to secure such beneficial use as the primary use of space, to the exclusion of weapons.

Some ideas, no matter how much they might serve the cause of peace, are brought forth at a time when States are not prepared to embrace them. They may be proposed, they may even be discussed, but they are then put aside to wait for a change in circumstances, leadership, technology, or perception. ISMA is one of those ideas. Perhaps now its time has truly come.

REDUCING TENSION IN SOUTH ASIA: NGO PROPOSALS

ANN HALLAN LAKHDHIR, Vice President for Program of the NGO Committee on Disarmament: This is the third panel discussion that we have held that has focused on South Asia. We will hold others in the future. As an American married to an Indian who has relatives in both Pakistan and India I have been highly conscious of the state of tension over many years between India and Pakistan. What seems very important is what our first speaker will be talking about, which is increasing the contacts, not just between governments but by ordinary people in both India and Pakistan. Our first speaker is Ilmas Futehally, who is with the International Center for Peace Initiatives, which is based in Mumbai, India. Her background is in the sciences and the environment. At the Center she has been organizing workshops with parliamentarians in South Asia to involve them in dialogue. She is the assistant editor of the bi-monthly journal, Peace Initiatives, and has been a visiting fellow at the Stimson Center for the last two months.

ILMAS FUTEHALLY: ...It is a great privilege and opportunity for me to be here to share my views on NGO efforts at peacemaking in South Asia with you. It is not as if we don't have NGOs and NGO activity aimed at peacemaking and conflict resolution in South Asia. We do. The objective of the **International Center for Peace Initiatives** is just that - to promote peace and peace-making activities in the region.

Interest in this area began at the time that the President of Bangladesh, Zia Ul Rahman, circulated a letter proposing the establishment of **SAARC**, the South Asian Association for Regional Cooperation, in 1980. The NGO community of South Asia reacted very positively to this. This was the beginning of a number of initiatives aimed at exchanges between countries. Some have involved academics, others retired government officials, and yet others have been aimed at specific groups, such as journalists, lawyers, women and environmental activists.

There are some initiatives that are outgrowths of the SAARC process. These include the **South Asian Association for Speakers and Parliamentarians** and the **SAARClaw** that is an association of lawyers. There is also an association of journalists and other groups.

Many of the NGO initiatives have been funded by US-based foundations, such as the Ford Foundation, or the W. Alton Jones Foundation. Last year, the USIS (the US Information Service) held a traveling seminar that brought about the exchange of journalists from India and Pakistan. This year in May there was an exchange of people working in the fields of air and water pollution. In November they are planning a seminar to explore environmental cooperation between India and Pakistan.

German, Japanese and Australian foundations have also played a catalytic role in bringing about an exchange of people in the region. There have been a number of cultural exchanges, of youth programs and conventions of grass-root level public interest groups that have sprung up in the last few years. Some of them have been useful in facilitating exchanges of information and ideas and for creating a sense of solidarity among groups working on common concerns.

One event that should be mentioned is the one organized by the **India Pakistan Forum for Peace and Democracy**. It is held every year. One year a hundred Pakistanis visit one of the cities in India and live with families there for the duration of the event. These meetings alternate between India and Pakistan. Unfortunately, for the last 18 months there has been no meeting held. Such organizations need to be strengthened. This is of special significance as participants fund their own travel and are guests of families in the other country. It is my firm belief that there can be no breakthrough in relations between the two countries until the people demand it. These kinds of meetings can help in quickening the demand.

Many Nepalese groups have been active in the field of the environment, while Pakistani human rights groups have been instrumental in promoting discussion of atrocities on South Asian women. Unfortunately many such groups have had limited impact because of organizational weaknesses. Similarly the efforts to organize parallel meetings with NGOs at the annual SAARC summit has not met with much success.

There are academic organizations in India, Pakistan and Bangladesh that work on strategic studies and analysis. The **Regional Center for Strategic Studies** was set up with the aim of networking and coordinating between these centers and in helping to identify and fill in some of the gaps that there are. Unfortunately, there are no such coordinating bodies yet in the NGO network, **if** what is present can be called a network at all. This is what really needs to be addressed. Mechanisms need to be set up that would help in informing NGOs what other NGOs are doing, so that instead of replication of projects, gaps can be filled in. This is what is lacking at the moment.

Track 2 diplomacy, involving the efforts of influential citizens for peacemaking through dialogues and meetings, have had two objectives - economic cooperation and conflict resolution. Mr. Parekh, a financial wizard, is credited with the initial effort at expanding economic cooperation in the 1960s. But the group that he set up was not able to achieve anything, as a war took place between India and Pakistan which resulted in the dismemberment of the group.

In the 1980s and 1990s the **Center for Policy Research** based in New Delhi played a role in analyzing and promoting regional cooperation. The **Coalition for Action for South Asia Cooperation** is an informal network that was set up by the Friedrich Ebert Stiftung. It has well-known personalities in all the South Asian countries who are leading initiatives.

In terms of Track 2 diplomacy, not research, where participants engage in a dialogue and arrive at solutions, the most successful initiative has been that of the **Independent Group on South Asian Cooperation**. Their report was released in April 1993 at the Heads of Government Summit at Dhaka.

But the efforts for economic cooperation in South Asia have been limited to scholars and the economic administration. The real actors, the business enterprises, have been generally left out of it. There have been some **exchanges between the Punjab-Haryana-Delhi Chambers of Commerce and Industry and the Federation of Chambers of Commerce and Industry in Pakistan**. There is a Ford Foundation-funded initiative that aims to bring together business leaders from the two countries at the end of the year in Dubai.

Some other initiatives need to be mentioned. The **Neemrana Process**, which began in 1995

310

when it was launched by the USIS, has now become independent. The last meeting was held in New Delhi last week and now the participants are hopeful of being able to raise money from the region to be able to fund the process. This is a big step forwards. It is vital that at some stage the resources come from within the region rather than from outside. This is the best way of developing a stake in the process. And only when people who have a stake in the process are involved can it go ahead.

There has also been an initiative to tap the younger generation of scholars. The idea of launching a summer school which would deal with subjects related to security, technology and arms control emerged about five years ago. This has been another success. Initially it was organized from Kings College in London, but it has now been handed over to the **Regional Center in Colombo** and the participants are drawn from all South Asian countries and China. It has also set up a winter workshop that deals with issues related to ethnicity, the environment and refugees.

More than anything else, this has been a channel of establishing communication links among the younger generation, and there is some chance that it would lead to joint projects. There is also an alumni association for this initiative that aims to keep participants of the workshops in touch with each other. The first issue of the newsletter should be in the mail now.

My organization, the **International Center for Peace Initiatives,** has been working on programs that would include the political leadership and political actors in peace-making and preventive diplomacy. We held a number of workshops for parliamentarians in South Asia: in Kathmandu in 1994; in the Maldives in 1995; in New Delhi in 1996. We are now in the stage of planning the next set of activities that came out of these deliberations.

But the most important question that needs to be answered is how effective is the role that NGOs can play in peace-making in the South Asian region? Most of the efforts described cannot be quantified by their contribution to peace and stability in the region. The fact that they have opened lines of communication that have not existed before is a big contribution. The study set up by the Ford Foundation argues that many of the dialogues in the region have significantly altered popular perceptions, countered prevailing stereotypes and enemy images, and have thus improved the atmosphere within which contentious issues in Indo-Pakistan relations are addressed. And they say that they are an expression of the growing assertiveness of civil society on both sides of the border.

If these initiatives are to be meaningful, they must involve not only the political decision-makers, but also the groups that are generally perceived to be against conflict resolution. It is easy to preach to the converted. Now it is time to go beyond.

NGO efforts in South Asia must also be extended to include the interests of other countries in the region. Most efforts so far have concentrated on India-Pakistan relations. While this is important, other countries should not be ignored. Nepal, Bangladesh, Bhutan and the Maldives have to be brought more to the forefront of these activities, and the problems of these countries must also be addressed.

Finally, the problems of financing affects all work in the non-governmental sector. While foreign foundations and institutions have been very forthcoming in funding initiatives, it is necessary to involve local resources and people who have a stake in peace and stability in the region in the process.

One question that I am always asked is, are you really able to achieve anything? How can a small group make a difference in what seems to be insurmountable problems between countries? Wouldn't it be better to focus on some sphere where you could see results more clearly? My answer is that we have to keep at it. And we have to involve more and more people in this kind of work. We need to build networks of people and organizations in the subcontinent, not only to know what the others are doing, but to be able to help in taking it ahead. There is a long way to go, and we are nowhere near the end as yet. This is not the time to give up on NGOs and NGO activity in peace-building in South Asia. It is the time to work along with them and build upon their work. Thank you.

ANN HALLAN LAKHDHIR: Our next speaker will be M.V. Ramana who is a physicist by training, working on issues related to nuclear weapons and energy in South Asia. He is presently at the Center for Energy and Environmental Studies at Princeton University. He is a founding member of the Alliance for a Secular and Democratic South Asia, a group that has been trying to combat growing religious bigotry in the subcontinent.

M.V. RAMANA: Since I am speaking barely a few months after the nuclear tests of May, 1998, I thought I would talk a little bit about the context in which these tests happened, and the context in which the emerging peace movements in South Asia are operating. So I will begin with a little bit of history and then go on to what is happening. The Indian nuclear program almost from its beginning had a bomb component. One rationale for the existence of the program was, in some sense, the possibility, which later turned into actuality, of the bomb. The shift in rationale in the last few years towards the military rationale has been much more prominent and there has been a hardening of stances which has marked the debate in the country.

Since 1967 and the negotiation of the Non-Proliferation Treaty, the official Indian government position has always been one that supported any non-discriminatory universal disarmament treaty. The NPT is obviously not. It divides states into five countries which have nuclear weapons and the rest cannot. This was discriminatory, clearly, and India opposed it. I am not saying it was only because India was in favor of universal treaties. It was also partly because India could not be part of the five nuclear weapon states in the NPT. That position has been maintained for 30 years.

It is only since the early nineties that we see the changes in this position among official circles. The causes for this can be traced in part to the strengthening of the so-called bomb lobby in the domestic Indian debate and also the growth of militant Hindu fundamentalism in regional and national politics which sets the context in which these kinds of ideas can be promulgated. The 1995 indefinite extension of the NPT was an important event. Hawks in the Indian nuclear debate argued that this was a signal that nuclear weapons were here to stay forever, and if India didn't want permanent second-class status, without nuclear weapons, while other countries had them, it should develop its nuclear weapons soon.

The first effect of this was the debate on the Comprehensive Test Ban Treaty in 1996. The treaty had originally been suggested by Prime Minister Nehru in 1954 and had been supported actively ever since then until the mid-1990s. Basically, in the context of the debate in India, the treaty was vilified and turned from one that was a universal treaty promoting disarmament to one which was a discriminatory treaty which India had to vote against. Of course, the reason why many of these people were arguing was because they supported India acquiring nuclear weapons, and India had to test if it wanted to develop nuclear weapons, so it could not possibly sign the CTBT.

Now I come to the present. It is interesting to observe who is saying what in the domestic debate in which decision-making happens. The very people who in 1996 had argued extensively against the Comprehensive Test Ban Treaty have turned around and said now India should sign the treaty. The reasons are twofold. One is to cut losses, in terms of sanctions and in terms of international prestige. The second, probably more important, is that they could now participate in the formulation of an Indian position of national policy and consolidate their hold on the domestic decision-making. You could say India's hawks are becoming its arms controllers.

It is in this context that NGOs and the peace movement are operating. The position of people in the peace movement and the NGO community has been far more principled and certainly not opportunistic. If they support the CTBT it is because they are opposed to nuclear weapons, period, and not because they want to get rid of sanctions or get foreign nuclear technology. Besides the people who have taken part in the debate in the past, after the tests in May we have seen a number of new voices, which previously were confined to a handful of people in some of the think tanks and government policy bureaus and the various departments of atomic energy and defense, the labs, etc. After the tests we have seen various journalists, film makers, scientists, artists, doctors, women, lower caste people, a plethora of other groups talking about it. For the first time we have a vibrant peace movement. We have seen people talking, taking this message to schools, to factories, to community centers, and so on.

On Hiroshima Day on August 6 there were rallies in most of the major Indian cities. The largest one was in Calcutta, where 400,000 people marched. This is a very welcome development. However, it is worth stepping back and looking a little bit at what exactly happened. For years we have wondered why there was no peace movement in India. The answer was the structure of Indian society itself. In 1996 a public opinion poll was conducted on the nuclear issue. It was mainly an elite poll among the top 2000 people. It is interesting to see the issues that people claimed they were most concerned about. The first was communalism, the second, poverty, third, economic stability, fourth, terrorism, fifth, Kashmir, sixth, global economic treaties like GATT, and the seventh was the nuclear issue. It was basically a non-issue, as far as most people were concerned. But now, after the testing, you see this coming much more into prominence. You have to look at who are the people who are now talking. The new faces in the debate are all people who have been involved in issues regarding social justice, environmental issues, and so forth.

The one journal which we have had in India which is sort of anti-nuclear is called Anumoti. Primarily it has focused on nuclear power and how it affects communities near these facilities. So you have to see beyond narrow treaties, the CTBT, and so on. You have to focus on the real goal, the abolition of nuclear weapons. It is on that level you have to engage. There have been a number of new initiatives which have combined some of these issues.

ANN HALLAN LAKHDHIR: Arundhati Roy, an Indian novelist, trained as an architect, who won the Booker award for her first book, has issued a statement on India's nuclear testing (appended). It is quite an unusual statement. It isn't full of physics, except on the first page, and it is an attack not only on India's nuclear testing but more generally on the program of the political party in control now. How effective do you think her argument is and with what part of the Indian electorate?

M.V. RAMANA: It is a very passionate argument, not logically reasoned out, x, y, z and therefore a, b, c kind of thing, but it is from the heart, and I think it speaks very well to a wide spectrum of people. There are people who are going to criticize it. I would add one thing to what Ann said. She is an architect by training, but her mother, Mera Kuti, was a well-known social activist in Kerala who has been involved in various education issues and issues regarding women, and it is with this background that Arundhati Roy comes into this. And you are going to see widespread linkages to other things happening in this society. To that extent I think she is going to be more effective.

ANN HALLAN LAKHDHIR: Our next speaker will be Rekha Datta, originally from Calcutta, India, who teaches at Monmouth University in New Jersey. Her special areas are international relations and the comparative politics of Asia and of developing countries in particular.

REKHA DATTA: ...I, having been raised in India, always wondered why in India we were growing up with the rhetoric of a kind of a hate-Pakistan mentality, so when I chose the topic for my dissertation I asked, what is it about Pakistan that elicits's India's concern? So I have been doing this kind of soul-searching and thinking alongside of my academic pursuit. I ended up writing a dissertation on the United States' military policy towards Pakistan because I realized that it perhaps is the source of much of the sentiment, particularly in the post-Independence period for India and the post-creation period for Pakistan, that has brewed over time. It has since been published as a book: *Why Alliances Endure: The United States-Pakistan Alliance, 1954-1971*. Recently I published another article which deals with United States' security policy in South Asia with regard to nuclear proliferation and non-proliferation. I had a very tough time deciding whether to call it non-proliferation or proliferation. I will try to put the question of nuclear tensions in South Asia in a larger context with a focus on other areas that sometimes get sidetracked. I thought of looking for some answers or solutions on how tensions could be reduced in South Asia.

Reducing tension in South Asia is a matter of global importance and urgency. The nuclear tests by India and Pakistan earlier this year, coupled with the historical rivalry between the two nations on the Kashmir issue, makes the search for security in South Asia urgent and imperative. The traditional rivalry that we witness between India and Pakistan is mired in historical, religious and territorial differences. There have been three armed conflicts between the two countries and all of these conflicts have some element of each of these traits. However, the real objectives or goals have never been addressed in clear terms. That is also part of the difficulty in looking for solutions. I think both countries are still searching for what is the goal.

When I teach from an introductory political science book there is the example of two conflicting countries in perfect agreement: they both want the same piece of land. In the case of India and Pakistan, regarding Kashmir, there is a similar kind of perfect agreement: both want Kashmir.

Since India and Pakistan have both tested their bombs there is no longer the possibility of putting them in the basement. We need to look at what the deciding factor of security in South Asia will be. Public opinion could go a long way in securing some kind of solution to the issues. To the extent that democratic processes are allowed in both these countries, we will find a renewed commitment from the leadership of both countries to refrain from using nuclear weapons and perhaps even a search for solutions to long-standing conflicts, such as the Kashmir problem. Furthermore, since regional stability in South Asia has in the last 50 years been a close handmaiden of Washington's security policy in the region, the role that Washington and other powers can play will be a vital one and thus ought to be carefully thought out.

In the context of the nuclear policy that both India and Pakistan have followed, where do we go from here? South Asia today is sitting on a powder keg. On May 18, 1974, India conducted what the Indian government had called at that time "a peaceful nuclear explosion." Since that time there have been numerous speculations about India's real intentions with nuclear weapons. Amidst border tension with Pakistan, and the Kashmir imbroglio, this speculation has bred criticism from outside India that the policy has led to an arms race in South Asia. In the post-Cold War period, when the world powers have renewed their pledge towards a non-proliferation regime, to be led by the existing nuclear powers, the nuclear policies of India and Pakistan continued to draw international criticism and concern. Therefore the May 11, 1998 tests, followed by five nuclear tests by Pakistan 17 days later, have given rise to the question of where this is going to lead both countries and the world.

For India, perhaps the most significant impact that the new government led by the Bharatiya Janata Party (BJP), a Hindu party, has had so far has been its decision to conduct nuclear tests. The BJP's posture toward Pakistan as a security issue is entangled with its commitment to Hindu nationalism and somewhat obfuscates the reality. The reality is that regardless of whether Pakistan is a Muslim state, the BJP looks at Pakistan as a security risk. It is made more complex because of Pakistan's role in Kashmir, so these issues have to be looked at more carefully when we look at the question of nuclear priority that the Hindu government has embarked on. The BJP has never made a secret of its desire to follow the nuclear program. In its manifesto it was very direct about the issue. It said, the BJP will re-evaluate the country's nuclear policy and exercise the option to induct nuclear weapons. This commitment to induct nuclear weapons was repeated and followed by the nuclear tests, so there was nothing secret about BJP's policy prior to the tests.

In Pakistan the government, led by Nawaz Sharif, also has a mandate to resolve the Kashmir issue such that Muslim Kashmir is under the suzerainty of Pakistan. With India's nuclear tests, the Pakistan government was urged by Washington not to follow suit, but that government felt that it was imperative that they do so, lest the public perceived them as weaker than India.

The events that have followed since then have been those of confusion leading to speculations, what does this really mean? Does this mean there is going to be a change in the balance of power? Does this mean that there is going to be parity between India and Pakistan? How is this going to help a search for solutions for issues like Kashmir? The issue of Kashmir could at any time flare up and there is ample cause for concern.

The issue of territory has brought India and Pakistan into conflict in 1947, 1965 and 1971. Kashmir, with a Muslim majority and proximity to Pakistan has been claimed by Pakistan. India claims that since the Maharajah signed the instrument of accession in 1948, Kashmir is part of India. In the last 50 years, Kashmir, once hailed as a haven for tourists, is now rife with neglect, civil conflict and economic stagnation. Meanwhile, secessionist forces are emerging, claiming an independent Kashmir. The questions that face Kashmir now are twofold: should there be a plebiscite in Kashmir to decide the fate of Kashmir, or should the crisis be mediated by a third party or mediated bilaterally?

So far as India is concerned, New Delhi rejects both, because the questions for New Delhi are now moot. Kashmir, for India, has an elected government, and rebels who seek to destabilize the situation need to be dealt with by force. This has, however, not prevented the outbreak of violence in the Kashmir valley. As late as August, 1998, violence, and the exchange of artillery fire across the line of control, resulted in deaths mounting to more than 100 on both sides of the border.

In light of the nuclear tests by India and Pakistan, and the violence that has continued in the Kashmir valley, the issue of Kashmir has reappeared on the global agenda with renewed importance. The United Nations has called for a bilateral solution to the crisis. India welcomes this, since this has been India's position for a long time. India does not want third party mediation on Kashmir.

Third party mediation or not, the need to find a solution is imminent, especially as the Pakistani Prime Minister has to deliver on the issue to his own people. According to Pakistan's Foreign Minister, Gowar Ayub Khan, Kashmir is the root cause of the tension between India and Pakistan, but the international community has ignored it. Elections were held in the Indian section of Kashmir, and in the Indian perception things are gradually returning to normalcy. Therefore India has no intention of keeping the Kashmir issue alive. On the other hand, Pakistan has made it a condition before it will sign any no-first-use pact with India. This being the context, what are the possible solutions which could lead to a future of security in South Asia?

Most reports since the nuclear tests were conducted by India and Pakistan suggest that there was initially widespread public support in both countries for the tests. The initial frenzy resulted from a feeling of newfound pride to be considered as one of the nuclear "haves." With time, however, public opinion in India has demonstrated a swing toward a more rational evaluation of the nuclear tests. The campaign against weaponization is fast gaining ground in India.

Two major conventions were held in New Delhi and Chenai (originally called Madras) in June and July of 1998. These two conventions shed light on the more substantial issues related to weaponization as an official policy. They contributed to a better understanding of the consequences of a nuclear outbreak on the environment, the increased risks of tensions in South Asia leading to a nuclear exchange, etc. Massive response to the convention, especially the one in Chenai, represented the shift in popular support that was now more critical of the tests than at the beginning.

Garnering public opposition to the weapons program will, I think, ensure popular discontent against the government's policies. To the extent that democratic processes are still in place in India, public opinion can and will go a long way in causing a shift in government policy. A critically conscious electorate can remind the government of its priorities, removing poverty, reducing population growth, ensuring basic education and health. All of these need to be the government's concerns, not nuclearization.

Much confusion, though, still persists among decision-makers in India. On the one hand, India has always favored disarmament only when the big powers also cooperate. India would not sign the NPT and CTBT because they were discriminatory. They seek to prevent the nuclear-have-nots from acquiring nuclear weapons while allowing the nuclear-haves to keep them, in India's eyes.

It seems that under the pressure of sanctions from the United States, and the international outcry against the May tests, the Indian Prime Minister declared at the United Nations in September that India is prepared, perhaps, to sign the CTBT next year. Strategically, the calculations seemed to be based on diverting the focus away from the Kashmir issue. By agreeing to sign the CTBT, the Comprehensive Test Ban Treaty, India will have scored points with countries such as the United States which will then refrain from pressuring India to resolve the Kashmir problem. I could be wrong, I would like to be wrong.

So the most important threat to peace in South Asia resolves around these issues. In the case of Kashmir the goals of India and Pakistan are not going to match, at least as they are now. Their objectives in signing the CTBT are also going to be different. The cards that these countries are going to play are going to be very crucial in seeking to restore the power balance in South Asia because the issues are still very confused.

In conclusion, India's position has been that since independence India has sought global disarmament and equal security for all. India now claims that she is sandwiched between two nuclear powers and that there is a vacuum in South Asia in the post-Cold War neglect of the region. Further, India questions, if nuclear deterrence has worked in the advanced world, why should it not work in South Asia? This may have been a valid point, but recent history has also demonstrated the price that the former Soviet Union has had to pay for that deterrent. So why does a country like India, or Pakistan, need to move in that direction?

Furthermore, by conducting the tests, India and Pakistan have lost their moral commitment to peace. Even though India has for decades claimed that the NPT and the CTBT regime are based on nuclear apartheid, it has committed nuclear suicide by treading the same road that it has so long lobbied against. For now, at least, the position that India is in is very critical. It will probably be able to immerse the Kashmir issue in the pledge to sign the CTBT, but that is no guarantee that Pakistan will allow Kashmir to continue to be a sleeping dog.

It is clear that both India and Pakistan have used the nuclear nationalism ticket and have made some short-term gains in domestic popular consent. When the economic sanctions begin to hurt, as they have already started doing in some areas, the popular mood will be far-removed from the initial euphoria. The national consensus that the two countries talk about was probably never there. I quote Arundhati Roy's questions in "The End of Imagination:"

> Is it possible for a man who can not write his own name to understand even the basic elementary facts about the nature of nuclear weapons? Has anybody told him that nuclear war has nothing at all to do with his received notions of war, nothing to do with honor, nothing to do with pride?"

Governments will do well to heed public opinion that is allowed to ferment and guide a democracy. The people of both India and Pakistan will be best served by democratic governments that reflect the spirit of the people, not the political agendas of any political party that seeks to create an artificial sense of unity and national pride by placing the country on a heap of enriched uranium or a critical mass. Finally, to borrow from Roy again:

"The nuclear bomb is the most anti-democratic, anti-national, anti-human outright evil thing that man has ever made." In light of all these considerations the governments of India and Pakistan must realize that in South Asia, a region associated with the Buddha, Gandhi, and the Dalai Lama, the recent nuclear tests, or any future association with nuclear weapons, will certainly not make the

Buddha smile again. Thank you.

ANN HALLAN LAKHDHIR: Our last speaker is Zia Mian, whom we have had as a panelist in the past. He is always guaranteed to keep everybody awake. He says it is enough to describe him as a peace activist and scientist currently at Princeton and an old friend of the NGO Committee on Disarmament. That doesn't really seem like enough to me. He was publishing a column in a newspaper in Islamabad, Pakistan when he was there with a research organization. It amazed me, what he was able to get published in a Pakistani newspaper that was critical of the Pakistan government. Last year he was with the Union of Concerned Scientists. I think he is in the process of writing at least one book while he is at Princeton. Zia.

ZIA MIAN: ...I want to start where Rekha left off with her quote from Arundhati Roy. She said that the nuclear bomb is the most anti-democratic, anti-human, immoral, appalling, disgusting thing that human beings have ever done. In a similar sort of vein, the former Canadian Ambassador for Disarmament, Douglas Roche, wrote a book entitled "The Ultimate Evil," about nuclear weapons.

It is a strange thing to say, but we talk about nuclear weapons in a century in which we have seen the gas chambers, where six million Jews were murdered, and yet it is the atom bomb that we now talk about as being the ultimate evil. It does reflect an important sensibility about where we have come, a sense of the depths to which human society, as we are familiar with it, is now capable of engaging with each other. Killing six million Jews was bad, but what we have come up with is even worse. And it is important to understand that this fundamentally anti-democratic, ultimately evil weapon was actually made here in the United States. It wasn't invented by some kind of appalling authoritarian brutal bloody-minded fascistic state. It was invented in the United States by the best scientists that the United States could bring to bear on this question. It was done with the consent of an American president.

Now you can say that it was under extraordinary situations - this was in the middle of World War II - but World War II ended in 1945. The United States continued and built 72,000 nuclear weapons. And it was an elected government after an elected government, Congress after Congress, president after president, who just kept giving money to do this. It has now been estimated that the United States has spent close to five and a half trillion dollars building nuclear weapons and the planes and missiles and bases that go with them as a way of fighting nuclear war. And it has been prepared and ready to fight nuclear war for 50 years.

On the way here from Princeton we caught the train to Penn station and took a cab from Penn station to here, because we were running late. It took about twenty minutes to cross Manhattan. Within that time the United States has the capability to launch 5,000 nuclear weapons. Fifteen minutes. And that is enough to destroy anybody, any opponent, any collection of possible opponents. And this, as I said, is what people with some degree of sensitivity talk about as the ultimate evil, this anti-democratic, anti-humane, immoral weapon. And it is an important question that faces South Asia now, the reason for having this meeting and all the other meetings that have been held on India and Pakistan, all the column inches that have been devoted to the terrible possibilities that are inherent in India and Pakistan having nuclear weapons. These are things that are done by turning ones back on the obvious facts of history and experience. It was a democratic society that developed nuclear weapons, and not just one. The British have had nuclear weapons for the better part of 50 years. And who would describe Britain as anything other than democratic. Or the French?

And so it seems that nuclear weapons and the capacity and readiness to invest money and be prepared to use them against others is something that democratic societies don't actually have a problem with, or at least some of them don't have a problem. And it is not as if they are poor and desperate and struggling. These are some of the wealthiest, the most powerful states in the world. And they don't have a problem.

Why don't they have a problem? I don't want to talk about NGOs in particular, because I think that is a bit of a misnomer when we are talking about peace movements, and that is really what I want to get to, the distinction between an NGO and a peace movement and the role that they can play and have played, and their connection with democracy and nuclear weapons.

You think of India and Pakistan, you think of third world societies, as being poor. Well, they are poor. The United Nations every year publishes the Human Development Index. They list all countries on the basis of their infant mortality, how many babies die before they are one, and their literacy rate, some other statistics, and they rank them from the highest to the lowest. Out of 173 or 174 countries Pakistan ranks number 138 and India ranks 139. Pakistan has a literacy rate of 37%. Just over one person in three can read. In India it is just over half. Now, to what extent is democracy possible in that kind of situation?

You can say there is really no fundamental connection between being able to read and understanding politics, and I agree with that. Many of the people who understand politics the least have Ph.D.s from Harvard and Princeton. And if you look at the way that people with Ph.D.s from Harvard and Princeton have gone around the world advising other countries on how to run their affairs, it becomes pretty clear that they don't understand much of the way the world works.

If you don't need a particularly good education to be able to understand democracy, what is clear is the fact that in both India and Pakistan, as well as many other third world countries, the vast majority of the poor, which is the vast majority of the population, is unable to translate their aspirations and their needs through a formal political process to make the government do what they want. You don't think that they vote to stay poor, but the question is, what happens in the political process that people who do come to power don't do anything about it? And it is not as though it happens once or twice. It has happened continuously for fifty years.

That same failure on the part of governments and states to address the needs and aspirations of the people is symptomatic of the absence of democracy, as far as I am concerned. Democracy is not about going to vote, it is about having your vote count, about what you want to happen in your life, your community, translating itself into some kind of action on the part of those whom you elect to represent you and to manage collective resources.

They fail to do this, so there is no presumption that having more democracy, or having that kind of activity will make those governments do anything about nuclear weapons. If they haven't done anything about poverty and feeding people and educating them, why should they do something about nuclear weapons, especially when nuclear weapons and big armies actually mean jobs and money for people who work for the state? It makes scientists important if they are involved in nuclear weapons programs. It makes generals important to have big armies because then they have lots of money and can shape policy.

I think the formal democratic process is not going to be able to get a grip on this in India and Pakistan any more than it has been able to get a grip in the United States or Britain or in France. If you can't do it, what on earth makes you think that we can do it, given the place where we start from?

And so we come to the question, what is possible? I think part of it has to do with the fact that the political structures that have been at work on the question of nuclear weapons in the United States have been largely single-issue-oriented. There has been a peace movement, but except for the 1960s anti-nuclear movement, it has been obsessed with the weapon, with the bomb, with the possibility of war, with the fear of dying in some cataclysmic end of the world situation, which it would have been and is a legitimate fear that exists as much now as it existed ten years ago or twenty years ago, because the weapons haven't gone away, even though there are no more communists running Russia.

It is because the institutions that manage nuclear weapons and are responsible for them have managed to gain such a phenomenal stranglehold on the policy-making process. When it came to the negotiations on the Comprehensive Test Ban Treaty, for example, the nuclear weapons laboratories in the US said, we don't like this idea of not having nuclear weapons tests, because that is what they do, they design and test nuclear weapons. We don't like it.

So what happened? Did the US government say shut up, we promised we would negotiate a treaty stopping nuclear tests? We have done that, so you will do what you are told. No. They said how much money do you want to agree to a Comprehensive Test Ban? The answer was four and a half billion dollars a year, which is what the US government now pays the weapons labs. So they can keep doing what they did before, but keep quiet and not complain about the Comprehensive Test Ban. That amount of money is not very different from what used to be spent on the labs in the middle of the Cold War, four and a half billion a year. And it reflects the incapacity of the political process to discipline these institutions that manage nuclear weapons.

If you can't do it here, what makes you think that in Pakistan, for example, which has had almost thirty years of military government? What makes you think that politicians can discipline those institutions and say we have a different set of priorities now, we don't want you to do this anymore?

The obsession with the nuclear weapon as a technology that has characterized the American peace movement, and peace movements around the world, has led to a certain inability to connect that to everybody else's issues. It hasn't been a bread and butter issue. It has become an issue that concerns those who were particularly sensitive to those kinds of concerns about fear and death as opposed to urban poverty or civil rights or the environment.

In the same way, in Pakistan and in India to a certain extent we have NGOs. An NGO is basically a way of people getting together to do something that the government should be doing but doesn't. So people try and do it themselves, like set up schools and clinics and hospitals and roads. It is not a substitute for government, though, because you will never have the capacity to really influence national policy. All you can do is take a little bit, a village here, a village there, and try and do as much as you can with it. And it is always dependent, from one year to the next, on a) the government allowing you to do what it is that you do, and b) somebody providing a little bit of money to do it, and a lot of support from the people you are trying to help.

It is precisely this that has stopped people from getting involved for a long time in these questions of huge levels of military spending and nuclear projects because it really was bread and butter issues, life and death issues, that they were concerned with, and what was the point of taking your attention away and thinking about the possibility of war in some future scenario when you had children dying because there wasn't clean water for them to drink?

It is the tests that have made them feel that we have to do something about this, but it won't last. It will last for three months, six months, a year, and then they will go back to worrying about children dying because there isn't clean water to drink because the kid will die, and nuclear war may happen next year or the year after, but in between how many children are you going to let die because you are worried about the bomb? So where does the capacity to do something about this lie if not in these already mobilized political actors? As I said, I don't think it is through the democratic process. I don't think they can manage that any more than others have managed that.

It really does seem to lie in the fact that there is now time to learn something about what democracy and the failure of democracy in the last 50 years has taught us, and that is that when it really comes to important issues, the democratic process does not deliver as presently constituted. It hasn't gotten rid of the bomb, it hasn't fed the poor. If you look at the Human Development Report, the top 20% of the richest people in the world, and let us be honest, a lot of them are here and in western Europe, consume 80% of the world's resources, and yet must of these countries that do this consumption are democracies, and it is not that they don't know, it is not even that they don't care. They just can't figure out how to go about doing something about it.

I think it is perhaps time to make the case for a much more thorough and determined rethinking of what the links need to be between movements in the powerful countries in the world, like the United States and western Europe and others, and movements in the Third World where the thing that they have in common is not the nuclear weapon or poverty but justice.

This is really what it comes down to. What we have in common is governments and processes for making decisions that have never listened to us. Therefore, basically, we should gang up against them and draw a different kind of line in the sand. Not the government of the United States talking to the Pakistan government about what it should do with its nuclear weapons, but the people of the United States and the people of Pakistan saying to both governments we don't want you or your damn weapons. Because by themselves they have proved incapable of addressing this question. Each government claims some sort of legitimacy, that it serves some kind of moral purpose to have them sit and make decisions on your behalf. Either they protect you or they lower your taxes or they make sure the trains run on time, although they don't from Princeton to New York.

There is fundamentally a question, have we reached the time when only a thorough-going, anti-systemic politics is required, not localized NGOs in South Asia, or small peace groups in the United States, or NGO Committee networks that bring little groups together once a year? Do we need far more thorough, deep-rooted, organized and systematic thinking about what it will take for people to realize that their problem is government and not each other? That is an anti-governmental proposal, an AGO is what we are really talking about. Thank you.

ANN HALLAN LAKHDHIR: Questions, comments?

MARY SHOIKET, SERVAS: Zia Mian was very provocative. What he had to say was you have a democracy, but it doesn't produce, it doesn't prevent hunger and it doesn't build schools instead of bombs. I have joined the Green Party because they stand for eliminating nuclear bombs but also for changing our structure into something which, we like to think, is more democratic, starting with reform of the moneys used to create candidates, and so on.

ZIA MIAN: Even though I am not sure I heard a question in that, let me use that to harangue you some more. It is enormously significant that the German Greens have finally come to power in a sort of way. Not very long ago these people were so far outside, they were beyond the fringe, as far as German politics was concerned and there was a determined attempt to keep them out. But they have fought their way into the German political process. Now the question will be how long they can stay there before they become part of the process of maintaining their own institutional capacity to be there. Once you are there, why should you leave?

And that is a question for the next generation of radical people to come along and say, you had your chance and you blew it. But it has to be more than just offering a different shade of politics. It has to be the kind of thoroughgoing systematic rethinking of the relationship of power between citizens and states, between citizens and elected officials. Until people are prepared to take that as the issue to their fellow citizens you are never really going to be able to construct the constituencies that can dig in and fight that battle.

REKHA DATTA: I would also like to respond to that but on a positive note. I think there is some hope. Democracies can redefine their priorities. I will mention two examples. In the United Nations we have a redefined notion of security, and that is called human security which leads on to the Human Development Index. This has become important in the post-Cold War period, but governments have still to heed that call. Related to that is the hopeful sign that Amartya Sen has won the Nobel prize for economics. He is on the forefront, arguing for justice and equality as a democratic priority, not liberalization and globalization per se, especially for developing countries.

MICHAEL NICOSIA, political science student at Monmouth University: First I want to commend the panel on a wonderfully informative presentation and discussion. My question is directed to Dr. Mian. I heard you get on the soap box of almost anti-democracy. I am curious if you have any solutions, or possibilities for the reduction of nuclear weapons, without requiring the overthrow of every government in the world?

ZIA MIAN: An international global revolution is much to be desired, given the state of the world. You might laugh, but 80% of the population of the world is having a shitty life and they don't like it and there is nothing right now that they can do about it. You have to take sides.

On the question on nuclear weapons, that is a lot easier, because there are only eight countries that have nuclear weapons, not 150. There is a convenient formalization that has crept into talk about nuclear weapons in recent years, and that is to talk about these rogue states who may have secret nuclear, chemical or biological weapons programs, but we know of eight rogue states, that is the United States, Britain, China, Russia, India, Pakistan and Israel, because they have built them and they are ready to use them.

And so it is actually a relatively straightforward question about what to do. The rest of the world is slowly going through the process of ganging up on them. Every year in this building there are resolutions calling for a treaty immediately to end all nuclear weapons. There is a treaty on biological weapons, and one on chemical weapons, and now it attracts the support of 115, 120 countries. There are about 22 countries that vote against it, basically led by the United States and its allies and a few countries that it buys off because they are so dependent on American aid. Do you think the Marshall Islands have a policy on nuclear weapons, considering how dependent they are on US aid?

As that process of building an international consensus against nuclear weapons and against the Nuclear Weapon States takes place, the key thing will be whether, within the Nuclear Weapon States, there are organized movements that demand that their governments change their policies. And there are movements in that direction. There are hopes and attempts to create a US campaign to abolish nuclear weapons, bringing together every group that has worked on this into one campaign...

Specifically, in the near future, there is great promise, but you have to realize that the obstacles lie basically in eight states, and out of those eight states, five, six, seven, actually claim to have representative democracy. Russia has multi-party elections, only China right now does not have multi-party elections. If in those seven countries citizens cannot become engaged on this issue, then I come back to my question as to where it is that we think the democratic process is, and what it implies, because if everybody else is working towards this, are the people in these seven countries going to stand outside and say we don't care what our governments are doing?

The US is increasingly isolated on these questions, like the International Criminal Court which the US is refusing to support, and the international convention on land mines, which the US tried to prevent getting through, but failed...It doesn't require war or revolution to get rid of nuclear weapons, it just requires the American people to tell their government to get rid of them.

DARYL KIMBALL, Director of the Coalition to Reduce Nuclear Dangers, which is an NGO coalition based in Washington...Zia's comments are something of a lightening rod. I would just notice, as a peace activist, while I agree with your final conclusions about what the peace movement needs to do to build stronger links with other constituencies outside the nuclear weapons arena, and your other comments, I think your analysis is a bit off. I think we must be careful not to confuse the ills of democracies as we define them, with capitalism and global resource inequities. I would say, not that democracy has so far failed in getting rid of nuclear weapons, but that we need to recognize that democracies may indeed lead to the existence of nuclear weapons. Democracy does not necessarily mean that you have no nuclear weapons.

This means that NGOs need to think about how we use our rights and our resources in those democracies to change policy. While the situation in the United States is in many ways far different from what it is in South Asia, there are some parallels that might be drawn. I think you sell the anti-nuclear movement short when you say it has focused just on nuclear weapons and that it has not succeeded. We would not have a test ban treaty if it were not for NGOs working in the US and all over the world for a test ban. The freeze movement in the US also had its successes.

My question is, given the difficulties that NGOs and citizens in South Asia face, with resource inequities, lack of literacy, what can be done, within the context of the situation there through the new peace movement that is emerging after the tests, what can be done in the near term, what can we hope for, and how can NGOs in other parts of the world assist people in South Asia who are trying to stop the arms race? I want to ask Ilmas and Rekha Datta to try and answer that question.

ILMAS FUTEHALLY: There are more and more linkages forming between Indians and Pakistanis on anti-nuclear issues. The India-Pakistan Forum for Peace and Democracy, soon after the Indian and Pakistani tests were conducted, held demonstrations in cities in India and Pakistan at the same time. I think more and more of these sorts of exchanges between people in both countries where there is a common interest have to be encouraged. I think that can go a long way, in showing the governments what the people are thinking.

REKHA DATTA: ...I will add to what Ilmas has just said. The need for dialogue is very crucial. We are a people that share a common history. We should not be thinking in confrontational terms. We do as a result of an accident of history, and we need to realize that. I think there is real hesitation in creating a dialogue and that has to be overcome. A dialogue between the people, not just among policy-makers, is essential. Whether or not Ambassadors and Foreign Ministers are shaking hands and discussing for two hours is really not going to make a difference. That is why I emphasize the role of public opinion, which has until recently not become engaged on this issue. I am also familiar with the book *Public Opinion and Nuclear Options*, in the context of India and the bomb. There has not been a concerted effort on this issue. For a person who is worried about where their next meal is going to come from, nuclear weapons are a remote issue. When nuclear weapons are very skillfully packaged as an issue of national pride, governments have been able to sell them to the people.

So people do need to gather forces around this issue. The world has changed significantly in the last 50 years, particularly in the last ten or so years. I think there is a real opportunity for both India and Pakistan to throw aside the historical baggage of another generation, the animosity that the partition caused. I think there is hope. We have a new Japan, we have a new Germany, why not a new South Asia? And I am still looking for answers to that question.

ZIA MIAN: ...I want to say something more pessimistic. There is a sense in which Rekha is right to talk about a younger generation and the possibility of change, because independence came within the lifetimes of the people who run these countries now. It wasn't something that happened two or three generations ago. But young people have grown up in exactly the kinds of environments and atmospheres that these people have created for them to grow up in and it has been shaped significantly by an emerging move towards extreme right-wing nationalistic politics in both countries. The party that is in power now in India, ten or fifteen years ago had two or three members of Parliament. And this is the party that can be traced back to the people who killed Mahatma Gandhi directly. And yet, 50 years later, they are now running India. That is how far the Indian political process has come toward the right in allowing these people to actually take office.

If you look at the kinds of people that they summon up for support, a lot of them are urban, a lot of them are young, and a lot of them are male, and these are the same kinds of people that you see in Pakistan supporting the Islamic fundamentalist groups. And so in one sense the politically most mobilized communities and groups in both societies are actually young but they are extremely hostile to each other and don't want to take part in these dialogues.

The Pakistan-India People's Forum for Peace and Democracy tries to bring people together from both sides of the country and it is done often at great odds. When they had their first meeting in Pakistan after the nuclear tests a friend of mine stood up and spoke about why Pakistan shouldn't test these nuclear weapons. He is a professor of physics. And a bunch of young men in their early twenties, bearded and all the rest that comes with Islamic fundamentalism, attacked him. They tore onto a stage like this one and they beat him up for daring to suggest in public that it was a mistake to test nuclear weapons and that Pakistan should not do it.

Much as we may like to pin our hopes on young people, there is this fact that the most mobilized and the most militant and the most willing to become involved in politics are right wing and violent in both countries. That is a problem to keep in mind when you think about the possibilities for practical, grass-roots politics for organizing and getting people together, either for an electoral process or signing petitions. You are going to do it in extraordinarily hostile conditions. They will still do it, because they realize it is the right thing to do, but it will be uphill all the way.

The way to make it easier for them to do it is to show them that there are people around the world who support them and people who will go to their own governments and ask why are you going off to talk to the Pakistani military and trying to deal with them on nuclear weapons? Why aren't you going out there and supporting the peace movement? And if you are supporting their peace movement, why don't you listen to us as well about our nuclear weapons? And that is really the way in which you are going to be able to make the equation that can push this forward.

M.V. RAMANA: As the one panelist who hasn't taken a crack at this and also because I work with Zia - we share offices, practically - I must say a couple of things. For all his pessimism, Zia actually does all these things. He is a founder member of this Pakistan-India Peoples Forum for Peace and Democracy. He is involved in talking and writing and doing all these things. By and large, these are the things which we know how to do, and we do it.

The difference which he is trying to project is that you have to have your eye on the ball when you are doing these things, and the ball is a big one. It is not just getting rid of nuclear weapons. It is also linked with social justice, it is also linked with environment issues, it is also linked with poverty, communalism. I think you can not be focused just on one thing and ignore everything else and hope that this will work out.

HANNAH WASSERMAN, Peace Links: I have been blown away by what Zia had to say because I have been feeling it, but I haven't been that articulate...I don't think one has to say one is against democracy but one has to say it has to become real. I think one piece of this is to make individuals feel more important. The center is everywhere and we all matter.

RICHARD RUSAK, a student of history and political science at Monmouth University: Does the money organizations in India and Pakistan receive from western foundations come with any political or ideological baggage attached to it, and if so, how does this limit the goals of these organizations on this particular question?

ILMAS FUTEHALLY: Generally when you are working with a western foundation for a grant for a particular project it tends to go back and forth between the NGO and the person who is financing the project. The foundation has its own agenda, the NGO has its, and you go back and forth to work out something that both feel is worth doing. It depends on the NGO and on the foundation.

ZIA MIAN: Having worked for one for a few years in Pakistan, it actually is quite a straightforward process. Foundations have money to give away because they want to make the world the way they think it should be. And they will find somebody who will do it. If you go to them and say we will do this they will give you the money. If you do other things as well as that, up to a certain point they won't mind. If you then turn around and attack them as part of the problem, not part of the solution, then they take the money away.

It is exactly like the World Bank. People with resources to dole out, inevitably take this position. Since they are paying you to do what they think needs to be done, if you tell them we would be further towards the solution without you, they will find somebody else to do it their way. And so there is a difficult political relationship and it is important to realize there are many key groups in India and Pakistan like the People's Forum for Peace and Democracy that refuse to take money from foundations or from anybody except those people who are members by subscription and membership only. Nobody from outside should be in a position to participate in that process except from a position of complete equality. And that may well be the way to go as these issues become increasingly contentious, and the pressures that are brought to bear very significant.

I will leave you with this one example. Never mind a poor little NGO which is full of kind, well-meaning people and tries its best. The World Bank has now told Pakistan that if it wants money from the World Bank it will have to change its constitution. They want reform of the civil service and changes in government rules which will have all kinds of ramifications which the Bank has not seen fit to discuss with anyone...

SCOTT WEIZACKER, an anthropology major at Monmouth University: I agree with Zia that in the democratic systems that we have now there is a lot of room for error. But this can be countered with knowledge, the people's most important tool. Don't you think that we are talking about bringing more humanitarianism, intellectualism, secularism into this? Don't you think it is time for a more populist movement?

ZIA MIAN: One should focus on as many things as one can, and that takes away from the focus. That is why I talk about it as anti-systemic. It is not a bit here, a bit there. There is a coherent pattern, and you have to challenge the pattern. What you say about knowledge is true. This fundamentally hinges on knowledge. Power creates the conditions that makes certain kinds of knowledge possible, and it disallows the possibility of other kinds of knowledge, as Noam Chomsky argues.

What you have to ask yourself is why, in the US or Britain or France, where you have a free media, universal literacy, the ability to express your opinion and to find out anything you want, why is it that the United States is in the position it is, and given its power in the world, why it has exercised its power in the way that it has chosen to exercise that power? I think in part it is that people have been taught to think about these things in particular ways. And the question is, how do you challenge ways of thinking? The structure of knowledge is what it comes down to, rather than knowing a particular fact. It is a long argument about how this process has worked its way through...

There are movements in India, not quite barefoot science, to reach the lowest levels of society and help them educate themselves so that they are better able to exercise their rights within society. There is a need to find ways of self-organization by citizens. I agree with the importance of that kind of organization...We have learned a lot since the 1960s of how to make organizations open and democratic and participatory. A lot of hard work has to be done, but you have to be clear about where you want to go and not be sidetracked onto some of the issues that are held up as immediate and valuable...You should be looking to cut down the tree rather than taking an apple.

JIM GARST: ...I am old enough to remember the days when important debates in the Security Council were broadcast live on television and radio. I have lost track of the year when they closed out the open processes in the Security Council...China has not been brought into the discussion. There are disputed borders between India and China which have been the subject of armed conflict in the past. What is the role of China and perhaps of other nations in South Asia?

M. V. RAMANA: Relations between India and China have been improving in the last decades since the 1962 war. China is relatively happy with the way the borders are. It is India which is the aggrieved party...They have signed agreements to demilitarize the border and have adopted other confidence-building measures. Regarding other countries, there have been some initiatives to make things better. India and Bangladesh had a long-standing dispute over the sharing of river waters, the Ganges especially, and that was resolved during the previous government's time. There are also some issues between Nepal and India which have been partially resolved. There are still some problems.

REKHA DATTA: China is significant. As late as 1987 there have been confirmed reports of the assistance that China has been given to Pakistan for its nuclear technology and weapons programs. China continues to be an important player in the region.I am not so sure about China's intentions with India. I think China is marking its time. China is very much a part of the nuclear issue.

DIANE PEARLMAN: I am a clinical psychologist with Psychologists for Social Responsibility. I think professionals have a job to do...Psychologists need to attack the pathology...It is obvious that cultures that are gender split are more violent...

ZIA MIAN: ...The nuclear test is an expression symbolically and scientifically in space and time of a nuclear program but the facilities that made this test possible have poisoned the environment and contaminated that land for at least one if not several generations and there will be dozens of workers who will have been affected and some may die. There has been enormous disrespect for people who work in and around nuclear facilities. In the case of nuclear programs which are done in complete secrecy, because they know no one will check, national security is at stake - and let us remember the United States did secret experiments on its own people during the Cold War involving nuclear testing, allowing clouds of radioactive fallout to drift over cities just to see what they would do.

ANN HALLAN LAKHDHIR: Our thanks to all the participants, including the many in the audience who participated. We welcome contributions from any who read this transcript. We intend to hold further discussions focusing on South Asia. We append a statement written jointly by Zia Mian and M.V. Ramana, and the statement of Arundhati Roy.

Appendix III: Stepping Away from the Nuclear Abyss: Some Proposals, by Zia Mian and M.V. Ramana, Center for Energy and Environmental Studies, Princeton University, an article soon to appear also in the INESAP Bulletin.

Following the examples set over the last fifty years by the US and the other nuclear weapon states, the governments of India and Pakistan have now clearly chosen to rely on weapons of mass destruction and terror as the basis for their relationship with each other and the rest of the world. The nuclear tests they conducted in May 1998 and the accompanying political and military crisis raise genuine fears for the future of the people of South Asia. It is important therefore to understand some of the motivations and linkages that policy makers in the two countries work with and seek steps towards a safer future.

India's current Bharatiya Janata Party can be distinguished from other Indian political parties and traditions by the fact that its politics are based on a violent intolerance of religious and ethnic minorities and determination to forge a new, Hindu, India. Just as it has not hesitated to use violence for achieving domestic ends, it regards the development of military might as the means to ensure that it gets its way in international affairs. This is at the core of its decision to move so decisively and quickly after coming to power and ordering the nuclear tests. The tests marked a rupture with over two decades of successive Indian governments supporting the nuclear weapons infrastructure but procrastinating about going the whole hog. Despite the many security-related justifications offered, for the BJP, the tests had as much to do with national pride as with other factors. In the words of India's Minister of Science and Technology, the tests "reflected India's endeavors to find a rightful place among the World's powers."

Such remarks coming from the highest levels of Indian government suggest that the BJP may not settle for anything less than a fully nuclear India, i.e., with deployed nuclear weapons. Reports of work on a new longer-range Indian missile and a nuclear submarine suggest the possibility that a real Indian nuclear force is being pursued. This, combined with the current levels of development of nuclear weapons and ballistic missiles, make it unlikely that India's quest for a nuclear arsenal will be ended anytime soon.

Only if the nuclear weapon states genuinely moved to eliminate nuclear weapons would any Indian government be likely to consider nuclear disarmament. For in that case, India would have a status equal to that of the "great powers." Indeed, shortly after the nuclear tests of May, the Indian government called for a convention banning nuclear weapons. More recently, as part of the South Asian Association for Regional Cooperation (SAARC), India and Pakistan, along with other SAARC countries, called for the elimination of all nuclear weapons.

It is this perspective that suggests that while supporting reductions in nuclear arsenals of the nuclear weapon states, Indian political leaders are unlikely to accept serious restraints on India's programs prior to a clear commitment by the nuclear weapons states that they are indeed disarming. It should be said, however, that there is a segment among India's nuclear hawks, who have consistently espoused acquiring a full-fledged nuclear arsenal and opposed any restraint, who now see value in participating in arms control agreements that they had previously decried. Such participation now would, in their view, consolidate the gains they feel India made by carrying out its nuclear tests. India's hawks may become its arm controllers.

The position of Indian opponents of nuclear weapons is a far more principled one. In a recent comment, Praful Bidwai, a leading anti-nuclear intellectual and activist, condemned India's nuclear tests as "strategically irrational, politically outrageous and morally repugnant" and then went on to argue that India "should avoid the temptation of looking for devious bargains that...perpetuate nuclear weapon-states hegemonies and legitimize machtpolitik."

Pakistan's leaders have far simpler motivations and far smaller ambitions. For decades they have engaged in fearful competition with India, no matter how self-destructive. Pakistan's nuclear weapons were presented first as a counter to India's nuclear weapons, but have since become seen also as an 'equalizer" against India's conventional military superiority. In the wake of India's tests and the attendant belligerence by the BJP government, Pakistan's leaders took the opportunity offered them, an opportunity some of them had long hoped for, and followed suit. It is now hard to see Pakistan's leaders giving up nuclear weapons without some sense of maintaining parity with India, and even insisting on creating such parity when it comes to conventional weapons. Pakistan's refusal to agree to the No-First-Use proposal offered by India is a result of this perceived imbalance.

It is in this light that the linkage Pakistan's leaders make between their nuclear weapons and the Kashmir dispute needs to be seen. Kashmir is undoubtedly a major flashpoint, one that has led to wars in the past. The recent shelling across the border indicates that the nuclear tests conducted by India and Pakistan have not stopped the low intensity battle there, only the stakes have been raised. A settlement of the Kashmir dispute therefore seems vital as a way of reducing the risk of conflict escalating, perhaps inadvertently, into nuclear war.

However, there is a lesson to be learned from the persistence of massive nuclear arsenals in the US and Russia after the collapse of the Soviet Union - even where the apparent source of conflict between two states is removed. If these states have nuclear weapons and the weapons remain, so does the danger. The settlement of the Kashmir dispute may leave the same legacy. Settling Kashmir will also not remove the risk of war. The last war between India and Pakistan had nothing to do with Kashmir, and resulted in the largest number of casualties in any Indo-Pakistan war, the creation of Bangladesh from the former East Pakistan and 90,000 Pakistani prisoners of war.

Despite these reasons, if India does put caps on its nuclear program, Pakistan may well be forced to follow suit. Pakistan's smaller infrastructure and economy is simply not capable of living up to the international pressure that is sure to ensue in the event that India acquiesces to the various arms control proposals suggested. The announcement of even limited sanctions after its nuclear tests was sufficient to trigger a near collapse of the Pakistani economy and has caused widespread hardship.

Seeking Pakistani participation in arms control through the imposition of sanctions and other punitive measures is, however, fraught with dangers. The last decade has seen Pakistan start to show signs of a deep crisis of legitimacy as a state and in its social order. The polity is fragmenting into warring religious and ethnic sectarian groups who battle out their differences on the streets of its cities amid collapsing infrastructure and lack of even basic social services. Sanctions have only led to further erosion of state authority and an increase in the popularity of religious nationalist groups.

In this context it is significant that the radical Islamist groups were the most vociferous in demanding that Pakistan conduct nuclear tests and they have subsequently adopted the bomb as their own. What is important is that many within the Pakistani state, the military and within the nuclear weapons program have sympathies with one or the other of these groups. In such a situation, the state may not be able to ensure control over its nuclear weapons.

The site of conflict may not be restricted to Kashmir, even though Pakistan's Islamist groups have played an increasingly important role there in the struggle against Indian occupation. They are also drawn to other profound and long-standing instances of injustice, such as the annexation of Palestine. More broadly, the sanctions which have devastated Iraq and the pressures on Iran, presented largely in terms of containing proliferation "risks," are widely seen as little more than a way of maintaining the dominance in the Middle East of a nuclear-armed Israel. In such an international environment, it seems inevitable, despite the government insisting that their nuclear weapons are not an "Islamic bomb."

In light of the Indian state's insistence on some kind of parity with the Nuclear Weapon States, and the compulsions on Pakistan to follow despite socio-economic collapse, the challenge to the nuclear weapon states and those who would propose nuclear policies to them is to accept explicitly the need for nuclear disarmament and to begin fighting for it. This is undoubtedly a difficult challenge. But not as difficult as it once was. The peace movement and the non-nuclear weapon-states, which have struggled for decades to be heard, now find their arguments echoed by the likes of the former head of Strategic Command, Lee Butler, and other senior military and political figures from the nuclear weapon-states. It is also worth noting that on May 28, 1998, following the first set of nuclear tests by Pakistan, President Clinton said, "I cannot believe that we are about to start the 21st century by having the Indian subcontinent repeat the worst mistakes of the 20th century, when we know it is not necessary to peace, to security, to prosperity, to national greatness or personal fulfillment." This is perhaps the closest any US president has come to officially stating, albeit grudgingly and not focusing on US policies, that it is terribly wrong to believe that nuclear weapons are necessary for peace or security.

Steps Forward: Following India's tests the Prime Minister declared a moratorium on further nuclear tests. After its tests Pakistan made the same announcement. The positions of the two governments on signing the CTBT have been fluctuating. Recently at the UN both indicated a willingness to sign the test ban and help it enter into force, provided sanctions were lifted, and other publicly unspecified conditions met. There is, however, a danger that refusal or delay in meeting India and Pakistan's demands may lead to another round of tests. In all likelihood, as with France and China, after testing there would be prompt accession to the CTBT.

The other arms control measure that India and Pakistan have been encouraged to participate in is the Fissile Material Production Cutoff. Recently the Conference on Disarmament seems to have reached a breakthrough in getting India and Pakistan to agree to start negotiations on the FMCT. India has agreed to drop its condition that the FMCT be linked to a time-bound program of nuclear disarmament and Pakistan has agreed to negotiate on a treaty that would not consider past stockpiles. This is surprising and it is still to be seen if India and Pakistan maintain this new stance once negotiations start. Even after the tests, Pakistan's ambassador at the Conference on Disarmament has said, "as regards the FMCT, for Pakistan this issue is now dependent on India's nuclear status, its degree of weaponization and size and quality of its fissile material stockpiles. Pakistan cannot afford to allow India to once again destabilize the balance of deterrence in future through asymmetry in the level of stockpiles."

In the atmosphere of distrust prevailing in South Asia, this divergence of interest in the FMCT makes the possibility of both countries signing the FMCT unlikely for some time to come. Since negotiations over such a treaty would take a long time, especially given the difficulties that are bound to arise in India and Pakistan over verification and inspections, starting negotiations alone is not sufficient.

A way around this problem is for the Nuclear Weapon States, as part of preparing the ground for abolishing nuclear weapons, to formalize their existing moratoria on fissile material production and begin to place significant fractions of their fissile material under international safeguards. This would address India's long-standing concerns that safeguards were discriminatory unless the nuclear weapon states allowed their facilities to be inspected. At the same time India could be asked to put its nuclear power reactors under safeguards. Without the possibility of running its power reactors at low burn-up, Indian capacity to produce large amounts of fissile material and so quickly build up its stocks is limited (see A.H. Nayyar, A.H. Toor and Z.Mian, "Fissile Material Production Potential in South Asia, *Science and Global Security*, Vol. 6, No.2, 1997). This step gains in importance if it can be done soon, since India is scheduled to start reprocessing power reactor fuel at the new Kalpakkam Reprocessing Plant in the near future. In exchange for such a restriction on India's fissile material production capability, Pakistan could be asked to not begin operation of its new plutonium production reactor at Khushab.

These agreements in themselves do little to reduce the immediate sense of danger to the people of the two countries. The most such measures could do is to restrict the potential devastation that they could wreak on each other. The other set of measures that should be pursued in parallel relate to the weapons themselves.

Over the last few years, it has been proposed that the nuclear weapon states take their deployed weapons off alert and introduce measures that increase the time it would take to launch a strike. In the case of South Asia, it is believed that India and Pakistan have not yet placed their nuclear weapons on missiles or otherwise deployed them. With this in mind, it is possible to build on proposals for a verified system of de-alerting the nuclear warheads of the nuclear weapon-states. It may be fruitful to invite India to participate in the verification of such de-alerting. This would meet some of its aspirations for recognition by engaging it in a process otherwise restricted to nuclear weapons states. India would be a participant-observer in the disarmament process. It may also put to rest some of the BJP government's claimed concerns about China.

For its part, India could be asked to make an unverified commitment to keep its nuclear weapons de-mated as well as stop the testing and deployment of missiles, in particular the Agni missile, which is under development and which may allow it to threaten China. The relatively small size of the Indian arsenal means that India may be unlikely to accept full reciprocity in verification. In the current climate, if Nuclear Weapon States demand reciprocal verification, India may well opt out.

An Indian agreement with the nuclear-weapon-states freezing further development and deployment of its long-range missiles is likely to be seen as irrelevant by Pakistan. The contiguous border and the size and shape of Pakistan ensure that nearly all its major cities and military installations are within range of India's short range Prithvi missile. There would therefore need to be a parallel but overlapping bilateral agreement between India and Pakistan covering such missiles. One possibility would be for India to stop manufacture of its Prithvi missiles and agree to move its existing missiles to monitored storage far away from the border. In exchange, Pakistan would commit not to test or deploy long range missiles, such as the intermediate range Ghauri - which is justified by Pakistan's government as a response to Prithvi. The difference in size between India and Pakistan means such an arrangement could remove the immediate threat to Pakistan's major cities, while ensuring that Pakistan could not threaten any major part of India. The value of such a step for India is that despite public rhetoric in Pakistan, it is highly unlikely, that with just one test conducted so far, the Ghauri would be ready for deployment; halting future missile tests would therefore be significant.

The limited means available to both states and the importance they still attach to ambiguity about the numbers of nuclear weapons and missiles make verification of such an agreement very difficult. However, the absence of even limited trust between the two states makes verification vital, especially since it is claimed Pakistan may have short-range Chinese made M-11 missiles which it has so far chosen not to deploy. One possibility would be for a single cooperative monitoring center, or two co-located ones, with international satellites providing Indians and Pakistanis identical high resolution imaging data from a several hundred km-wide swath on both sides of the border. The exact width of the swath could be such as to ensure that neither Prithvi nor the M-11 could be deployed close enough to the border to be able to threaten significant areas of the other state without being detected.

Since both India and Pakistan could deliver their nuclear weapons by aircraft, any arrangement would have to cover not just missile development and deployment, but also airbases. India and Pakistan could simply agree to monitor activity at airbases through inspections. This proposal, again, is only likely to create stability until the next crisis. The only certain way to prevent the deployment and possible use of nuclear weapons in South Asia as elsewhere is the absolute and unconditional abolition of nuclear weapons.

Appendix IV: Excerpts from "The End of Imagination" by Arundhati Roy, author of *The God of Small Things*, which won the Brooker prize, on India's Nuclear Bomb, as published in Outlook, a magazine published in India, on August 3, 1998

"My world has died. I write to mourn its passing."

"The desert shook," the Government of India informed us (its people).

"The whole mountain turned white," the Government of Pakistan replied.

"By afternoon the wind had fallen silent over Pokhran. At 3:45pm, the timer detonated the three devices. Around 200 to 300 m deep in the earth, the heat generated was equivalent to a million degrees centigrade - as hot as temperatures on the sun. Instantly, rocks weighing around a thousand tons, a mini mountain underground, vapourised...shock waves from the blast began to lift a mound of earth the size of a football field by several metres. One scientist on seeing it said 'I can now believe stories of Lord Krishna lifting a hill'." - India Today.

May 1998. It'll go down in history books, provided, of course we have history books to go down in. Provided, of course, we have a future. There's nothing new or original left to be said about nuclear weapons. There can be nothing more humiliating for a writer of fiction to have to do than restate a case that has, over the years, already been made by other people in other parts of the world, and made passionately, eloquently and knowledgeably.

I am prepared to grovel. To humiliate myself abjectly, because in the circumstances, silence would be indefensible. So those of you who are willing: let's pick our parts, put on these discarded costumes and speak our second-hand lines in this sad second-hand play. But let's not forget that the stakes we're playing for are huge. Our fatigue and our shame could mean the end of us. The end of our children and our children's children. Of everything we love. We have to reach within ourselves and find the strength to think. To fight.

Once again we are pitifully behind the times - not just scientifically and technologically (ignore the hollow claims), but more pertinently in our ability to grasp the true nature of nuclear weapons. Our Comprehensive of the Horror Department is hopelessly obsolete. Here we are all of us in India and in Pakistan, discussing the finer points of politics, and foreign policy, behaving for all the world as though our governments have just devised a newer, bigger bomb, a sort of immense hand grenade with which they will annihilate the enemy (each other) and protect us from all harm. How desperately we want to believe that. What wonderful, willing, well-behaved, gullible subjects we have turned out to be. The rest of humanity (Yes, yes, I know, I know, but let's ignore Them for the moment. They forfeited their votes a long time ago), the rest of the rest of humanity may not forgive us, but then the rest of the rest of humanity, depending on who fashions its views, may not know what a tired, dejected, heart-broken people we are. Perhaps it doesn't realise how urgently we need a miracle. How deeply we yearn for magic.

If only, if only, nuclear war was just another kind of war. If only it was about the usual things - nations and territories, gods and histories. If only those of us who dread it are just worthless moral cowards who are not prepared to die in defence of our beliefs. If only nuclear war was the kind of war in which countries battle countries and men battle men. But it isn't. If there is a nuclear war, our foes will not be China or America or even each other. Out foe will be the earth herself. The very elements - the sky, the air, the land, the wind and water - will all turn against us. Their wrath will be terrible.

Our cities and forests, our fields and villages will burn for days. Rivers will turn to poison. The air will become fire. The wind will spread the flames. When everything there is to burn has burned and the fires die, smoke will rise and shut out the sun. The earth will be enveloped in darkness. There will be no day. Only interminable night. Temperatures will drop to far below freezing and nuclear winter will set in. Water will turn into toxic ice. Radioactive fallout will seep through the earth and contaminate groundwater. Most living things, animal and vegetable, fish and fowl, will die. Only rats and cockroaches will breed and multiply and compete with foraging, relict humans for what little food there is.

What shall we do then, those of us who are still alive? Burned and blind and bald and ill, carrying the cancerous carcasses of our children in our arms, where shall we go? What shall we eat? What shall we drink? What shall we breathe?

The Head of the Health, Environment and Safety Group of the Bhabha Atomic Research Centre in Bombay has a plan. He declared in an interview (The Pioneer, April 24, 1998) that India could survive nuclear war. We take the same safety measures as the ones that scientists have recommended in the event of accidents at nuclear plants. Take iodine pills, he suggests. And other steps such as remaining indoors, consuming only stored water and food and avoiding milk. Infants should be given powdered milk. "People in the danger zone should immediately go the ground floor and if possible to the basement."

What do you do with these levels of lunacy? What do you do if you're trapped in an asylum and the doctors are all dangerously deranged?

Ignore it. It's just a novelist's naivete, they'll tell you, Doomsday Prophet hyperbole. It'll never come to that. There will be no war. Nuclear weapons are about peace and not war. 'Deterrence' is the buzz word of the people who like to think of themselves as hawks. (Nice birds, those. Cool. Stylish. Predatory. Pity there won't be many of them around after the war. Extinction is a word we must try and get used to.) Deterrence is an old thesis that has been resurrected and is being recycled with added local flavor. The theory of Deterrence cornered the credit for having prevented the Cold War from turning into the Third World War. The only immutable fact about The Third World War is that if there is going to be one, it will be fought after the Second World War. In other words, there's no fixed schedule, we still have time. And perhaps the pun (The Third World War) is prescient. True, the Cold War is over, but let's not be hoodwinked by the ten-year lull in nuclear posturing. It was just a cruel joke. It was only in remission, it wasn't cured. It proves no theories. After all, what is ten years in the history of the world? Here it is again, the disease. More widespread, and less amenable to any sort of treatment that ever. No, the Theory of Deterrence has some fundamental flaws.

Flaw Number One is that it presumes a complete, sophisticated understanding of the psychology of your enemy. It assumes that what deters you (the fear of annihilation) will deter them. What about those who are not deterred by that? The suicide bomber psyche - the "We'll take you with us school" - is that an outlandish thought? How did Rajiv Gandhi die? In any case who's the 'you' and who's the 'enemy'? Both are only governments. Governments change. They wear masks within masks. They molt and re-invent themselves all the time. The one we have at the moment, for instance, does not even have enough seats to last a full term in office, but demands that we trust it to do pirouettes and party tricks with nuclear bombs even as it scrabbles around for a foothold to maintain a simple majority in Parliament.

Flaw Number Two is that Deterrence is premised on fear. But fear is premised on knowledge. On an understanding of the true extent and scale of the devastation that nuclear war will wreak. It is not some inherent, mystical attribute of nuclear bombs that they automatically inspire thoughts of peace. On the contrary, it is the endless, tireless, confrontational work of people who have had the courage to openly denounce them, the marches, the demonstrations, the films, the outrage - that is what has averted, or perhaps only postponed nuclear war. Deterrence will not and cannot work given the levels of ignorance and illiteracy that hang over our two countries like dense, impenetrable veils. (Witness the vhp wanting to distribute radioactive sand from the Pokhran desert as prasad all across India. a cancer yatra?) The Theory of Deterrence is nothing but a perilous joke in a world where iodine pills are prescribed as a prophylactic for nuclear irradiation.

India and Pakistan have nuclear bombs now and feel entirely justified in having them. Soon others will too. Israel, Iran, Iraq, Saudi Arabia, Norway, Nepal (I'm trying to be eclectic here), Denmark, Germany, Bhutan, Mexico, Lebanon, Sri Lanka, Burma, Bosnia, Singapore, North Korea, Sweden, South Korea, Vietnam, Cuba, Afghanistan, Uzbekistan...and why not? Every country in the world has a special case to make. Everybody has borders and beliefs. And when all our larders are bursting with shiny bombs and our bellies are empty (Deterrence is an exorbitant beast), we can trade bombs for food. And when nuclear technology goes on the market, when it gets truly competitive and prices fall, not just governments, but anybody who can afford it can have their own private arsenal - businessmen, terrorists, perhaps even the occasional rich writer (like myself). Our planet will bristle with beautiful missiles.

There will be a new world order. The dictatorship of the pro-nuke elite. We can get our kicks by threatening each other. It'll be like bungee-jumping when you can't rely on the bungee cord, or playing Russian roulette all day long. An additional perk will be the thrill of Not Knowing What To Believe. We can be victims of the predatory imagination of every green card-seeking charlatan who surfaces in the West with concocted stories of imminent missile attacks. We can delight at the prospect of being held to ransom by every petty troublemaker and rumour-monger, the more the merrier if truth be told, anything for an excuse to make more bombs. So you see, even without a war, we have a lot to look forward to.

But let us pause to give credit where it's due. Whom must we thank for all this?

The Men who made it happen. The Masters of the Universe. Ladies and gentlemen. The United States of America! Come on up here folks, stand up and take a bow. Thank you for doing this to the world. Thank you for making a difference. Thank you for showing us the way. Thank you for altering the very meaning of life.

From now on it is not dying we must fear but living. It is such supreme folly to believe that nuclear weapons are deadly only if they're used. The fact that they exist at all, their very presence in our lives, will wreak more havoc than we can begin to fathom. Nuclear weapons pervade our thinking. Control our behaviour. Administer our societies, inform our dreams. They bury themselves like meat hooks deep in the base of our brains. They are purveyors of madness. They are the ultimate colonizer. Whiter than any white man that ever lived. The very heart of whiteness.

All I can say to every man, woman and sentient child here in India and over there, just a little way away in Pakistan, is, Take it personally. Whoever you are - Hindu, Muslim, urban, agrarian, - it doesn't matter. The only good thing about nuclear war is that it is the single most egalitarian idea that man has ever had. On the day of reckoning, you will not be asked to present your credentials. The devastation will be indiscriminating. The bomb isn't in your backyard. It's in your body. And mine. Nobody, no nation, no government, no man, no god, has the right to put it there. We're radioactive already, and the war hasn't even begun. So stand up and say something. Never mind if it's been said before. Speak up on your own behalf. Take it very personally...

(*Arundhati Roy was not in India at the time of the nuclear tests.*)...I returned to India. To what I think/thought of as home. Something had died, but it wasn't me. It was infinitely more precious. It was a world that has been ailing for a while, and has finally breathed its last. It's been cremated now. The air is thick with ugliness and there's the unmistakable stench of fascism on the breeze.

Day after day, in newspaper editorials, on the radio, on TV chat shows, on mtv, for heaven's sake, people whose instincts one thought one could trust - writers, painters, journalists - make the crossing. The chill seeps into my bones as it becomes painfully apparent from the lessons of everyday life that what you read in history books is true. That fascism is indeed as much about people as about governments. That it begins at home in drawing rooms, in bedrooms, in beds. "Explosion of self-esteem,""Road to Resurgence," "a Moment of Pride," these were headlines in the papers in the days following the nuclear tests. "We have proved that we are not eunuchs any more," said Mr. Thackeray of the Shiv Sena. (Whoever said we were? True, a number of us are women, but that, as far as I know, isn't the same thing.) Reading the papers, it was often hard to tell when people were referring to Viagra (which was competing for second place on the front pages) and when they were talking about the bomb - "We have superior strength and potency." (This was our Minister for Defence after Pakistan completed its tests.)

"These are not just nuclear tests, they are nationalism tests," we were repeatedly told.

This has been hammered home, over and over again. The bomb is India, India is the bomb. Not just India, Hindu India. Therefore, be warned, any criticism of its is not just anti-national, but anti-Hindu. (Of course, in Pakistan, the bomb is Islamic. Other than that, politically, the same physics applies.) This is one of the unexpected perks of having a nuclear bomb. Not only can the Government use it to threaten the Enemy, they can use it to declare war on their own people. Us.

In 1975, one year after India first dipped her toe into the nuclear sea, Mrs. Gandhi declared the Emergency. What will 1999 bring? There's talk of cells being set up to monitor anti-national activity. Talk of amending cable laws to ban networks "harming national culture" (*The Indian Express*, July 3). Of churches being struck off the list of religious places because "wine is served" (announced and retracted, *The Indian Express*, July 3, *The Times of India*, July 4). Artists, writers, actors, and singers are being harassed, threatened (and succumbing to the threats). Not just by goon squads, but by instruments of the government. And in courts of law. There are letters and articles circulating on the Net - creative interpretations of Nostradamus' predictions claiming that a mighty all-conquering Hindu nation is about to emerge - a resurgent India that will "burst forth upon its former oppressors and destroy them completely." That "the beginning of the terrible revenge (that will wipe out all Moslems) will be in the seventh month of 1999." This may well be the work of some lone nut, or a bunch of arcane god-squadders. The trouble is that having a nuclear bomb makes thoughts like these seem feasible. It creates thoughts like these. It bestows on people these utterly misplaced, utterly deadly notions of their own power. It's happening. It's all happening. I wish I could say "slowly but surely" but I can't. Things are moving at a pretty fair clip.

Why does it all seem so familiar? Is it because, even as you watch, reality dissolves and seamlessly rushes forward into the silent, black and white images from old films - scenes of people being hounded out of their lives, rounded up and herded into camps. Of massacre, of mayhem, or endless columns of broken people making their way to nowhere? Why is there no sound-track? Why is the hall so quiet? Have I been seeing too many films? Am I mad? Or am I right? Could those images be the inevitable culmination of what we have set into motion? Could our future be rushing forward into our past? I think so. Unless, of course, nuclear war settles it once and for all.

When I told my friends that I was writing this piece, they cautioned me. "Go ahead," they said, "but first make sure you're not vulnerable. Make sure your papers are in order. Make sure your taxes are paid." My papers are in order. My taxes are paid. But how can one not be vulnerable in a climate like this? Everyone is vulnerable. Accidents happen. There's safety only in acquiescence. As I write, I am filled with foreboding in the country. I have truly known what it means for a writer to feel loved (and to some degree, hated too). Last year I was one of the items being paraded in the media's end-of-the year National Pride Parade. Among the others, much to my mortification, were a bomb-maker and an international beauty queen. Each time a beaming person stopped me on the street and said "You have made India proud" (referring to the prize I won, not the book I wrote), I felt a little uneasy. It frightened me then and it terrifies me now, because I know how easily that swell, that tide of emotion, can turn against me. Perhaps the time has come. I'm going to step out from under the fairy lights and say what's on my mind.

It's this. If protesting against having a nuclear bomb implanted in my brain is anti-Hindu and anti-national, then I secede. I hereby declare myself an independent, mobile republic. I am a citizen of the earth. I own no territory. I have no flag. I'm female, but have nothing against eunuchs. My policies are simple. I'm willing to sign any nuclear non-proliferation treaty or nuclear test ban treaty that's going. Immigrants are welcome. You can help me design our flag.

My world has died. And I write to mourn its passing. Admittedly it was a flawed world. An unviable world, a scarred and wounded world. It was a world that I myself have criticised unsparingly, but only because I loved it. It didn't deserve to die. It didn't deserve to be dismembered. Forgive me, I realise that sentimentality is uncool - but what shall I do with my desolation?

I loved it simply because it offered humanity a choice. It was a rock out at sea. It was a stubborn chink of light that insisted that there was a different way of living. It was a functioning possibility. a real option. All that's gone now. India's nuclear tests, the manner in which they were conducted, the euphoria with which they have been greeted (by us) is indefensible. To me, it signifies dreadful things.

The end of imagination. The end of freedom actually, because, after all, that's what freedom is. Choice.

On the 15th of August last year we celebrated the fiftieth anniversary of India's independence. Next May we can mark our first anniversary in nuclear bondage. Why did they do it?

Political expediency is the obvious, cynical answer, except that it only raises another, more basic question: Why should it have been politically expedient? The three Official Reasons given are China, Pakistan and Exposing Western Hypocrisy. Taken at face value, and examined individually, they're somewhat baffling. I'm not for a moment suggesting that these are not real issues. Merely that they aren't new. The only new thing on the old horizon is the Indian Government. In his appallingly cavalier letter to the US President (why bother to write at all if you're going to write like this?) Our Prime Minister says India's decision to go ahead with the nuclear tests was due to a "deteriorating security environment." He goes on to mention the war with China in 1962 and the "three aggressions we have suffered in the last fifty years (from Pakistan). And for the last ten years we have been the victim of unremitting terrorism and militancy sponsored by it...especially in Jammu and Kashmir."

The war with China is thirty-five years old. Unless there's some vital state secret that we don't know about, it certainly seemed as though matters had improved slightly between us. Just a few days before the nuclear tests General Fu Quanyou, chief of General Staff of the Chinese People's Liberation Army, was the guest of our Chief of Army Staff. We heard no words of war.

The most recent war with Pakistan was fought twenty-seven years ago. Admittedly Kashmir continues to be a deeply troubled region and no doubt Pakistan is gleefully fanning the flames. But surely there must be flames to fan in the first place? Surely the kindling is crackling and ready to burn? Can the Indian State with even a modicum of honesty absolve itself completely of having a hand in Kashmir's troubles? Kashmir, and for that matter, Assam, Tripura, Nagaland - virtually the whole of the Northeast - Jharkhand, Uttarakhand and all the trouble that's still to come - these are symptoms of a deeper malaise. It cannot and will not be solved by pointing nuclear missiles at Pakistan.

Even Pakistan can't be solved by pointing nuclear missiles at Pakistan. Though we are separate countries, we share skies, we share winds, we share water. Where radioactive fallout will land on any given day depends on the direction of the wind and rain. Lahore and Amritsar are thirty miles apart. If we bomb Lahore, Punjab will burn. If we bomb Karachi - then Gujarat and Rajasthan, perhaps even Bombay, will burn. Any nuclear war with Pakistan will be a war against ourselves.

As for the third Official Reason: Exposing Western Hypocrisy - how much more exposed can they be? Which decent human being on earth harbours any illusions about it? These are people whose histories are spongy with the blood of others. Colonialism, apartheid, slavery, ethnic cleansing, germ warfare, chemical weapons - they virtually invented it all. They have plundered nations, shuffled out civilizations, exterminated entire populations. They stand on the world's stage stark naked but entirely unembarrassed, because they know that they have more money, more food and bigger bombs than anybody else. They know they can wipe us out in the course of an ordinary working day. Personally, I'd say it is more arrogance than hypocrisy.

We have less money, less food and smaller bombs. However, we have, or had, all kinds of other wealth. Delightful, unquantifiable,. What we've done with it is the opposite of what we think we've

338

done. We've pawned it all. We've traded it in. For what? In order to enter into a contract with the very people we claim to despise in the larger scheme of things, we've agreed to play their game and play it their way. We've accepted their terms and conditions unquestioningly. The ctbt ain't nothin' compared to this.All in all, I think it is fair to say that we're the hypocrites. We're the ones who've abandoned what was arguably a moral position, i.e.: We have the technology, we can make bombs if we want to, but we won't. We don't believe in them.

We're the ones who have now set up this craven clamouring to be admitted into the club of Superpowers. (If we are, we will no doubt gladly slam the door after us, and say to hell with the principles about fighting Discriminatory World Orders.) For India to demand the status of a Superpower is as ridiculous as demanding to play in the World Cup finals simply because we have a ball. Never mind that we haven't qualified, or that we don't play much soccer and haven't got a team. Since we've chosen to enter the arena, it might be an idea to begin by learning the rules of the game. Rule number one is Acknowledge the Masters. Who are the best players" The ones with more money, more food, more bombs.

Rule number two is Locate Yourself in Relation to Them, i.e.: Make an honest assessment of your position and abilities. The honest assessment of ourselves (in quantifiable terms) reads as follows:

We are a nation of nearly a billion people. In development terms we rank No. 138 out of the 175 countries listed in the UNDP's Human Development Index. More than 400 million of our people are illiterate and live in absolute poverty. Over 600 million lack even basic sanitation and over 200 million have no safe drinking water.

So the three Official Reasons, taken individually, don't hold much water. However, if you link them, a kind of twisted logic reveals itself. It has more to do with us than them.

The key words in our Prime Minister's letter to the US President were "suffered" and "victim." That's the substance of it. That's our meat and drink. We need to feel like victims. We need to feel beleaguered. We need enemies. We have so little sense of ourselves as a nation and therefore constantly cast about for targets to define ourselves against. Prevalent political wisdom suggests that to prevent the State from crumbling, we need a national cause, and other than our currency (and, of course, poverty, illiteracy and elections), we have none. This is the heart of the matter. This is the road that has led us to the bomb. This search for selfhood. If we are looking for a way out, we need some honest answers to some uncomfortable questions. Once again, it isn't as though these questions haven't been asked before. It's just that we prefer to mumble the answers and hope that no one's heard.

Is there such a thing as an Indian identity? Do we really need one? Who is an authentic Indian and who isn't? Is India Indian? Does it matter?

Whether or not there has ever been a single civilisation that could call itself "Indian Civilisation," whether or not India was, is, or ever will become a cohesive cultural entity, depends on whether you dwell on the differences or the similarities in the cultures of the people who have inhabited the subcontinent for centuries. India, as a modern nation state, was marked out with precise geographical boundaries, in their precise geographical way, by a British Act of Parliament in 1899. Our country, as we know it, was forged on t he anvil of the British Empire for the entirely unsentimental reasons of commerce and administration. But even as she was born, she began her struggle against her creators. So is India Indian? It's a tough question. Let's just say that we're an ancient people learning to live in a recent nation.

What is true is that India is an artificial State - a State that was created by a government, not a people. a State created from the top down, not the bottom up. The majority of India's citizens will not (to this day) be able to identify her boundaries on a map, or say which language is spoken where or which god is worshiped in what region. Most are too poor and too uneducated to have even an elementary idea of the extent and complexity of their own country. The impoverished, illiterate, agrarian majority have no stake in the State. And indeed, why should they, how can they, when they don't even know what the State is? To them, India is, at best, a noisy slogan that comes around during the elections. Or a montage of people on government TV programmes wearing regional costumes and saying Mera Bharat Mahan.

The people who have a vital stake (or more to the point, a business interest) in India, having a single, lucid, cohesive national identity are the politicians who constitute our national political parties. The reason isn't far to seek. It's simply because their struggle, their career goal, is - and must necessarily be - to become that identity. To be identified with that identity, if there isn't one, they have to manufacture one and persuade people to vote for it. It isn't their fault. It comes with the territory. It is inherent in the nature of our system of centralised government. a congenital defect in our particular brand of democracy. The greater the numbers of illiterate people, the poorer the country and the more morally bankrupt the politicians, the cruder the ideas of what that identity should be. In a situation like this, illiteracy is not just sad, it's downright dangerous. However, to be fair, cobbling together a viable pre-digested "National Identity" for India would be a formidable challenge even for the wise and the visionary. Every single Indian citizen could, if he or she wants to, claim to belong to some minority or the other. The fissures, if you look for them, run vertically, horizontally, layered, whoried, circular, spiral, inside out and outside in. Fires when they're lit race along any one of these schisms, and in the process, release tremendous bursts of political energy. Not unlike what happens when you split the atom.

It is this energy that Gandhi sought to harness when he rubbed the magic lamp and invited Ram and Rahim to partake of human politics and India's war of independence against the British. It was a sophisticated, magnificent, imaginative struggle, but its objective was simple and lucid, the target visible, easy to identify and succulent with political sin. In the circumstances, the energy found an easy focus. The trouble is that the circumstances are entirely changed now, but the genie is out of the lamp, and won't go back in. (It could be sent back, but nobody wants it to go, it's proved itself too useful.) Yes, it won us freedom. But it also won us the carnage of Partition. And now, in the hands of lesser statesmen, it has won us the Hindu Nuclear Bomb.

To be fair to Gandhi, and to other leaders of the National Movement, they did not have the benefit of hindsight and could not possibly have known what the eventual, long-term consequences of their strategy would be. They could not have predicted how quickly the situation would careen out of control They could not have foreseen what would happen when they passed their flaming torches into the hands of their successors, or how venal those hands could be.

It was Indira Gandhi who started the real slide. It is she who made the genie a permanent State Guest. She injected the venom into our political veins. She invented our particularly vile local brand of political expediency. She showed us how to conjure enemies out of thin air, to fire at phantoms that she had carefully fashioned for that very purpose. It was she who discovered the benefits of never burying the idea, but preserving their putrid carcasses and trundling them out to worry old wounds when it suited her. Between herself and her sons she managed to bring the country to its knees. Our new Government has just kicked us over and arranged our heads on the chopping block.

The BJP is, in some senses, a spectre that Indira Gandhi and the Congress created. Or, if you want to be less harsh, a spectre that fed and reared itself in the political spaces and communal suspicion that the Congress nourished and cultivated. It has put a new complexion on the politics of governance. While Mrs. Gandhi played hidden games with politicians and their parties, she reserved a shrill convent school rhetoric, replete with tired platitudes, to address the general public. The B.J.P., on the other hand, has chosen to light its fires directly on the streets, and in the homes and hearts of people. It is prepared to do by day what the Congress would do only by night. To legitimise what was previously considered unacceptable (but done anyway). There is perhaps a fragile case to be made here in favour of hypocrisy. Could the hypocrisy of the Congress Party, the fact that they conduct their wretched affairs surreptitiously instead of openly, could that possibly means there is a tiny glimmer of guilt somewhere? Some small fragment of remembered decency?

Actually, no. No. What am I doing? Why am I foraging for scraps of hope?

The way it has worked in the case of the demolition of the Babri Masjid as well as in the making of the nuclear bomb - is that the Congress sowed the seeds, tended the crop, then the B.P. stepped in and reaped the hideous harvest. They waltz together, locked in each others' arms. They're inseparable, despite their professed differences. Between them they have brought us here, to this dreadful, dreadful place.

The jeering, hooting young men who battered down the Babri Masjid are the same ones whose pictures appeared in the papers in the days that followed the nuclear tests. They were on the streets, celebrating India's nuclear bomb and simultaneously condemning Western Culture by emptying crates of Coke and Pepsi into public drains. I'm a little baffled by their logic. Coke is Western Culture, but the nuclear bomb is an old Indian tradition?

Yes, I've heard the bomb is in the Vedas. It might be, but if you look hard enough, you'll find Coke in the Vedas too. That's the great thing about all religious texts. You can find anything you want in them - as long as you know what you're looking for.

But returning to the subject of the non-vedic nineteen nineties. We storm the heart of whiteness, we embrace the most diabolical creation of western science and call it our own. But we protest against their music, their food, their clothes, their cinema and their literature. That's not hypocrisy. That's humour. It's funny enough to make a skull smile. We're back on the old ship. The S.S. Authenticity & Indianness. If there is going to be a pro-authenticity/anti-national drive, perhaps the government ought to get its history straight and its facts right. If they're going to do it, they may as well do it properly.

First of all, the original inhabitants of this land were not Hindu. Ancient though it is, there were human beings on earth before there was Hinduism. India's tribal people have a greater claim to being indigenous to this land than anybody else, and how are they treated by the State and its minions? Oppressed, cheated, robbed of their lands, shunted around like surplus goods. Perhaps a good place to start would be to restore to them the dignity that was once theirs. Perhaps the Government could make a public undertaking that more dams like the Sardar Sarovar on the Narmada will not be built, that more people will not be displaced.

But, of course, that would be inconceivable, wouldn't it? Why? Because it's impractical. Because tribal people don't really matter. Their histories, their customs, their deities are dispensable. They must learn to sacrifice these things for the greater good of the Nation (that has snatched from everything they ever had).

Okay, so that's out. For the rest I could compile a practical list of things to ban and buildings to break. It'll need some research, but off the top of my head, here are a few suggestions.

They could begin by banning a number of ingredients from our cuisine: chillies (Mexico), tomatoes (Peru), potatoes (Bolivia), coffee (Morocco), tea, white sugar, cinnamon (China)...they could then move into recipes. Tea with milk and sugar, for instance (Britain). Smoking will be out of the question. Tobacco came from North America. Cricket, English and Democracy should be forbidden. Either kabaddi or kho-kho could replace cricket. I don't want to start a riot, so I hesitate to suggest a replacement for English (Italian...? It has found its way to us via a kinder route: Marriage, not imperialism). We have already discussed (earlier in this essay) the emerging, apparently acceptable alternative to democracy.

All hospitals in which western medicine is practised or prescribed should be shut down. All national newspapers discontinued. The railways dismantled. Airports closed. And what about our newest toy - the mobile phone? Can we live without it, or shall I suggest that they make an exception there? They could put it down in the column marked 'Universal'? (Only essential commodities will be included here. No music, art or literature.)

Needless to say sending your children to university in the US, and rushing there yourself to have your prostate operated upon will be a cognizable offence. The building demolition drive could begin with the Rashtrapati bhavan and gradually spread from cities to the countryside, culminating in the destruction of all monuments (mosques, churches, temples) that were built on what was once tribal or forest land. It will be a long list. It would take years of work. I couldn't use a computer because that wouldn't be very authentic of me, would it?

I don't mean to be facetious, merely to point out that this is surely the shortcut to hell. There's no such thing as an Authentic India or a real Indian. There is no Divine Committee that has the right to sanction one single, authorised version of what India is or should be. There is no one religion or language or caste or region or person or story or book that can claim to be its sole representative. There are, and can only be, visions of India, various ways of seeing it - honest, dishonest, wonderful, absurd, modern, traditional, male, female. They can be argued over, criticised, praised, scorned, but not banned or broken. Not hunted down.

Railing against the past will not heal us. History has happened. It's over and done with. All we can do is to change its course by encouraging what we love instead of destroying what we don't. There is beauty yet in this brutal, damaged world of ours. Hidden, fierce, immense. Beauty that is uniquely ours and beauty that we have received with grace from others, enhanced, re-invented and made our own. We have to seek it out, nurture it, love it. Making bombs will only destroy us. It doesn't matter whether we use them or not. They will destroy us either way.

India's nuclear bomb is the final act of betrayal by a ruling class that has failed its people.

However many garlands we heap on our scientists, however many medals we pin to their chests, the truth is that it's far easier to make a bomb than to educate four hundred million people.

According to opinion polls, we're expected to believe that there's a national consensus on the issue. It's official now. Everybody loves the bomb. (Therefore the bomb is good.)

Is it possible for a man who cannot write his own name to understand even the basic, elementary facts about the nature of nuclear weapons? Has anybody told him that nuclear war has nothing at all to do with his received notions of war? Nothing to do with honour, nothing to do with pride. Has anybody bothered to explain to him about thermal blasts, radioactive fallout and the nuclear winter? Are there even words in his language to describe the concepts of enriched uranium, fissile material and critical mass? Or has his language itself become obsolete? Is he trapped in a time capsule, watching the world pass him by, unable to understand or communicate with it because his language never took into account the horrors that the human race would dream up? Does he not matter at all, this man? Shall we just treat him like some kind of a cretin? If he asks any questions, ply him with iodine pills and parables about how Lord Krishna lifted a hill or how the destruction of Lanka by Hanuman was unavoidable in order to preserve Sita's virtue and Ram's reputation? Use his own beautiful stories as weapons against him? Shall we release him from his capsule only during elections, and once he's voted, shake him by the hand, flatter him with some bullshit about the Wisdom of the Common Man, and send him right back in?

I'm not talking about one man of course. I'm talking about millions and millions of people who live in this country. This is their land too, you know. They have the right to make an informed decision about its fate and, as far as I can tell, nobody has informed them about anything. The tragedy is that nobody could, even if they wanted to. Truly, literally, there's no language to do it in. This is the real horror of India. The orbits of the powerful and the powerless spinning further and further apart from each other, never intersecting, sharing nothing. Not a language, Not even a country.

Who the hell conducted those opinion polls? Who the hell is the Prime Minister to decide whose finger will be on the nuclear button that could turn everything we love - our earth, our skies, our mountains, our plains, our rivers, our cities and villages - to ask in an instant? Who the hell is he to reassure us that there will be no accidents? How does he know? Why should we trust him? What has he ever done to make us trust him? What have any of them ever done to make us trust them?

The nuclear bomb is the most anti-democratic, anti-national, anti-human, outright evil thing that man has ever made. If you are religious, then remember that this bomb is Man's challenge to God. It's worded quite simply. We have the power to destroy everything that You have created. If you're not (religious), then look at it this way. This world of ours is four thousand six hundred million years old. It could end in an afternoon.

RELIGIOUS LEADERS SPEAK ON NUCLEAR WEAPONS

MODERATOR: SEN. DOUGLAS ROCHE of Canada: This afternoon we will focus on the moral questions raised by the continuation of nuclear weapons in the modern world. We have assembled here religious leaders who will address this topic. There is what one might call ecumenical concern about the moral issues that humanity must deal with regard to nuclear weapons, and it will be well worth our attention. I call on Dr. Vendley, the Secretary General of the World Conference on Religion and Peace, a primary sponsor of this event, to open it.

DR. WILLIAM VENDLEY: Mr. Moderator, distinguished members of the panel, and friends, it is my pleasure to open this symposium which signals the depth of the on-going collaboration on the issue of the non proliferation of nuclear weapons. This panel before you today is a result of the combined efforts of the NGO Committee on Disarmament, Pax Christi International, the Interfaith Center of New York, Franciscans International, and the World Conference on Religion and Peace. It demonstrates our grave moral concern that the proliferation of nuclear weapons endangers the life and security of all humankind, threatens global and regional stability, and undermines peaceful coexistence among states.

Permit me to introduce our moderator. Senator Douglas Roche was Canada's Ambassador for Disarmament from 1984 though 1989. He was elected Chairman of the United Nations Disarmament Committee, a main UN body dealing with political and security issues at the 43rd General Assembly. During the course of his career, Senator Roche has contributed significantly to the field of disarmament and it is a great honor to have him lead our discussion this afternoon. Thank you, and now I give the floor to our moderator, Senator Roche.

DOUGLAS ROCHE: Thank you, Dr. Vendley. I have the honor first to present His Excellency Archbishop Renato Martino, Permanent Observer of the Holy See to the United Nations since 1987. I can assure you not many Ambassadors survive thirteen years in this arduous posting. Archbishop Martino has intervened on disarmament questions in the First Committee of the UN and is a committed promoter of disarmament, starting of course with nuclear weapons, as well as a range of other issues on which he expresses his views.

The second speaker will be Rabbi Arthur Hertzberg, the Bronfman Professor of Humanities at New York University, Professor Emeritus of Religion at Dartmouth College in New Hampshire and past President of the American Jewish Congress. He will be followed by the Venerable Dr. Chung Ok Lee, Abbess of the Won Buddhist Temple of New York, and the Main Representative of Won Buddhist International to the United Nations. Dr. Lee will be followed by Dr. Anand Mohan, Professor of Philosophy and Social Science at Queens College of the City University of New York, who is active in the Hindu community and Secretary of the Adhyayana Universal Mission. Dr. Gamel Badr, our final speaker, is Adjunct Professor of Islamic Law at New York University, a former member of the Board of the Egyptian Bar Association, former Justice of the Supreme Court of Algeria and former Director of the Office of Legal Affaires at the United Nations. Archbishop Martino.

ARCHBISHOP RENATO MARTINO: Thank you, Senator Roche. It's a pleasure to participate in this ecumenical seminar at an important moment in the international community's long struggle to free itself from the bonds of nuclear weapons. The preparations now being made for the 2000 Review of the Non Proliferation Treaty will signal whether we can go forward to progress through the NPT Process. Despite all the difficulties - well known to those attending this seminar - the Holy See never wavers from what it has said on several occasions:

Nuclear weapons are incompatible with the peace we seek for the 21st Century. They cannot be justified. They deserve condemnation. The preservation of the Non Proliferation Treaty demands an unequivocal commitment to their abolition. This is a moral challenge, a legal challenge, and a political challenge. That multiple-based challenge must be met by the application of our humanity.

The Non-Proliferation Treaty is the preeminent instrument to bring about the complete elimination of nuclear weapons. The indefinite extension of the NPT in 1995 was accompanied by a Programme of Action which called, in the main, for a Comprehensive Nuclear Test Ban Treaty (CTBT), the "early conclusion" of negotiations on a ban on production of fissile material for nuclear weapons, and "systematic and progressive efforts to reduce nuclear weapons globally, with the ultimate goal of eliminating those weapons."

Since then, the CTBT has been signed by 152 States, but its ratification by the requisite number of States and hence entry into the force is far from certain. The negotiations for a fissile ban are still dragging. And "systematic" progress to nuclear disarmament is hard to discern, since START II is not yet in force and most of the Nuclear Weapons States have refused to begin comprehensive negotiations for elimination. The present picture of nuclear disarmament is not a bright one. Nuclear testing by new States reveals the weakness of the non-proliferation regime.

Continued high military spending in virtually every region of the world weakens the will for disarmament. The picture is worsened by the resurgence of militarism in the resolution of the dispute over Kosovo and the continued intransigencies in Iraq. And one must not forget the many conflicts ravaging Africa. Enormous human suffering, atrocities, and forced deportations of peoples are an unacceptable scourge. The gross violations of human rights and human dignity are intolerable and must be stopped. There can never be peace in the world while such injustices abound. The legal structures for peace, slowly taking form through the development of the UN system and the regional organizations, must once more be re-asserted. The application of international law must be the international community's highest priority as we prepare to enter the new millennium.

While militarism of all kinds must be checked, the abolition of nuclear weapons is the prerequisite for peace in the 21st century. What has been promised for a long time by the Non Proliferation Treaty must be achieved. Therefore, the present difficulties must be overcome. The Nuclear Weapon States and the non-nuclear weapons States must together work to establish measured progress to the ultimate goal. The preparatory process for the 2000 Review must be able to look forward as well as backward to determine both the processes to be used and periods of time during which successive phases of nuclear disarmament can take place.

In order for the "road map" to be clearer, the Holy See favors a new set of "Principles and Objectives for Nuclear No Proliferation and Disarmament" to be adopted at the 2000 Review. The new Principles and Objectives, building on the 1995 work, should reinforce the political accountability that is critical to the vitality and viability of the NPT process.

At the same time, the Conference on Disarmament should help the NPT process by commencing substantive discussion on nuclear disarmament issues. This could encourage and expand the START process, which all the Nuclear Weapon States should join.

Here the work of the New Agenda Coalition can be particularly fruitful. This new network of middle-power states has already identified the most pressing areas of progress through their important resolution presented to the General Assembly in 1998. The resolution, noting frankly that the Nuclear Weapons States have not fulfilled speedily and totally their commitment to elimination called on the Nuclear Weapons States to demonstrate an "unequivocal commitment to pursue in good faith and bring to a conclusion" negotiations leading to elimination.

As it continues its work, the New Agenda Coalition deserves even wider support from the international community, particularly Western states who share the goals of the New Agenda Coalition. All this work will be helped immensely by the continued devotion and hard work of civil society. The Middle Power Initiative is a promising effort to bring together like-minded governments and the leading element of wide-ranging non governmental organizations. The continued work of ecumenical groups, so evident here today, is bound to enhance the common effort to rid the world of "ultimate evil," represented by nuclear weapons, which are an offense to God's creation.

As we are gathered here as believers, I would like to conclude with the reference to what Pope John Paul II said just yesterday in St. Peters Square, as he spoke on the "dialogue with the great world religions." Such a dialogue "must not be limited to the search for a lowest common denominator" but rather must "render a courageous service to the truth."

In this way, believers are called to contemplation in order to "penetrate more deeply into the mystery of God" Along these lines, the activities of believers in the field of disarmament are a blessing and a service to humanity. Amidst the difficulties of achieving this noble goal are new signs of hope. When we build on signs of hope, we are taking part in God's love of creation.

RABBI ARTHUR HERTZBERG: I am particularly moved and delighted to be part of this meeting precisely for the reason that Archbishop Martino has given at the very end. We in the religious communities owe it to ourselves that we do this work together. My own studies in the history of religion has convinced me that, both theoretically and in actual historical practice, we have done too much of the reverse. We have talked too much division, justified too many quarrels which have taken to arms and therefore we have not done enough to bring all of humanity together. In this century we must redress that imbalance. The fact that all the major religious traditions of mankind are in this room is a move in that direction.

I have been asking myself for a long time, working as scholar and historian, what is it that set all of this in motion. I found the key to it not in the texts that I usually read but in some stone age anthropology. Back to the stone age, according to the best anthropologist that I am able to find, the people who lived in one little community persuaded themselves that they were the chosen people, that they were humanity and all people outside their circle were lesser people and therefore it was all right to do very means things to them, including killing them. After all, the biblical tradition has at least three versions of the chosen people and their representatives are all sitting here. The bible tells us over and over again, love the stranger because you were once strangers in the land of Egypt, and on the other hand, it tells us some very fierce things about that we should do to the infidels, to the pagans, to those who have traduced the faith or are dangerous to it. And so that struggle continues to exist within the human soul between those who will define humanity as only the people who will agree with them as the people in the right, and those who would define our obligation to humanity as total, every one is one of us.

When I was in my early middle years I wrote a monograph on the enlightenment. Of course when you write a monograph on the enlightenment you go to Voltaire. I discovered that, apart from the fact that Voltaire thought the Jews were a lesser breed with fanaticism built into their hearts, Voltaire, and I think this is not widely known, invested in stocks in the slave trade. One investment has been proved. He found it possible to do this by declaring Negroes to be an intermediate stage between monkeys and human beings.

What made it possible for PHDs from Heidelberg, not merely the SS, to throw my grandfather and all my uncles and aunts and their children into a gas chamber was the notion the Jews were an inferior race, that you can pronounce Jews outside of humanity and therefore cleaning house of them was like using a flit gun on bugs. We have been too busy for too many centuries justifying ourselves as humanity, that is, whatever fraction thereof we happen to be, and to looking at others and saying we owe them less. In this century, when weapons of mass destruction became technologically feasible, it became possible to use them or to threaten their use. And it is not only atom bombs, it's biological warfare, chemical warfare, and gas chambers. It is our capacity to make war against each other, our capacity to be very kind to our own children and to use other people's children for target practice which is an issue. And it is an issue so long as the most respectable, the most decent, the most morally responsible element of humanity, we, the women and the men of religion, do not tear this out by its very roots from all of our traditions.

And that I think is indeed what has been going on. It has been going on because we have stared at the abyss. We saw it at Auschwitz, we saw it in Hiroshima, we are staring at it day after day in wars all over the world. We are staring at the abyss, at the capacity to destroy humanity. We are trying to say together, here in this room and every room in which we can get together, no, no, all of God's children, all of God's creation are our responsibility. And we must to do everything that is within our power to say there are no kosher weapons of mass destruction, no kosher weapons in general. They cannot be used against the "lesser breed without the law" in good conscience.

To conclude, it seems to me that the very worst thing that has happened in the world for lo these many centuries is that we can do wicked things to other people in good conscience. We can drop an atom bomb and say, well, we have saved lives by shortening this war. We can do terrible things, I am not going to give you a very long list of them or even a short one. But we are setting here at this table, people of the traditions, most of whom have not been at peace with one another for lo these many centuries, and we are reaching beyond that, towards our joint responsibility.

May I give you my formula for it? To defend the defenseless, whoever they may be, to keep them from harm. And the defenseless are not monkeys on the way to becoming human beings in our imagination, or heretics, or traducers of the truth. They are simply our brothers, our sisters and our children everywhere in this world.

And so, in this building dedicated to peace, we speak, not in the name of religion, how dare we, but as religious people who have been brought up in various traditions. We are saying we long for peace, we long for reaching each other, we long for putting into the past that part of all our histories which has justified or made possible or at least forgiven war and hatred. That we are doing this together under the leadership of the several organizations which have called these meetings. This is being emphasized and reemphasized, and yes, as the Archbishop said, it is the doing God's work.

DR. CHUNG OK LEE: Nuclear weapons are a key topic in the Korean Peninsula where I grew up. Today Korea is the only country in the world divided by political ideology, the North is communist socialist and the South democratic capitalist. I grew up with a fear of war, in an intense military presence. I often had nightmares of a nuclear holocaust. It is not a healthy environment for the young to grow up with this kind of fear and insecurity. Based on my personal experience, and the experience of all Koreans, in every possible way we need to stop developing or using nuclear weapons.

I believe that nuclear weapons are morally, ethically and spiritually wrong. Nuclear weapons as mass destruction weapons used through either accident, intent or terrorism will wipe out all forms of life, not just your targeted enemies but other innocent people, animals, plants, and other forms of life. The first precept of Buddhism is do not kill life. We believe all forms of life have sacredness. Without other forms of life humans are unable to sustain their lives. We as human beings have ethical, moral and spiritual responsibility to protect them. In addition, it is morally wrong to keep silence about the production and testing of nuclear weapons which will slaughter the innocent and destroy the environment.

Secondly, it is legally wrong if it applies unequally. Some countries insist that nuclear weapons are essential for their security and for that of their allies. Why then deny the same right to others? It is discrimination, it is an injustice and illegal. Everyone should be equal before the law. As Senator Douglas Roche proposes, "States must treat other States as they wish to be treated." in this modern era we have to make the United Nations more democratic. In this modern era, we have to make more democratic the United Nations and all member States must practice equality and the justice of the international law.

Thirdly, the production and testing of nuclear weapons are politically wrong. Governments must reflect their people's concerns in policy-making. Democratic practice and participation must be reflected in policy making. Nuclear weapons production and testing damages and harms the very people that governments claim to protect because it results in extensive health and environmental damage in the nuclear-weapons States. In addition, the earth community and all human beings should not be in jeopardy because of the arrogance or misbehavior of a few in power.

We need new approaches for the old problems of tragic nuclear weapons. I want to suggest a few new approaches. First we need a new vision. The vision we have is no longer effective because it is based on Western civilization and dualism. We are suffering because of division and separation. This division induces people to conquer the other. We need a new vision to create a new civilization and new consciousness. In order to create a new vision to embrace all., we must change our minds.

Buddhists believe all problems begin from the human mind. The human mind is expressed in words and behaviors. Therefore, we must find ways to overcome a dualistic world view which divides

348

us and them, men and women, human beings and nature. Buddhist philosophy emphasizes the interdependency and interconnectedness of all. You cannot protect your people by the production and testing of nuclear weapons. You are part of whole. If you want to damage others, you will harm your people at the same time. We cannot separate us and them. Dualistic approaches will not work any more. In this new vision, there are no boundaries of our people and your people or us and them. As a good example, environmental pollution does not have any boundaries between us and them.

Secondly, we need a new paradigm. We need to create a new paradigm at the United Nations. Global society is tired of top-down policy making. A new paradigm may come from a bottom-up movement at the United Nations by mobilizing middle power states and small states. I am happy with the Middle Power Initiative. This Middle Power Initiative and small states can unite to create a new way of working together for international affairs. This bottom-up movement of small states may be assisted by civil societies and NGOs. Due to the development of democracy, people's power becomes stronger and influential in policy-making. In this new paradigm, group consciousness is important because the whole group must participate and be conscious of contributing for the larger whole. In this new paradigm, a hero does not play an important role but everyone becomes small heros to make life better. Therefore, each one of us has a crucial role to play in this new paradigm.

Thirdly, we need a new spirituality. In the past, to be spiritual meant to be nice and gentle. Thus the religious and spiritual community kept silence in the face of injustice, aggression and mass destruction. In this new era we need a new spirituality to stop aggression and injustice in advance. A new spirituality must participate in the international debate and contribute to deal with the global issues. The religious and spiritual community have an enormous capacity to reach out to people.

Finally, we need a new definition of security. The security of states no longer will be effective with the old fashioned concept. We need a new definition of security which does not mean sovereignty or independence of the nation. We need a holistic approach to security. In this new definition. We must focus on the earth's security or life's security. I believe human security is not enough. We have to change our mind that human beings have authority to control nature. This pattern of thoughts has created irreversible environmental degradation.

I hope these suggestions may provide the United Nations ways to improve and become more democratic to solve issues around nuclear weapons. I join in with the previous speakers for a united voice of the religious and spiritual community saying that nuclear weapons are wrong, wrong for human health and for the environment and ecology.

ANAND MOHAN: Let me observe at the outset that the Hindu tradition of political realism does not subscribe to any absolute ethic. With that in mind, I should like to step back into history a little, because that explains why we are where we are today. I am sure all of you know that the church in Medieval Europe, as well as all the other religious traditions, had demanded that if there was war at all it should always be a just war. This very conception of a just war was eclipsed three hundred years ago by a new way of looking at war which was essentially rational. War which was looked upon in moral and immoral terms, was now simply reduced to being either a rational enterprise or an irrational adventure. And the same principles that held valid for economics, that is, a kind of a cost-benefit analysis, now characterized war. War was a rational enterprise and in the age of reason, whatever was rational ipso facto became also moral. So the distinction between what was rational and moral was obliterated, and it is that heritage that we have all inherited.

Now first of all, its demonstration effect was to universalize this new western ethic, if I may so put it. The proliferation of nuclear weapons is nothing more than telling the nuclear "haves" by the nuclear "have nots" that imitation is the sincerest form of flattery. Whatever the West does would apparently pass muster with the non Western societies also. The notion that some countries are "more equal" than others has resulted in inscribing into the very fabric of the Charter of the United Nations the privileges of the five permanent members of the Security Council, who are by definition above the law because the Charter does not control them. The Charter actually empowers them to do the things they have done. And now for us to turn round a three hundred year, tradition that some are more powerful than others, and that power is itself a justification for whatever they seek to do, is not easy. Therefore my optimism is considerably tempered by the necessity to look at the facts. We ought to make a distinction between facts and values. The Pax Christi conclusions which are given as moral conclusions are really not moral conclusions at all, they are factual conclusions. The policy of nuclear deterrence is being institutionalized, that's a simple fact.

Second, the role of nuclear deterrence has been extended in the post Cold War era, which is also a fact. Lastly, the nuclear powers have no intention of adopting a policy position of eliminating these weapons entirely is also a simple statement of fact.

Now, how can we turn a factual statement into a value statement?

We simply cannot. We are talking about these facts, irrefutable facts. The sovereignty of these brute facts stares in our eyes and we cannot simply pretend that we can change these attitudes by preaching and moralizing. It seems to me that the abolition of nuclear weapons is impossible in the immediate future and there is no purpose served by ignoring this and looking at pie in the sky.

The policy MAD, Mutual Assured Destruction, although the acronym assured us it was mad, it certainly was not; it served a rational purpose, a rational purpose of deterrence, a rational purpose which was supported by religious establishments in all the countries of the world for fifty years.

These nuclear weapons became accepted and were rendered acceptable. And we ourselves, if we want to reverse that tendency, can honestly admit that perhaps there was a period of time when these nuclear weapons had a purpose and A role to play but that the quantitative destruction that they can bring about has made a qualitative difference to our discussion and therefore the new universe of discourse in which we are all participating may well be said to have made the use of nuclear weapons utterly immoral. That's why I started out with saying that the Hindu ethical tradition is a relativistic tradition and though we could make a good case for nuclear weapons at an earlier time, we can no longer make that case today. In that sense we should really adopt the position that they are immoral.

But if they are indeed immoral, they should be immoral for all of the human race, for all the countries of the world. For three hundred years we have been told that the most foundational principle of international law was the sovereign equality of nations; and that principle has been flouted by nothing other than the United Nations Charter itself.

Now if we cannot get rid of these nuclear weapons, and as I said it would be impossible to

350

do that in the immediate future, then the other two measures which have been proposed are perfectly rational, sensible and moral. One is that every country in the world, nuclear powers included, should declare there will be no first use of nuclear weapons under any circumstances whatsoever. We should make that a categorical moral imperative of a Kantian type. Now if we do that, there is an enormous amount of conventional military power which all the great, middle and the other powers have which is considerable enough to act as a deterrent. We simply cannot make a case that only nuclear weapons can deter; certainly the conventional weapons that we all have, that all the great nations have, are so enormous that they do have a deterrent capacity and we don't need nuclear deterrence.

And the second measure is de-alerting. De-alerting also can be accomplished universally without discrimination. Once those two are accomplished then I believe that we can expect to have some incremental change, though no great revolutionary change. Over time, the building of confidence, and confidence-building measures, may create a new sense of trust and accomplish what we are attempting to do.

And in all of this of course the nuclear powers must indeed take the lead. Because whether within a country or within the world as a whole, it is the dominant elites which impose moral standards and ethical standards. So far it is the nuclear weapons which have imposed the current impasse, as a dominant elite, on the whole world. And the reversal of this trend must take place among the nuclear powers before it can take place anywhere else.

I am reminded of Mr. Dalai Steven son, who was the American Ambassador to the United Nations. In the 1952 election he was very fond of repeating that the purpose of power should never be lost in the fact of power. Unfortunately in the last fifty years that is precisely what has happened in the world. We have lost the purpose of power. We gloat in the fact of power, and to the extent that we are oblivious of the distinction between the two we may be accused of being both irrational and immoral. Consider the fact that nations spend billions and billions of dollars on defense when there is no money for health, no money for education, no money for social well-being. This is indeed immoral. It is downright immoral that such a state of affairs should exist in the most affluent and most powerful nation on earth.

It seems to me that if there is going to be a moral revolution it should start at the grassroots level in every individual country. It is only then that we can attempt to change the behavior of nations. But these nation states dealing with each other, with a long history of mistrust, with a long history of not being under the law, but as being above the law. That cannot easily change. Therefore I would like to submit that the principles of universality and equality which have been ignored and which have rendered the United Nations itself peripheral and quite marginalized, must be reasserted and restored.

What is attempted to be done in Kosovo today should have been done in the United Nations, one month ago, three months ago. And now when this policy has failed, its the United Nations which is supposed to bail them out. So the immorality is in the uses of power. I am not particularly concerned about the position of power or the fact of power; bur it is the uses of power that render it moral or immoral.

DR. GAMEL BADR: One of the important teachings of Islam is that the preservation and promotion of the welfare of all mankind is an important activity and every Muslim is required, under the rules of his religion, to do whatever he or she can be able to do to preserve and promote the welfare of everyone else. And at least to abstain from doing anything that would affect negatively the welfare of mankind. Now this being the general rule, it is obvious anything that negatively affects the welfare of mankind is considered illegitimate under Islamic rule. Everything that promotes the welfare of mankind is considered appropriate and welcome. Not only does this relate to the possession and the eventual use of weapons of mass destruction, especially nuclear weapons, but even with regard to the traditional weapons of older times. The rules of war in Islam prevent a combatant from one country indiscriminately inflicting injury or death on his enemies. Violence in war should be used only to the extent that the purpose that is expected is achieved. But any wanton or indiscriminate killing or injuring of the enemy is unlawful and this is related to traditional weapons so you can imagine how this rule can apply to a world where weapons of mass destruction, and especially nuclear weapons, abound. That is why Muslims were chagrined last year to see one of their countries enter into a race to manufacture and store nuclear weapons and we all hope that the efforts that have been done since then to solve this crisis will ultimately result in the Islamic country I have in mind relinquishing this unlawful and un-Islamic objective of obtaining nuclear weapons.

Now, if I may become a bit more technical with regard to how to Islamic law and Islam in general regard the question of weapons of mass destruction and in particular nuclear weapons, let me say that in Islamic jurisprudence, no rule of law can be lawful and applicable unless it meets one of the following five criteria. Such a rule of law should protect or promote one of these five values, which are the goals or objectives of Islamic law. The first value is human life. Any rule that does not protect human life or exposes human life to wanton danger is not lawful. The second value is faith. A person's faith has to be protected.

The third value among these five is the person's intellect. Anything that affects a person's intellect, for example narcotics, is prohibited. They effect an individual's intellect. The fourth is the value of progeny, the children, one's sons and daughters. Anything that protects their interests is lawful, anything that goes against is unlawful. Finally, the fifth goal of Islamic law is an individual's material assets. Anything that promotes and protects the assets is lawful, anything that goes against is unlawful. So when you think of the rights, of the five values of Islamic law, when you think what nuclear weapons can do to mankind I think it would be abundantly clear that under Islamic law and Islamic conception, nuclear weapons are illegitimate and should be removed or done away with.

Now, what we can hope for is that maybe over time, and thanks to the efforts done among nation states and by NGO's on the other, a time will come that everyone will realize that humanity's future is definitely linked to elimination of mass destruction weapons and particularly of nuclear weapons.

ADDRESSES OF NGO PANELISTS (except for the NPT presenters, that are listed after their presentations):

Dr. Gamel Badr, 18 Peter Lynes Ct., Tenafly, NJ 07670; tel: 201-569-5874

Bruce Blair, The Brookings Institution, 1775 Massachusetts Ave., NW, Washington, DC 20036; tel:202-797-6237; fax: 202-797-6003;

Loretta Bondi, Human Rights Watch, 1630 Connecticut Ave NW, Suite 500, Washington, DC 20009; tel: 202-612-4321; fax: 202-612-4333; E-mail: bondil@hrw.org

Merav Datan, International Physicians for the Prevention of Nuclear War, 727 Massachusetts Ave, Cambridge, MA 02139, tel: 617-868-5050; fax: 617-868-2560; E-mail:mdatan@ippnw.org   web site: http://www.ippnw.org

Prof. Rekha Datta, Monmouth University, Dept. of Political Science, West Long Branch, NJ 00764; tel: 732-571-4438; fax: 908-571-3656

Jonathan Dean, Union of Concerned Scientists, 1616 P St., NW, Suite 310, Washington, DC 20036; tel: 202-332-0900; fax: 202-332-0905; E-mail: jdean@ucsusa.org

Prof. Alan Dowty, University of Notre Dame, 0313 Hesburgh Center, Notre Dame, IN 46556; Tel: 219-631-5098; fax: 219-631-6973; E-mail: Alan.K.Dowty.1@nd.edu

Prof. Colleen Driscoll, Common Heritage Institute, P.O. Box 1748, Doylestown, PA 18901; tel: 215-230-4276; fax: 215-348-5502; E-mail: CMDriscoll@prodigy.net

Prof. Steve Fetter, School of Public Affairs, University of Maryland, College Park, MD 20742-1821; tel: 301-405-6355; fax: 301-403-8107; E-mail: sfetter@wam.umd.edu;   http://puaf.umd.edu/papers/fetter.htm

Prof. Harold Feiveson, Center for Energy and the Environment, Princeton University, Princeton, NJ 08544; tel: 609-258-4676; fax: 609-258-3661; E-mail: feiveson@princeton.edu

Randall Caroline Forsberg, Institute for Defense and Disarmament Studies, 675 Massachusetts Ave, Cambridge, MA 02139; tel: 617-7337; fax: 617-354-1450; E-mail: forsberg@idds.org

Ilmas Futehally, International Center for Peace Initiatives, C-306 Montana, Lokhandwala Complex, Andheri West, Mumbai 400 053 India; Tel: 91-22-610-5282; E-mail: icpi@giasbm01.vsnl.net.in

Daryl Kimball, Coalition to Reduce Nuclear Dangers, 100 Maryland Ave, Suite 200, NE Washington, DC 20002; tel: 202-546-0795, fax: 546-5142; E-mail: dkimball@clw.org

Thomas Graham Jr., Lawyers Alliance for World Security, 1901 Pennsylvania Ave, NW, Suite 201, Washington, DC 20006; tel: 202-745-2450; fax: 202-745-0444; E-mail: disarmament@lawscns.org

Jonathan Granoff, 124 Colwyn Lane, Bala Cynwood, PA 19004; tel: 610- 668-5470; fax: 610-668-5455; E-mail: JGG786@aol.com

Rabbi Arthur Hertzberg, Temple Emmanuel, 147 Tenafly Rd., Engelwood, NJ 07631

Joost Hiltermann, Human Rights Watch, 1630 Connecticut Ave NW, Suite 500, Washington, DC 20009; tel: 202-612-4321; fax: 202-612-4333; E-mail: jhiltermann@hrw.org

Ven. Dr. Chung Ok Lee, Wong Buddhist Temple, 431 East 57th St., New York, NY 10022; tel: 212-750-2774

Lora Lumpe, PRIO (International Peace Research Institute), Fuglehaugatta, N-0260 Oslo, Norway; tel: 47-22-54.7700; fax: 47-22-54.7701; E-mail: lora@prio.no (Lora Lumpe may be back in the US by the end of 1999, but PRIO should be able to tell you where she is.)

Arjun Makhijani, Institute for Energy and Environmental Research, 6935 Laurel Ave., Suite 204, Takoma Park, MD 20912; tel: 301-270-5500; fax: 301-270-3029; E-mail: ieer@ieer.org

H.E. Archbishop Renato Raffaele Martino, Permanent Observer Misison of the Holy See to the UN, 25 East 39th St., new York, 10016-0903; tel: 212-370-9622

Saul Mendlovitz, Rutgers Law School, and the World Order Models Project, 475 Riverside Drive, Rm.246, New York, NY 10115; NY tel: 212-870-2391; fax: 212-870-2392; NJ tel: 973-353-5585; fax: 973-353-5074; E-mail: womp@igc.org cgcg@andromeda.rutgers.edu

Dr. Anand Mohan, 130-53 229th St., Laurelton, NY 11413-1838; 718-723-4641

Zia Mian, Center for Energy and Environmental Studies, Princeton University, Princeton, NJ 08544; tel: 609-258-6468; fax: 609-258-3661; E-mail zia@princeton.edu

John Pike, Federation of American Scientists, 307 Massachusetts Ave., NE, Washington, DC 20002; tel: 202-675-1023; fax: 202-675-1010; E-mail: johnpike@fas.org

M.V. Ramana, Center for Energy and Environmental Studies, Princeton University, Princeton, NJ 08544; tel: 609-258-1761; fax: 609-258-3661; E-mail: ramana@princeton.edu

Michael Renner, World Watch Institute, 1776 Massachusetts Ave, NW, Washington, DC 20036; tel: 718-956-7615; fax: 202-296-7365; E-mail: mrenner@worldwatch.org

Senator Douglas Roche: 8923 Strathearn Drive, Edmonton, Alberta T6C 4C8 Canada; tel: 403-466-8072; fax: 403-469-4732; E-mail: roched@sen.parl.gc.ca

Jonathan Schell, 108 Reade St., New York, NY 10013; tel at The Nation: 212-209-5400; fax: 212-982-7193; E-mail: jschell@wesleyan.edu

Bill Sulzman, P.O. Box 915, Colorado Springs, CO 80901;

Admiral Stansfield Turner, 1320 Skipwith Rd., McClean, VA 22101; tel: 703-528-2023; fax: 703-528-0942;E-mail: admturner@aol.com

Hiro Umebayashi, Pacific Campaign for Disarmament and Security, Peace Depot/PCDS International Office, 3-3-1 Minowa-cho, Kohoku-ku, Yokohama 223-0051 Japan tel: 81-45-563-5101; fax: 81-45-563-9907; E-mail: CXJ15621@niftyserve

William F.Vendley, World Conference on Religion and Peace, 777 United Nations Plaza, new York, NY 10017; Tel: 212-687-2163; fax: 212-983-0566; wvendley@WCRP.org

Alyn Ware, Lawyers Committee on Nuclear Policy (LCNP) , 211 E.43rd St., 12th floor, New York, NY 10017; tel: 212-818-1861; fax: 212-818-1857; E-mail for LCNP: lcnp@aol.com. E-mail for Alyn Ware, who is no longer in the NY office : alynw@ibm.net

Jim Wurst, the Middle Powers Initiative, LCNP, 211 E. 43rd St., 12th floor, New York, NY 10017; tel: 212-818-1861; fax: 212-818-1857; E-mail: jhwurst@aol.com

The area code for New York City is about to change, so some of the telephone numbers will be affected.

USEFUL INTERNET SOURCES:

A great many more NGO web sites - nearly 150, and we will add more - and some governmental sources are found in the NGO Committee on Disarmament's web site, **http://www.peacenet.org/disarm**

The web site for the United Nations is **http://www.un.org** If you click onto "Peace and Security" and then onto "Disarmament," you will be able to access the UN Department for Disarmament Affairs web pages, including reportage on the First Committee, the link to the Conference on Disarmament, the one multilateral negotiating body that negotiated the Chemical Weapons Convention (CWC), the Comprehensive Test Ban Treaty (CTBT) and the link to the UN Institute for Disarmament Research (UNIDIR). And the time of writing the link to the Disarmament Commission was not yet up. From the UN Department for Disarmament Affairs site you can also link to the NPT site and the Demining data base and find very current information on conventional weapons, particularly small arms .

The Organization for Prohibition of Chemical Weapons is **http://www.opew.nl** The International Atomic Energy Agency, IAEA, is **http://www.iaea.org** The Comprehensive Test Ban Treaty Organization is http://www.ctbto.org

The United Nations Studies program at Yale, an excellent source, is **http://www.library.yale.edu/un/index.html** The official texts of disarmament treaties are also available on-line through the Fletcher program in International Studies at Tufts University at **http://www.tufts.edu/fletcher/multilaterals.html** including the CTBT, the CWC, the NPT and the Convention on Certain Conventional Weapons which may be Deemed to be Excessivly Injurious or Having Indiscriminant Effects (CCCW), the Land Mines Treaty.

Some other sites:

http://www.napf.org/abolition2000	Abolition 2000, which has many sites
http://www.gn.apc.org/acronym	The Acronym Institute, UK, reportage & analysis of the First Committee, Disarmament Commission, Conference on Disarmament, NPT & events affecting arms control, disarmament.
http://www.arias.or.cr	Arias Foundation for Peace & Human Progress - Costa Rica (in Spanish)
http://www.armscontrol.org	Arms Control Association - Washington, DC
http://worldpolicy.org/	Arms Trade Resource Center and World Policy Journal
http://www.bicc.uni-bonn.de	Bonn International Center for Conversion
http://www.basicint.org	British American Security Information Council has recent NPT documents
http://www.brook.edu	The Brookings Institution - Washington, DC thinktank
http://www.caat.demon.co.uk/	Campaign Against the Arms Trade
http://www.ceip.org	Carnegie Endowment for International Peace - USA
http://www.cartercenter.org	The Carter Center - USA
http://www.armscontrol.ru/	Center for Arms Control, Energy and Environmental Studies - Russia
http://www.princeton.edu/~cees	Center for Energy and Environmental Studies - Princeton University - USA
http://www.fsk.ethz.ch	Center for Security Studies and Conflict Research - Zurich, Switzerland
http://www.crnd.org	Coalition to Reduce Nuclear Dangers - Washington, DC
http://www.cdi.org	Center for Defense Information - Washington, DC
http://www.stanford.edu/group/CISAC	Center for International Security and Arms Control - Stanford Univ.
http://www.miis.edu	Center for Non-Proliferation Studies at Monterey
http://hdc-www.harvard.edu/cfia/.	Center for Science and International Affairs - Harvard University
http://www.nyu.edu/cwpnm/	Center for War, Peace and the News Media at New York University
http:// www.cbaci.org	Chemical and Biological Arms Control Institute
http://www.ncf.carleton.ca/ip/global/coat/	Coalition to Oppose the Arms Trade - Canada
http://www.cwihp.si.edu/default..htm	Cold War International History Project
http://www.clw.org	Council for a Livable World - US
http://www.amacad.org	Com'tee on Intern'l Security Studies, Amer. Acad. of Arts & Sciences
http://www.ecaar.org	Economists Allied for Arms Reduction
http://www.grip.org	Europ'n Instit. for Research & Inform'n on Peace & Security (GRIP) - Belgium

http://www.fas.org	Federation of American Scientists. Outer space, biological weapons, plus
http://www.fourthfreedom.org	Fourth Freedom Forum
http://www.fcnl.org/	Friends Committee on National Legislation - USA
http://twics.com/~antiatom/	Gensuikyo -Japan Council Against A & H Bombs
http://www.globalactionpw.org	Global Action to Prevent War
http://www.gci.ch	Green Cross International, one of the sites of the Gorbachev Foundation
http://www.haguepeace.org	Hague Appeal for Peace, 1999
http://fas-www.harvard.edu80/~hsp/	Harvard/Sussex Program on CBW Armament and Arms Limitation
http://www.stimson.org	Henry L. Stimson Center - Washington, DC thinktank
http://www.idds.org/	Institute for Defense and Disarmament Studies, Cambridge, Mass., USA
http://www.ieer.org	Institute for Energy and Environmental Research - Maryland, USA
http://www-igcc.ucsd.edu/	Institute of Global Conflict and Cooperation - Univ. of California, San Diego
http://www.iansa.org	International Action Network on Small Arms
http://www.international-alert.org	International Alert - UK/Norway
http://www.ddh.nl/org/ialana	International Association of Lawyers Against Nuclear Arms
http://www.icbl.org	International Campaign to Ban Land Mines
http://www.isn.ethz.ch/iiss	International Institute of Strategic Studies - United Kingdom
http://www.th-darmstadt.de/ze/ianus/inesap.htm	Internat'l Network of Engineers & Scientists Against Proliferation
http://www.healthnet.org/IPPNW/	Intern'l Physicians for the Prevention of Nuclear War
http://www.ipb.org	International Peace Bureau
http://www.tau.ac.il/jcss	Jaffee Center for Strategic Studies - Israel
http://www.lawscns.org	Lawyers Alliance for World Security - USA
http://www.lcnp.org	Lawyer's Committee for Nuclear Policy
http://www.lasg.org	Los Alamos Study Group - USA
http://www.igc.org/nrdc/	Natural Resources Defense Council - Washington, DC
http://www.nautilus.org	Nautilus Institute for Security and Sustainable Development - California, USA
http://www.nisat.org	Norwegian Initiative on Small Arms Transfers
http://www.wagingpeace.org	Nuclear Age Peace Foundation - USA
http://www.nonviolence.org/pcusa	Pax Christi USA
http://www.webcom.com/peaceact/	Peace Action - USA
http://osiris.colorado.edu/SOC/ORGS/peace.html	The Peace Studies Association
http://www.pircenter.org	PIR - Center for Policy Studies - Russia
http://www.prif.org	Peace Research Institute, Frankfurt, Germany
http://www.ecn.cz/temelin/english.html	Prague International Anti-Nuclear Office (PIANO)
http://www.ploughshares.ca/index.html	Project Ploughshares - Canada
http://www.soton.ac.uk/~ppnn	Programme for Promoting Nuclear Non-Proliferation
http://www.qmw.ac.uk/pugwash/archive/describe.html	Pugwash Conference on Science and World Affairs
http://www.princeton.edu/~ransac/	Russian-American Nuclear Security Advisory council (RANSAC)
http://www.acdisweb.acdis.uiuc.edu/homepage_docs/resource_docs/test_docs/india.html	Program in Arms Control, Disarmament & Internat'l Security - Univ. of Illinois, has India documents, plus
http://www.rand.org	RAND Corporation, USA
http://www.sfcg.org	Search for Common Ground , Washington, DC, focus on the Middle East
http://www.mnet.fr/aiindex/	South Asian Citizens Web. From this site you can reach others, including the Movement in India for Nuclear Disarmament (MIND) and South Asians Against Nukes
http://www.sipri.se	Stockholm International Peace Research Institute
http://www.toda.org	Toda Institute for Global Peace & Policy Research - Japan
http://www.ucsusa.org	Union of Concerned Scientists - USA
http://www.fhit.org/vertic/	Verification Technology Information Center
http://www.ipcs.org/	Institute of Peace and Conflict Studies, New Delhi, India
http://www.webwombat.com.au/intercom/newsprs/index.htm	- not an NGO, but very useful. At this site you can access newspapers throughout the world